"Information through Innovation"

Using *Microsoft Works 3.0* for *Windows*

An Introduction to Computing

Gwynne Larsen
Kenneth D. Shaw
Kathryn A. Marold
Metropolitan State College of Denver

bf

boyd & fraser publishing company

I(T)P An International Thomson Publishing Company

Danvers • Albany • Bonn • Boston • Cincinnati • Detroit • London • Madrid • Melbourne
Mexico City • New York • Paris • San Francisco • Singapore • Tokyo • Washington

Acquisitions Editor: Anne E. Hamilton
Project Manager: Christopher T. Doran
Production Manager: Patty Stephan
Production Services: Elm Street Publishing Services, Inc.
Composition: TSI Graphics
Cover: Mike Fender/Mike Fender Design
Manufacturing Coordinator: Tracy Megison
Marketing Manager: Daphne Snow

Printed in the United States of America

This book is printed on recycled, acid-free paper that meets Environmental Protection Agency standards.

For more information, contact boyd & fraser publishing company:

boyd & fraser publishing company
One Corporate Place • Ferncroft Village
Danvers, Massachusetts 01923, USA

International Thomson Publishing Europe
Berkshire House 168-173
High Holborn
London, WC1V 7AA, England

Thomas Nelson Australia
102 Dodds Street
South Melbourne 3205
Victoria, Australia

Nelson Canada
1120 Birchmont Road
Scarborough, Ontario
Canada M1K 5G4

International Thomson Editores
Campose Eliseos 385, Piso 7
Col. Polanco
11560 Mexico D.F. Mexico

International Thomson Publishing GmbH
Konigswinterer Strasse 418
53227 Bonn, Germany

International Thomson Publishing Asia
221 Henderson Road
#05-10 Henderson Building
Singapore 0315

International Thomson Publishing Japan
Hirakawacho Kyowa Building, 3F
2-2-1 Hirakawacho
Chiyoda-ku, Tokyo 102, Japan

1 2 3 4 5 6 7 8 9 10 BN 8 7 6 5 4

Library of Congress Cataloging-in-Publication Data

Larsen, Gwynne.
Using Microsoft Works 3.0 for Windows : an introduction to computing / Gwynne Larsen, Kenneth D. Shaw, Kathryn A. Marold.
p. cm.
Includes index.
ISBN 0-87709-845-X
1. Integrated software. 2. Microsoft Works for Windows. I. Shaw, Kenneth, 1937-. II. Marold, Kathy, 1944-. III. Title.
QA76.76.I57L37 1994 94-21639
005.369—dc20 CIP

Text with 3.5" student data disk: ISBN 0-87709-287-7

1 2 3 4 5 6 7 8 9 10 BN 8 7 6 5 4

Brief Contents

Contents

Preface

Using Microsoft Works 3.0 for Windows is intended for students who are interested in learning about IBM personal computers and ways to increase their personal computer productivity. This book combines an exploration of fundamental computer information systems concepts with comprehensive, hands-on tutorials for using *Works 3.0 for Windows*.

The book differs substantially from typical computer literacy texts in two important ways. First, whereas the technical terminology spans a broad spectrum, the level at which these terms are discussed is suitable for a beginning student in any discipline. Second, using *Works 3.0 for Windows* features and exercises are integrated throughout the book, making using the computer easier to learn and understand.

Each chapter is organized into the following parts:

- Chapter objectives
- Concepts related to the chapter
- Description and overview of the chapter's software module and its functions and commands
- Tutorials that cover both mouse commands and toolbar icons to create complete documents and that explore concepts relating to the software. Interrelated tutorials use a personal financial management case study throughout the text.
- Chapter summary
- Review section including key terms, chapter questions, and additional, unsolved software problems to reinforce learning

Distinguishing Features

The authors, Larsen, Shaw, and Marold, are experienced writers in the computer field. The coverage of the book is comprehensive. It presents the essential DOS commands and *Windows* functions. Information systems concepts appear throughout the text; students learn much more than they could from the cookbook-style strings of keystrokes found in many tutorial texts.

One can easily move among the different *Works* applications—spreadsheet, word processor, graphics, database, and communications—using a common set of commands. Many of the icons and menu selections are the same throughout the software, one of the major benefits of using an integrated application. The integrated theme culminates in Chapter 13, which spans all of the concepts learned throughout the text. The instructor may use this material as final evidence of concepts learned and skills acquired.

The book leads novice users of *Works 3.0 for Windows* step by step through each *Works* application at their own pace. Later they can tackle many exercises to apply the information they have learned. For some exercises, files are supplied on the student data diskette to keep the time spent keying in text or data to a minimum. Tutorial assignments and software exercises build on everyday, personal financial management topics that should interest students of any age.

Numerous photos and drawings of concepts and equipment being discussed, software screen displays, and an extensive review section filled with key terms, concept questions, and additional unsolved software problems all enhance dynamic learning.

A five-step guideline for purchasing a personal computer is the subject of Chapter 14. This chapter will help anyone considering purchasing or upgrading a microcomputer for personal use.

Computer crime, viruses, security, and ethics are covered in Chapter 15; piracy and viruses are dealt with at length. This valuable information is found in few other texts.

The numerous software exercises at the ends of the chapters were developed with four different learning methods in mind. Some are based on the concepts in each chapter; some build on the work completed in the step-by-step tutorials; some come from the student software diskette enclosed with the book; and some are more open-ended and challenging.

A comprehensive *Instructor's Manual* includes sections on each chapter's purpose; vocabulary words; chapter objectives; lecture outline; teaching suggestions keyed to the lecture outline; answers to chapter review questions; answers to chapter exercises; test questions in the true/false, multiple choice, fill-in-the-blank, and matching formats; and transparency masters. A diskette that covers most sections using the *Works* format accompanies the manual. Chapter coverage can be tailored to meet individual requirements.

Supporting Materials

A 3.5-inch student data disk is packaged with the textbook. It contains files the student needs to complete some of the exercises and assignments.

The *Instructor's Manual* includes its own 3.5-inch diskette with supporting materials.

Hardware and Software Requirements

An IBM or compatible microcomputer with a hard disk, graphics capability, and 4MB of memory is necessary. DOS, *Windows 3.1* (or higher), and *Works 3.0 for Windows* are the software required for the book.

Acknowledgments

The authors wish to thank all who have contributed to the development and production of this text, in particular, our families, who were so encouraging and supportive during this long process. We give a special thanks to Randy Larsen for helping with the tutorials; to Marcia Hydusko for helping with the test questions; to the people at boyd & fraser—Jim Edwards, Chris Doran, and Patty Stephan—for overseeing the publication process; and to Nancy Shanahan and Kelly Spiller of Elm Street Publishing Services for helping with the many production details.

Many thanks to the following people for reviewing the manuscript and for the helpful comments suggestions:

JoDane Autry, Collin County Community College
Gay Getz, Kingwood College
Robert Landrum, Jones County Junior College
Gerald Mellenthin, William Raney Harper College
Daryll Rhoads, Rio Hondo College
Jim Swanson, Lenoir-Rhyne College

Gwynne Larsen
Kenneth D. Shaw
Kathryn A. Marold
September 1994

Part 1

Beginning Concepts

Chapter 1

Introduction to the Personal Computer

Objectives

After studying this chapter you will be able to:

- *Define the term* computer system
- *Classify computers by their uses*
- *Explain the different kinds of input and output hardware*
- *Describe personal computer hardware components*
- *Explain the differences among the several microprocessor chips used in IBM and compatible personal computers*
- *Explain the difference between application and systems software*
- *Explain the difference between integrated and stand-alone software*
- *Explain the functions of systems software and identify the major microcomputer operating systems*

Computer Systems in General

A computer is an electronic tool for storage, manipulation, and retrieval of data. It operates by joining hardware with software to enable people to generate text, automate record-keeping, complete various mathematical operations, and communicate the results of these operations to others. A computer does not create information; it is a tool that helps people produce information. The development of that tool has irrevocably changed our lives.

Computers have been around since the 1940s. We typically divide computers into classes. **Supercomputers** have many processors (which perform the actual computing) that work together to help solve complex problems. **Mainframes** are large, expensive, powerful systems that require their own physical facilities. **Minicomputers** are business-oriented machines used for slightly smaller operations. Finally, **microcomputers** are even smaller systems whose operations are controlled by **microprocessors** (integrated circuits etched on very small pieces of silicon that are usually referred to as **chips**). In the past, supercomputers, mainframes, minis, and micros were distinguished by their physical size differences, the power of their central processing units, the amount of data they could retain in temporary memory, and the speed with which they could compute.

This classification into clear-cut categories of supercomputers, mainframes, minis, and microcomputers is becoming blurred as technology gets more and more sophisticated. A modern desktop microcomputer may feature several processors that make it many times more powerful and faster than an early main-

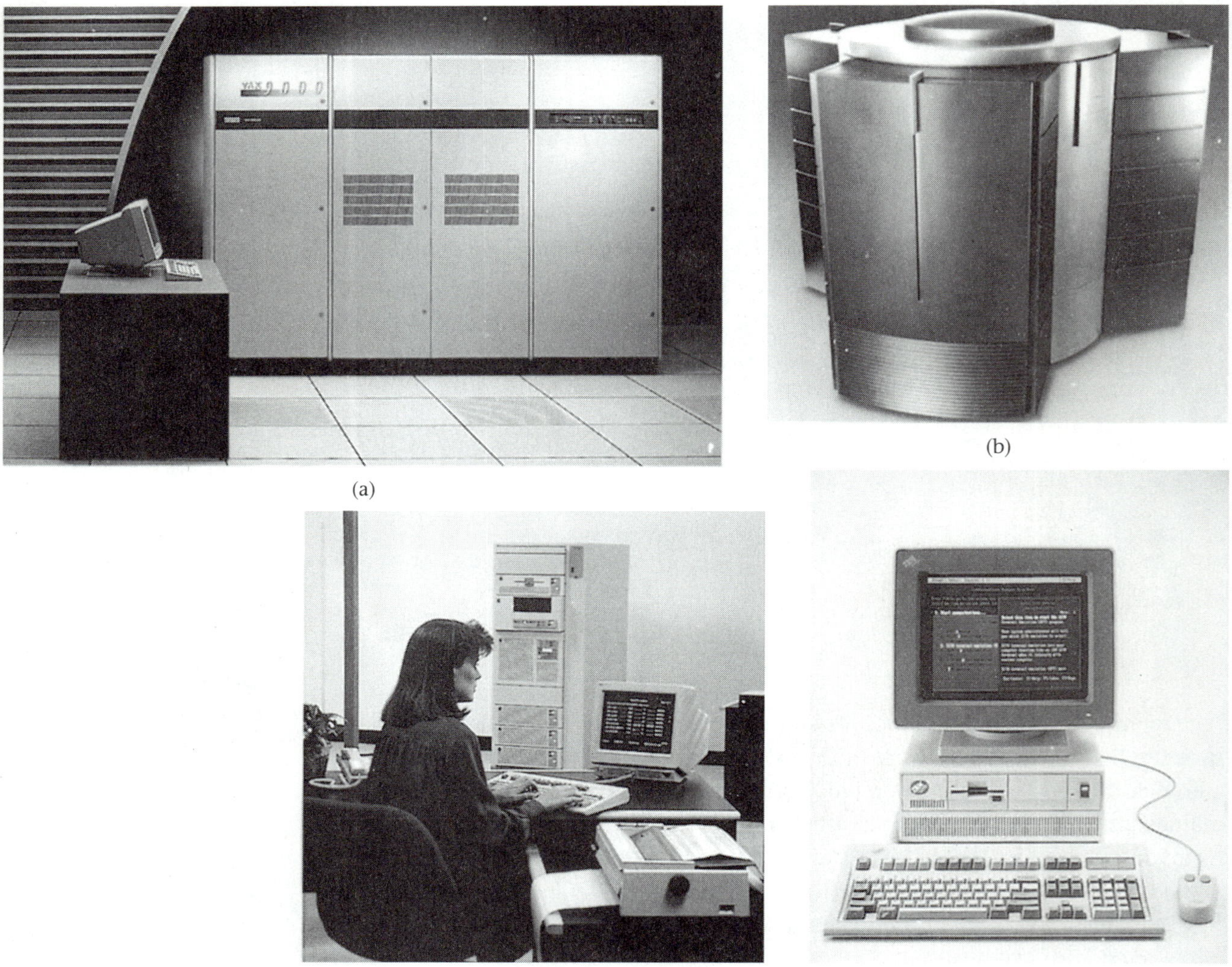

(a) (b) (c) (d)

Figure 1.1

Four Types of Computers—(a) Mainframe, (b) Supercomputer, (c) Minicomputer, and (d) Microcomputer

frame, which typically took up a whole floor of an office building. Likewise, today a relatively inexpensive microcomputer can handle as much data as a costly mainframe could handle in the past.

Therefore, it is better now to classify these machines, not by their cost, power, speed, and so forth, but by how they are used. Supercomputers, mainframes, and minicomputers are still used mostly for medium to large business and scientific applications, while microcomputers are often used as personal information systems. Recently, users have begun increasingly to link them with other microcomputers into networks that can act like large business systems. When we speak of a **personal computer**, we refer to a microcomputer that is used as a personal information system to help people do their own personal work (in an office or at home) more efficiently. Figure 1.1 shows examples of the four types of computer systems.

Personal Computer Systems

All computers are systems composed of multiple elements. We usually think of a personal computer as consisting of **hardware** (the system's physical components), **software** (its programs or coded instructions), and **data** (raw facts or coded information that programs process). Of course, none of these elements would function without a further essential component—you, the user. Figure 1.2 shows a typical microcomputer-based personal computer system.

Figure 1.2

A 486 Microcomputer System

A personal computer system is a tool that you can use for many different applications. For example, you could use your system to write letters and reports, keep track of your checkbook balance, graph personal tax deductions, file an inventory of household items, and even receive stock quotations from an information service. By changing the software, or the instructions the computer follows, you can change the type of task you do without changing the hardware. This makes the computer a many faceted tool, truly a general problem-solving aid.

Personal Computer Hardware

Input Hardware

The physical components of a personal microcomputer system can be divided into input, output, processing, and storage hardware. In order for the computer to operate upon your data, you must first enter the data into memory—a temporary storage area—to await processing. We refer to those hardware elements that allow you to enter data as **input hardware**. The **mouse** and the **keyboard** are the two major input devices for microcomputers.

Mouse

The mouse is an electronic pointing device that operates by the movement of a ball imbedded underneath a palm-sized, maneuverable unit that is attached to the system unit. This device is part of most newer personal computer systems because it greatly facilitates selection of menu items and speeds user operations. The mouse was not the first input device; the keyboard was the dominant initial input hardware. The mouse became commonplace less than a decade ago, but it is rapidly replacing the keyboard as the primary selection device for personal computers. You direct the mouse arrow or rectangle shown on the screen (the mouse indicator) by rolling the mouse along a mouse pad until the indicator reaches the desired selection on the screen. Then you press (or *click)* a mouse button to confirm the selection of the highlighted item. This operation is the equivalent of using the keyboard's directional arrow keys to position the cursor where you wish, then pressing the ENTER key.

You may use the mouse with *Works 3.0 for Windows* to indicate and select desired menu alternatives, to select blocks of text in word processing, and to do many other useful tasks. To use the mouse, you must have the physical hardware itself, as well as special software, called a *driver,* to control it, and the software program you are using must support mouse operations. More and more new programs are making use of this handy piece of hardware. Further details on its operation are explained in Chapter 2 along with an introduction to the *Windows* and *Works 3.0 for Windows* software.

Keyboard

The keyboard allows you to enter text and numbers much as you would on an ordinary typewriter. The computer keyboard has additional keys, however, that allow you to predefine keystrokes, change specific characters in the character set (the total, fixed set of characters that the monitor can display), and perform some

Figure 1.3

Standard Keyboard

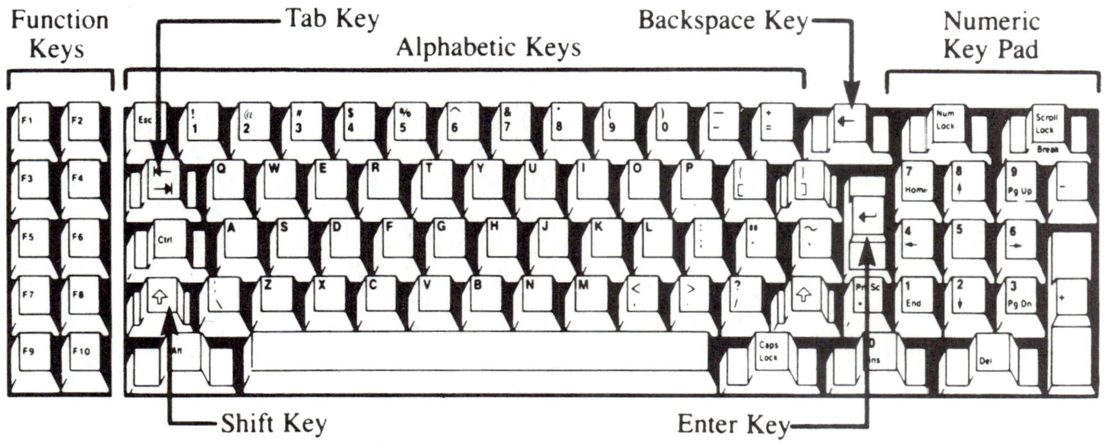

general editing operations. A standard keyboard is illustrated in Figure 1.3. An enhanced keyboard is shown in Figure 1.4.

For alphabetic and numeric characters, both keyboards have the same basic layout as a conventional typewriter. On the enhanced keyboard, the special-purpose keys, such as the **function keys**, the ENTER or RETURN key, the CTRL key, the ALT key, the directional arrow keys, the DEL key, the TAB key, and the cursor placement keys are more numerous and arranged differently. Moving from a standard keyboard to an enhanced keyboard requires only a minor adjustment in finger placement on the keyboard.

Figure 1.4

Enhanced Keyboard

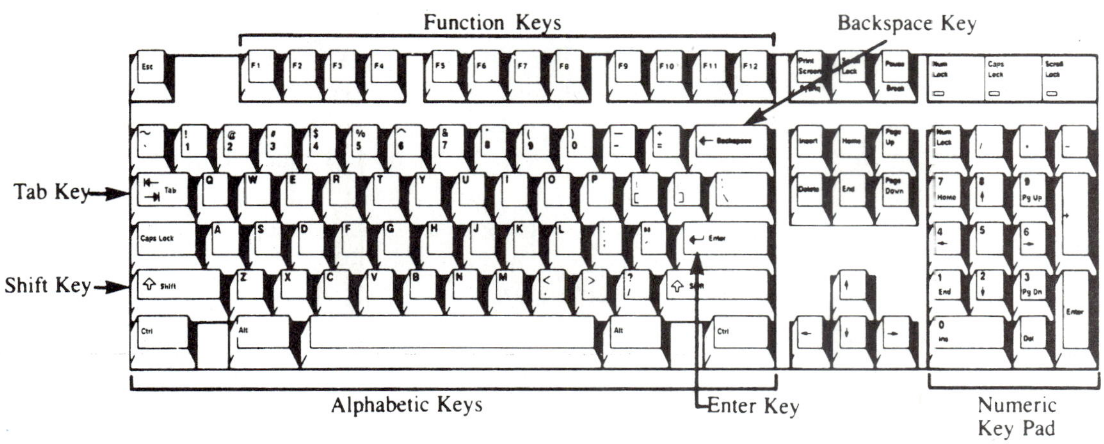

Although keys may be placed in different areas on different keyboards, their functions are the same with all personal computer keyboards. ENTER and RETURN are interchangeable labels for the key by which you signal to the operating system that it should accept and act on a given instruction. A keyboard may have neither word printed on the key, but only an arrow pointing down and to the left [ ] to indicate the accept key. Pressing the ENTER key signals the end of a command or input, or confirms an operation, much as the click of the mouse does. It also functions in the same way as the carriage return key on a typewriter. Also, it has further uses that you will see when you begin working with software.

Special Keys The function keys are numbered from F1 through F12. (Older keyboards may have only ten function keys.) The function keys have different meanings, depending on the functions for which they are programmed in specific software packages. You will soon discover, however, that many specific programs use the same function key for the same basic purpose. F10 is often a save key, F1 is often a help key, and so forth.

The NUMLOCK key enables you to use the numeric keypad, located on the right side of the keyboard, to enter a series of numbers quickly without using the top row of the standard character set. When NUMLOCK is not on (on some keyboards, indicated by a light to designate whether the key is on or off), those same keys move you around the screen—left, right, up, or down. This operation is referred to as **scrolling**. If you know the ten-key calculator pad, you will find the numeric keypad a real time saver. When NUMLOCK is on, you can enter many numbers very quickly.

The PRINT SCREEN (or PRTSCR) key is used to print the information currently displayed on your monitor. On some keyboards, you must hold down the SHIFT key, then press the PRTSCR key to activate a printout of the screen. This sends the 25 lines displayed on your monitor to the printer for a hard copy printout of the screen's contents. Screen characters that cannot be printed on your printer will be replaced with other symbols from the printer character set. Therefore the screen display will not appear the same as the output that you get when you choose a Print command from a **menu** (list of selections) in a regular program. The PRINT SCREEN key does not function as an immediate screen display when the *Windows* software is running; instead, the screen contents are stored in a **buffer**, or temporary storage area. This will be explained in Chapter 2.

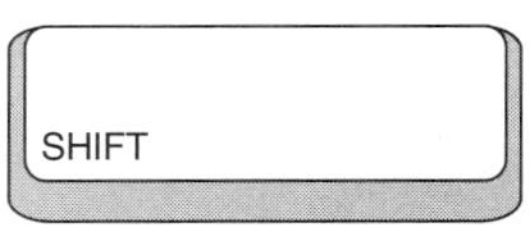

The SHIFT key is labeled with an open arrow [ ] or the word *Shift.* The two SHIFT keys operate in a similar fashion to the SHIFT keys on a typewriter. They change from lower-case to upper-case characters. However, like so many of the other special keys, they can also change the character set in issuing commands, that is, the meaning of a command changes, according to the special key you press along with a character. Thus the combinations SHIFT + M, ALT + M, and CTRL + M all mean something different from just typing the letter *M.* By combining special keys with regular character keys, you can represent many more alternatives with the same number of keys on the keyboard. If you could not use special keys in combination with regular keys, you would need a keyboard that was longer than the desktop on which your computer sits!

If you want several characters capitalized, as in a manuscript title, you may use the CAPS LOCK key to type all text in upper case. You must still use the SHIFT key to enter alternative characters for any key that has a double set of characters printed on it, such as the question mark (?), double quotes ("), numbers, or other special characters. Finally, if you press the SHIFT key while the CAPS LOCK is on, the alphabetic character pressed returns to lower case.

The TAB key is used to move to tab settings, just as on a typewriter. It can also be used to move from option box to option box in the *Works 3.0 for Windows* program. Option boxes are rectangles that offer a variety of choices to the user. The TAB key is likewise used in many other programs, including *Windows* itself, to move to a different selection area on the screen. You will become more familiar with the TAB key as you progress through the chapters of this book.

The ALT (or Alternate) key is a special key that does not appear on a standard typewriter keyboard. The ALT key was one of the first special keys placed on personal computer keyboards. Like the SHIFT key, it is used in combination with other character keys to select commands when using *Works 3.0 for Windows,* and other programs, as well. You can move in and out of the command line menu (the set of text choices at the top of the screen) with the ALT key if you do not wish to use the mouse.

The CTRL key is another special-purpose key that is unique to a computer keyboard; a typewriter does not have one. The CTRL key changes the character set; thus it is always used in conjunction with another key, just as the ALT and SHIFT keys are. The CTRL+BREAK or PAUSE+BREAK key combinations (depending on which keyboard you have) cancels whatever function the system is performing. (The plus sign here indicates that you hold down the CTRL key while you press the second key.) The CTRL+NUMLOCK combination, or the PAUSE key, halts whatever the system is doing until you press another key. Usually this combination of keystrokes freezes the screen display when information is scrolling too quickly to read comfortably. The CTRL key sometimes combines with letters, such as B for boldface and U for underline, for shortcut keystroke commands.

Because the CTRL and SHIFT keys must be used in conjunction with other keys, if you mistakenly press one or the other, nothing will happen. Simply release the key and no harm is done. In *Works 3.0 for Windows,* if you press the ALT key by mistake, you invoke the command line menu at the top of the screen.

The **ESC key** will soon become one of your best friends. In most programs (but not all), it is the "oops" key; it cancels the prior command. Thus, if you mistakenly enter a command, you can back out of it by pressing the ESC key. This key is always placed in the upper-left area of the keyboard, away from the regular character set so that you will not strike it inadvertently and cancel a process you did not want to cancel. As you begin to master *Works 3.0 for Windows,* you may be using the ESC key a lot. For example, if you press ALT instead of SHIFT when entering an upper-case letter, simply press the ESC key, and your command will be canceled. You may now proceed to use the correct key combination, or select with the mouse.

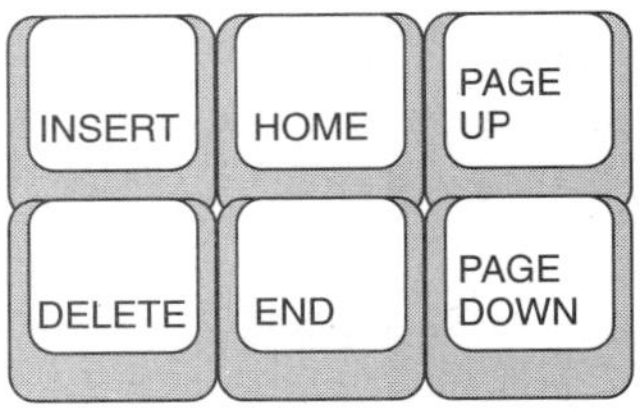

If you look closely at the keyboard illustrations (Figures 1.3 and 1.4), you will notice other special-purpose keys—the PAGE UP, PAGE DOWN, HOME, END, DELETE, INSERT, directional arrow (←, →, ↑, ↓) and BACKSPACE (←) keys. These keys aid in navigation through screens. They are often referred to as *editing keys* because they allow you to quickly position your **cursor**, or insertion point—the flashing input prompt that indicates where you are on the display and waits for a response from you. For example, in word processing, pressing PAGE UP will take you upward, or backward, one screenload or 25 lines of text. It will also take you backward one screen in a spreadsheet or database file.

The BACKSPACE key allows you to cancel one or more keystrokes that you have just entered. It backs up the insertion point one space and deletes the character in that space. Touch typists often know intuitively when they press incorrect keys. Having the BACKSPACE key conveniently located directly above the right-hand position allows them to quickly cancel typing errors and continue typing without breaking rhythm. You will soon find the easiest way for you to delete an unwanted character, by either pressing the BACKSPACE key immediately after you have made the error or waiting to use the DELETE key.

The DELETE key deletes the character to the right of the insertion point when you press the key. It deletes just one character at a time, so it is handy for correcting minor errors. Also, for a beginner, it is safer than working with blocks, or multiple lines, of text. You can do less harm if you delete characters one at a time with the DELETE key than you could selecting and deleting large blocks of text. To delete a number of characters, or even a whole sentence, you can hold down the DELETE key and it will quickly delete the characters to the right of the insertion point, one after another. Because holding down the key causes its action to repeat, the DELETE key is called a **repeating key**.

The INSERT key is used to insert text at a certain point in a word processing document. In many word processing applications, this key allows you to **toggle** (turn off or on) between an **insert mode** (in which new characters add to existing text) and a **typeover mode** (in which you replace existing characters by writing over them). *Works 3.0 for Windows,* however, is automatically in the insert mode when you open a file, and beginning users rarely move from the insert mode to the typeover mode. They simply type in the correct text at the spot where they wish, then delete any extraneous, incorrect text.

You will soon become very proficient at using these special keys, no matter which keyboard you use. If you have an **editing keypad** as well as the **numeric keypad,** as on an enhanced keyboard, you have a duplicate set of editing keys and can choose whichever is more comfortable for you. If you are just beginning with a computer, use the darker gray editing keypad and directional arrows to the left of the numeric keypad; reserve the numeric keys to enter numbers by leaving the NUMLOCK key in the ON position.

In *Works 3.0 for Windows* the special keys just covered perform the following tasks:

- TAB moves from one option, box, or field to another, in addition to moving to the traditional tab settings in word processing.
- ALT, used singly, activates menus; in combination with another key, it allows you to bypass the three-step menu selection process.
- CTRL is used with another key for quick commands:
  +HOME takes you to the top of a file, the first record in a database, etc.
  +END takes you to the bottom of a file, or the last record or row
  +PAGE UP takes you one record up in a database form
  +PAGE DOWN takes you one record down in a database form
  +ENTER forces a manual page break in word processing
- ESC backs you out of a command and cancels the operation.

Figure 1.5

Alternatives to a Keyboard; Four Common Types of Input Devices. (a) A mouse moves the cursor on the screen when the ball inside comes in contact with a flat surface. (b) The trackball is a real benefit for a crowded workspace! (c) The light pen is used to draw or issue commands when it touches the video monitor screen. It is commonly used for computer-aided drafting, (CAD). (d) This hand-held scanner is an efficient way to input both photos and text. (e) All you need is a pen with a notepad computer. These computers can read your handwriting.

(a)

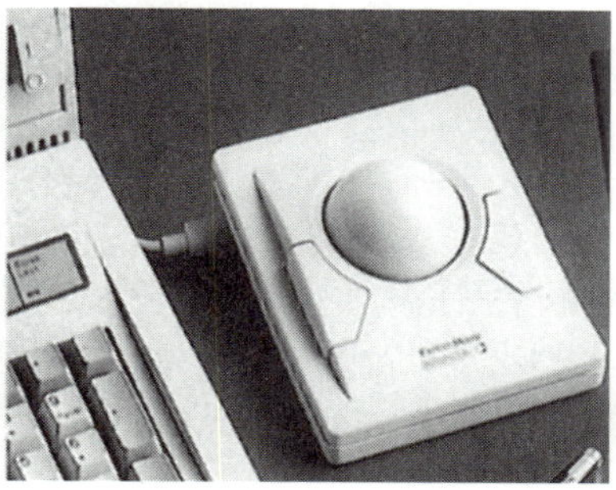

(b)

(c)

(d)

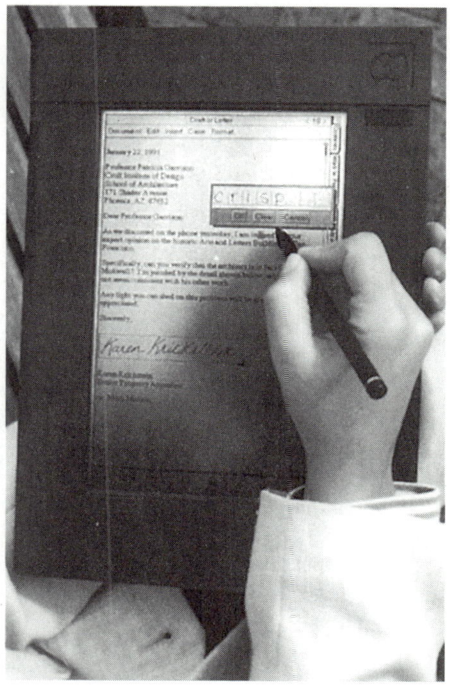

(e)

Scanner

Another familiar input device, the **scanner**, can interpret text or an image via a laser beam and translate it into a pattern that the computer can process. A scanner can recognize printed words, graphic illustrations, or even photographs and store the computer equivalent for future use, if you have a program that can manipulate the resulting pattern. The scanner operates in much the same way as a copy machine.

Although scanners can greatly speed entry of information and even allow you to incorporate photographs into documents, not many personal computer users employ these input devices at present. Scanners are relatively expensive, and their use takes up a lot of computer memory (a topic we will cover in a later section). Nevertheless, as more word processing packages incorporate features of **desktop publishing** (software that generates text and graphics in the same document), personal computer users are adding scanners as optional input hardware.

If you are not familiar with common input hardware, refer to Figure 1.5 and locate the items. The only essential input hardware for a personal computer is, of course, a keyboard. A mouse is required to use all of the options in *Works 3.0 for Windows,* and it certainly is recommended for all *Windows* software packages, but it is possible to use a personal computer without a mouse.

Output Hardware

Output hardware refers to the physical devices that allow the computer to display the results of input and processing. The most common output devices in personal computer systems are **monitors** and **printers**.

Monitor

The monitor is a visual display unit, resembling a television screen, that is attached to the system unit of the computer. Whether it contains a cathode ray tube like a television screen, or a liquid crystal or gas plasma display, it allows you to see the results of your input and processing. Video displays have improved markedly as personal computers have become more sophisticated. The first **monochrome** (literally, one-color) monitors have been replaced by **color graphics adapter (CGA)** displays, but systems also offer **enhanced graphic adapter (EGA)** displays, **video graphics array (VGA)** displays, and even very-high-resolution monitors, or **extended video graphics array (XGA)** monitors. The number and quality of **pixels,** or picture elements, on a screen affect its resolution. As the number of pixels in a monitor increases, the resolution of a screen display becomes higher.

The screen display is composed of a number of dots, or picture elements, that form the characters and pictures you see on the screen; the density of these dots is determined by the display adapter (a circuit board that is connected to the CPU, as discussed below). The density of pixels determines the resolution of the screen. The screen resolution is measured by the number of pixels horizontally by the number of pixels vertically. For example, a low-resolution screen would measure 320 pixels horizontally by 200 pixels vertically. A very-high-resolution monitor available today might measure 1,024 pixels by 768 pixels. Table 1.1 shows the various displays and their corresponding resolution levels.

Table 1.1 Monitor Resolutions

Display	Pixels
CGA	640 x 200
EGA	640 x 350
VGA	800 x 600
XGA	1,024 x 768

As mentioned before, displays can show output in several colors or one color, as white on black, or black on white, green, or amber. In a monochrome monitor, each pixel is represented by one dot. In a color monitor, each pixel is represented by three dots: red, green, and blue; electronically mixing these colors produces many colors.

Printer

Although it is not absolutely necessary for a personal computer system, if you want a hard copy or printout of what you produce with the microcomputer, you will need a printer. A wide range of printers is available for the personal computer today. The least expensive, impact-action **dot matrix printers**, form characters on paper by placing closely grouped collections of ink dots. Such a printer may have as few as nine pins on its printhead. Many today have 24 pins, which produce crisper characters. At the other extreme, in both cost and image quality, very sophisticated nonimpact laser printers transfer characters to paper by heat and pressure from a drum that contains toner which adheres to the paper by electrostatic charge.

Dot matrix printers are probably the most commonly used personal computer printers. They are inexpensive and fast, though they are criticized for noisy operation. Such printers have one of two types of **tractor feeds** that feed fanfolded, perforated paper across their printheads—either push or pull tractors. A **push tractor feed** conserves paper, is easier to operate, and allows you to scroll the paper backward without turning off the printer and readjusting the paper. Either type of tractor feed has spokes that catch the perforated strips on the side of each sheet of paper as it is fed onto the roller. Almost all dot matrix printers can also be used in **cut-sheet mode**, where one piece of paper is fed at a time. Dot matrix printers are very useful for multipart forms, such as NCR paper. Almost every dot matrix printer offers a lower-quality draft mode and a **near letter quality (NLQ) mode**, where the printhead goes over the array of dots several times. This produces a much higher quality of hard copy.

Ink jet printers and **laser printers** produce very clear, almost typeset-quality hard copy quickly and quietly. They are popular options today, when high-quality output is desired. Both of these types of nonimpact printers are page printers, and they require a great deal of memory to produce each printed page. Ink jet printers operate by ejecting ink from a nozzle to form a character. Ink jet printers are moderately priced and they produce good print quality, although they are almost always slower than dot matrix printers.

Although still somewhat expensive and temperamental, laser printers have allowed personal computer systems to produce high-quality documents. Laser printers combine photo-copier technology and printer technology; they operate by a light source reflecting images onto a photosensitive drum via mirrors. Particles of toner adhere to the drum, and characters are formed on paper by transferring those particles to the paper. Most personal computer laser printers can output about four pages a minute, but some can print up to ten pages a minute. This is much slower than the commercial laser printers that have been used in businesses for some time, but the print quality of both classes of laser printers is excellent.

Color printers are available with both laser and ink jet technology; some dot matrix printers can even produce color output. Color ink jet printers are popular and affordable color printers used with personal systems today. Tastefully selected color output can be very impressive, and the cost of color ink jet printers is reasonable. Color laser printers and six-color pen plotters are still used almost exclusively in business systems.

Figure 1.6

(a) An Ink jet Printer, (b) A Laser Printer, (c) A Dot Matrix Printer

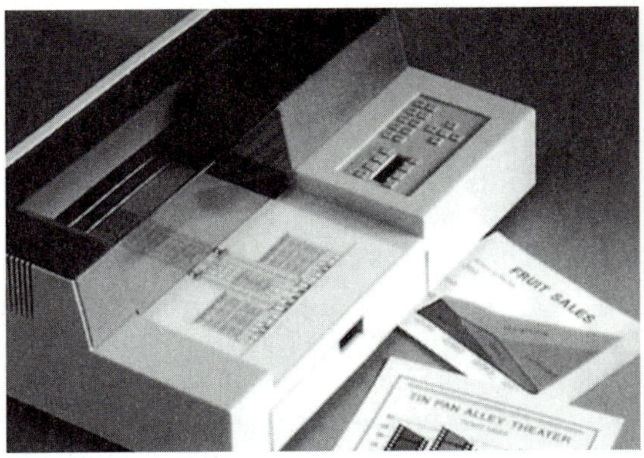

(a)

(b)

(c)

You can spend as much time and money selecting a printer as for the system unit itself. Various types of printers are illustrated in Figure 1.6.

Personal computer systems may include other input/output devices, as well. Sometimes one piece of hardware can double for both, as a touch-screen monitor can. Joysticks, light pens, and bar code readers are also used with personal systems. For now you need only to remember that input hardware allows you to enter data into the computer, while output hardware allows you to display that data in some form.

Processing Hardware

Processing hardware is the equipment that accepts input, stores it, and then performs various operations on it prior to output.

CPU

The heart of any computer system is the **central processing unit (CPU)**. A personal computer uses a microprocessor for its central processing unit. A microprocessor chip contains many integrated circuits on a quarter-inch silicon wafer. The actual work, or processing, of a computer system takes place here. IBM or compatible personal computers began with Intel's 8088 microprocessor, perhaps with an 8087 math coprocessor to help speed up mathematical calculations. They progressed to the more powerful 80286 microprocessor chip, and then to the 80386/SX chip, which could manipulate more internal data. The true 80386 chip could manipulate more data both internally and externally, and the 80486 chip increased operating speeds further, as high as 33/66 megahertz (a measure of the speed of a computing cycle, in millions of cycles a second). Finally, Intel's new Pentium chips and the PowerPC processor (a chip by Motorola that will run both Apple and IBM computers) contain approximately 3 million transistors. CPUs have become faster and more powerful with each new generation of micro-

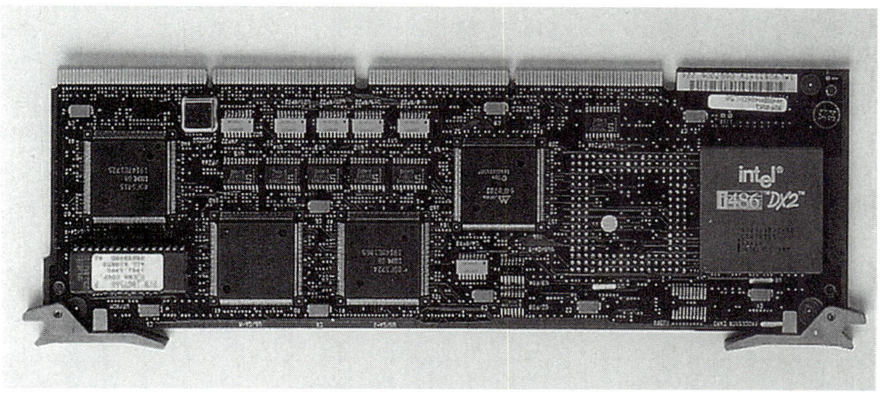

Figure 1.7

Top View of a PC's Motherboard

processor. As the appetite for more sophisticated and more graphically oriented computing grew, the power of central processing units had to grow, as well. The capabilities of these various microchips will become more clear as you become more computer literate.

You will find it helpful to pull the cover off a system unit as shown in Figure 1.7 and explore the **motherboard** (the main circuit board) as you read about processing hardware, memory, and storage devices. What seems to be very complex and unfamiliar now will become remarkably simple upon further investigation. For now, just know that the capacity and speed of your computing depends on the type of CPU the computer contains.

Main Memory (RAM)

Most of the data that awaits processing by the central processing unit is stored in the computer's **RAM (random access memory)**. RAM is composed of a number of integrated circuits; their number and capacity determine the amount of memory a system has. RAM provides temporary storage of programs and data while the computer has power. RAM is called memory because data must be stored here before it can be processed; no computing can be done without such a storage area in which to place instructions and information. Memory is immediately accessible to the CPU; data in **secondary storage** (on magnetic disks) must be moved to RAM before it can be processed.

RAM is volatile, limited, and relatively expensive. The term *volatile* means that if you trip on the cord connecting your computer to the electrical outlet so that power is cut off, everything in RAM is gone instantly! RAM is also limited; older personal computers have only 640K (the equivalent of about 640,000 characters, or bytes) of RAM; newer models often have up to 16 MB (the equivalent of about 16 million characters) and they can go as high as 64 MB. **Bytes** are the basic units of measurement in computer memory. Each byte is composed of eight **bits**, or binary digits; together they represent a character or number to the computer. Figure 1.8 illustrates the 0/1 representation scheme that is used in all computers. Now 2 million characters may seem like a great deal of memory, but loading several large programs may leave only a relatively small amount of room for data. There is a limit to what you can store in the memory of a personal computer.

Figure 1.8

Bits and Bytes

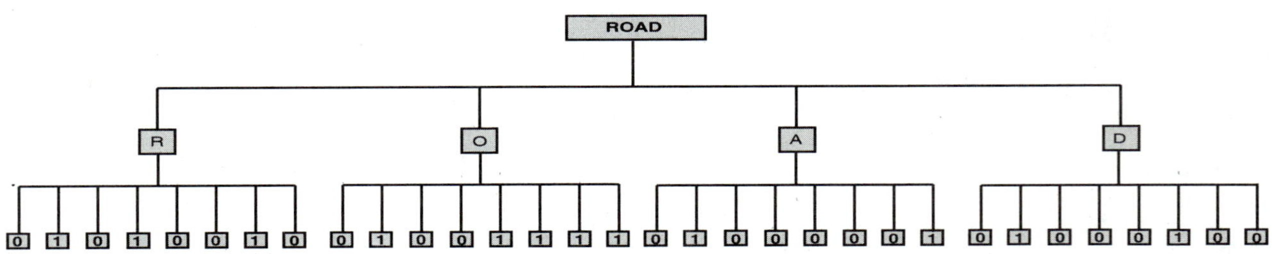

8 bits = 1 byte = 1 character

Read Only Memory (ROM)

The motherboard of a personal computer offers another, more permanent type of memory that uses a different kind of microchip. This is **ROM (read only memory)**. As its name suggests, the material in ROM is meant only to be read and not written to, or changed, once installed. Certain programming instructions necessary for the computer to function correctly are included on ROM chips. All of the material in ROM is permanent in the sense that turning off the machine does not remove the information included on those microchips. It can be read and executed over and over again when the machine is turned on, but it cannot be changed without replacing the ROM chips themselves.

Cache Memory

Some microcomputers exploit another type of memory called *cache memory.* This is a small amount of very fast RAM that lies between main memory and the CPU. Cache memory was added to microcomputer designs when microprocessors went beyond 20 MHz to improve transfer rates and raise processor speeds by helping system memory to keep up with processors. The cache unit stores copies of recently read instructions and other data. When the correct data is found in the cache (known as a *hit*) the processor does not have to go to memory for it (as it does in a *miss*). The further developments of 486 technology have gotten even more complicated with internal and external caches, but that is beyond our scope. Suffice it to say that cache memory is extremely important in the processing speed of modern microcomputers.

Input/Output Ports

On the rear of the system unit of a personal computer are **ports**, which resemble sockets into which you can plug peripherals (external components like a printer or a mouse). The ports can be either **serial ports** (transporting data one bit at a time), or **parallel ports** (transporting data eight bits, or a byte, at a time). A mouse or an external **modem** (modulator–demodulator for communications between computers) plugs into a serial port; a printer often plugs into a parallel port.

Expansion Slots

Your personal computer probably has several **expansion slots**, or openings where you can insert extra circuit boards to add components such as more memory, an internal modem, a hardcard (a hard disk equivalent mounted on a circuit board), or other peripherals. Expansion slots allow your computer system to grow along with your expertise and needs.

A completely new motherboard can be installed if you wish to expand beyond the two or three slots included with the original system.

Modem

A modem is a piece of hardware that accommodates computer-to-computer communications across geographic distances. As we have stated, the term stands for *modulator–demodulator.* Computers can connect to each other over public telephone lines through this piece of hardware. Many computers sold today include modems.

A modem translates the digital I/O code of the computer to the **analog**, or continuous, wave patterns that travel over telephone lines. The receiving modem then demodulates, or retranslates, the signal to the **digital** (on/off, discrete) code that the computer uses. A software communications program is also required for computers to "talk" to one another. You will study different types of modems and software settings when we discuss data communications in detail in Chapter 12.

Secondary Storage Hardware

The preceding discussion touched on the limitations of primary memory, or RAM, and the need for a solution to the data storage dilemma. That solution is secondary storage. You cannot permanently store any computer information for eventual reuse without access to an alternative medium, such as magnetic tape, a magnetic disk, or an optical disk. Writing information to such a medium requires storage hardware. **Disk drives** allow for secondary storage by writing to and reading from magnetic disks.

Floppy Disk Drive

Most personal computers have at least one **disk drive** that writes information permanently to a **floppy disk** (also called a **diskette**). (The term *floppy* arose because the first diskettes, the 8 inch size, were flexible rather than rigid.) A floppy disk drive contains at least one **read/write head** similar to the mechanical devices that read or record cassette tapes. They transfer information in main memory to a more permanent, reliable form on a magnetic medium. They also transfer data from diskette back to RAM. This hardware, then, allows a more stable, inexpensive, and less limited computing environment.

Floppy disk drives allow you to write information to a medium that is portable. They come in several sizes for personal computers, from 5.25-inch drives to 3.5-inch drives, even to 2-inch drives. The corresponding diskettes differ in appearance, size, and construction, but their function is the same—to store information in a more permanent form than RAM, and to allow it to be copied into memory for action by the central processing unit.

Density refers to how compactly data is stored on the surface of the medium—how many bytes can be stored on a diskette. Floppy disks for IBM and compatible microcomputers come in two densities, double density and high density. Double-density diskettes cannot hold as much data as high-density diskettes. A double-density drive cannot read data from a high-density diskette; however, a high-density drive can read data from a double-density diskette. Diskettes are clearly marked to indicate the densities they are capable of storing, but disk drives are usually not marked as either high-density or double-density drives. Microcomputers still commonly have mixtures of double-density and high-density drives in school, home, and business settings; the lower-density disk will work in all settings, whereas the high-density disk restricts you to high-density drives.

Hard Disk Drive

Personal computers sold today also include **hard disk drives**, or fixed disks. A hard disk drive is a high-speed, large-capacity secondary storage unit. A hard disk can hold many times more data than a floppy disk, and the read/write heads can access that data much faster. A hard disk in a typical system usually holds from 80 to more than 200 MB of data. Figure 1.9 shows the interior of a hard disk drive, including the read/write head that performs the mechanical actions of reading data into memory or writing it to disk.

Figure 1.9

Interior of a hard disk drive showing read/write heads

Hard disks are also more resistant to data loss and damage than floppy disks because the hard disk is hermetically sealed. The entire drive operates inside a metal or plastic case, where it is relatively safe from dust, smoke, magnetic charges, and other threats to the storage medium. One disadvantage of a hard disk is that the medium and the information stored on it cannot be removed from the system unit and taken from the site for safekeeping. Removable hard disks do exist, but they are not common in personal computer systems. Therefore, users must make **backup**, or reserve, copies of the contents of the disk regularly. We will discuss backing up your disks in more detail in Chapter 3, when you are ready to learn the operating system commands to perform this task.

The medium, or storage material, to which floppy disk drives write and from which they read, is coated with magnetic oxide so that the read/write heads can record or read spots of positive or negative polarity on the surface. Hard disks, as you have already seen, have this material sealed within the disk drive. A coating of magnetic oxide is also present on all floppy disks or diskettes.

Drive Configurations

As was noted, two kinds of disk drives are common—hard drives and diskette drives. Figure 1.10 illustrates the possible disk drive configurations found in personal computers. Most systems today include one hard drive and one or two diskette drives. If you purchase a computer today with a hard drive and two diskette drives, the diskette drives will most likely be of different sizes and capacities. One will accept 3.5-inch diskettes capable of holding approximately 720 KB (double-density diskettes) or 1.44 MB (high-density diskettes), and the other will accept 5.25-inch diskettes capable of holding approximately 360KB (double-density diskettes) or 1.2 megabytes (high-density diskettes).

Figure 1.10

Typical Microcomputer Case with 1 Hard Drive and Two Floppy Drives and an External CD-ROM Drive

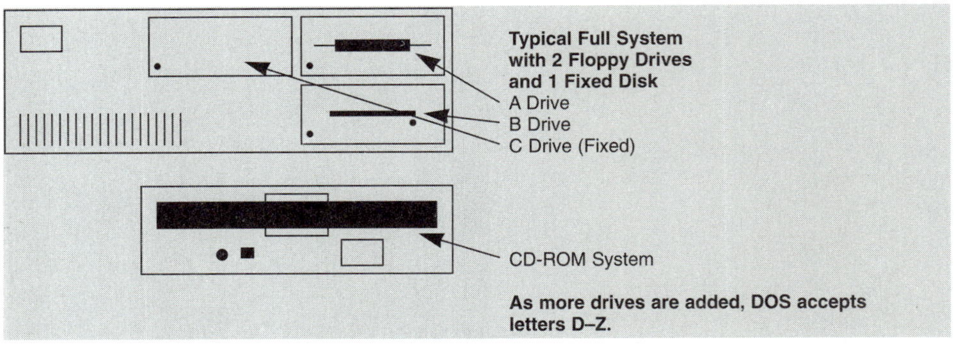

Optical Disk Drive

In the past decade optical technology has brought the **CD-ROM** (Compact Disk-Read Only Memory) drive to personal computers. CD-ROM drives read laser-generated compact disks on which information is already permanently written. The information cannot be written over; it can only be read. Data is stored on the disk by burning a pattern of bubbles on the surface with a laser beam. You can purchase compact disks containing encyclopedias, general databases, clip-art pictures for use in desktop publishing, and even **multimedia** presentations (which can combine text, graphics, video images, sound, animation, and interactive programming) such as a video of an event, complete with sound.

WORM (write once, read many times) **drives** allow you to write to an optical disk and preserve it for future use. We still do not have reliable erasable optical drives for personal computers, which would allow users to rewrite to the surface many times but that advance is expected within the decade.

Compact disks can store many times more information than a floppy diskette; a 640 to 650 MB capacity is standard. An entire 20-volume set of encyclopedias can be stored on one CD-ROM disk. Thus, it is very efficient to store information that is not going to change over time on a compact disk and retrieve it at will with a CD-ROM drive. Now that multimedia software is available, CD-ROM drives are becoming more popular with personal computer users, even though access to the data is somewhat slower than with magnetic hard disk drives.

When you add a CD-ROM drive to your system, it should be accompanied by several other pieces of hardware. Multimedia software requires speakers along with a sound card plugged into an available expansion slot for quality audio output, a super VGA monitor, and perhaps even a microphone for recording. In addition, to use a CD-ROM drive, you must have a software driver that recognizes the existence of the foreign storage device; the operating system software (DOS) does not recognize CD-ROM drives without a special software program. Adding the multimedia capability to a system's hardware takes the personal computer user to a whole new level of computing. CD-ROM drives are rapidly becoming standard fixtures on new personal computer systems.

Multi-media computer

Personal Computer Software

We have spent a good deal of time discussing the physical elements, or the hardware, of a personal computer system. A computer system is much more than its physical components, however. Without instructions, or software, the most elaborate collection of hardware can do nothing. Thus, we now turn to the second major component of computer systems—software.

All computers, from mainframes to micros, are **digital processing devices**; they process only the binary digits (bits) that we discussed in connection with RAM. Humans cannot readily process a series of zeroes and ones. Thankfully, however, we have software, or stored sets of instructions, to do this for us.

Software programs are saved to a medium (disk) so that the series of instructions can be repeated upon the demand of the computer user—you. Although it is possible to write your own software programs, save them to disk, and run them for specific tasks, most personal computer users purchase commercial software packages to help them perform specific tasks such as writing letters, figuring home budgets, or keeping track of music collections. The availability of many different types of commercial software makes the computer a flexible, general problem-solving tool.

Application Software

The programs, or series of instructions, that allow us to do a specific type of task on a personal computer are called *application software.* This category of software includes word processing programs, spreadsheet programs, database programs, presentation graphics programs, and even the games we play on the personal computer. Even nonusers of computers are familiar with the names of some of the more popular applications. We can further divide application software into integrated and independent, or stand-alone, packages.

Examples of popular applications software packages

Integrated Software

Software programs that combine more than one type of application or module in a single package are referred to as **integrated software**. Most of the integrated programs have, at the very least, a word processor to generate text; a spreadsheet to manipulate, store, and retrieve numbers; and a database application to keep records. The integrated package you will use with this book, *Works 3.0 for Windows,* has five main components—a word processing program, a spreadsheet program, a graphing program to visually represent spreadsheet numbers, a database program, and a communications program to allow your computer to communicate with other computers.

An integrated package has the same main menu, or beginning list of selections, for all modules. This makes the package much easier to learn than a string of unrelated applications. Many of the submenus, or lists of more specific selections, also correspond. In an integrated package, it is very easy to move from one module to another, say from a spreadsheet into a word processing document, because the paths you follow to perform similar functions are familiar. The **interface**, or layer of dialog between you and the program that allows you to interact with it in a user-friendly manner, is consistent throughout all modules in an integrated package. In *Works 3.0 for Windows,* the interface takes the form of pull-down windows that present command choices for selection. **Option boxes** list choices framed in rectangles on the screen, and **dialog boxes** present clear, simple messages to the user.

In an integrated package, the keystrokes you use to create a document in the word processor are the same as the keystrokes you use to construct a worksheet in the spreadsheet module; they are common to similar functions in all of the modules. For this reason, the integrated package is a wise choice. The *Windows* utility program under which *Works for Windows* runs is based on this same integrated philosophy; many of the same tasks are repeated in various parts of the *Windows* interface using the same keystrokes, viewing the same basic layout.

Stand-Alone Applications

A **stand-alone,** or independent, **application** is dedicated to one general computing task—whether it be word processing to create text files or database management to store and retrieve records in many different ways. Independent applications are distinguished by their power and sophistication. Even the best integrated package is not as powerful or multifaceted as its independent counterparts. The stand-alone application is usually more expensive and more technically advanced than the integrated application. When you are ready to dedicate the major portion of your computing time to spreadsheets, for example, you may decide to purchase *Excel* or *Lotus 1-2-3.*

If you perform a variety of tasks on your personal computer, but never go into great depth in any one application, you may prefer to stay with an integrated package indefinitely. On the other hand, if you submit manuscripts for publication or do a great deal of accounting, you will undoubtedly move to an independent, more powerful word processing or spreadsheet application. Once you learn the basic concepts of personal computing, you can select software that suits your needs, because the principles apply to other applications.

The newest type of application packages offers **suites** of applications programs that combine different functions in an attempt to give the user the best of both software choices—the ease of integrated packages and the power of standalone applications. Packages such as Microsoft *Office for Windows, WordPerfect Office,* or *Lotus SmartSuite* offer independent word processing, spreadsheet, database, and communication applications boxed together.

Systems Software

The user's freedom of choice with application software does not apply to **systems software**—the instructions that allow application software to work with hardware to produce a meaningful product. Application software is optional; systems software is not. You must have the proper systems software for your particular hardware, or you can do no computing. Systems software performs tasks like managing the input/output (I/O) of data, managing the allocation of main memory, and managing the many files on a disk. It is the traffic cop of the personal computer system.

While systems software includes several types of programs, you will be concerned primarily with the **operating system** (the topic of Chapter 3). In your case, it is a version of DOS (Disk Operating System): either PC-DOS for an IBM machine, or MS-DOS for an IBM-compatible personal computer. Of the several different operating systems for personal computers, DOS is by far the most common. The newer IBM and compatible personal computers with 80386 or greater microprocessors may also use the new *OS/2* operating system. It allows multitasking operations (running numerous programs simultaneously) and multithreading (running numerous segments within each program simultaneously). Microsoft *Windows NT* is another new operating system that promises better performance in business environments. A new version of *Windows* for personal computers, code name *Chicago*, is on the drawing board.

Although we have stressed your range of choice in application software, this faces one important limitation: the application program that you use must run with the operating system for your particular computer. That is why you cannot take the *Works 3.0* program from a Macintosh computer, which runs the Systems 7 operating system, and run it on an IBM-compatible machine.

There is a specific version of DOS for the Apple line of personal computers. There is also a special version of Unix (a popular operating system for larger computers) for the AT&T microcomputers. The point is that you must use the operating system written for your particular hardware system, and you must purchase application programs that run on that operating system. To run *Works 3.0 for Windows,* you must have version 3.1 or later of MS-DOS or PC-DOS. Although many users have termed *Windows* an operating system, it is not. It is a component of systems software, an interface. *Windows* cannot run without an operating system; it relies on DOS or *OS/2* for operation. We restrict this text to personal computers that use DOS.

Systems software is concerned with the system operations of your computer, that is, the primitive operations of the computer that allow the hardware to read from or write to disk, store certain data in specific memory locations, manage the way information is sent to a printer, and so forth. Unlike application programs, systems software is necessary for computing. The operating system must be present in memory during the entire computing session; it underlies all application software, which depends on it for the primitive tasks like those listed. The operating system is the first software to be loaded into memory and the last to be cleared when turning off the machine.

All operating systems have command interpreters that allow them to perform tasks at the command of the user, like preparing a disk for use, deleting files, and so forth. You will learn some of the more important DOS commands when you study Chapter 3. You will also learn how to access these commands from the *Windows* File Manager. The operating system performs many other tasks in the background of which you are never aware, nor do you need to be concerned with them. The ever vigilant operating system manages your computing session so that applications programs do not interfere with each other. It also keeps track of where each data item is stored in memory.

Other types of systems software besides operating systems perform a range of functions. Systems software includes programming languages, with or without **compilers** (systems software that translates specific programming code into machine-readable form) and **utility programs** that diagnose hardware problems and optimize storage of files on disk. Other systems programs can back up (make additional copies of) the contents of an entire hard disk in a minute or two. In addition, special interface systems programs, such as *Windows,* alter the operating system's user interface. Although personal computer users are often not as aware of systems software as of application software, nor as well-versed in its operation, it is the necessary software for the operation of a computer.

All of these components—the hardware, the software, the unique data that you input into the personal computer system, and of course, you, the user—must work together as a team to derive any benefit from a microcomputer. This working group of components makes the personal computer an efficient tool for handling today's information needs.

Chapter Summary

A personal computer is a microcomputer system that consists of (1) hardware (physical components), (2) software (instructions), (3) data, and (4) the user—the human who uses the computer system as a general problem solving tool.

Hardware consists of input, output, processing, and storage components. Software consists of systems software, such as the operating system, and application software. The operating system performs the primitive operations of a computer. It controls input, output, and processing. Application software enables the user to do specific tasks on the computer.

Integrated application software is easier for a beginner to learn and use. Such a package generally combines a word processor, spreadsheet, and database with a common user interface. It is often the only software package many personal computer users will ever need to learn because it serves all of their needs.

Independent application software refers to stand-alone programs that are dedicated to specific tasks, such as word processing. While they can perform more functions than integrated software packages, they are usually more complex than necessary for a beginner.

Suites offer independent applications that share a common user application interface. The user stores individual units of work created with an application in files on secondary storage such as floppy disks.

The personal computer is one of our newest and most useful tools to handle information.

KEY TERMS

- American Standard Code for Information Interchange
- analog
- ASCII
- backup
- bit
- buffer
- byte
- CD-ROM
- central processing unit
- CGA
- chip
- color graphics adapter
- common user application
- compiler
- CPU
- cut-sheet mode
- data
- density
- desktop publishing
- dialog box
- digital
- digital processing device
- disk drive
- diskette
- DOS
- dot matrix printer
- editing keypad
- EGA
- enhanced graphics adapter
- ESC key
- expansion slot
- extended video graphics array
- floppy disk
- function key
- gigabyte
- hard disk drive
- hardware
- ink jet printer
- input hardware
- insert mode
- integrated software
- interface
- keyboard
- laser printer
- letter quality printing
- mainframe
- main memory
- menu
- microcomputer
- microprocessor
- minicomputer
- modem
- monitor
- monochrome
- motherboard
- mouse
- multimedia
- near letter quality mode
- NLQ
- numeric keypad
- operating system
- option box
- output hardware
- parallel port
- personal computer
- pixel
- port
- printer
- push tractor feed
- random access memory
- RAM
- read only memory
- read/write head
- repeating key
- ROM
- scanner
- screen dump
- scrolling
- secondary storage
- serial port
- software
- stand-alone application
- suite
- supercomputer
- systems software
- toggle
- tractor feed
- typeover mode
- utility program
- VGA
- video graphics array
- WORM drive
- XGA

REVIEW QUESTIONS

1. What is a computer system?
2. Explain the differences between a microcomputer, a minicomputer, a mainframe, and a supercomputer.
3. Describe the physical components that make up a personal computer system.

4. List some of the personal computer hardware that is used for input.
5. Explain the use of function keys.
6. What is a mouse? When would you find a mouse useful?
7. What is a scanner? What purpose does it serve?
8. Define VGA, and XGA. How do the resolution levels of these monitor types differ?
9. Explain the difference between impact and nonimpact printers.
10. What is the difference between near-letter-quality and letter-quality printing? Describe a situation in which each type of print quality would be acceptable.
11. Recall the differences in cost, operation, and print quality between dot matrix, ink jet, and laser printers.
12. List the different microprocessor chip model numbers for IBM and compatible computers. How do their capabilities differ?
13. Define RAM and ROM. Explain what they contribute to a computer.
14. Explain the concept of a byte. How are bytes used to represent data in a computer?
15. What is the source of the word *modem,* and what function does this device perform?
16. Define the meaning and use of cache memory.
17. Explain the functions performed by expansion slots.
18. Explain the difference between hard disks and floppy disks in terms of (a) capacity, (b) density, and (c) retrieval speed.
19. Explain the differences between an integrated and a stand-alone software package. Compare and contrast each of these to a suite of programs.
20. Name and describe the purposes of the main categories of (a) application software, and (b) systems software.

FIELD EXERCISES

For each of the following software exercises, make arrangements with your instructor, or visit your campus library or a local computer store. Each exercise requires a report or sketch. A presentation or discussion may be substituted for the report, at your instructor's discretion.

Exercise 1.1

1. View the inside of a computer's system unit. Sources of sample machines include your campus lab, your instructor's office computer, a local computer store, or your library's copy of *PC World* or *PC* magazine ads featuring system units.

2. Sketch the motherboard. Identify ROM, RAM, CPU, expansion slots, serial and parallel ports, power supply, hard disk, and floppy disk drives in your sketch.

Exercise 1.2

1. Compare VGA, and XGA color monitors.
2. Write a short report on the differences in resolution (picture clarity) and cost you found between each of these monitors.

Exercise 1.3

1. Compare 486SX, DX, DX2 and DX4 microprocessors to the Pentium chip in terms of operational speed and cost.
2. Write a short report on your findings.

Exercise 1.4

1. Research the differences in communicating with a personal computer via a mouse or keyboard.
2. Write a short report on your findings.

Exercise 1.5

1. Compare the resolution of hard copy produced by 9-pin dot matrix, 18/24-pin dot matrix, ink jet, and laser printers.
2. Write a short report on the differences you observed.

Exercise 1.6

1. View a demonstration of a color dot matrix printer and a color ink jet printer.
2. Write a short report on your findings.

Exercise 1.7

1. Examine an exposed personal computer CPU under a magnifying glass, or research the internal characteristics of the CPU chip in the library.
2. Write a short report about what you saw or discovered.

Exercise 1.8

1. Compare the keyboard offered with an IBM personal computer with those offered by at least two IBM-compatible computer manufacturers. What similarities and differences did you note with regard to features, number and position of keys, touch, and price?
2. Write a short report on your findings.

Exercise 1.9

1. Compare an internal and an external modem.
2. Write a short report about the advantages and disadvantages of each.

Exercise 1.10

1. View a scanner demonstration.
2. Write a short report about how this device works and its usefulness as an input device.

Chapter 2

Introduction to *Works 3.0 for Windows* and the *Windows* Interface

Objectives

After studying this chapter you will be able to:

- *Define the term* interface
- *Explain the purpose and characteristics of an interface*
- *Describe the two types of interfaces*
- *Install* Works 3.0 for Windows *on a microcomputer*
- *Navigate comfortably through the* Windows *interface*
- *Load* Works 3.0 for Windows *into memory for use*
- *Use the* Works 3.0 for Windows *help function*
- *Use the* Works 3.0 for Windows *tutorial*
- *Execute the keystrokes that move you through the* Works 3.0 for Windows *menus*
- *Execute the keystrokes to exit from* Works 3.0 for Windows

Application Program Interfaces

Definition

Every program written for the personal computer user includes an interface, or intermediary layer between the user and the actual functions of the application. This is a layer of presentation on top of the actual technical characteristics of the program. How the program appears to you on the screen, how you move between applications, how you enter menus, how you enter or cancel commands—all of these characteristics depend on the interface of the particular program you are using.

Purpose

The purpose of the interface is to make the program more user friendly. (That can be a very relative term for beginning computer users!) The quality of the interface determines how easily you can learn and operate a program and how smoothly you can use it once you are familiar with it. The interface, then, is concerned entirely with you, the user, and has no bearing on how powerful or complex the program is. The interfaces of application programs have improved tremendously since the first personal computer programs were developed. Software designers have invested much time and money in developing interfaces that are more intuitive and natural, and thus easier to use, than the programs of their competitors. Integrated programs, in particular, since they are aimed at beginning computer users, usually have more highly developed interfaces.

Characteristics of Interfaces

Menus

Every application program has some type of **menu system** that drives the program. The user chooses from a list of selections to enter a specific command. You may choose by clicking the mouse after pointing to a choice (the point and click technique), typing a number, or highlighting a selection with the mouse or directional arrows to change the display to **reverse video** (the opposite contrast, with the background light and the foreground letters dark blue or another contrasting color). You may even double-click an icon (a picture). All of the new presentation system programs like *Windows*, the *DOS SHELL*, and *Presentation Manager* for OS/2 have menu selection systems, based on either icons or text.

Top-Down Design

The menu system in a program has an order, or hierarchy, of commands that is often referred to as **top-down design**. When this term is applied to an interface, it means that the program is designed to take you from the general to the specific as you make your selections. You go from one general selection (maybe the File menu in *Works*) to a more specific selection (maybe the Open command), and proceed in this way until you reach the exact task you wish to perform (maybe choosing the file LETTER1.WPS to open). This type of organization in a program makes it easier to navigate through the menu system and to move back out when you finish a task. Layers are sequenced from the most general to the most specific, in true hierarchical form.

Windows/Displays

The display you see on the monitor while using an application program is usually in the form of a **window**, or rectangular box. Several, variously sized rectangles may appear on the screen, as in the *Windows* interface, or one rectangle may occupy the entire viewing surface. Each rectangle will have a frame, or border that identifies it.

Interfaces vary widely in the forms that their presentations take. Some programs have pull-down windows, like *Works*. Some have command line menus at the top or bottom of the screen; some have cascading windows that lie one on top of another; some split the screen into several different areas. *Works* has pull-down windows of submenus under the headings in the main menu across the top of the screen. It also has a **tool bar** of **icons** (pictures, or graphic representations of objects and functions) from which you may choose options.

Usually an interface will have, at the minimum, an area of display that is a menu, an area that is a status and/or message line, and a work area where your work is displayed. The type of interface your program has will determine what form your selection will take, but areas will be reserved for certain functions, and those areas will stand out in some way or another from the rest of the screen. You input your choice with a point and click of the mouse, or with keystrokes. Figure 2.13 on page 55 shows a **tile** arrangement in the *Windows* interface.

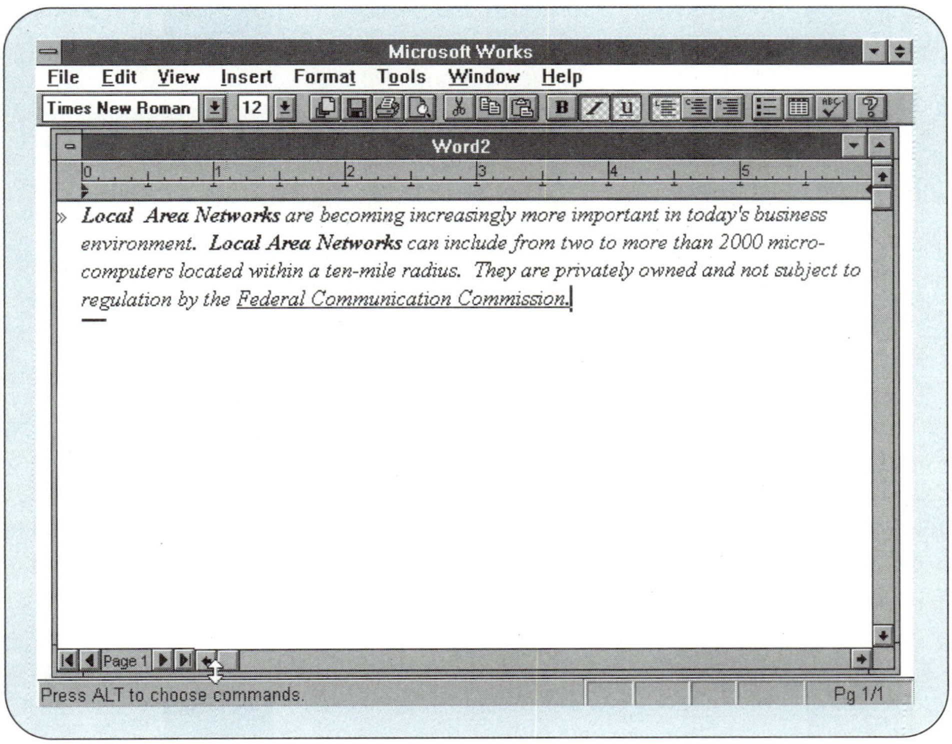

Figure 2.1

A Document Containing Underlining, Bold, and Italics

An increasingly popular feature of application program interfaces is the **WYSIWYG**, or "what you see is what you get," display. This type of display shows you exactly how your text will look when it is printed; this is a particularly useful feature for word processing. You see the text underlined on the screen if you have used the underline format in your document. If you have used superscript (text or numbers raised one-half line above the rest of the text, and usually in a smaller type size), the small numbers will be raised on the screen, away from the rest of the text. *Works 3.0 for Windows* has a WYSIWYG interface. Figure 2.1 shows a word processing document that includes italics, underlining, and bold type.

Some programs have **view**, or **preview**, options that allow you to preview a file, page by page, exactly as it will appear when it is printed. This is another feature that depends on the particular interface of the program. The preview option allows you to page forward or backward, or even **zoom** in by magnifying the display by 100 percent or 200 percent.

Default Settings

Interfaces of all application programs assume some basic formats or commands. These **default settings** are choices made for you. If you do not change them, the program will assume that those settings satisfy you, and you can proceed with your task without making a choice on every single specification. For instance, *Works* assumes that a word processing document will print on 8.5-inch by 11-inch paper with 66 lines, 55 of which contain text that is single spaced with normal-sized characters. These are default settings. You do not have to make decisions on paper size, line spacing, font size, and so forth if you want to accept the default settings.

Default settings are always the most common characteristics, whether for the width of a column in a spreadsheet or the size of print in a word processing document. You will discover in Chapter 3 that DOS and the *Windows* File Manager have many default settings. Defaults make life easier and programs much more user friendly for beginning computer users. When you are more proficient at using a program, you can change these default settings if you wish.

Special Keys

Most programs use at least a few of the keyboard's function keys to automate some commands. You have already seen in Chapter 1 that *Works* makes use of some **special keys**. Many times, the software author will use a function key to perform the same automated task that that key performs in other programs. This is true of *Works*, as well. The F2 key, for instance, is commonly used as an edit key in many applications, from spreadsheets to databases. Most program interfaces make similar uses of the HOME, DELETE, PAGE UP, PAGE DOWN, and END keys. The set of preprogrammed choices of certain keys is a characteristic of a program's interface.

The ESC key is used to cancel a command in *Works*, and in many other programs, as well. It allows for a graceful exit should you change your mind about a chosen process; you can back out of a command. It is also used to move out of the menu into the work area in some spreadsheet programs. The F1 function key is almost universally a way of moving into on-line help systems.

On-Line Help

On-line help is one of the newest and most user friendly attributes of software applications. It offers tutorial and reference material about your particular program. Rather than stopping work to look up the procedure for a particular task in the printed documentation (user manual), you can press the F1 key or click on Help in the menu bar and receive instructions on the screen.

Most programs, like *Works*, have indexes to guide you to the particular help you need. All the while, your document waits in the background, still in memory, until you return to it.

Additional Hints

Interfaces in application programs often have other on-screen aids, or prompts to guide users. These may take the form of message lines at the bottom of the screen, prompts that appear when the mouse is clicked or a keystroke is issued, or navigation lines to guide the user's choice of the next command. You may even see the window cue card (explained in the exercises below) or a prompt that changes automatically as the task changes, without a special request for help from the user.

Icon Explanations

Icons have proven to be very popular features of **GUIs** (or **graphical user interfaces**, as explained below). Because there are so many icons, *Works* includes a feature known as Tool Tips—descriptive text which appears under each icon as the mouse pointer stops on that icon.

You can probably think of other features of a program interface that make it more user friendly for you. Some programs have more of these cosmetic features than other, perhaps more powerful, programs. Whatever its characteristics, the interface allows you to have a dialog with the program and accomplish your chosen task.

Types of Interfaces

There are basically two types of interfaces available today: the graphical user interface (mentioned earlier) and the **text-based user interface (TUI)** or **command line interface**. A graphical user interface always presents icons to depict individual programs, directories, files, etc. It typically uses a mouse and has multiple windows that you can move into and out of quickly with the click of the mouse button. On color monitors, a GUI makes liberal use of various colors for emphasis. *Works 3.0 for Windows* and the *Windows* program itself both use GUIs.

A text-based interface, while it may also have windows that can be sized (increased or decreased) with a mouse, is character-based. You choose the desired menu item, file, directory, format, or whatever, from a list of words instead of graphical symbols. The character-based text interface is the oldest interface, and it is still frequently used in application programs for personal computers. A text-based interface is much easier to design and takes far less memory to run. Table 2.1 shows an example of a menu in a text-based interface.

Table 2.1

An Opening Menu in a Text-Based Program

```
                    MAIN MENU

Select appropriate number for task you wish to do:

            0:   EXIT
            1:   ORGANIZE YOUR FILES
            2:   WORK ON PATIENT RECORD
            3:   WORK ON DAYSHEET
            4:   PRINT A REPORT
            5:   CREATE QUARTERLY FILES

Enter the desired number selection:___
```

GUIs are becoming the standard primarily because proficient users can quickly adapt to any interface, whereas true beginners face steep learning curves and appreciate more intuitive interactions with the computer. Without a doubt, although they have been criticized for their screen clutter, the GUIs of modern programs are much more attractive than text-based interfaces.

The *Works 3.0 for Windows* interface allows you to work very quickly once you master a few simple icons, learn to point and click, size your windows, and drag objects on the screen. Many of the same features of *Windows* are common to *Works* and to many other applications.

Quick Tour of Windows

Before we review how to install *Works 3.0 for Windows* on your personal computer, you should become familiar with a few basics of the *Windows* interface. *Windows* is fairly simple and intuitive, so it does not require extensive, detailed instructions. However, a screen covered with many foreign graphic symbols and the need to manipulate a mouse can intimidate a beginner. A few simple exercises will put you in control by making you familiar with opening and closing windows, minimizing and maximizing displays, layering windows, and discovering the tools at your disposal within the *Windows* program.

Although the *Windows* interface makes the program appear simple, this image belies a very complex and powerful package. A quick tour will familiarize you with the basics, but you will master other useful *Windows* operations as you become more computer literate. The most common DOS operating system commands will be covered in Chapter 3 when the *Windows* File Manager is introduced. For now we will review only the most commonly used operations in *Windows* as an introduction.

Windows *Operations*

A major advantage of *Windows* is its capability to have several programs open and running at the same time. This is called **multitasking**. Another advantage is that you can **cut**, or copy, information from one application and **paste** it into another application. (You will have a practice session doing that.)

Disadvantages of *Windows* are its appetite for memory—it needs 6 megabytes or more—and it requires at least an 80386 microprocessor to adequately run several programs at once. With any processor less capable than an 80386DX, *Windows* and *Works 3.0 for Windows* are fairly slow.

Windows includes a built-in communications module that allows you to communicate with another computer via a modem. To use the *Windows* communications software at home or work, you would select Accessories, Terminal and follow the screen prompts. *Works 3.0 for Windows* includes its own communications tool, which we will cover in Chapter 12. The Write command, Recorder (which creates macros), Notepad, Calculator, Calendar, Cardfile, Clock, Media Player, and Sound Recorder are some other available tools that you might want to explore.

Starting Windows

If *Windows* is not already running on your computer:

1. Be sure your current drive is the C drive (or the one on which *Windows* resides).
2. Have the DOS prompt C:\> showing.
3. Type **WIN**.
4. Press **ENTER**.

When *Windows* is activated your screen should resemble Figure 2.2, with the Program Manager and its icons displayed. Don't be concerned if it is not exactly the same, however, because different software may be loaded. The *Windows* program contains rectangular areas where you work with applications and documents, called *windows*.

Figure 2.2

Program Manager Icons

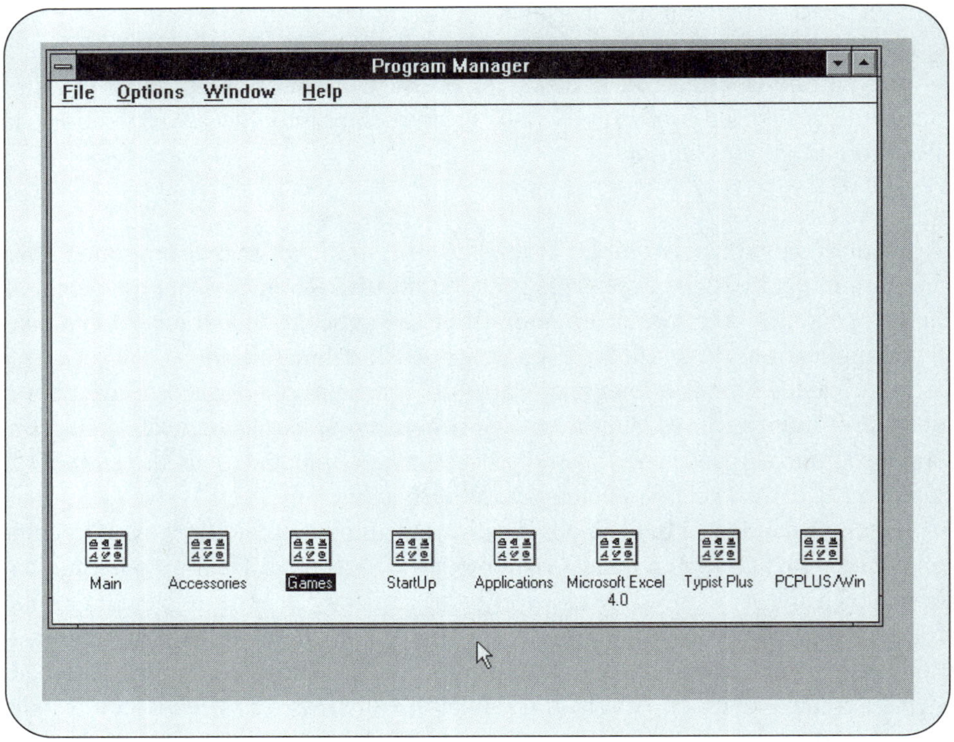

Program Manager

The Program Manager is exactly what the name implies—a manager. The Program Manager directs and manages the flow of data, and it keeps track of the software applications that are running and the documents that belong in each window. It also controls the computer's hardware such as the printer, the monitor, memory, and disk drives. When you exit the Program Manager, your *Windows* session is terminated.

Identifying Windows *Components*

Notice that the Program Manager window has various parts or components. A number of important tasks can be performed by selecting one of those components with either the mouse or combinations of keystrokes. As you work with *Windows*, you will see that each window has the same basic components. Once you learn to execute a particular function in one window, you will be able to use the same technique in another window, which helps make your learning curve less steep. The components of a window are identified in Figure 2.3 and described in the following text.

- **Desktop**. The amount of screen space *Windows* covers is the **desktop**. It is similar to the surface of a desk. You can move items around (software and documents, in the forms of icons), adding new ones and deleting old ones.
- **Window borders**. The outside edges of the window are called *borders*.

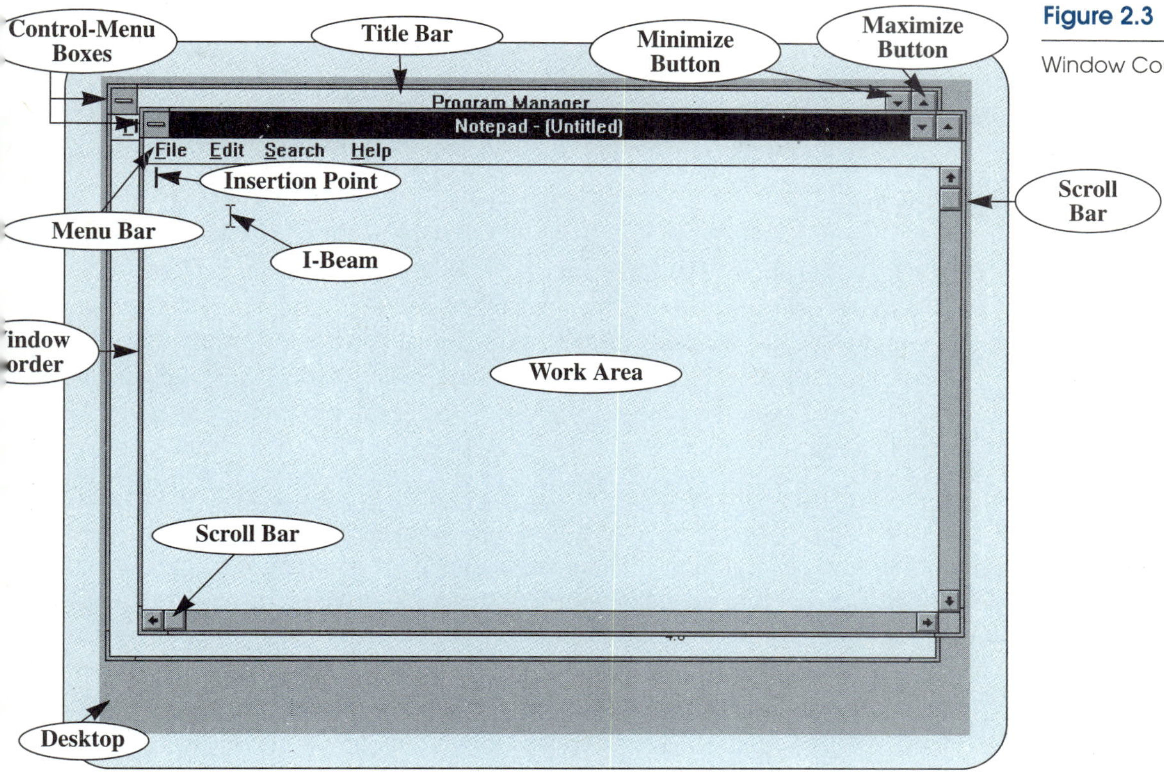

Figure 2.3

Window Components

- **Title bar**. The first line of the window that identifies the name of the application and document is called the **title bar**. If more than one window is open, the title bar for the active window is a different color than the other windows' title bars.
- **Control menu box**. In the upper, left-hand corner of each window is a small box with a dash inside, called the **control menu box**. This box has a pull-down menu with commands that allow you to control the size of the window, to terminate the program, or close a document.
- **Sizing buttons**. A pair of side-by-side arrows (one pointing down, one pointing up) in the upper, right-hand corner of the window are called **sizing buttons**. The downward arrow is the minimize button; when selected it reduces a window into an icon at the bottom of the desktop. The upward arrow, the maximize button, expands the window to the maximum size of the desktop.
- **Menu bar**. Directly below the title bar, the **menu bar** lists the primary commands of the specific application. Most applications have at least File, Edit, and Help menu options.
- **Icons**. **Icons** are graphic symbols that represent documents and programs when those programs are not currently opened into windows.

- **Insertion point**. The **insertion point** is a flashing vertical bar that denotes your place on the screen, much as a cursor does in text-based applications.
- **Mouse pointer**. The **mouse pointer** takes on several different appearances: a single-headed arrow, a double-headed arrow, a four-headed arrow, and an I-beam when inserted in text. You can move the insertion point by positioning the mouse pointer in the desired location and clicking.
- **Program groups**. The Program Manager window is organized into **program groups** displayed as icons at the bottom of the window. Several programs can be included in one group. When you open a group into a window, it displays additional icons. These icons, called *items*, represent applications that you can run. Choosing one of the program icons starts the application.

Windows comes with several predefined program groups: Main, Accessories, Games, *Windows* Applications, and Non-*Windows* Applications. Each of these groups contains several items. This graphical way of handling applications and documents helps you to organize your work and allows you to group your applications together in ways that make sense to you. As mentioned before, your computer's Program Manager may look different from others because of the different programs installed on various systems. However, the process for using the programs is the same.

Using the Mouse

Usually the most efficient way to give *Windows* a command or instruction is to use the mouse. The mouse moves the pointer as it slides across a flat surface such as a mouse pad. As the ball inside the mouse moves, the mouse pointer (indicated as an arrow on the screen) moves in the same direction. A slight movement of the mouse will move the mouse pointer a great distance on the screen. Should you run out of space on the desktop, simply pick up the mouse, reposition it, and begin sliding it again.

A mouse may have two buttons or three. The left button is the primary mouse button that you will use in *Works 3.0 for Windows*. If your mouse has three buttons, you will not use the middle button. To make a selection using the mouse, move the mouse pointer to the desired item and gently press and release the left mouse button once quickly. This is referred to as *clicking*. This method is sometimes referred to as **point and click**.

Two additional terms arise when using the mouse. **Double clicking** means quickly pressing and releasing the left mouse button twice; the motion should be gentle. **Dragging** means holding down the mouse button while moving the mouse.

Conventions Used in This Text

The use of the mouse as a selection device is emphasized throughout this text, although occasionally the keystroke equivalents will also be covered. When a command is first introduced, the text will show how to access it through the menu. Later uses of the command will access it through the toolbar icon. In most instances, the toolbar is the fastest way of accessing commands. The mouse equivalent of keystrokes in the *Works* program uses only the single click of the left mouse button. Selecting a command can be accomplished by rolling the mouse so the mouse pointer is positioned at the desired menu selection, then clicking the left mouse button once.

When keys are to be pressed simultaneously, the plus symbol (+) joins the keystrokes. For example, to go to the top of a document, press CTRL + HOME. This indicates that you should hold down the CTRL key while pressing the HOME key.

When commands to perform a function are given in the description sections of the chapter, they are preceeded by bullets. These steps are to be read only and then referred to, when necessary, to complete the assignments.

For example, to copy text:

- Select the text to be copied by highlighting it.
- Click on Edit-Copy.
- Move the insertion point to the destination of the text.
- Click on Edit-Paste.

In the tutorials, the steps to be performed at the computer are numbered. **Bold** text indicates input to be typed by the student. Names of documents or files are also shown in boldface. When you must select or click on two commands, one after the other, a hyphen will separate the two.

For example, to open a named file:

1. Click on File-Open.
2. Select **Inslet.wps** as the file to open.
3. Click on OK, or press ENTER.
4. Type **Mr. John Dysert**

In the following exercise you will open a group icon into a window.

Exercise

1. Position the mouse pointer anywhere on the Accessories group icon.
2. Click the left mouse button once.

   The icon menu appears, as shown in Figure 2.4.
3. Position the mouse pointer on the Restore option.
4. Click the left mouse button once.

   The Accessories window appears, as shown in Figure 2.5.

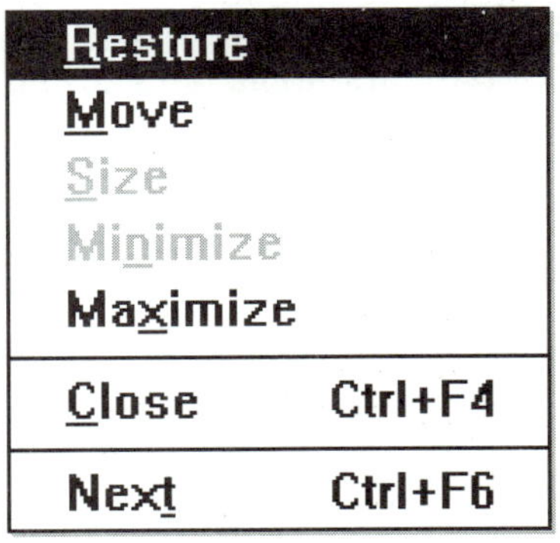

Figure 2.4

The Icon Menu

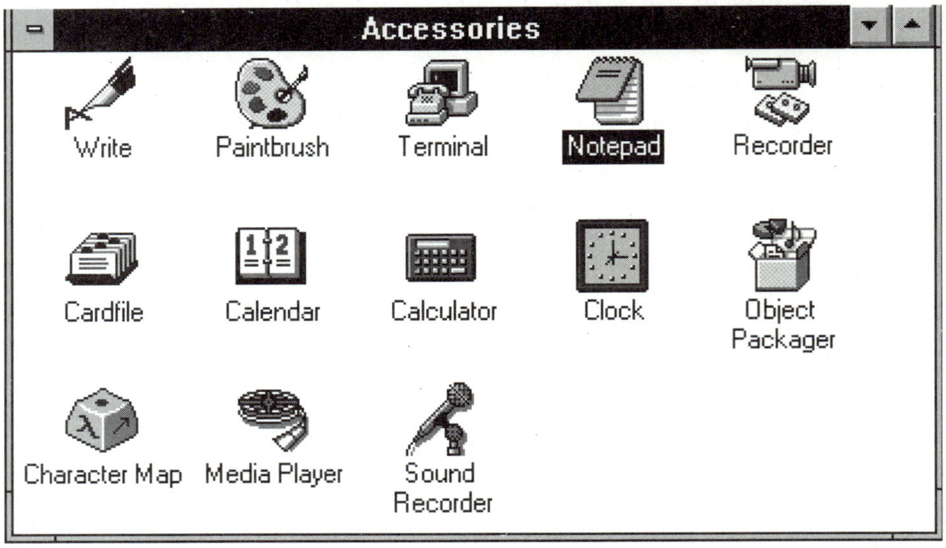

Figure 2.5

The Accessories Window

Note that the screen may be larger or smaller than the one in the figure, depending on the size of the window the last time it was activated. Also, your Accessories window may be ordered differently from Figure 2.5 and it may have a different group of icons. Notice that the Accessories window has most of the same components as the Program Manager—title bar, control-menu box, minimize and maximize buttons, and icons.

The Program Manager is an example of an application window that allows you to open several document windows (called *group windows*) in its application work area. If you have the Accessories window open, notice that it does not have a menu bar. It is a document window, and the Program manager lets you open several document windows or group windows in its application work area. Leave the Accessories window open for the time being.

Canceling a Menu Feature

When using a mouse, you may inadvertently select the wrong feature. If you activate the wrong menu, just move the mouse pointer somewhere on the desktop and click the left mouse button once. (You could press the ESC key twice to achieve the same effect.)

Exercise

1. Position the mouse pointer on the Window menu option on the menu bar of the program manager.
2. Click the left mouse button once.

   A pull-down menu appears as shown in Figure 2.6. (Remember that your screen may differ from the figure.)

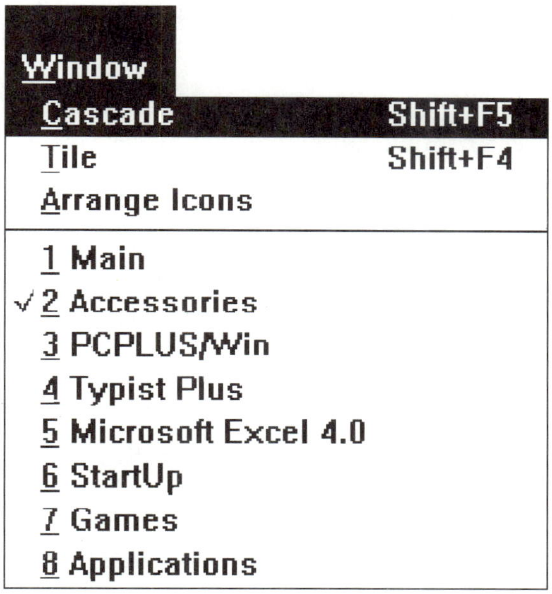

Figure 2.6

The Window Menu

To close the pull-down menu:

3. Position the mouse pointer anywhere on the desktop outside the menu and click the left mouse button once.

   The Window pull-down menu closes.

4. Position the mouse pointer on Options in the menu bar.
5. Click the left mouse button once.

   The Options menu shown in Figure 2.7 appears.

Notice that a checkmark precedes Save Settings on Exit. This option instructs *Windows* to save the arrangement of the Program Manager windows and icons when exiting. A checkmark preceding a command denotes that the option is activated. To deactivate the option, click on it.

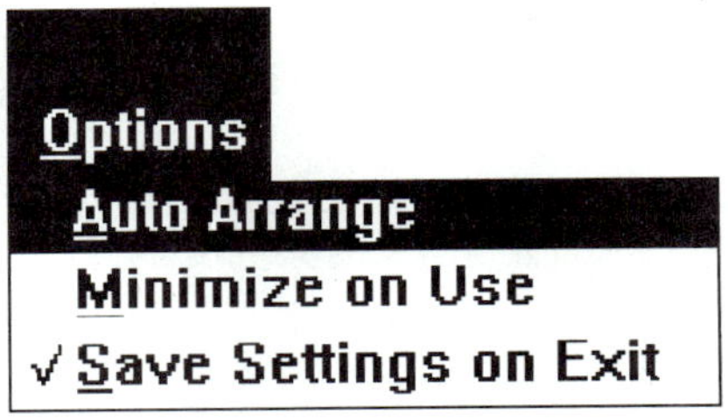

Figure 2.7

The Options Menu

Once you have your desktop the way you want it to appear each time you load *Windows*, activate Save Settings on Exit in the Options pull-down menu and then exit *Windows*. The next time you run *Windows*, deactivate the Save Settings on Exit in the Options pull-down menu, so the original settings will remain regardless of any changes you make during future editing sessions.

Selecting a Menu Feature

You may use either the mouse or the keyboard to activate an option from the menu bar or a pull-down menu. To use the mouse, position the mouse pointer on the option and click the left mouse button once. To choose an option from the Menu Bar using the keyboard, press ALT plus the underlined letter of the menu option. Once the pull-down menu is open, type the underlined letter of the desired option. Because it is very unlikely that you would use *Windows* without a mouse, only the mouse approach for making selections will be shown.

Opening a Program Group Window

As previously mentioned, the Program Manager displays several group icons. Each group icon can contain several application icons, which are graphical representations of application programs that you may run. The easiest way to start an application is to open the group icon and then select the desired application icon. To open or restore a program group, position the mouse pointer on the icon and click the left mouse button once. A pop-up menu appears. Click on the Restore option.

In the following exercise, you will restore the Paintbrush icon into a window. You currently have the Accessories window open. As a shortcut, you can restore group icons and program icons to a window by double clicking on those icons. If you have difficulty double clicking on the icon to execute an application, click on the icon once to highlight the name of the icon an then press ENTER.

Exercise

1. Double click on the Paintbrush icon.

   The Paintbrush icon is restored to a window.

Moving a Window

As you may have noticed when you had several windows open, they stack on top of each other. You can easily move one of these windows by:

- Positioning the mouse pointer in the title bar
- Pressing and holding down the left mouse button while dragging the window to the desired position
- Releasing the mouse button

To cancel the move:

- Press ESC before releasing the mouse button

Two windows are now open on your desktop. In the next exercise, you are going to practice dragging a window to another position on the desktop.

Exercise

1. Position the mouse pointer in the Paintbrush title bar.
2. Keeping the left mouse button depressed, drag the window to the upper, left-hand corner of the screen and then release the mouse button.

Changing a Window's Size

When working with multiple applications on the screen, you might want to reduce the size of an application's windows without minimizing it or enlarge the window without maximizing it to fill the entire screen. *Windows* gives you this capability.

You may have noticed in the previous exercises that the shape of the mouse pointer changed to a double-headed arrow when you moved the pointer over a window border. The double-headed arrow allows you to change a window's size. When the mouse pointer changes to a double-headed arrow as you cross a border, press the left mouse button and drag the border until the window is the size you want. You can see the border move as you drag it even though the window size does not actually change until you release the left mouse button. With the pointer positioned at a corner, the sizes of two borders can be changed at one time.

In this exercise, you will change the size of a window.

Exercise

1. Move the mouse pointer slowly over the right border of the Paintbrush window until the pointer's shape changes to a double-headed arrow.
2. Press and hold the left mouse button. Move the border inward about one-half inch before releasing the mouse button.
3. Move the mouse pointer slowly over the lower, right-hand corner until the pointer becomes a double-headed arrow.

4. Press and hold the left mouse button. Drag the border to the right-hand corner of the desktop before releasing the button.

If you minimize or maximize your window, when it is restored, the window will be the same size and in the same location as it was before being minimized or maximized.

Activating a Window

As you can see, *Windows* allows you to have several windows open with applications running at the same time. However, only one window may be active at any given time. When you open a new window, that window automatically becomes the foreground or active window. When several windows are open at the same time, the active window appears in front, and the title bar changes color to distinguish it from the other windows. To activate a window, move the mouse pointer anywhere within its perimeter and click the left mouse button once.

***Background* Windows** All windows that are open but not active are in the background. The background windows get smaller shares of the computer's processing time; therefore, their applications run more slowly. For example, if you are performing a database search in the background while you work on word processing in the active window, the search will take longer than it would have taken if you had performed it in the active window. In your current desktop, the Paintbrush window is the active window—it appears in front of all other windows and its title bar is a different color.

CTRL+ESC* and *ALT+TAB Sometimes the window for the program you want to activate is covered up on the desktop, and sometimes the program you want may already be open. To see what programs are open, press CTRL+ESC to bring up the Task List, shown in Figure 2.8. You can then highlight the program you want and select Switch To. It is also possible to close a program using End Task. Pressing ALT+TAB will cycle through all currently open programs.

You will now make the Accessories window active.

Exercise

1. Position the mouse pointer anywhere within the Accessories window. (You may have to move the Paintbrush window and click on the minimize button in the upper, left-hand corner, or press CTRL+ESC, to get to it.)
2. Click the left mouse button once.

   The Accessories window is now the active window. Now make the Paintbrush window current.
3. Position the mouse pointer somewhere within the Paintbrush window.
4. Click the left mouse button once.

   The Paintbrush window is now the active window.

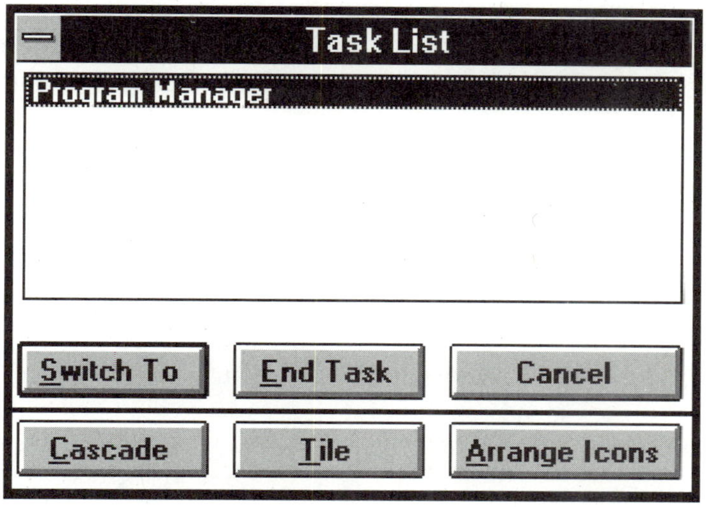

Figure 2.8

The Task List Option Box

Closing a Program Group Window

When you no longer want a Program Group window open, you may reduce it to an icon by selecting Close in the Control menu box of the window to be closed. Another way to close a Program Group window is to double click on the Control menu box. Recall that the Control menu box is just left of the title bar. (refer to Figure 2.3.)

In this exercise, you will reduce the Paintbrush window to an icon.

Exercise

1. Position the mouse pointer on the Paintbrush Control menu box. (You may have to reposition the Paintbrush window to see the control menu box.)
2. Click the left mouse button once to display the Control menu.
3. Click on Close.

Opening a Program

As we mentioned earlier, the icons in a program group window are graphical representations of application programs. To execute an application program, double click with the mouse pointer on the icon.

In this exercise, you will execute the Clock application by double clicking on the icon. The Accessories window should still be restored to a window on your desktop.

Exercise

1. Position the mouse pointer on the Clock icon.
2. Double click the left mouse button.

   An hour glass icon appears while the Clock program is being loaded. (This icon always signals that the processor is working; you will see it many times during your *Windows* sessions.) The clock may display in Analog or Digital; it depends on the way it was last viewed. Notice that the Clock window has the same components as the Program Manager—a title bar, which indicates the name of the application, a Control menu box, minimize and maximize buttons, and a menu bar. Because the Clock is an application, it has a menu bar.

3. Click on the Settings title bar.
4. Click on either Analog or Digital, whichever is not currently marked.

Maximizing a Window

Maximizing an application window expands the window to cover the entire desktop. When you begin working with applications such as *Works 3.0 for Windows,* Calendar, or Cardfile, it is easier to view and edit documents using the full screen as a window. There are two ways to maximize a window:

- Click on the Control menu box and choose the Maximize option.
- Click on the Maximize button.

In this exercise, you will maximize the Clock window using the Control menu box.

Exercise

1. Position the mouse pointer on the Clock's Control menu box.
2. Click the left mouse button once.

   The Control menu appears.
3. Click on the Maximize option.

   Notice that the Clock window expands to fill the entire screen.

Restoring a Window

There are two ways to restore a window to its original size:

- Click on the Control menu box and select the Restore option.
- Click on the double-sided arrow in the upper, right-hand corner of the screen. The Maximize button changes to a double-sided arrow to indicate that the window is maximized.

In this exercise, you will restore the Clock window to its original size using the Control menu box.

Exercise

1. Position the mouse pointer on the Clock's Control menu box.
2. Click the left mouse button once.

   The Control menu appears.
3. Click on the Restore option.

Minimizing a Window

To clear more room on your desktop, *Windows* gives you the option of minimizing a window, that is, shrinking it into an icon. When an application, such as the Clock, is minimized, the program remains operational in the background. A program continues to operate until you close it. This is an advantage when you need to look up information such as a date on your calendar or a phone number of a client, but you may not want many windows to be cluttering up your desktop.

There are two ways to minimize a window:

- Click on the Control menu box and select the Minimize option.
- Click on the Minimize button.

In this exercise, you will minimize the Clock to an icon using the Minimize button. You will then close the application.

Exercise

1. Click on the Minimize option.
2. Press CTRL+ESC.
3. Click on Clock.
4. Click on Switch To.

   The Clock is now an active window
5. Position the mouse pointer on the Clock window's Control menu box.
6. Double click the left mouse button. The Clock application is now closed.

   Notice that the Accessories group is still open. To close the Accessories group:
7. Double click the left mouse button on the Control menu box. The Accessories group is closed and the Program Manager window is the active window.

Using the Accessories

One of the accessories in the *Windows* package, Notepad, is really a text editor that allows you to create, save, and print ASCII files, that is, files that contain no formatting commands. These are also called *DOS text files*. Notepad can be used to write short notes or memos. Notepad has only minor word processing capabilities, such as word wrap, insert/delete, cut, copy, paste, change margins, find, and headers and footers. (You will be familiar with all of these word processing functions when you have completed Chapters 4 and 5. To keep the text from extending beyond the window, you activate the word wrap option.) Notepad automatically assigns a .TXT extension to its file names.

Cut and Paste

It is possible to move or copy material from Notepad, Cardfile, or Paintbrush, among others, by cutting or copying it and then opening your destination program, such as *Write*, and pasting it in place. As explained earlier, when the mouse pointer is used to select commands, it has the shape of an arrow; when it is moved into text, it becomes an **I-beam**; when you click the mouse button, an insertion point (a flashing vertical bar) appears.

To cut and paste, you must first select the text you want to cut or copy. There are several ways to select text:

- Place the I-beam at the beginning of the text, click the mouse button to activate the insertion point, hold down and drag to the end of the material, and release the button.

  OR
- Place the insertion point at the beginning of the text, use the arrow key to mark the text.

  OR
- Place the insertion point at the beginning of the text, move the mouse pointer to the end of the text to be selected, press and hold the SHIFT key, and click the left mouse button.

Text that is selected will appear in reverse video, or white characters on a black or dark background.

To paste desired text into a file, open the destination program (or another area in the same program, if you desire), then:

- Position the insertion point at the desired location.
- Click on Edit.
- Click on Paste.

Again, you will be doing many of these same copying and moving functions when you begin to study word processing in Chapter 4. These same procedures will also apply to text in the *Works* program.

Clipboard

Clipboard is a powerful *Windows* tool that lets you store information that has been cut or copied from one application until it can be pasted into another. It is a buffer, or temporary storage area, as discussed in Chapter 1. Material pasted into Clipboard remains there until you move in a new selection, you clear the material in Clipboard, or the system is turned off. Thus, you can paste the same material from Clipboard many times. As was noted in Chapter 1, in the discussion of the PRT SCRN key, printing an exact copy of the screen directly to the printer is not possible in *Windows*. However, you can copy the screen by pressing the PRT SCRN key (or possibly ALT + PRT SCRN, or CTRL + PRT SCRN) which automatically puts a copy of the screen in Clipboard. From there it can be pasted into another application or saved as a file. It is possible to view material in Clipboard by opening the Clipboard window. The material will be displayed on the screen. Save it to a file by selecting File, Save As, and entering a file name.

Saving a File

When a file is saved the first time, or when you want to assign a new name or new directory (covered in detail in Chapter 3), you should select the File pull-down menu and then select Save As and name the file. To merely resave a file with the same name, select File, Save. The file will be saved without any further action from you.

If you attempt to leave an application after making changes to a file, you will be prompted to "Save Changes?" If you select No, the latest version of the file will not be saved; if you select Yes, it will be saved. These same options appear in the *Works 3.0 for Windows* program, as well as other Microsoft programs.

In the following exercise you will open Notepad, activate word wrap, insert the current date, and type some material. You will then select it and copy it to the Clipboard, paste it into the Write module, and print it.

Exercise

1. Double click on Accessories.
2. Double click on Notepad.
3. Select Edit.

   The Edit menu displays, as shown in Figure 2.9.

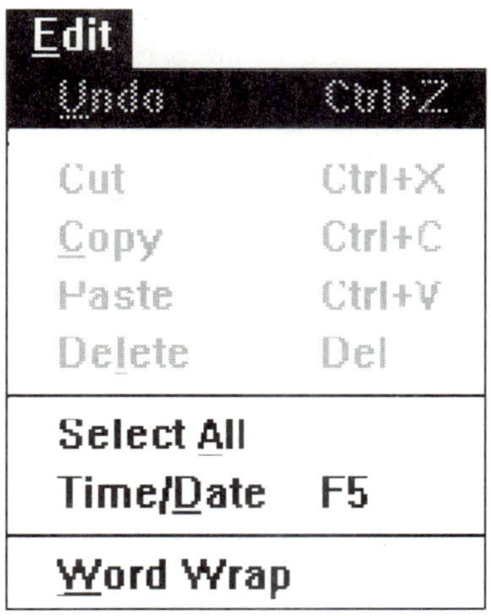

Figure 2.9

The Edit Menu

   To activate the Word Wrap feature:

4. Click on Word Wrap.

   To insert the current time and date in your document:

5. Click on Edit again.
6. Click on Time\Date.
7. Press ENTER twice.
8. Type the following material:

   To select text with the mouse, position the I-beam at the beginning of the text to be selected, press and hold down the left mouse button, drag the mouse to the end of the text, and release the mouse button.

   You can also select text with the arrow keys.

9. Using the mouse, highlight the entire document.
10. Click on Edit-Copy. (If you choose Cut, the material will be deleted from your file.)

    The text is automatically stored in *Windows'* Clipboard.

11. Click anywhere within Notepad to deselect the text.
12. Close Notepad (double click the Control menu box).
13. Double click on Write (the fountain pen icon).

    To insert the material onto the screen in the Write program, position the insertion point at the top of the Write screen.

14. Click on Edit.
15. Click on Paste.

    Your text will appear in the Write program. To print it:

16. Click on File.

    The File menu displays as shown in Figure 2.10

Figure 2.10

The File Menu

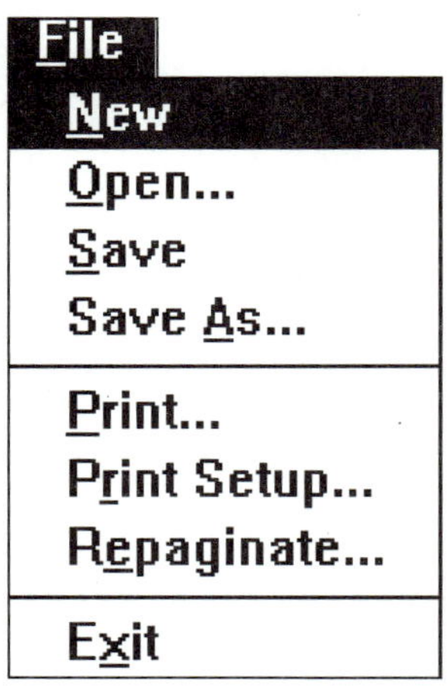

17. Click on Print.

    Note: If this is the first print procedure you have done on your computer system, make sure you are familiar with the basic operations of your printer. Take a few minutes to check the functions of switches, how to feed the paper, and how to take the printer off line for manual control so that you can line feed and form feed if desired, and turn it back on line so that the computer has control. You will learn how to save a file in the next chapter.

    To leave the Write program:

18. Click on File.
19. Click on Exit.

Rearranging Windows

You can choose among several possible arrangements of windows on your desktop: cascade, tile, and unarranged. In this exercise, you will open several windows and arrange them.

Exercise

1. The Accessories group should be open.
2. Open the Games group, if it is available on your computer. (Double click on the Games icon.)
3. Open the Main group icon.

   Notice the disorganized arrangement of the windows on your desktop, as shown in Figure 2.11.

4. Click on Window in the menu bar of the Program Manager.
5. Click on Cascade.

   Notice how the windows arrange themselves in layers on the screen, as shown in Figure 2.12

6. Click on Window, Tile.

   Your windows now appear in squares or rectangles on your screen, with the title bars visible, as shown in Figure 2.13.

Figure 2.11

Unarranged Windows

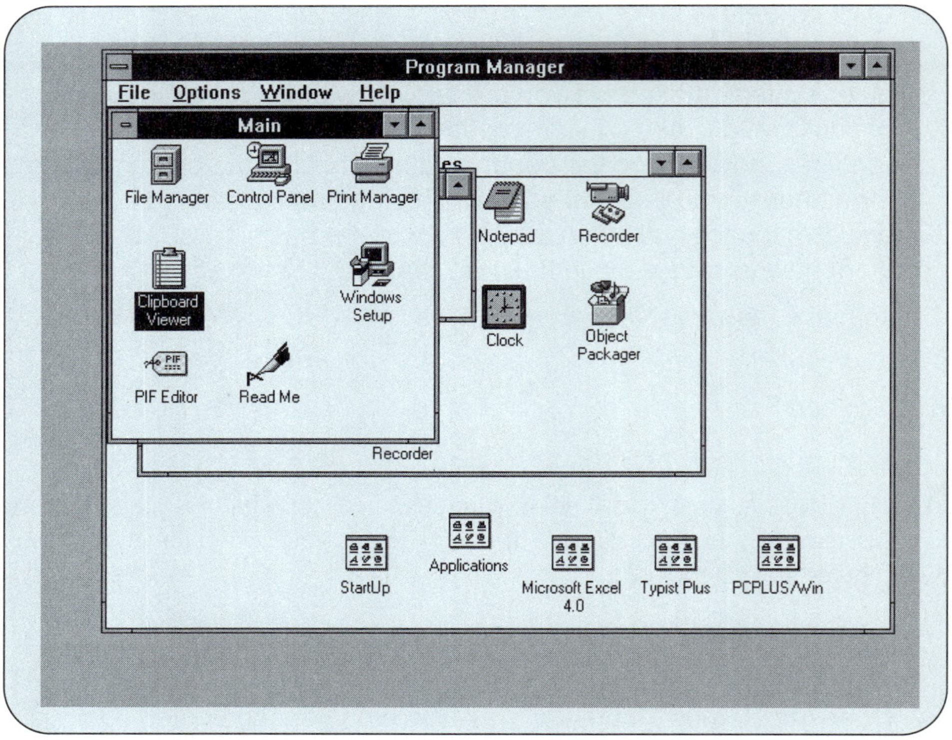

Figure 2.12

Windows Arranged in Cascade Mode

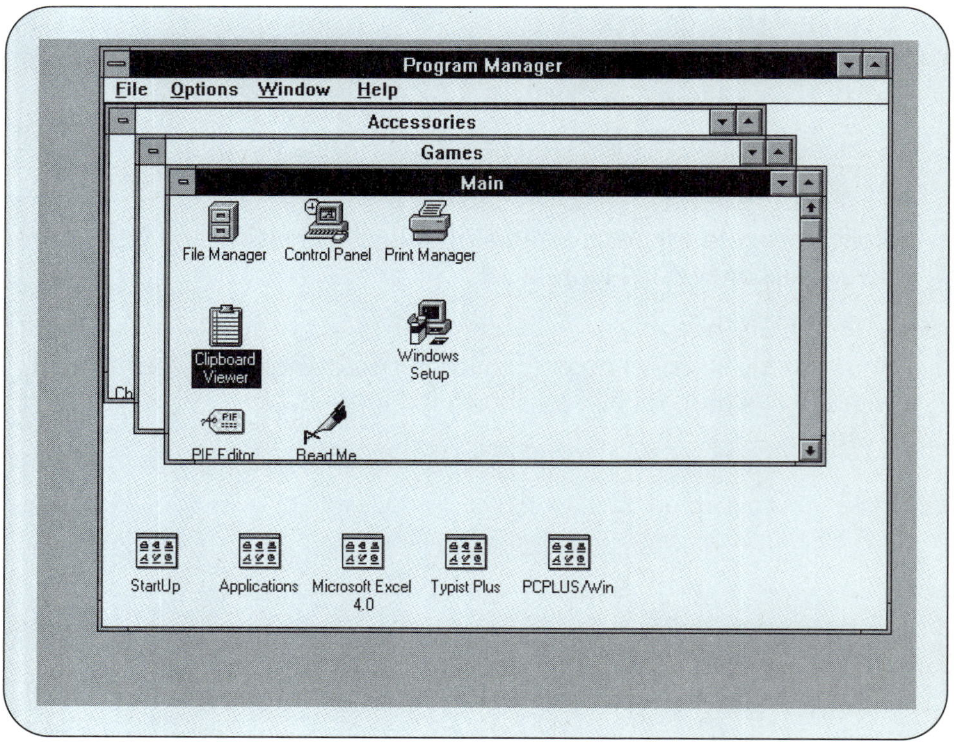

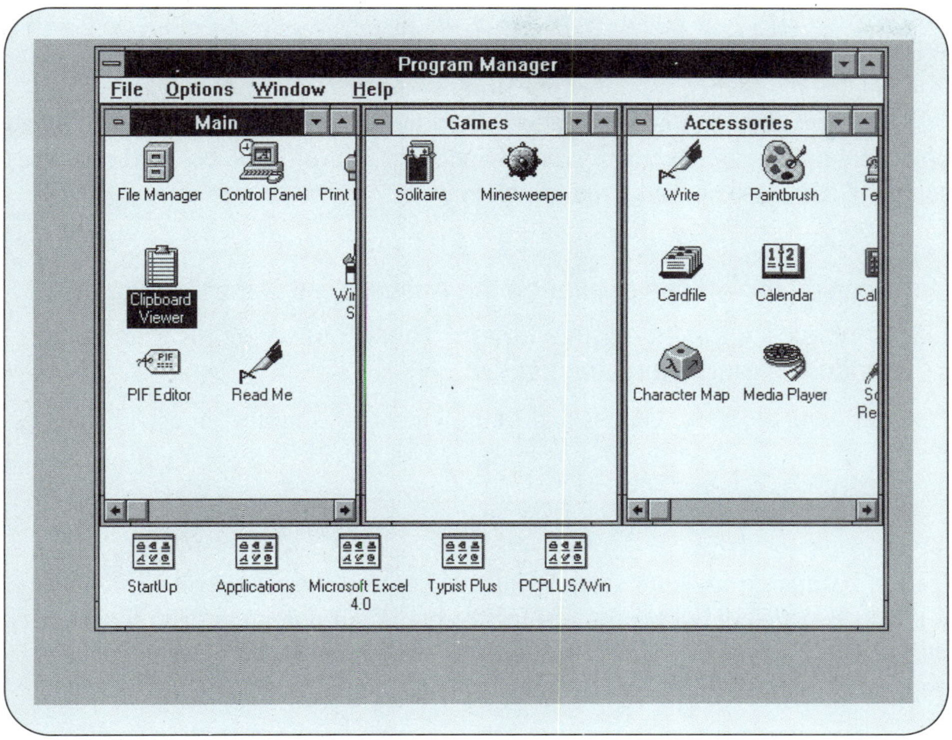

Figure 2.13

Windows Arranged in Tile Mode

Closing a Program

To exit or close an application program, choose the Close option from the Control menu box. (For keyboard shortcut, press ALT+F4.) Remember, that closing an application program is different from minimizing its window. If a program is minimized, it continues to run in the background and it remains instantly available. If a program has been closed, you must reactivate the program and, in some instances, load the desired file.

Exiting Windows

In most situations, when you are finished using *Windows,* it is important that you return to the DOS prompt before turning off your computer. The screen will be blank except for C:\> (or whatever your drive indicator is).

You will do some work from the DOS prompt in Chapter 3 when we discuss operating systems. If any unsaved files remain, *Windows* will ask you if you want to save them. Check with your instructor before you exit *Windows*, because many computers in school labs are left on until the labs close.

Otherwise, there are two ways to exit *Windows:*

- Click on the File menu of the Program Manager and select the Exit *Windows* option.
- Click on the Program Manager's Control menu box and select Close (or double click on the Control menu button). (Shortcut: Press ALT+F4.)

If you inadvertently exit *Windows*, you may have to reboot the computer. Press Reset or CTRL+ALT+DEL to perform a reboot. (We will discuss this operation in Chapter 3 when we cover operating systems.)

Now close the open group window, by double clicking on the Control menu box. Remember, double clicking on a window's Control menu box is the same as selecting the Close option in the Control menu box.

Exercise

1. Position the mouse pointer on the Accessories Control menu box.
2. Double click the left mouse button. The Accessories program group window is reduced to an icon.

On your own, close the Games and Main windows using the mouse or the keyboard.

Getting Started with Works 3.0 for Windows

If the *Works* program is not already installed on the computer you will be using, it must be installed and configured for the particular computer. You must verify that your system satisfies certain hardware requirements before you run *Works* on your chosen machine.

Minimum Hardware and Software Requirements

The *Works 3.0 for Windows* program, as it is covered in this text, requires an IBM or compatible personal computer that uses an 80386 or higher CPU, with at least 2 megabytes of RAM (the more the better). Version 3.1 or later of MS-DOS or PC-DOS is required, with *Windows* 3.1 or a later version installed.

Your computer must have an internal hard drive for secondary storage to run *Works*; in addition it should have at least one floppy drive of either size or density. The *Works 3.0 for Windows* program will take about 14 megabytes of memory on your hard drive.

You need to have a VGA color monitor to run *Works 3.0 for Windows*. A mouse is not absolutely necessary to run the *Windows* interface, but a Microsoft compatible mouse is required to run the latest version of *Works*. If you wish to use the communication portion of the program, you will need to have a Hayes-compatible modem installed, as well. Of course, you don't have to have a printer to run the program, but you cannot print your work without one.

Installing Works 3.0 for Windows

If you want to install your own copy of the *Works 3.0 for Windows* program at home, you will find a Setup diskette included with the application program diskettes. You will install the program on your computer by running a very simple, menu-driven setup program stored on the setup disk. It will prompt you when to insert the other diskettes. You will run this program from drive A or B and follow the prompts it gives you. You may need to know: (Many times the system can determine what your hardware setup is)

- The type of monitor display you have
- The type and name of printer, if you have one
- The type and name of the mouse you have

You must turn on the machine and have DOS and *Windows* loaded into main memory.

(Note: If you are loading *Works* on your own computer, you may get an error message stating that the program SHARE.EXE is required. SHARE.EXE is a DOS program and should be in your DOS directory. You may have to include it in your path statement in your AUTOEXEC.BAT file.)

The Run program will automatically create a *Works* subdirectory on your hard drive unless you choose not to do so. In this subdirectory, the setup routine will install and copy the program. It is best to keep *Works* in its own directory. A screen display will indicate what percentage of the program is installed as the disks are being copied and the program is configured for your computer.

Install *Works* on your computer as follows:

- Place the Setup diskette in drive A or B.
- In the Program Manager window, click on File.
- Click on Run.

In the Command Line text box:

- Type **A:\setup** or **B:\setup** and press ENTER or click on OK.
- Follow the prompts on the screen.

The setup routine offers a default choice for every item. It asks if you wish to install *Works* in the \WORKS subdirectory. If you agree with the default choices, just press ENTER or click on OK, and the program will be set up on your hard drive. You will be prompted to insert each diskette as necessary, so that the program, the help and tutorial programs, the spelling dictionary, and other necessary files can be copied. The program will recognize a color monitor and a mouse, and ask you to verify its view of the hardware.

Finally, it will ask you to choose a printer for your system. If you do not find your specific printer in the large list of printers the program recognizes, choose the one closest to yours. Perhaps your printer's manual has a list of printers that are compatible with yours. A standard TTY chosen from the list will most certainly be compatible, although it may prevent you from using some extra fonts or formatting capabilities of your printer. Once the program is installed on your computer, you are ready for a quick tour of *Works*.

Backing Up the Program

When you have set up *Works* on your hard drive system, you should store the original copies of the program away from your computer. If something should happen to your hard drive, you can always install *Works 3.0 for Windows* from your original program disks. You may also wish to make backup copies of the original program disks as an extra precaution. See Chapter 3 if you need instructions on how to make backup copies.

Brief descriptions of the four modules that will be covered in this text follow.

Word Processing Application

The **word processing** module is used to generate text; the files you produce with this module are called **documents**. This module would be used to write letters, reports, memos, and so on.

Spreadsheet Application

The **spreadsheet** module in *Works* is useful for "number crunching"—adding, subtracting, multiplying, and dividing numbers. Balance sheets, income and expense statements, statements of cash flow, and checkbook reconciliation are some of the many uses for a spreadsheet program. **Charting**, a subprogram of the spreadsheet application, lets you create charts (sometimes called *graphs*) from the numbers you enter in the spreadsheet module. Charts display graphically the data entered in the spreadsheet. Several different types of charts can be created using the same data.

Database Application

The **database** in *Works* lets you enter information about people, places, and things. Later, you can create reports by extracting specific pieces of information from your database. You can also put information from the database into the word processor to create form letters.

Communication Application

You can use the **communication** feature in conjunction with a modem to communicate with other computers and external information services. It is also possible to send electronic messages (E-mail) within your company, your city, or across the nation.

Tour of Works 3.0 for Windows

When *Works 3.0 for Windows* is successfully installed on your computer, a Microsoft Solutions group window will automatically be created, with an individual icon. You may drag this icon to another group if you wish, such as an application window where all of your programs are accessed. The drag instructions you reviewed in the quick tour of *Windows* will help you move the icon where you wish it to be.

Works *Startup Screen*

After an opening Welcome Screen flashes, the Works Startup Screen appears, as shown in Figure 2.14. You can choose to create a new file, open an existing document, use a template, use a WorksWizard, or obtain further instructions.

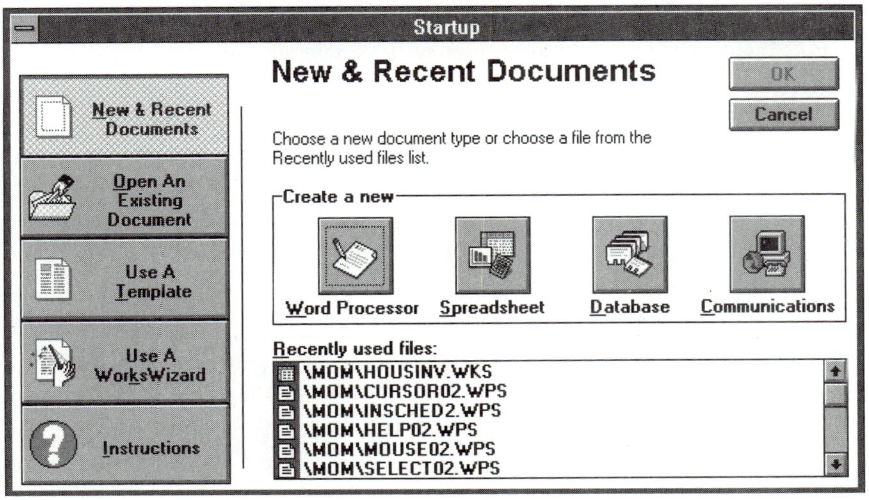

Figure 2.14

Works Start Up Screen

Creating a New File To create a new file, choose the application in which you want to create the file: word processor, spreadsheet, database, or communications. Simply click on the specific *Works* tool you wish to use.

Open an Existing Document If you have already created (and saved) a file, to retrieve it:

- Select the file name in the file list box

  OR
- Type the name of the file in the File Name text box.
- Click on OK.

If the file is in a different directory:

- Click on the correct directory to get a list of files.
- Click on the file name.
- Click on OK.

If the file is on a different drive:

- Click on the down arrow in the Drives list box.
- Click on the new drive, as A:, B:, D:, etc.
- Click on the file name.
- Click on OK.

The last six files you have used will appear at the bottom of the "Recently used files" list box; double click on one of them, and that document will be loaded on the screen. You will be placed in the program that created the file, either the word processor, spreadsheet, and so on. The file folder icon appears to the left of each file name. This graphic symbol changes from a closed file folder to an open file folder when a specific file is being used.

Use A Template Choosing Use a Template lets you select a predefined file supplied with your program. Templates are master documents already created and ready for you to enter desired information. In Works, AutoStart templates are quick ways to create documents using predefined, ready-to-go documents. The four major groups are: AutoStart Business, AutoStart Personal, AutoStart Education, and Custom. Within each group, several categories are available and within each category several templates are available. For example, in the AutoStart Personal group the categories available are Addresses, Documents, Household Management, and Personal Finances; in the Personal Finances category, a Mortgage Loan Analysis template is available.

Use a WorksWizard If you choose Use a WorksWizard, you open a *Works* feature that streamlines your activities. **WorksWizards** are part of a new, interactive feature which simplifies some common functions; for example, it can ask you questions and then create the document or find a file for you. Some of the tasks made easier with WorksWizards include making a personalized address book, mailing labels, and form letters. We will cover some of the WorksWizards features in Chapter 13.

Instructions Selecting Instructions from the opening screen gives you a detailed explanation of each of the topics just mentioned, as shown in Figure 2.15. You may abandon your entry into the *Works* program by double clicking on the Cancel command.

After you make your selection and one of the specific programs launches, you choose the menu or tool bar item you want by pointing to it with the mouse and clicking the left mouse button. You move in an out of all menus in *Works* in exactly the same fashion. To cancel a selection at any time, just choose Cancel or press the ESC key twice.

Notice that the *Works* interface is very similar to the *Windows* interface that you just toured. Many of the same tasks can be performed with the same series of commands.

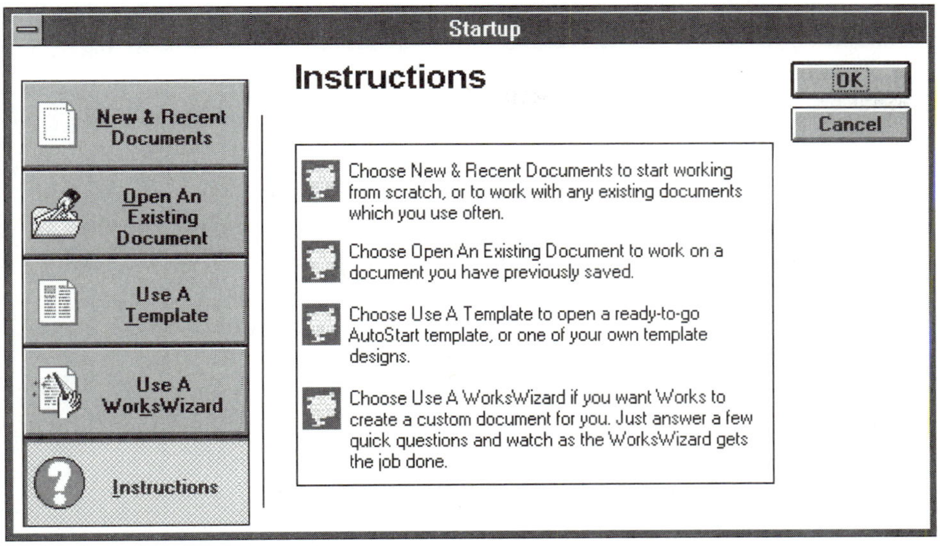

Figure 2.15

Instructions About Works Topics

Main Menu

The main menus for all applications in *Works* look the same, although the contents of each of their submenus differ somewhat. This similarity of menus is one of the nicest features of an integrated program. Once you learn the meanings of menu items in one application, you know they will have similar, if not identical, meanings in the other applications. This tremendously increases the proficiency of a beginner, because your knowledge is portable from one application to the next.

If you choose the word processing program, the blank screen that appears is your **work area**, as shown in Figure 2.16. This is where you actually compose your document.

There is a work area for every application in *Works.* At the top of the work area, the menu bar lists available selections for the particular application. The menu bars are almost identical in all four applications. You reach the menu bar by pointing to the text selection you wish and clicking with the left mouse button. Until you access the menu, the mouse pointer, which can be in the form of a rectangle or an arrow, is shown in your work area, and a solid bar (__) indicates the end of your document.

Directly below the menu bar, a toolbar contains the most commonly used commands in each module to make it easier and faster to select commands. As we said earlier, if you rest the mouse pointer on a particular icon in the toolbar for a few seconds, *Works 3.0 for Windows* flashes an explanatory title in yellow

Figure 2.16

Annotated Word Processing Screen

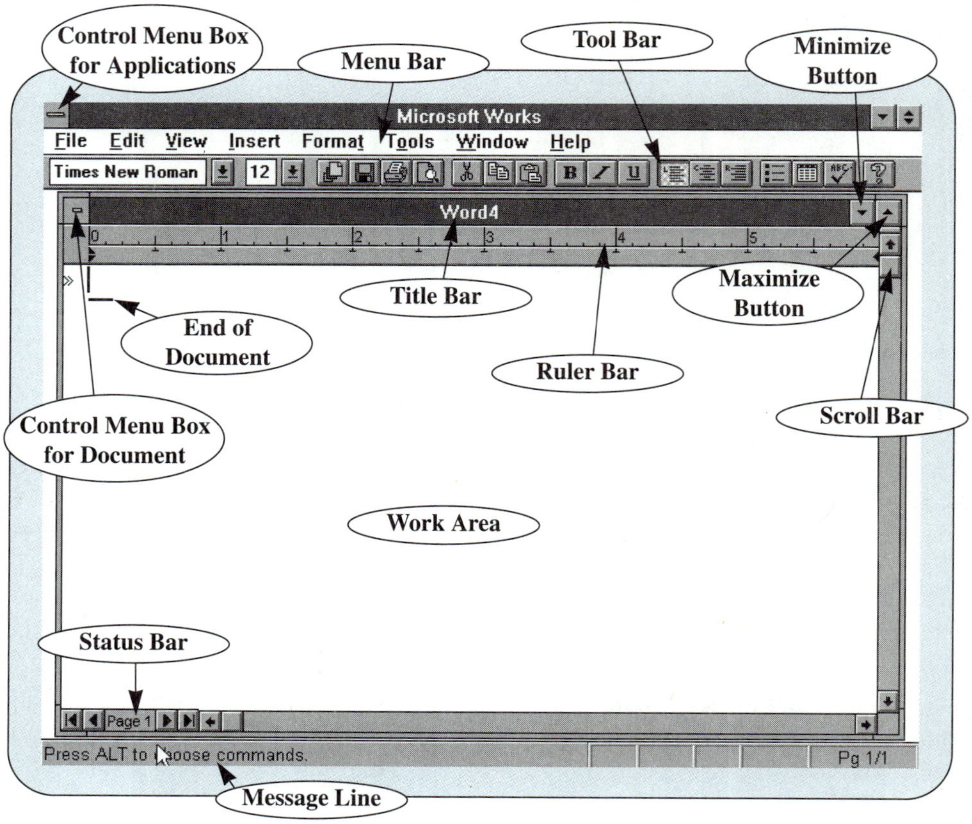

(a tooltip) to help you understand its function; if you notice the message line, you will see a longer description of the icon. Because the toolbar is different for each application, it will be further discussed later in the text.

Right below the toolbar, the title bar displays the name of the document currently in use. Until you name and save your document, the name will reflect the program you are in, as word4 in the word processing module.

A **ruler** displays next. It shows the left and right margins, and any tabs and indents that have been set.

At the bottom of the screen, a **message line** says "Press ALT to choose commands." However, the message changes with whatever task you are performing. Remember to watch this line for hints on how to execute the specific command you select. On the right side of the message line, the current page number and the total number of pages in the document are displayed.

Also at the bottom of the screen, above the message line, the **status bar** indicates the page number of the material currently in the display. You can click with the mouse on **scroll bars** on the right side of the screen to move forward and backward in your document. You can also use the PAGE UP, PAGE DOWN, or arrow keys to move forward or backward in your document.

As you use *Works,* you will find that all applications look pretty much the same, which is encouraging. The simple, clear interface in *Works* allows you to gain proficiency in each of the specific applications without undue emphasis on learning specific keystrokes.

Each time you click on a selection followed by three dots, a **pull-down window** with more selections appears. The selections in these windows, in turn, lead to other option boxes or dialog boxes that allow you to interact with the program. Because the File menu, the Help menu, and the Window menu are similar in all the applications, those will be introduced here.

Help Menu A real advantage in *Works* is its **context sensitive** help feature. When you are trying to use a command and need some help, if you select help, the screen will display information about the command you are using. To activate the help menu, click on Help or press the function key F1. The list of choices will be covered in more detail in the *Works* tutorial.

File Menu To activate the File menu, click on File with the mouse. You may choose any of the commands that do not appear faded and gray. These selections are described below:

- Create New File (opens a new, blank screen)
- Open Existing File (opens a file previously created and saved)
- WorksWizards
- Templates
- Close (closes a file without saving)
- Save (saves after the first time)
- Save As (for first-time saves or to save a second copy with a new file name)
- Page Setup (sets top, bottom, left, right, header, and footer margins)
- Printer Setup (to choose a printer)
- Print Preview (to see a document in a full-page image with *very* small letters, called a *Greeked* image.)
- Print (to set the number of copies and area to print)
- Exit Works

You may select any of the features in the File menu by pointing with the mouse and clicking. You may also select by pressing the highlighted letter and then pressing ENTER. Another selection method is to use the down arrow to highlight the whole line, and then press ENTER. This is true throughout the *Works* program.

Shortcut keystrokes can perform some functions by combining the ALT or CTRL keys with letter keys, indicated in this book by ALT + and CTRL +; hold down the first key while pressing the second key and then let go of both keys.

For example, CTRL+ B marks text for bold type. In another kind of shortcut (designated as ALT, letter) you press and release the ALT key, and then press and release the letter key. For example, ALT, F displays the File menu. Because *Works 3.0 for Windows* is a mouse-driven program, we will show the mouse commands and any short-cut keys that are available. Appendix A shows the most-used shortcut keys.

Figure 2.17

Works Window Menu

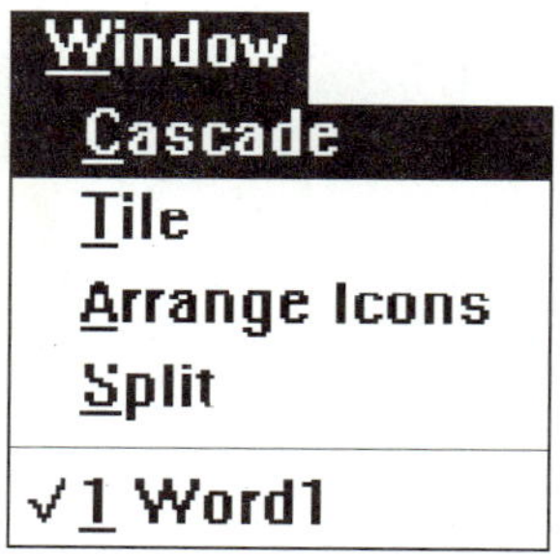

Window Menu In your tour of *Windows*, you used the Window menu to cascade and tile your windows. You can do the same thing in *Works*. In addition, you can go from one window to another by clicking on the open document you wish to make active. The Window menu is shown in Figure 2.17. As many as eight windows can be open at one time, and they will all be listed in the Window pull-down menu.

To change document windows:

- Click on Window.
- Click on the new document name.

The following exercise will help to acquaint you with an overview of the individual *Works* programs. Note: If your computer system does not allow you to enter an application such as *Works* unless a formatted disk is in drive A or B, refer to Chapter 3, page 95, to learn how to format a disk.

Exercise

1. Click on the Microsoft *Works* icon.

   The opening Welcome Screen may show briefly, and then the Startup screen displays. (Review Figure 2.15.) The default is New & Recent Documents—Create a New Word Processor.

2. Press ENTER or click on Word Processor.

   The Word Processor program opens, as shown in Figure 2.16.

   Notice the menu bar, toolbar, the title bar (showing *Word4*), and the ruler bar. The blinking insertion point lies at the beginning of the document and the horizontal bar designates the end of the document. The I-beam (or mouse pointer) is somewhere on the screen. The CueCards screen also displays as shown in Figure 2.18.

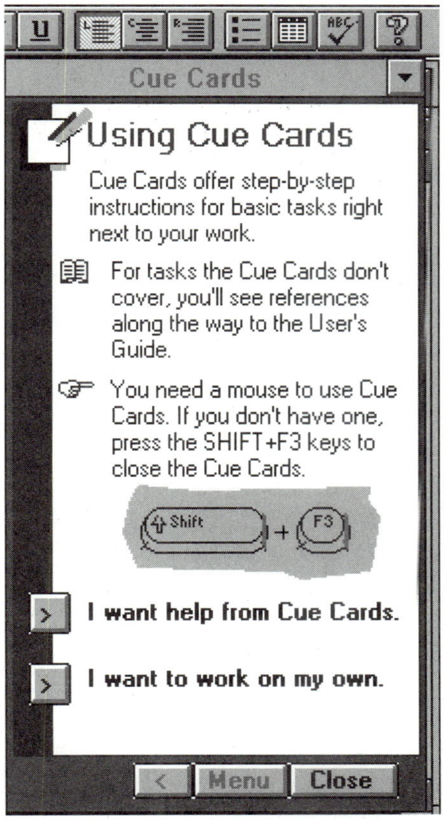

Figure 2.18

Word Processing Cue Cards

3. Move the I-beam to the menu bar. (It becomes a mouse pointer.)
4. Click on File.

   The File menu displays, as shown in Figure 2.19. It shows many of the same commands that were available in the opening screen.

Figure 2.19

The File Menu

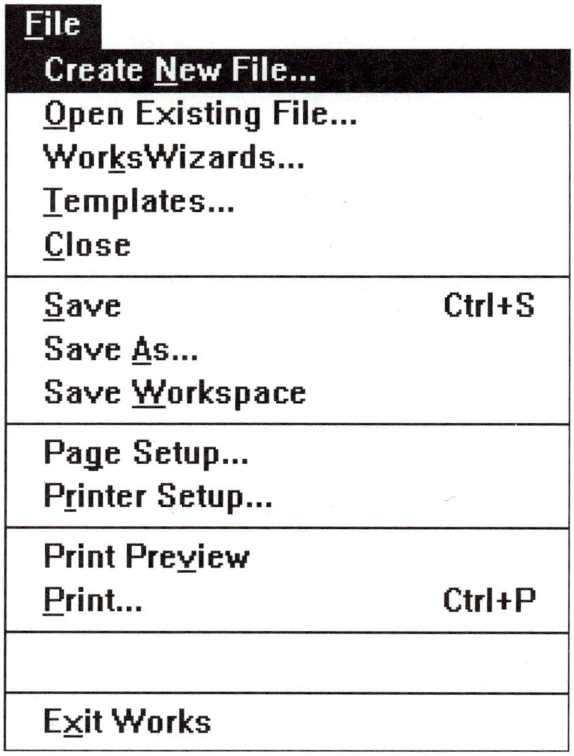

5. Click outside the menu to close it.
6. Click on Help.

   The Help menu displays, as shown in Figure 2.20.

Figure 2.20

The Help Menu

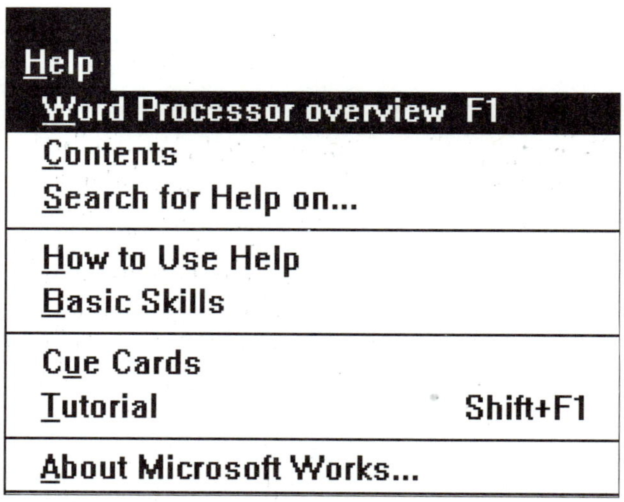

7. Click on Word Processor overview.

   Information about the word processing module displays.

8. In the Help window, click on File, then click on Print Topic.

   Read the topics you print and keep them for later reference.

9. Click on File in the Help screen.
10. Click on Exit.

    You can click outside the Help screen to exit, but it remains in memory, and does not actually close. You must still close it at some later time.

11. Click on File, then click on Close.

    You are returned to the Startup screen.

12. Click on the Spreadsheet icon.

    The spreadsheet screen displays, as shown in Figure 2.21.

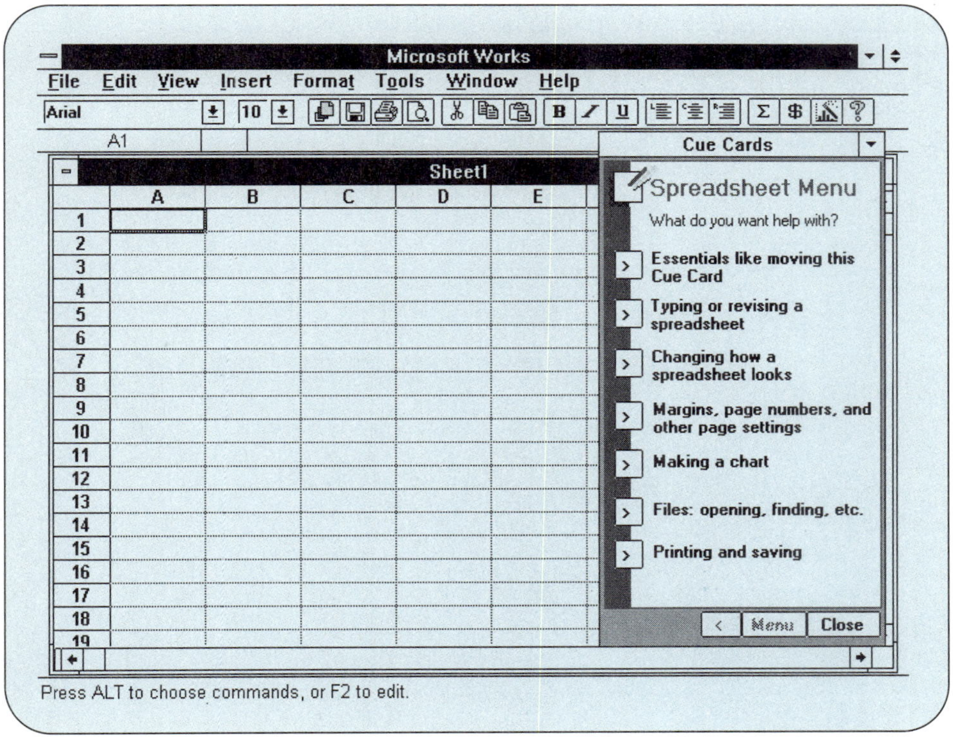

Figure 2.21

The Spreadsheet Screen

13. Click on Help-Spreadsheet overview.
14. Click on File in the Help menu bar.
15. Click on Print Topic.

16. Click on File in the Help menu bar.
17. Click on Exit.

    When you actually use the program you will probably want to deactivate the cue cards as they take up a large portion of your screen, blocking the material behind them. To deactivate cue cards, if they are displayed:
18. Click on Close at the bottom of the cue card screen.

    You get a "Before You Close" message.
19. Click on the Close Cue Cards button, or click on Close again.

    To activate cue cards in the future, click on Help-Cue Cards.

    To close the spreadsheet program:
20. Click on File, then click on Close.

    To open the database program:
21. Click on Database.

    The database screen displays, as shown in Figure 2.22.

    If you get a startup message:

Figure 2.22

The Database Screen

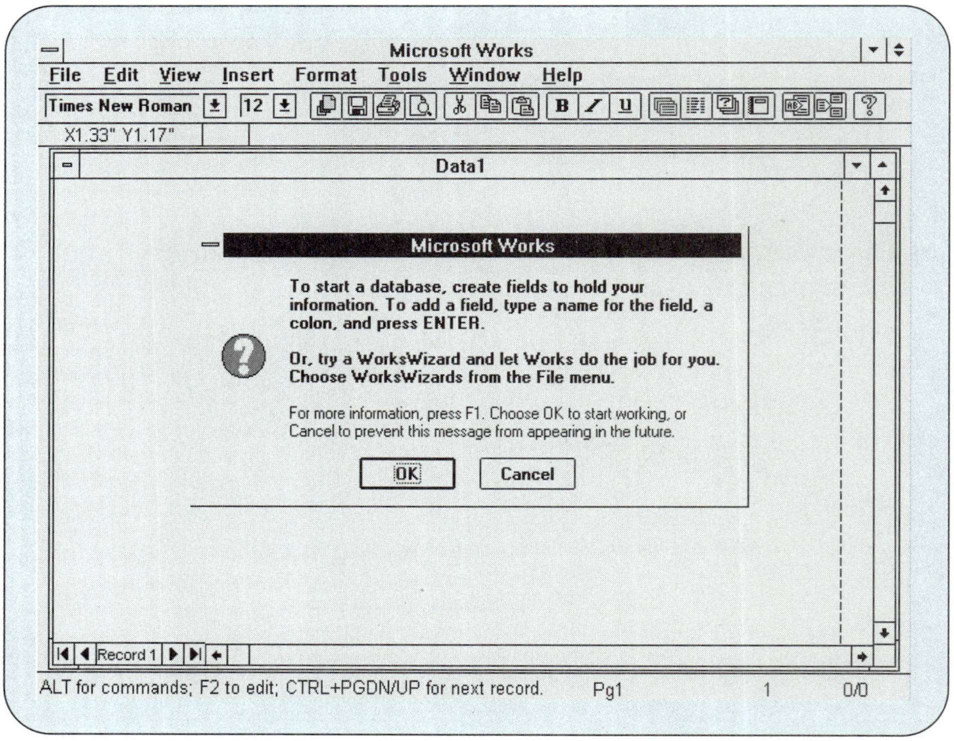

22. Click on OK.

    You can cancel the startup message later.

23. Click on Help.
24. Click on Search for Help On.
25. In the text box, type **Report**.
26. Click on Show topics.
27. Click on Database overview.
28. Click on Go To.
29. Click on File, then click on Print Topic.
30. Click on File, then click on Exit in the Help screen.

    To practice activating the cue cards:

31. Click on Help.
32. Click on Cue Cards.

    A message about the cue cards displays.

33. Click on "I want help from Cue cards."

    The cue cards will remain active until you close them again.

34. Click on file in the Database screen, then click on Close.
35. Click on Communication.

    The Communication screen displays, as shown in Figure 2.23.

36. Click on Cancel in the Easy Connect screen.
37. Click on Help.
38. On your own, print the communication overview, close the Help screen, and close the Communication program.

    Notice in each of the Help topics you printed out a *See also* cross-reference at the bottom of the page and a list of topics that can be accessed for future information.

39. On the Startup screen, click on Cancel.
40. Click on File.
41. Click on Exit *Works*.

Figure 2.23

The Communication Screen

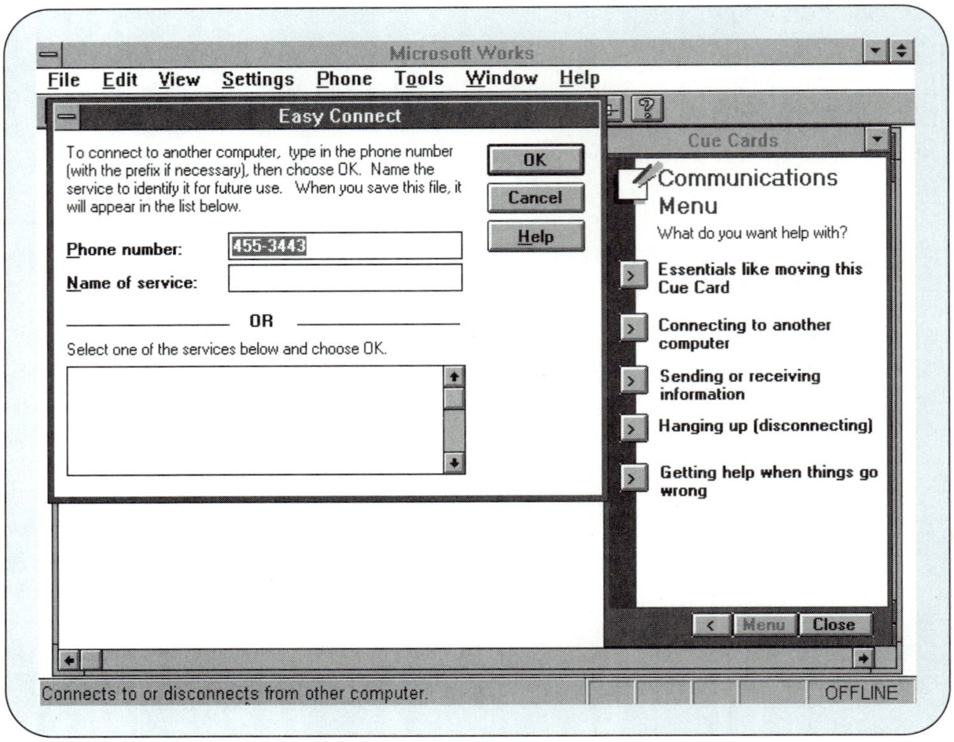

Cue Cards

In the *Works 3.0 for Windows* tour, you have seen one of the newest additions to all of the new Microsoft program interfaces. Called **cue cards**, these are attractive overlaid windows that give helpful hints for execution features as you work on them. The cue card occupies 10 to 15 percent of the screen and changes automatically as your task changes. It gives you a cue, or on-line help in the form of a brief but immediate prompt. As we have noted in the exercises, once you have mastered many of the basics of *Works 3.0 for Windows,* you may wish to turn off the cue cards option. By default cue cards appear in all individual tools of *Works*, as you might have noticed when you opened each of the programs.

RTS and Interfaces

In your quick tour of the *Works* program, you probably noticed that the screen often presents explanatory information in the message areas, and it often prompts you for input. The best advice a beginner can receive when learning to use a personal computer is **RTS**, which stands for **Read the Screen.** User manuals, on-line help, tutorials, and explanatory textbooks all are very useful for a beginner, but many times if you carefully read the screen and follow the directions that it gives you, you can master an application much more easily than you first imagined. When developing an interface for an application program, software companies take great care in designing user-friendly screen directions and prompts. You should watch for these messages and try to follow any specific directions the screen gives you; the cue cards in the *Works* program change to pertain to the task you are performing. All of these on-screen aids will help you more than any external documentation could.

In the beginning, it takes special effort to focus your attention on the messages that are displayed on the screen. They are not always in the same area for every program, and sometimes you focus so intently on the work area of the screen that you ignore helpful screen directions. The message line at the bottom of the *Works* screen display offers a wealth of valuable information, including explanatory text when you pause on an icon in the toolbar, and Help commands that indicate what action to take next; it even gives a description of the command you have just selected. All of these helpful messages, directions, and prompts are there for you if you will only Read the Screen.

Chapter Summary

An interface is characterized by the way it presents a program to you, the user. There are graphic interfaces, text interfaces, and hybrids of the two presentation styles. User-friendly interfaces make a program easier for a beginner to learn. They can also speed operation of your input, even after you master the program, especially if you use a mouse. Generally, a better developed interface allows smoother operation of a program.

This chapter introduced you to the Microsoft *Windows* graphical user interface and to the *Works 3.0 for Windows* program. To use the IBM and compatible *Windows* version of *Works,* you must have 2 MB of main memory, a hard drive with 14 MB of free space, a VGA monitor, a mouse, and 3.1 or later versions of DOS and *Windows*. Installing and running *Works* is a simple, menu-driven process. The basic tasks you perform in *Windows* are very similar in the *Works* program.

In this chapter, we took you on a quick tour of *Windows* and *Works 3.0 for Windows* to make you familiar with their menu system before mastering the specific applications.

KEY TERMS

box	database	I-beam
charting	default setting	icon
command line interface	desktop	insertion point
communication	document	menu bar
context sensitive	double clicking	menu system
Control menu box	dragging	message line
cut and paste	graphical user interface	mouse pointer
cue card	GUI	multitasking

on-line help
point and click
preview
program group
pull-down window
read the screen
reverse video
RTS
ruler
scroll bar
sizing button
special key
spreadsheet
status line
text-based user interface
tile
title bar
toolbar
top-down design
TUI
view
window
word processing
work area
WorksWizards
WYSIWYG
zoom

REVIEW QUESTIONS

1. Define the word *interface.*
2. Explain the purpose of an interface.
3. List and define the characteristics of an interface.
4. Explain the differences between GUIs, TUIs, and hybrid interfaces.
5. Which kind of interface is generally preferred by (a) experienced users? (b) novice users?
6. What is an icon? Why do icons need text explanations?
7. Identify the major advantage of *Windows.*
8. Review the role that the Program Manager plays in *Windows.*
9. List and describe each of the components of a window.
10. Explain the purpose and use of the mouse in the *Windows* environment. What are the differences between clicking, double clicking, and dragging?
11. Briefly explain how to accomplish each of the following tasks: (a) select and cancel a menu feature, (b) move a window, (c) change a window's size, (d) make an inactive window active, (e) close a program group window, (f) open a program, (g) maximize a window, (h) minimize a program, (i) cut and paste, (j) use the clipboard.
12. To save a file, explain when it is best to use Save As and when Save will do.
13. Illustrate the several possible arrangements of windows on your desktop.
14. List the minimum hardware requirements for using *Works 3.0 for Windows.*
15. List the major steps to install *Works 3.0 for Windows* on a hard disk system.
16. Briefly describe the purpose of each of the four major *Works 3.0 for Windows* applications.
17. Briefly explain what a template is and name any three templates

available in each of the word processor, spreadsheet, and database program modules.

18. What is the purpose of the WorksWizards?
19. Briefly describe what you see on a typical *Works* work area screen. Begin with the top of the work area and proceed downward.
20. Explain the difference between Help and context-sensitive Help.
21. What is a cue card? How could you use it?
22. What does RTS mean? Why is this the best advice a beginning computer user can receive?

SOFTWARE EXERCISES

Exercise 2.1

1. Start *Windows* (if it is not already started).
2. On the Program Manager menu bar, click on Help.
3. Click on Windows Tutorial.
4. Type **M** to begin the Mouse lesson.
5. Hand write or type your answers to the following questions: (a) What is the shape of the pointer that moves across the screen as you move the mouse on a flat surface? (b) What action are you performing when you click the mouse? (c) With which button do you perform this action? (d) What is another way to make a selection? (e) Describe what you are doing when you drag and drop an item on the screen.
6. Click on No if you are asked if you want to change the default mouse button to be the right button.
7. Exit the tutorial.
8. Exit *Windows* (unless you are suppose to leave *Windows* on the screen in a lab).

Exercise 2.2

1. Start *Windows* (if it is not already started).
2. On the Program Manager menu bar, click on Help.
3. Click on Windows Tutorial.
4. Type **W** to begin the *Windows* lesson.
5. Hand write or type your answers to the following questions: (a) What starts every time you start *Windows*? (b) What does each icon in the Program Manager window represent? (c) What happens when you open a group? (d) What does each icon in a group window represent? (e) How do you start an application? (f) What button enlarges a window so that it fills the screen, and what is its shape? (g) What

button restores a window to its previous size, and what is its shape? (h) What button minimizes a screen, and what is its shape? (i) How do you move a window to another place on the screen? (j) How do you change the size of a window? (k) Where is the menu bar and what does it contain? (l) How do you open a menu on the menu bar? (m) How do you close a menu without choosing a command? (n) When you choose a command that is followed by three dots, what happens? (o) What are the two ways to select a file? (p) What are four ways to provide information to a dialog box? (q) What is the name of the window in which you are working? (r) How do you make an inactive, open window active? (s) How do you close a window?

6. Exit the tutorial.
7. Exit *Windows* (unless you are suppose to leave *Windows* on the screen in a lab).

Exercise 2.3

1. Start *Windows* (unless it is already started).
2. Click on Program Manager Help.
3. Click on About Program Manager . . . and hand write or type your answers to the following questions: (a) What version of *Windows* are you using? (b) To whom is it licensed? (c) What percentage of your system resources remain free?
4. Click on OK.
5. Minimize all group windows on the desktop to make them icons (if they are not already icons).
6. List the group icons.
7. Open the Accessories window (if the window is not already open).
8. List the program item icons that you see in the Accessories window.
9. Open the Main window (if the window is not already open).
10. List the program item icons that you see in the Main window.
11. Click on Window-Cascade.
12. Which group window is active.
13. Click on Window-Tile.
14. Sketch what you now see in both windows.
15. Minimize the Main window.
16. Minimize the Accessories window.
17. Click on File-Exit Windows . . . (unless you are suppose to leave *Windows* on the screen in a lab).

Exercise 2.4

Start by loading *Works 3.0 for Windows* into RAM.

1. You are going to use the arrow keys to explore in turn each of the three main menu choices—File, Tools, and Help.
   (a) If the Startup screen is showing, click on Cancel.
   (b) If the File menu isn't on your screen, click on file.
   (c) Read the first entry under File along with the explanation of the entry at the bottom of the screen on the message line. Briefly note the entry and message.
   (d) Press the down arrow and repeat Step (c) until you have read all of the File entries.
   (e) Press the right arrow key to move to the Tools menu. Press the down arrow to highlight the Options . . . menu if it is not already highlighted. Press ENTER. Briefly note each of the entries in the Options window. Click on Cancel.
   (f) Click on Help. Read the first entry under Help along with the brief explanation of the entry at the bottom of the screen on the message line. Use the down arrow key to read each entry in turn until you have read all of the Help entries. Briefly note each entry and message.
   (g) Press the left arrow until you see the File menu.
   (h) Press the up arrow or the down arrow repeatedly until Exit Works is highlighted.
   (i) Press ENTER to leave *Works*.
2. Hand write or type the notes on what you saw.

Exercise 2.5

Start by loading *Works 3.0 for Windows* into RAM.

1. You are going to use the mouse to explore in turn each of the three main menu choices—File, Tools, and Help.
   (a) If the Startup screen is showing, click on Cancel.
   (b) If the File menu is not showing, select it by moving the mouse so that the arrow on the screen is pointing at File and click (press) the mouse button (usually, the left button).
   (c) Read the first entry under File (Create New File) along with the explanation of the entry at the bottom of the screen on the message line. Briefly note the entry and message.
   (d) Click (press) and hold down the mouse button. Drag (move) the mouse downward so that the name of each command in turn is displayed. Continue until you have read all of the File entries. Briefly note each entry and message.

(e) Without releasing the mouse button, move the mouse up and to the right to open the Tools menu. Pull the mouse down so that Options . . . is highlighted. Release the mouse button. Briefly note each of the entries in the Options window. Click on Cancel.
(f) Click on Help. Without releasing the mouse button, move the mouse down so that the name of each command in turn is displayed. Continue until you have read all of the Help entries. Briefly note each entry and message.
(g) Without releasing the mouse button, move the mouse up and to the left so that the File menu is displayed.
(h) Move the mouse pointer to the Exit *Works* entry.
(i) Release the mouse button to exit *Works*.

2. Hand write or type the notes on what you learned.

Note: You held down the button continuously in this exercise to avoid selecting unwanted choices. Normally, you position the mouse pointer on the menu choice you want and click the mouse button to make that choice.

Exercise 2.6

Start by loading *Works 3.0 for Windows* into RAM.

1. You are going to use the letter keys to explore in turn a few of the three Main menu choices—File, Tools, and Help.
   (a) If the Startup screen is showing, click on Cancel.
   (b) If the File menu doesn't show on your screen, press ALT, then press F.
   (c) Press N for the Create New File entry. Briefly note the screen. Press ESC.
   (d) Press ALT, F; then press O for the Open Existing File entry. Briefly note the screen. Press ESC.
   (e) Press ALT, O, and O again to open the Tools, Options menu. Briefly note the screen. Press ESC.
   (f) Press ALT, then press H to open the Help menu. Press C to open the Table of Contents menu. Note the main headings and the subheadings. Use the down arrow to view the entire screen. Press ALT, F, and then press X for exit.
   (g) Press ALT, then press F to open the File menu; Press X to exit *Works*.
2. Hand write or type your notes.

Exercise 2.7

1. To familiarize yourself with the *Works 3.0 for Windows* help system, bring up the *Works 3.0 for Windows* Main menu. The Main menu lists File, Tools, and Help across the top of the screen.

2. If the startup menu is showing, click on Cancel.
3. To select Help, click the mouse on Help; then click on Contents.
4. Use the Help Table of Contents screen to answer the following questions:
   (a) For what categories does Microsoft *Works* provide on-screen information? (List the categories found on the screen, beginning with Step-by-Step Help.)
   (b) How do you get help information (or instructions) as you work, or task-related help, in *Works 3.0 for Windows*? (Hint: Click on Search from the Help Table of Contents menu; type the word **help**; click on Help: Getting Instructions as You Work; click on Show Topics; click on Getting Instructions from Cue Cards as You Work; Click on Go To; make notes about how to get task-related help from cue cards.
   (c) When you are done making notes about using cue cards, move the mouse pointer to the left of the Help screen and click once to close the Help screen.
   (d) Click on File, Exit *Works*.
5. Hand write or type your answers to the questions.

Exercise 2.8

Start by loading *Works 3.0 for Windows* into RAM.

1. Make arrangements with your instructor to familiarize yourself with the *Works* tutorial. You can get to this from the Help menu by selecting Tutorial. Click on Fundamentals.
2. Make notes about what was covered in each of the following sections:
   (a) Introducing Computers
   (b) Working with Windows
   (c) Introducing *Works 3.0 for Windows*
3. Hand write or type the notes about what you learned.

Chapter 3

Introduction to Systems Software

Objectives

After studying this chapter you will be able to:

- *Define the term* systems software
- *Explain how disk operating systems work*
- *Describe how DOS functions within* Windows
- *Explain the purpose of each primary DOS command*
- *Explain the syntax of each primary DOS command*
- *Describe the result of using each primary DOS command*
- *Use common DOS commands from within* Windows
- *Write syntactically correct commands from the DOS command line*

Systems Software

We noted in Chapter 1 that systems software performs the more primitive functions of computing. Systems software regulates memory, determines where and how data is stored both in RAM and on secondary storage media, manages I/O (input and output), and generally monitors the computing session. As a beginning computer user, you will be exposed to interface systems software, in this case *Windows,* and operating system software, a version of *DOS* (disk operating system).

Windows is the layer of software that is immediately obvious to the user, the software that lies between you and the disk operating system. Indeed, many consider *Windows* an operating system in itself because they interact only with it, even when issuing DOS commands. We will explain how to use the operating system from within *Windows* and also from the command line (which the *Windows* icon describes as the *DOS Prompt*).

In Chapter 2, you learned about *Windows* as an interface. In this chapter, you will learn how it joins with DOS to perform operating system commands.

Operating System Concepts

As you have already seen in Chapter 1, an operating system is software that is necessary to run a personal computer. Practically speaking, you cannot compute without an operating system, although it is quite possible to accomplish some computing tasks without an application program.

An operating system is a collection of software programs that enables a computer to perform specific functions. The primary function of an operating system is to control the use of computer resources, which includes memory, secondary storage, and input/output (I/O) devices. The operating system also provides a standard command interface through which application programs access the computer's hardware and it provides for continuous operation of the computer. The operating system is the first software program copied into RAM and the last program remaining before the computer is turned off.

The operating system of a personal computer is usually not apparent when you are generating text, constructing a spreadsheet, or using another application program. However, it resides continually under all application programs, performing primitive functions when called upon by an application program. Many application programs provide access to DOS without leaving the applications. You can sometimes execute DOS functions without exiting application programs. This feature saves you considerable time.

Windows provides most of the DOS file management commands from within the **File Manager**, including commands to copy files, delete files, rename files, create directories, remove directories, copy disks, format (prepare for use) disks, and set the system date and time. You will explore some of these functions later in this chapter when you do the exercises. Application programs written specifically for *Windows* often have their own File Managers. *Works 3.0 for Windows* has a **File Organizer** in the WorksWizards menu that allows you find a file, copy it, rename it, move it, and so forth without exiting to DOS or to the *Windows* File Manager.

This approach provides a more user-friendly interface that allows you to make menu selections by clicking the mouse rather than having to type DOS commands, all the while leaving the application program running.

DOS Defined

DOS (which stands for **disk operating system**) is the operating system developed for the IBM PC and compatible computers.

IBM and compatible personal computers currently run many different versions of DOS. These versions range from the 1.x series up to the most recent release, DOS 6.2. Most application programs today require at least version 3.0 of DOS. Application programs that are written to work specifically in conjunction with *Windows* require DOS 3.1 or greater. The differences in the various versions of DOS are significant enough that you should take care to format diskettes with the same operating system that you will use later. Just as the density of a diskette makes a difference, the version of DOS you use to back up your hard drive must be the same version that you use when you restore files (copy back to the hard drive). Each new version of DOS offers more capabilities to the user.

Loading DOS

As with any operating system, DOS must be copied into RAM before any specialized computing can be done. This step can be accomplished by a **cold boot** (loading the system instructions stored in ROM by turning the power on) or a **warm boot** (clearing RAM and reloading the operating system—in effect, starting over without shutting down the power). The bootstrap loader, a special set of instructions in ROM, locates the system files and places a copy of these files into RAM. (The term *boot* is derived from the old expression "pulling oneself up by the bootstraps.") To use *Windows,* these files must exist on a hard disk for the computer to boot.

Cold Boot When a hard disk computer system is turned on, the following sequence of events occurs:

- The CPU (central processing unit) runs a diagnostic check program from ROM. If this check detects errors, the booting process is terminated and an error message appears on the screen. The memory in RAM is checked, address by address.
- Next, the computer searches for the DOS system files. The computer will start looking for the DOS system files first on drive A and then on drive C. When the computer locates the files, it copies them into RAM. If the system is unable to find the files, you will get an error message. If you see the error message "Non-System disk or disk error. Replace and press any key when ready" you probably have a diskette of your own in drive A. Simply take out the disk in drive A and press any key.
- The CPU then searches the drives for a file called CONFIG.SYS, which is optional and created by the user. If located, the CPU processes the instructions in this file, which contains commands that customize the system.
- The CPU then searches for a file called COMMAND.COM. This is the file that contains DOS's internal commands, which we will discuss later in this chapter. (Note: Since COMMAND.COM contains the internal DOS commands in one file, they will not list out when you are using the directory listing command covered later in the chapter.)

- The CPU then searches for a file called AUTOEXEC.BAT, which is another optional, user-created file to automatically perform some tasks. If located, the commands contained in this file are executed. They may further customize the system or establish a **path** to disk directories.
- Upon execution of the previous steps, either the DOS prompt appears or *Windows* loads automatically and the Program Manager with the available icons representing applications appears, indicating that the computer is ready to execute DOS commands and software applications. The screen display depends on the operating system you are using and the contents of the AUTOEXEC.BAT file.

Warm Boot An occasion may arise when you need to reload DOS and *Windows.* For example, your system may lock up or freeze, and fail to respond when you try to remedy the situation by pressing ESC or CTRL + BREAK. When this happens, you don't need to turn off the system and then turn it on again. If you hold down the CTRL and ALT keys while pressing the DELETE key (or, on some machines, by pressing a reset button on the front of the system unit) all data in the computer's memory will be cleared and DOS will be reloaded into RAM. This process of loading DOS is called a *warm boot.* The system files are immediately copied, and the *Windows* interface is reloaded. Just keep in mind that when you perform a warm boot, RAM is completely cleared, just as if you had just turned the power on to begin a computing session. Anything that is not saved to disk when you initiate the warm boot will be lost.

Loading DOS from a Hard Drive If your computer is not already running, be sure you don't have any diskettes in drive A or B. If you do, remove them.

- Turn on the monitor.
- Locate the on/off switch on the system unit and push it to the 1 (on) position.

During the boot process you may notice some text and numbers appearing on your monitor. This is part of the diagnostic operation. If the AUTOEXEC.BAT file that we mentioned above does not contain a command to load *Windows,* you will see the C> prompt. If the AUTOEXEC.BAT file contains directions to display the date and time, as they often do, your screen may look similar to this:

```
C:\win\Monday Jan 01 1996 09:00:00>
```

You could proceed to do any operating system tasks (file management, etc.) from the command line of DOS, using procedures explained in the DOS command line exercises below. You could also load the *Windows* program and issue commands from within the GUI Program Manager, as you practiced in the exercises in Chapter 2. Whichever you choose, DOS is now loaded into main memory.

If Windows is not already running:

- Type **Win** and press ENTER to load the *Windows* program.

Your monitor will flash the Introductory screen, and within a second or two the Program Manager will appear with the now familiar choices: File, Options, Window, and Help.

Default Drive

When a computer is first started (booted), the **current drive**, or **default drive**, is the drive from which DOS was copied, usually the hard drive, that is, the C drive. Therefore, after booting, if *Windows* is not automatically loaded, the screen will most likely contain the C:\> prompt in some variation, indicating that the C drive is the active or default drive. A computer with a hard drive also has one or two diskette drives. The diskette drives can be made current by typing **A:** or **B:** and pressing ENTER. This changes the default, or currently logged drive.

***Setting the Default Drive in* Works** Before you begin working on the applications you have available, it is a good idea to set the default drive, where the system will store and retrieve your files. Once you start doing some work in the applications, you will want to read and write your own files to a specific drive. If you are using your own computer and want everything stored on the same drive where your program is stored (drive C, usually), this step is not necessary.

Most often, however, you want to keep a separate diskette to store your assignments. Perhaps you are using a network system in a lab and you must use either drive A or drive B for your own files. Many users do not use the computer's hard drive to save personal files, even on their own computers. This saves housekeeping, or clearing extraneous files that can clutter a drive, and protects data files from loss if the hard drive should fail. If you want to save on diskettes, you need to learn now how to change the default drive of *Works* to read and write to your selected drive.

From the opening screen in *Works:*

- Select Open an Existing Document.
- Click on the down arrow in the Drives list box.
- Click on A or B, depending on which type of floppy drive you use.
- Click on Cancel.

The program will reflect the change by listing your chosen drive in the Drives text box. Any files contained on the diskette in your chosen drive will be listed in the first option box. You may select the file to open by scrolling through this listing, which is organized alphabetically within each application.

Once you have changed the default drive you do not have to think twice when saving or retrieving a file; the system will read from and write to the selected drive. This enables you to simply type the name of the file you wish to use on the first line in the Open File display; no drive prefix is necessary. You will practice changing to a new drive in Chapter 4 before you save a word processing file.

Internal and External DOS Commands

After DOS is loaded, it is ready to respond to your commands. The commands you issue can come from a series of more than 66 verbs that actually are names of small programs, or subroutines of instructions. These short programs can either reside in memory constantly (sometimes called **internal commands**), or they can wait on disk to be accessed when needed then cleared from memory when they have finished executing. (The latter are sometimes called **external commands**.) Just remember that some DOS commands, such as COPY, DEL, and DIR are always present in memory; other commands such as FORMAT, BACKUP, or CHKDISK are external and must be loaded into memory each time you issue them.

If you need to distinguish between internal and external commands or wish a comprehensive list of all available DOS commands, a DOS users' manual or a DOS reference book can guide you. We will cover only a small portion of the available DOS commands, those that most beginners use.

Structure of DOS Commands

DOS is systems software that is composed of many individual programs. It possesses a syntax or structure that requires careful adherence. Just as sentences are composed according to the syntax of a language, a DOS command has its own syntax, too. The DOS sentence begins with the command itself, such as COPY. It may also specify subjects and objects; these are the **source drive** and destination or **target drive**, designated by letters such as A, B, or C. Each source or destination drive is indicated by a unique letter followed by a colon. The DOS command may also specify **parameters**, or boundaries; these are sometimes optional and may give further information or instructions. Finally, the command may include **delimiters**, which separate components of the commands.

The skeleton, or underlying structure of a DOS command, is:

```
COMMAND [SOURCEDRIVE:] (parameter) [TARGETDRIVE:] (parameter)
```

A text-based command to copy a file named oldfile.txt from the A drive to the B drive with a new name of newfile.txt is:

```
COPY A:oldfile.txt B:newfile.txt
```

One or more of these parts is often unnecessary; the only part that's always there is the command. Although it is valuable to know the sequence of elements in DOS commands, you will use this knowledge only if you issue your DOS commands from the DOS prompt. In the File Manager in *Windows,* issuing a command is as easy as selecting it with a click of the mouse, and specifying the letters of the source drive and the target drive.

HELP Command in DOS

Any time you are stuck and need help, you can easily get it in two ways. You can select the *Windows* Help function by clicking the mouse within the File Manager, then using the index to select a command with which to view information. In

DOS (version 5.0 or higher), you can invoke the **HELP command** from the DOS prompt by typing the word **help**, followed by the command with which you want help. Since you may need to issue DOS commands from both the File Manager and the text command line (DOS prompt), we encourage you to learn both ways.

Common DOS Commands

FORMAT Command

The disk (the magnetic medium on which computers store files) must be initialized, or prepared, for any computer system to be able to use it. That is because disks are manufactured for general use, with no particular operating system in mind. In initializing, or formatting, the computer marks a disk to correspond to the requirements of the operating system. This process can be compared with putting a blueprint or a template upon the medium so it can be identified and used by DOS.

The DOS **FORMAT** command performs three functions:

- It "cleans" the disk, setting every bit to zero. This cleaning process erases anything that is currently on the disk.
- It defines tracks, sectors, and cylinders on the disk.
- It sets up an empty internal directory called a **FAT (file allocation table)** on the disk. This directory records the physical locations of files on the disk.

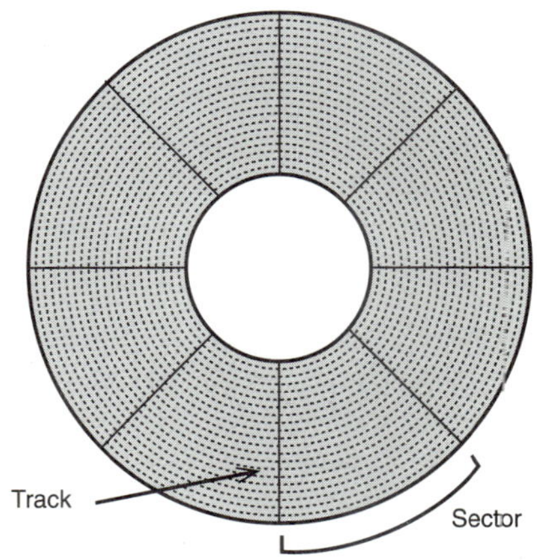

A Formatted Disk Showing Tracks and Sectors

Tracks are concentric circles that define areas on the disk. **Sectors** are pie-shaped divisions of tracks. See the above figure showing a formatted disk with tracks and sectors. A **cylinder** refers to the same location on a track, regardless of surface, on a multisurface hard disk. All the like-numbered tracks on all surfaces of a single disk pack are a cylinder. This organization gives a scheme by which the operating system can identify every area of the disk precisely. It assigns data to specific locations, or **addresses**, on the disk and records these addresses on the file allocation table.

You must format all new diskettes before you use them, unless you purchase preformatted diskettes, which have become available in the last several years. You can reformat a used diskette, but keep in mind that any data on it will be erased in the process. In later exercises, you will get instructions on formatting a diskette both ways.

First, however, you need to know how to insert the medium into the disk drive. If you have a 5.25-inch drive, insert the diskette into the drive with the exposed read/write oval first and the label on top. Figure 3.1 shows how to insert diskettes. Close the door of the drive. You must manually open the drive door to remove the disk when you are through using it.

Figure 3.1

Inserting a Disk Into a Disk Drive

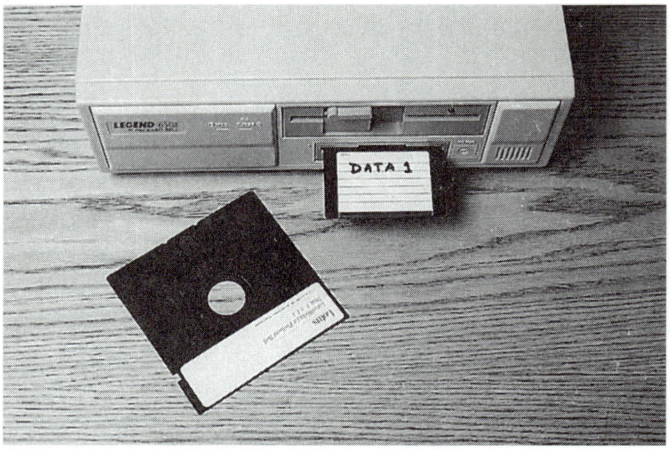

If you have a 3.5-inch drive, look for the arrow embossed on the plastic cover of the diskette. The arrow indicates the direction in which the diskette should be inserted, with the sliding metal window covering the read/write area inserted into the machine first. The diskette will click into place automatically; press the release tab next to the drive to release the diskette when you are finished.

Copying Files and Disks

Two of the earliest DOS commands you need to master are those that allow you to duplicate one or more files. Frequently, you will want to copy one file at a time with the COPY command, but it is often convenient to use a command that will copy the entire contents of one disk onto another in one operation (DISKCOPY). The COPY and DISKCOPY commands are easy to master and are very useful. DISKCOPY requires you to identify source and target drives. Both commands are methods of duplicating files for storage.

COPY Command

To copy a file from one disk to another, you type the **COPY** command followed by the exact file name of the source, including the extension (if any). If you wish to make a copy of a file on the same disk, the name of the copy must be different from the original by at least one character. If you are copying a file from the default drive and directory, you needn't include the name of the drive and directory. It will not hurt to do so, but it is simply superfluous.

Notice in Figure 3.2 that you can use **global** and **wildcard** options to copy multiple files. Wildcards are symbols that can be used in place of characters in filenames or extensions. The two wildcards for DOS are a question mark ? and an asterisk *. The ? can take the place of one unknown character and the * can take the place of several unknown characters. They can be used globally—throughout the entire directory. The global option, indicated by *.*, means you want to copy all files with all extensions. The wildcard option means you want all files that contain the typed characters in their file names. For example, you could specify either *.wps or letter?.wps to copy letter1.wps, letter2.wps, and letter3.wps because the asterisk stands for any number of characters up to the eight for file names and three for extensions, and the question mark stands for any one character.

Figure 3.2

COPY/DISKCOPY Options

`copy *.* a:`	Copies all files in the current directory to drive A.
`copy c:letter.wps a:`	Copies letter.wps to drive A.
`copy c:\graphics\budget\analysis.wps c:\safplace`	Copies analysis.wps from one directory to another.
`copy inventry.wdb a:stock.wdb`	Copies inventry.wdb from the default drive to drive A and renames it.
`copy c:\wordproc\custltr b:`	Copies all the files in the custltr directory to drive B.
`diskcopy a: b:`	Copies all the files from the disk in drive A to the disk in drive B.
`diskcopy a: a:`	Copies all the files from the disk in drive A, called the source disk, to a second disk in drive A called the target disk. You follow the screen prompts regarding the switching of source and target disks.

Although the COPY command is easy, straightforward, and relatively safe, you need to be careful about one thing. Remember that each file name must be unique. If you copy a file from one disk to another and a version of that file already exists on the destination disk, the existing version of the file will be overwritten with the newly copied file. Most of the time that is just what you intend, to replace an old destination file with the newest version. Sometimes, however, you may not want to replace the old file with a newer one (such as when you are doing research notes and final papers). In such a case, when copying files to another disk, always change the file name by at least one character.

Also, make sure that that character is significant. For instance, copying C:Shakespeare1.wps to A:Shakespeare2.wps is not going to do the trick, since the computer stores only the first eight characters before the file extension. Therefore the file is really Shakespe.wps in both cases, and your original file is overwritten!

The COPY command adds to the files already on a destination disk. Therefore you don't need an empty disk; you may simply keep copying files onto a destination disk until it is full. Sooner or later, you may get the ominous message "Disk Full" or "Insufficient Disk Space 0 Files Copied" after entering the command in DOS. This message simply means that the destination disk does not have enough room to copy your file. Replace the destination disk with another formatted disk, and repeat your command. (If using the command line from the DOS prompt, pressing the function key F3 will repeat the command for you, and eliminate retyping, if you wish.) If you are uncertain how much room remains on the destination disk, you can always issue a DIR command (discussed below) before copying to check the number of bytes that are free.

XCOPY Command

The **XCOPY** command enhances the older COPY command by speeding up the process of copying groups of files. It also allows you to copy subdirectories and their contents, if any; the COPY command cannot do this. Type XCOPY /s to copy all nonempty subdirectories in the current directory. Type XCOPY /s/e to copy all subdirectories, even empty ones.

DISKCOPY Command

DISKCOPY allows you to make a duplicate copy of a diskette. The entire diskette is copied, sector by sector and file by file, in exactly the same pattern as on the original diskette. If the target (destination) diskette isn't formatted, DOS will format it before copying. You can perform a DISKCOPY in *Windows* File Manager or at the DOS prompt.

Beginners should approach the DISKCOPY command with caution, since it writes over the target diskette with the new material from the source (original) diskette. It is sometimes confusing to keep track of which diskette drive is the source drive and which is the target drive, leading to the common error of incorrectly inserting the source diskette into the drive where the target diskette should be.

Suppose that you type:

DISKCOPY A: B:

when you have put the blank diskette in drive A and the diskette with all of the files you wish to copy in drive B. If the diskette in drive B has no **write protection** (a way to prevent data from going on the disk), it will be written over with the contents of the diskette in drive A—nothing—and you will have lost the contents you intended to copy!

Also, DISKCOPY is limited to the capacity of the target disk. And you cannot use DISKCOPY on disks of different sizes.

If you have only one floppy drive, you should enter:

- **DISKCOPY A: A:**
- Press ENTER.
- Follow the screen prompts to insert both source and target disks, several times as the system requires.

If you have two floppy drives, you should type the command as:

DISKCOPY A: B:

Heed one warning, however, DISKCOPY copies any bad sectors (corrupt areas on your disk) from the source disk to the target disk. Although you must approach the DISKCOPY command with caution, it is an excellent, quick way to copy an entire disk, such as an application program that you have purchased. You can make a working copy of the program and then put the original in a safe place should you need it again. This procedure is explicitly recommended by the manufacturers of some software packages.

DEL or ERASE Command

Being able to delete, or erase, certain files is just as important as being able to duplicate them with a COPY command. Deleting files frees space on your disk that you may then reuse. It also is simply good housekeeping to clear unneeded files and keep your data organized. Searching through a directory of 25 word processing files and guessing which one contains the document you need (or actually opening each one) is time-consuming. It is much easier to delete unneeded files regularly, as soon as they are no longer useful. Files seem to multiply like rabbits. If you do not periodically remove the unneeded ones, you will soon have a crowded, unmanageable disk.

The **DEL** and **ERASE commands** can be used interchangeably to remove a file from a disk. You may delete one file at a time by issuing the command and specifying the drive and directory where the file is located, or you may use globally the wildcard characters—question mark (?) and asterisk (*)—to delete several files at one time. The asterisk can represent up to eight characters of a filename, and up to three characters of an extension. The question mark replaces only one character in a particular position of a file name or extension. You will practice the DEL and ERASE commands in the exercises below.

If you have DOS 5.0 or a later version, you have the option of using the **UNDELETE command** in special instances. Although it is not always possible, this command in the later versions of DOS may allow you to reverse your action when you have deleted a file by mistake. This is a savior in those instances when you have not thought carefully before clicking the mouse button and have erased a file that you did not intend to remove from disk.

DOS requires no confirmation granting permission to erase a single file from the DOS prompt.

Conventions for File Names

Every operating system has definite rules on how to name files created and stored by it. DOS has an eight-character limit on **file names**, with an optional three-character **extension** following a period (e.g., filename.ext). If you assign a name that is longer than eight letters, the computer will store only the first eight letters. This combination allows you to describe the file contents by unique names. Each file must have a unique name, even if only its extension differs from other files. As a general rule, you will want to assign names that represent what files contain to keep the job of remembering file contents easier. Thus you might choose letterl.wps, letter2.wps, and letter3.wps for three files that are successive versions of the same letter.

Naming Files and Directories File and directory names can contain letters, numbers or any of a group of special characters (~` ! @ # $ ^ & ( ) _ - { } '). Note that file names cannot contain spaces. Even though special characters and numbers are allowed in file and directory names, we suggest that you create names made up mostly of letters that either spell words or are abbreviations of words.

A file extension, the one to three optional characters following a file name and period, often reveal as much as the file name itself. Extensions of .com and .exe always mean files that are executable—they can run by themselves without other programs in memory to drive them. These commonly used file extensions can often help you to identify your files.

As you progress through this book, you will find that *Works* automatically adds file extensions as you save your work. *Works* adds the extension .WPS to word processing files, .WKS to spreadsheet files, .WDB to database files, and .WCM to communication files. You will soon learn to recognize what these extensions mean, and they will help you organize your personal collection of files.

Commands Relating to Directories

You will often want to view the directory, or listing of the names of the files residing on a drive, using the DOS **DIR** command. The directory is much like the directory in the lobby of an office building, which lists the names of the companies that occupy office space. To view the directory, simply type **dir**. Your screen will then display a list of files stored on the disk in the active directory. The display includes:

- The name of each file
- The size (in bytes) of the file
- The date and time the file was created or last changed

It also includes a count of the number of files on the disk and reports how much free storage space remains on it. It is a good practice to verify the available storage on each disk periodically before using it.

Directory Structures

Although you could save all of your files in a single directory, you would soon find the DIR listing unwieldy and perhaps even bewildering, especially for a large hard disk. It is more efficient from the beginning to practice orderly file management in which you keep related files in separate directories. To put it another way, a hard disk is much like an empty file drawer. It provides storage, but no organization. To make it easier to find items, you create separate directories to hold your files. Such detailed organization is rarely needed for diskettes.

The DOS directory structure is hierarchical (ordered top-down, from general to specific). The main or top level directory is called the **root directory**. The root directory is designated in DOS with a backslash (\). When a computer with a hard drive is turned on or rebooted, the default or active directory is the root. Your DOS prompt looks like C:\>. The C: indicates that drive C is current and the backslash indicates that the root directory is also the current directory. The root directory cannot, like other user-created directories, be re-named or removed. A brand new hard drive would contain only one directory—the root.

The directories that you create branch out from the root, much as children branch out from parents. Just as children can eventually become parents themselves, each directory you create can have a number of other directories beneath it. Each directory is a **subdirectory** to the directory that precedes it in the hierarchy. Each directory can both be a subdirectory and have its own subdirectories.

For instance, in the inverted-tree structure shown in Figure 3.3, the top level is the root directory (\). Below the root directory are three directories—SPSHEET, HOBBY, and WP. These three directories are subdirectories of the root directory. The directory HOBBY has one subdirectory called ANTIQUES. WP has one subdirectory called REPORTS and one named LETTERS. SPSHEET has no subdirectories.

The directory that encompasses a subdirectory is called the *parent directory*. The only directory that does not have a parent is the root. In Figure 3.3, the parent of the ANTIQUES directory is HOBBY. The parent of HOBBY is the root. The parent of SPSHEET is also the root. The parent of REPORTS is WP and the parent of WP is the root.

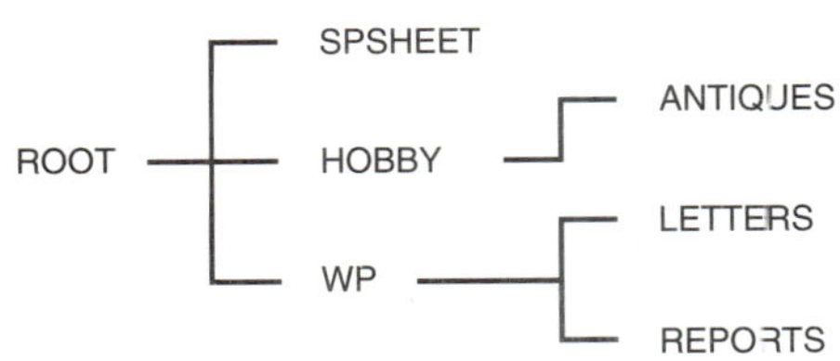

Figure 3.3

Inverted Tree Structure of Directories and Subdirectories

The only directory that is guaranteed to be found on a fixed disk is the root directory. Other subdirectories can be created and will no doubt vary in name and structure from disk to disk. After a directory has been created, files can then be placed in it.

Making Directories

The DOS **make directory command** is **MD** followed by the name of the directory or subdirectory. When you make a subdirectory, as **MD Letters** with a space between the command and the subdirectory, the subdirectory will be made in the directory you are currently in. When you make a subdirectory with a backslash between the command and the subdirectory, as **MD\Letters**, the subdirectory will be made in the root directory (C:\> on the hard drive and A:\> on the A drive). For example, at the C:\> prompt, the command **MD Letters** would make the subdirectory in the root directory. However, if you were in a word processing subdirectory as C:\>Wordproc, the command **MD Letters** would put the subdirectory Letters in the Wordproc directory, but the command **MD\Letters** would put the subdirectory Letters in the root directory. Stop and think what directory you are in when you make a subdirectory and where you want that subdirectory to go. As in file names, a directory may contain eight characters, but no extension.

There are numerous advantages to organizing your hard disk with directories:

1. System organization. Unless you use directories, your software programs, user data files, DOS files, and utility programs will all be mixed helter skelter, making it difficult to locate files and determine what is on the disk.
2. Addition and deletion of software programs. Organized directories allow you to add or remove program and data files more easily. Many programs create their own directories when they are installed on disk.
3. Ease of updating software. You can easily convert to new releases of software if you keep each application in its own directory.
4. Keeping user files separate. If more than one person uses a computer, a directory for each user will eliminate confusion. Each of you can edit your own files, without confusing them with another user's files that might have similar names.

There is no limit to the number of levels of subdirectories you can create, but a practical limit is about four or five. Beyond five subdirectories, a directory structure becomes too complex and confusing.

Changing Directories

When you first boot your computer, the root directory is usually current; however, you can change the current directory. The DOS **change directory command, CD**, is used to change the current directory. When you use the CD command, you must give DOS the path (similar to a road map) instructing DOS where to find the directory to which you want to move. The rules about spaces and backslashes apply just as in making a directory. The path for a directory begins at the root directory and follows with the subdirectory name. If the path includes additional subdirectories, each one's name must be separated by a backslash (\). For example, if you wanted to delete a file named Expenses in the Reports Subdirectory of the WP Directory, you would type at the C:\> prompt: DEL C:\WP\Reports\Expenses. You will practice changing directories, both from the File Manager and from the DOS command line, following in the exercises below.

TREE Command

The **TREE command** is useful for refreshing your memory when you have created several directories and subdirectories. It displays the path name for each directory, followed by a list of subdirectories contained in the directory, if any. The command TREE/F will show you not only the subdirectories, but also the names of the files in each. You can issue the TREE command either from the File Manager or from the DOS prompt. The TREE command gives you a breakdown of your hard disk's structure.

Removing Directories

On occasion you will no longer need a directory and the files contained in it. In that case, you may want to clean house by removing it. To do so, use the **remove directory command, RD**, followed by the path and directory name.

Two restrictions limit your ability to remove directories. First, the directory must be empty. You must delete the files in a directory before you can remove it. The second restriction is that the directory to be removed may not be the current directory. In other words, you cannot remove a directory that you are currently using—you must change directory to another directory. To remove several layers of subdirectories, you must remove the lowest level first and then proceed to the next previous level, removing one level at a time. You will practice removing a directory in the exercises below.

RENAME (REN) Command

A file can be renamed any number of times without changing its contents by the DOS **RENAME (REN) command**. Renaming is often desirable, whether to make a file name more mnemonic (easier to associate with the file's contents), to correct a spelling error in the original name, or to make a duplicate of the same file on the same disk. As we have indicated, a file cannot be copied beside itself, that is, you cannot have two files with the same name on the same drive and directory. However, you may give one copy of the file a different name and duplicate it. You will rename a file in the following exercises.

TYPE Command

One of the most helpful of the DOS commands, the **TYPE command**, allows you to see the contents of a file without going into the application program that generated it. TYPE is evoked from the DOS prompt.

The display of a text file will be very readable. Displays of spreadsheet, word processing, and graphic files are not so readable from a TYPE command. Spreadsheet and graphic files contain so many control characters and machine symbols that your columns and rows will barely be distinguishable from all of the hearts, smiley faces, stars, and other machine characters if you issue a TYPE command from the DOS prompt. However, being able to reveal the contents of a text file from the operating system without going into a word processing, spreadsheet, or other application program is still very convenient.

TYPE is a good browsing command; you cannot change the file in any way, but you may view its entire contents as it scrolls by on the screen. To review a file that is longer than one screenful, press CTRL+NUMLOCK, PAUSE, or CTRL+S to freeze the display at any point, or type **TYPE¦MORE** to see one screenful at a time. Then press any key to resume viewing the file.

The CHKDSK Command

You can use the CHKDSK command on both floppy disks and hard disks. It is good practice to run CHKDSK on the hard disk periodically. Among other items the information displayed will be the total amount of disk space, the number of directories assigned, the number of user files, and the number of bytes still available on the disk. It will also list the number of total bytes of memory (RAM) and the number of bytes of RAM free or available for use by the programs.

You will not use all of the DOS commands we have explained all of the time, nor have we discussed all of the commands included in DOS. We have focused on those most commonly used by beginning computer students, or most in need of explanation. There are DOS prompt commands to clear the screen **(CLS)**, change the appearance of the prompt you see at the operating system level **(PROMPT)**, direct output to the printer **(PRINT)**, identify your version of DOS **(VER)**, and change the date **(DATE)** or time **(TIME)** in the computer, among other functions. To get help in using the commands we have reviewed, or any of the DOS commands or their parameters, remember to use the on-line DOS help function. For a more detailed explanation of the DOS commands, consult a book that deals specifically with this subject.

Now you will have an opportunity to try out some of the common DOS commands for your own use. Remember that DOS is not as user friendly as most application programs. DOS has definite structural rules for its commands. Thus it may take two or three tries before you type in a command in the correct form. If you get an error message, simply retype the command, paying close attention to all of the spaces, colons, file extensions, and so forth. (The computer doesn't know how many tries it takes you to succeed!)

As we mentioned, several different disk drive sizes and capacities are available. The following exercises assume you are using an IBM or compatible computer with one hard drive and one 3.5-inch, high-density diskette in the A drive. If you have a different configuration, your instructor will give you additional instructions.

This exercise also assumes that your computer is turned on, that *Windows* is active, and that DOS is represented by an icon in the *Windows* screen. DOS accepts commands in either upper or lower case. We will state commands in lower case in these exercises. As in all exercises and tutorials in this book, material that you should type is shown in **bold face**. You will be using some files that are on a student data disk in the back of your book. Instructions will indicate when to insert the data disk.

Warning: Do not attempt to insert or remove your diskette while the diskette drive light is lit. Doing so may damage your disk or disk drive.

From the DOS Command Line: Exercises

In the following exercises, you will practice some of the more commonly used DOS commands, such as DIR, DIR/P, DIR/W, DIR A:, CLS, FORMAT, COPY, RENAME, CHKDSK, and DEL (or ERASE). Also, you will make directories and subdirectories and put files in them.

1. Double click on the DOS icon.

   You should have C:\> showing on the screen. To see the directory of the files on the C drive (the default drive):

2. Type **dir**
3. Press ENTER.

   Notice that the files scroll quickly off the screen so that all you see is the end of the listing with the number of files and bytes used, and the number of bytes free. To see one screen of files at a time, showing the date and time each was created and the number of bytes in each, add the **/P switch** (for *pause*):

4. Type **dir/p**
5. Press ENTER.

   The display stops after filling the screen and prompts you to press any key to continue.

6. Press any key on the keyboard to continue displaying the files. Press CTRL+C whenever you want to interrupt the display and return to DOS.

   To see all the files, but without the date, time, and size information, add the **/W switch** (for *wide*):

7. Type **dir/w**
8. Press ENTER.

   The files are displayed in a wide format.

9. Type **cls**
10. Press ENTER.

    Your screen is cleared.

You want to make a copy of the student data disk at the back of your *Works* textbook and put the original away in a safe place.

1. Insert a **blank**, unformatted, 3.5-inch diskette in drive A.
2. Type **format a:**

   Caution: Be very careful with the FORMAT command. Typing **format** without specifying a drive formats the default drive, in this case, drive C. Also, remember that any files on the formatted disk will be deleted.

3. Press ENTER.
4. Follow the instructions on your screen.
5. Press ENTER if/when you are asked for a label.
6. Type **N** or **NO** when asked if you want to format another diskette.

Now you want to make an identical copy of your data disk, using the DISKCOPY command. (Actually, this exercise does not depend on the previous one because DISKCOPY will also format a disk, if necessary.) Remember, any files on the disk would be deleted.

1. Type **diskcopy a: a:**

   You are prompted to insert your source diskette (in this case the data diskette from your book) in drive A and press ENTER. When a portion of the disk has been copied into memory, you are asked to insert your target (blank) diskette and press ENTER. You must repeat these steps several times until all the data has been copied onto your new disk. Leave your newly copied disk in drive A.

2. Type **dir a/w:**

   Your screen should look similar to the one in Figure 3.4. Do not be concerned if your screen differs somewhat from the figure. You would like to have a paper printout of the files contained on the disk, as you will be using them for later assignments.

3. Hold down the SHIFT key and press the PRT SCRN key.

Figure 3.4

The dir/w Command

```
A:\>dir/w
Volume in drive A has no label
Directory of A:\

CHARTER.WPS   VACATON.WPS    WILL.TXT      README        NETWRTH.WKS
RETIRE.WKS    INDXFND.WKS    PERFM.WKS     ADDRES.WDB    PTR.WDB
OUTBRD.WDB    INSFRMLR.WDB   REQUIRE.WPS   SURVEY.WPS    MILITARY.TXT
ESSAY.WPS     README.BAT     CORECTIN      JLERROR       GLERROR.TXT
GLERROR.WPS   WKS2ERRS.WPS   INSCHED.WPS   ABSTRACT.WPS  FIGURES
HELP02.WPS    MOUSE02.WPS    CURSOR02.WPS  SELECT02.WPS
       29 file(s)     143037 bytes
                      572416 bytes free

A:\>
```

This will print a copy of your screen on the printer. (Note: Check with your instructor to see if you can access the C drive for the next step in this exercise. Skip it if you can't have access to the C drive.) Now you will use the COPY command to copy two of the files on the diskette to the C drive. They will be stored on the root directory of drive C, but you will soon delete them.

4. Type **copy a:select02.wps c:**
5. Type **copy a:mouse02.wps c:**

   To see the files:
6. Type **dir/w**

   You do not want to leave the files on the C drive, so you will delete them. You can use either the DEL command or the ERASE command. Be sure the prompt is C:\>.
7. Type **del select02.wps**
8. Type **erase mouse02.wps**
9. Do a directory of C again to see if the files were removed.
10. Clear the screen (CLS).

In the next exercise, you will make the A drive the default drive, rename a file, and check the disk for errors.

1. Type **a:**
2. Press ENTER.

   The default drive changes from drive C to drive A, as shown in Figure 3.5.
3. Type **ren help02.wps assist02.wps**

```
C:\a:
A:\>
```

Figure 3.5

Changing from Drive C to Drive A

4. Press ENTER.
5. Type **dir**

   The file help02.wps has been renamed assist02.wps. It may be necessary to check the number of bytes unused on a diskette and to see if it includes any bad spots. The CHKDSK command does this. You are still on the A drive.
6. Type **chkdsk**
7. Press ENTER.

   Your screen should look similar to that in Figure 3.6. Do not be concerned if your screen differs somewhat from the figure.

Figure 3.6

The CHKDSK Command

```
A:\>chkdsk

      730112  bytes total disk space
      157696  bytes in 29 user files
      572416  bytes available on disk

        1024  bytes in each allocation unit
         713  total allocation units on disk
         559  available allocation units on disk

      655360  total bytes memory
      581264  bytes free

A:\>
```

In the next set of exercises you will use the MAKE DIRECTORY (MD), CHANGE DIRECTORY (CD), REMOVE DIRECTORY (RD), and TREE commands.

1. Type **md wordproc**
2. Press ENTER.
3. Type **md spread**
4. Press ENTER.
5. Type **md database**
6. Press ENTER.
7. Type **dir**
8. Press ENTER.

You have now made three directories on your disk in drive A. In the directory listing, they are designated by <DIR>. To make a subdirectory in any of those directories you will use the MD command again. You will make two subdirectories in the wordproc directory—letters and reports. First, you must change directories (with the CD command) to enter the wordproc directory.

1. Type **cd wordproc**

   You are in the wordproc subdirectory.
2. Type **md letters**
3. Type **md reports**
4. Type **cd..** (cd period period)

   This command takes you backward (or upward) one subdirectory level.

5. Press ENTER.

   You are back in the root directory, from which you will copy two files into the reports subdirectory.

6. Type **copy select02.wps a:\wordproc\reports**
7. Type **copy cursor02.wps a:\wordproc\reports**

   Now to see what your directory structure looks like:

8. Type **tree**
9. Press ENTER.

Figure 3.7 shows the directories and subdirectories you created. It does not show any files. In the following exercise, you will move downward and backward within the directory structure.

```
A:\>tree
Directory PATH listing
Volume Serial Number is 13F6-1734
A:.
├───WORDPROC
│   ├───LETTERS
│   └───REPORTS
├───SPREAD
└───DATABASE

A:\>
```

Figure 3.7

The Tree Command

1. Type **cd wordproc**
2. Press ENTER.

   Your prompt now reads A:\WORDPROC>.

3. Type **cd reports**
4. Press ENTER.

   Your prompt now reads A:\WORDPROC\REPORTS> because you are one directory level below WORDPROC.

5. Type **cd..**
6. Press ENTER.

   Now your prompt reads A:\WORDPROC>.

   Recall that the \ indicates the root directory. You can type **cd** to get to the root or **cd** plus the name of the directory and path under the root to which you want to go.

7. Type: **cd\spread**

8. Press ENTER.

   You see the A:\SPREAD> prompt.

You are now going to remove each subdirectory. Remember you must first remove the files, if any.

1. Type **cd\wordproc**
2. Press ENTER.
3. Type **cd reports**

   You want to delete all the files in the current subdirectory.

4. Type **del *.***

   Caution: Be careful with the global DEL command. Never use it without making sure you are in the correct directory.

5. Press ENTER.

   You see a message explaining that all files in the current directory will be deleted and asking "Are you sure (Y or N)?" Make it a habit to take your hands off the keyboard and check the directory you are in before you type **Y** for *Yes*. You are in the reports directory, but you cannot remove the current directory.

6. Type **cd..**
7. Type **rd reports**
8. Press ENTER.
9. Type **rd letters**
10. Press ENTER.
11. Type **cd**
12. Press ENTER.
13. Type **rd spread**
14. Press ENTER.
15. Type **rd wordproc**
16. Press ENTER.
17. Type **rd database**
18. Type **Exit** to return to the *Windows* screen.

Within the Windows File Manager: Exercises

Sometimes it is easier to perform DOS commands through *Windows* instead of exiting to DOS. In the following exercises, you will issue some of the same DOS commands as you did earlier, but from the *Windows* File Manager. Put your data disk in the A drive. All the *Windows* icons should be displayed on the screen.

1. Double click on the Main icon.
2. Double click on File Manager.

   Your screen will look similar to that in Figure 3.8. The left window lists the directories on the C drive, with the Windows directory open. (The icon is an open file folder.) The right window lists the directories and files in the Windows subdirectory.

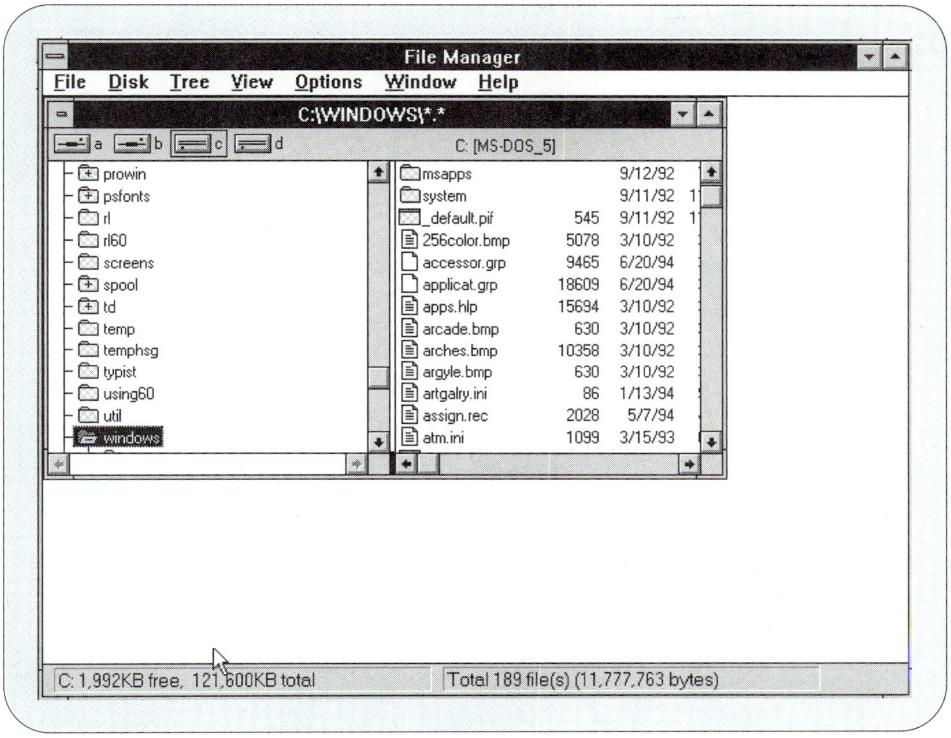

Figure 3.8

Windows File Manager

3. Move the mouse pointer to prowin in the left window and double click on it.

   It becomes the active directory and the right window displays the files in that directory. To change to the A directory:

4. Click on the A directory file icon in the upper, left-hand corner.

   The files on your data disk display in the right window. You can see the number of bytes in each file and date and time each was created. (You may have to drag the scroll bar to the right or click on the right arrow to see all of this information.) Notice also that the bottom, left-hand side of the status bar shows the number of bytes free and the total number of bytes available; the right-hand side of the status bar shows the total number of files and the total of storage bytes occupied by those files.

5. Click on the cursor02.wps file to select it.
6. Click on File.

   The File pull-down menu, shown in Figure 3.9, appears.

Figure 3.9

The File Menu

7. Click on Copy.

   The copy screen displays, as shown in Figure 3.10. You will copy the cursor02.wps file to the C drive.
8. In the To text box type **C:**
9. Click on OK.

   To see the file:
10. Click on the C drive icon, then click on C:\

    Use the scroll bar to locate the cursor02.wps file, as shown in Figure 3.11. Now, to delete it from the C drive:
11. Select cursor02.wps.
12. Click on File.
13. Click on Delete.

    The File Delete dialog box displays.

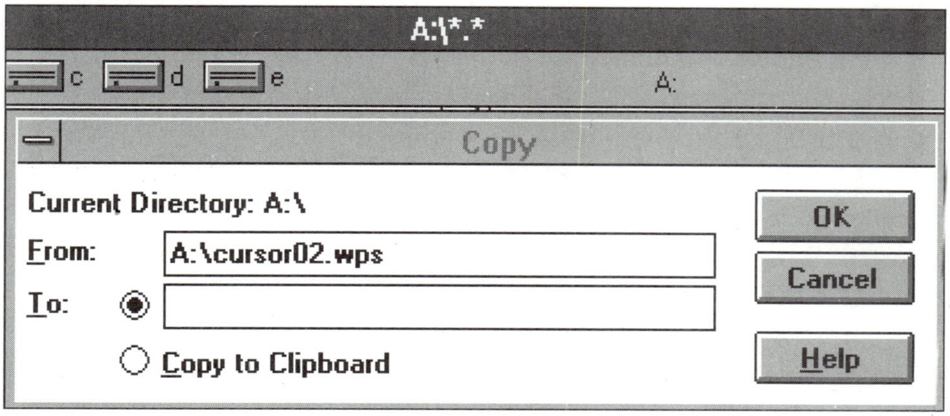

Figure 3.10

The Copy Option Box

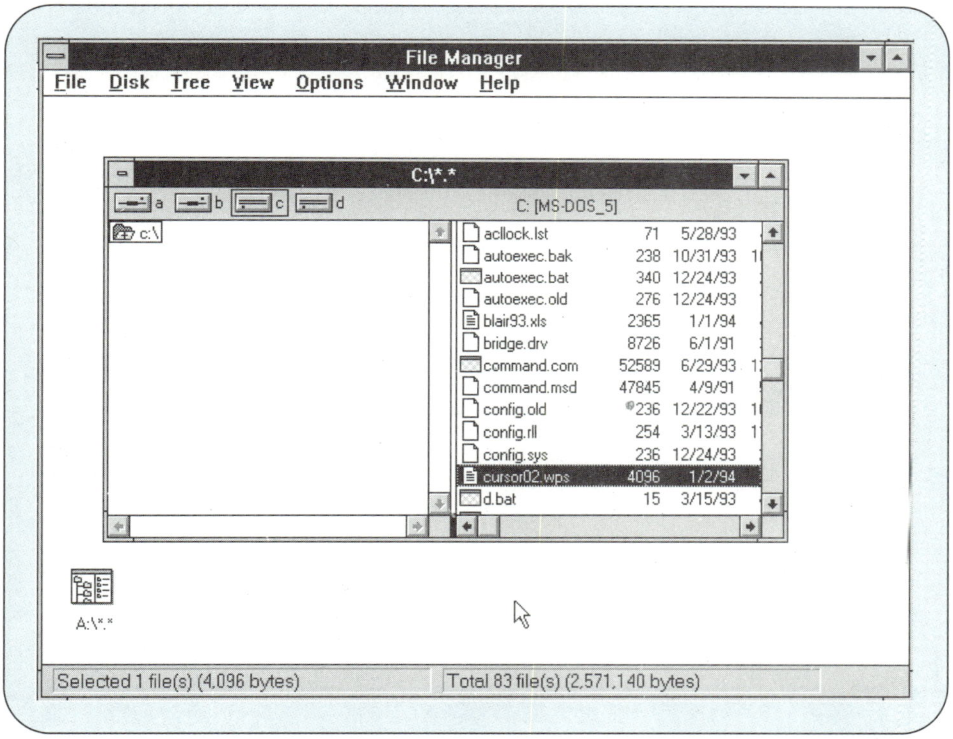

Figure 3.11

Files on the C Drive

14. Click on Yes.

    You see a Confirm? prompt.

15. Click on OK.

You will now rename the assist02.wps file as help02.wps.

1. Click on the A drive icon.

2. Click on assist02.wps in the right text box
3. Click on File-Rename.

   The Rename option box displays, as shown in Figure 3.12.

Figure 3.12

The Rename Option Box

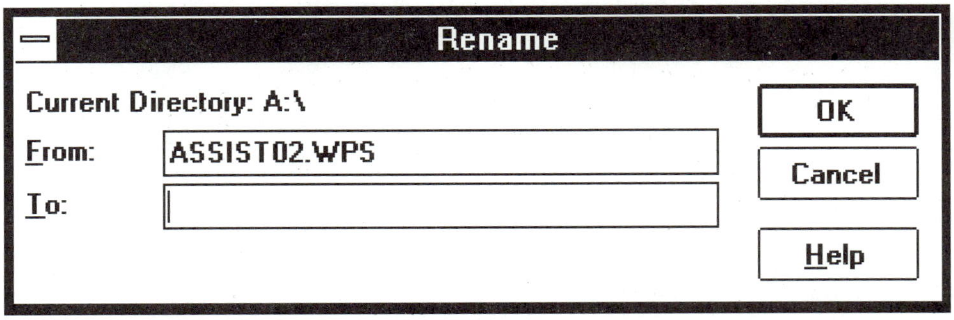

4. In the To text box, type **help02.wps**
5. Click on OK.

You will now make a new directory, wordproc, and two subdirectories, reports and letters. The A directory should be displayed on your screen.

1. Click on File-Create Directory.

   The Create Directory option box displays, as shown in Figure 3.13.

Figure 3.13

The Create Directory Option Box

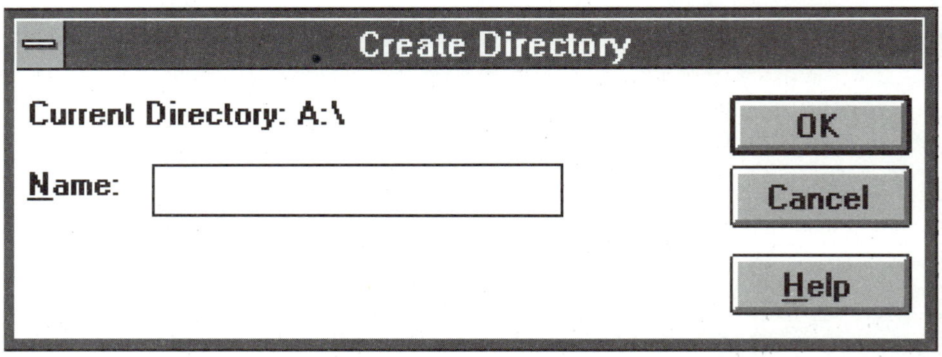

2. In the Name text box, type **wordproc**
3. Click on OK.
4. Click on wordproc in the left-hand window.
5. Click on File-Create Directory.

   The Create Directory box shows A:\WORDPROC
6. In the Name text box, type **reports**, then click on OK.
7. On your own, create a letters subdirectory in wordproc.

You can copy files from one directory to another using the mouse. Use the *Windows* Help feature to find out how.

1. Click on Help.

   The Help pull-down menu displays, as shown in Figure 3.14.

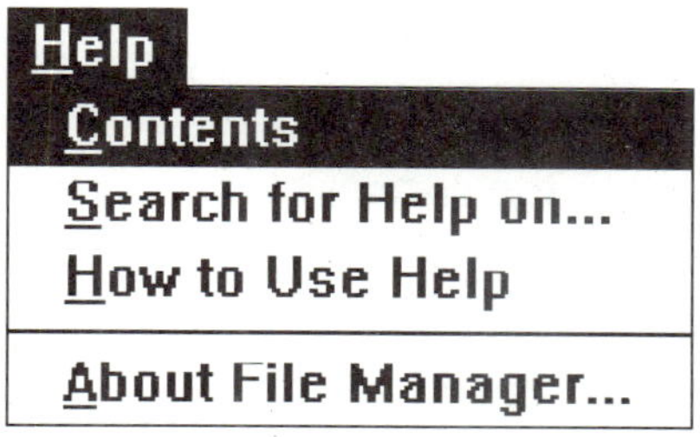

Figure 3.14

The Help Menu

2. Click on Search for Help on.

   The Search menu displays, as shown in Figure 3.15.

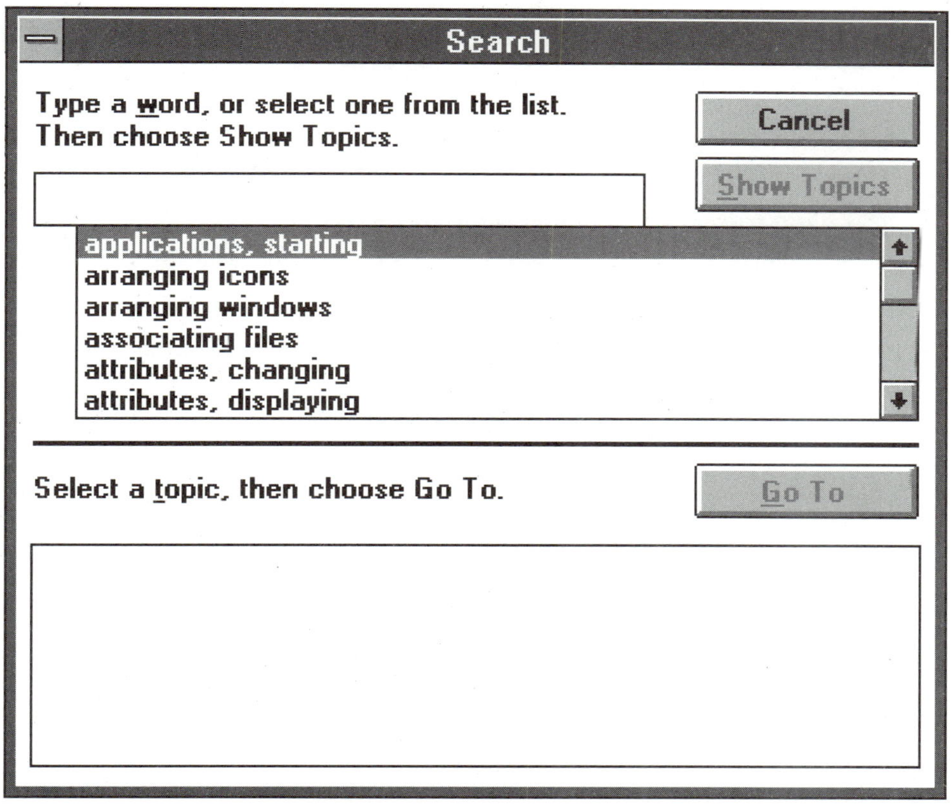

Figure 3.15

The Search Menu

3. In the text box, type **copying files**
4. Click on Show Topics.

5. Click on Go To.

   Information with the heading “Copying Files and Directories” displays.

6. Click on File-Print Topic in the Help window.
7. Click on File-Exit to exit the Help window.

   Read the printed information to find that you can copy a file by holding the CTRL key as you drag the icon.

8. If the subdirectory names are not displayed, click on wordproc in the left-hand window to display letters and reports.
9. Click on the up-arrow icon in the right-hand window to display the files on the A drive.
10. Hold down the CTRL key, click on cursor02.wps, and drag it to the reports directory.

    A rectangle will surround reports as a Confirm option box displays.

11. Click on Yes.

Now copy the mouse02.wps file using the *Windows* Copy function.

1. Select mouse02.wps.
2. Click on File-Copy.
3. In the To text box, type **wordproc\reports**

   You must give the complete path name.

4. Click on OK.
5. Click on the reports icon.

   The list of files will show in the right-hand list box.

In the next exercise, you will delete the wordproc, letters, and reports directories and the mouse02.wps and cursor02.wps files.

1. Click on the wordproc icon.
2. Click on File-Delete.

   A Delete confirmation box asks you to confirm that you want to delete reports, letters, and the two files. In other words, it prompts you to confirm deletion of all files and subdirectories under the chosen directory.

3. Click on Yes to confirm these deletions.

You have already formatted a disk and copied your data disk onto it. However, to format another disk in *Windows*, you would follow these steps:

1. Click on Disk.

   The Disk pull-down menu displays, as shown in Figure 3.16.

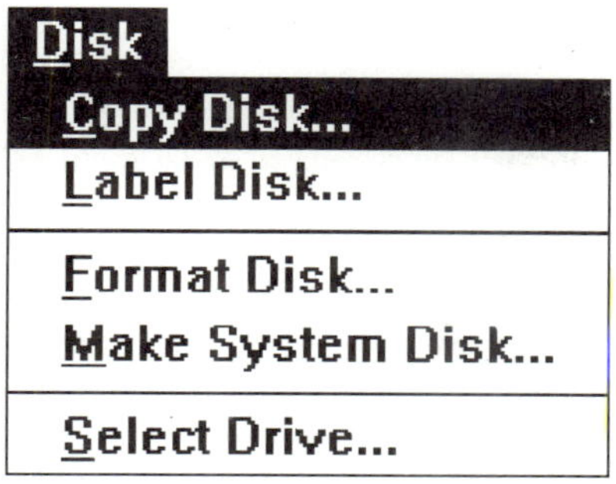

Figure 3.16

The Disk Menu

2. Click on Format Disk.

   The Format Disk option box displays, as shown in Figure 3.17.

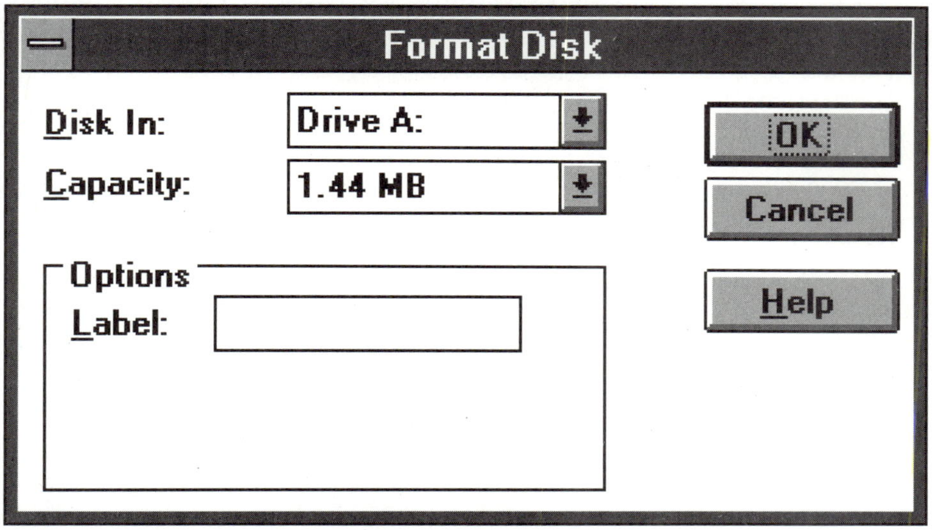

Figure 3.17

The Format Disk Option Box

3. Click on the Disk In arrow to select drive A or B.
4. Click on Capacity to select 1.44MB or 720K for a 3.5-inch disk, or 360K or 1.2MB for a 5.25-inch disk drive.
5. Click on OK and Yes in response to several confirm messages.

To make an exact copy of a disk, you would:

1. Click on Disk-Copy Disk.

   The Copy Disk option box displays, as shown in Figure 3.18.

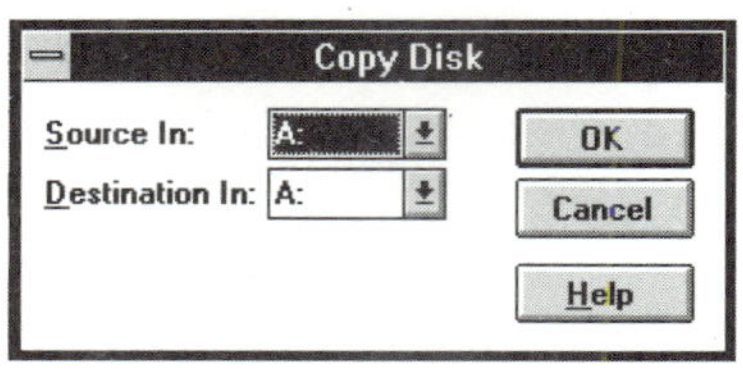

Figure 3.18

The Copy Disk Option Box

2. Click on OK and follow the screen prompts.

   One advantage of copying a disk through *Windows* is that you put each disk in only one time, as opposed to several times through DOS.

3. Click on File-Exit to exit the File Manager.

Note that one command you issued in DOS that you cannot access in *Windows* is CHKDSK. To perform that command you must exit to DOS.

Challenge Exercise: Student Macro

This exercise may be beyond the scope of some beginning students, but it explores the only way to create macros in *Works*. In this exercise, you will create a macro to reproduce your name, your instructor's name, space for an assignment number, and space for a date due in the *Works* word processor screen. This may seem a complicated way to save keystrokes, but once they are saved, they can be replayed at any time. Also, many, more complicated sets of keystrokes can be saved in the same way.

1. Double click on Works, then click on Word processor.
2. Minimize the screen.

   (Click on the down arrow on the right-hand side of the Word processor title bar.)

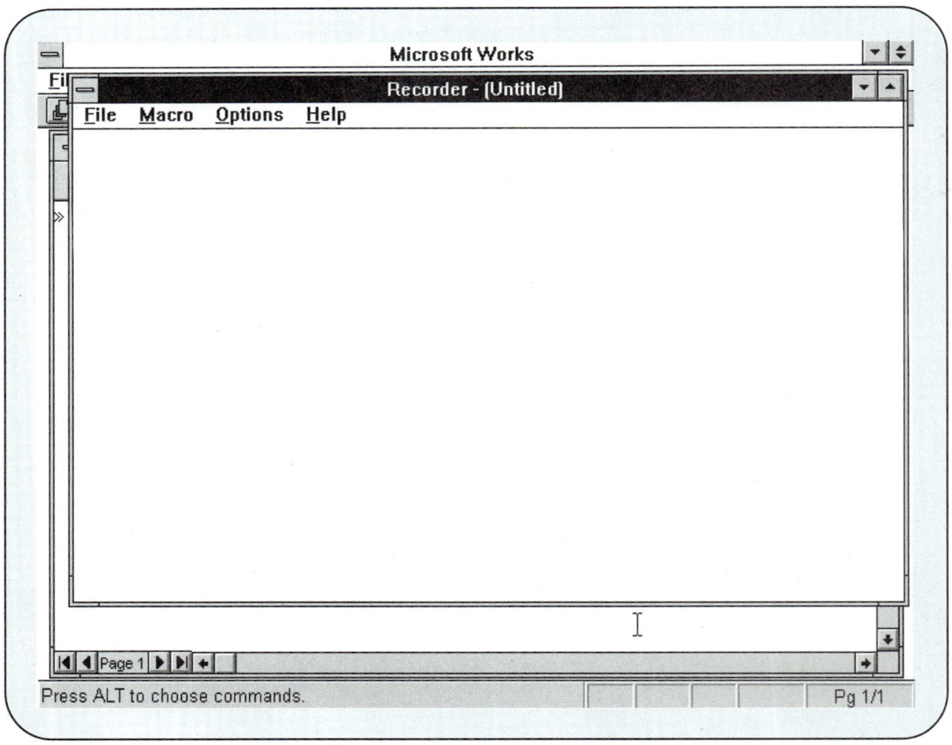

Figure 3.19

Windows Recorder Feature

3. Double click on Accessories.
4. Double click on Recorder.
5. Minimize Recorder.
6. Press CTRL+ESC, then select Microsoft *Works* and click on Switch to.

   You should now be in the *Works* word processor screen, where you want to place your information.
7. Press CTRL+ESC, then select Recorder and click on Switch to.

   The Recorder screen appears, as shown in Figure 3.19.
8. Click on Macro.

   The Macro pull-down menu appears, as shown in Figure 3.20.
9. Click on Record.

   The Record Macro dialog box appears, as shown in Figure 3.21. The insertion point should be in the Record Macro Name text box. You will assign the shortcut keys CTRL+O to begin your macro.
10. Type **Assign**
11. Tab to the Shortcut Key box and type **o**
12. Click on the Ctrl box, if it is not already marked.
13. Click on Start.

    You return to the *Works* word processor screen. (If not, press CTRL+ESC and Switch to Works.)

Figure 3.20

The Macro Menu

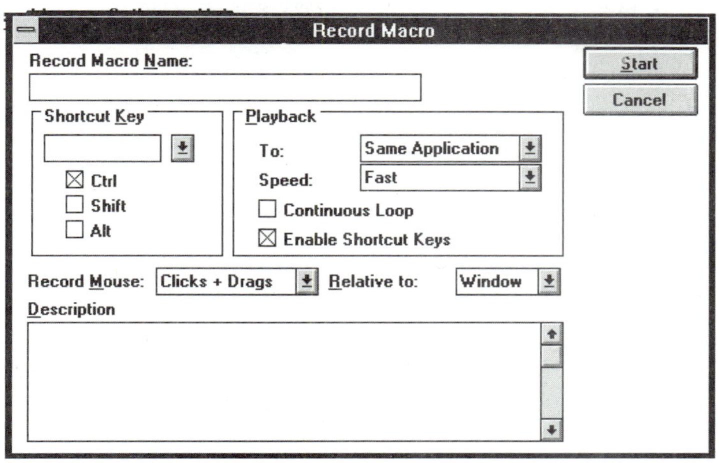

Figure 3.21

The Record Macro Dialog Box

14. Type the following:

    Your name

    Your instructor's name

    Assignment No.________________________

    Date________________________

15. Press ENTER twice.
16. Press CTRL+BREAK (the Pause key on the far right of the top row).

    An option box, shown in Figure 3.22, displays.

Figure 3.22

The Save Macro Option Box

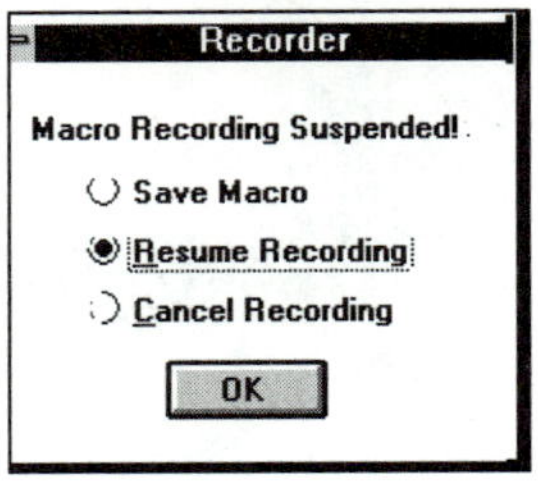

17. Click on Save Macro.
18. Click on OK.

    You must save the macro in a file for future use.

19. Press CTRL+ESC, then click on Recorder-End Task.

    An option box asks if you want to save your changes.

20. Click on Yes.

    The File Save As dialog box displays.

21. In the File Name text box type **assign.rec**
22. Click on OK.

You will now play the macro. Close the *Works* document without saving and open a new word processor screen.

1. Press CTRL+ESC and Switch to Recorder.

   The screen Recorder–ASSIGN.REC displays, as shown in Figure 3.23.

2. Click on File-Open.

   The File menu appears, as shown in Figure 3.24, with the assign.rec file shown in the file list box.

3. Select assign.rec-OK.
4. Switch back to your word processor screen. (CTRL+ESC)
5. Select and delete the text on the screen.

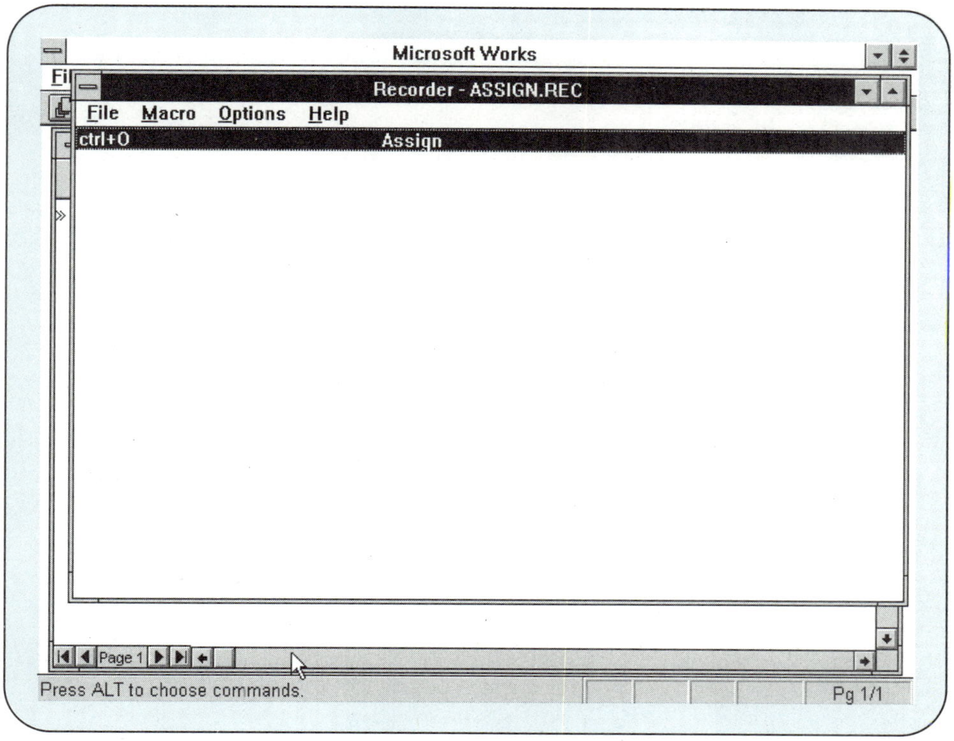

Figure 3.23

The Assign Recorder Screen

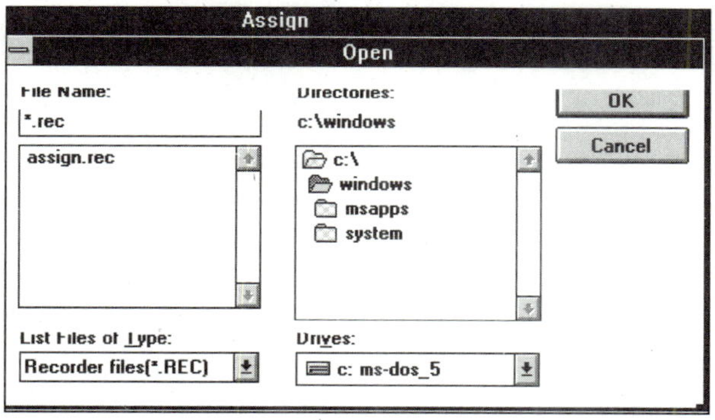

Figure 3.24

The Recorder File Open Option Box

6. Press CTRL+O.

   Your screen should look similar to that in Figure 3.25.

You will be able to use the macro by pressing CTRL+O until you exit the *Windows* program. To activate this macro for use when you open *Windows* again, just click on Accessories-Recorder-Open File-Assign.rec.

Figure 3.25

The Created Macro

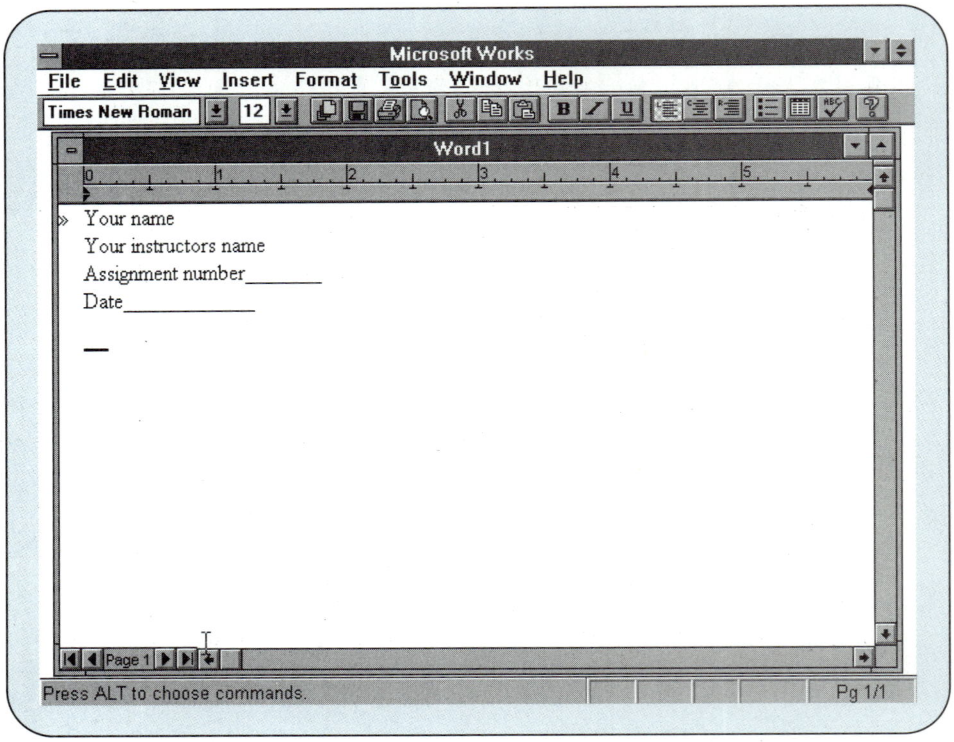

Chapter Summary

Systems software is concerned with management and maintenance of computer system components. It includes interfaces, such as *Windows,* utility programs that back up hard disk files, or operating systems, such as DOS.

Operating system software is the traffic cop of the personal computer system. It is necessary for the operation of a computer because it manages resources, peripherals, programs, and data; it keeps track of all the primitive functions that go on during a computing session. DOS is one example of an operating system. It is the program that works with the hardware of an IBM or compatible computer, your application programs, your files, and you.

DOS must be copied into RAM each time you turn on the computer. DOS always underlies any application program that you use. Each application program constantly calls upon DOS for input/output management.

The many functions of DOS vary from formatting a disk for use on a particular type of machine, to controlling nearly every function of the computer. Although DOS is not readily apparent to most users, especially when overlaid with the *Windows* interface software, a rudimentary knowledge of its purpose, functions, and commands is necessary for even the beginning user.

KEY TERMS

address
BACKUP command
change directory
CD
CLS
cold boot
COPY
current drive
cylinder
DATE
default drive
DEL
delimiter
DIR
disk operating system
DISKCOPY
ERASE
extension
external
FAT
file allocation table
File Manager
File Organizer
file name
FORMAT
global
HELP
internal command
make directory
MD
MORE
/P switch
parameter
path
PRINT
PROMPT
RD
REN
RENAME
remove directory
root directory
sector
server
source drive
subdirectory
target drive
TIME
track
TREE
TYPE
UNDELETE
VER
/W switch
warm boot
wildcard
write protection
XCOPY

REVIEW QUESTIONS

1. Is *Windows* an operating system? Explain your answer.
2. What does the term *operating system* mean?
3. What function(s) does an operating system perform?
4. Define *DOS*.
5. On what general class of computer (microcomputer, minicomputer, mainframe, or supercomputer) is DOS designed to run?
6. Explain why users support a number of versions of DOS.
7. Explain the concept of booting a computer.
8. Explain the difference between a warm and a cold boot.
9. List the keys you would press to initiate a warm boot.
10. If *Windows* does not load automatically when a computer boots, what do you type to load the *Windows* program into RAM?
11. Explain the meaning of the term *default drive*.
12. Explain how to set a directory in *Works*.
13. Explain the meaning of (a) internal DOS commands and (b) external DOS commands.
14. Why are some DOS commands internal and other commands external?

15. Briefly review the structure of DOS commands.
16. How can users of DOS 5.0 (or higher) get on-line help for commands they can't quite remember?
17. What three functions does FORMAT perform?
18. Compare and contrast the COPY, XCOPY, and DISKCOPY commands.
19. What command(s) remove unneeded files from disks? Briefly explain how these commands are used.
20. DOS recognizes two wildcard characters—the asterisk and the question mark. Explain how each of them is used.
21. What command in DOS 5.0 or higher might allow you to reverse a mistaken deletion of a file?
22. What rules govern naming DOS files and directories?
23. Identify the correct file names and extensions from the following list: (a) incometax.93, (b) budget.ken, (c) budget.harriet, (d) finances, (e) ltrhome.94.
24. Explain why you can't delete or rename the root directory.
25. Briefly explain a few of the advantages you can gain by organizing your hard disk with directories.
26. BACKUP and RESTORE should be done with the same version of the operating system. Explain why.
27. Recall when you might want to use the ¦MORE command.
28. Briefly explain the syntax and function of each of the following DOS commands: DIR, DIR/P, DIR/W, DIR *.*, MD, CD, RD, COPY, DISKCOPY, BACKUP, RESTORE, DEL or ERASE, REN, TYPE, CLS, PROMPT, PRINT, VER, and TREE.

SOFTWARE EXERCISES

The following exercises assume that you are seated in front of an IBM or compatible computer equipped with a hard drive and a 3.5-inch diskette drive with DOS copied into RAM.

Exercise 3.1

1. Repeat the tutorials in this chapter until you have learned the commands.

Exercise 3.2

1. Buy one or more diskettes and format them from the C:\> prompt.
2. If prompted on the screen, enter up to 11 characters for a volume label (your name, initials, or a course name or number) or press ENTER for no label.

3. Upon completion of the format operation, the screen will display a summary of disk statistics; note these statistics for each formatted diskette, or print them out using the PRT SCRN key.

Exercise 3.3

1. Buy one or more diskettes and format them using the File Manager in *Windows*. Be careful to choose the correct drive and disk size for the diskette you are formatting.
2. Upon completion of the format operation, the screen will display a summary of disk statistics; note these statistics for each formatted diskette, or print them out using the PRT SCRN key.
3. Type or write a summary of the steps you took to successfully complete this assignment. For example, you had to be in *Windows*, you had to select the Main icon from the Program Manager, and so on.

Exercise 3.4

1. To get a file copy of the extensive list of DOS commands and the help available for each of them, put a formatted diskette in drive A.
2. At the C:\> prompt, type **help > a:help.txt** and press ENTER. (Leave a single space before or before and after the > symbol.)
3. To view the file's contents on your screen, type : **a:help.txt¦more** and press ENTER. Press any key to view each screen.
4. To get a print out of the file, type **print a:help.txt** and press ENTER. If you get a message that says "Name of list device [PRN]," press ENTER.
5. Choose any three DOS commands from your list and get a help screen on each. To get help on a specific command, type **help** followed by the command name.
6. Summarize (a) the total number of DOS commands for which you can get help, and (b) what you learned from each of the three help screens you viewed. Hand write or type your notes.

Exercise 3.5

Note: Don't attempt to do this exercise if your machine is connected to a network.

1. Put a formatted diskette in drive A.
2. Turn the computer on or, if it is already on, warm boot it by simultaneously pressing and holding the CTRL, ALT, and DEL keys.
3. Note the screen's response.
4. Remove the diskette from drive A and follow the directions on the screen.

5. Note the result.
6. Hand write or type a short paragraph about what happened and why it happened.

Exercise 3.6

1. Turn the print screen function on by pressing the CTRL and PRT SCRN keys simultaneously.
2. At the C:\> prompt, display the directory (a) without stopping the display, (b) by stopping the listing near the top of the page, (c) by page, (d) across the page.
3. Turn the print screen function off by pressing the CTRL and PRT SCRN keys simultaneously.
4. Briefly summarize the differences you see in the listings produced by a through d above.
5. Type or hand write your notes.

Exercise 3.7

1. At the C:\> prompt, clear the screen by typing CLS.
2. Turn the print screen function on.
3. Check the version of DOS installed on the machine you are using by entering **VER**.
4. Check the date function by entering **DATE** at the C:\> prompt. If the date displayed is not current, enter the current date in the format displayed on the screen and press RETURN; if the date is current, simply press ENTER.
5. Check the time function by entering **TIME** at the C:\> prompt. If the time is not current, enter the current time, in the form HH:MM for hours and minutes, and press ENTER; otherwise, simply press ENTER. (Note: DOS versions before 4.0 require the time after noon to be entered using the 24-hour clock. For example, to indicate 2:30 in the afternoon, you would enter **14:30**. DOS versions 4.0 or later allow an alternative to the 24-hour clock. You can simply append the letter *a* or *p* to the time to stand for *AM* or *PM*. Thus, you would enter 2:30 in the afternoon as **2:30p**.)
6. Turn the print screen function off.

Exercise 3.8

1. At the C:\> prompt, change to the DOS directory. At the C:\DOS> prompt, display all files that have the extension *.exe*.
2. Use the print screen function to print out the names of the .exe files found on the C:\DOS> directory.
3. At the C:\DOS> prompt, copy any three .exe files to a formatted disk in drive A.

4. Use the DIR command and print screen function to print a copy of the files on drive A.
5. Erase the .exe files from your diskette in drive A.

Exercise 3.9

1. From the *Windows* Main group, open the File Manager.
2. Click on the DOS subdirectory on the C drive.
3. From View, click on Directory Only.
4. From View, click on Sort by Type.
5. Identify any three files with the .exe extension and copy them to your formatted disk in the A drive. (To obtain help in doing this, click on Help, Search for Help on . . . In the Search dialog box, type the word **copy**, click on copying files, click on Show Topics, and click on Go To to select Copying files and directories.)
6. Use the DIR command and print screen function to print a copy of the files on drive A.
7. Erase the .exe files from your diskette in drive A.
8. Click on File-Exit to exit from the File Manager.

Exercise 3.10

1. At the C:\> prompt, change to the DOS directory. At the C:\DOS> prompt, enter **CHKDSK** and press ENTER. Note (a) the number of bytes of total disk space, (b) the number of bytes in hidden files, (c) the number of bytes in directories, (d) the number of bytes in directories, (e) the number of bytes in user files, (f) the number of bytes available on disk, (g) the number of bytes in each allocation unit, (h) the number of bytes in total allocation units on the disk, (i) the number of bytes of total memory, and (j) the number of bytes free.
2. Put a formatted diskette in drive A.
3. At the C:\DOS> prompt, type **A:** and press ENTER.
4. At the A:\> prompt, enter **CHKDSK** and press ENTER. Note the data for (a) through (j) above. Note: (b) and (e) are not applicable.

Exercise 3.11

Note: This exercise requires you to have the COUNTRY.SYS file available in your DOS subdirectory. If COUNTRY.SYS is not available, please substitute any file you have with the .SYS extension.

1. At the C:\> prompt, change to the DOS directory. At the C:\DOS> prompt, enter **type country.sys** and press ENTER.
2. Note the response on the screen.
3. Insert the student diskette that accompanies the text in drive A.
4. At the C:\DOS> prompt, enter **type a:charter.wps** and press ENTER.

5. Note the response on the screen.
6. Hand write or type a short paragraph about the differences you saw between the first and second uses of the TYPE command. What do you think accounts for the difference?

Exercise 3.12

1. Put a formatted diskette in drive A.
2. At the C:\> prompt, change to the A drive.
3. At the A:\> prompt, use the make directory (MD) command to create the following directory/subdirectory system:

```
wp
   letters
      home
      friends
   reports
      English
      history
      science
   memos
      work1
      work2
sp
   budget
      personal
      house
   checks
      Jan
      Feb
db
   address
   collect
```

4. Use the TREE command to display your system of directories.
5. Use the PRT SCRN key to make a copy of your diagram.
6. Use the remove directory (RD) command to remove each subdirectory and directory from the diskette.

Exercise 3.13

1. Put a formatted diskette in drive A.
2. From the *Windows* Main program group, open the File Manager.

3. From the *Windows* Accessories program group, open Write. Use ALT + TAB to move back to the Program Manager, if necessary.
4. Use ALT + TAB to move to the File Manager.
5. Click on the A drive icon.
6. Use the File-Create Directory command to create the directory/subdirectory system outlined below. (Be certain to click on View-Tree and Directory if Tree and Directory is not already checked.)

   - wp
     - letters
       - home
       - friends
     - reports
       - English
       - history
       - science
     - memos
       - work1
       - work2
   - sp
     - budget
       - personal
       - house
     - checks
       - Jan
       - Feb
   - db
     - address
     - collect

7. Press the PRT SCRN key to make a copy of your diagram for the Clipboard. (On some keyboards, you must press the SHIFT and PRT SCRN keys together.)
8. Use ALT + TAB to move to the Program Manager; open the Main program group screen, if it is not already open.
9. View the captured screen by double clicking on Clipboard Viewer. If the captured screen of your directories is displayed, continue by closing the clipboard View and closing the Main group. If your captured screen of directories is not displayed, return to the File Manager and try the PRT SCRN capture process again.

10. Use ALT + TAB to move to Write.
11. In Write, click on Edit-Paste.
12. Click on File-Print to print out your A diskette directories.
13. Exit Write without saving the file, and close Accessories.
14. Return to the File Manager.
15. Use the File-Delete command to remove each subdirectory and directory from the A drive diskette.
16. Exit File Manager.

Exercise 3.14

1. At the library, research the difference between the various versions of DOS. Begin with DOS 1.0 and work up to the current version.
2. Hand write or type your findings.

Exercise 3.15

1. At the library, research the difference between the IBM and compatible *Windows* user environment and the Macintosh user environment.
2. Hand write or type your findings.

Exercise 3.16

1. Arrange with your instructor to take a DOS tutorial (if your campus offers one).
2. Note the topics covered.
3. Hand write or type a summary of those topics.

Part 2

Learning the Applications

Chapter 4

Beginning Word Processing

Objectives

After studying this chapter you will be able to:

- *Define the term* word processing
- *Briefly review the history of word processing*
- *Explain typical word processing documents*
- *Load the* Works 3.0 for Windows *word processor module into memory*
- *Identify the various parts of the* Works *document screen*
- *Describe the uses of beginning word processing features*
- *Create a new document*
- *Easily move the cursor wherever you want it to be*
- *Format characters, words, or paragraphs*
- *Use the Toolbar or shortcut keys to increase your productivity*
- *Set a directory to the A or B drive and save a document onto your own diskette*
- *Open and modify an existing document*
- *Close a file and exit* Works 3.0 for Windows

Word Processing *Defined*

One of the most useful applications that has been developed for the personal computer is word processing. Word processing is the ability to generate text using a special editing computer program. A text file, called a *document*, is created and saved to a disk.

The development of word processing software for computers has allowed you to type in text once and never have to type the original material again. You simply edit, or change, the contents. You may decide to rearrange the order of the text, or improve upon the document by expanding or deleting parts, and you may format it (change its form or appearance) so that it looks like you want it to look. The original draft can be reworked many times before it is finally produced in its finished form. This advantage frees you from typing successive drafts of the same text over and over again, as typewriters used to require.

With a laptop computer and your favorite word processing program, work can be done anywhere.

As you can see, word processing has eliminated much of the drudgery of developing long and complex manuscripts. The end result is a better product that is produced much more quickly and more easily than in the days when several drafts of the same document had to be typed. Also, with all of the different printers available today to print the finished document, the final copy is often superior to the same text typed on a typewriter, even by a professional typist.

History of Word Processing

Word processing began before there were personal computers. In 1964, IBM pioneered the development of what was to become a major improvement in office systems by introducing the IBM Magnetic Tape Selectric Typewriter (MT/ST). This was the first step toward electronic word processing, though these single-purpose electronic machines could process only text.

The electronic generation of text proved to be so popular that word processing soon became widely available on large-scale dedicated word processing machines, and on large, general-purpose computer systems, as well. It is not surprising that when the microcomputer arrived, one of the first applications developed was word processing. **Turnaround** for generation of business documents (the amount of time from the beginning to completion) was becoming very short; that same service was one of the first things users of microcomputers wanted for their personal use. The illustration in Figure 4.1 shows some of the more popular independent word processing applications for personal computers.

Figure 4.1

There are a number of different independent word processing applications; personal preferences dictate your choice.

Types of Word Processing Documents

The variety of documents that you can generate using a personal computer word processing program is as great as the number of unique, text-dependent tasks you can conceive. Most word processing applications are capable of functions that even the best executive secretary of 30 years ago would have found challenging. You can use the word processing application on a microcomputer to do everything from an informal half-page letter, requiring little or no revision, to a long term paper that requires a rough draft, many revisions, footnotes, and a bibliography. Figure 4.2 shows samples of some types of documents commonly produced by word processing.

Multiple-Draft Documents

Many documents require several revisions for proper development. A document in a business setting requires an average of three revisions before reaching its final, finished form. Personal documents often require more than that. Because revisions are so much easier with a word processor, you need not hesitate to correct and recorrect your work. Because the word processor helps you with the format, you can concentrate on the content and then adjust the format as an easy, minor task.

With new laptop computers and modems to access research material, you can create an excellent research paper without pencil ever touching paper. You do, of course, need a high level of organization, knowledge of the keystroke sequences to format the document, and a mind that can create at the keyboard. After developing these skills, you, in teamwork with hardware, word processing software, and data, will be able to create a high-quality document in the most efficient manner.

Obviously, the word processor cannot create the document itself. That is where you are indispensable. The computer is still just a tool to help you with your multiple-draft document, but it is a fantastic tool. Figures 4.2a and 4.2b show a typical business letter and a page from a research document.

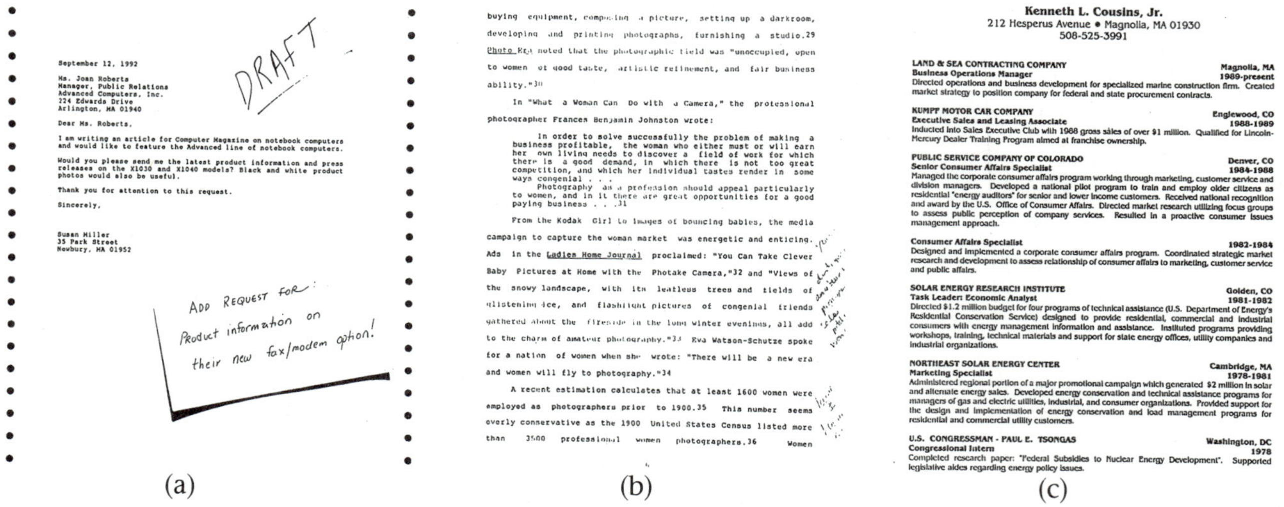

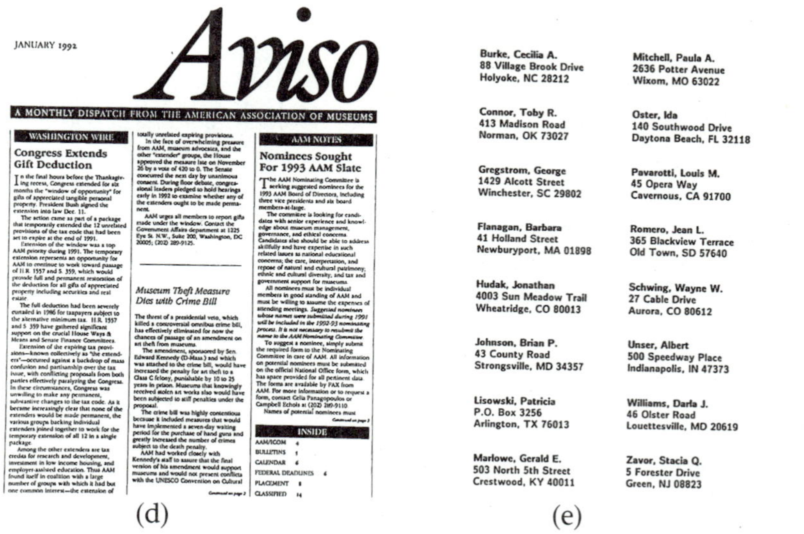

Figure 4.2

With word processing, text changes are easily accomplished without retyping, such as in (a) a business letter, (b) a research paper, (c) a multi-draft document, (d) a newsletter, and (e) a mailing list.

Repetitive and Archived Documents

Many documents need to be prepared one time, revised and updated periodically, and produced in large quantities after each revision. Policy manuals, procedure manuals, family histories, class notes, and resumes are documents of this type. They are much easier to produce with a word processing program than with a typewriter. You can revise and update them at will, retaining as much of the original text as needed. With this repetitive material archived (saved as a file on a disk), it is convenient to make the revisions. You simply edit the document and then overwrite the original file, or save the material to a new file. You can have several documents open at one time, to move material from one into another, for even greater efficiency. Figure 4.2c shows one type of repetitive document, a resume.

Highly Structured Documents

Often word processing users need to produce text that is highly formatted. It may contain many tables, columns, rows of numbers, bulleted lists, and so forth. The document may still be primarily text, making a spreadsheet inconvenient despite the need to calculate numbers, yet a measure of material must be structured in a specific, predefined way.

Text that needs to be formatted in columns across the printed page is cumbersome to edit and revise manually. A word processing program allows you to add and delete columns without having to retype the entire table. Even a simple newsletter or bulletin is much easier to produce with a word processor than with a typewriter. *Works* and other word processing programs allow you to create **newspaper columns** (columns that snake across the page) by completing one column of typing and beginning at the top of the next column automatically, with no further formatting. Figure 4.2d shows a sample of a highly formatted document.

Lists of Names and Items

Lists of employees, clients, and customers can easily be kept in a word processing file. When you do not need a true record-keeping system, such as a database application, but still need to keep names, addresses, and demographic information for future use, a word processing file is the answer. Such files can be sorted alphabetically, selected to use only a portion of the list, and even merged with other documents, such as form letters, to create individualized mailings. The list is easily updated with necessary changes. Names can be added and deleted at will, leaving the rest of the file intact. Parts of the list can be printed, leaving the rest in the file for another time.

When you get to Chapter 13 ("Integrating the Applications"), you will have an opportunity for some hands-on experience with mailing lists. Figure 4.2e shows a mailing list similar to the one you may produce when you use **mail merge**—the process of joining a **boilerplate** (standard) letter with a list of names and addresses to produce personalized letters for many people.

The most complex type of document is one that requires a desktop publishing program that combines text and graphics. The format of the text of a document prepared in a desktop publishing program, that is, the presentation of the content, is often more important than the content itself. We will discuss desktop publishing in Chapter 5. The newer word processing applications, including *Works 3.0 for Windows*, have drawing packages, libraries of **clip art** (predrawn pictures that you may insert into your documents), and many other graphics capabilities.

Loading the Works Word Processor

The word processor is the default selection for *Works*, which means that the program assumes that you will use the word processor unless you indicate differently. It also assumes that you will create a new file.

After *Works* is loaded, you can choose Create a New Document from the opening menu:

- Click on the New and Recent Documents button
- Click on the Word Processor button

See Figure 2.15 in the tour of *Works* in Chapter 2 if you need to review the Startup dialog box for *Works 3.0 for Windows*.

Since the word processor is the default selection, simply pressing ENTER will bring you to the word processor screen. The blank document screen will be presented, with the command line menu at the top, and the toolbar below it. Inside the Word1 window, the ruler line will show. A thick horizontal bar symbol marks the end of a new document (▁), and the insertion point is blinking to indicate its readiness on the blank work area. The status line at the bottom of the screen indicates that you are on page 1/1 of the document called WORD1, and the message "Press ALT to choose commands" is displayed. All is ready to begin a new document.

Editing Features

The *Works 3.0 for Windows* word processing application provides most of the same features as independent application programs. In most instances, *Works* features are invoked, or chosen, by single clicking on one of the menu selections with the left mouse button. You can also invoke these formatting and editing features by pressing the ALT key to reach the command line, and then selecting the command you desire, either Edit, Insert, Format, or View. The editing and formatting features discussed in the following sections are generic, in the sense that all word processors offer them. The terminology may vary a little, and the mouse procedures or keystrokes used to invoke them will differ, but the effects are the same.

Insertion Point Movement

The insertion point is the blinking vertical bar symbol that indicates your place in a document. (This is called the *cursor* in text-based interfaces.) You can use the control keys (directional arrows, HOME, END, PAGE UP, and PAGE DOWN) to move the insertion point around in your document. These keys do not delete or move text as the space bar and ENTER key do.

It takes a few sessions to get used to entering spaces just like characters and to remember that those spaces are as important to the document as the text symbols. In *Works 3.0 for Windows* it may help the new user to invoke the **All Characters** choice in the View menu. This will cause those reserved spaces to appear on screen as dots (. . . .) wherever the space bar has been pressed.

Just remember that you can move the insertion point location by pointing with the mouse or pressing the directional arrow keys or the other insertion point control keys on the right-hand side of your keyboard. The chart in Table 4.1 shows how to move the insertion point with keys and how to scroll rapidly through your document.

Table 4.1 Insertion Point Control Keys

To Move	Press
Left one character	LEFT ARROW
Right one character	RIGHT ARROW
Up one line	UP ARROW
Down one line	DOWN ARROW
Left one word	CTRL + LEFT ARROW
Right one word	CTRL + RIGHT ARROW
Up one paragraph	CTRL + UP ARROW
Down one paragraph	CTRL + DOWN ARROW
To beginning of line	HOME
To end of line	END
To beginning of document	CTRL + HOME
To end of document	CTRL + END
Up one screen	PAGE UP
Down one screen	PAGE DOWN
To beginning of screen	CTRL + PAGE UP
To end of screen	CTRL + PAGE DOWN

INSERT/DELETE/BACKSPACE Keys

Works is an insert program; the default setting for the program is the **insert mode**. This is the opposite of the **typeover mode**, which allows you to write over, or replace, existing text as you type. In insert mode, when you begin to type at the insertion point, the existing text moves to the right, making room for the new text. This is safer for beginning users. You can toggle, or switch, back and forth from insert to typeover mode as you edit.

Inserting text within *Works* is as simple as putting the insertion point where you want text to appear and beginning to type. Any amount of text can be inserted this way; the existing text will continue to move down to allow room for what you are typing. To change to typeover mode, press the INS key or choose Typing Replaces Selection in the Tools-Options menu.

Works offers three ways to delete text. First, if you make a mistake as you type a word processing document, you can use the BACKSPACE key to delete the mistake immediately and then continue typing. Second, to delete previously typed text, place the insertion point to the right of the first character to be deleted and press the DELETE key. Like certain other keys on the keyboard, DELETE is a repeating key, so it can remove a string of characters rather rapidly.

The third way to delete text, which is especially useful for larger amounts, is to select a **block** (any number of characters selected for further action) and delete it. You can do this by positioning the mouse pointer where you wish to begin, then clicking and dragging the mouse to the end of the block. (Refer to Chapter 2 if you need to review the dragging process.)

You can also select a block by holding down the SHIFT key while pressing the directional arrows or the F8 function key the desired number of times. Pressing F8 once selects the character at the insertion point. Pressing it twice selects the word; pressing it three times selects the sentence; pressing it four times selects the paragraph; pressing it five times selects the whole document.

You can delete a whole block at one time by pressing the DELETE key, or by cutting it to the Clipboard for later use, as you practiced in Chapter 2. To cut a block of text in *Works 3.0 for Windows*:

- Select the block by any of the above means.
- Click on Edit.
- Click on Cut.

If you wish to remove a block for which you have no further use:

- Select the block of text by any of the above means.
- Press the DELETE key.

Selection of blocks of text for further action is a basic word processing function. Of course, if you have the *Works* Typing Replaces Selection feature from the Tools-Options menu marked, the old material will be deleted as soon as you start typing new material. In the future, you will be using these same methods of block selection to apply many different formatting features to text that you have previously typed.

Word Wrap

When using a word processor, you should not press ENTER when you reach the end of a line, as you would press the carriage return when using a typewriter. As you type, the words that will not fit within the right margin of your screen will automatically be moved to the following line. This feature is called **word wrap**. Just type in the text, and the lines will arrange themselves within the margins you have selected. If you add or delete text, word wrap will rearrange your material within the margins for you.

Works has an additional feature called **Wrap for Window** under the View menu. When you are using a small **font** (style and size of type) that allows more text on a line than you can see on the screen, Wrap for Window will wrap the text on the edge of the screen to the next line allowing you to view all of your document without scrolling left and right. A mark is placed beside the command name on the View menu to indicate when it is activated. It's a toggle, so just click on it to select the command again.

- Click on View.
- Click on Wrap for Window.
- Click on OK, or press ENTER.

In a few cases, you will press ENTER at the end of a line, including when you intend to let a line run short, end a paragraph, or insert a blank line in your text. When you press ENTER to end a line or paragraph, you create a **hard return**. A hard return functions exactly like a carriage return on a typewriter. If you have chosen the Show All Characters selection from the View menu, your hard returns will be indicated on the screen by paragraph symbols.

A **soft return** is the line break that occurs when the *Works* program moves text to the next line automatically as part of word wrap. No symbol appears on the screen in a *Works* document to indicate a soft return.

Undo Editing

The **Undo Editing command** reverses the last thing you did. If you choose it immediately after making a change, you can reverse editing (move, copy, or delete), formatting (bold, italic, or underline), and all changes made during a spell check.

- Click on Edit.
- Click on Undo Editing (or press ALT + BACKSPACE).

The Undo Editing feature is offered in all of the applications in the *Works 3.0 for Windows* program, and it functions the same way. You may undo the last change you made, whether you are in a word processing document or a database file.

Formatting Features

The *Works* word processor offers a variety of styles of type. You may choose some of these simply to improve appearance, while some will serve more functional purposes, such as to make a word or phrase stand out from the surrounding text.

Toolbar and Shortcut Keys

As mentioned in Chapter 2, *Works* has a toolbar that can be used with the mouse to make formatting easier. The commands and results available from icons in the word processing toolbar are indicated in Figure 4.3. If the icon is not immediately obvious to you, rest the insertion point on the icon for a moment, to display a tool tip.

The formatting options are toggles—you click on them where you want the specific format to begin and click on them again where it should end. You can also type the material first, highlight it, and then click on the formatting option. For the Font and Point options, you must put your pointer on the down arrow when you click.

The toolbar will display when you open the program. If you do not want it to show on your screen:

- Click on View.
- Click on Toolbar.

Figure 4.3

Icons on Word Processing Toolbar

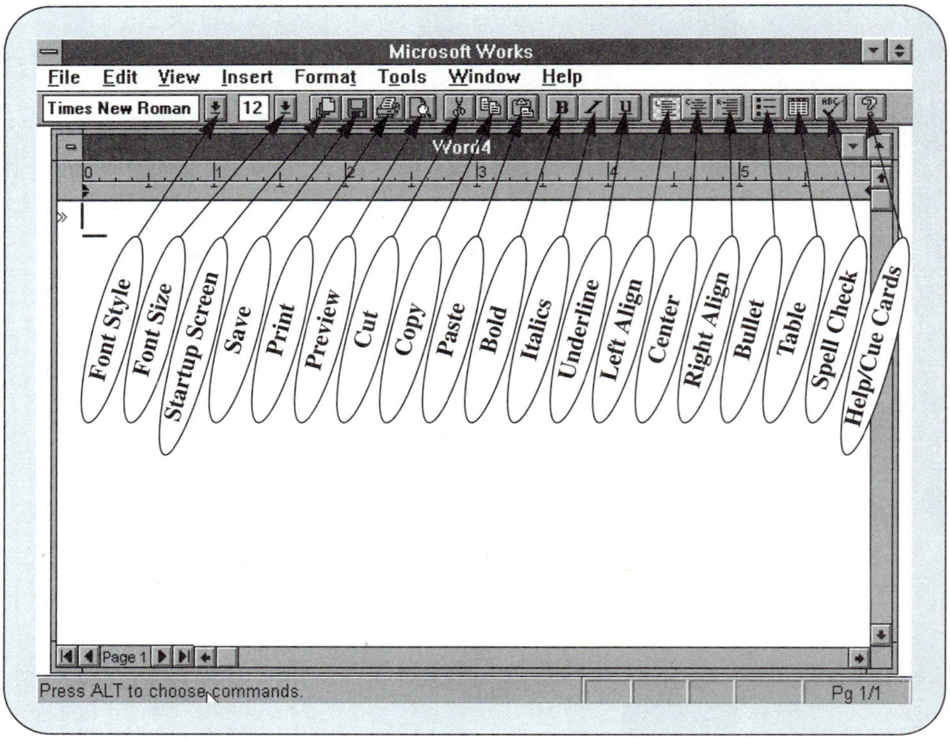

You can customize your toolbar in *Works* and add other features that you use often in your word processing tasks. You can also remove icons that you never use. To customize your toolbar:

- Click on Tools.
- Click on Customize Toolbar.
- In the Categories list, click on a menu name.
- Drag one of the available icons up to the Toolbar by pointing to it, holding down the button on your mouse, and moving the mouse pointer.

The toolbar is a great help to the beginner; it will speed your learning and allow you to be productive even as a novice word processing student. How much you use it, and whether you customize it to fit your needs, are strictly individual decisions. You will practice modifying the toolbar in Chapter 5.

It is also possible to use the ALT key, plus the appropriate underlined letter in a pull-down command window. We will indicate only the mouse clicks and some shortcut keystrokes, such as CTRL plus a letter (CTRL + B for bold). Your word processing efficiency will increase when you use the mouse instead of keystrokes. Modern word processing software offers many different ways to accomplish many tasks. You will soon find which way suits you best.

Underline/Bold

One of the ways to add emphasis in documents is to underline or boldface specific words. You may also use italic type; the principles are the same. To use the menu to underline text before it is typed:

- Click on Format.
- Click on Font and Style.

  In the Style Box:

- Click on Underline (or press CTRL + U, or click on the underline icon).
- Click on OK.
- Type the word or words.

To discontinue underlining:

- Click on Format.
- Click on Font and Style.
- Click on Underline again to remove the check mark (or press CTRL + SPACEBAR)
  (or click on the underline icon).

In effect, you turn underlining on before you type and turn it off after you type.

If you wish to go back and underline some text after is has been entered:

- Select the block of text.
- Click on Format.
- Click on Font and Style.
- Click on Underline (or press CTRL + U or click on the underline icon).

If you wish to make the text you are typing appear in boldface or italic type, follow the same procedure as above, but select Bold or Italic instead of Underline from the Format-Font and Style window. You can also use the shortcut keys CTRL + B for bold or CTRL + I for italics. CTRL + SPACEBAR will return text to plain text, or you can click on the italic or the bold icon to turn these formats on and off. **Boldface** formatting is a way of emphasizing part of your text by printing it darker than the surrounding text.

You can choose the Bold option before typing the text, or go back and use it after the text has been entered. Just remember, if you have invoked the Bold command before typing in text, you must turn it off again or your whole document will end up in boldface, giving your chosen text no emphasis at all!

You can execute a *Works* command in three ways: (1) simply highlight the word of your choice in the pull-down menu by clicking the left mouse button on it, or press ALT and then the desired highlighted letter, followed by ENTER, (2) press the ALT key together with the character that stands for the desired option, or (3) use shortcut keys or toolbar icons when available. The method you use is up to you. The second and third methods are faster, but beginners often prefer highlighting entire words until they become more proficient. Figure 4.4 shows a block of text that is highlighted in reverse video (white text on a dark background).

Figure 4.4

Example of Selected Text in Reverse Video

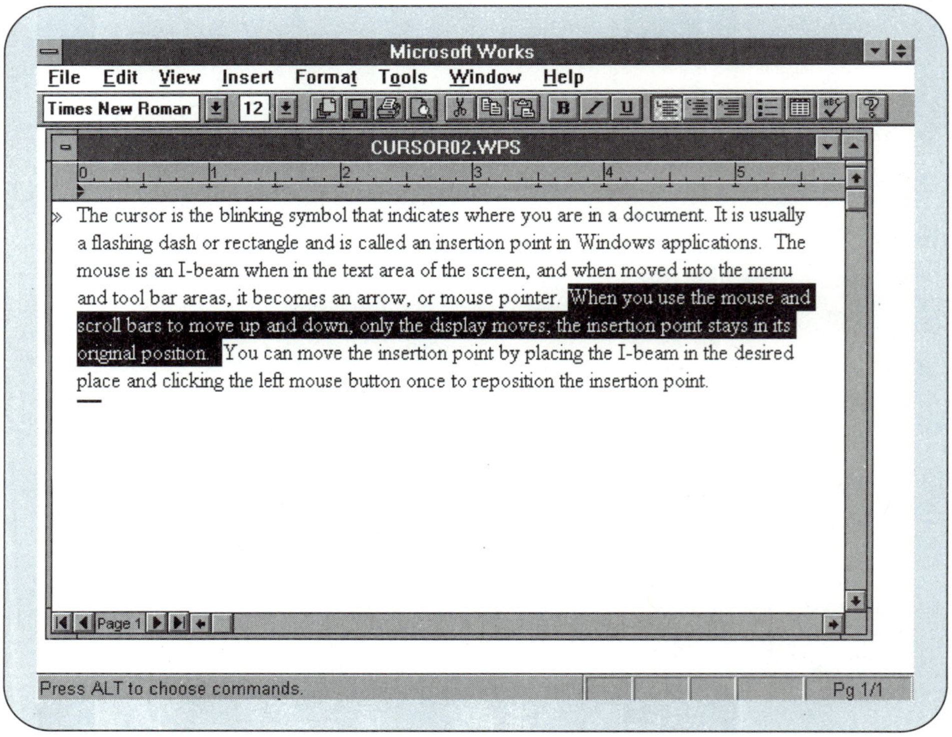

Hard Spaces

Certain conventions, or established standards, guide creation of documents using word processing programs, whether the hardware is a mainframe computer or a microcomputer. We will discuss some of these standards in this chapter and the next. We will not discuss all of the available features, only the most common ones. Hard spaces, or **nonbreaking spaces**, are among these conventions.

When typing dates and times, it is not correct to separate the day from the month, or the hour from the minutes. In the Insert-Special Character menu, *Works* offers a Nonbreaking space choice that enters a type of space that will prevent two words from being divided. For example, when typing *July 2,* you want the month and the day to remain together on the same line of the document, even if it means moving both words to the next line. (You may have heard hard, or nonbreaking, spaces referred to as *sticky spaces*; this term hints at their function of keeping two words stuck together.)

To assure a nonbreaking space in the *Works* program:

- Click on Insert.
- Click on Special Character.
- Click on Nonbreaking space.
- Click on OK.
- Type the next word you wish to remain on the same line as the previous word. Now even if your document is edited later and text is inserted or deleted, you are assured that the two words will remain together on the final copy.

Setting Tab Stops

As with most other word processing programs, when *Works* is activated, it presets tab stops every five spaces, or 0.5 inch. These are default settings. You cannot delete these tab stops in *Works*; however, when you set your own tab stops, *Works* ignores all default settings to the left of them.

To set a new tab stop:

- Click on Format.
- Click on Tabs.
- Click on (or press TAB to go to) the Position box.
- Type the position number of the desired stop.
- Click on Insert.
- Click on OK.

Because *Works* assumes that every measurement is stated in inches, you do not have to enter the inch symbol.

Tabs can employ diverse options. You can select right, left, centered, or decimal alignment (the last lines up numbers) of tab material. You can place **leaders** (repeated leading symbols, such as === or . . . .) before your tabbed material, so that the reader's eye follows easily from one column of text to the next. The *Works* tab options allow you to customize your document, giving it a more professional appearance and making it easier to read. The default tab alignment is left, without leaders, unless you change the leader option. You may also delete all of your previous tab settings in a document and begin anew. Simply click on the Delete All button in the Tab dialog box.

Paragraph Styles

By default, *Works 3.0 for Windows* will produce a normal text paragraph format, without any special indenting or symbols. You signal the end of a paragraph by pressing the ENTER key. If you wish, you may press the TAB key to begin a paragraph with an indent. It is simple, however, to format paragraphs with special styles, such as bulleting or hanging or quotation styles.

Bulleted List A **bulleted list** places a solid mark before each line of a listing, to add emphasis. A Bullet icon allows you to choose this format before typing a paragraph, or to format a paragraph this way after it has been typed. If you wish, you may also use the Format menu to do the same thing. To choose the bulleted list format:

- Click on Format.
- Click on Paragraph.
- Click on Bullet in the Quick Format Style area.
- Click OK.

Now you may type the paragraph and *Works* will automatically begin a new line with a bullet each time you press ENTER.

Quick Paragraph Formats *Works* offers several **quick paragraph format** styles to help you generate a document with a desired appearance. Producing a number of different paragraph styles within a single document is as simple as clicking on the Paragraph option from the Format menu, or on the correct toolbar icon if you have customized the toolbar. In a **hanging paragraph**, all of the lines except the first are indented. In a **quotation** paragraph, *Works* indents the text one-half inch from both the right and left margins. We discussed the bullet paragraph above. A first-line indent paragraph style automatically tabs the first line of every paragraph you type.

All of these paragraph formats can be reached from the Format-Paragraph commands at the top of your screen. If you use one of the paragraph formats more frequently than the bulleted style, you can customize your toolbar to include that style, and delete the icon for the bullet style that is included in the default toolbar that is present when you install *Works 3.0 for Windows*. The sample pane in the Quick paragraph window shows an example of the selected format.

File Handling Features

In Chapter 3 you learned about the need to assign names to your files so that the system can retrieve them when you want to work on them again. Let's see how the principles apply to word processing documents.

Save As versus Save

Until you save a new file, your text exists only in the computer's memory (RAM). Because this memory is cleared when the computer is turned off, you must store the material on a disk (hard or floppy) to save it permanently.

When you first create a file, *Works* automatically names it WORD1. The first time you save your document to disk, you choose a unique name for it using the Save As selection from the File menu, or you can click on the toolbar Save icon and type in the new file name. If you do not change the default name from WORD1, the next time you save a word processing file, *Works* will write over the previous one with the new material.

To save a file the first time:

- Click on File.
- Click on Save As.
- The Save As dialog box appears.
- Type the name of your file in eight characters or less. (If you have not changed your directory from the Open Dialog box prior to first saving a file, and you wish to save it on a floppy drive, A or B, type that drive plus a colon before you type the file name.)
- Click on OK or press ENTER.

Do not type an extension, as *Works* will add .wps for you. As your file is saved to disk, the drive light will light.

Once a document has been named and saved to disk, you will save updated versions of it that will write over the old version. To save a file after the first time:

- Click on File.
- Click on Save.

  OR
- Click on the toolbar's Save icon.

Previewing a File

One of the most useful developments in word processing applications in the last several years is the **preview mode**. The preview mode allows you to see what the printed page will look like before actually printing it out on the printer. It is truly a WYSIWYG ("what you see is what you get") view that displays a picture of the page with all margins and special formatting represented. This feature is a real time-saver, and it is economical as well because you can correct errors in formatting and layout before you send the document to the printer to produce a hard copy.

To see how your document will look before you print it on the printer, use the *Works* Print Preview icon from the toolbar, or:

- Click on File.
- Click on Print Preview.

In a second or two, your screen will display the page of the document in which the insertion point appeared. The display will look almost exactly like the printed document, though type will be "Greeked," so small that you probably won't be able to read the text. For a multipage document, the preview will identify the page on the top, right-hand Page button.

Zoom Previews To see more of a previewed document:

- Click on Previous or Next to see more than one page.

- Click on Zoom In to magnify the page 100 percent.
- Click on Zoom In again to magnify it 200 percent.
- Click on Cancel to return to your document.

The **zoom** button allows you to actually read the contents of the previewed page. Often the type is so small on a preview page that you cannot read it clearly, yet the page layout is clearly shown. The zoom feature zooms in on the text, leaving the rest of the page layout behind.

This is a very useful feature of most new word processing packages that have graphics capabilities. The maximum magnification of a *Works* preview is 200 percent, or two clicks on the Zoom button.

Closing a File

When you finish working with a file, you close it to clear it from the screen. Closing a file also removes it from the computer's main memory. If you have made any changes to the file since you last saved it, *Works* will ask if you want to save the changes.

To close a file:

- Click on File.
- Click on Close.
- Click on the Yes button, or press ENTER, to save changes.

  OR
- Click on the No button to abandon the changes.

The document will be erased from the screen, and you may continue your word processing session with another document, if you wish. If you decide not to close the file, abandon the command:

- Click on Cancel to return to the document.

Now that you have read about some basic word processing functions, and how to execute them in *Works 3.0 for Windows*, you may follow the chapter tutorial to put some of these concepts into practice. You will enter the required text via the keyboard, format the text, and save the finished document to the work diskette you formatted in Chapter 3.

The hardware, the software, and you, the user, will work together to produce a document. Remember that what you are to type is shown in bold type; when you are to click on several commands in a row, they will be separated by hyphens.

Word Processing Tutorial No. 1

Suppose that you have recently purchased a new computer and decide you must get insurance for it. You are going to type a letter to the insurance company to check on your current coverage. Before starting, be sure to have a formatted work disk in drive A or B. Also, when you name your document, you must designate the drive if you have not already changed the directory to either A or B, as explained in Chapter 3 and noted above. For example, to name the letter *INSLET*, if your disk were in drive A, when first saving the letter you would type **a:inslet** and then press ENTER or click on OK. If you set the directory, as you do in the beginning of this tutorial, you needn't type the drive designation; your document will automatically be saved to the disk in the drive to which you set the directory.

We assume that you have turned the computer on and have the *Windows* screen showing. Type the letter just as directed, including errors—you will correct them later. Caution: As you work through the assignments, carefully check that the insertion point is exactly where you want a command to take effect before you invoke the command. It is very easy to inadvertently move the insertion point and produce unintended effects.

1. Double Click on the Microsoft Works icon.
2. The *Works* Startup screen displays.

   To change your directory to the A or B drive:
3. Click on Open an Existing Document.
4. The Open file dialog box displays as shown in Figure 4.5.

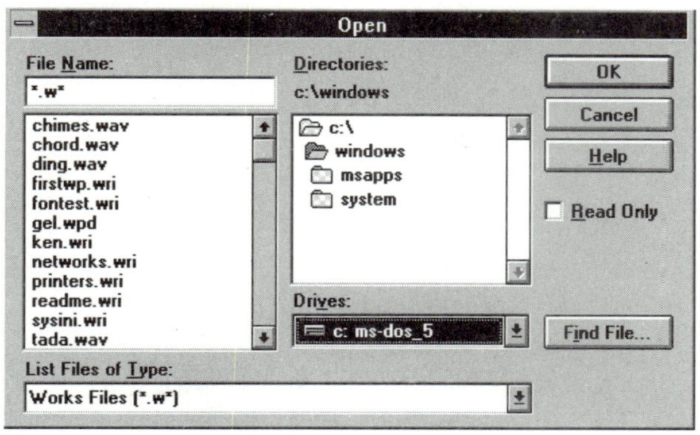

Figure 4.5

The Open File Option Box

5. Click on the down arrow in the Drives list box.
6. Click on a: or b:, depending on which floppy drive you use.
7. Click on Cancel.

   Your files will be saved on the designated drive until you exit *Works* at the end of this session. Try to remember to specify a drive at the beginning of each *Works* session. Note: Use a new formatted disk which we will refer to as a work disk to save your files on. Do not save files onto the student data disk. In fact, you might want to write-protect it by moving the black square in the slot.

8. Click on Word Processor (or press ENTER).

   The blank Word Processor screen displays, as shown in Figure 4.6. If the cue cards are displayed, hide them by clicking first on Help, then on Cue Cards. For now you want to see your spaces, tabs, and returns on the screen. You can hide them later, if you like.

Figure 4.6

The Word Processor Opening Screen

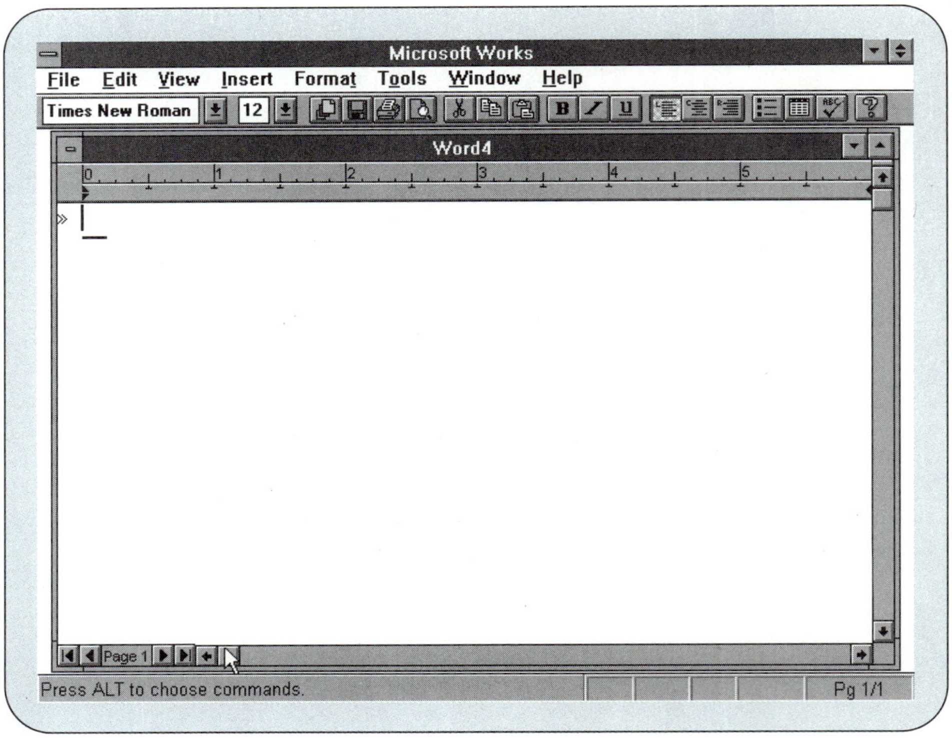

9. Click on View.

   The View menu displays (Figure 4.7).
10. Click on Show All Characters.
11. Press ENTER four times.
12. Type **January 22, 1995**
13. Press ENTER four times.
14. Type **Fred Abercrombie**
15. Press ENTER.
16. Type **National Insurance Company**
17. Press ENTER.
18. Type **8080 E. Indianapolis**
19. Press ENTER.

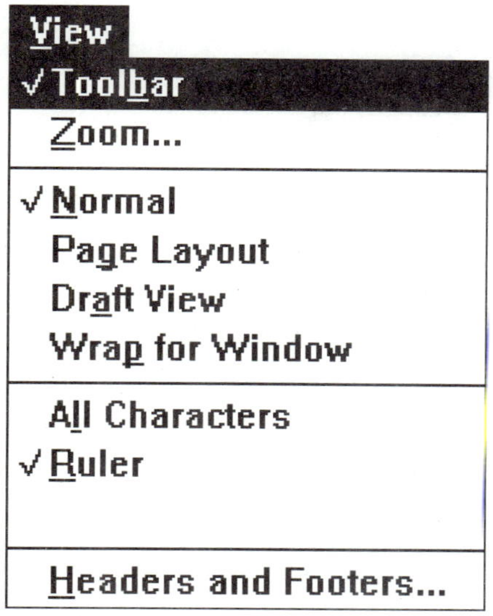

Figure 4.7

The View Menu

20. Type **Wichita, KS 67207**
21. Press ENTER two times.
22. Type **Dear Mr. Abercrombie**:
23. Press ENTER two times.
24. Type the following paragraph, remembering not to press ENTER until the end (let it word wrap) and to make the error:

    I would like to receive a detailed printout that shows my coverage wiht your company and the value of the perosnal property that I have insured. I recently purchased an

    To bold the next phrase:
25. Click on Format.

    The Format menu displays, as shown in Figure 4.8.
26. Click on Font and Style.

    The Font and Style option box displays, as shown in Figure 4.9.
27. In the Style box, click on Bold-OK (or click on the bold icon in the toolbar, or press CTRL + B).

    Notice that, regardless of how you select bold, underlined, or italics formatting, the icon on the toolbar changes colors when the feature is active.
28. Type **IBM PS/2 model 77**

    To turn off bold:
29. Click on Format-Font and Style-Bold-OK (or click on the bold icon in the toolbar, or press CTRL + SPACEBAR).

Figure 4.8

The Format Menu

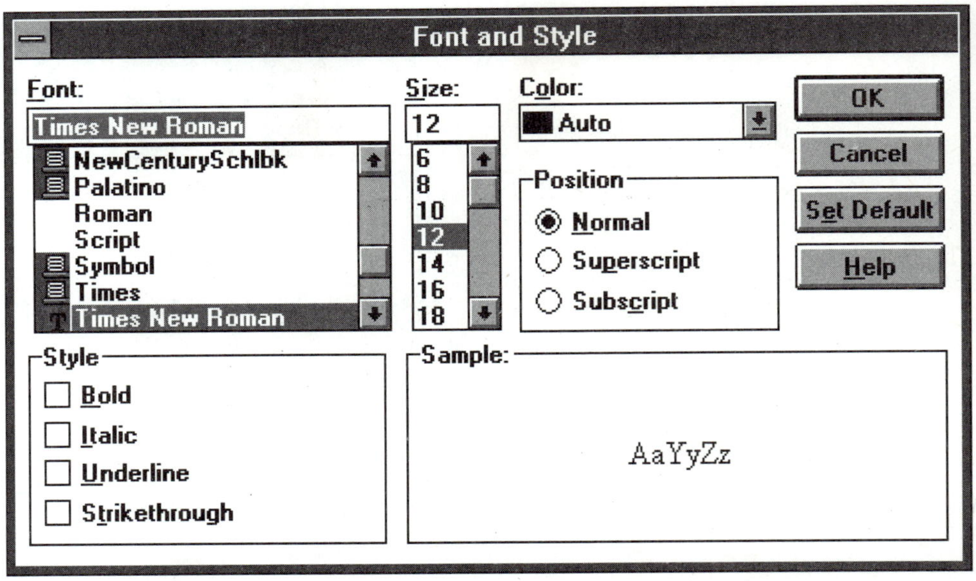

Figure 4.9

The Font and Style Menu

30. Continue typing the paragraph:

    and I want to make sure that it is covered under my

    To underline the next word:

31. Click on Format-Font and Style-Underline (or click on the underline icon in the toolbar, or press CTRL + U).
32. Type **existing**
33. Click on Format-Font and Style-Underline-OK (or click on the underline icon in the toolbar, or press CTRL + SPACEBAR).
34. Continue typing:

    policy. Also, please check to see if the following items are covered:

    You want to make a bulleted list of the items. If you make a mistake and add an unwanted bullet, you cannot delete it, you must place the insertion point at the beginning of the line affected and click on Format-Paragraph-Quick Format-Normal.

35. Press ENTER twice.
36. Click on Format-Paragraph.

    The Paragraph dialog box displays, as shown in Figure 4.10.

37. If it is not already selected, click on Quick Formats.
38. In the Style box, click on Bulleted.

Figure 4.10

The Paragraph Dialog Box

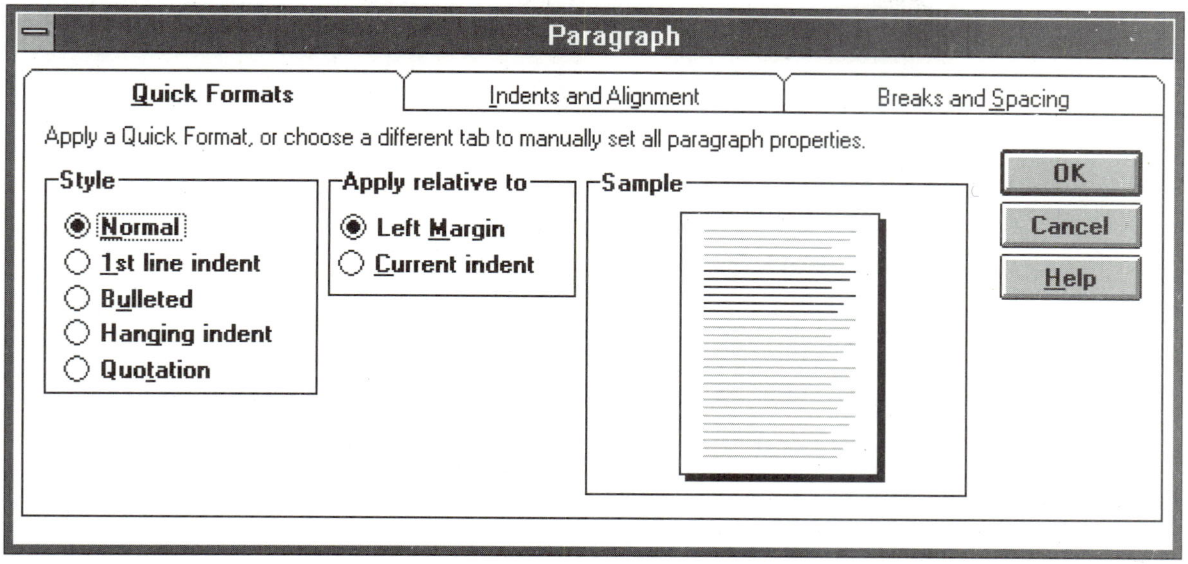

39. Click on OK.

    A bullet displays.

40. Type **a pool table valued at $1,000**
41. Press ENTER, and another bullet displays. Type a bulleted list of the next three items:

    3 gold watches, total value $5,000
    1 Camcorder valued at $800
    a coin collection valued at $10,000

    To end the bullets after the last bulleted line:

42. Press ENTER.
43. Click on Format-Paragraph-Normal-OK.
44. Press ENTER again to leave a blank line.
45. Finish typing the paragraph:

    Our personal property including the computer totals about $20,000. If my existing policy does not cover this amount, please sned insurance quottes to me by February

    (Do not press the SPACEBAR; you want to insert a hard space to keep the date February 1 together on one line.)

46. Click on Insert.

    The Insert menu displays, as shown in Figure 4.11.

Figure 4.11

The Insert Menu

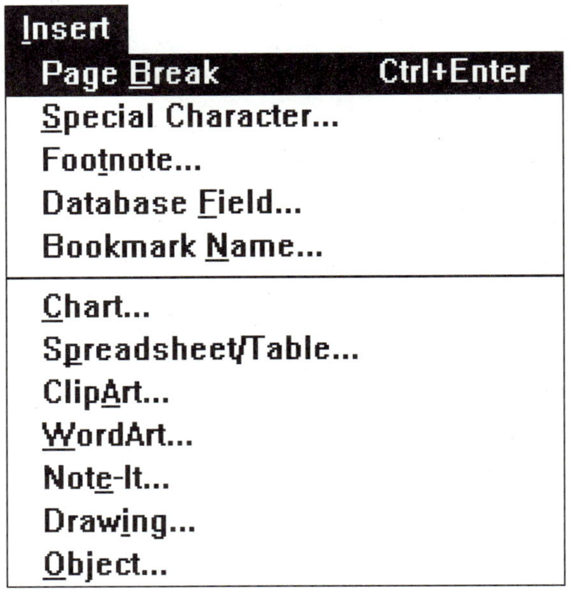

47. Click on Special Character.

    The Special Character menu displays, as shown in Figure 4.12

Figure 4.12

The Special Character Menu

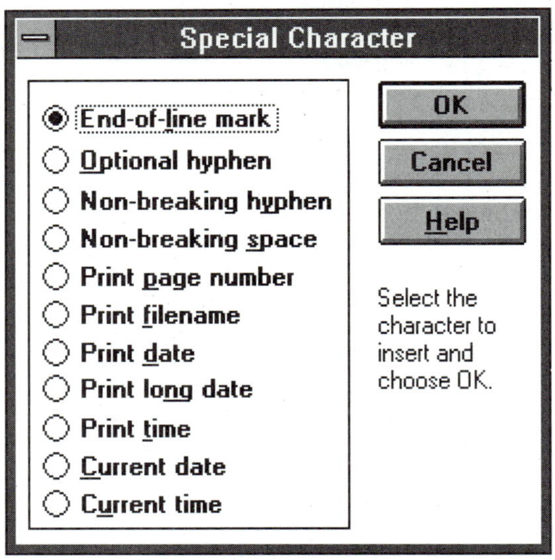

48. Click on Nonbreaking space-OK.
49. Type **1 at the following address**:

50. Press ENTER.

    You want the address in italics, tabbed in 2.5 inches.

51. Click on the toolbar's italic icon.
52. Click on Format-Tabs.

    The Tabs dialog box displays, as shown in Figure 4.13.

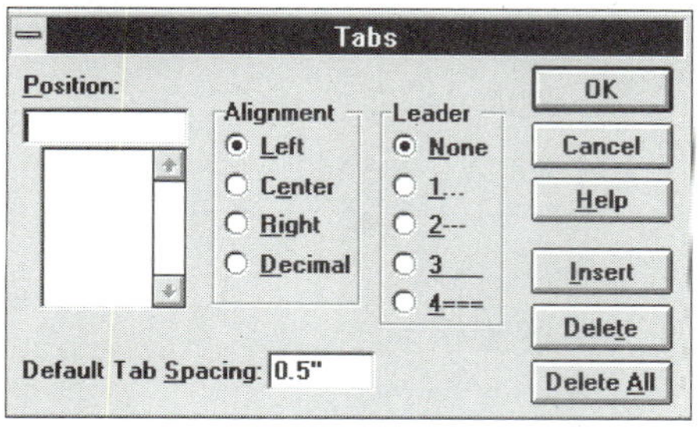

Figure 4.13

The Tabs Dialog Box

53. In the Position text box, type **2.5**
54. Click on Insert.
55. Click on Close.

    Notice that all the tab stops to the left of 2.5 inches are deleted.

56. Press TAB.
57. Type **your name**
58. Press ENTER.
59. Press TAB.
60. Type **your street address**
61. Press ENTER.
62. Press TAB.
63. Type **your city, state, Zip**
64. Click on the toolbar's italics icon.
65. Press ENTER two times.
66. Type **Thank you for your attention in this matter.**
67. Press ENTER two times.
68. Type **Sincerely,**
69. Press ENTER four times.
70. Type **your name**

    If you like, use the assign macro you created in Chapter 3 to put your name and assignment number on the bottom of the letter, or on a separate page. Refer to page 108. To save your document on your work disk:

71. Click on File.

    The File menu appears, as shown in Figure 4.14.

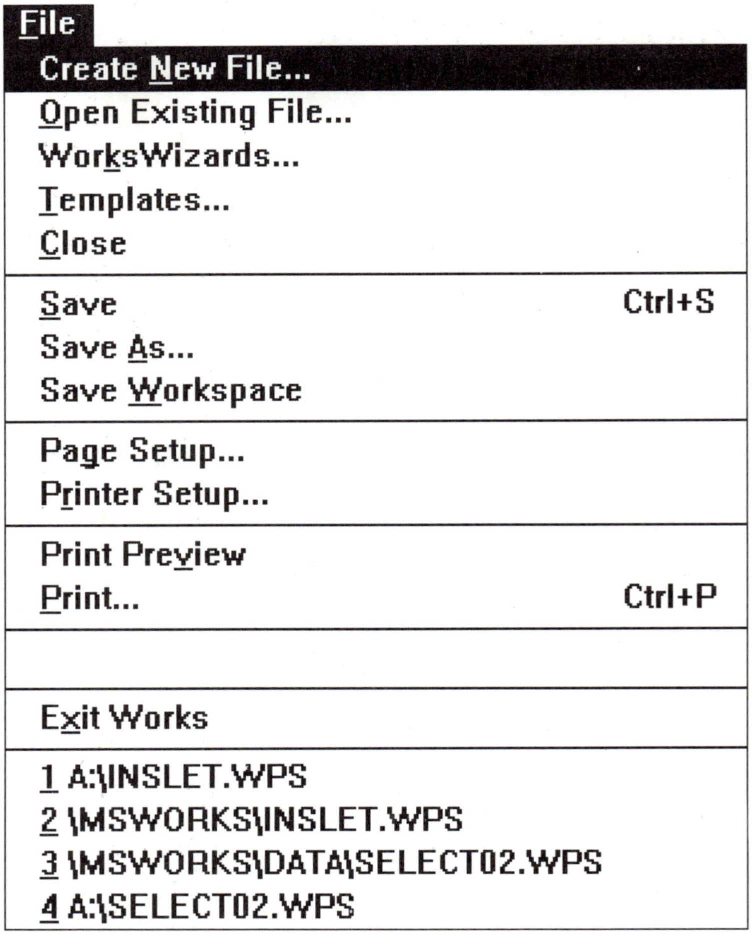

Figure 4.14

The File Menu

72. Click on Save As.

    The Save As option box appears, as shown in Figure 4.15

73. Type **inslet**
74. Click on OK.

    Works automatically adds a .WPS extension to your file name. Before you print your letter, preview it to see how it looks on the page.

75. Click on File-Print Preview.

    The letter is Greeked (so small you cannot read it). To read it, click on Zoom. You can print a document from the Preview menu, or you can print from the File menu.

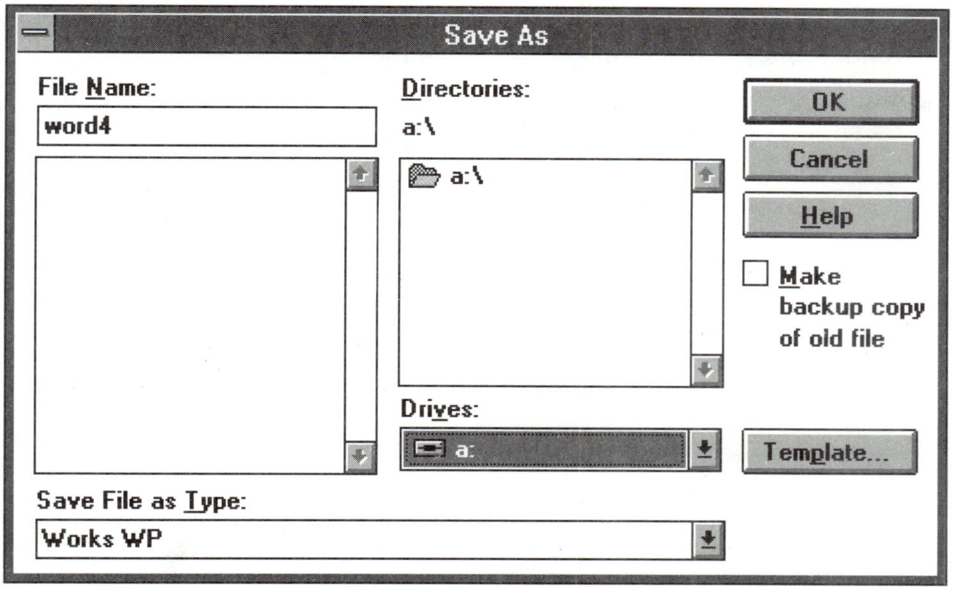

Figure 4.15

The Save As Option Box

76. Click on Print.

    The Print dialog box displays, as shown in Figure 4.16.

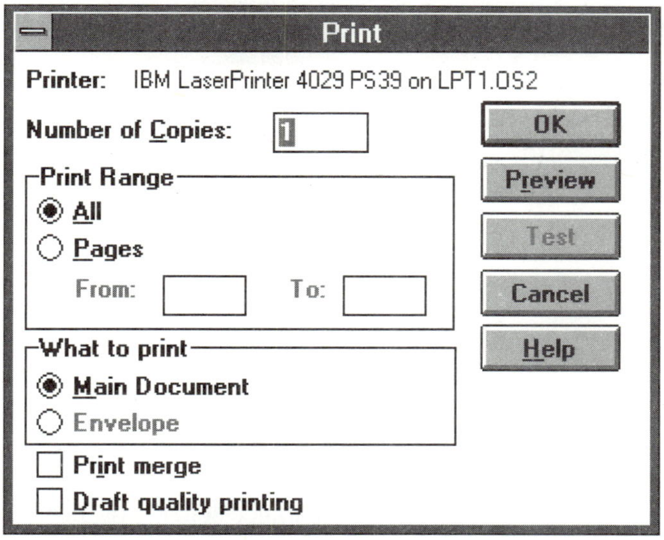

Figure 4.16

The Print Dialcg Box

The following choices should be marked:

Number of Copies—1

Print Range—All

What to print—Main document

77. Click on OK.

    Your document should look similar to that in Figure 4.17.

    Obviously, the tab stops, return symbols, and space markers will not show. To leave the document:

Figure 4.17

inslet.wps Document

January 22, 1995

Fred Abercrombie
National Insurance Company
8080 E. Indianapolis
Wichita, KS 67207

Dear Mr. Abercrombie:

I would like to receive a detailed printout that shows my coverage wiht your company and the value of the perosnal property that I have insured. I recently purchased an **IBM PS/2 model** 77 and I want to make sure that it is covered under my existing policy. Also, please check to see if the following items are coverd:

- a pool table valued at $1,000
- 3 gold watches, total value $5,000
- 1 Camcorder valued at $800
- a coin collection valued at $10,000

Our personal property including the computer totals about $20,000. If my existing policy does not cover this amount, please sned insurance quottes to me by February 1 at the following address:

your name
your street address
City, State Zip

Thank you for your attention in this matter.

Sincerely,

your name

78. Click on File-Close.

    To leave *Works*:

79. Click on File-Exit *Works*.

In order to finish your insurance letter, you need to know some additional word processing techniques. Remember, the underlying principle of word processing is to type text once and then rearrange its form according to present need. This requires that you learn what some of your options are and how to execute them.

File Handling: Open an Existing Document

A document that already exists, saved to a disk, can be retrieved and loaded into RAM when you wish to add, change, or delete material in the file. When you open a file, it remains open until you close it or exit the program. To open an existing file:

- Click on Open an Existing Document.
- Click on Drive-Directory, if necessary.
- Click on File Name.

When using the *Works* program you can have up to eight files open at one time. Once you have closed a file, however, to work on the document again you must first open it, and that requires looking up its location. The program needs your help to locate the document that you intend to retrieve and edit, because personal files are often not stored in the same place on the disk as the *Works* program itself.

If you are accessing *Works* from a network or from a hard drive, you must indicate the drive and directory where your own documents are stored, as we explained in Chapter 3. You may do this from the File menu when you choose File-Open an Existing Document. The option box that appears has a directory setting in the middle area of the Open File window. Click on or TAB to that area and highlight the drive of your choice with the mouse or the directional arrows, then click on OK to set the correct directory.

If you have forgotten how to change the default drive, refer to Chapter 2. It can be disappointing to have your files end up on the hard disk when you do not intend them to be stored there—or worse, to have them saved to a network server, where they can be promptly deleted without warning. Files saved to network servers are almost never regained. Rather than risk losing your work, or at best, spending time trying to find it, make a habit of designating a drive when you first open *Works 3.0 for Windows*.

At the start of every computing session, you should designate the directory to which you wish to save files and from which you wish to retrieve them. This allows you to bring a current file into memory for additional work simply by selecting File-Open, after which you click on or TAB to the file name and select it from the List box on the left side of the screen, then click on OK or press ENTER. Your file will be loaded into RAM and it will appear on the document screen, ready to be modified. File names are listed alphabetically in the far left pane of the Open box. The file extension indicates the type of file: .wps for word processor, .wks for spreadsheet, and so on. If your file does not appear in the listing, check the middle box to see which directory the program is reading.

More Formatting Features

Before continuing with your hands-on work, let's look at more ways you can control the appearance of your document. The center and find and replace functions will be shown in the tutorial in this chapter and copy/move and changing margins will be covered in the tutorial in Chapter 5.

Centering a Block of Text

You can center any amount of text within a document's margins. As with the other formatting options, you may center as you type. To do this:

- Press CTRL + E, or click on the center icon in the toolbar.
- Type the text.
- Click on the left align toolbar icon, or enter CTRL + L from the keyboard.

The text you type next will return to normal alignment. If you have already typed the text you wish to center, you must first go back and select it for further action in any of the following ways:

1. Hold the SHIFT key and press arrow keys.
2. Press F8 once and use the arrow keys to extend the highlighting of text as far as you want, then press CTRL + SPACEBAR to deactivate F8 (extend).
3. Press the F8 function key two, three, four, or five times to select text.
4. Drag the mouse over the material.

After the text has been selected in a block, click on the center icon in the toolbar, or press CTRL + E, as noted above. The selected text will be centered within the right and left margins.

After the text has been centered, it remains highlighted. Click outside the selected area to deselect the text. (Don't forget to return to left alignment.)

Moving and Copying Text

Two of the most useful features of word processing applications are the ability to move, or relocate, portions of text and to copy, or duplicate, portions of text. You use *Works'* Cut command and its Paste command to move text from one place in the document to another. This removes the text from its original location, and places it only in the new location. With the Copy command, you duplicate the desired text; it remains in its original location and appears in the new location, as well. You use Copy and Paste to duplicate text.

Think carefully about which command you want before you access the Edit command or click on the Copy or Cut toolbar icons. Both operations involve selecting the text to be cut or copied, invoking the Edit command, and finally indicating the new location by clicking on Paste while the I-beam marks the insertion point at the desired spot in the document.

To cut or copy:

- Select the text to be cut or copied.
- Click on Edit.

- Click on Copy or Cut.

  OR
- Click on the Copy or Cut icon in the toolbar.
- Position the insertion point at the desired new location.
- Click on Edit.
- Click on Paste.

  OR
- Click on the Paste icon.

The previously selected text will be cut or copied from its original location to appear at the indicated destination.

You can cut or copy any amount of text in this manner. Just be certain of which command you want, and be sure to position the insertion point at the desired destination before clicking on Paste to finish the command. You cannot, of course, cut or copy text beyond the end of the document, so you may have to press ENTER to insert several hard returns before using the Copy command or the Cut and Paste commands. Also, once you begin the cut or copy operation, you must finish it (or press ESC more than once to terminate the command) before you can return to the word processing application. You do not, however, have to paste the text immediately. Just remember that you cannot invoke another Cut or Copy command until you complete the first one.

Changing Margins and Paper Size

Margins are the spaces between the edges of a page and the printed area. You can change the area that accommodates printing by changing the margins. When you enter *Works*, the default paper size is 8.5 inches by 11 inches, and the margins are 1.0 inch on the top and bottom, 1.25 inches on the left and right sides. It is very easy to change these margins, and even the size of the paper, to customize your document.

To change the margins:

- Click on File.
- Click on Page Setup.

  The Margin section is at the left of the Page window.
- Click on the margin you wish to set—top, bottom, left, or right.
- Enter the new measurement.
- Click on OK or press ENTER.

(Remember, you do not have to type the symbol for inches unless you change the units of measurement.)

You can control header and footer margins in this Page Setup window, as well. We will discuss headers and footers in Chapter 5.

Margins are saved with your document when it is saved to disk. Margin and page layout settings are unique to each file, and do not have to be reset every time you retrieve the document. They are saved along with your text in the document.

If you wish to format one copy of the document for 8.5-by-11-inch paper and regular margins, and another copy for 3-by-5-inch notecards with no margins, you can save two separate copies of the original document (each with a unique name, of course). Each can have its own margin and page layout settings. To merely try out an alternative layout, you can retrieve the document, change the settings, print it, and close it without saving those new margin settings.

Find/Replace

A unique feature of word processing applications is the ability to search for (Find in *Works*) a certain word and replace it throughout your document with another word. This handy feature can save hours of editing with a few keystrokes. If you have misused a word throughout a 50-page paper and wish to correct it, the **Edit command** will give you the menu to accomplish this. The Edit menu gives you the choice of **Find**, which merely searches and locates the sequence of characters that forms the word, and **Replace**, which allows you to replace that sequence with another.

If you choose Replace, you can specify whether you want to replace all occurrences of the word without confirming each change (a global replacement), or you can isolate each occurrence and confirm the replacement individually. You also may choose case-sensitive replacement, which replaces the text only if the occurrence matches the capitalization you specify. (The default is case-insensitive, which replaces all occurrences in both upper case and lower case.)

Finally, you may specify that you want to replace only a whole word. That way you will not need to add spaces before or after the characters you type in to avoid replacing parts of a word. (If you asked to replace *the* with *a* without this option, every word that contained the sequence *the* would be altered. Thus *theater, their, them, themselves*, and *there* would be changed to *aater, air, am, amselves*, and *are*; this is not the intended result.)

In most cases, to effectively replace text, you must be at the top of the document (get there by pressing CTRL + HOME) before you access the Edit menu. You generally want to find and replace text from the top of a document to the end (called a *global search and replace*), ignoring the case.

To perform the Find function (merely to locate a word or string of words):

- Click on Edit.
- Click on Find.
- Select options if desired:
  Match whole word
  Match upper/lower case
- Click on OK.

To perform the Find/Replace function (to identify a word or string of words and replace it with another):

- Click on Edit.
- Click on Replace.
- Enter the Find and Replace texts.
- Select options, if desired:

  Match whole word

  Match upper/lower case
- Select Replace, if you want to stop at each occurrence.

  OR
- Select Replace All, to replace globally without stopping.
- Click on the Close button when you finish entering the Find and Replace information.

Printing a File

Most users want to print word processing documents and retain hard copies. In fact, most documents are printed several times before they are considered complete.

If you are on a network, your printer is probably already selected. If not,

- Click on File.
- Click on Printer Setup.
- Click on the printer you wish to use from the list presented.

To print one copy of a *Works* document:

- Click on File.
- Click on Print.
- Click on OK or press ENTER for the default choice of one copy.

  OR
- Click Number of Copies box and type any number.

To print a portion of the whole document:

- Click on the Pages round (radio) button.

To print a single page, as page 3:

- Type From: **3** To: **3**

To print a continuous range of pages, as pages 3 through 6:

- Type From: **3** To: **6**
- Click on OK.

The Main Document option is selected by default. The **draft quality** option allows you to print with less clarity than near-letter quality, and print more quickly; this is often desirable for a preliminary copy. Besides increasing printing speed, this feature allows you to use less ink in the ink cartridge in an ink-jet or laser printer.

If you click on the toolbar Print icon, you will bypass all of the print selections and send your document directly to the printer with the default settings of one copy, all pages, printed in letter quality. This is a quick way to print a document without going through the menu options. Likewise, you could simply invoke the Print menu and press ENTER twice. The first few documents you print will probably use the default settings of *Works*. In this case:

- Click on File-Print.
- Press ENTER twice.

If your printer is **on-line** (turned on, ready to go with paper loaded, and under automatic rather than manual, control) one copy of the entire document will begin to print.

As a beginner, you will benefit by spending a few minutes familiarizing yourself with your particular printer, including reviewing its manual. Printing becomes much easier with practice; those early paper jams, slipping tractor feeds, off-line printers, and worn ribbons or cartridges will soon be in your past.

Exiting Works

When you are finished using *Works*, you can exit the program in one step if you made no changes, and in two steps if you made changes:

- Click on File.
- Click on Exit.
- If you made changes, click on Yes to save them.
- If you made no changes, or you don't want to save any, click on the No button.

WORD PROCESSING TUTORIAL NO. 2

In the following tutorial you will retrieve your inslet.wps file, change the left and right margins, center the date and closing lines, correct your spelling errors manually (you will use a spelling checker in the next chapter), replace the word *computer* with *personal computer*, and copy a line.

Before you begin, make certain that the work disk containing your inslet.wps file is in the A or B drive.

1. Double click on the Microsoft *Works* icon.
2. In the Startup screen, click on Open an Existing Document.
3. Select inslet.wps (or type **a:inslet.wps** in the File Name text box).
4. Click on OK (or double click on inslet.wps).

5. Save the file as inslet2 to keep the original intact. (File-Save As-type **inslet2**-OK.)

   To change the left and right margins, verify that the insertion point appears at the top of your document, then:

6. Click on File-Page Setup.

   The Page Setup option box displays, as shown in Figure 4.18.

Figure 4.18

The Page Setup Option Box

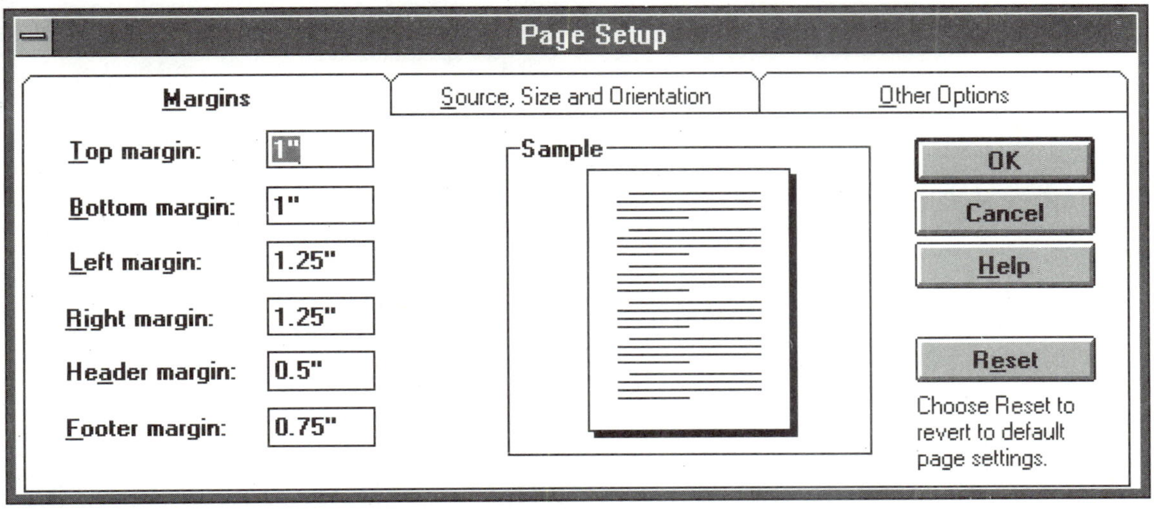

7. Click on Margins, if it is not already selected.
8. TAB to Left Margin.
9. Type **1.5**
10. TAB to Right Margin.
11. Type **1.5**
12. Click on OK.

    To center the date:

13. Select the date (highlight it with the mouse).
14. Click on Format-Paragraph-Indents and Alignments.

    The Indents and Alignments dialog box displays, as shown in Figure 4.19.

15. In the Alignments list box, click on Center.
16. Click on OK.
17. Deselect the text by clicking outside the selected area.

    In the first sentence, position the I-beam to the left of the *h* in *wiht* and click on the mouse to activate the insertion point.

Figure 4.19

The Indents and Alignments Dialog Box

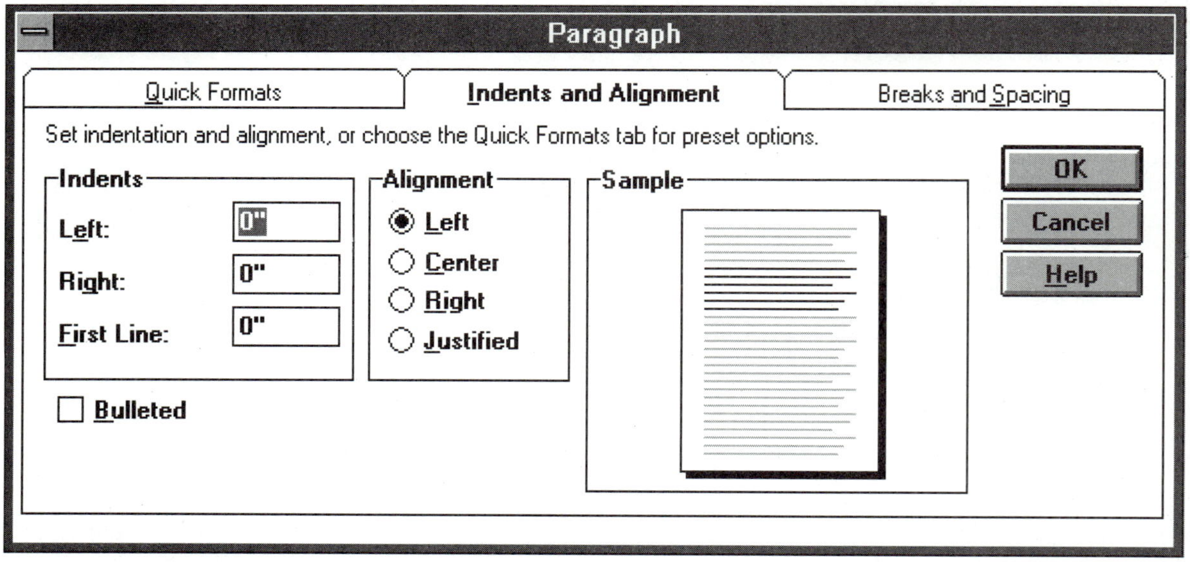

18. Press the INS key.

    The prompt on the bottom, right-hand side of the status line should read “OVR” for *strikeover*.
19. Type **th**
20. Move to the left of the *o* in *perosnal* and type **so**
21. Move the insertion point to the right of *77*.
22. Press the INS key.
23. Press the SPACEBAR, then type **computer**
24. In the last line of the paragraph, type an **e** in *coverd*.
25. In the third paragraph type over *sned* with **send**

    (Remember to press the INS key.)
26. Move the insertion point between the two *t*s in *quottes*.
27. Press the BACKSPACE key.

    To center the closing lines:
28. Select the text from *Sincerely* through your name (highlight it with the mouse).
29. Click on the Center icon.
30. Deselect the text.

You will now find *computer* and replace it with *personal computer*.

31. Press CTRL + HOME.
32. Click on Edit.

    The Edit menu displays, as shown in Figure 4.20.

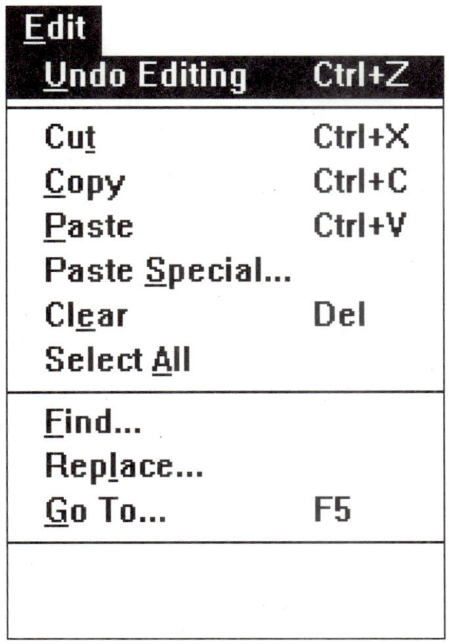

Figure 4.20

The Edit Menu

33. Click on Replace.

    The Replace dialog box displays, as shown in Figure 4.21.

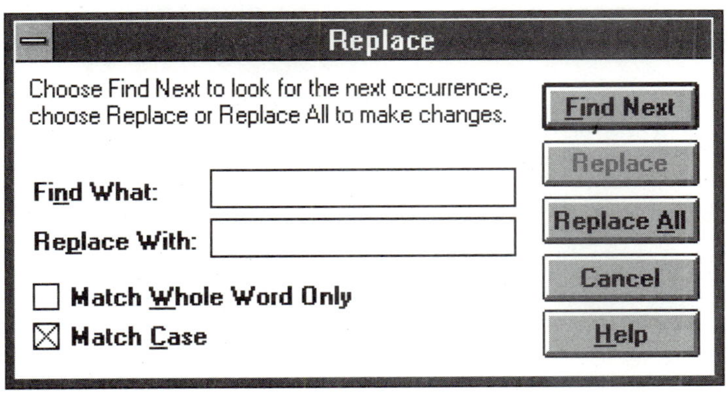

Figure 4.21

The Replace Dialog Box

34. In the Find What text box, type **computer**
35. TAB to the Replace With text box and type **personal computer**

36. Click on Replace All, then click on Close.

    Check to see if the replacement was successful.

37. Save, print your letter, and exit *Works*.

    Your document should look like the one in Figure 4.22.

Figure 4.22

inslet2.wps Document

January 22, 1995

Fred Abercrombie
National Insurance Company
8080 E. Indianapolis
Wichita, KS 67207

Dear Mr. Abercrombie:

I would like to receive a detailed printout that shows my coverage with your company and the value of the personal property that I have insured. I recently purchased an **IBM PS/2 model 77** personal computer and I want to make sure that it is covered under my existing policy. Also, please check to see if the following items are covered:

- a pool table valued at $1,000
- 3 gold watches, total value $5,000
- 1 Camcorder valued at $800
- a coin collection valued at $10,000

Our personal property including the personal computer totals about $20,000. If my existing policy does not cover this amount, please send insurance quotes to me by February 1 at the following address:

your name
your street address
City, State Zip

Thank you for your attention in this matter.

Sincerely,

your name

Chapter Summary

Word processing is the process of generating and correcting text using of a special editing program for computers. It is one of the most useful applications developed for the personal computer. Its most important advantage is that it reduces the need for retyping documents.

Word processing was among the first applications developed for personal computers. Today's powerful word processors allow relative novice users to generate many different document types, using easily learned features.

In this chapter, you learned the history of word processing; the types of word processing documents; the *Works* editing, formatting, and file handling features; how to load the *Works* word processor into RAM; how to create, save, and print a document; and how to close a file and exit *Works*.

KEY TERMS

block
boilerplate
boldface
bulleted list
clip art
draft quality
Edit command
Find
font
hanging paragraph
hard return
insert mode
leader
mail merge
newspaper column
nonbreaking space
on-line
preview mode
quick paragraph format
quotation
Replace
All Characters
soft return
typeover mode
turnaround
Undo Editing command
word wrap
Wrap for Window
zoom

REVIEW QUESTIONS

1. Define the term *word processing.*
2. Explain several advantages of using word processing for document creation, as compared with older forms of writing.
3. Briefly outline the history of word processing.
4. Complete this statement: "The variety of documents that can be generated using a word processing program is . . ."
5. The cost of a personal computer, printer, and word processing software can run into hundreds or even thousands of dollars. Justify this expenditure (a) for personal use and (b) for business use.
6. List and define features found in all word processors.
7. When would it be useful to choose the View-All Characters function from the word processing menu?
8. Name at least eight insertion point control keys and the movements they produce.
9. Explain the three ways to delete material in *Works.*
10. Briefly explain the concept and advantage of word wrap.
11. *Works* has two ways to add emphasis to type in a document. What are they? How do you use them?
12. When is it useful to keep two words or letters together on a line? How is this done in *Works*?

13. Suppose you want to set three tabs at intervals of eight spaces each from the left margin. List the steps you would take to accomplish this task.
14. List and briefly explain the several quick paragraph formats available in *Works 3.0 for Windows*.
15. Explain when you would use the Save As command as opposed to the Save command.
16. WYSIWYG stands for "what you see is what you get." Discuss the usefulness of this concept and briefly describe how to invoke it in *Works*.
17. Explain the purpose and technique of closing a file.
18. Explain (a) what the Toolbar contains, (b) where it is located on the screen, (c) how to show or hide it, and (d) the advantage of using it, as compared with using a menu.
19. Explain (a) the importance of setting a directory when you first begin using the *Works* word processor, and (b) how to set a directory to save your own files on a floppy disk in the B drive.
20. Briefly describe how you would accomplish the following tasks in the *Works* word processor: (a) center a three-line block of text, (b) move the second paragraph to just below the fourth paragraph, (c) change the margins from their default settings to 2 inches from the right and left sides of an 8.5-by-11-inch sheet of paper.
21. Explain the purpose and use of the zoom feature.
22. Suppose you wrote a paper about the Mississippi River. Instead of typing the name of the river over and over, you typed the characters *MSX* instead. Explain how you could quickly find each occurrence of *MSX* and replace it with the word *Mississippi*.

SOFTWARE EXERCISES

Exercise 4.1

1. Make arrangements with your instructor to familiarize yourself with the *Works* word processing tutorial.
2. Make notes about what was covered in each of the following sections:

   (a) Introducing the word processor

   (b) Entering text
3. Use *Works 3.0 for Windows* to type your notes about what you learned.
4. Save your work as tutwp4.
5. Print tutwp4.wps.
6. Close tutwp4.wps and exit *Works*.

Exercise 4.2

1. In this exercise, you will type a letter to an insurance company.
2. Open a new word processing file.
3. Set the left and right margins at 2 inches.
4. Set a single tab at 2. inches.
5. Using Figure 4.23 as a reference, type in your return address in place of the one in the figure.

2643 S. Oneida

Wheat Ridge, CO 80033

December 24, 1994

American Family Insurance Co., Inc.

One Insurance Square

Minneapolis, MN 40801

Ladies and Gentlemen:

I am interested in purchasing a term life insurance policy. I am twenty-one years of age, a male, and a nonsmoker.

Please send me a quotation on a five-year renewable term life policy with a value of $100,000.

Sincerely yours,

Ken Shaw

Figure 4.23

lifeltr1.wps Document

6. Substitute the current date for the one in the figure.
7. Type the rest of the letter, substituting your own age and sex for those in the figure.
8. In the complimentary close, TAB to the stop you set and type **Sincerely yours**; leave three or four lines and TAB to the stop you set and substitute your name for the one in the figure.
9. Save the letter as lifeltr1.
10. Print the letter.
11. Close lifeltr1.wps and exit *Works*.

Exercise 4.3

1. Open the lifeltr1.wps file that you created in Exercise 4.2, or complete Exercise 4.2 before continuing.
2. Click on View-All Characters to Show All Characters, if not already displayed.
3. Change the margins to 1.3 inches on the left side and 1.2 inches on the right side.
4. Tab your return address and the current date to the existing 2" tab setting.
5. Select the paragraphs; set a tab .8 inch from the left margin.
6. Indent each paragraph .8 inch (.8) from the left margin if not already indented .8 inch.
7. Change the entire letter from double spacing to single spacing, with double spacing between paragraphs.
8. Save the letter as lifeltr2.
9. Print the letter.
10. Close the lifeltr2.wps file and exit *Works*.

Exercise 4.4

1. Open the lifeltr1.wps file that you created in Exercise 4.2, or complete Exercise 4.2 before continuing.
2. Change the entire letter from double spacing to single spacing, with double spacing between paragraphs. Remove the paragraph indention, if necessary.
3. Center the inside address and the date (your address and the current date) and the closing.
4. Remove your age, your sex, and the claim to be a nonsmoker from the body of the letter and put each one on a separate line following a bullet. Single space each bulleted line, but insert one extra line before the bulleted lines and after them. Edit the bullets as necessary.

5. Save the letter as lifeltr3.
6. Print the letter.
7. Close the lifeltr3.wps file and exit *Works*.

Exercise 4.5

1. Open the lifeltr1.wps file that you created in Exercise 4.2, or complete Exercise 4.2 before continuing.
2. Change the entire letter from double spacing to single spacing with double spacing between paragraphs. Return to the block style with no indentions.
3. Change the name of the insurance company from American Family Insurance Company, Inc. to Allstate Insurance Company, Inc.
4. Change the existing company street address to 1009 11th Ave.
5. Change the existing company city, state, and Zip to Greeley, CO 80631.
6. Add the following new paragraph: **Also include a quotation on the same policy with a value of $250,000.**
7. Add an extra blank line between the added paragraph and the one preceding it so you have double spacing between paragraphs.
8. Save the letter as lifeltr4.
9. Print the letter.
10. Close the lifeltr4.wps file and exit *Works*.

Exercise 4.6

1. Open the lifeltr1.wps file that you created in Exercise 4.2, or complete Exercise 4.2 before continuing.
2. Use search and replace to replace term life with whole life throughout the document.
3. Change the entire letter from double spacing to single spacing.
4. Save the letter as LIFELTR5.
5. Print the letter.
6. Close the LIFELTR5.WPS file and exit.

Exercise 4.7

1. Open the file inslet2.wps from this chapter's tutorial.
2. Change the type of computer from an IBM PS/2 model 77 to an Applied Computer Technology DX2/66 personal computer.
3. Add a value for the Applied Computer Technology personal computer of $3,000 to the sentence so that it now reads, "I recently purchased an Applied Computer Technology personal computer valued at $3,000.00 and I . . ."

4. Change the worth of the personal property from $20,000 to $25,000.
5. Preview the letter on the screen. Zoom in, as needed.
6. Save the letter as inslet3.
7. Print inslet3.wps.
8. Close inslet3.wps and exit *Works*.

Exercise 4.8

1. Open the file inslet2.wps from this chapter's tutorial.
2. Add and center your return address.
3. Change the margins to 1.8 inches on the left and 1.7 inches on the right.
4. Begin the first sentence of each paragraph by indenting (tabbing) one-half inch.
5. Remove the double spacing between paragraphs.
6. Change the emphasis on IBM PS/2 model 77 from bold to underline.
7. Preview the letter.
8. Save the letter as inslet4.
9. Print inslet4.wps.
10. Close inslet4.wps and exit *Works*.

Exercise 4.9

1. Open the file named vacation.wps on the student data diskette that accompanies this text.
2. Replace the existing return address with your own return address and center it; center the current date below your return address.
3. Change the margins to 1.8 inches on the left and 1.7 inches on the right.
4. Begin the first sentence of each paragraph by indenting (tabbing) one-half inch.
5. Remove the double spacing between paragraphs.
6. Change the body of the letter to double spacing.
7. Use your own name and the current date.
8. Change the duration of your proposed stay from one week to two weeks.
9. Change the dates of your proposed stay to reflect an added week and make the dates current with the year when you would travel.
10. Preview the letter.
11. Save the letter as vacaton1.
12. Print vacaton1.wps.
13. Close vacaton1.wps and exit *Works*.

Exercise 4.10

1. Open the file named charter.wps on the student data diskette that accompanies this text.
2. Add the current date, your own return address, and your own name after the complimentary close.
3. Change the letter to block style with left justification (everything lined up on the left margin).
4. Change the body of the letter from double spacing with indented paragraphs to single spacing with no indents for paragraphs, but with double spaces between paragraphs.
5. Add the following paragraph: **In addition, we would like to know the additional cost of having a captain and cook accompany us on the charter.**
6. Preview the letter.
7. Save the letter as charter1.
8. Print charter1.wps.
9. Close charter1.wps and exit *Works.*

Exercise 4.11

1. Use the WorksWizard to create a letterhead. Personalize it with your name, address, city, state, Zip, and telephone number. Experiment with the letterhead style; select the one you like best. Align your letterhead in the way that most suits you. Click on neither when asked if you would like to add a decorative border or picture.
2. Compose a letter on your letterhead to an insurance company asking for a quote on disability insurance. State the following facts in your letter: your current age, sex, state of your own general health, and effective immediately. Use the same company address (for National Insurance Company) from Tutorial No. 1 along with your own name, home address, and current date.
3. Choose top, bottom, and side margins and tab settings that place your letter properly on the page.
4. Preview your letter.
5. Save your letter as inslet5.
6. Print inslet5.wps.
7. Close inslet5.wps and exit *Works.*

Exercise 4.12

1. Use the WorksWizard to create a letterhead. Personalize it with your name, address, city, state, Zip, and telephone number. Experiment with the letterhead style; select the one you like best. Align your letterhead in the way that most suits you. Click on neither when asked if you would like to add a decorative border or picture.

2. Compose a letter on your letterhead to a mutual fund asking for the following: a health care sector prospectus, minimum initial investment, minimum monthly investment, and whether or not the fund charges a sales load on a purchase, a redemption fee, an exchange fee, or a 12b–1 fee. Address your letter to: Fidelity Investments, 82 Devonshire Street, Boston, Massachusetts 02109.
3. Choose top, bottom, and side margins and tab settings that place your letter properly on the page.
4. Preview your letter.
5. Save your letter as fundltr.
6. Print fundltr.wps.
7. Close fundltr.wps and exit *Works*.

Exercise 4.13

1. Use the WorksWizard to create a letterhead. Personalize it with your name, address, city, state, Zip, and telephone number. Experiment with the letterhead style; select the one you like best. Align your letterhead in the way that most suits you. Click on neither when asked if you would like to add a decorative border or picture.
2. Compose a letter of complaint on your letterhead to a recreational equipment outfitter. Make the following points: the backpack you ordered from them for carrying your school books and supplies came apart at the seams in less than 30 days of normal use; you want the backpack replaced or repaired free of cost to you. Address your letter to Recreational Equipment, Inc., P. O. Box 88125, Seattle, WA 98138–2125.
3. Choose top, bottom, and side margins and tab settings that place your letter properly on the page.
4. Preview your letter.
5. Save your letter as complain.
6. Print complain.wps.
7. Close complain.wps and exit *Works*.

Chapter 5

Working With Long Documents

Objectives

After studying this chapter you will be able to:

- *Compose complex documents*
- *Design documents with complex layouts and styles*
- *Customize the Toolbar with your most frequently used icons*
- *Use different paragraph styles and line spacing*
- *Use a spelling checker or thesaurus*
- *Compose footnotes in* Works
- *Explain the use of the window feature*
- *State the primary reason for using a text file*
- *Save a* Works *file in a text format*
- *Identify the three general levels of document preparation*
- *Describe the purpose and use of desktop publishing*
- *Use Note-it and clip art to improve your documents*

Once you have mastered relatively simple, sequential documents on a word processing application, you are ready to learn how to produce more complex documents. Chapter 4 explained the types of documents that you can format on the microcomputer word processing applications available today. All but the most complex documents, which require desktop publishing packages, can be produced with the *Works* word processing module. In this chapter, you will experiment with adding graphics to your word processing documents, formatting columns and wrapping text around pictures, and other desktop publishing techniques that are now commonplace in most word processors.

This chapter concentrates on the formatting used in complex documents. It also shows you the extra tools that word processing packages provide, such as the spelling checker, the thesaurus, and footnote feature.

Page Layouts in More Structured Documents

When we introduced formatting in the last chapter, we said that it refers to the way your document appears on the page. Formatting involves controlling **margins** (top, bottom, left, and right), **line spacing**, paragraph indents, and paragraph **alignment**. In addition to the way your document is set up on the page, the text or characters can also have different styles or fonts. Long documents may require headers and/or footers and page numbers. All of these options are used to create a more structured, and often, more aesthetically pleasing document.

Using the Ruler

A word processor typically displays a **ruler line** at the top of the screen. This line shows basic margin and tab formatting that you have defined for the document. Any default settings, such as the default tab stops, are also visible. The ruler line helps you control the structure of your document. Most ruler lines can be toggled off, so that they do not display on the screen if you would rather not see them. They are helpful, however, for beginners and seasoned word processing students alike.

The *Works* ruler line extends the length of the right and left margin settings, as shown in Figure 5.1. The ruler appears as a scale across the top of the screen, showing the length of the line, the indents, and the tab stops for the paragraph in which the cursor lies. The default settings are 1.25 inches for both the left and right margins. This leaves a 6 inch writing line and approximately 1.3 inches of white space on both sides of the text when it is printed on an 8.5-by-11-inch piece of paper. If you wish, you may change those margins in a specific document by going to the File-Page Setup menu and changing the settings.

Figure 5.1

The Ruler Line

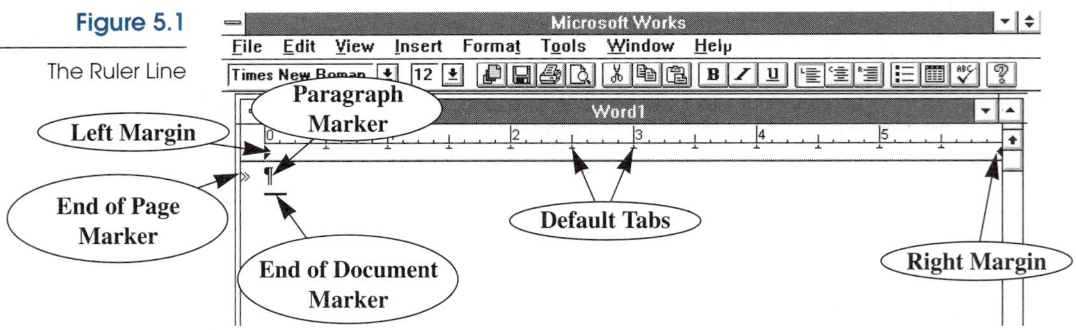

To change those default margins:

- Click on File-Page Setup.
- Click on, or TAB to, the desired margin.
- Type a new number.
- Click on OK, or press ENTER.

Each time you change the margins, the new settings will be reflected in the ruler line at the top of the word processing screen. If you do not wish to refer to the ruler line as a guide when using the *Works* word processor, turn it off with the following commands:

- Click on View.
- Click on Ruler.

This is a toggle command, which means that you turn it off or on each time you complete the above selection process. A small check mark (√) will appear alongside the Ruler choice when the ruler is turned on. The check mark disappears when the ruler is turned off.

Indenting Text

An **indent** is a space between the left or right margin and the beginning or end of a line. The Normal paragraph style has no indents. To change the indents for a paragraph, use the Paragraph Format dialog box from the Format menu. To see the indents you have created, display the ruler and move the cursor anywhere in the paragraph. The ruler shows left and right indents with tiny left- and right-pointing triangles, and it shows user-defined tabs and other formats with broken arrows.

Paragraph Formats

Paragraph formats determine the appearance of a document's paragraphs. Variables include alignments, indents, line spacing, tab settings, and borders. When you press ENTER, you create a paragraph ending, though the paragraph may consist of only part of one line. These forced line endings are often referred to as *hard returns*, because you determine where the line will end, instead of allowing the program to do so through its word wrap function. In *Works*, if you have the All Characters option turned on (from the View menu), you will see a paragraph symbol (¶) wherever you have pressed ENTER.

As with the other formatting options in *Works*, you can either select a paragraph and format it after typing, or choose formatting options before typing the paragraph. Remember, as well, that *Works* stores all paragraph formats in the paragraph mark at the end of each paragraph. If you delete a paragraph mark, the text joins with the next paragraph and takes on the format of that paragraph.

The Paragraph menu selection from the Format command offers a submenu of three selections. As we discussed in Chapter 4, the quick formats can define five specific styles. Indents and alignment formats allow numerical settings; paragraph break and spacing options allow you to format the lines between paragraphs, or to keep a paragraph together on one page. This protects against what is sometimes referred to in journalism and publishing as **widow and orphan** sentences and paragraphs. Widows and orphans are short lines of text that are left alone at the tops of pages, or at the bottoms of pages, distracting the reader from the text as a whole. The widow and orphan sentence concept applies to paragraphs, as well. Sometimes you may wish to keep a paragraph all together on one page. When using the last option of the Format-Paragraph menu, the Breaks and Spacing command, you needn't force a page break to keep a paragraph together. *Works* will recognize the text to be kept together and automatically format your pages accordingly. The commands to do this are discussed later in the chapter, under borders.

Aligning Text

Paragraphs may be left-aligned (normal), right-aligned (the reverse of left-aligned), justified, or centered, as shown in Figure 5.2. They may have first line indents, hanging indents, or quotation indents, as you learned in the last chapter. You will experiment with different text alignment styles in the tutorials in this chapter.

Figure 5.2

Sample of Four Alignment Styles

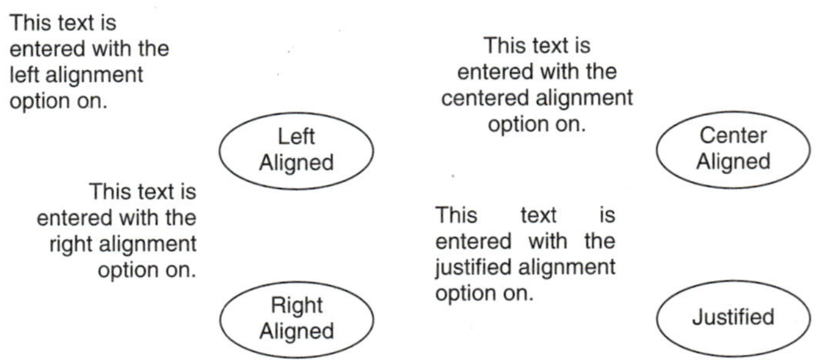

You can enter the commands for alignment before you type, or you can select the material after it has been typed and then enter the commands.

The lines of a justified paragraph are evenly aligned at both the right and left indents or margins. To justify a paragraph:

- Click on Format-Paragraph.
- Click on the middle Indents and Alignments area.
- Click on the Justified choice.

You may also use the quick keystroke combinations:

- Press CTRL + J.

Many word processing packages use the term *justification* for all types of alignment. They allow for left, right, and full justification. CTRL + J will give you what others term *full justification*.

A right-aligned paragraph is aligned along the right indent or margin; text on the left edge is uneven, or "ragged." Some uses for right alignment might be headings, dates, return addresses, and so on. To right-align a paragraph:

- Click on Format-Paragraph.
- Click on the Indents and Alignments area.
- Click on the Right Alignment choice.

Alternately, you may:

- Select the R icon from the toolbar.

  OR

- Press CTRL + R.

A left-aligned paragraph lines up all text evenly along the left margin or indent. Paragraphs are usually left-aligned, so to undo all other paragraph alignment, apply left alignment. To left-align a paragraph:

- Click on Format-Paragraph.
- Click on Indents and Alignments.
- Click on the Left Alignment choice.

Alternately, you may:

- Select the L icon from the toolbar.

  OR

- Press CTRL+ L.

A centered paragraph places text horizontally in the middle of the page. One line, several lines, or a whole paragraph can be centered. To center:

- Click on Format-Paragraph.
- Click on Indents and Alignments.
- Click on the Centered Alignment choice.

Alternately, you may:

- Select the C icon from the toolbar.

  OR

- Press CTRL + C.

Changes in alignment remain in place until you change to another setting. To return to normal:

- Click on the Format-Paragraph menu selections.
- Click on Quick Formats.
- Choose Normal from the list of styles.

  OR

- Select the L icon from the toolbar.

Left alignment is the default for *Works 3.0 for Windows*.

Figure 5.3 shows the various ways paragraphs can be formatted in *Works*. A hanging indent can be used to set off the first line of a paragraph from the rest of the paragraph. The rest of the paragraph "hangs" below it, indented on the left side only. This format is especially useful for entries in a bibliography, among other uses.

Figure 5.3

Works Paragraph Indenting Styles

***Works* Indenting Styles**

Normal

You can also turn on Select mode (by pressing F8) and then use the directional keys to highlight the text to be affected. Alternatively, after pressing F8 you can press a key to extend the selection to the chosen character. Unlike the other two methods, Select mode will not replace the selected text with the characters you type. To deselect text that has been selected, either press F8 again or click the mouse anywhere in the work area.

First Line Indent

To edit, replace, delete, cut, or copy text, you must first select the text to be edited. To select text, move the mouse pointer in the text area; the pointer turns into an I-beam. Position the I-beam in front of the text to be edited, press the left mouse button and drag the mouse until the desired text is highlighted, then release the mouse button.

Bulleted

In addition to dragging the mouse and using the shift-and-click method, you can also select various quantities of text with the mouse as follows:

- One word — double-click on the word
- One sentence — triple-click on the sentence
- One paragraph — Quadruple-click on the paragraph

Hanging Indent

1. An alternative to dragging, called shift-and-click, requires you to position the insertion point at the beginning of the text to be selected, move the I-beam to the end of the text, press and hold the Shift key while clicking the left mouse button. The text between the insertion point and the I-beam is then selected.

Shaw, Kenneth D., Gwynne Larsen, and Kathryn A. Marold, *Using Microsoft Works* (Danvers, Mass.: Boyd & Fraser, 1994), 512 pp.

Quotation

> The cursor is the blinking symbol that indicates your position in a document. Usually a flashing dash or rectangle, the cursor is called an *insertion point* in Windows applications. The mouse is an I-beam when in the text area of the screen; when moved into the menu and toolbar areas, it becomes an arrow, or mouse pointer.

To align a paragraph with indents from the regular page margins on both sides, choose the quotation style from the Format-Paragraph menu selections; this indents each line of a paragraph one-half inch from the left and one-half inch from the right. You might use this choice to set off a direct quotation or other citation from the rest of the text in a research paper.

To indent the first line of a paragraph:

- Click on Format-Paragraph.
- Select First Line Indent from the Style choices in the Quick Format area.

This last selection allows your quick format to apply to the entire page, or just to the paragraph on which you are currently working. A small window will display the view of the layout you have chosen. This choice eliminates the need to press the TAB at the beginning of each paragraph.

- Click OK or press ENTER.

  To indent all lines in a paragraph:
- Click on Format-Paragraph.
- Click on Indents and Alignments.
- Click on the Left Indent, Right Indent, or First Line box.
- Type a number.
- Click on OK or press ENTER.

To remove indents:

- Click on Format-Paragraph.
- Select Indents and Alignments.
- Replace existing numbers with zeroes.

Obviously, there are many different ways of creating paragraph styles and alignments. You could create hanging paragraphs by using the above option. After pressing ENTER, you could choose the quick format Hanging Style choice from the Paragraph window. For another method, you could use the quick keys CTRL + H to begin an indented paragraph and CTRL + G to return to the normal format. You could even use the TAB key to create hanging paragraphs alongside bullets.

As we have noted, in *Works* you can format a paragraph before or after typing it. Remember, the format commands are stored in the paragraph mark that appears when the View-All Characters option is turned on.

To format before you type:

- Click on Format-Paragraph.
- Select the desired paragraph format.

  OR

- Choose the Bullet icon from the toolbar.
- Type your text.

To format after you have typed a paragraph:

- Select the paragraph by dragging the mouse.
  OR
- Select the paragraph first by pressing F8 three times.
  OR
- Hold down the SHIFT key while pressing the arrow keys.
- Click on Format-Paragraph.
- Select your choice of formats.

Remember that paragraphs will continue to use the designated format until you specify another format. You can return to the Normal paragraph format by accessing the quick formats from the Format-Paragraph menu option.

Once you have created a complex paragraph format, you do not have to go through the process of designing the format again if you wish to use that same format at a later point in the document. You can use the Copy command in the Edit menu simply to copy the previously defined format to the new text you wish to format. This is very convenient when switching from one paragraph format to another, as in a research paper. You can use the normal paragraph format, then switch to a previously defined quotation paragraph format whenever you need to insert a quotation longer than a sentence or two. To do this:

- Select the paragraph whose format you want to copy.
- Click on Edit-Copy.
- Select the paragraph where you want to apply the format.
- Click on the Edit-Paste Special command.

  A dialog box appears with either Character or Paragraph options, as Figure 5.4 illustrates.

Figure 5.4

The Paste Special Menu

- Click on the Paragraph-Format button.
- Click on OK or press ENTER.

If the same paragraph format remains in the Clipboard buffer and you do not replace it with newer contents, you may repeat the Paste Special process each time you wish to use the format. Paragraph format is the default choice in the dialog box that appears when you issue the Paste Special command. After you have typed the text you need in the special format, as always, you need to issue the Format-Paragraph-Quick Formats-Normal command to return to the regular format.

Defining Text Styles

Fonts

As we noted earlier, the term *font* refers to a size and style of type. Technically, a font is a complete set of characters of one design in a specific style and size. When printers first began to set type in the mid-1400s, a font was a "pouring" of typeset letters. We now loosely refer to a font as a size and style of typeface. The style could be bold, underlined, italics, or shadowed. It could be superscript, raised one-half line above the regular line, or subscript, lowered one-half line below the regular text. There are screen fonts to control how text appears on the screen, and printer fonts to control how text appears in a hard copy.

Most newer applications for *Windows* support many different fonts. Word processing applications, in particular, support a large range, including Times Roman, Optima, Courier, London, Sans Serif, Helvetica, and many other styles. Modern **True Type fonts** take more memory because they are vector produced, or generated as needed according to prewritten sets of instructions. True type fonts appear the same on both screen and printer; they remain unchanged even if you move your file to another personal computer and print the file from a different system. They are **scalable fonts**, meaning that they can be scaled to any size.

Size also affects the selection of fonts. The size of a font determines how much text you can fit on one page. The size of a font is measured in either **points** or **pitch**. One point is 1/72 of an inch. If your program measures type size in points, a larger number indicates a larger print size, and a smaller number indicates smaller letters. *Works* measures fonts in points. Most word processing packages convert from point to pitch automatically, so you needn't be concerned with conversion techniques. Pitch is measured in characters per inch. If the program measures fonts by pitch, a larger number indicates smaller type, with more of it fitting in a given space.

To emphasize certain elements of a document or to control its use of space, you might compose a document that would contain several different fonts (although rules of good design specify no more than 2). Figure 5.5 illustrates several different fonts available with *Works*. Of course, your printer must be capable of producing these fonts if you choose them for your printed document.

To format a font, you can access the bold, italics, or underline icons from the toolbar, as was noted in the last chapter, or you may:

- Click on Format-Font and Style.
- Use the scroll bar to locate the desired font and size.
- Click on OK.

Figure 5.5

Typical Fonts—Typeface, Style, and Size

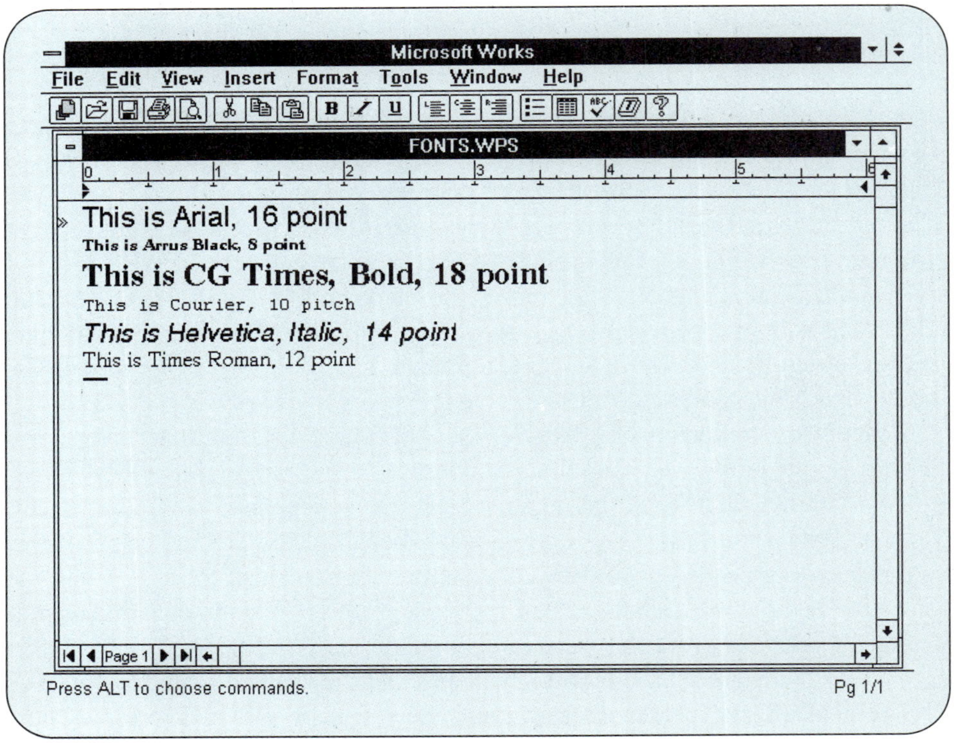

You may now type the text you wish to appear in the chosen font. If you are changing the font of text that has been typed:

- Select the block of text whose font you wish to change.
- Click on Format-Font and Style.
- Use the scroll bar to select a font, size, or style.
- Click on OK.

The selected text will be converted to the desired font.

The Position option refers to the location of the font. As we noted in Chapter 4, the name and size of the current text font is always displayed on the far left of your toolbar, unless you have changed the toolbar.

Superscripts and Subscripts

As was noted, **superscripts** and **subscripts** raise or lower text in relation to the regular line of text. You needn't worry about a superscript when composing footnotes, because *Works 3.0 for Windows* automatically formats them as superscript. Superscripts and subscripts are useful for other reasons, however.

Mathematical formulas, chemical compositions, or any time you wish to raise or lower the position of text for whatever reason, you may use the Position option in the Font and Style menu. A Normal position option allows you to return to the original line position. Beginners often overlook this step, resulting in a document with large blocks of the text raised or lowered after the superscript or subscript command was invoked! It is also important to remember that your printer must support the chosen font size option. If it does not, you must be certain to double space your document, or the superscript or subscript will interfere with the line of text above or below. To raise or lower text:

- Click on Format-Font and Style.
- Click on the Superscript or Subscript Position option.
- Click on OK.
- Type the desired superscript or subscript material.

When you are ready to return to the normal line position:

- Click on Format-Font and Style.
- Click on Normal Position.
- Click on OK.

You may also format text as superscript or subscript after typing it by selecting it in any of the traditional ways, then following the above steps. Once the text is highlighted, it can be formatted as a superscript or a subscript.

Thesaurus and Spelling Checker

When creating a document you may not be able to think of a word that means just what you want to say; *Works* has a feature that helps you be more precise. Its **thesaurus** can help you to find a synonym (another word with a similar meaning) and replace an unsatisfactory word.

To use the thesaurus:

- Select the word you want to replace.
- Click on Tools-Thesaurus.
- With the arrow keys, select the Meaning for which you want to see synonyms.
- The synonyms change as you change Meanings.
- Click on the Meaning you want.
- Select the synonym you want.
- Click on Suggest to see Meanings of the synonym.

You can switch from Meaning to Synonym and back again several times until you find the word you wish to use. When you find it:

- Click on Change.

You can cancel the command any time you wish if you decide that your original word was the best choice after all. *Works* has a built-in 100,000-word dictionary that is used for the thesaurus and the **spelling checker** program. If the dictionary does not list a word that you use frequently, you may add it. The spelling checker lets you check for incorrectly spelled words, words capitalized or hyphenated incorrectly, and repeated words, such as *the the*.

It is a very simple matter to check one word or a whole document with the spelling checker. In fact, it is so simple that you should never finish a document without first running a spelling check.

To check spelling:

- Move the cursor to where you want to begin (or press CTRL + HOME to go to the beginning of the document).
- Click on Tools-Spelling.
- A dialog box displays with the misspelled word selected.
- To leave the word spelled as it is, click on Ignore or Ignore All.

If you choose Ignore All, further instances of this same word will be bypassed as the spelling check continues.

For most questionable words, the screen presents a list of suggestions. If the Suggestions windows shows nothing:

- Click on Suggest

If the program identifies any suggestions, they will show. Otherwise, "No Suggestions" may show in the Suggestion window.

- To manually change the word, edit it in the Change To: box.
- To replace a misspelled word with a suggested word, click on Change or Change all.

Change All will correct all future instances of the word.

- To add a word to the dictionary, click on Add (but be sure it's spelled correctly).

After you choose Ignore, Add, or Change, *Works* selects the next questionable word and continues through the document in this fashion, stopping at each possible misspelling. To stop the spelling check at any time:

- Click on Cancel

When the entire document has been checked and you have taken action on each possible misspelling, a dialog box indicates that the spelling check is completed.

- Click on OK.

You will return to your document. Make sure to save it to disk again after correcting all of the spelling errors.

Spelling checkers are not foolproof; they are no substitute for good proofreading. For example, the spelling checker will ignore incorrectly used homonyms (words that sound the same, but have different spellings) or other words that are spelled correctly, but appear in the wrong setting. It will not distinguish between *sale* and *sail* for instance, or between *desert* and *dessert*, nor will it signal use of, say, *and* where *end* is appropriate. Therefore, to avoid nonsense in your important documents, you still must proofread. Still, spelling checkers have relieved many authors who are not intuitive spellers of an enormous burden.

WORD PROCESSING TUTORIAL NO. 3

You are going to modify the toolbar; open a document on your data disk; change the top margin; center, bold, and change the font of the heading; align the paragraphs; run a spelling check; and use the thesaurus. Before beginning this tutorial, position the mouse pointer on each toolbar icon for a few seconds and read the "tooltip." Take note of the name and shape of each icon.

1. Open Works-Word Processor.
2. Click on Tools-Customize Toolbar.

   The Customize Toolbar option box displays, as shown in Figure 5.6. You want to remove the Font Name and Point Size from the toolbar.

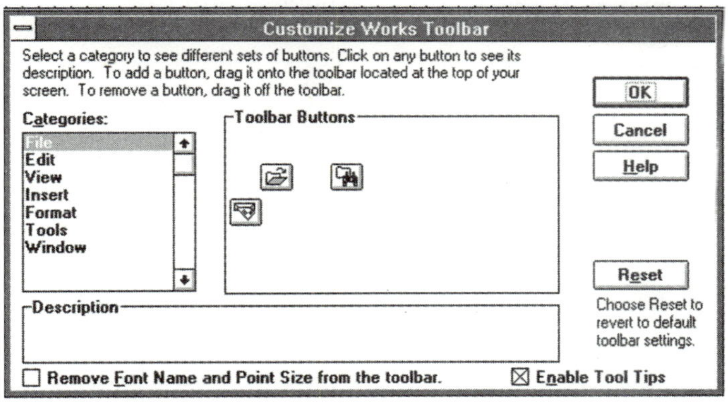

Figure 5.6

Customize Works Toolbar

3. Click on Remove Font Name and Point Size at the bottom of the option box.
4. With File categories selected, click on the Toolbar Button icons until you find the one for Open Existing Document.
5. Drag it up to the toolbar to follow the Startup icon.
6. Click on Tools.
7. Drag the Thesaurus icon (a book with a *T* on the cover) to the toolbar at the right of the Spelling Checker icon.
8. Click on OK.
9. Click on the newly added Open Existing File icon.
10. Close word1.
11. Open the existing document insched.wps on your student data disk.

12. Save it as insched2.wps to retain the original file.

    To keep your student data disk unchanged for future use, take the disk out after you open the file and put in your work disk. When you save the file, Click on File-Save As and type **A:\filename**. It's good practice to make two copies of your files in case something happens to your work disk. In the future repeat the foregoing command each time you finish a document and save it on another (formatted) disk.

13. Print the file to keep it for reference.

    To change the top margin:

14. Click on File-Page Setup.
15. In the Margins list box, click on, or TAB to, Top Margin (if the insertion point is not already there).
16. Type **2** then click on OK.

    To enhance the heading:

17. Select all three lines, beginning with *Part 1* and ending with *Coverage BB*.
18. Click on the Bold and Center icons.

    To change the size and type of the font:

19. Click on Format-Font and Style.

    The Font and Style dialog box appears, as shown in Figure 5.7.

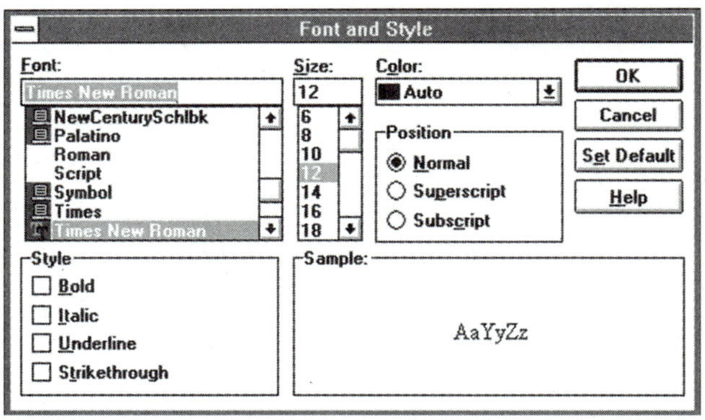

Figure 5.7

The Font and Style Dialog Box

20. In the Font box, scroll until Arial displays, then click to select it.
21. In the Size box, click on 14.

    Notice that the small window at the bottom, right-hand corner of the screen shows how your text will look.

22. Click on OK.

    Note that Arial is a sans serif font—it includes straight letters with no extra embellishment. Text in Times Roman has extra embellishments on the characters. You want to line up the paragraphs in the hanging indent style so the lines after the numbers align evenly.

23. Select paragraph number 1 under *Additional Payments.*
24. Click on Format-Paragraphs-Hanging Indent, then click on OK.

    The lines are evenly indented five spaces in from the number 1.

25. On your own, align paragraphs number 3 and 4.

    To run a spelling check on the document:

26. Click on Tools.

    The Tools menu displays, as shown in Figure 5.8.

27. Click on Spelling.

    The Spelling dialog box displays, as shown in Figure 5.9. The first word the check identifies, *coverages*, is an insurance term that does not appear in the *Works* dictionary; however, it is spelled correctly. To add it to the dictionary:

28. Click on Add.

    The check stops next at *ohers.*

29. Click on Suggest.

    Others is suggested.

30. Click on Change.
31. The next stop is *testin.*

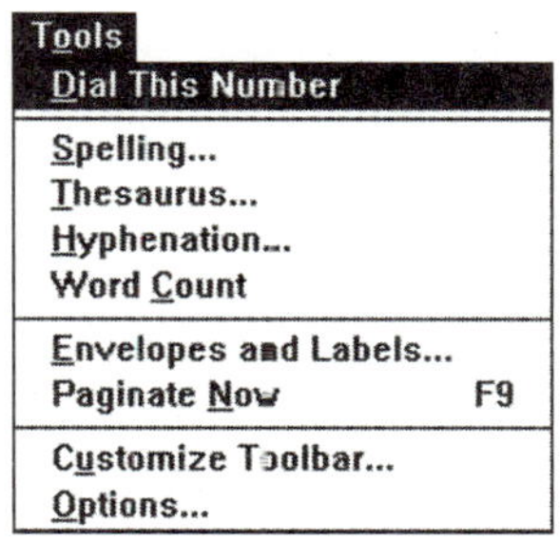

Figure 5.8

The Tools Menu

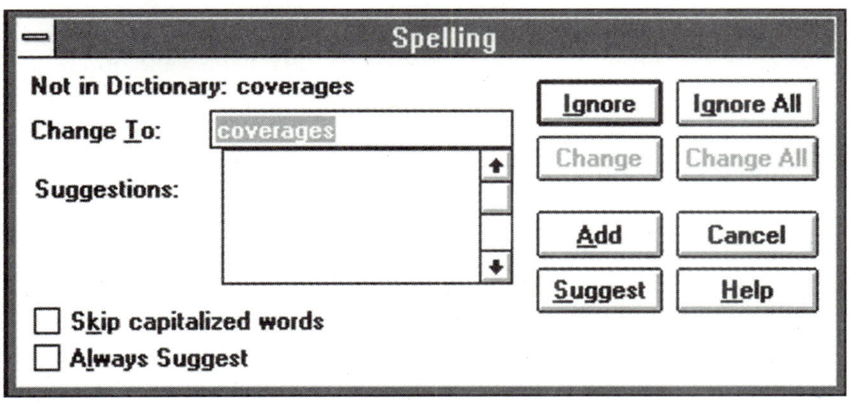

Figure 5.9

The Spelling Dialog Box

32. Click on Suggest-Change to change the word to *testing.*

    The check stops next at *co-workers* because it is hyphenated.

33. Click on Ignore.
34. On your own, correct *reasonabley*, *inteded*, and *liiability.*

    A prompt signals the end of spelling checking.

35. Click on Yes.

    You would like to find other words to replace *obligated*, *available*, and *designed.* To use the thesaurus:

36. Place the insertion point in *obligated* in the first sentence.
37. Click on the thesaurus icon.

    The Thesaurus dialog box displays, as shown in Figure 5.10. Suppose that you don't like any of the suggested replacements.

Figure 5.10

The Thesaurus Dialog Box

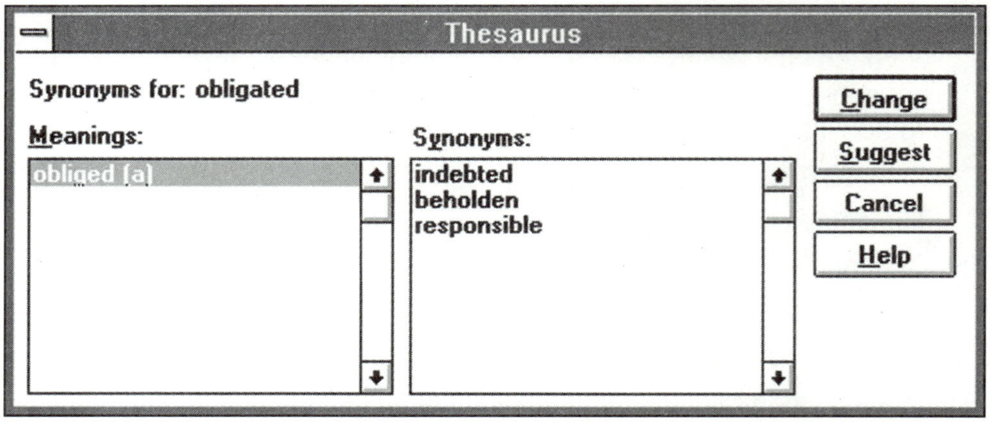

38. Click on Cancel.
39. Place the insertion point in *available* under *Insured Autos*, paragraph number 3. (Hint: Click on Edit-Find and type in *available*, then click on Find Next.)
40. Select *convenient.*
41. Click on Change.

    You aren't pleased with the choice.

42. Click on Edit-Undo.

    The original word, *available,* returns.

43. In paragraph number 4, replace *designed* with *made.*
44. Save and close the document.

Formatting Text

Page Breaks

A page break is a command to the printer to end one page and begin another. You can cause **manual page breaks** to force a new page, or the program can create **automatic page breaks**.

Works automatically inserts a page break at the end of 55 lines if you leave the page size at the default size of 8.5 by 11 inches. The automatic page break is designated by two small greater than symbols at the left edge of the text (>>). As you insert or delete text, *Works* automatically adjusts page breaks to reflect these changes. Automatic page breaks cannot be deleted individually. You must use the Tools menu selection Paginate Now to repaginate the whole document.

Often, however, you will want to force a page break and begin a new page of text before you fill the normal number of lines. This is called a **manual page break** because you create it "by hand" when needed. Manual page breaks remain where they are unless you delete them manually. They are not automatically adjusted to accommodate inserted or deleted text. A manual page break is designated by a series of dots across the page.

To insert a manual page break:

- Position the cursor where the break should occur.
- Click on Insert-Page Break.

A series of dotted lines appears across the page.
You can also use a quick page-break command; simply:

- Press CTRL + ENTER

To delete a manual page break:

- Place insertion point on the row of dots.
- Press DELETE.

Headers, Footers, and Page Numbers

When you want a specific notation to appear on every page of your document, it is efficient to include that text in a header or footer. Header text will appear at the top of every page of the document, wherever you place it horizontally on the page; footer text will appear at the bottom of every page. We will discuss headers and footers together.

A **header** is text that is repeated at the top of every page of a document. It is defined once, at the beginning of the document, or at the top of the first page where you wish the header to begin. A **footer**, also defined just once, is text that is repeated at the bottom of every page of a document. Sometimes it includes only a page-number placeholder, but it may include other text, as well.

There are many different types of headers and footers. *Works* users place footers most frequently to insert **page numbers** at the bottom of document pages.

Headers often state the titles of documents, dates, draft versions, or authors' names. You can, however, define any text to be repeated in either a header or a footer.

Headers, footers, and page numbers are formatting features that give your document a more professional appearance. Headers and footers can be formatted like regular text, perhaps including tab marks, or appearing centered or aligned at the right margin.

You can even change the default distance between the top of the page and the top of the header or the bottom of the page and top of the footer. To do so, choose File-Page Setup-Margins-Header margin or Footer margin and enter a new measurement. The default for Header is .5" and for footer, .75":

Works offers two types of headers and footers—standard and paragraph.

Standard Headers and Footers Standard headers and footers are limited to one line of text. You type that line in the Header and Footer option box as follows:

- Position the cursor at the top of the document (CTRL + HOME).
- Select View-Headers and Footers.
- Fill in the first two lines in the option box.
- Click on OK or press ENTER.

The following codes can be entered in the Header and or Footer boxes and the corresponding information will print accordingly:

Table 5.1 Codes That Can be Included in Header and or Footer Option Box

Code	Meaning
&l	Align characters that follow on the left margin
&c	Center characters that follow
&r	Align characters that follow on the right margin
&p	Print the page number
&f	Print the name of the file
&d	Print the date
&n	Print the date in long format
&t	Print the time
&&	Print an ampersand

To insert a page number in a standard footer:

- Click on View-Headers and Footers.
- Click to toggle off Use Header and Footer Paragraph Bullet, if necessary.
- Click on the Footer box.
- Type **&p** with any desired text before or after (as *Page &p*).
- Click on OK or press enter.

Paragraph Paragraph headers and footers can have multiple lines of text and can include a drawing if desired. Works automatically inserts a page-number placeholder (*page*) in the footer; however you can cut it from the footer and paste it in the header or delete it entirely. To create a header or footer paragraph:

- Position the cursor at the top of the document (CTRL+HOME).
- Click on View-Header and Footer.
- Click on the Use Header and Footer Paragraphs option.

Notice that the standard header and footer lines are now no longer available.

- Click on OK or press ENTER.

Works inserts an H for header at the top of the document and an F for a footer that appears at the bottom of the document. You then enter the information directly into the document:

- Move the cursor to the *H* or *F* marker in your document.
- Press TAB once to center or twice to right-align the header or footer text.
- Type the desired text.
- If you want more than one line, press SHIFT + ENTER and type the additional line.
- Press ENTER.

The View-Header and Footer menu also allows you to choose whether to print a header or footer on the first page of a document. Common practice omits both a header and a footer from the first page of a formal document. To do this, within the Header and Footer option box:

- Click on No Header on 1st Page.
- Click on No Footer on 1st Page.
- Click on OK or press ENTER.

If you use an ink-jet or laser printer and you get the error message "Footer too tall," you need to increase the footer margin in the File menu's Page Setup and Margins option box to 1.0 inch before printing your document.

The important thing to remember is that you insert a header or footer only once, at the top of the document, and *Works* repeats it automatically for you. Figure 5.11 shows header and footer marks in a document.

Header and footer paragraphs are available only in the word processing application, but the header and footer lines are available in all of the *Works* applications. Your document will be printed with whatever text you specify in your header and footer. Even if your document runs to 50 pages, if you have the *page* marker entered in your footer definition, each page will be correctly numbered when printed. If you have entered anything else in a header or footer definition, it will be printed on each page of your finished document.

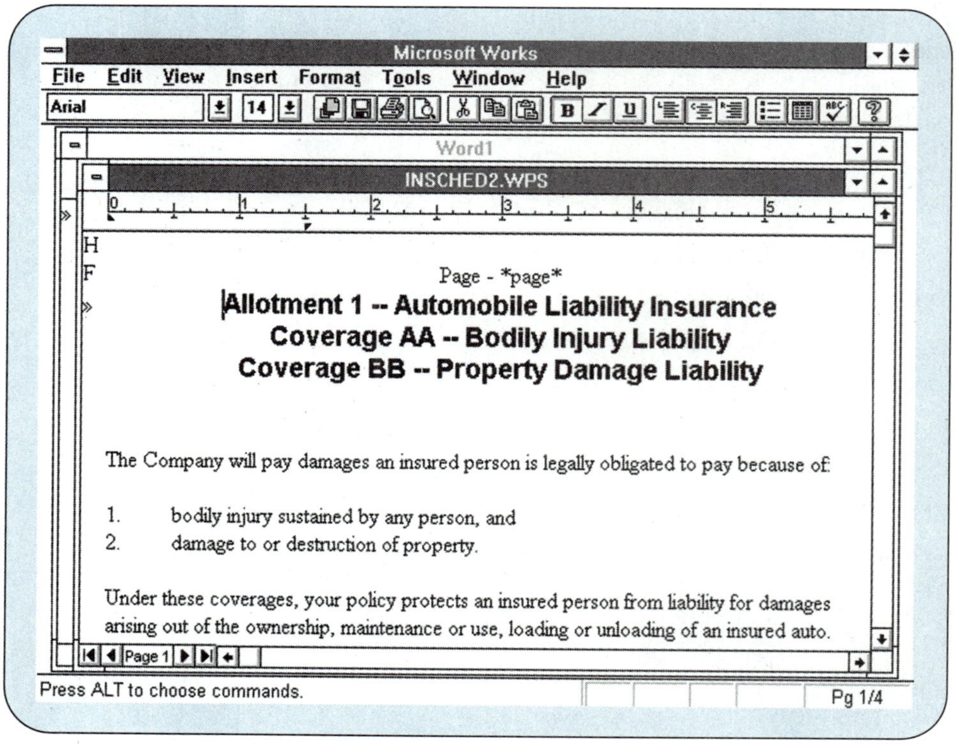

Figure 5.11

Example of Header and Footer Paragraph Style

Line Spacing

The *Works* word processor offers several line spacing options. Besides single and double spacing, these include spacing at 1.25, 2.5, and 3 lines as well. To specify the spacing you want, you fill in the number of spaces between each line.

To change to single or double spacing:

- Click on Format-Paragraph.
- Select Breaks and Spacing in the Paragraph window.
- Click on or TAB to the Spaces between Lines box.
- Enter the number of spaces you want between lines.
- Click on OK or press ENTER.

The term *Auto* means that *Works* will automatically adjust the line height within a paragraph. You can also use quick keystroke combinations to define line spacing. To double space:

- Press CTRL + 2.

To return to single spacing:

- Press CTRL + 1.

You should already be familiar with techniques for customizing the toolbar. You will probably switch from single to double spacing frequently when you are composing documents; therefore, adding the Single and Double Spacing icons to your toolbar makes sense. To ensure that you can quickly specify either single or double line spacing in your word processing sessions:

- Click on Tools-Customize Toolbar.
- Select the double and single spacing icons from the Toolbar-Format options by dragging the desired icons to your toolbar.
- Click on OK.

Now you can switch back and forth from single to double spacing simply by clicking on the proper toolbar icon.

Window within Windows

A time might arise when you would like to move material from one document into another document. You have already seen how to cut and paste to move blocks of text, and how to copy text within one document. The *Windows* Clipboard has simplified this operation so that you can perform the formerly complex processes of moving material from one file to another as simply as cutting and pasting through the now familiar technique. To perform this operation you need to have both documents open at the same time. In fact, you can have as many as eight documents open at once by using the Window menu of *Works*. Figure 5.12 shows the Window menu with four windows open at once.

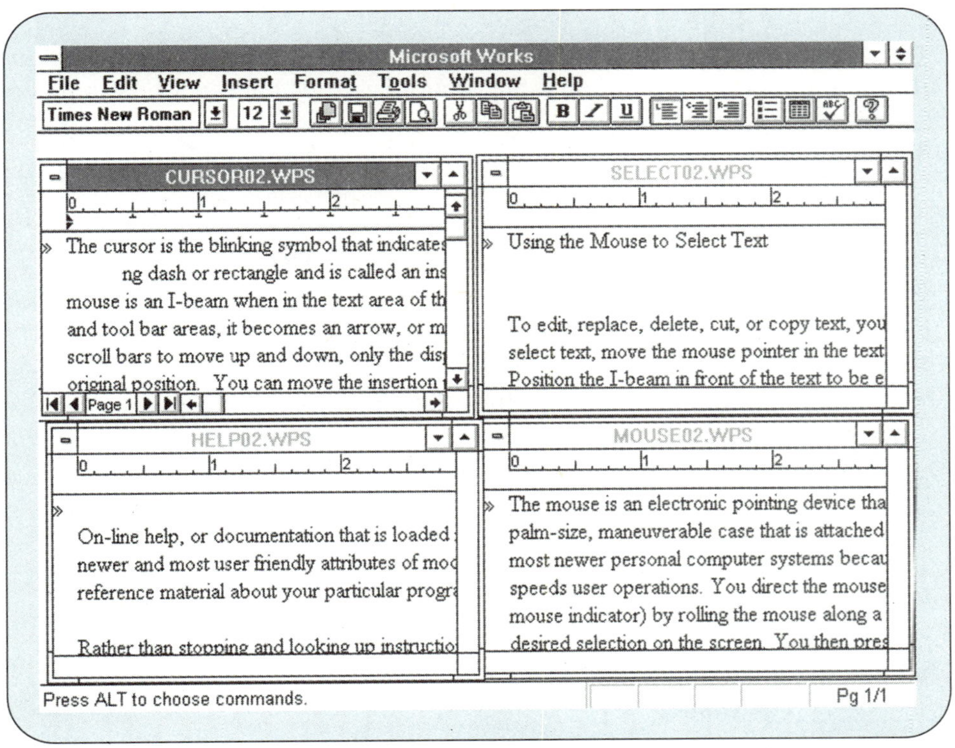

Figure 5.12

Four Files Open at One Time

Each window is a view into a different open file. You merely open the files you want to work on without closing any of them; the Window pull-down menu keeps track of them by both number and name. You can then copy data between any of the open files without having to continually close and open them.

The **active window** is the one where you are currently working. On a color monitor, the active window has double top border lines and scroll bars in a different color. The active window always contains the cursor. As we said, the Window menu lists all open files, numbered in the order you opened them.

To make a different window the active one:

- Click on Window.
- Select the number of the document to which you wish to move, using the mouse or directional arrows.

For an external copy, the Copy and Cut commands function just as they do within a single document. To copy from one file to another:

- Click on File-Open and open each document.
- Select the text you wish to copy or move.
- Select Edit-Copy or Edit-Cut.
- Switch to the Window with the receiving file.
- Position the cursor where the text should appear.
- Click on Edit-Paste to complete the copy or move.

Because *Works* is an integrated package, you will soon find yourself moving and copying items from different applications into documents. This is one of the most powerful features of *Works 3.0 for Windows*; it is the main topic of Chapter 13.

Borders

To enhance the attractiveness of your document, you can draw a **border** around a single paragraph, several paragraphs, or a whole page. The border can consist of single or double lines; the lines can box all sides of the chosen text or mark just the top, bottom, left, or right; the lines can be in boldface or color. A border runs from the left margin to the right margin. To insert a border:

- Highlight each paragraph to be included (or the whole page).
- Select Format-Border.
- Mark the desired options.
- Click on OK or press ENTER.

To delete a border:

- Highlight the text within the border.
- Select Format-Border.
- Click to remove marks from all of the options.
- Click on OK or press ENTER.

Keep Text Together on a Page

When you create a table or some other special material, you may not want it split between two pages. Just as you may not want widow or orphan sentences or paragraphs, you do not want page breaks within specially formatted material. You prevent tables, pictures, and charts from splitting between two pages in exactly the same manner as keeping paragraphs or sentences from becoming widows or orphans:

- Highlight the material.
- Click on Format-Paragraph-Breaks and Spacing.
- Select Don't break paragraph, or Keep paragraph with next.
- Click on OK or press ENTER.

WORD PROCESSING TUTORIAL NO. 4

You have worked with the insurance schedule file. On the last page of that file, you will create a double spaced payment schedule using dot leaders and decimal tabs, and surrounded by a border. You will copy the schedule into a new document and print it for reference.

1. Open the file insched2.wps.

   To go to the bottom of the document and insert a page break:

2. Press CTRL + END.
3. Click on Insert.

   The Insert menu displays, as shown in Figure 5.13.

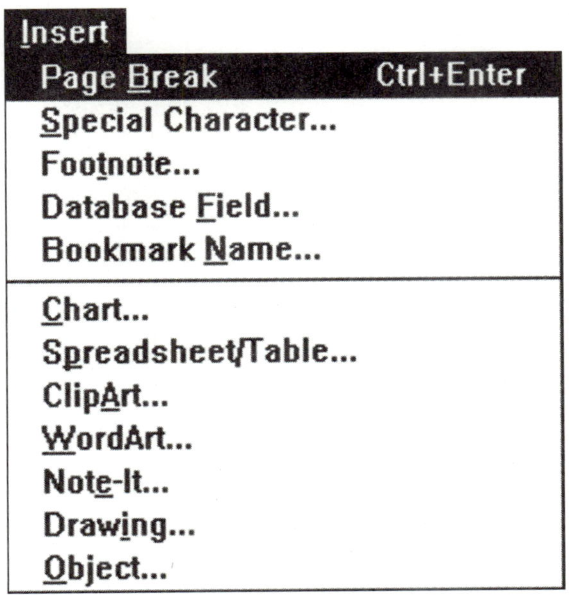

Figure 5.13

The Insert Menu

4. Click on Page Break (or press CTRL + ENTER).

   A dotted line appears across the screen. To change to double spacing:

5. Click on Format-Paragraph-Breaks and Spacing.

   The Breaks and Spacing dialog box displays, as shown in Figure 5.14.

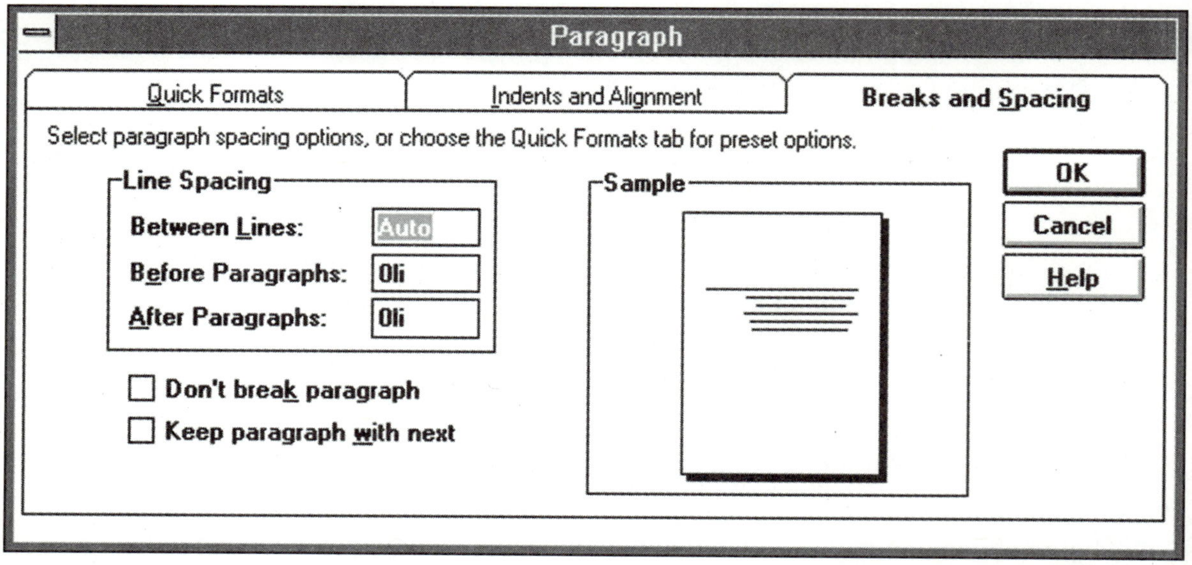

Figure 5.14

The Breaks and Spacing Dialog Box

6. Under Line Spacing, TAB to the Between Lines box.
7. Type **2**
8. Click on OK.
9. Click on the center and bold icons.
10. Type **Payment Schedule** in Arial, 14 point (Format-Font and Style)

    To go back to the default type, press ENTER, then:

11. Click on the bold and left justify icons, and select Times New Roman 12 point.

    To change the tabs to decimal, dot leader format at 5.5 inches: Be sure the ruler line is displayed. Delete all existing tabs. Note: you can position the mouse pointer on the tab arrow on the ruler bar, click, and drag it off the ruler to delete.

12. Click on Format-Tabs.

    The Tabs dialog box displays, as shown in Figure 5.15.

13. In the Position box, type **5.5**
14. In the Alignment box, click on Decimal.

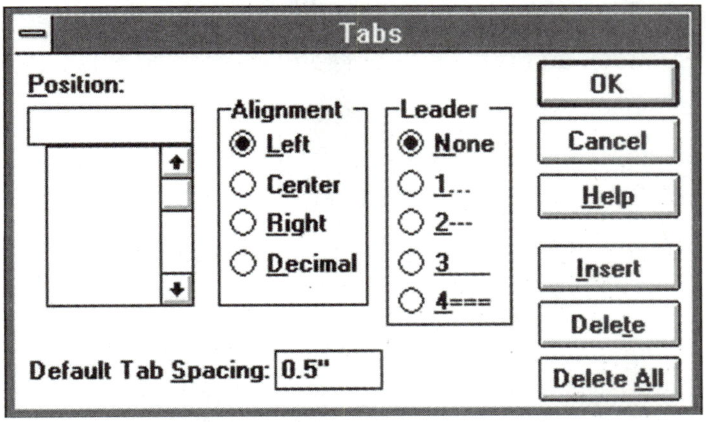

Figure 5.15

The Tabs Dialog Box

15. In the Leader box click on 1.
16. Click on Insert.
17. Click on OK.
18. Type **One Year**
19. Press TAB.
20. Type **$1,200.00**
21. Press ENTER.
22. Type **Twice a Year (tab) 600.00**
23. Press ENTER.

    To set a tab at .5 inches, position the mouse pointer on the bottom ruler line directly below the .5 marker and click.
24. Set a tab at 0.5 inches.
25. Press TAB.
26. Type **Service Charge (tab) 4.50**
27. Finish typing the table in Figure 5.16.

Payment Schedule

One Year..$1,200.00
Twice a Year..600.00
    Service Charge..4.50
Monthly..100.00
    Service Charge..9.24

Figure 5.16

paysched.wps Document

To keep the table from ever being divided on two pages (which is a good practice when typing tables):

28. Select the title and the schedule.
29. Click on Format-Paragraph-Breaks and Spacing.
30. Click on Don't break this paragraph-OK.

    To put a border around the table:

31. Select the table, including its title.
32. Click on Format-Border.

    The Border option box displays, as shown in Figure 5.17.

Figure 5.17

The Border Option Box

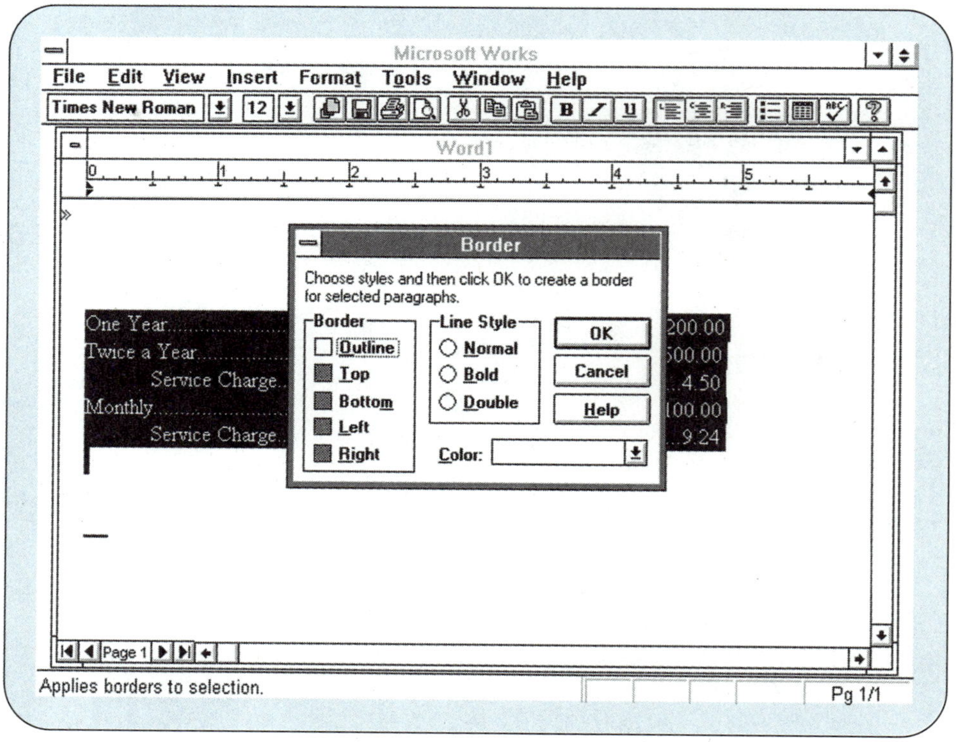

33. In the Border box, click on Outline.
34. In the Line Style box, click on Double.
35. Click on OK.
36. Click on the Save icon.

    You now want to make a separate copy of the payment schedule so you can refer to it later. You will open another file (by creating a new document) and copy only the payment schedule into that document, then you will save it under the file name paysched and print it.

37. Remain in the current document, **insched2**.
38. Click on the Startup icon.

39. Press ENTER for Word Processor.

    A blank screen opens, titled Word1.

40. Select Window.

    The Window menu displays, as shown in Figure 5.18.

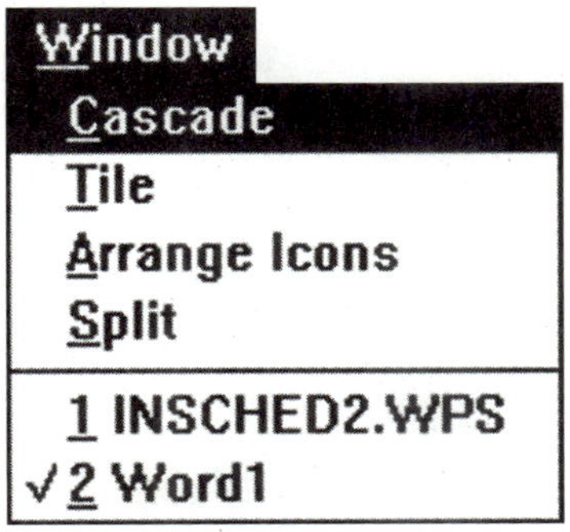

Figure 5.18

The Window Menu

41. Click on 1 insched2.wps

    The insched2 document opens on the screen.

42. Move the insertion point to the left of the *P* in *Payment*.

    Hint: If you are not already at the schedule, search for *Payment* with the Edit-Find command.

43. Select the title and the schedule.
44. Click on the Copy icon.
45. Click on Window.
46. Click on 2 (1)Word1.wps
47. Click on Paste.

    The payment table displays on the screen.

48. Click on File-Save As
49. Type **paysched** then click on OK.
50. Print and close the pay schedule document.

    It should look similar to the screen in Figure 5.16. You want to add a header, Auto Insurance, to your insurance document and a footer with a centered page number.

51. Click on View-Headers and Footers.

    The Headers and Footers option box displays, as shown in Figure 5.19.

52. In the Header text box, type **Auto Insurance**
53. In the Footer text box, type **&cPage &p**

Figure 5.19

The Headers and Footers Option Box

54. Mark No Header on first Page.
55. Mark No Footer on first Page.
56. Click on OK.
57. Click on Print Preview to see if your document looks correct.
58. Save and print insched2.wps; then close and exit.

    Your document should look similar to the one in Figure 5.20.

Figure 5.20

insched2.wps Document

Part 1 -- Automobile Liability Insurance
Coverage AA -- Bodily Injury Liability
Coverage BB -- Property Damage Liability

The Company will pay damages an insured person is legally obligated to pay because of:

1. bodily injury sustained by any person, and
2. damage to or destruction of property.

Under these coverages, your policy protects an insured person from liability for damages arising out of the ownership, maintenance or use, loading or unloading of an insured auto.

We will defend an insured person sued as the result of a covered auto accident, even if the suit is groundless or false. We will choose the counsel. We may settle any claim or suit if we believe it is proper. We will not defend an insured person sued for damages which are not covered by this policy.

Additional Payments the Company Will Make

When we defend an insured person under this Part, we will pay:

1. up to $50 a day for loss of wages or salary if we ask that person to attend hearings or trials to defend against a bodily injury suit. We won't pay for loss of other income. We will pay other reasonable expenses incurred at our request.
2. court costs for defense.
3. interest accruing on damages awarded. We will pay this interest only until we have paid, offered or depositied in court the amount for which we are liable under this policy. We will only pay interest on damages not exceeding our limits of liability.
4. premiums on appeal bonds and on bonds to release attachments, but not in excess of our limit of liability. We aren't required to apply for or furnish these bonds.

We will repay an insured person for:

1. the cost of any bail bonds required due to an accident or traffic law violation involving the use of the insured auto. We won't pay more than $300 per bond. We aren't required to apply for or furnish these bonds.
2. any expense incurred for first aid to others at the time of an auto accident involving the insured auto.

Figure 5.20 Continued

insched2.wps Document

Auto Insurance

Insured Persons

1. While using your insured auto:
   a. you,
   b. any resident, and
   c. any other person using it with your permission
2. While using a non-owned auto:
   a. you,
   b. any resident relative using a four wheel passenger auto or utility auto.
3. any other person or organization liable for the use of an insured auto if the auto is not owned or hired by this person or organization, provided that the use is by an insured person under 1, or 2, above.

Insured Autos

1. Any auto described on the declarations page. This includes the four wheel private passenger auto or utility auto you replace it with.
2. An additional four wheel private passenger auto or utility auto you become the owner of during the policy period. This auto will be covered if we insure all other private passenger autos or utility autos you own. You must, however, tell us within 60 days of acquiring the auto. You must pay any additional premium.
3. A substitute four wheel private passenger auto or utility auto not owned by you or a resident relative with the owner's permission. This auto must not be available or furnished for the regular use of an insured person.
4. A trailer while attached to an insured auto. The trailer must be designed for use with a private passenger auto or utility auto. This trailer can't be used for business purposes with other than a private passenger auto or utility auto.

Definitions

1. "The Company," "We," "Us," or "Our" -- means the company shown on the declarations page of the policy.
2. "Auto" -- means a land motor vehicle designed for use on public roads.
3. "Bodily Injury" -- means bodily injury, sickness, disease, or death.
4. "Resident" -- means a person who physically resides in your household with the intention of continuing residence there. Your unmarried dependent children while temporarily away from home will be considered residents, if they intend to resume residing in your household.

Page 2

Figure 5.20 Continued

insched2.wps Document

Auto Insurance

5. "Utility Auto" -- means an auto of the pick-up body, sedan delivery, or panel truck type. This auto must have a gross vehicle weight of 10,000 pounds or less, according to manufacturer's specifications.
6. "You" or "Your" -- means the policyholder named on the declarations page and that policyholder's resident spouse.

Exclusions--What Is Not Covered

The Company will not pay for any damages an insured person is legally obligated to pay because of:

1. Bodily injury or property damage arising out of the use of your insured auto while used to carry persons or property for a charge, or any auto you are driving while available for hire by the public. This exclusion does not apply to :
   a. shared-expense car pools.
   b. the occasional rental of your insured motor home or travel-trailer to ohers for personal use if a rental premium is shown on the declarations page.
2. bodily injury or property damage arising out of auto business operations such as repairing, servicing, testing, washing, parking, storing, or selling of autos. However, coverage does apply to you, resident relatives, partners, or employees of the partnership of you and a resident relative when using your insured auto.
3. bodily injury or property damage arising out of the use of a non-owned auto used in any business or occupation of an insured person. However, this exclusion does not apply while you, your chauffeur, or domestic servant are using a private passenger auto or trailer.
4. bodily injury to an employee of any insured person arising in the course of employment. This exclusion does not apply to your domestic employee who is not required to be covered by a workers' compensation law or similar law.
5. bodily injury to a co-worker injured in the course of employment. This exclusion does not apply to you.
6. bodily injury to any person related to an insured person by blood, marriage or adoption and residing in that person's household.
7. bodily injury or property damage which may reasonably be expected to result from the intentional or criminal acts of an insured person or which are in fact intended by an insured person.
8. bodily injury or property damage which would also be covered under nuclear energy liability insurance. This applies even if the limits of that insurance are exhausted.

Page 3

Figure 5.20 Continued

insched2.wps Document

Auto Insurance

Payment Schedule

One Year..$1,200.00

Twice a Year.. ....600.00

Service Charge..4.50

Monthly......... ....100.00

Service Charge..9.24

Page 4

Text Enhancement

Footnotes

Footnotes usually serve two purposes—to cite references or to offer explanatory text. There are several different styles of footnotes, from the parenthetical documentation style that simply encloses the reference in parentheses in the main text, to **endnotes** that are printed at the end of the document, to the traditional footnote with a superscript in text that references material at the bottom of a page. *Works 3.0 for Windows* allows all three versions.

Both traditional footnotes and endnotes are relatively simple to produce. You needn't worry about changing the font; that is automatically done for you when you choose the footnote command. Also, if you delete a footnote or add another in the middle of your document, *Works* will automatically renumber all of your footnotes for you. (You may also choose not to number footnotes, but to use another character to mark them.) If you insert text that moves the footnoted text to the next page, the footnote will move with it.

Creating footnotes with *Works'* word processor is a simple way to avoid ever again retyping a page of a footnoted paper because a planned footnote will not fit at the bottom of a page. To create a footnote:

- Position the insertion point where the footnote's text reference should go.
- Click on Insert-Footnote.
- Click on Numbered or Character mark (insert mark).
- Click on OK.

The proper number will appear above the text it references, and the insertion point will move down to the Footnote window.

- Type in the desired text.
- Press F6 to return to the main body of the document or move the I-Beam to the document and click.
- To close the footnote window, click on view-footnotes.

Figure 5.26 shows the option window that appears when you select the Insert-Footnote command. There is also a Footnote option in the WorksWizards tool that is accessible from the Startup menu. The WorksWizard can help you construct a footnote, even if you do not know the proper form or accepted style. When you enter the reference information, it constructs the footnote, puts it in the accepted order, and inserts it in the footnote window of your document.

Note-It

Within the last decade, America has become enamored of the ubiquitous, yellow, sticky note that the 3M Company first developed. Post-It Notes™ often serve as temporary reminders about something pertaining to a document. They are now a standard fixture in both our offices and our homes.

Works 3.0 for Windows offers an electronic equivalent called **Note-It**. It allows you to post a short memo on a word processing document and keep it for future reference, or delete it when you no longer need it. The end-user documentation department of the *Works* division of the Microsoft Corporation is fond of telling how this added option to the new versions of *Works* was developed by a young summer intern. It is now standard in the *Works 3.0 for Windows* program.

To post a note on one of your *Works* documents:

- Click on Insert-Note-It.
- Three areas of the Note-It window appear.
- Click on a picture to indicate the Style of note you desire.
- Click on Caption and type a title.
- Type a message in the Message box.
- Click on Big if you wish the text to be larger.
- Click on OK to complete the note.

Your note form appears on the document. The title you specified in Caption appears below it, but without any text. To see the note's message:

- Double click on the note.
- The text of the message appears.
- Click anywhere else on the screen to hide the message.

The note remains on the document, ready to reveal its contents again whenever you double click on it. If you do not wish a caption to appear below the note, delete the text in the Caption box. Delete the direction "type your message here," as well, if you do not want it to appear in the finished note.

The note will appear on a hard copy printout of a document; you must remove it from the file before printing if you wish it to be an on-screen reminder only. Still, this is a handy addition to the word processing tool that does not require complex formatting; it can be very useful for shared files.

Saving Text in a Different Format

You can save a *Works* word processing file in straight ASCII code (DOS text) with no special formatting characters that are unique to *Works*. This creates a straight **text file**, with no bolding, indents, page numbers, footers, and so forth.

The ability to produce a file that is straight text, rather than formatted for a particular word processing program, is very valuable because it makes the file portable. You can move the file into another word processing program without retyping the document simply to change software. It is unrealistic to think that you will always be able, or even want, to use the same word processing program. Saving and retrieving straight text, or ASCII, files provides a way around this difficulty. Merely adding special formatting characters to a 50-page paper that you wish to access with another word processing program is a small inconvenience; retyping the entire 50-page paper is a major job. You can achieve the underlying objective of word processing—to type text just once—even if you change software.

You can even begin a document in one word processor, save it as a straight text file, and then move it into another microcomputer word processing program and complete it. The flexibility works both ways; *Works* also allows you to convert files from other word processing programs to the *Works* format.

To save a file as a text file:

- Click on File-Save As.
- In the File Name option box, type a file name.
- In the Save File as Type box, scroll to the Text or Text [DOS] formats.
- When the format you want appears, release the mouse button.
- Click on OK or press ENTER.
- The Lose Formatting? box appears.
- Click on OK or press ENTER.

Notice that *Works* can save in many file formats. You could save a file in formats of *Word, WordPerfect*, the older DOS versions of *Works*, and other popular word processing packages. Of course, if you know the specific package to which the *Works 3.0 for Windows* file will be imported, this is a good idea; *Works* will automatically convert the formatting to match the package you indicate.

However, you cannot go wrong with an ASCII text file. It is as portable as you can get on an IBM or compatible computer. A DOS text file is the option to choose if you wish to move your file to another IBM or compatible microcomputer file; a plain text file is the option to choose if you wish to upload the file to another architecture, such as a mainframe or minicomputer.

If you are using a word processing file that has formatting from a program other than *Works*, upon opening it, you may convert it to the *Works* format by the following sequence:

- Select File-Open Existing File.
- Type the file name and extension in the box provided.
- In the List Files of Type box, scroll to the type of file you are converting.
- Click on OK or press ENTER.

Works will flash a dialog box to report that it is converting the file to a *Works* format. The file is automatically converted and can then be saved again in the *Works 3.0 for Windows* format.

Notice that you can even convert a file from Macintosh *Works* or *Word* in this way. Use the Save As option and give the file a new name if you wish the file to remain in the original format and also create a copy in the *Works 3.0 for Windows* format. Remember that the two separate files cannot have exactly the same name. *Works* will add the .wps extension to distinguish its version if you do not add your own extension.

Print Options

The Printing function in *Works* presents many options to control your printed output. After reviewing your document on the screen with the File-Print Preview option, you can change the margin settings, the orientation (direction of printing) of the page, and the size of the paper in the File-Page Setup-Source, Size and Orientation dialog box. By selecting File-Print, you can print specific pages identified in the Print Range area; you can also print envelopes you have created, or form letters created in WorksWizards or in the regular word processing tool, by checking Print merge. We will cover mail merge in Chapter 13. As mentioned in Chapter 4, the Print menu offers a draft-quality setting to print material that is unfinished, or not in final form. This saves ink, toner, or ribbon by printing a rough copy of a document instead of a finished-quality copy. You can explore the various print options as you become more proficient with word processing.

Desktop Publishing

The most sophisticated means of document preparation using a microcomputer is **desktop publishing**—software that allows the personal computer user to combine text and graphics into highly structured and aesthetically pleasing documents. There are three general levels of document creation: word processing, which has limited typefaces and fonts; desktop publishing, which can integrate text and graphics on the screen and in the printed document; and electronic or conventional publishing, which is the epitome of professional document creation.

In office environments, word processing has been used as an interface to conventional publishing for some time. Text could be keyed in, revised, and typed in final form; the keystrokes could then be transferred to a phototypesetter via a magnetic disk or over a phone line via a modem; the typesetter had only to insert the codes that would control the text formats and leave spaces for the graphs and art work.

Desktop publishing programs have allowed personal microcomputer users, to integrate text on the screen with graphics and photographs, and output the result to a laser printer, which must be flexible enough to print high-quality graphics and a wide range of fonts. *Aldus Pagemaker, Adobe, Quark,* and *Ventura* are some of the more popular personal computer software packages for desktop publishing.

In desktop publishing, the first step is the same as in conventional publishing—preparation of text on a word processor. The newest desktop publishing programs allow you to enter the text directly in the DTP program bypassing a word processing package. However, once the file is entered into the DTP program, whether via a stand-alone word processing package or directly into the desktop publishing program, the work is far from finished. You must now assign type specifications such as font size, column width, and justification settings; the program places the text into columns of the desired width. Graphic images can be imported from various graphics programs and placed appropriately in the text;

even photographs may be included through the use of an optical scanner. See Figure 5.21 for an example of a document that was prepared via a desktop publishing program.

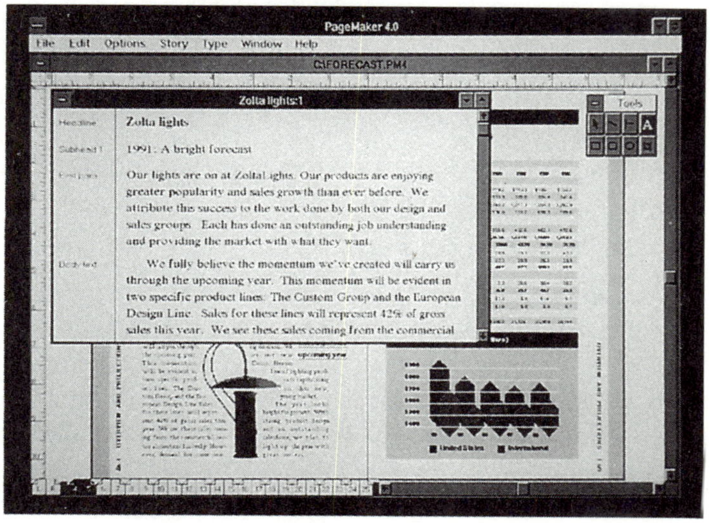

Figure 5.21

A Desktop Publishing Software Package

The text and graphics can be checked on the screen and corrections made, if necessary. Desktop publishers display documents in true WYSIWYG format; the document will print out the way it looks on the screen. The entire document is then output to a laser printer. The pages that come from the printer can serve as the final document or, if a large number of copies are needed, the pages can be sent to an offset printing supplier.

Desktop publishing software has become very popular in recent years. However, it is wise to master the rudiments of word processing before tackling the complexities of desktop publishing. Also, although desktop publishers are valuable aids that give the user an economical way to produce very professional-looking documents, they require some artistic sense in order to produce truly elegant products.

More Advanced Features

Column Formats

Although *Works 3.0 for Windows* is definitely not a desktop publishing package, some of its graphics and layout features resemble the features available in larger desktop publishing programs. It is possible to create newspaper columns, as we discussed in the last chapter. Recall that this creates snaking columns that wrap to the next column as the text reaches Line 55. This allows a newsletter or newspaper format with a user-defined number of columns on a page, but without complex tab settings. To create a page with a column layout:

- Click on Format-Columns.

  The Column window offers choice of number of columns.
- Type in the number of columns you wish.

  The sample page layout changes to represent your choice.
- Mark or unmark the choice to place a Divider line between the columns you have created.
- Click on OK or press ENTER.

  If you do not have Page Layout displayed, a dialog box will appear to ask if you wish to display it.
- Click on OK or press ENTER.

The column measures will be indicated by tiny triangles in the ruler. You may now proceed to type your text. The first column will fill to Line 55 before the text wraps to the next column, and so on. When all columns are filled, the program will insert an automatic page break and the column format will continue on Page 2. Note that, when you format columns, the entire document is affected. You may not mix the column format with other paragraph formats in the same document. Titles that must cross columns are formatted as headers.

Clip Art and Wrap around Text

As we noted in Chapter 4, clip art is a collection of predrawn figures that may be inserted into word processing documents. *Works 3.0 for Windows* has an extensive collection of pictures. To insert a picture from the clip art gallery, position your insertion bar where you wish to paste the picture, then:

- Click on Insert-Clip Art.
- Click on a topic, and the available figures will display.
- Click on the picture you wish to insert.
- Click on OK or press ENTER.

The picture will be inserted into your document. You may size the picture, increasing or decreasing it by clicking on the corner border and dragging the mouse until the picture is the size you wish.

It is possible to wrap text around the picture, as newspaper articles often do. To do this:

- Click on the picture to select it.
- Click on Format-Picture/Object.
- Click on the Text Wrap option.
- Click on Absolute for placement.
- Select a Horizontal option, either Center, Top, or Bottom.

  OR
- Type the distance from the left margin where you wish the picture to appear.

- Select a Vertical option, either Center, Top, or Bottom.

  OR
- Type the distance from the top margin where you wish the picture to appear.
- Click on OK or press ENTER.

The text wraps around the clip art as it is typed.

The above layout options, and the Draw option and Text box that we will introduce in Chapter 13, enable you to produce attractive, professional-looking documents without a desktop publishing program. *Works 3.0 for Windows* offers diverse graphics tools within the word processor.

WORD PROCESSING TUTORIAL NO. 5

In the next tutorial you will open a file called columns.wps on your student data disk, change that document into two columns, insert a clip art image into the document, size the image, set the text to wrap around the image, and create a footnote. When working with columns and adding art, you should switch to Page Layout format.

1. Open the file columns.wps on your data disk.
2. Save it as columns2.wps.

   To switch to the Page Layout mode:
3. Click on View-Page Layout.

   To format your document in two columns:
4. Click on Format-Columns.

   The Columns dialog box displays, as shown in Figure 5.22.

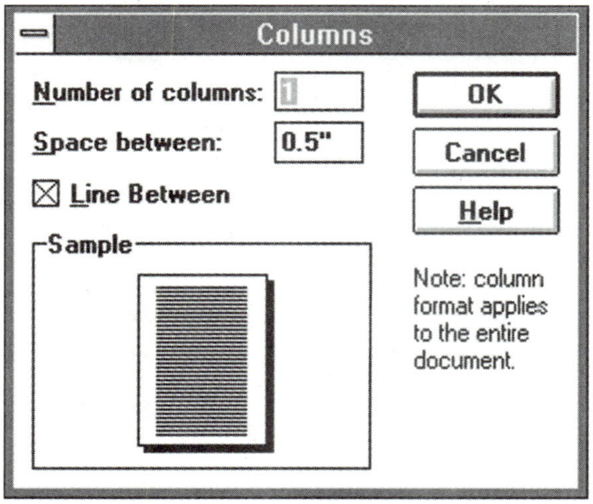

Figure 5.22

The Columns Dialog Box

5. In the Number of Columns box, type **2**
6. If it is not marked, click on Line between Columns.
7. Click on OK.

   Your document is now in two columns. You want to insert a clip art drawing in the right column. Move the insertion point to the left of the paragraph that begins, "The mouse is an . . . "
8. Click on Insert-Clip Art.

   The Clip Art option box displays, as shown in Figure 5.23.

Figure 5.23

The Clip Art Option Box

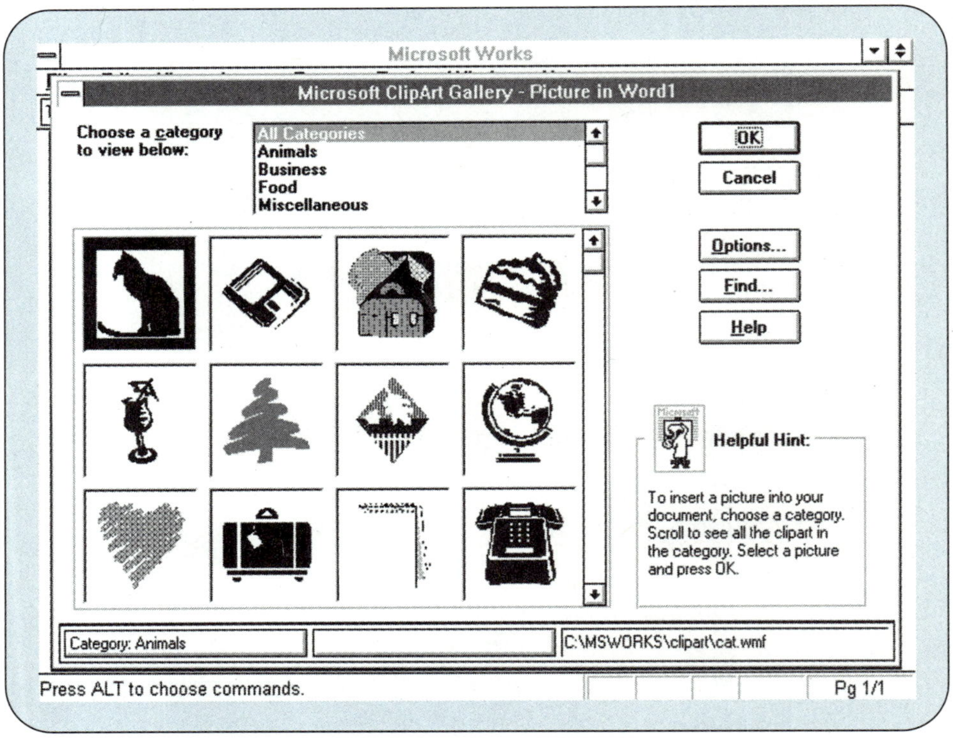

9. Click on the cat.
10. Click on OK.

    The cat is inserted, but it is a little large. To make it smaller:
11. Move the I-beam onto the cat and click.

    A square with sizing handles around the border surrounds the cat.
12. Click on Format-Picture/Object.

    The Picture/Object dialog box displays, as shown in Figure 5.24.
13. In the Size box, tab to the Width text box and type **1.5**
14. Tab to the Height box and type **1.5**

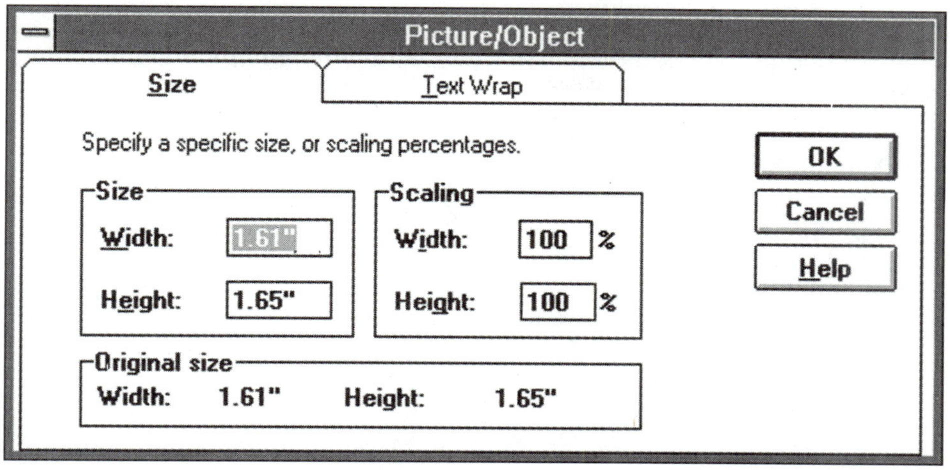

Figure 5.24

The Picture/Object Dialog Box

15. Click on OK.

    The size of the cat is reduced. Now you want the text to wrap around the cat.

16. Click on Format-Picture/Object-Text Wrap.

    The Text Wrap dialog box displays, as shown in Figure 5.25.

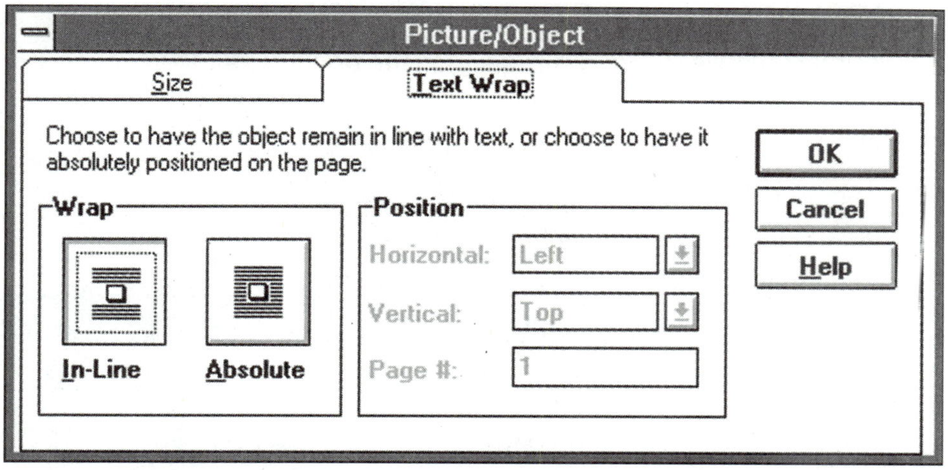

Figure 5.25

The Text Wrap Dialog Box

17. Click on Absolute.
18. Click on OK.

    The cat would look better further down in the paragraph.

19. Click on the cat and drag it downward a few lines.
20. Save the columns2 document.

    You will now insert a footnote at the end of the document.

21. Press CTRL + END.

22. Click on Insert-Footnote.

    The Footnote dialog box displays, as shown in Figure 5.26.

Figure 5.26

The Footnote Dialog Box

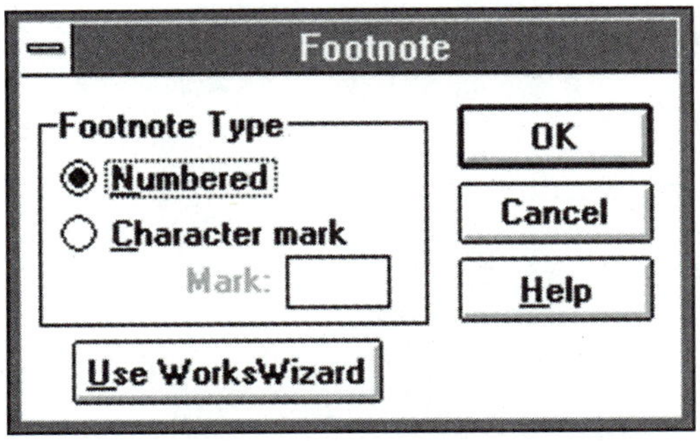

23. If it is not marked, click the Numbered radio button.
24. Click on OK.
25. Type the following footnote in the footnote pane; the system will enter the two superscript 1s. (Don't be concerned if the lines are short; they will fit in one column.)

    Shaw, Kenneth, Gwynne Larsen, Kathryn Marold, click on the Italics icon, **Using Microsoft Works,** click on the Italics icon again, **(Danvers, Mass.: Boyd & Fraser, 1994), 512 pp.**

    Your last step is to insert a Note-It on the document. Move your cursor up into the end of the document area from the footnote area.

26. After the superscript 1, press ENTER three times.
27. Click on Insert-Note It.

    The Note-It dialog box displays, as shown in Figure 5.27.

Figure 5.27

The Note-It Dialog Box

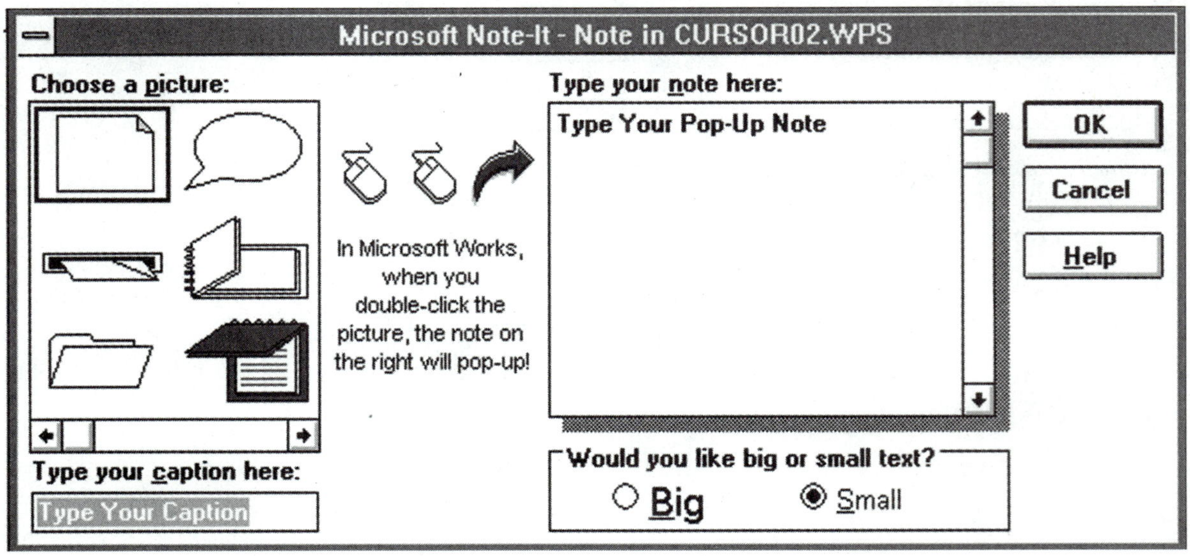

28. Click on the square Post-It Note™ form.
29. In the Caption text box, type **Reminder**
30. TAB to the Note text box and type **First Draft,** press ENTER, type **CG Times**, press ENTER, type **10 point**
31. Click on OK.

    The Note-It is inserted into your document, but not the text of the note. To read it, double click on the Note-It. The note without the text will show in your document when printed.
32. Save and print columns2.wps.
33. Close your document and exit *Works.*

    Your document should look similar to that in Figure 5.28.

To edit, replace, delete, cut, or copy text, you must first select the text. To select text, move the mouse pointer in the text area; the mouse turns into an I-beam. Position the I-beam in front of the text to be edited, press the left mouse button and drag the mouse until the desired text is highlighted, then release the mouse button. If you accidentally highlight the wrong text, move the I-beam away from the selected text and click the left mouse button once.

An alternative to dragging is called shift-and-click, which means to position the insertion point at the beginning of the text to be selected, move the I-beam to the end of the text, and press and hold the Shift key while clicking the left mouse button. The text between the insertion point and the I-beam is then selected.

In addition to dragging the mouse and using the shift-and-click method, you can also select various quantities of text with the mouse as follows:

One word - double-click on the word
One sentence - triple-click on the sentence
One paragraph - Quadruple-click on the paragraph

You can also turn on Select mode (by pressing F8) and then use the directional keys to highlight the text to be affected. Alternatively, after pressing F8 you can press a key to extend the selection to that character. For example, if your insertion point is at the beginning of a sentence, you can turn on Select and type a period. The text from the insertion point to the first period will be highlighted. Unlike the other two methods, Select mode will not replace the selected text with the characters you type. To deselect text that has been selected, either press F8 again or click the mouse anywhere in the work area.

The mouse is an electronic pointing device that operates by moving a ball underneath a palm-sized, maneuverable

case that is attached to the system unit. This device is used with most newer personal computer systems because it facilitates selection of menu items and speeds user operations. You direct the mouse arrow or rectangle shown on the screen (the mouse indicator) by rolling the mouse along a mouse pad until the indicator reaches the desired selection on the screen. You then press (or click) a mouse button to confirm the selection of the highlighted item. This operation is the equivalent of using the keyboard's directional arrows to position the cursor where you wish, then pressing the Enter key.

You may use the mouse with the *Works 3.0* program to select desired menu alternatives, select blocks of text in word processing, and perform many other utilitarian tasks.

On-line help, or documentation that is loaded into RAM with the program, is one of the newest and most user friendly attributes of modern interfaces. It offers tutorial and reference material about your particular program.

Figure 5.28

columns2.wps Document

Figure 5.28 Continued

columns2.wps Document

Rather than stopping and looking up instructions for executing a particular task in the printed documentation (user manual) for your particular program, you can press the Fl key and receive assistance. Most programs, like *Works*, have indexes to guide you to the particular help you need. All the while, your document remains in the background, still in memory, waiting for you to return to it. Almost every application program written today offers on-line help. It requires personal computers to have more main memory than before, but it has proved to be one of the most popular features of today's interfaces.

The cursor is the blinking symbol that indicates your position in a document. Usually a flashing dash or rectangle it is called an *insertion point* in *Windows* applications. The mouse is an I-beam when in the text area of the screen; when moved into the menu and tool bar areas, it becomes an arrow, or mouse pointer. When you use the mouse and scroll bars to move up and down, only the display moves; the insertion point stays in its original position. You can move the insertion point by placing the I-beam in the desired place and clicking the left mouse button once to reposition the insertion point.[1]

Reminder

---

[1]Shaw, Kenneth, Gwynne Larsen, Kathryn Marold, *Using Microsoft Works (Danvers, Mass: boyd & fraser, 1994) 512 pp.*

Chapter Summary

In this chapter we discussed advanced word processing topics such as page layouts, defining text styles, the thesaurus and spelling checker, formatting text, text enhancement, desktop publishing, and some additional, advanced features.

The discussion of page layout included use of the ruler, how to indent text, paragraph formats, and aligning text. The discussion of defining text styles included use of boldface, italics, superscripts, subscripts, and footnotes in longer, more complex documents.

The discussion of formatting text included how to use page breaks, more about page numbers, control of single and double spacing, windows within *Windows*, borders, and how to keep text together on one page. We also discussed how to save text in ASCII, and how to preview your work on the screen before it is printed.

The next topic in the chapter was desktop publishing, which combines text and graphics into one document. This kind of program offers the most sophisticated means of document preparation available on microcomputers. Several graphics options and the available column layouts introduced the student to some desktop publishing concepts.

KEY TERMS

active window
alignment
automatic page break
border
desktop publishing
endnote
external copy
footer
footnote
header
indent
line spacing
manual page break
margin
Note-It
page number
pitch
point
ruler line
scalable font
spelling checker
subscript
superscript
text file
thesaurus
True Type font
widow and orphan

REVIEW QUESTIONS

1. Describe how to use the ruler to change the layout of a page.
2. Explain how to add, change, hide, or delete the ruler.
3. Describe (a) how to set margins, and (b) how to indent text.
4. Paragraphs can be formatted before and after you type them. What are the two different ways of accomplishing this?
5. Briefly discuss the concept of a widow or an orphan.
6. What is the difference between left, right, justified, or centered alignment?
7. Explain the difference between (a) a hanging paragraph and (b) a quotation style paragraph. Explain how to construct each type of indent in *Works*.
8. Discuss the ways in which fonts contribute to defining text style.
9. State the difference between superscripts and subscripts. How is each inserted into a document?
10. Explain how a spelling checker and a thesaurus can help a writer.
11. State the difference between automatic and manual page breaks. How is each of these accomplished?
12. Distinguish between the terms *header and footer*. How are each of these inserted into a document?

13. Some documents are entirely single spaced. Others are entirely double spaced. Still others combine these line spacing formats. Review the technique in *Works 3.0 for Windows* to accomplish each of these formats.
14. Discuss the use of the window within *Window* feature in *Works*. How do you move selections from one document to another?
15. Why would you use a border in a document? How do you put a border around a single paragraph?
16. How do you prevent specially formatted text from being separated by a page break?
17. What is the difference between a footnote and an endnote? How are each of these inserted into a document?
18. Briefly explain the purpose of a Note-It in a document. How would you insert one?
19. What is the primary reason for saving a document as a text file?
20. How can the Print Preview option help you produce a document?
21. Explain the use(s) for desktop publishing.
22. Recall the functions of columns in a document. How are columns created in *Works?*
23. Briefly explain the uses of clip art and wrap around text.

SOFTWARE EXERCISES

Exercise 5.1

1. Make arrangements with your instructor to familiarize yourself with the *Works* word processing tutorial.
2. Make notes about what was covered in the section on formatting characters.
3. Use *Works 3.0 for Windows* to type your notes about what you learned.
4. Run a spelling check on your report.
5. Save your work as tutwp5.
6. Print tutwp5.wps.
7. Close tutwp5.wps and exit *Works.*

Exercise 5.2

1. Type the report in Figure 5.29 with these settings:
   (a) Left margin 1.3 inches, right margin 1.2 inches
   (b) Centered heading followed by a blank line
   (c) Single space the entire report.
2. Run a spelling check on the entire report.

3. Save the report as report1.
4. Print the report.
5. Close report1.wps and exit *Works.*

Figure 5.29

Computer Viruses

Computer Viruses

Computer viruses are nothing more than small segments of program code. This code is designed to replicate itself, attach itself to other files, and change the behavior of the computer that has the virus.

The first known virus program was written in 1983. The author was Fred Cohen. As a Ph.D. candidate at USC, Fred set out to prove that such a program could be written successfully. He presented his findings at a seminar on computer security. Later, his work became the basis for his doctoral dissertation.

Viruses have evolved since that time. This evolution has been caused by the use of antivirus programs, which seek to find and destroy known viruses.

Viruses originate from all over the world. Patricia M. Hoffman's *Virus Information Summary List* lists 33 countries from which viruses have originated. The United States has originated the most, with 41 strains, Bulgaria is second with 38 strains, and the former Soviet Union is third with 26 strains.

Exercise 5.3

1. Open report1.wps, or complete Exercise 5.2 before continuing.
2. Create a cover sheet that includes the centered title in all capital letters and in bold, along with your name and the current date in normal type. Put the centered title about 15 lines from the top of the page and your name and the current date about 2 inches from the bottom of the page.
3. Change the heading of the document to bold with all capital letters.
4. Center the heading if it is not already centered.
5. Double space the entire report.
6. Save the report as report2.
7. Print the report.
8. Close report2.wps and exit *Works.*

Exercise 5.4

1. Open report1.wps, or complete Exercise 5.2 before continuing.
2. Change the left margin to 1.8 inches and the right margin to 1.7 inches.
3. Double space the entire report.
4. Format the heading in boldface.
5. Change the heading to all capital letters, if not already in capital letters.
6. Create a footer to print page numbers on each page of the document so that the number appears centered at the bottom of the page.
7. Add the following reference as footnote 1 to the end of the last sen-

tence in the report: **"On Guard: 20 Utilities that Battle the Virus Threat,"** ***PC Magazine 10*****, no. 18 (October 29, 1991), p. 201.**

8. Save the report as report3.
9. Print the report.
10. Close report3.wps and exit *Works*.

Exercise 5.5

1. Open report1.wps, or complete Exercise 5.2 before continuing.
2. Double space the entire report.
3. Add the following sentence to the third paragraph: "Follow these tips to safer computing:"
4. Add the following text as a single-spaced, hanging indent section between the third and fourth paragraphs following the inserted sentence:

   (a) Put write-protect tabs on all program disks before using them to install new software.

   (b) Don't install software on your machine that is not shrink-wrapped.

   (c) Back up all of your work frequently.
5. Add endnote number 1 so that it is keyed to the end of the sentence "Follow these tips to safer computing:" **"On Guard: 20 Utilities that Battle the Virus Threat,"** ***PC Magazine*** **10, no. 18 (October 29, 1991), p. 201.**
6. Insert a manual page break after the last sentence in the last paragraph.
7. Center the word *ENDNOTE* at the top of the last page.
8. Run a spelling check on the report.
9. Save the report as report4.
10. Print report4.wps so that the endnote is printed at the end of the document and not at the bottom of the page where its reference appears.
11. Close report4.wps and exit *Works*.

Exercise 5.6

1. Open the file insched2.wps, completed during this chapter's tutorials.
2. Change bold to italics throughout the document.
3. Change the right and left margins to one inch.
4. Exchange the section on Insured Persons with the section on Insured Autos.

5. Create a cover sheet with the title "Automobile Liability Insurance" in all capital letters and in bold type. Center this title about one-third of the way down the page from the top.
6. Add a footer to print "Page-" (that's *Page*, hyphen) and the page number on every page except the first one (the cover).
7. Run a spelling check on the entire document.
8. Save the file as insur.
9. Print insur.wps.
10. Close insur.wps and exit *Works*.

Exercise 5.7

1. Open the file essay.wps on the student data diskette that accompanies the text.
2. Add a cover page with the heading centered in all capital letters and in bold type. Position this heading about one-third of the way down from the top of the page.
3. Center your name about 2 inches from the bottom of the page.
4. Center the current date one line below your name.
5. Indent each paragraph eight spaces from the left margin.
6. Double space the entire document.
7. Change the title to bold.
8. Put your name in a right-justified header.
9. Number each page except the cover page in a footer. Put the page number in the center of each page.
10. Run a spelling check on the entire document.
11. Preview the essay.
12. Save the essay as essay1.
13. Print essay1.wps.
14. Close essay1.wps and exit *Works*.

Exercise 5.8

1. Open the file essay.wps on the student diskette that accompanies the text.
2. Change the right margin to 1.6 inches and the left margin to 1.5 inches.
3. Indent each paragraph ten spaces from the left margin.
4. Double space the entire document.
5. Add a cover page with the title of the essay centered in bold type. Center your name 2 inches from the bottom of this page in regular type.

6. Add a table of contents with dot leaders preceding the page numbers.
7. Change each subheading in the essay by making it bold.
8. Number each page except the cover pages in a footer and center the page number.
9. Run a spelling check on the entire document.
10. Preview your work.
11. Save your essay as essay2.
12. Print essay2.wps.
13. Close essay2.wps and exit *Works*.

Exercise 5.9

1. Open the file essay.wps on the student data diskette that accompanies the text.
2. Save essay.wps as a text file; name it essaytxt.
3. Close essay.wps and exit *Works*.
4. Open essaytxt in another word processor. Follow Steps 2 through 11 in Exercise 5.7 to complete this assignment.
5. Print the essay using the other word processor.
6. Save the file in the format of the other word processor.
7. Close the file and exit.

Exercise 5.10

1. Use *Works 3.0 for Windows* to load the text file will.txt from the student data diskette.
2. Remove the many end-of-line characters that are presently in the wrong places. Click on View-All characters to see the end-of-line characters, if necessary.
3. Double space the entire document.
4. Add a footer to center the page number on each page.
5. Center the heading in bold.
6. Run a spelling check on the entire document.
7. Save the document as will.
8. Print will.wps.
9. Close will.wps and exit *Works*.

Exercise 5.11

1. Use *Works 3.0 for Windows* to load the text file military.txt from the student data diskette.

2. Remove the many end-of-line characters that are presently in the wrong places.
3. Double space the entire document.
4. Indent paragraphs five spaces.
5. Add a footer to center the page number on each page.
6. Center the title in bold, capital letters.
7. Run a spelling check on the entire document.
8. Save the file as military.
9. Print military.wps.
10. Close military.wps and exit *Works*.

Exercise 5.12

1. Open the file lethal.doc on the student data diskette that accompanies the text. This essay was first written and saved on a Macintosh computer. Later the Macintosh was used to resave it in WordPerfect 5.1 format. It can now be read into *Works 3.0 for Windows* which will automatically translate it into the *Works* word processing format.
2. Change the margins to 1.3 inches on the left side and 1.2 inches on the right side.
3. Change the heading to all capital letters and bold.
4. Remove the original author's name, class, and date from the upper, right-hand corner.
5. Add a header with your name, class, and current date. Print the header in every page except the cover page.
6. Add a footer to center "Page-" (that's *Page*, hyphen) on every page except the cover page.
7. Add a cover page with the title centered and in bold about one-third of the way down the page. Center your own name about 2 inches up from the bottom of the page, and center the current date right under your name.
8. Change the spacing of the document from single to double spacing.
9. Change all paragraphs so that the margin is aligned only on the left instead of justified on both the right and left.
10. Run a spelling check on the entire document.
11. Save the document in *Works* format as lethal.
12. Print lethal.wps.
13. Close lethal.wps and exit *Works*.

Exercise 5.13

1. From the *Works 3.0 for Windows* Startup screen, choose Use a Template.
2. Choose AutoStart Business from the template group, Documents from the category group, and Three Column Newsletter from the template section.
3. Click on Show Instructions Cue Cards, if not already selected.
4. Click on OK.
5. Follow the cue card directions for a three-column newsletter by replacing the filler you see (in English and in Latin) with your own material and art work.
6. Run a spelling check on the entire document.
7. Save the document in *Works* format as 3colnews.
8. Print 3colnews.wps.
9. Close 3colnews.wps and exit *Works*.

Exercise 5.14

You arrive home from work more angry than you can ever remember. Your boss has done it again. You have had enough of your boss and your present job. You decide to write your boss a letter of resignation, effective two weeks from today.

1. Open a new word processing document in *Works 3.0 for Windows*.
2. Use your own return address and the current date.
3. Address your letter to your current or an imaginary boss.
4. Write the body of the letter in such a way that the person who receives it will know how angry you are. Let him or her know you are quitting. Give the customary two weeks' notice and state a date two weeks from the present date.
5. Close with "Sincerely yours," and type your name five lines below the closing.
6. Run a spelling check on the entire document.

   After writing this letter, you decide to think for a week before sending it. As a reminder to yourself, put a Note-It on the letter.
7. Put the cursor on the last paragraph. Choose Insert-Note-It.
8. Click on the picture that looks like a file. Delete the instruction "Type your caption" and type **File in pending** as a caption.
9. Delete the instruction to "Type your pop-up note here" from the dialog box and type the following message: **File this letter in the PENDING folder for one week while I think it over.**

10. Click on Big text and on OK.
11. Double click on the file folder object to check the message.
12. Print the letter.
13. Save the letter as quitjob.
14. Close quitjob.wps and exit *Works*.

Exercise 5.15

1. Use *Works 3.0 for Windows* to write a paper on the subject of computer viruses, or on a subject of interest to you or assigned by your instructor.
2. Center and bold the heading.
3. Underline the heading for each major section.
4. Add appropriate footnotes.
5. Add a footer to center the page number.
6. Run a spelling check on the entire document.
7. Save your file as paper.
8. Print paper.wps.
9. Close paper.wps and exit *Works*.

Exercise 5.16

1. Use *Works 3.0 for Windows* to complete a word processing assignment for an outside class.
2. Use all of the techniques you have learned so far to enhance the appearance of your work.
3. Save your file as outside.
4. Print outside.wps.
5. Close outside.wps and exit *Works*.

Chapter 6

Beginning Spreadsheets

Objectives

After studying this chapter you will be able to:

- *Indicate the uses of spreadsheets*
- *Explain the basic components of spreadsheets*
- *Describe how to construct a good spreadsheet*
- *Use special formats in a spreadsheet*
- *Master entry of labels, values, and formulas*
- *Use the spreadsheet toolbar to facilitate your work*
- *Employ the concept of a range to total, copy, or move a cell or group of cells*
- *Recall the cause and cure for the CIRC error message*
- *Demonstrate the sorting of spreadsheet rows*
- *Know the order of operations in spreadsheet calculations*
- *Save and print a spreadsheet*

Spreadsheet software is one of the most widely used types of application packages. Many users rely on this kind of software for decision making support. A spreadsheet is a tool for analyzing data through mathematical operations. It gives you a logical form in a ledger format where you can assemble data and solve problems. It also gives you a method for organizing, calculating, and presenting financial, statistical, and other numerical data as a basis for decision making. Spreadsheets have long been used by professionals, managers, sales and accounting personnel, and support staff. This was one of the first kinds of packages developed for the personal computer and its popularity has increased with the development of more powerful, easier-to-use packages. Figure 6.1 shows typical spreadsheet technology prior to the development of spreadsheet software.

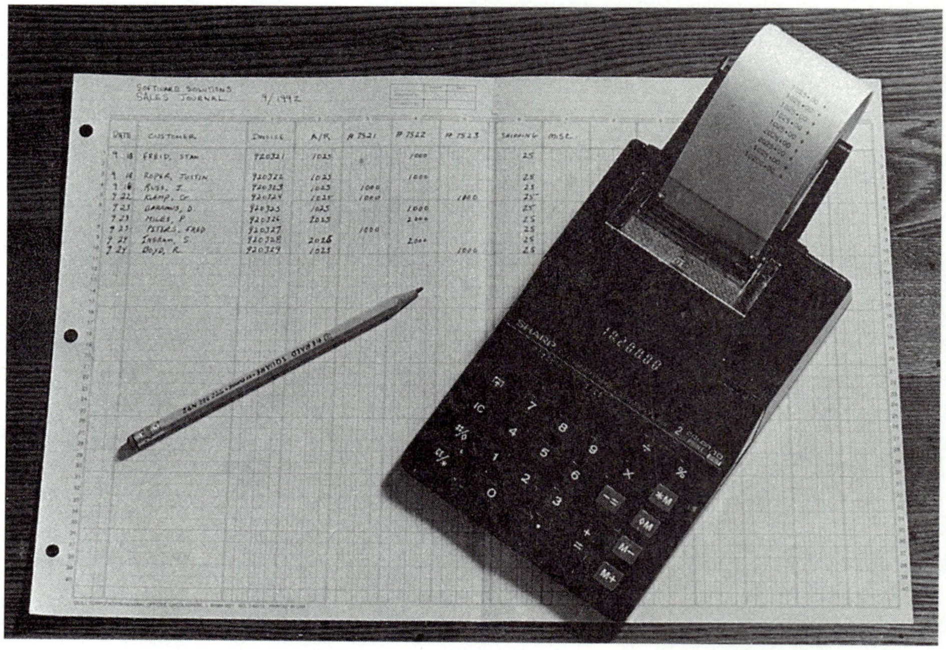

Figure 6.1

Electronic spreadsheet programs are modeled on the columnar arrangement of manual ledger forms.

What a Spreadsheet Does

Spreadsheets allow users to manipulate numbers electronically instead of with pencils and paper. You can use them simply to list and summarize data, but you can also use them to analyze and spot trends. Finally, you can use them to forecast, or predict, the consequences of actions.

It is this last use of spreadsheets that has caused them to become so popular. They are especially useful for "what if" analysis, to answer questions such as "What if sales were 50 percent of the estimate?" or "What if sales were 200 percent of the estimate?" These types of questions can be answered swiftly and accurately by entering values, formulas, and labels into a spreadsheet. The values can then be changed and the results recalculated almost instantly. In this way, you can try out many values, see at once what their effects would be, then quickly return to the original numbers, all without redesigning the spreadsheet. Since all of the tedious calculations are done for you immediately, you can experiment with many courses of action.

Some of the possible uses for spreadsheets are:

- Budgets and forecasts
- Checkbook reconciliation
- Simple financial models
- Financial analysis
- Investment analysis

- Financial statement preparation
- Tax estimation
- Present value determination
- Marketing analysis and projection
- Statistical analysis

History of Spreadsheets

Spreadsheets for the personal computer began with Frankston and Bricklin's *VisiCalc* for the Apple II personal computer. Based on their familiarity with spreadsheets for large computer systems, the authors devised *VisiCalc* for their master's thesis project at The Harvard Business School in 1979. *Supercalc* followed for the IBM personal computer.

Lotus 1-2-3 stormed the personal computer market when it introduced its companion **charting** application that supported graphical representation of worksheet numbers. *Lotus* is somewhat expensive at a cost of about $100 to $200, depending upon the version. (*Windows* versions of software applications are generally more expensive.) Some software clones have entered the market, however, such as *VP Planner* and *Joe Spreadsheet*, that cost only nominal amounts. *Excel*, by the publisher of *Works*, is a very popular spreadsheet program that is also available for Macintosh computers. *Quattro Pro* is another spreadsheet program that has become popular in recent years. The suites of software applications that are now becoming popular within the *Windows* environment (such as Microsoft's *Office*) include powerful spreadsheet programs.

The *Works* spreadsheet is not as large or powerful as some of the stand-alone spreadsheet programs, but it is often adequate for the smaller applications of most personal computer users. In addition, the spreadsheet gives you the advantage of the familiar interface from the word processing application that you just covered. Moving to a specific accounting or financial computer application often requires a basic knowledge of spreadsheet computing. Therefore, even if you do not stay with the *Works* spreadsheet, knowledge of its operation will provide rudimentary skills that you can build upon as your computer literacy level increases.

Elements of a Spreadsheet

A spreadsheet is composed of **columns** (vertical dividers), lettered from A to Z, and **rows** (horizontal dividers), numbered from 1 to more than 4,000. A **cell** is the intersection of a row and a column. A **matrix** is the combination of all rows and columns; its size is expressible as a total number of cells. For example, a matrix of 200 columns by 2,000 rows would produce 400,000 cells. In a manner similar to accountant's ledger paper, the matrix organizes numerical data.

Spreadsheet cells contain **labels**, **values**, and **formulas**, the last of which can be **functions**, or predefined formulas that are supplied for you by the authors of the spreadsheet program. Labels are text composed of letters or numbers. (They are **alphanumeric data**.) Labels cannot be used in calculations; they usually serve as column headings and row descriptions. Values, by contrast, are numbers that are entered in cells; they are the raw material used in calculations. (Sometimes they are, in fact, the products of calculations, entered not by you, but by the program.) Values that you enter are sometimes referred to as **constants** because, unlike the numbers that result from formulas, they remain the same unless you change them in the spreadsheet.

Formulas are the recipes, or algorithms, for mathematical operations. You can write your own mathematical formula for an operation, or you can choose a function from those supplied with the program. In the latter case, you simply enter the **parameters**—cell addresses (locations) or constant numbers—where the function finds data to carry out its operation. If you use a function, you do not have to figure out the process involved in a computation and write the formula; you simply plug in the numbers, or references to numbers in other cells. Each function has an **argument** enclosed in a set of parentheses ( ) where you enter the parameters. For example, the Sum function =SUM (A1:A6) totals the values in all the cells from A1 to A6, saving you the time to list each cell with a plus sign. You simply entered cell addresses within the argument. You could also enter constant values within the argument to execute an addition operation that would return a value such as =SUM(3,4,5). Figure 6.2 shows the layout of the *Works* spreadsheet screen, and identifies the title bar, the menu bar, the formula bar, and column and row labels.

Figure 6.2

Spreadsheet Layout

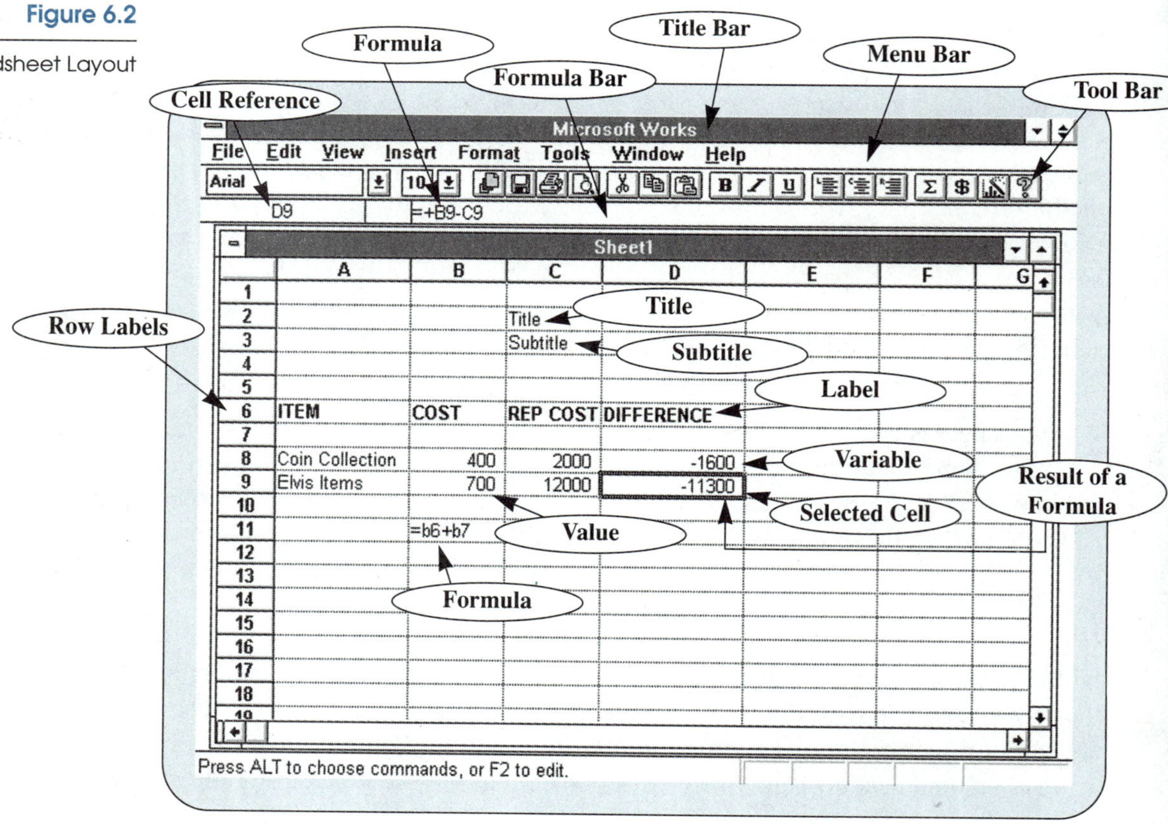

Designing a Spreadsheet for Problem Solving

It would be a serious mistake for you to open the spreadsheet application of *Works* and simply begin to construct a **worksheet** (the application's "scratch pad," or spreadsheet in memory) without first thinking about the problem you wish to solve. Good spreadsheets are not created casually. Instead, they are carefully thought out and planned. You must decide what you wish to accomplish—what problem you want to solve—and how best to organize a solution. You should also think about the cosmetic appearance of the spreadsheet; how can you best present the numerical data so that a printout of the spreadsheet will be easy to read and understand. This result, too, takes some prior planning.

After you have carefully identified what you want to include in the spreadsheet, whether you use paper and pencil or the worksheet displayed on the monitor itself to design the spreadsheet is immaterial. What is important is that you do design it carefully first. Decide which labels to include and where to place them, which formulas or functions to use, where to enter the values that the spreadsheet will manipulate. If you design or lay out the organization of the spreadsheet first, your job of actually constructing it will be a lot easier, and you will do less revising. First designing a **template**—an empty spreadsheet containing only labels and formulas—will improve your final product and save you time in the long run.

Critically Examining Your Spreadsheet

Perhaps the greatest danger in the use of spreadsheets is the tendency to unquestionally accept the results. With all of those figures neatly arranged in rows and columns, and all of the formulas and functions included, it is easy to believe what you see. But a spreadsheet is really helpful only if it is accurate. Does it do what it is supposed to do? Are the calculations correct? Maybe an incorrect formula was entered. Or perhaps it referenced the wrong cells. Incorrect values may have been entered because of errors in data entry. The slogan GIGO (garbage in, garbage out) was never truer than with spreadsheet construction. The computer will not calculate incorrectly unless it is mechanically malfunctioning, but it will certainly return erroneous data if you make an error putting information in the spreadsheet. Therefore, all spreadsheets should be checked carefully before being accepted.

To put it another way, spreadsheets are wonderful tools for analysis and decision making; however, they work only as well as their designs, input, and interpretation. Misrepresenting a problem, intentionally or not, can have major repercussions, so check your spreadsheets carefully. Perform a few calculations manually to make sure that all is well before simply accepting that neatly printed page and its companion graph. The greatest advantage to spreadsheet computing, carrying out complex computations instantly, is also its greatest threat because it is too easy to assume that the spreadsheet gives the correct answers. Users often forget to check results carefully.

Rules for Designing a Layout

Certain conventions guide most spreadsheet designers when formatting their worksheets. The **home area**, composed of Cell A1 and the few columns and rows adjacent to it, is most often reserved for identification of the contents, author, and date of the spreadsheet. The reader needs to know the subject of the spreadsheet, what it deals with, who wrote it, and so forth. The first available column below the home area, beginning around Cell A4, is most often used for labels and descriptive text of some sort. The first several rows usually contain labels, as well. The actual numbers and formulas are placed below and to the right of these initial rows and columns.

Double lines (================), single lines (----------), and empty rows separate text from values. Also rows or columns are often totaled both horizontally and vertically to allow cross-checks of sums. See Figure 6.3 for a typical spreadsheet layout.

Figure 6.3

Spreadsheet design benefits from setting aside general functional areas in the matrix.

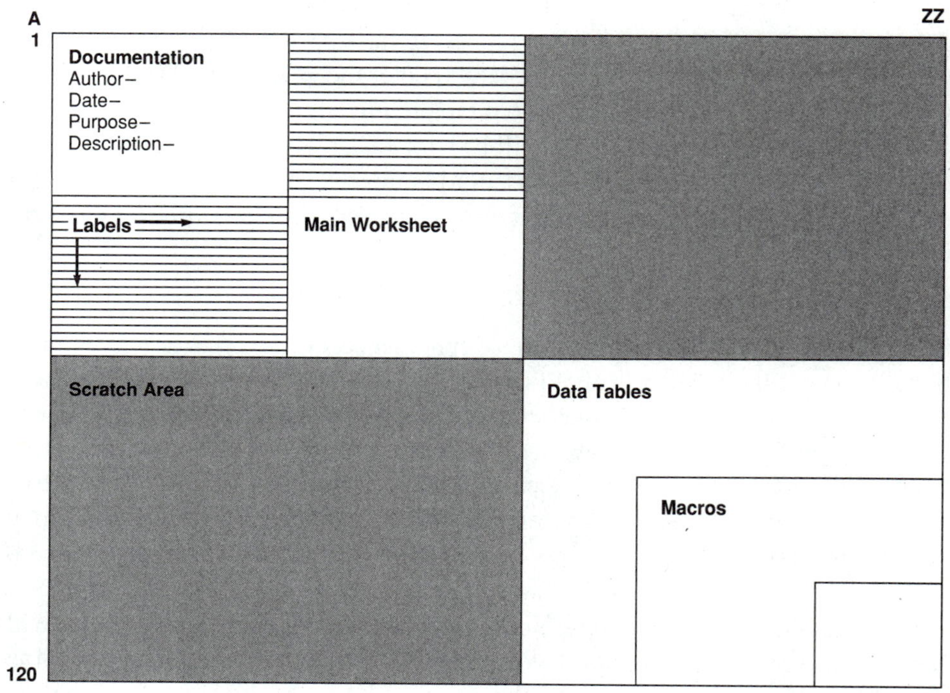

In addition, spreadsheets often contain documentation, or very brief text explanations of what problem is being solved and how it is executed. If the spreadsheet contains **macros** (series of stored keystrokes that can be replayed at will by issuing single commands), they will be set apart from the main worksheet in another area of the matrix, and usually they contain their own documentation. You will be creating very simple spreadsheets with limited numbers of rows and columns, and no macros. Nevertheless, you should design them with the same care as large spreadsheets.

Building the Spreadsheet

After you have decided what to include in your spreadsheet and how it will look, you can begin by entering the labels. Next, you can enter any formulas you will use, if you know the cell locations where the formulas can find appropriate data. If not, enter the values into cells first, then enter the formulas or functions, including the addresses, or cell location references, for the values they must use.

In a formula, you connect the cell addresses by **operators** consisting of + (plus), - (minus), * (multiplication), and / (division). For example, to total three cells in a *Works* spreadsheet, you might enter the formula =B6+B7+B8. The mathematical symbols are the operators, and the cell references are the **operands**, or what is being calculated.

Works has 76 functions (see Appendix B) that perform common tasks such as adding the numbers in a group of cells (SUM), calculating a fixed rate of interest (RATE), or finding an average (AVG). For example, if you want to add a column of six numbers, it is much faster to use the function =SUM(B1:B6) than to type =B1+B2+B3+B4+B5+B6. Both will work, however. (Don't forget to type the = sign in front of either a formula or a function.)

To use a function, such as the SUM ( ) function, you enter the relevant cell addresses within the parentheses (the argument portion) of the function. In our example, the notation (B1:B6) stands for all cells in the **range** B1 through B6.

Relative and Absolute Cell References

When using formulas, cell references are critical. If you want the formula to reference a particular cell, regardless of how many rows and columns are inserted or deleted, and regardless of whether the formula is copied to another location, you must include an **absolute reference**. This denotes the address of the row or column, or both, that must remain constant. An absolute cell reference is preceded by a dollar sign ($). For example, if the Social Security rate must remain in Cell D6, without changing locations you enter the reference in a formula as D6. That will assure that the cell reference will not change as you insert, move, or delete rows and columns.

If you do not state a cell address as an absolute reference, the address changes with the cell's location, making it a **relative reference**. That is, if you insert, delete, move, or copy contents of cells, you do not have to change relative references; the program adjusts them for you. For example if you were copying the formula =B3+B4 to the third column (Column C), the formula would be automatically changed to read =C3+C4. This default setting of the *Works* spreadsheet will adjust the new location automatically for you, and change the address. It is one of the most valuable, time-saving features of all spreadsheet programs, allowing you to edit your worksheet without worrying about changing all of the addresses of moved items.

Just be aware that sometimes you do not want a relative reference to change; then you must remember to include the $ symbol to indicate that the address should not change with editing. Most spreadsheet programs use the same symbol, the $ sign, to indicate an absolute reference.

Format and Design in Works *Spreadsheets*

Spreadsheet Toolbar The process for formatting worksheets and controlling their layouts is similar in most spreadsheet programs. This section will give formatting tips for a *Works* worksheet, but the process is very similar to that of any other spreadsheet program. As in the word processing module, a toolbar at the top of the screen offers many commands or tools to make your selection easier. Figure 6.4 shows the three icons in *Works* that are different from the word processing toolbar identified: the SUM icon, the Currency icon, and the Chart icon.

Figure 6.4

Specific Spreadsheet Icons

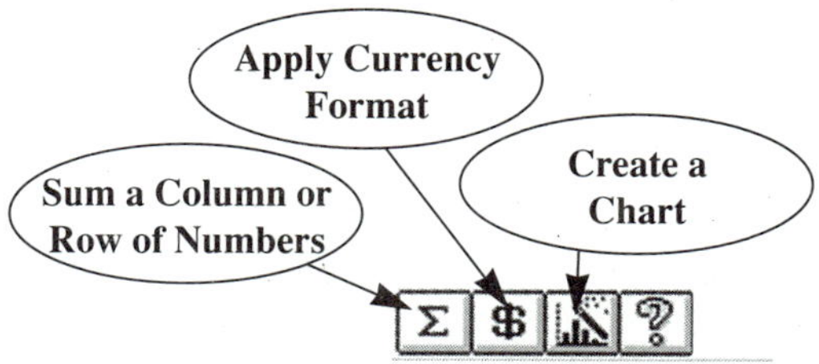

The options available on the spreadsheet toolbar are similar to the icons introduced in the word processing toolbar. Notice the familiar Startup Dialog, Save, Print, View, Cut, Copy, and Paste icons after the Font style and size windows, with their scroll options (see Figure 6.2). The remaining icons perform some familiar functions, and some new ones:

- B—Make the highlighted entry bold
- *I* —Make the highlighted entry italic
- U—Underline the highlighted entry
- L—Left align cell contents
- C—Center cell contents
- R—Right align cell contents
- Σ—(Sigma) Activate the autosum option
- $ —Format cell contents as currency
- Bar Chart icon—Display a new chart
- ? —Help

As we mentioned when describing the *Works* interface, if you rest the mouse pointer on a toolbar selection for a moment, a descriptive term (tool tip) will flash on the screen to help identify the icon. As you become more proficient with the *Windows* interface, you will see the advantage to using the toolbar rather than the pull-down menu selections at the top of the screen. Toolbar selection is quick and efficient; you will want to use it as much as possible when making selections in all of the *Works* applications.

We will cover all of the cell **formats**, or appearances below; however, notice that the toolbar contains the currency icon, which allows you to change the appearance of selected cells to show values in dollars and cents. Since this is often the choice of a user when defining a spreadsheet, it is included in the default toolbar.

The Greek sigma (Σ) is the symbol for "the sum of." You may invoke the spreadsheet's **autosum** feature by clicking on this icon. If you select the cell at the end of a column or the bottom of a row of numbers and choose the autosum icon, the total of those values will be inserted in the cell. To complete this action, you must approve the suggested summation by pressing ENTER or clicking on the Enter box. Otherwise the =SUM( ) function will be inserted with an empty argument, and you may insert the cell references you desire.

The chart icon in the toolbar lets you begin a new chart, or graphical representation of a spreadsheet's numbers, using the current spreadsheet. We will cover charting in detail in Chapter 8, where you will learn eight different styles of charts. However, the charting application in *Works 3.0 for Windows* is a subset of the spreadsheet application, since you must have spreadsheet data in order to create a chart. The default chart type for *Works* is the bar chart; that is what you will see if you choose this icon from the toolbar.

You may customize your toolbar in the spreadsheet application, just as you learned to customize the word processing toolbar to simplify selection of the quotation paragraph format or other heavily used features. You may add icons to, or delete them from, the toolbar as you desire. The most frequently used features of the spreadsheet application already have icons in the default toolbar. You will probably be satisfied with these options until you master simple spreadsheets.

Styles of Labels You have already seen that text in the labels on your spreadsheet can be styled in some of the same ways as word processing documents with the Format-Style command. You can use bold, underline, and italic type to emphasize text, as follows:

- Select the cell or cells.
- Click on Format.
- Select Font and Style.
- Click on any of the following: Bold, Underline, Italic.
- Choose any of the available fonts for you printer.
- Click on OK.

Column Widths The column width determines how many characters can fit in one cell. The default setting in the *Works* spreadsheet is 10. Suppose that you enter more than ten characters. If the cell to the right is empty, *Works* will continue the current cell's contents into the adjacent cell. Otherwise, it will display no more than ten characters. It will indicate that a number or date is too large for the cell by displaying a series of number signs (#) in the cell. You can let *Works* determine the correct column width by selecting the Best Fit Option.

To widen a cell:

- Select a cell in the column you want to change.
- Click on Format-Column Width.
- Type a number between 0 and 79 for the width, or check the Best Fit check box.
- Click on OK.

Notice that there is an option for row height, as well. It is possible to format a spreadsheet with rows that are two or three lines high. We will experiment with this technique in Chapter 7.

Entering Text, Numbers, and Formulas

You make cell entries by selecting cells and simply typing in text, dates, or numbers. To enter a formula, you must type an equals sign (=) first and then the formula. As you create the formula, it appears in the formula bar in the upper, left-hand corner of the spreadsheet. You can backspace, delete, and move the cursor with the arrow keys until you get the formula the way you want it; then press ENTER. If you want a number to appear as a label, such as 1994, type a quotation mark (") in front of it.

In the command menus, a mouse pointer determines your location. In the spreadsheet itself, it is an intersecting **cross bar**. When you move the cross bar to a cell and click with the mouse, this active cell is outlined with a dark, double border. As you select cells for future operations, the first cell of the series remains clear; the others are highlighted in reverse video (white on black, usually). We will usually refer to the *cross bar* or to *selecting* a cell in our discussion of spreadsheets.

To enter text, numbers, and formulas into a cell:

- Select the cell.
- Type the text, number, or formula.
- Press ENTER.

Design Enhancements As you type data into a cell, text is left-aligned and dates and numbers are right-aligned. You can format characters as bold, underlined, or italic in your spreadsheet. To change character styles or alignment:

- Select a cell or range.
- Click on Format-Font and Style.
- Select the desired option in the Style box.
- Click on OK.

Selecting, Clearing, and Deleting Spreadsheet Elements

A cell is automatically selected when you move the cross bar into it and click the mouse button. To select a whole row:

- Move the cross bar into the row number.
- Click on the row number.

To select a whole column:

- Move the cross bar into the column letter.
- Click on the column letter.

You can also use F8 or SHIFT + directional arrows to select cells. You can click and drag with the mouse, or even use the Edit menu, Select Row or Select Column options to select entire rows or columns.

This process requires a word of caution, though. Be certain that you wish to select a whole row or column for your task. If you are changing the appearance, or format, of a row or column, selecting in this manner is appropriate. If you are copying material, take care to select only the cells to which you wish to copy material; otherwise, you could fill entire sections of the matrix (4,000 rows or 256 columns) with material when you wish to fill only 20 or 30 cells! Carefully select your range of cells.

Concept of Range

A range can be any cell or rectangular group of cells—a single cell, a column, a row, a block of cells, or an entire spreadsheet. Ranges can have names that can replace more cumbersome cell references, simplifying some tasks. A range begins in the upper, left-hand corner and ends in the lower, right-hand corner of the desired number of cells. To select a range:

- Select the upper, left-hand corner cell.
- Depress the mouse button and drag to highlight the desired cells.

As an alternative, you may use the menu to select an entire row or column:

- Select a cell in the row or column.
- Click on Edit-Select Row or Edit-Select Column.

When you **clear** a cell or range (sometimes called *blanking* or *erasing)*, you remove the contents, but the formatting (bold or centered, for example) remains. To clear cells:

- Select a cell or range.
- Click on Edit-Clear.

To clear a single cell, press BACKSPACE and then press ENTER.

When you delete a row or column, everything in the selected area is removed. Follow these steps to delete:

- Select a cell in the row or column.
- Click on Insert-Delete Row/Column.
- Click on Row or Column-OK.

An Undo selection in the Edit menu will reverse your decision if you should inadvertently delete the wrong range. Be certain to Undo your error immediately, though; as you may recall, the Undo function applies only to the last action you performed. A shortcut method of undoing your last change can save time: simply press CTRL + Z.

To make corrections in a cell (edit its contents), you can either replace the entry by retyping the contents or press F2 and edit the cell contents in the formula bar, as follows:

- Select a cell.
- Press F2.
- Use any of the editing keys shown in Table 6.1.
- Press ENTER to confirm or ESC to cancel.

Table 6.1 Editing Keys for *Works 3.0 for Windows*

Go to the beginning of the formula bar	HOME
Go to the end of the formula bar	END
Go left one character	LEFT ARROW
Go right one character	RIGHT ARROW
Delete the character to the left of the cursor	BACKSPACE
Delete the selected character	DELETE

To go to a cell reference or range—that is, to jump directly to a chosen cell or range:

- Click on Edit-Go To, or press F5.
- Type the cell reference in the Go To box.

  OR
- Select the range name in the Names box.
- Click on OK.

Totaling Columns or Rows

As we noted above, the autosum icon in the toolbar lets you quickly total a series of numbers. You can access this same automatic function through the Edit menu. This is a quicker way than entering a formula to add a row or column:

- Highlight the cell at the end of the row or column that you want to total.

- Click on Edit-Autosum.
- Click on OK.

Works will add the cells above or to the left. If it does not recognize the range you wish to sum, it will allow you to type in a range in the empty argument.

Copying Cells and Ranges

You can copy the contents of cells to another location, or to the right or down to an adjacent location in the spreadsheet. To copy a cell's contents to adjacent cells:

- Select the cell, column, or row you wish to duplicate.
- Extend the selection to the right or down where you want to place the copied cells.
- Click on Edit-Fill Right, or Edit-Fill Down.

To copy to nonadjacent cells:

- Select a cell or range to copy.
- Click on Edit-Copy, or press SHIFT + F3.
- Select the cell or range where you want to place the copy.
- Select Edit-Paste.

  OR
- Click on the Copy and Paste icons.

To repeat a copy:

- Select the cell or range where the duplicated information goes:
- Press SHIFT + F7.

Periodically, when working with your spreadsheet, you should save what you have done. The layout, or template, of your design is very valuable, even if no values have been entered yet. When all of the text, formulas, functions, and values have been entered into your worksheet, save it once again. The familiar Save As and Save commands are in the same place in the spreadsheet's File menu as they were in the word processing application. A final step is to test your spreadsheet and carefully examine its results.

Circular References

In entering a formula, you may get an error message that reads, "Circular Reference." This means the formula refers to itself, instead of to other cells. In *Works*, "CIRC" will display in the status line. Check your formula again to be certain that it does not reference itself.

Testing Your Design

As the author of a spreadsheet, you are responsible for testing it with several different sets of data. You should convince yourself that the calculations are correct, that all formulas and functions reference the correct cells, that the formulas and functions are the proper ones to use, and so forth.

Many spreadsheet authors prefer to use **manual calculation** mode (in which the spreadsheet must be given a command before it will calculate formulas) while they are building and testing worksheets. Most spreadsheet programs use **automatic calculation** by default; whenever a value or a formula is edited or copied, the entire worksheet is recalculated. If you have a **math coprocessor** (an additional chip to help the CPU perform calculations) or a more powerful computer, this is done so rapidly that you barely notice the wait. For very large worksheets or slower models of computers, however, it can be frustrating to wait for all of the formulas to be recalculated, especially if you have more numbers to edit and the process will be repeated for every new number you enter. In this case, you may turn off the automatic calculation feature and direct the program to **recalculate** only when you give the command.

To change the automatic recalculation mode in *Works*:

- Click on Tools-Manual Calculation.

When you wish to recalculate:

- Click on Tools-Calculate Now.

Do not forget to toggle back to automatic calculation before you save the spreadsheet and exit the program. Otherwise, you may forget to calculate all of the formulas again after a change; this would risk saving incorrect results. The next time you open the spreadsheet, you may not remember that you had toggled manual calculation on, and your additions will not be computed.

You will create a simple spreadsheet in this chapter's tutorial, and then compare it with a model printout to be sure you have constructed it correctly. Careful evaluation of the worksheet is the last step, but one of the most important ones in completing any spreadsheet.

SPREADSHEET TUTORIAL NO. 1

You are now going to complete an inventory of your household items for your insurance company. You will need to change the width of the first column to 20 characters to accommodate your description, and you want to title your spreadsheet, as well as center and bold your column headings. Use the mouse or the arrow keys to move the cross bar. Start by loading the *Works* program, and then proceed with the steps below:

1. From the Startup screen, click on Spreadsheet.

   The spreadsheet matrix appears on your screen, as shown in Figure 6.5. If Cell A1 is not selected (marked with a bold outline):

2. Move the cross pointer to Cell A1 and click to select it.

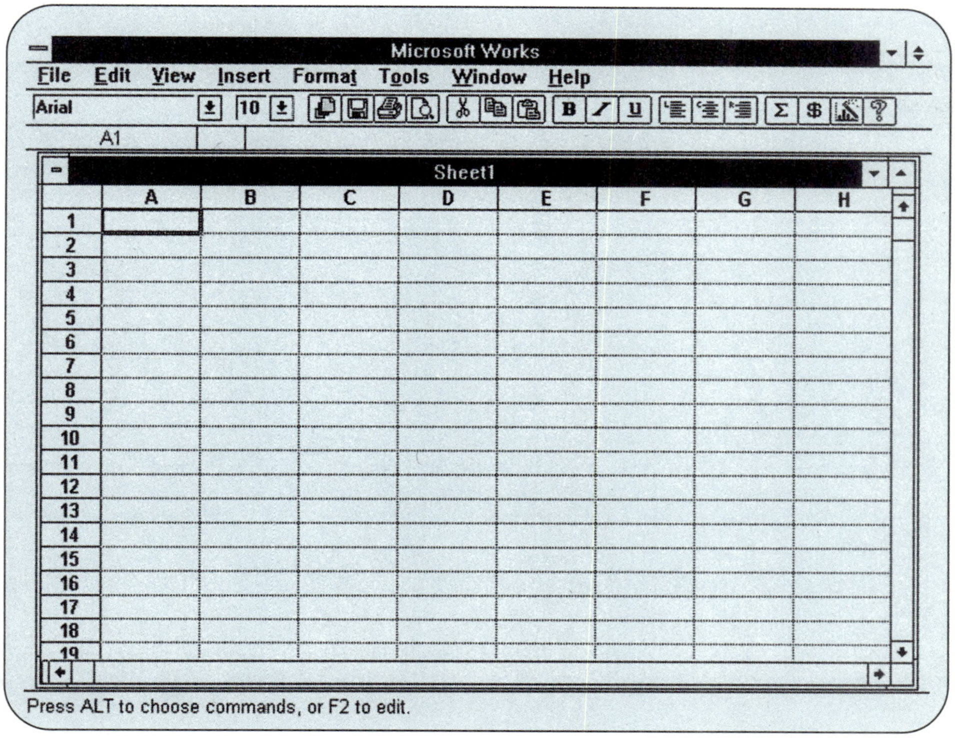

Figure 6.5

The Spreadsheet Matrix

3. Click on Format.

   The Format menu displays, as shown in Figure 6.6.

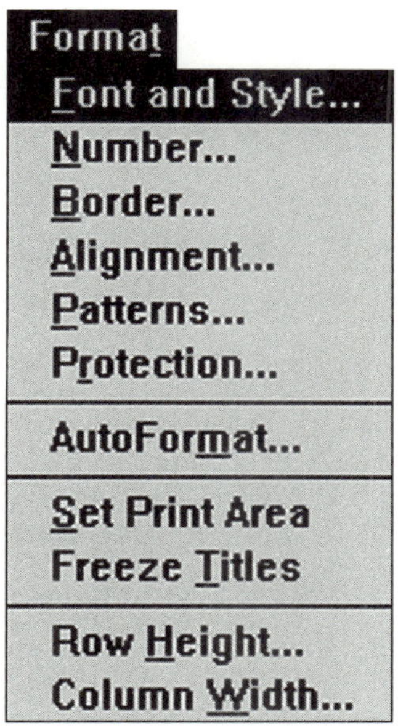

Figure 6.6

The Format Menu

4. Click on Font and Style.

   The Font and Style menu displays, as shown in Figure 6.7.

Figure 6.7

The Font and Style Menu

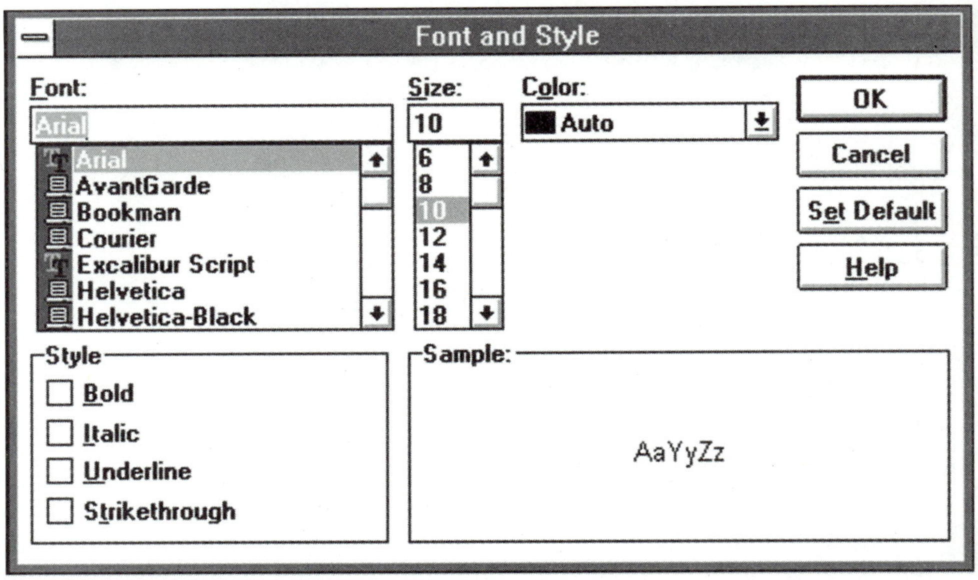

5. In the Font list box, click on the down arrow or drag the scroll bar to select a different font of your choice.
6. In the Size list box, click on 14, if it is available.
7. In the Style box, click on Bold.
8. Click on OK.

   You want to center the title across Columns A1 to E1 in the spreadsheet.
9. Click on Cell A1 and drag to select through E1.
10. Click on Format-Alignment.

    The Alignment option box displays, as shown in Figure 6.8.
11. Click on Center across selection.
12. Click on OK.
13. Deselect the columns by pressing the left arrow key once.
14. Type **Household Inventory List**

    The first letters are hidden as you type. To insert the title:
15. Click on OK.

    Your title should be centered.

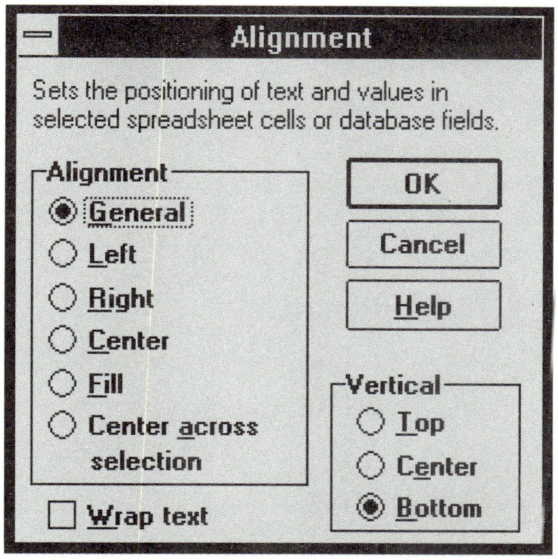

Figure 6.8

The Alignment Menu

16. Select Cell A2.
17. Type your first and last name, then press ENTER.
18. Center your name across Cells A2 to E2, as you did the title.

    To change the width of the first column:
19. Place the cross pointer in the first column (Cell A3) and click to select it.
20. Click on Format.
21. Click on Column Width.

    The Column Width dialog box displays, as shown in Figure 6.9.

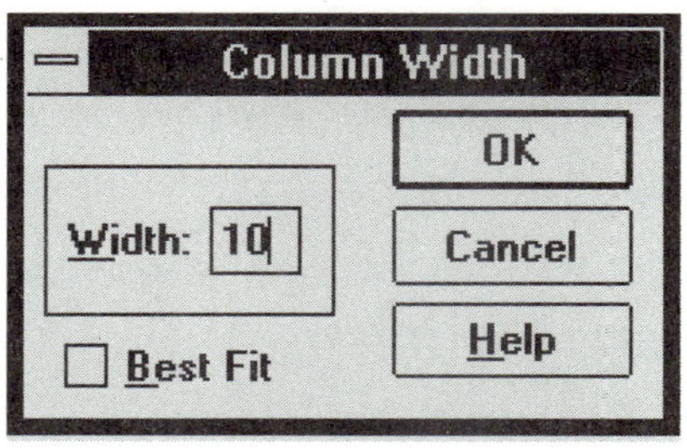

Figure 6.9

The Column Width Dialog Box

22. Type **20**
23. Click on OK.

    The first column is now 20 characters wide. Now enter the column headings:
24. Select Cell A4.

25. Type **Item**
26. Select Cell B4 (by pressing the right arrow key once).
27. Type **Cost**
28. Select Cell C4.
29. Type **Rep Cost** (short for *replacement cost*).
30. Select Cell E4.
31. Type **Difference**

    To center and bold your headings:

32. Select Cell A4 and press SHIFT + RIGHT ARROW to select all headings in Cells A4 to E4. (The first selected cell is white and rest are black.)
33. Click on the Center icon.
34. Click on the Bold icon.
35. Click outside the text to deselect it.

    You now want to save what you have done so far:

36. Click on File-Save As.

    The Save As dialog box displays, with the title Sheet1 in the name text box. Beginning with a floppy drive designation, if needed:

37. Type **houseinv**

    Works adds the extension .wks.

38. Click on OK.

    To enter data into the spreadsheet:

39. Select Cell A6.
40. Type **Sony Camcorder**
41. Press RIGHT ARROW once (or TAB) to Cell B6.
42. Type **780**
43. Press RIGHT ARROW once (or TAB) to Cell C6.
44. Type **1000**
45. Press RIGHT ARROW twice (or TAB) to Cell E6.

    You want to enter a formula that will calculate the difference between the item's original cost and its replacement cost. You also want to insert this formula only once, and then copy it down the column for later entries, but you don't know how to enter a formula in *Works*. See if the Help function can explain.

46. Click on Help.

    The Help menu displays, as shown in Figure 6.10.

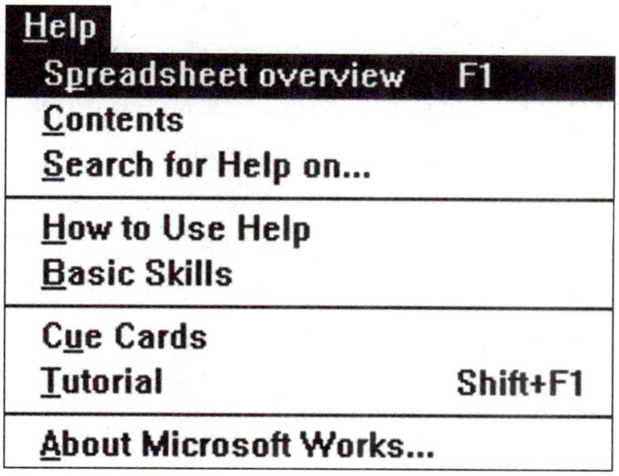

Figure 6.10

The Help Menu

47. Click on Contents.

    The Help Contents menu displays, as shown in Figure 6.11. In the command button bar:

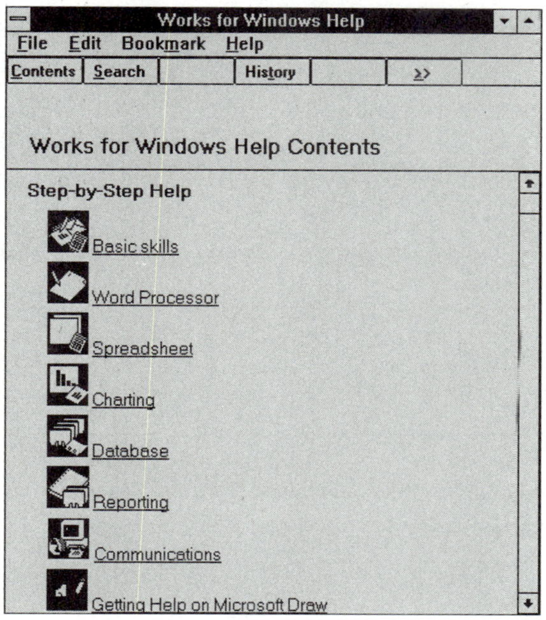

Figure 6.11

The Help Contents Menu

48. Click on Search.
49. In the text box, type **formulas**
50. Click on Show Topics.
51. In the Select a Topic window, click on Formulas SS.

52. Click on Go To.

    The Formulas help guide displays.

53. In the Help menu bar, click on File-Print Topic.
54. Click on File-Exit to exit Help.

    You can click outside the Help screen to remove it; however, it remains open on the desktop and takes up memory.

The Help information instructs you to do the following to create a formula:

- Select the cell in which the formula is to appear.
- Type =
- Type the formula.
- Click on OK.

Works displays the formula in the formula bar and the result of the formula in the selected cell. You want to enter a formula to subtract the replacement cost (C6) from the cost (B6):

55. In Cell E6, type **=B6-C6** (in either upper or lower case).
56. Click on OK.

The difference for the first row of your spreadsheet is a -220; in other words, the replacement cost is higher than the original cost. Notice that the result of the formula is all that appears in the worksheet; the formula itself is visible only in the formula bar at the top, left-hand corner of the screen when the cursor is located on cell E6. On you own, fill in the data for the items shown in Table 6.2. *Do not fill in the Difference column, yet.* You will do that later by copying the formula.

Table 6.2

Item	Cost	Rep Cost	Difference
IBM PS/2	3795	2800	
Pool table	4500	5495	
Stamp collection	300	1200	
Coin collection	50	2000	
Elvis items	700	12000	
Honda lawnmower	1000	1200	
Ham radio	1299	1500	
Jade figurine	200	800	
Jewelry	2000	4000	

Do not include commas or dollar signs when you enter the numbers. If you want dollar signs, commas, percentage signs, etc., you will have the opportunity to add them later with the Format-Number command. You can TAB or press the arrow keys to go from cell to cell; HOME takes you to the first cell in a row, and END takes you to the last cell in a row. CTRL+HOME takes you to the beginning of the worksheet, and CTRL+END takes you to the end of the worksheet.

When you have finished entering the data, you need to save the worksheet again:

57. Click on the Save icon.

    You will now total the second and third columns.

58. Select Cell A17.
59. Click on the Bold icon.
60. Press the SPACEBAR three times and type **Total**
61. Select Cell B17.

    Now you want to enter the function into the proper cell (Recall that a function is a specific formula, such as average, abbreviated *AVG*, sum several cells, abbreviated *SUM*, and so on.)

62. Type **=SUM(B6:B15)**

    Note: You could also click on the autosum icon and then press the ENTER key or click on the ENTER box in the formula bar.

63. Press ENTER.

    The total, 14624, is shown.

64. Select Cells B17 through C17.
65. Click on Edit.

    The Edit menu displays, as shown in Figure 6.12.

66. Click on Fill Right.

    The total of 31995 displays on the screen. On your own, use the Fill Down command in the Edit menu to copy the difference formula to the rest of the cells in Column E. Don't forget to select Cells E6 through E15.

67. Save the spreadsheet again, and print, but do not close.

Figure 6.12

The Edit Menu

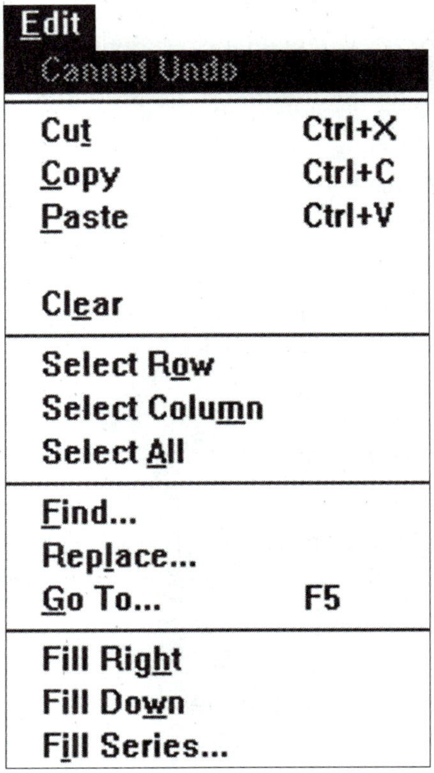

Saving and Printing Spreadsheets

In the tutorial you just completed, you designed a small, simple spreadsheet that can easily fit across a single 8.5-by-11 inch piece of paper. Soon you will need to break up your displayed spreadsheet and print it on several different pages, or change the printout to condensed print. Perhaps you will want to add headers and footers. It is even possible to print spreadsheets sideways. All of these printing controls help you produce a more readable, understandable spreadsheet. You will learn in the next chapter how to enhance your printed spreadsheets, and in Chapter 8 how to graph them, as well.

Until your work is saved to a spreadsheet file, it exists only in memory. Once it is saved to disk, *Works* automatically gives it the .wks extension and it becomes a file. That file must be retrieved into the worksheet, or scratch pad, to be modified. The file includes print controls and graphs, as well as the data you enter. These are saved along with the file and are retrieved with it when you open an existing spreadsheet. They do not exist separately. Therefore, remember to save the spreadsheet once again after you make any changes such as adding headers, changing to condensed print, or defining graphs, as you will do in Chapter 8.

Sorting Rows

A spreadsheet can perform many database-related tasks. You cannot query, or question, a spreadsheet in *Works*, as you can in *Lotus 1-2-3*, but you can look up and sort, or rearrange, rows of cells. Sorting is one of the more popular advanced procedures available with the spreadsheet application in *Works*.

If you wish to rearrange cells in numerical or alphabetical order, you can do so with the Sort Rows command. You can even sort within another sort, if you wish. You sort rows according to the contents of columns. You can sort on up to three columns, in either **ascending order** (A to Z or 0 to 9) or **descending order** (backward, from Z to A or 9 to 0).

To sort cells in a spreadsheet:

- Position the cross bar at the row and column to sort.
- Click on Tools-Sort Rows.
- The selected column letter is in the first sort choice.
- If this is correct, TAB to Ascend or Descend and select.
- Move to the second and third column choices, if desired.
- Repeat the Column and Order choices.
- Click on OK to complete the command.

The selected rows will be rearranged. This is especially handy for grouping names into alphabetical order, or putting numbers, such as salary rates, into consecutive order. You will learn many more methods of manipulating data when you study the database tool of *Works*. However, sorting in a spreadsheet allows you to maintain a primarily mathematical file and still perform some database functions.

It is possible to sort some columns and not others. If you want to reorder the information in a range of cells, you should select the entire area to be sorted before performing the sort.

You have been exposed to a small part of the complex and powerful world of spreadsheets. As with all of the applications, the more you work with spreadsheets the more proficient you will become. The growth in popularity of this tool for "what if" analysis is not surprising. It has given the layman the tools of the professional in a simple and easily mastered form.

Hierarchy and Order of Operations

Spreadsheets perform calculations according to the rules of order shown in Table 6.3. This **hierarchy of operations** is not unique to *Works*; all spreadsheet programs follow the same general rules, which are universal in the mathematics world. Refer to Table 6.3 and try to determine why the following formulas will yield different answers:

=B1+B2*.06　　　　=(B1+B2)*.06

Table 6.3 Hierarchy of Mathematical Operations

Operator		Order of Evaluation
()	Parentheses	First
^	Exponent	Second
*	Multiplication	Third
/	Division	Third
+	Addition	Fourth
-	Subtraction	Fourth
=	Equals	Fifth

As you can see, you must be very careful when entering formulas and functions. The computer will do exactly what you tell it to do, whether that is what you meant or not.

In spreadsheets, every formula and function must be preceded by an operator. In *Works*, this is the same symbol for both formulas and functions, the equals (=) sign. If you do not precede a formula or function with an equals sign, the *Works* program will store what you are entering as text instead of as a formula, because the first letter is text, not a value. Obviously, no calculation can take place with text. Omitting the equals sign from a formula is a very common error among beginning users of spreadsheets.

If your spreadsheet does not yield the results you expect, verify that you followed the hierarchy of operations and that you preceded each formula with an equals sign. Keeping these rules in mind can help you **debug**, or find the mistakes in, your spreadsheets.

SPREADSHEET TUTORIAL NO. 2

You have thought of one more item to add to your insurance spreadsheet. You want to sort the items alphabetically, shade the total row, and enter a footer with your name.

1. Click on Cell A8.
2. Click on Insert.

   The Insert menu displays, as shown in Figure 6.13.
3. Click on Row/Column.

   The Row/Column option box displays.
4. Click on Row-OK.

   A blank row is added, beginning in Cell A8.
5. Add the item **GE VCR**, cost **500**, rep cost **300**

   The formula will not appear in Cell E8.

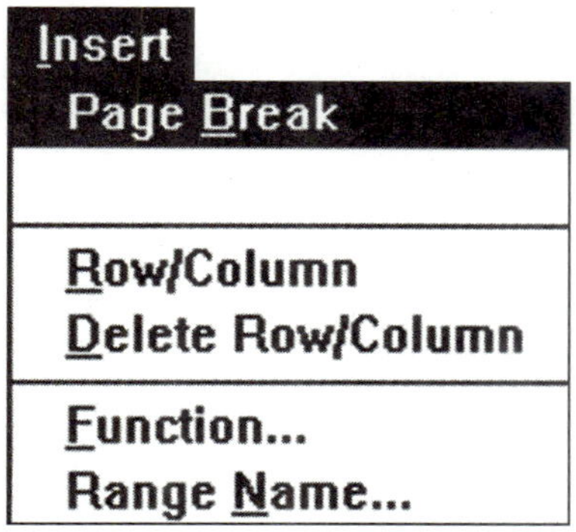

Figure 6.13

The Insert Menu

6. Select Cells E7 and E8 and click on Edit-Fill Down.

   Notice that the totals changed automatically to reflect the addition. To sort the items alphabetically:
7. Select the items (Cells A6 through 16).
8. Click on Tools.

   The Tools menu displays, as shown in Figure 6.14.

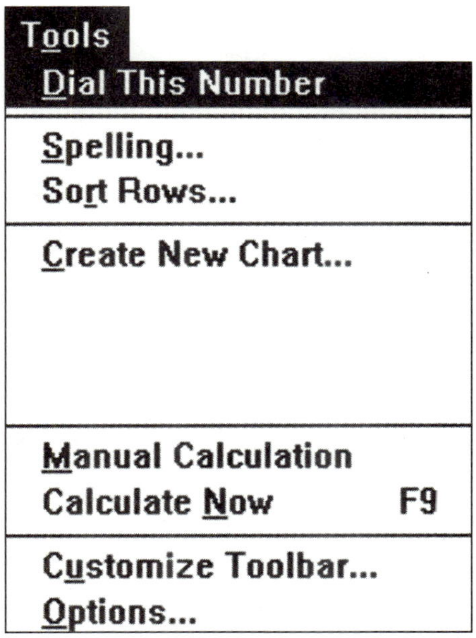

Figure 6.14

The Tools Menu

9. Click on Sort Rows.

   The Sort Rows dialog box displays, in Figure 6.15.
10. If not shown, type **A** in the 1st Column text box and click on Ascend A.

Figure 6.15

The Sort Rows Dialog Box

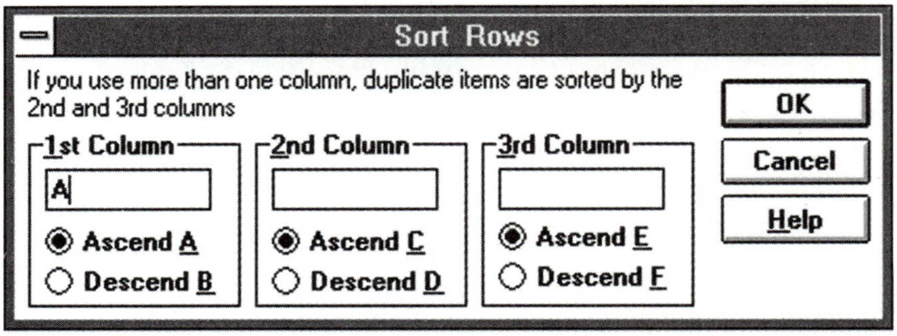

11. Click on OK.

    The items are arranged in alphabetical order. To shade the total cells:

12. Select Cells A18 to C18.
13. Click on Format-Patterns.

    The Pattern dialog box displays.

14. In the Pattern box, click on the down arrow once to see a partial list of available patterns.
15. Click on the pattern that is presently second from the bottom.

    Your screen should look similar to that in Figure 6.16.

Figure 6.16

The Patterns Dialog Box

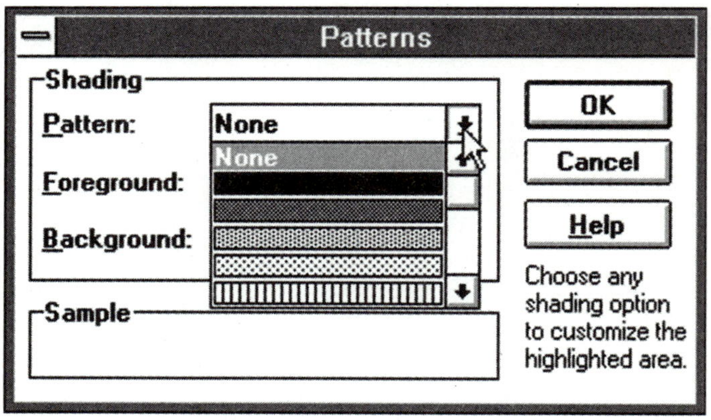

16. Click on OK.

    To enter a footer with your name for future assignments:

17. Click on View-Headers and Footers.
18. In the Footer text box type **&Lyour name**

19. Click on OK.

    When printed, your name will be aligned on the left margin. Note: You can add a header to your work instead of a footer, if desired.

20. Save your file.

    You want to print two copies of the spreadsheet.

21. Click on File-Print.

    The Print menu displays as shown in Figure 6.17.

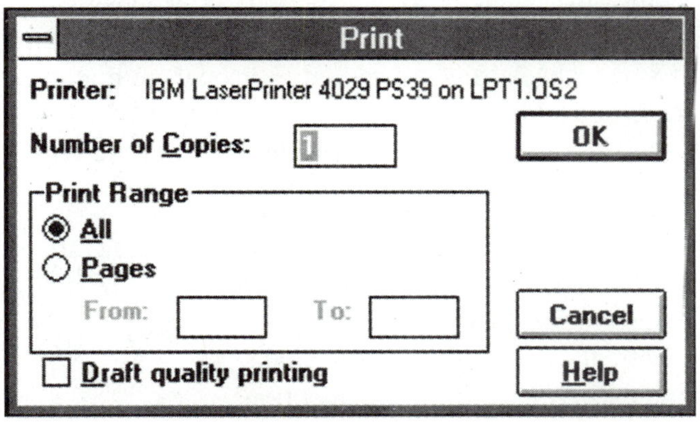

Figure 6.17

The Print Menu

22. In the Number of Copies text box type **2**
23. Click on OK.

    Your document should look similar to that in Figure 6.18.

24. Close and exit *Works*.

Figure 6.18

Sample Spreadsheet Document

Household Inventory List

First Last Name

Item	Cost	Rep Cost	Difference
Coin collection	50	2000	-1950
Elvis items	700	12000	-11300
GE VCR	500	300	200
Ham radio	1299	1500	-201
Honda lawnmower	1000	1200	-200
IBM PS/2	3795	2800	995
Jade figurine	200	800	-600
Jewelry	2000	4000	-2000
Pool table	4500	5495	-995
Sony Camcorder	780	1000	-220
Stamp collection	300	1200	-900
Total	**15124**	**32295**	

Chapter Summary

Spreadsheets are an application tool to help you organize, calculate, and present numerical information. A spreadsheet is a matrix organized into columns and rows that contain labels, values, or formulas (including functions). By supporting "what-if" analysis, spreadsheets help predict future developments electronically without the tedium of manually repeating complex mathematical operations with pencil and paper.

Spreadsheets have long been used in business and government, by professionals, managers, sales and accounting personnel, and support staff.

Spreadsheets are created by personal computer users for everything from home budgets to forecasting stock dividends. Spreadsheets that are carefully designed and meticulously examined after they are completed can help solve many complex problems.

KEY TERMS

absolute reference
alphanumeric data
argument
automatic calculation
autosum
cell
charting
clear
column
constant
cross bar
debug
format
formula
function
hierarchy of operations
home area
label
macro
manual calculation
math coprocessor
matrix
operand
operator
parameter
range
recalculate
relative reference
row
template
value
worksheet

REVIEW QUESTIONS

1. Electronic spreadsheets have become the most popular microcomputer decision support tool. Explain the reason(s) for this.
2. Explain the meaning of "what if" analysis as it applies to spreadsheets.
3. Name five uses for spreadsheets that were listed in this chapter. Add three more uses of your own.
4. Briefly recall the history of spreadsheets.
5. How does stand-alone spreadsheet software compare with the *Works* spreadsheet: (a) for personal use, and (b) for business use?
6. List and briefly define the major spreadsheet elements.
7. What is the primary difference between a formula and a function?
8. Most spreadsheets have eight common features. Name any five of these.

9. Explain the slogan *GIGO* as it pertains to spreadsheet construction.
10. What is the difference between an absolute and a relative reference?
11. The spreadsheet toolbar presents a number of standard icons. List and briefly define the purposes of any six of them.
12. What is the default column width in a *Works* spreadsheet?
13. What character is displayed in a cell that is too small to hold the data entered in it?
14. Explain how the *Works* program distinguishes between a formula and text in a cell.
15. What does the cursor look like in the spreadsheet? Is this the same as or different from its appearance in a word processor document?
16. When you selected text in the word processor, the selected text was highlighted. How do selected cells appear in the spreadsheet?
17. Text is left-aligned and numbers and dates are right-aligned. Explain what this means.
18. Define the concept of a range.
19. Explain how a range is defined in *Works.*
20. You see the word *CIRC* displayed on the status line. What caused this to occur? What action should you take to correct the problem?
21. What is the difference between manual and automatic calculation?
22. When might you want to set the spreadsheet to calculate manually rather than automatically?
23. Testing a spreadsheet is very important. Review the reason(s) for this.
24. Of what use is the ability to sort spreadsheet rows? How is this done?
25. Apply the hierarchy of operations rules to the following formula and list the operations that occur first, second, third, and so on: =A4^2*B4-C4+(D4-E4)/2.

SOFTWARE EXERCISES

Exercise 6.1

1. Make arrangements with your instructor to familiarize yourself with the *Works* spreadsheet tutorial.
2. Make notes about what was covered in each of the following sections:
   (a) Introducing the spreadsheet
   (b) Entering text and numbers

Use *Works 3.0 for Windows* word processor module to type your notes about what you learned.

3. Save your work as tutsp6.
4. Print tutsp6.wps.
5. Close tutsp6.wps and exit *Works*.

Exercise 6.2

1. Construct a spreadsheet from the data presented in Table 6.4; use formulas for total income and total outlay.

Table 6.4

CASH FLOW	
INCOME	
Wages, salary, and commissions	26950
Dividends and interest	1600
Child support and alimony	0
Annuities, pensions, and Social Security	0
Rents	0
Other	100
TOTAL INCOME	28650
OUTLAY	
Taxes	6130
Housing	5400
Food	5000
Clothing	600
Transportation	4980
Utilities	600
Insurance	1140
Education	600
Child care	0
Entertainment	1200
Vacations	3000
Professional fees	0
Gifts, donations	0
Miscellaneous	0
Savings	0
TOTAL OUTLAY	28650

2. Make the following headings bold: INCOME, TOTAL INCOME, OUTLAY, TOTAL OUTLAY.
3. Add a column to the outlay section of the spreadsheet entitled "Outlay as a % of Income." Put this heading on two lines and change the column width to 11.
4. Enter a formula into the new column on the outlay row for Taxes to compute the percentage of outlay to income (taxes/total income).
5. Copy this formula down through the rest of the new percentage columns.
6. Format all dollar amounts with commas and zero decimal places and all percentages with percent signs and two decimal places.
7. Format the Total Income and Total Outlay columns with a light colored pattern of your choice.
8. Save the spreadsheet as cashflo.
9. Print the cashflo.wks spreadsheet.
10. Click on Formulas from the View menu to show the formulas.
11. Print cashflo.wks again.
12. Click on Formulas from the View menu to hide the formulas.
13. Close cashflo.wks and exit *Works.*

Exercise 6.3

1. Open cashflo.wks, or complete Exercise 6.2 before continuing.
2. You are going to substitute your own data for the data given for the first quarter of the year.
3. Add rows as needed in the income and outlay sections so that the spreadsheet fits your own situation.
4. Add the following heading in row one: CASH FLOW DATA FOR THE FIRST QUARTER; use the Format, Alignment, Center across Selection command to center your heading.
5. Add the following heading in row two: your name and the current date; use the Format, Alignment, Center across Selection command to center your heading.
6. Clear all the data in the column headed "Outlay as a Percentage of Income."
7. Leave the third row blank.
8. Put the following headings into Cells A4, B4, C4, D4, and E4: ITEM, JANUARY, FEBRUARY, MARCH, TOTAL; center align these headings.

9. Enter your own data for the months of January, February, and March.
10. Total each row by quarter.
11. Format all numerical cells as currency with no decimal places.
12. Save the spreadsheet as cashflo1.
13. Print cashflo1.wks.
14. Click on Formulas from the View menu to show the spreadsheet's formulas.
15. Print cashflo1.wks. again.
16. Click on Formulas from the View menu to hide the formulas.
17. Close cashflo1.wks and exit *Works*.

Exercise 6.4

1. Open cashflo.wks, or complete Exercise 6.2 before continuing.
2. Add two columns to the outlay section of the spreadsheet. The first one will show the average household's percentage outlay for various categories for a single person, age 25 with $30,000 in income, as shown in Step 3. The second column will show the dollar amount of the total $30,000 income that goes for taxes, housing, and so on.
3. Enter the following data for the first new column: Taxes—33%; Housing—15; Food—8; Clothing—4; Transportation—9; Utilities—3; Insurance—9; Education—3; Child care—0; Entertainment—4; Vacations—3; Professional fees—2; Gifts, donations—2; Miscellaneous—5; Savings—0; Total—100%.
4. Add a third new column to the outlay section.
5. Enter a formula into the new column on the outlay row for taxes to compute the difference between your percentage outlay and the average percentage outlay.
6. Copy this formula down through the rest of the Difference columns.
7. Format all dollar amounts with commas and zero decimal places; format all percentages with percent signs and two decimal places.
8. Add the following title on line 2: "My Cash Flow compared with a Single Twenty-five year olds Cash Flow"
9. Close the format, alignment command to center the existing heading "Outlay as a % of Income" across cells D16 through E17.
10. Add the following bold headings to cells D18, E18, F18, and G18 respectively: MINE, AVERAGE, DIFFERENCE, % DIFFERENCE.
11. Save the spreadsheet as cashflo2.
12. Print cashflo2.wks.

13. Click on Formulas from the View menu to show the formulas.
14. Print cashflo2.wks again.
15. Click on Formulas from the View menu to hide the formulas.
16. Close cashflo2.wks and exit *Works*.

Exercise 6.5

1. Open the netwrth.wks spreadsheet file on the student data diskette.
2. Make the following headings bold: NET WORTH FOR, TOTAL ASSETS, TOTAL LIABILITIES, LAST YEAR, and THIS YEAR.
3. Underline the following headings: Cash and Equivalents, Personal Property, Real Estate, Investments, Current Bills, Amount Owed on Loans, Taxes Due, and Other.
4. Add your name and the current date in Cells C3 and C4, respectively.
5. In Cell E6, add the bold title DIFFERENCE.
6. Subtract last year's data from this year's and put the result in Column E.
7. Format all numbers as currency with no decimal places.
8. Save the spreadsheet as netwrth1.
9. Print the netwrth1.wks spreadsheet.
10. Click on Formulas from the View menu to show the formulas.
11. Print netwrth1.wks again.
12. Click on Formulas from the View menu to hide the formulas.
13. Close netwrth1.wks and exit *Works*.

Exercise 6.6

1. Open the netwrth.wks spreadsheet file on the student data diskette.
2. Substitute your own data for the data given. Add or delete rows under ASSETS and LIABILITIES as needed to make the spreadsheet fit your situation.
3. Put your name and the function =NOW() in Cells C3 and C4, respectively. Note: =NOW() is a function that will print a number that represents the current date every time the spreadsheet is run.
4. With the date cell selected, format the contents as a date, which prints the day, month, and year as numbers separated slashes (/).
5. Add two columns to the right of the existing spreadsheet. Title the first column CHANGE and the second column % CHANGE.
6. Enter into the CHANGE column a formula that subtracts the amount in the LAST YEAR column from the amount in the THIS YEAR column.

7. Copy this formula down to the appropriate cells in the CHANGE column.
8. Enter into the % CHANGE column a formula that computes the percentage change from last year to this year.
9. Copy this formula down to the appropriate cells in the PERCENTAGE CHANGE column.
10. Format all dollar amounts with commas, and zero decimal places and all percentages with percent signs and two decimal places.
11. Save the spreadsheet as netwrth2.
12. Print netwrth2.wks.
13. Click on Formulas from the View menu to show the formulas.
14. Print netwrth2.wks again.
15. Click on Formulas from the View menu to hide the formulas.
16. Close netwrth2.wks and exit *Works*.

Exercise 6.7

1. Choose Use a Template from the Startup menu. Open the Mortgage and Loan Analysis form from the Personal Finances, AutoStart Personal template group.
2. Assume that you want to borrow $12,400 for three years to finance a new car and that the interest rate is 8 percent. You will make 12 payments each year. Use the numerical form of the current month/year for the start date.
3. Complete the template by following the directions given in the cue card that accompanies this template. (Note: Click on Help, Cue Cards if the cue card is not showing.)
4. Format the dollar amount fields as currency with two decimal places.
5. Select Cells D2 through G2; add the following to the selected row: **For Your Name**
6. Center For Your Name across the selection.
7. Print the template.
8. Save your work as morttem.
9. Close morttem.wks and exit *Works*.

Exercise 6.8

1. Open houseinv.wks from the tutorial in this chapter.
2. Add the following items, costs, and replacement values to houseinv.wks: Bassett bedroom suite, 2500, 4000; Oak computer disk, 650, 850; Brass table lamp, 150, 180; Leather office chair, 1050, 1295; Stonehill living room set, 3500, 4500.

3. Complete the spreadsheet by moving or copying formulas as needed.
4. Sort the items in the spreadsheet into descending order by difference.
5. Format the dollar amounts as currency with no decimal places.
6. Save as inventr1.
7. Print inventr1.wks.
8. Click on Formulas from the View menu to show the formulas.
9. Print inventr1.wks again.
10. Click on Formulas from the View menu to hide the formulas.
11. Close inventr1.wks and exit *Works*.

Exercise 6.9

1. Construct a spreadsheet that keeps track of your monthly allowance and what you spent it on for the past three months. Assume you recive $100 per month, or use your actual allowance, if it is different for $100. Use your actual expenditures, or invent some.
2. Put an appropriate title at the top of the spreadsheet along with your name, the date (with the month written out in full) and the year for which you are keeping a record.
3. Center and bold the headings over Columns A through E.
4. Leave two blank rows after the date and year row.
5. Add the following subheadings to Columns A, B, C, D, and E, respectively: EXPENDITURES, MONTH1, MONTH2, MONTH3, TOTAL. Note: Change MONTH1, MONTH2, and MONTH3 to the previous three months from the date of the spreadsheet and widen the columns as necessary.
6. Total each row and column.
7. Shade the column totals for each month.
8. Format the dollar amounts as currency with two decimal places.
9. Save the spreadsheet as allowanc.
10. Print allowanc.wks.
11. Click on Formulas from the View menu to show the formulas.
12. Print allowanc.wks again.
13. Click on Formulas from the View menu to hide the formulas.
14. Close allowanc.wks and exit *Works*.

Exercise 6.10

1. Construct a spreadsheet that keeps a record of the deposits made and the checks written on your checking account for one month. Provide a means to keep a running balance.
2. Put an appropriate title at the top of the spreadsheet along with your name and the month and year for which you are keeping a record.
3. Save the spreadsheet as currbal.
4. Print currbal.wks.
5. Click on Formulas from the View menu to show the formulas.
6. Print currbal.wks again.
7. Click on Formulas from the View menu to hide the formulas.
8. Close currbal.wks and exit *Works*.

Exercise 6.11

1. Construct a spreadsheet that records 12 courses you have taken to date along with numbers that represent the grades you received. Use 4 for A grades, 3 for B grades, 2 for C grades, 1 for D grades, and 0 for Fs. Also compute your cumulative GPA for these courses.
2. Put an appropriate title at the top of the spreadsheet along with your name and the current date.
3. Save the spreadsheet as gpa.
4. Print gpa.wks.
5. Click on Formulas from the View menu to show the formulas.
6. Print gpa.wks again.
7. Click on Formulas from the View menu to hide the formulas.
8. Close gpa.wks and exit *Works*.

Chapter 7

More on Spreadsheets

Objectives

After studying this chapter you will be able to:

- *Explain the function of ranges and range names*
- *Recall the reason for hiding cells*
- *List the spreadsheet formats available in* Works
- *Describe the difference between printing spreadsheets in landscape mode and portrait mode*
- *Describe several different ways to view large spreadsheets*
- *Recognize when to use a function*
- *Demonstrate how to print a selected area of a spreadsheet*
- *Explain how to protect cell contents*
- *Explain why cell contents might need protection*
- *Apply the intermediate and advanced spreadsheet concepts in this chapter to the solutions of typical spreadsheet problems*

As the most popular decision support application for the personal computer, spreadsheets have advanced from use as simple budget or checkbook summaries to serve a wide variety of more sophisticated uses. Many of these, such as "what if" analysis of projected situations, were originally developed for business. With only an elementary knowledge of mathematical operations, however, the personal computer user can take advantage of the many benefits of spreadsheets. For example, larger spreadsheets with comparison information can be created and updated annually. Net income statements, profit and loss statements, and even tax returns can be prepared on spreadsheets. Investment portfolio records can be kept on spreadsheets, as well.

Now that you have mastered some of the basics of constructing a spreadsheet and learned how to plan one properly, you can move on to study the details that will help you construct more useful spreadsheets. We will not cover all of the options that spreadsheet software offers; that is a very rich field, indeed. If you will be using the spreadsheet application of *Works* more than any other application, or if you will be moving to an independent spreadsheet application like *Lotus 1-2-3*, you can explore the more advanced techniques on your own after taking these intermediate steps.

Simple spreadsheets can help organize your personal finances and help keep your balances current.

Working with Ranges

In the last chapter, you learned that a range is a group of cells. A range can contain anything from one cell, to a single row or column, to a larger, rectangular block of cells. Spreadsheet users refer to ranges by the addresses of their corners, from the upper, left-hand cell to the lower, right-hand cell. Thus B3 is a range; so is B1 through B20, which is a column of cells. A3 to M3 is a range composed of a row across several columns. A3:M20 is also a range; it is a block of cells that extends both vertically and horizontally. The naming of ranges is a topic we will discuss a little later.

Selection for Further Action

In any spreadsheet program, you must select a cell or range of cells in order to carry out further action. A program may require you to select the range after you issue the editing command. In *Works*, however, you must often select cells before you issue a command.

You select cells for further action by highlighting them. To do this, you can use the mouse to click and drag, you can select an entire row or column by clicking on its number or letter, or you can use the Select command in the Edit menu. You can also select cells using the F8 key, or you can highlight a range of cells by pressing the SHIFT key plus an arrow key. You can choose to select only certain cells, select by row or by column, or select the entire worksheet with the All command. The Edit menu also offers the **Go To** option (activated by the F5 key).

To access Select from the Edit menu:

- Click on Edit-Select Row or Select Column.

You may also select cells by clicking on the first cell of the intended range and dragging the mouse until the block is highlighted. This is similar to "draw" techniques in other spreadsheet programs. The first, leftmost cell will not be highlighted; instead, a border will indicate that it is the first cell in the range. Figure 7.1 shows a selected range.

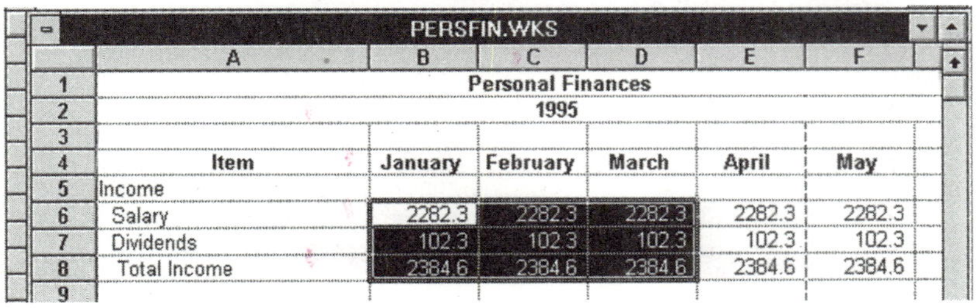

Figure 7.1

Example of a Selected Range

Inserting, Formatting, Moving, and Copying

When you wish to insert another row or column into your spreadsheet, you must select where to add the cells. *Works*, like other spreadsheet programs, always inserts rows and columns above and to the left of a selected area. After selecting a location by the procedure just described, you may insert as many rows or columns as you need. Recall that, when you inserted rows and columns in the last chapter, you learned not to worry about changing cell references in formulas and functions in the subsequent cells because *Works* adjusts them automatically relative to their new locations.

To insert a row:

- Click to the right of and below the spot of insertion.
- Click on Insert-Row/Column.
- Click on Row or Column.
- Click on OK.

A new, empty row or column appears and the subsequent rows or columns are renumbered

Formatting Ranges One purpose for which you may select a range of cells is to change their formats, or appearances. You have already changed the width of a cell from the Format menu. We will talk about the other choices offered by the Format menu in the next section of this chapter. For now, just remember that you must select the range before you can change the cell's format.

Moving Ranges When you move information from one place to another, *Works* adjusts all references to the moved cells. Moving spreadsheet ranges is similar to moving text in a word processor. You can copy the material, or you can cut it to the clipboard and paste it elsewhere, if you wish. The first technique replicates material; the second relocates it. You first select the range you wish to move; you then invoke the Edit-Cut or Edit-Copy commands. The material enters the clipboard buffer. To paste it, place the cursor at the desired location and issue an Edit-Paste command.

Relocating requires a Cut command. To move a cell or range:

- Select the original cell(s) or range(s).
- Click on Edit-Cut, or press CTRL + X.
- Select the target cell(s) or range(s).
- Click on Edit-Paste, or press CTRL + V.

To duplicate a column or row:

- Select the original column(s) or row(s).
- Select Edit-Copy, or press CTRL + C.
- Select the target column(s) or row(s).
- Click on Edit-Paste, or press CTRL + V.

Copying Cells and Ranges You can perform several different types of copy processes with spreadsheets. With the simple copy command, you can copy whatever is in the cell, either text, a formula, a function, or a value that you have entered. You performed a simple copy in the last chapter.

Sometimes, however, you will want to copy only a value produced by a formula or function in a cell. You can do this with the Edit-Paste Special command. This special copy procedure can carry cell contents between separate spreadsheets, and even between applications, such as from the spreadsheet to a word processing document. (To do this, you use the Window command. Chapter 13 concentrates on these external moves.)

You can copy the contents of cells to nonadjacent locations, or you can copy to the right or downward to adjacent locations. This is the Fill command. The procedure for a fill to adjacent cells is:

- Select the cell, column, or row you wish to duplicate.
- Extend the selection to the right or downward to include the cells to be repeated.
- Click on Edit-Fill Right or Fill Down.

Take care not to select an entire column or row when you intend to paste many fewer cells. *Works* will do exactly what you command it to do. As was noted before if you select a whole column or row, and then Fill Right or Fill Down, the entire spreadsheet matrix will be filled with the highlighted formula or value. Almost always, you wish to fill just a portion of the matrix.

To immediately repeat a copy:

- Select the next cell or range where you want information to appear.
- Press CTRL + V.

If you wish to copy the range to another open worksheet, use the above procedure, then:

- From the Window menu, select the name of the open file where you will place the copied cells.
- Select the cell or range where you want the copied information to appear.
- Click on Edit-Paste.

Your range is copied to the receiving worksheet, and you may then return to the source worksheet:

- Click on Window.
- Click on the worksheet to which you want to return.

As we mentioned, you may frequently wish to copy the results of formulas in a range of cells, or values, and not the underlying formulas or functions. For example, if you are importing figures from one spreadsheet to another, you probably will not want the formulas or functions from the original location, but only the values that those calculations produced. In this case, you copy with the Paste Special command:

- Select the range you wish to copy.
- Select Edit-Cut or Copy.
- Select the cells in which to place information.
- Click on Paste Special.
- An option box appears.
- Select Values only.
- Click on OK.

Notice that you can also add values in the clipboard to or subtract them from the values present in the target cells. A running total between two different spreadsheets can be created in this way. Figure 7.2 shows the Paste Special option box.

Figure 7.2

The Paste Special Option Box

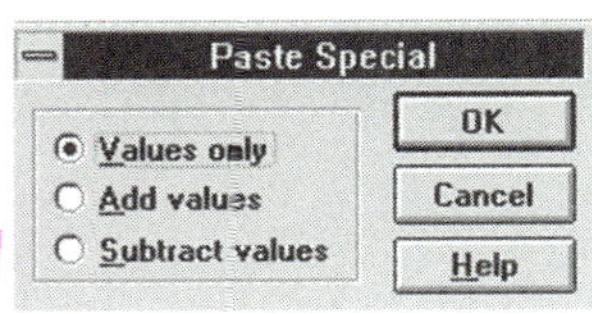

When copying and moving, the destination does not matter; *Works* will adjust the addresses of the target worksheet accordingly. Copying cells relative to their locations means that you can construct a column full of intricate formulas and functions, and then simply copy those same formulas and functions to the rest of your spreadsheet. This is one of the true time-savers built into all spreadsheet programs. In addition, copying or moving the values resulting from formulas to another location, instead of creating new formulas gives you even more flexibility.

Naming Ranges in a Spreadsheet

By now, you should have a good idea of what a range is and how to select a range for future action. Spreadsheets also allow you to assign a **range name** and then use that name instead of specific addresses in your commands. In this way, you can go to a precise location on a spreadsheet and set a specific range for printing, or use that range in formulas and functions, without having to remember the specific addresses of the chosen cells. This feature simplifies editing and saves a great deal of time. (In this text, we will not cover the construction of **macros** in spreadsheets. They allow you to save strings of keystrokes; however, you must know how to name a range in order to construct a macro.)

Assigning a name to a range can be very helpful. If you assign the name *Expenses* to a range of cells, in subsequent commands you can refer to that range by name instead of having to remember, let's say, A3:F10. You can, for example, set the print area in the Print menu by that name instead of by addresses. If you want to go directly to the named section of your spreadsheet, you can press the F5 function key and respond with the word *Expenses*, and your cursor will immediately go to the chosen location. You never have to scroll to that area of the worksheet, find out the addresses, and then return and type in those addresses in order to complete a command.

Naming ranges of cells is also a method of self-documentation. If you use range names, instead of actual cell addresses, in formulas and functions your spreadsheet will be much clearer. You will not forget what you were doing if you pick up that same spreadsheet next month, or even next year. For example, the formulas =Income - Expenses or =SUM (Expenses) is much clearer than =B14 - F11 or =SUM(F1:F10). Incidently, if you cannot remember what you named a range, you can always issue the Edit-Go To command and review the names of your ranges in the Names option box. They will all be listed, and you can select the one you want.

To name a range:

- Select the range.
- Click on Insert-Range Name.
- Type a name from 1 to 15 characters in length.
- Click on OK.

You may also delete range names through the Name option box. Suppose that you no longer want to identify a block of cells with a certain name, have misspelled the name, or want to delete the name of the range for any other reason. All you need to do is select the Delete option in the Name option box, which lists all of the range names that you have defined for the current spreadsheet, together with the cells that each named range includes. To delete a range name:

- Click on Insert-Range Name.
- Select the name in the Name option box.
- Click on the Delete option.
- Click on OK.

Before you delete the name of a range, make sure that none of your existing formulas, functions, print areas, and so forth contain the name of the range you are deleting: if they do, deleting the name will introduce an error into the worksheet. Also, note that deleting a range name merely removes a label that you had applied to the range. It has no effect on the contents of the cells in the range.

When you include a range name in a formula or function, that text or name substitutes for actual cell addresses. This is the only kind of text that can appear in a formula or function. If you enter any text that is *not* a range name into a formula, you will get an error message because text cannot be used in calculations. However, the contents of cells that stand behind the named range can be used in calculations, because they are being referenced in the same way as a cell address (like B4) references a value.

Spreadsheet Formats and Styles

As we noted in Chapter 6, the appearance of a cell's contents is referred to as its *cell format*. You need to distinguish carefully between the format and the contents of a cell. A cell with a currency format will still have only a value, or number, as its contents (45.00, for instance), even if that number is displayed, or formatted, as $45.00.

Some formats affect font and style. You used these formats in Chapter 6. **Number formats** refer to symbolic notations of values. Numerical values can have up to seven decimal places and can be displayed in nine formats. Table 7.1 describes these formatting choices. The default in *Works* is the general format, although that format could quickly be changed by using the currency icon in the spreadsheet toolbar.

Table 7.1 Formatting Choices for Spreadsheets

Number Format	Characteristics
General	Displays a value as precisely as possible as an integer (123), as a decimal fraction (1.45), or, if the number has too many digits to fit into the cell, in exponential notation (1.23E+75).
Fixed	Displays a specified number of decimal places, rounding if necessary.
Currency	Precedes the value with a $ sign and inserts a comma every three places ($3,444.45).
Comma	Inserts a comma every three places.
Percent	Shows a number as a percentage; for example, 0.56 becomes 56%, or 56.00% if you specify two decimal places.
Exponential	Shows a number in exponential (scientific) notation.
Leading Zeros	Maintains any zeros that precede a number, as 03456. (In general format, leading zeros are dropped.)
Fraction	Shows a number in fraction form, as 15 3/4.
True/False	Causes cells to display logical values. All cells whose values are zero display *FALSE* and all nonzero cells display *TRUE*.
Date	Lets you choose from several date formats
Time	Lets you choose from several time formats
Text	Displays a value as text, so that a truly alphanumeric number, such as a Zip code, phone number, etc., is displayed appropriately.

You can define as many different formats for different cells in a spreadsheet as you wish, and you can format before or after entering data. Remember, changing a format does not change the value. To change a number format:

- Select the cell or range you want to format.
- Click on Format-Number.
- Select the desired format from the displayed list.
- If you choose fixed or currency format, type the number of decimal places you desire.
- If you choose time or date format, select a particular format.
- Click on OK.

To change the formatting for every cell in the spreadsheet in one operation, select All from the Edit menu. This approach is comparable to what other spreadsheet packages call a **global** change. It is usually easier to begin by formatting the spreadsheet globally in the predominant format (such as currency), and then format any special ranges (such as percentages, times, or dates) individually to override the global norm.

The general format (the default) is often satisfactory for all but date displays. The computer stores months in a date as numbers, such as 06 for June, 07 for July, and so on; therefore, you must format them as time or date displays in order to read the date properly. Always format a cell that uses the DATE( ), DAY( ), MONTH( ), YEAR( ), or NOW( ) functions (mentioned at the end of this chapter and explained in Appendix B), as time or date, and choose the specific display you wish. Otherwise, your date will simply look like a large number, 33569, for example.

Formatting Cell Widths

As you have seen, *Works* sets the width of spreadsheet cells to ten spaces by default, but often you will want to change that width. You can make *Works* spreadsheet cells up to 79 spaces wide. You may need to widen a column to accommodate text labels, or you may want to decrease the width of a column that needs only a space or two to fit more columns across your screen display. Remember that if you see number signs (####) in a cell, it means that the cell is not wide enough to display the values entered in it. Text entries do not display as number signs if the cell is not wide enough for them. If the cell to the right is empty, the leftover characters will display in that cell. If the cell to the right does contain text, numbers, or formulas, however, there will be no spillover. Instead, the entity that is too wide will simply be **truncated**, or cut off, at the width of its cell.

Hiding Cells

In certain cases, you may want to set a cell width to zero. The effect is to prevent display of the contents of the cell. This feature can be useful if you wish to enter sensitive or private data for spreadsheet calculations, yet not have this information display to the viewer. You might conceal wage rates for employees, or other numbers that convey personal information, in this way. To hide a column of cells:

- Click on Format-Column Width.
- Type **0**
- Click on OK.

When you wish to redisplay hidden cells, you must use the Go To command (F5) and type in their addresses in order to widen the column again. *You cannot manually move your cursor into cells that are hidden on the screen.*

Easier Viewing of Larger Spreadsheets

As your spreadsheets become larger, you will not be able to see all of their columns and rows on the screen. It takes time to scroll back and forth, across and down, a worksheet, and it can be confusing when constructing or viewing a spreadsheet. The Go To command (F5 key) is helpful, but *Works* offers two other ways to make viewing easier.

Freezing Row and Column Titles

The first feature that helps you control the display is the ability to **freeze**, or fix, column and row titles to keep them in the window while you scroll through the rest of the spreadsheet. This is a very helpful feature of all spreadsheet programs, and it is well worth the effort to learn. Freezing affects all rows above and to the left of the highlighted, or active, cell.

To freeze a row or column in *Works*:

- Move the cross bar below the rows, or to the right of the columns, you want to freeze.
- To freeze only columns, move the cross bar to Row 1; to freeze only rows, move the cross bar to column A.
- Click on Format-Freeze Titles.

A check mark appears in front of the option when titles are frozen.

Although freezing titles is generally a helpful feature, you do not want to leave them frozen at the end of your work session because you cannot access frozen titles with the cursor. A common beginning mistake is to freeze titles and save to disk, then bring up the spreadsheet at a later time and try to access the text in the frozen area. You may forget that the titles are frozen and spend some frustrating minutes trying to figure out why you cannot move to a title cell and change its contents. The spreadsheet is stored as it appeared when you saved to disk and exited, frozen titles and all. It is, therefore, a good practice to unfreeze titles before saving a worksheet to disk.

To unfreeze a row or column:

- Click on Format-Freeze Titles.

The check mark in front of the option disappears, indicating that the option has been toggled off. You can always tell very quickly if the freeze titles option is toggled on by looking at the Format menu.

Splitting Worksheets

Another feature of most spreadsheet programs is the ability to split the worksheet area into different windows, or areas of display. *Works* allows you to split both horizontally and vertically within one worksheet to define four areas of display, or **panes**, on the screen at the same time. This feature is invaluable for large spreadsheets. You can see four different areas at the same time, and you can scroll within each of those areas. To split your worksheet into windows:

- Click on Window-Split.
- Move the vertical and horizontal cross bars to the points at which you wish to divide the display, then click.

You may then use the F6 function key or click with the mouse to move the cursor from one window to another in clockwise rotation. See Figure 7.3 for an illustration of a spreadsheet that is split into four different panes.

Figure 7.3

Example of Spreadsheet Split into Four Panes

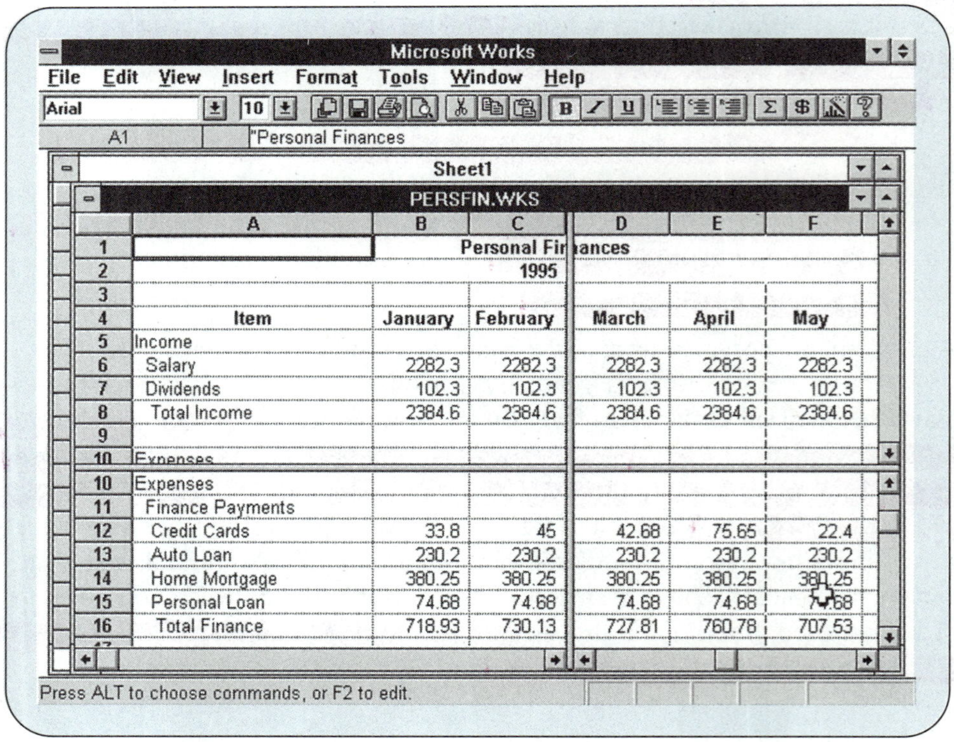

To unsplit the windows, reverse the process. Select the Window-Split command and move the cross bar back to the far left and top of the screen, then click. You *must move the bars back to the edge of the screen before leaving the screen.*

More on Printing Spreadsheets

Works offers certain options to enhance its printing function for spreadsheets: printing more than one copy, printing certain pages only, previewing a spreadsheet's printed appearance, printing in draft quality, and printing sideways. Most of these options were covered in the word processing section, and they remain the same for spreadsheets. Follow familiar steps to perform one or more of the following functions:

- Click on File-Print, Page Setup, or Print Preview.
- Select printing options.
- Click on OK.

Printing Specific Areas

Besides printing an entire spreadsheet, you can also print designated parts of it. This is often desirable with a large spreadsheet to control the appearance of the hard-copy printout, or simply to print only a portion of the spreadsheet. To set the print area:

- Select the portion of the spreadsheet you want to print.
- Click on Format-Set Print Area.
- Click on OK in the dialog box.

Inserting Page Breaks

Another way to control the printout of a spreadsheet is by inserting page breaks and then printing specific pages. If you do not insert page breaks and wish to print the entire spreadsheet, *Works* will break the material according to the number of columns that fit on an 8.5-by-11-inch piece of paper. Inserting a horizontal page break enables you to print only certain rows of a spreadsheet. Inserting a vertical page break enables you to print only certain columns.

To insert a page break:

- Select the column or row where you wish to place a break.
- Click on Insert-Page Break.
- Choose Row or Column from the dialog box.
- Click on OK.

You may delete these page breaks any time you wish. To do so:

- Click on Insert-Delete Page Break.

With page breaks established, you can control exactly what portions of the spreadsheet are printed by typing page numbers into the From: and To: boxes in the Print Range option box from the File-Print menu.

Spreadsheets must be constantly checked for accuracy; user errors can result in misleading analyses.

Landscape Mode versus Portrait Mode

Works has a specific command to print your spreadsheet sideways, in **landscape mode**, instead of the default **portrait mode** (which prints text vertically). If your printer supports landscape printing, enter the Page Setup option box in the File menu and go to the **orientation** option. You will then be able to print your spreadsheet sideways. To do this:

- Click on File-Page Setup.
- Click on the Size, Source, and Orientation area.
- Click on Landscape Orientation.

Notice that the program reverses the width and length settings of the page. The sample now appears sideways.

- Click on OK.

Even if your printer cannot print in landscape mode, a wide-carriage printer using 15-inch paper can print 132 characters across the page in the portrait orientation. With the condensed print features of some printers, you can increase this to 264 characters across the widest available paper, to include the maximum number of columns. You may also decrease the margin settings in the Margins area of the Page Setup option box to as low as 0.3 inches. This leaves a larger printing area. Another possibility is to change the font to a smaller size, such as 6 or 8 point.

SPREADSHEET TUTORIAL NO.3

You decide you would like to have a listing of your income and expenses for the last six months.

1. Double click on the *Works* icon.

2. Click on Create a New Spreadsheet.

   The spreadsheet screen displays. You want to type a heading and a subheading in bold, and center both across the columns that contain data for the first six months of the year.
3. Select Cells A1 through G2.
4. Click on the Bold icon.
5. Click on Format-Alignment-Center across selection-OK; deselect the cells.
6. In cell A1, type **Personal Finances**
7. Click on OK.

   The new heading should be in bold type and centered across the previously selected columns.
8. In Cell A2, type **1995** and press ENTER.
9. Change the width of Column A to 25 (Format-Column Width-25-OK).

   Now you want to select Row 3 and format all of its cells in bold type, centered.
10. Select Cells A3 through G3.
11. Click on the Bold icon.
12. Click on Format-Alignment-Center-OK.
13. Press HOME.

    The cursor moves to Cell A3.
14. Type **Item**
15. In Cell B3, type **January**
16. Select Cells B3 through G3.
17. Click on Edit-Fill Series.

    The Fill Series option box displays, as shown in Figure 7.4.

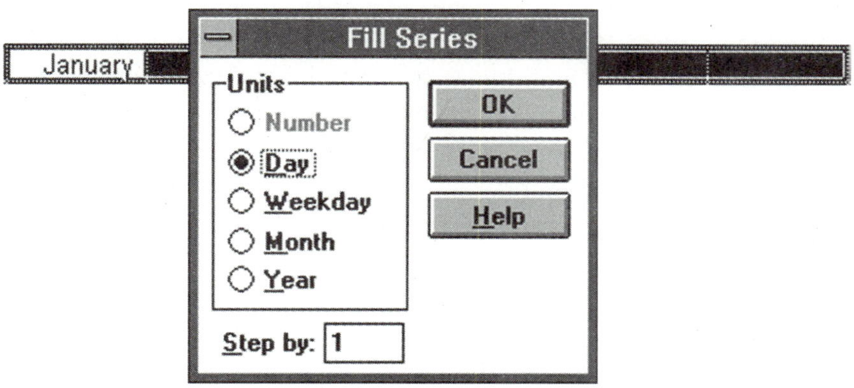

Figure 7.4

The Fill Series Option Box

18. Click on Month-OK.

    The system inserts the names of the months incrementally.
19. Press the DOWN ARROW once and then press HOME.
20. In Cell A4, type **Income**
21. In Cell A5, press SPACE BAR twice and type **Salary**
22. In Cell B5, type **2282.30** and press ENTER.

    Now you will copy the salary amount to each cell from B5 to G5.
23. Select Cells B5 through G5.
24. Click on Edit.
25. Click on Fill Right.
26. Save the spreadsheet as persfin
27. In Cell A6, space two times and type **Dividends**
28. Enter **102.30** for every month.
29. In Cell A7, space three times and type **Total Income**

    Enter the formula to add Salary and Dividends.
30. In Cell B7, type **=B5+B6** and press ENTER.
31. Select Cell B7.
32. Press F8 to extend the selection.
33. Press the RIGHT ARROW five times.
34. Click on Edit.
35. Click on Fill Right.
36. Finish typing the spreadsheet shown in Figure 7.5.

To repeat a number or formula, select the cells and use Edit-Fill Right or Fill Down. To total columns, use a formula such as =sum(b10:b13). You will add some blank rows between categories later. *Save frequently*! (Remember, you can click on the save icon on the toolbar.) If you need to make a correction in a cell, either type over the existing contents, or press F2 to edit, and use the arrow keys to move to the place for the correction. (Hint: To compute net income, you must first add your total expenses, including subtotals or finance, insurance, and miscellaneous expenses. Then subtract total expenses from total income to get the net income (or loss).

After you finish typing, you decide to move auto expenses to the row after groceries.

37. Select Auto Expenses.
38. Click on Edit.
39. Click on Select Row.

    The entire row is highlighted.

Figure 7.5

Example of the Printed Spreadsheet

Personal Finances
1995

Item	January	February	March	April	May	June
Income						
Salary	2282.3	2282.3	2282.3	2282.3	2282.3	2282.3
Dividends	102.3	102.3	102.3	102.3	102.3	102.3
Total Income	2384.6	2384.6	2384.6	2384.6	2384.6	2384.6
Expenses						
Finance Payments						
Credit Cards	33.8	45	42.68	75.65	22.4	56.43
Auto Loan	230.2	230.2	230.2	230.2	230.2	230.2
Home Mortgage	380.25	380.25	380.25	380.25	380.25	380.25
Personal Loan	74.68	74.68	74.68	74.68	74.68	74.68
Total Finance						
Insurance Payments						
Home Insurance	43.2	43.2	43.2	43.2	43.2	43.2
Auto Insurance	65.6	65.6	65.6	65.6	65.6	65.6
Life Insurance	28.3	28.3	28.3	28.3	28.3	28.3
Medical Insurance	30	30	30	30	30	30
Dental Insurance	22.12	22.12	22.12	22.12	22.12	22.12
Total Insurance						
Miscellaneous Payments						
Groceries	208.2	189.43	216.34	220.16	175.43	202.56
Clothing	30	38	56	70	45	16
Entertainment	40	25	34	22	30	48
Cable TV	29.5	29.5	29.5	29.5	29.5	29.5
Auto Expenses (gas)	32	34	29	27	31	28
Total Miscellaneous						
Total Expenses						
Net Income (loss)						

40. Click on Edit-Cut.

    Do not be concerned if you get an ERR message in your total columns.

41. Move the cursor to the Clothing row.
42. Click on Edit-Paste.

    You would like to see what your spreadsheet looks like so far.

43. Click on File-Print Preview.

    You decide that your spreadsheet would look better with some blank rows. (An inserted row will appear above a selected row.)

44. Click on Cancel in the Preview screen.
45. Select any cell in Row 3.

46. Click on Insert-Row/Column.

    The Insert option box displays.

47. Click on Row-OK.

    A blank row is inserted above the months.

48. Insert blank rows above Expenses, Insurance Payments, Miscellaneous Payments, and Net Income (Loss).

49. Print, save, and close the file.

Figure 7.6

Example of Data in Spreadsheet

NOTE: We have printed the row and column letters and numbers so you can check to see that the data in your spreadsheet is identical to that in Figure 7.6. Make any needed adjustments to your spreadsheet before continuing.

(Page 1) **(Page 2)**

	A	B	C	D	E		F	G	H
1	**Personal Finances**					**1**			
2	**1995**					**2**			
3						**3**			
4	**Item**	**January**	**February**	**March**	**April**	**4**	**May**	**June**	**Total**
5	Income					**5**			
6	Salary	2282.30	2282.30	2282.30	2282.30	**6**	2282.30	2282.30	13693.80
7	Dividends	102.30	102.30	102.30	102.30	**7**	102.30	102.30	613.80
8	Total Income	2384.60	2384.60	2384.60	2384.60	**8**	2384.60	2384.60	14307.60
9						**9**			
10	Expenses					**10**			
11	Finance Payments					**11**			
12	Credit Cards	33.80	45.00	42.68	75.65	**12**	22.40	56.43	275.96
13	Auto Loan	230.20	230.20	230.20	230.20	**13**	230.20	230.20	1381.20
14	Home Mortgage	380.25	380.25	380.25	380.25	**14**	380.25	380.25	2281.50
15	Personal Loan	74.68	74.68	74.68	74.68	**15**	74.68	74.68	448.08
16	Total Finance	718.93	730.13	727.81	760.78	**16**	707.53	741.56	4386.74
17						**17**			
18	Insurance Payments					**18**			
19	Home Insurance	43.20	43.20	43.20	43.20	**19**	43.20	43.20	259.20
20	Auto Insurance	65.60	65.60	65.60	65.60	**20**	65.60	65.60	393.60
21	Life Insurance	28.30	28.30	28.30	28.30	**21**	28.30	28.30	169.80
22	Medical Insurance	30.00	30.00	30.00	30.00	**22**	30.00	30.00	180.00
23	Dental Insurance	22.12	22.12	22.12	22.12	**23**	22.12	22.12	132.72
24	Total Insurance	189.22	189.22	189.22	189.22	**24**	189.22	189.22	1135.32
25						**25**			
26	Miscellaneous Payments					**26**			
27	Groceries	208.20	189.43	216.34	220.16	**27**	175.43	202.56	1212.12
28	Auto Expenses (gas)	32.00	34.00	29.00	27.00	**28**	31.00	28.00	181.00
29	Clothing	30.00	38.00	56.00	70.00	**29**	45.00	16.00	255.00
30	Entertainment	40.00	25.00	34.00	22.00	**30**	30.00	48.00	199.00
31	Cable TV	29.50	29.50	29.50	29.50	**31**	29.50	29.50	177.00
32	Total Miscellaneous	240.20	223.43	245.34	247.16	**32**	206.43	230.56	1393.12
33	Total Expenses	1148.35	1142.78	1162.37	1197.16	**33**	1103.18	1161.34	6915.18
34						**34**			
35	Net Income (loss)	1236.25	1241.82	1222.23	1187.44	**35**	1281.42	1223.26	7392.42

Advanced Spreadsheet Concepts

In this section we will look more closely at spreadsheet formats, and investigate some functions that you may access. We will also discuss protection of cell contents and sorting of rows.

Autoformat

As spreadsheet programs get more sophisticated, and personal computer hardware allows you to create more cosmetically appealing products, you can choose among many more options when creating spreadsheet templates. It is now possible to create presentation-quality spreadsheets with *Works 3.0 for Windows* using the **autoformat** option. This choice allows you to create three-dimensional styles and financial formats similar to the highly sophisticated products of large business applications.

Works will automatically apply some generally accepted standards for slide presentations and stock portfolio spreadsheets for you if you wish. If you have a color printer, or are presenting the spreadsheet by projecting it on a high-quality monitor or overhead projector, the results can be striking. *Works* can even create materials for professional presentations. To access these general, global formats:

- Click on Format-AutoFormat.
- Choose one of the styles from the Table format.
- A sample of your spreadsheet in that format will appear.
- Click on OK when you are satisfied.

That is all there is to it. *Works* has automatically formatted your entire spreadsheet in a professional manner. If you have the necessary hardware, it will appear this way when printed or projected.

Common Functions

Works includes 76 functions, or predefined formulas, for your convenience in constructing spreadsheets and databases. As discussed in the previous chapter, functions are especially useful as substitutes for long formulas. For example, instead of typing A1+A2+A3+A4 . . . +A10 you could simply type =SUM(A1:A10). You have already used several of the simpler functions. Most spreadsheet users never use more than five or six, but as you can judge by the number available, they can choose from a great variety.

We have already discussed the autosum function that *Works 3.0 for Windows* provides in the toolbar. This function automatically totals a series of cells by simply clicking on the check mark when the Sigma icon (Σ) is selected from the toolbar.

The functions supplied by *Works* can be divided into several types. There are *mathematical* functions such as SUM( ), COUNT( ), ROUND( ), INT( ), and SQRT( ), along with time/date functions such as DATE( ), NOW( ), DAY( ), MONTH( ), YEAR( ), and HOUR( ). There are also *trigonometric* functions, such as SIN( ), TAN( ), and COSIN( ). *Statistical* functions such as AVG( ), STD( ), MAX( ), MIN( ), and VAR( ), are frequently used as are *financial* functions such as NPV( ), RATE( ), PYMT( ), and IRR( ). *Logical* functions, such as IF( ), TRUE( ), and ISNA( ), allow you to set up conditions and select alternative paths for calculations. An extensive array of *text functions* allows you to manipulate character strings, such as LENGTH( ), TRIM( ), and VALUE( ). Finally, functions such as CHOOSE( ), and VLOOKUP ( ) or HLOOKUP( ) select out cells for calculations. Indeed, almost any calculating task you have can be made easier through the use of a function. Appendix B contains a complete list of the functions available with *Works*. As you become more proficient with spreadsheets, you will want to explore new functions.

Every function returns a value. Even TRUE( ) returns 0 or 1, which is evaluated as false or true. Even as a beginner, you should exploit the power of these predetermined formulas. They can save you much work in constructing your spreadsheets. If you have a choice of using your own formula or a function, it is usually better to use a function. Not only has it been thoroughly tested, but, like a range name, it tends to be self-documenting. When you return to your spreadsheet much later, it is easier to remember what you were trying to accomplish when you see a function instead of a long series of cell addresses connected by mathematical operators.

Protecting Cell Contents

Works has a feature that allows you to protect the contents of cells so that they cannot be written over or changed. This device is very helpful when preparing templates, or partially completed spreadsheets, with highly formatted labels and many formulas and functions. The Tools menu gives access to a Set Protection option box where you can choose to lock or unlock a range that you have selected. Locking and protecting cells is a precaution to guard against accidental or unauthorized changes.

By default, *Works* locks all cells; however, the lock has no effect until the user turns on protection. When a cell is locked and protection is on, you cannot format the cell, change its contents, or unlock it. *Works* initially locks all cells by default. After the material is designed, you can turn protection on at any time and avoid inadvertently changing the contents of cells when the cursor ends up where you didn't intend it to be.

To lock or unlock a cell or range:

- Select the cell or range you want to lock or unlock.
- Click on Tools-Protection.
- Turn on or off the Locked option.
- Turn on or off the Protect Data option.
- Click on OK.

SPREADSHEET TUTORIAL NO.4

In this tutorial you will freeze the titles so you can look at the last line of expenses and the item and month headings at the same time. You will also practice protecting your data, changing the formats of your numbers, changing to Formula view, selecting cells and applying range names, using manual calculation mode, inserting page breaks, and experimenting with autoformat.

1. Open persfin.wks.
2. Press CTRL +HOME.
3. Select Cell B6.
4. Click on Format.

   The format menu displays, as shown in Figure 7.7.
5. Click on Freeze Titles.
6. Scroll down to Groceries under Miscellaneous Payments and scroll over to the month of June. Notice that the item and month headings stay on the screen.
7. Press CTRL + HOME.
8. Click on Format-Freeze Titles to go back to normal.

   You decide to turn on the cell protection feature so that the contents of the cells cannot be changed inadvertently.
9. Click on Format-Protection.

   The Protection option box displays, as shown in Figure 7.8.

Figure 7.7

The Format Menu

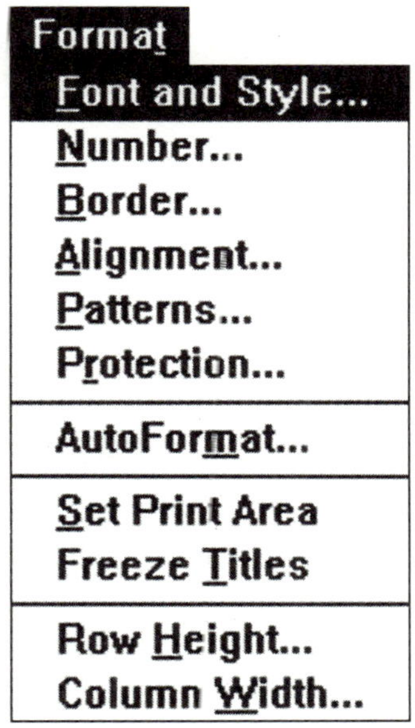

Figure 7.8

The Protection Option Box

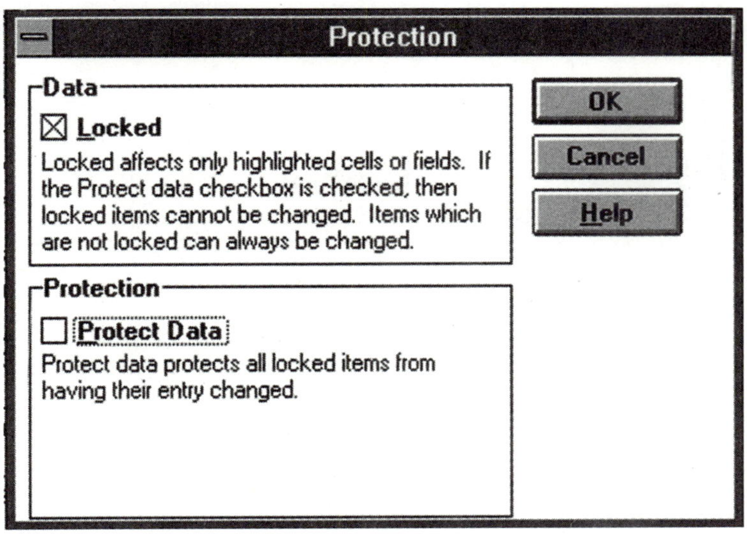

10. Click on Protect Data-OK.

    To see if it worked:

11. Move the cursor to January's credit card payment.
12. Type **55** and press ENTER.

    You get the message "Cannot Change: Locked." After you read the message, click on OK. To reverse the protection procedure:

13. Click on Format-Protection-Protect Data-OK to remove the check mark.

    Now you want to change the spreadsheet to include dollar signs and commas in the numbers.

14. Highlight the rows and columns where numbers appear.
15. Click on Format.
16. Click on Number.
17. The number option box displays, as shown in Figure 7.9.

Figure 7.9

The Currency Option Box

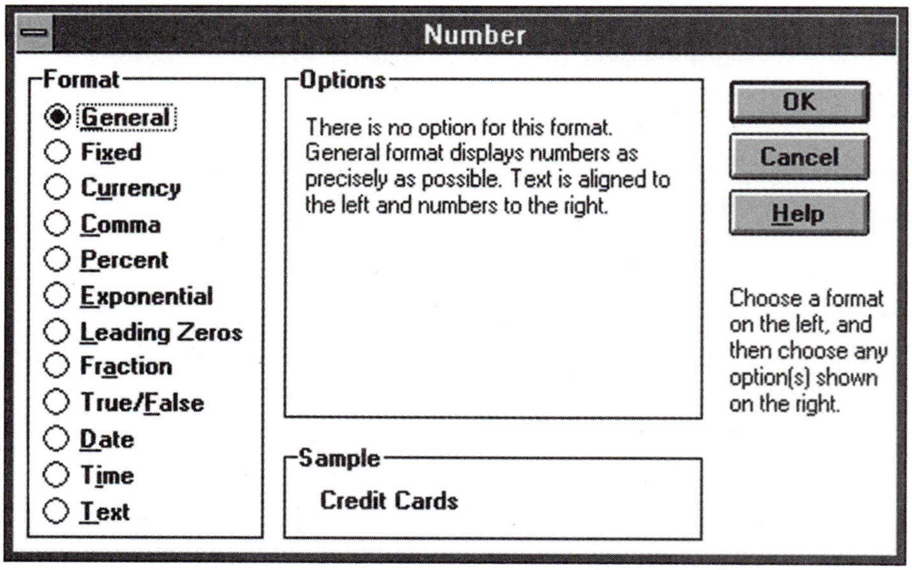

18. Click on Currency.

    The Currency option box appears.

19. Click on OK to accept 2 for Number of Decimals.

All the numbers are now preceded by dollar signs ($) with commas every three places. You may notice that the year in Cell D2 and the months January through June changed to dollar amounts as a result of globally formatting the spreadsheet as currency. Don't worry; you will fix the problem soon.

You decide to remove the inappropriate dollar signs and commas while the spreadsheet is still selected.

20. Click on Format-Number-Fixed.
21. Click on OK to confirm two decimal places.

    The year and the months are still displayed as numbers, reflecting the numerical values under which dates are stored in *Works.* (You will notice a 30-day or 31-day difference between consecutive months.)
22. Select Cell B4 and click on the number 4 at the left edge of the row.
23. The entire row is selected.

    Be aware that every column in Row B4 has now been selected; we present this technique of clicking on the left edge of a row so that you know about it, rather than to use it at this point in the tutorial.
24. Click on Format-Number-Date.

    The date options are shown in Figure 7.10.

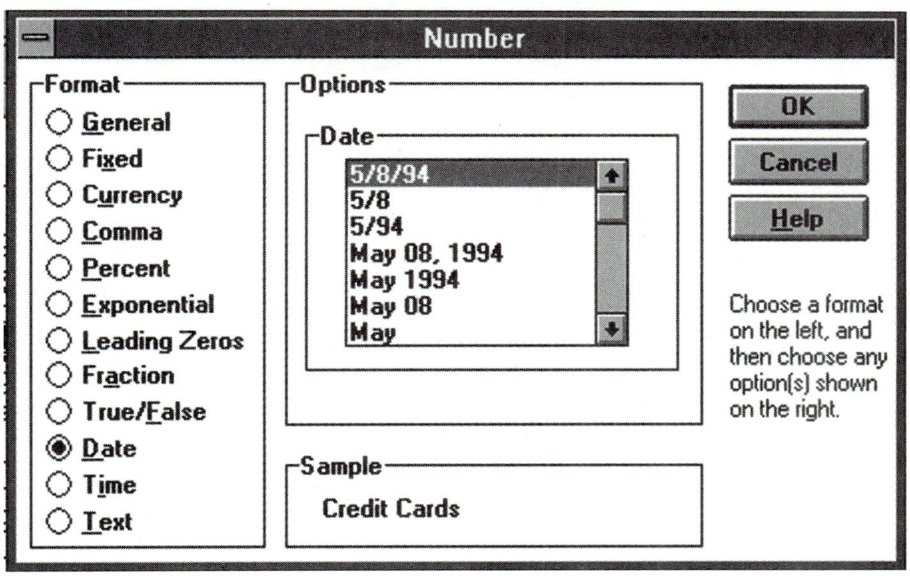

Figure 7.10

The Date Options

25. Click on the name of the month alone as January.

    (The month name will vary depending upon when you complete this assignment.)
26. Click on OK.

    The months are again correct.
27. Click on the number 2 in the second row to select the row that contains the year.

Figure 7.11

The Range Name Option Box

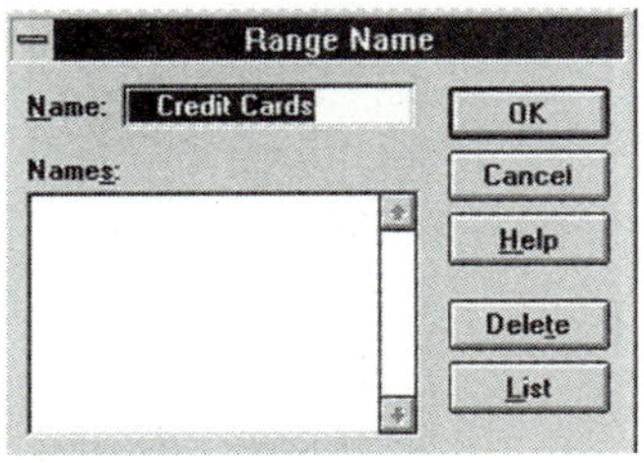

28. Click on Format-Number-General-OK.

    Your next step is to select the various expense categories and give them range names.

29. Place the crossbar in Cell A12. (This cell contains the words *credit cards.*)
30. Press F8 (for extend) and select through Cell G15. (Be careful not to include totals.)
31. Click on Insert-Range Name.

    The Range Name option box displays, as shown in Figure 7.11.

32. Type **Finance**

Figure 7.12

Example of List in The Name Box

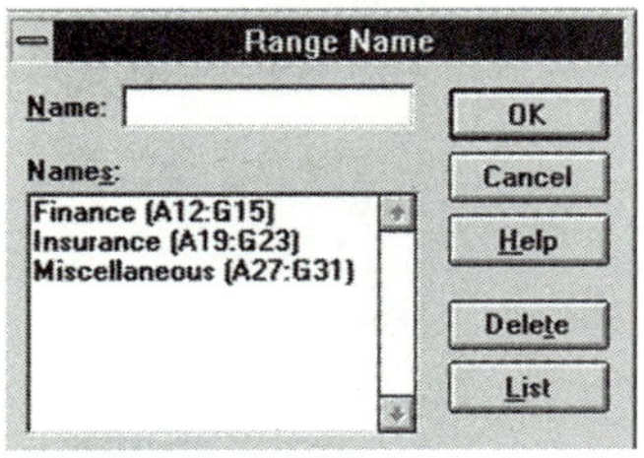

33. Click on OK, then deselect the text.

    On your own, create and name ranges for Insurance and Miscellaneous. (Be careful not to include totals.) The list in your name box should look like Figure 7.12.

    You will enter a total column after the June data to sum each item for the six-month period, changing the calculation mode to manual while you are adding the new items.

34. In Cell H4, type **Total** and press ENTER.
35. Click on Tools-Manual Calculation.
36. Select Cell B6 and freeze the titles (Format-Freeze Titles).
37. Move the cross bar to Cell H6.
38. Enter a formula to add Cells B6 through G6.

    The total is entered in the cell.

39. Select Cell H6.
40. Select the remainder of the column.
41. Select Edit-Fill Down.

    Notice that the formulas are copied, but the calculations are not correct and some of the cells contain zeros.

42. Select Tools-Calculate Now.

    Notice how swiftly all calculations are made. Now you want to change back to automatic calculation after each entry.

43. Select Tools-Manual Calculation.
44. Press ENTER.
45. Unfreeze the titles.
46. Delete the zeros in those cells that have them.

    (The fastest way to delete groups of zeros in adjacent columns is to select the cells and click on Edit-Clear.)

47. Save the spreadsheet.

    You may sometimes want to see all the formulas you have entered. To do that:

48. Click on Edit-Select All.
49. Click on View.

    The View menu displays, as shown in Figure 7.13.

Figure 7.13

The View Menu

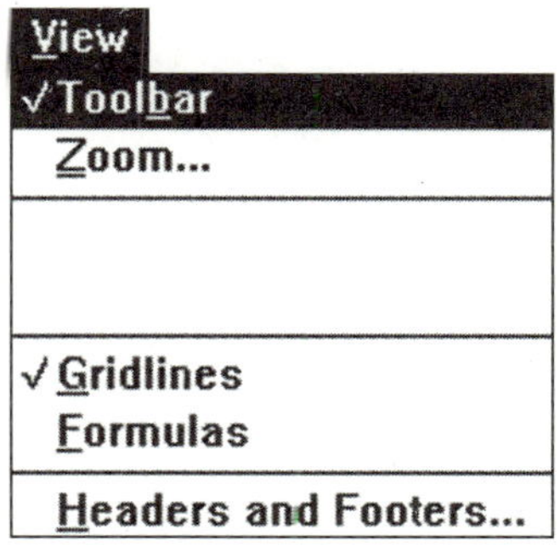

50. Click on Formulas.

    The formuals, rather than the resulting values, display, and the spreadsheet occupies several pages. You want to print just the item headings and January data, which are on Page 1.

51. Click on File-Print.

    (Do not use the Print icon because you want to change the selection.) The Print menu displays, as shown in Figure 7.14.

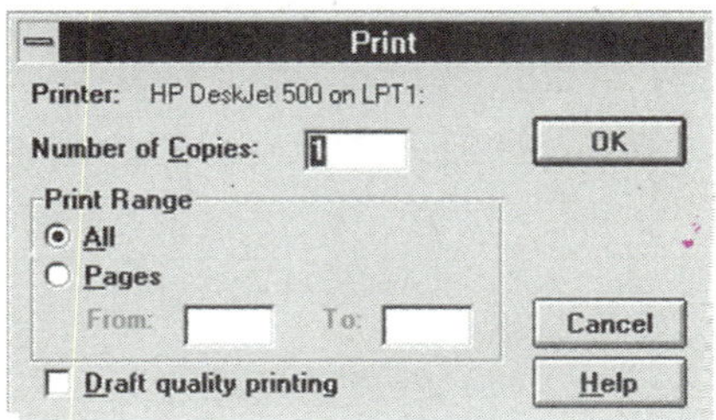

Figure 7.14

The Print Menu

52. Click on the Pages radio button.
53. TAB to the From: text box.
54. Type **1**
55. TAB to the To: text box.
56. Type **1**

    Columns A and B print with formulas, as shown in Figure 7.15. (We printed row and column letter and number)

57. Click on OK.
58. Deselect the current text by pressing any arrow key.
59. Click on View-Formulas.

    The spreadsheet toggles back to values. A page break can be inserted after a row, a column, or both. You want to insert a page break between Columns E and F.

60. Select Cell F1.
61. Click on Insert-Page Break.

    The Insert Page Break option box displays.

Figure 7.15

Example of Printed Columns A and B

	A	B
1	**Personal Finances**	
2	**1995**	
3		
4	**Item**	**34335**
5	Income	
6	Salary	2282.3
7	Dividends	102.3
8	Total Income	=B6+B7
9		
10	Expenses	
11	Finance Payments	
12	Credit Cards	33.8
13	Auto Loan	230.2
14	Home Mortgage	380.25
15	Personal Loan	74.68
16	Total Finance	=SUM(B12:B15)
17		
18	Insurance Payments	
19	Home Insurance	43.2
20	Auto Insurance	65.6
21	Life Insurance	28.3
22	Medical Insurance	30
23	Dental Insurance	22.12
24	Total Insurance	=SUM(B19:B23)
25		
26	Miscellaneous Payments	
27	Groceries	208.2
28	Auto Expenses (gas)	32
29	Clothing	30
30	Entertainment	40
31	Cable TV	29.5
32	Total Miscellaneous	=SUM(B27:B28)
33	Total Expenses	=B16+B24+B32
34		
35	Net Income (loss)	=B8-B33

62. Click on the Column radio button (if it is not already marked).
63. Click on OK.

    A dotted line separates Columns E and F. To view your worksheet:
64. Click on File-Print Preview.
65. Click on Next to see Page 2.
66. Click on Print-OK.

    The spreadsheet will print on two pages, as shown in Figure 7.16. The *Works* AutoFormat feature will automatically change the formatting of your file. Just for fun, try some of the various formats.
67. Save your spreadsheet as persfin2.
68. Select your entire spreadsheet with the mouse, or F8 and the arrow keys.

Figure 7.16

Example of Printed Spreadsheet

(Page 1) **Personal Finances 1995** (Page 2)

Item	January	February	March	April	May	June	Total
Income							
Salary	2282.3	2282.3	2282.3	2282.3	2282.30	2282.30	13693.80
Dividends	102.3	102.3	102.3	102.3	102.30	102.30	613.80
Total Income	2384.6	2384.6	2384.6	2384.6	2384.60	2384 60	14307.60
Expenses							
Finance Payments							
Credit Cards	33.8	45	42.68	75.65	22.40	56.43	275.96
Auto Loan	230.2	230.2	230.2	230.2	230.20	230.20	1381.20
Home Mortgage	380.25	380.25	380.25	380.25	380.25	380.25	2281.50
Personal Loan	74.68	74.68	74.68	74.68	74.68	74.68	448.08
Total Finance	718.93	730.13	727.81	760.78	707.53	741.56	4386.74
Insurance Payments							
Home Insurance	43.2	43.2	43.2	43.2	43.20	43.20	259.20
Auto Insurance	65.6	65.6	65.6	65.6	65.60	65.60	393.60
Life Insurance	28.3	28.3	28.3	28.3	28.30	28.30	169.80
Medical Insurance	30	30	30	30	30.00	30.00	180.00
Dental Insurance	22.12	22.12	22.12	22.12	22.12	22.12	132.72
Total Insurance	189.22	189.22	189.22	189.22	189.22	189.22	1135.32
Miscellaneous Payments							
Groceries	208.2	189.43	216.34	220.16	175.43	202.56	1212.12
Auto Expenses (gas)	32	34	29	27	31.00	28.00	181.00
Clothing	30	38	56	70	45.00	16.00	255.00
Entertainment	40	25	34	22	30.00	48.00	199.00
Cable TV	29.5	29.5	29.5	29.5	29.50	29.50	177.00
Total Miscellaneous	240.2	223.43	245.34	247.16	206.43	230.56	1393.12
Total Expenses	1148.35	1142.78	1162.37	1197.16	1103.18	1161.34	6915.18
Net Income (loss)	1236.25	1241.82	1222.23	1187.44	1281.42	1223.26	7392.42

Caution: Again, remember not to use Select All, as that selects all available rows and columns. It takes a long time to process, you usually run out of memory, and a very large matrix results.

69. Click on Format-AutoFormat.

The AutoFormat option box displays, as shown in Figure 7.17. A preview of your selection displays in the small window in the feature screen.

Figure 7.17

The AutoFormat Option Box

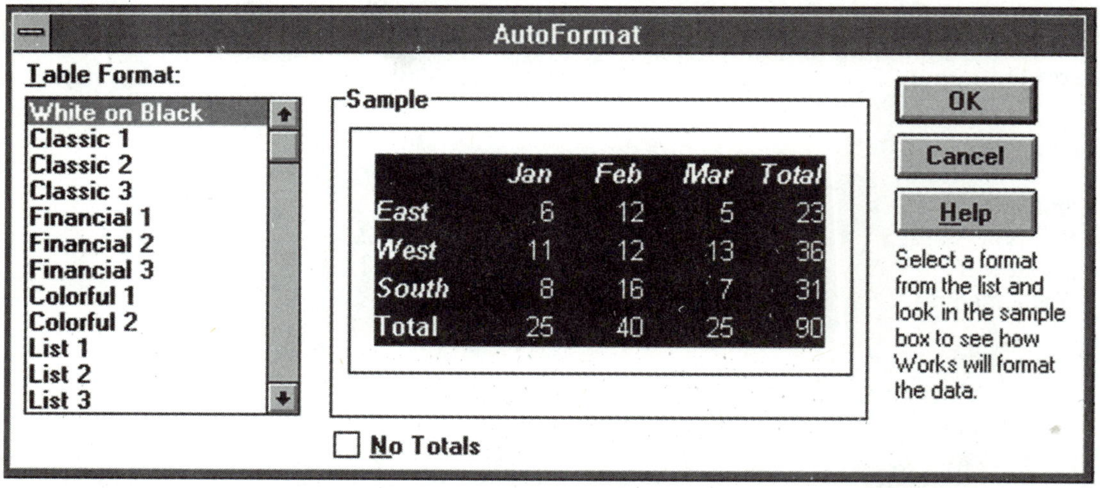

70. Click on Colorful 1-OK.

    You don't like that one.

71. Click on Edit-Undo (or press CTRL+Z).
72. Click on Format-AutoFormat.
73. Select 3D Effects 2-OK.
74. Save and print only the first page of the spreadsheet.

    Your print out should look similar to the one in Figure 7.18.

75. Close persfin2.wks.

    You forgot to include any documentation on your original spreadsheet, so you will add that to your original copy now.

76. Open persfin.wks.
77. Select Cell A37.

    To format the cell to wrap text so you can enter more than one line:

78. Click on Format-Alignment-Wrap Text-OK.
79. Type the following text:

    This spreadsheet was created on July 1, 1995, and contains data for all income and expenses for the last six months.

    Note that the text will disappear as you enter it until you press ENTER or an arrow key. You want to put a border around the text so it will stand out from the rest of the spreadsheet.

Figure 7.18

1995				
Item	January	February	March	April
Income				
Salary	2282.30	2282.30	2282.30	2282.30
Dividends	102.30	102.30	102.30	102.30
Total Income	2384.60	2384.60	2384.60	2384.60
Expenses				
Finance Payments				
Credit Cards	33.80	45.00	42.68	75.65
Auto Loan	230.20	230.20	230.20	230.20
Home Mortgage	380.25	380.25	380.25	380.25
Personal Loan	74.68	74.68	74.68	74.68
Total Finance	718.93	730.13	727.81	760.78
Insurance Payments				
Home Insurance	43.20	43.20	43.20	43.20
Auto Insurance	65.60	65.60	65.60	65.60
Life Insurance	28.30	28.30	28.30	28.30
Medical Insurance	30.00	30.00	30.00	30.00
Dental Insurance	22.12	22.12	22.12	22.12
Total Insurance	189.22	189.22	189.22	189.22
Miscellaneous Payments				
Groceries	208.20	189.43	216.34	220.16
Auto Expenses (gas)	32.00	34.00	29.00	27.00
Clothing	30.00	38.00	58.00	70.00
Entertainment	40.00	25.00	34.00	22.00
Cable TV	29.50	29.50	29.50	29.50
Total Miscellaneous	240.20	223.43	245.34	247.16
Total Expenses	1148.35	1142.78	1162.37	1197.16
Net Income (loss)	1236.25	1241.82	1222.23	1187.44

80. Select the cell again.
81. Click on Format-Border.
82. Select the last border in the row (the thick line).
83. Click on OK.
84. Save and print Page 1 of your spreadsheet.
85. Close the spreadsheet and exit *Works*.

Chapter Summary

In this chapter, we concentrated on the most popular intermediate to advanced spreadsheet concepts. These included: ranges and range names, spreadsheet formats and styles, simplified viewing of large spreadsheets, alternatives to printing entire spreadsheets, common functions, and cell content protection.

KEY TERMS

autoformat
freeze
global
Go To
landscape mode
locked cells
number format
macro
orientation
pane
portrait mode
protection
range name
truncate

REVIEW QUESTIONS

1. Explain the concept of a range and a range name; when might you find these useful?
2. Why might you select cells and what are some of the ways you can do this?
3. List and briefly explain how the several different copy processes for spreadsheets work.
4. As mentioned above, it is possible to give a range of selected cells a name. Relate how to do it.
5. List and explain the purposes of at least 5 of the 11 formats covered in this chapter.
6. Explain the difference between a local and a global format change. What is the simplest way to select the entire spreadsheet?
7. You have just entered data into a cell and pressed the ENTER key when you see a string of number signs (#####) appear in the cell. What does this symbol mean and how would you deal with the situation?
8. Explain (a) why you might want to hide a cell or column, (b) how to do this, and (c) how to redisplay those hidden cells.
9. Recall the several different ways to view a large spreadsheet.
10. State the reason(s) why you might print a specific area of a spreadsheet instead of the whole thing.
11. Describe the steps you must take in order to print a selected area.
12. Relate the advantage(s) of using autoformat.
13. Identify the purpose of a function. Summarize the major types of functions.
14. State why you might want to lock a cell.

15. Explain why locking a cell alone does not protect it from changes.
16. Recall the reason(s) for changing a spreadsheet from automatic calculation to manual calculation. How do you make this change?
17. What is the difference between the portrait and landscape modes of printing a spreadsheet?

SOFTWARE EXERCISES

Exercise 7.1

Your school club has an annual opportunity to run the concession stand for a school sports event.

1. Load the *Works* program.
2. Create a new spreadsheet that computes the club's total profit based upon the data in Table 7.2 by filling in the empty columns with formulas.
3. Change the heading from "Football Game Income" to refer to whatever sport interests you. Change the club name to the name of a club you are in, or invent one that suits you.
4. Center the club heading, your name, and the date on which you created the spreadsheet across the columns the spreadsheet occupies.
5. Test your spreadsheet. When it is operational, go to Step 6.
6. Format Sold for, Profit, Total Profit, and Total cells with dollar signs and two decimal places.
7. Save your spreadsheet as club.
8. Print club.wks.
9. Click on View-Formulas to show the formulas.
10. Print club.wks again.
11. Click on View-Formulas again to hide the formulas.
12. Close club.wks and exit *Works*.

Table 7.2

Football Game Income
Varsity Sports Club
Income Statement Prepared by your name
current date

Food:	**Burgers**	**Pizza**	**Pop**	**Candy**	**Total**
Number	450	233	800	150	
Cost us	1.00	1.50	0.30	0.25	
Sold for	1.75	2.25	1.00	0.50	
Profit					
Total profit					

Exercise 7.2

1. Load the *Works* program.
2. Open the club.wks file that you created in Exercise 7.1, or complete Exercise 7.1 before continuing.
3. Format the first and second lines of the heading in bold.
4. Copy the portion of the spreadsheet that starts from just below the date row to four rows below the last line of the existing spreadsheet.
5. Center the following subheading across the columns two rows above the copied version of the spreadsheet: 10% Increase in Food Sales.
6. Calculate a 10 percent increase for the number of food items sold. Hold all other numbers constant.
7. Insert a page break between the two versions of the spreadsheet.
8. Save your spreadsheet as club1.
9. Print club1.wks.
10. Click on View-Formulas to show the formulas.
11. Print club1.wks again.
12. Click on View-Formulas again to hide the formulas.
13. Close club1.wks and exit *Works*.

Exercise 7.3

1. Load the *Works* program.
2. Open the buyrent.wks file from the student data diskette.
3. Widen the columns, if necessary.
4. Assign the name *RENT* to the range with the lines headed Rent, Renter's, Insurance, and Utilities.
5. Assign the name *BUYEXP* to the range with the lines that deal with a buyer's expenses.
6. Assign the name *BUYSAV* to the range with the lines that deal with a buyer's savings.
7. Use these range names in the spreadsheet formulas.
8. Save your spreadsheet as buyrent1.
9. Print buyrent1.wks.
10. Click on View-Formulas to show the formulas.
11. Print buyrent1.wks again.
12. Click on View-Formulas again to hide the formulas.
13. Close buyrent1.wks and exit *Works*.

Exercise 7.4

1. Load the *Works* program.
2. Open the buyrent.wks file from the student data diskette. Widen the columns, if needed.
3. Select all the cells with numbers in the RENT range of your spreadsheet.
4. Unlock all the selected cells in the RENT range of your spreadsheet.
5. Select all the cells with numbers in the BUY EXPENSES range.
6. Lock and protect all the selected cells in the BUY EXPENSES range.
7. Attempt to enter new data into the RENT and the BUY EXPENSES ranges of your spreadsheet.
8. Note the results of these attempts.
9. Click on Format-Protection-Protect Data to make it possible to change the data again.
10. Change the data in the spreadsheet to reflect your own situation, or one that you invent.
11. Save your spreadsheet as buyrent2.
12. Print buyrent2.wks.
13. Insert a page break after the rent section, the buy–expenses section, and the buy–savings section.
14. Print buyrent2.wks again.
15. Close buyrent2.wks and open a new *Works* word processor file.
16. Use *Works* to type up your notes from Step 8 above. Append these notes to your printouts.
17. Save your notes as locknote.
18. Close locknote.wps and exit *Works*.

Exercise 7.5

Assume that you are now 20 years of age, and that you intend to save $2,000 per year in an IRA until you retire at age 65. The built-in *Works* function =FV(Payment, Rate, Term) gives the future value of an ordinary annuity of equal payments, earning a fixed interest rate per term, compounded over several terms. Your goal is to accumulate $500,000 in your IRA by the time you retire.

1. Open a new *Works* spreadsheet file.
2. Enter the title "IRA ACCOUNT FOR" on the first line.
3. Enter your name on the second line.

4. Construct a spreadsheet using the FV function; use the spreadsheet to test different values for the rate of interest until you find one that gives a final value close to or slightly greater than $500,000.
5. Based upon your calculations above, fill in the blanks in the following sentence: To have $_____ by the time I am 65 years of age, I must earn _____% on my $2,000 per year deposit. NOTE: Enter the sentence on several lines of the spreadsheet.
6. Format the cells that represent dollars with the currency format and no decimal places.
7. Save your spreadsheet as ira.
8. Print ira.wks.
9. Close ira.wks and exit *Works*.

Exercise 7.6

Your goal is to accumulate $500,000 in your IRA by the time you retire. Use your current age to compute the term in the *Works* FV function: =FV(Payment, Rate, Term).

1. Open the existing ira.wks spreadsheet file (completed in Exercise 7.5), or complete Exercise 7.5 before continuing.
2. Add to the heading a third line that reads: "beginning at age (your current age here)."
3. Add a fourth line to the heading, but leave it blank.
4. Test different interest rates and payment amounts until you find a combination that is close to or slightly greater than $500,000.
5. Save your spreadsheet as ira1.
6. Print ira1.wks.
7. Close ira1.wks and exit *Works*.

Exercise 7.7

You have decided that you would like to purchase a home that costs $120,000. You can finance 80 percent of its value ($96,000) for 30 years at 8 percent. You want to know how much the monthly mortgage payment will be and how much cumulative interest you will pay over 30 years. You can finance the same $96,000 at 7.5 percent for 15 years. How much higher is the monthly payment for the 15-year loan, and how much interest do you save by paying off the loan in 15 years instead of 30 years?

1. Open a new *Works 3.0 for Windows* spreadsheet.
2. Center an appropriate title on Row 1.
3. Center your name on Row 2.
4. Center the current date on Row 3.

5. Use the function =PMT(Amount Borrowed, Rate/12, Term in Months) to compute the payment amounts that the exercise requires. The term in months is 360 for the 30-year loan and 180 for the 15-year loan.
6. Construct other formulas as needed to compute the total amount of interest paid [(monthly payment x Number of months) - 96,000] for each length and percentage of loan.
7. Add text to explain what the formulas mean. Add text below the work you have just completed to clearly answer the questions posed at the beginning of this exercise.
8. Save your work as loan.
9. Print loan.wks.
10. Click on View-Formulas to show the formulas.
11. Print loan.wks again.
12. Click on View-Formulas again to hide the formulas.
13. Close loan.wks and exit *Works*.

Exercise 7.8

1. Open the existing file persfin.wks, which you completed in this chapter's tutorial.
2. Sort the rows in Column A that contain amounts other than totals.
3. Save the spreadsheet as persfin1.
4. Print persfin1.wks.
5. Select only what will print on one page.
6. Click on Format-Set Print Area.
7. Print the selected portion of the spreadsheet.
8. Reset the entire spreadsheet as the print area. (Hint: Click on Format and use the DOWN ARROW to highlight Set Print Area, then press F1 for Help on the Set Print Area command.)
9. Close persfin1.wks and exit *Works*.

Exercise 7.9

1. Open the existing file persfin.wks, completed in this chapter's tutorial.
2. Carry out the following steps at the bottom of the existing spreadsheet.
3. Use the function =MAX(RangeReference0, RangeReference1, . . .) to find the largest expense item.
4. Use the function =MIN(RangeReference0, RangeReference1, . . .) to find the smallest expense item.
5. Split the screen so you can see these functions, as well as most of the expense area.

6. Save the spreadsheet as persfin3.
7. Remove the splits from the screen.
8. Print the entire spreadsheet.
9. Click on View-Formulas to show the formulas.
10. Print persfin3.wks again.
11. Click on View-Formulas again to hide the formulas.
12. Close persfin3.wks and exit *Works*.

Exercise 7.10

1. Open the retire.wks spreadsheet file from the student data diskette.
2. Change the existing heading to all caps and bold.
3. Add a second line with your name and the current date.
4. Add a blank line between the second and third lines.
5. Format all dollar values in the currency format with zero decimal places.
6. Widen column A to best fit.
7. Substitute your own data on each line.
8. Save your spreadsheet as retire1.
9. Print retire1.wks.
10. Close retire1.wks and exit *Works*.

Exercise 7.11

Assume that you are part of a two-income household.

1. Open the retire.wks spreadsheet file from the student data diskette.
2. Change the spreadsheet heading to reflect a two-income household; type the heading in all capital letters and make it bold.
3. Add a second line with your family name and the current date.
4. Add a blank line between the heading and the first line of data called "Current Income."
5. Substitute your own two-income data on each line by putting your data in Column B and your partner's data in Column C. Place the sum of Columns B and C in Column D.
6. Save your spreadsheet as retire2.
7. Print retire2.wks.
8. Click on View-Formulas to show the formulas.
9. Print retire2.wks again.
10. Click on View-Formulas again to hide the formulas.
11. Close retire2.wks and exit *Works*.

Exercise 7.12

1. Use *Works 3.0 for Windows* to complete a spreadsheet assignment for an outside class or for a club or personal project of interest to you.
2. Use all of the techniques you have learned so far to enhance the quality and appearance of your work.
3. Save your file as othersp.wks.
4. Print othersp.wks.
5. Close othersp.wks and exit *Works*.

Chapter 8

Creating Graphics from Spreadsheets

Objectives

After studying this chapter you will be able to:

- *Define the term* graphics
- *Explain the uses of graphics*
- *Summarize the history of graphics programs*
- *List the characteristics and proper uses of the different types of charts*
- *Use the toolbar symbols in place of menu choices*
- *Explain the importance of the chart titles, labels, and legends*
- *Create, view, print, and save a chart*
- *Customize charts with 3-D effects, colors, patterns, and markers*

Definition and Use of a Graphics Program

It is important to make all of the spreadsheets you complete with your personal computer as clear and understandable as you can. As you make your presentation more understandable, you make your communication more effective. Graphics can help you improve your presentations. With graphics, you can represent pictorially the sometimes complex numerical information you produce in a spreadsheet. A **graphics program** is software that allows the computer user to create, edit, display, and print graphic images such as bar graphs, pie charts, or scatterplots.

We live in a very visually oriented culture; if detailed data can be translated into a simpler, more understandable format, it can be more readily understood by someone who is not accustomed to reading columns and rows of numbers. The effectiveness of your communication can improve dramatically when enhanced by adding properly chosen graphics to your spreadsheets. The *Works* spreadsheet application, like many other spreadsheet applications, allows you to choose different forms of graphical presentation for your spreadsheet data. The types of charts that you can create are the subject of this chapter.

Graphs can make it much easier to look at an entire picture, to spot a trend, to evaluate a relationship, or to see what part something is of a whole. Graphs are so common in business that a day rarely passes when at least one graph does not appear on the business page of any newspaper. Graphs can help make important decisions easier, and thus spreadsheet programs in general, and charts in particular, are often used in decision making. They clarify the data so that the final choice is easier to make. Analyzing, evaluating, and choosing an alternative with the help of a chart simplifies decision making.

Graphics programs to chart spreadsheet data have been around for some time. Large statistical programs have long supported graphical presentation of data on minicomputers and mainframes. You learned in Chapter 6 that the first spreadsheet program for a personal computer was *VisiCalc*. It did not have a graphics companion. *Lotus 1-2-3* was introduced with a companion graphics program; the reception of the *Lotus* spreadsheet program is now history. *Lotus 1-2-3* became a phenomenal best-seller in the microcomputer world, its success due largely to its graphics program, which allowed the PC user to represent the figures in a spreadsheet pictorially, much as programs for large systems could do.

Projecting spreadsheets and accompanying charts directly from your computer display is an easy way to share financial information.

Graphics programs have evolved into very sophisticated packages that may even be purchased separately from spreadsheet applications. These application programs are commonly referred to as **presentation graphics software**. Such popular programs as *Harvard Graphics*, *Persuasion*, *Corel Draw!*, *Freelance Plus*, and *Draw Applause* fit into this category of software. You may **import** (bring in) a spreadsheet from another program and graph it in this kind of package. Presentation graphics programs are often used to produce high-level reports for business meetings and customer presentations. Figure 8.1 shows part of a slide presentation that uses charts prepared with a presentation graphics program.

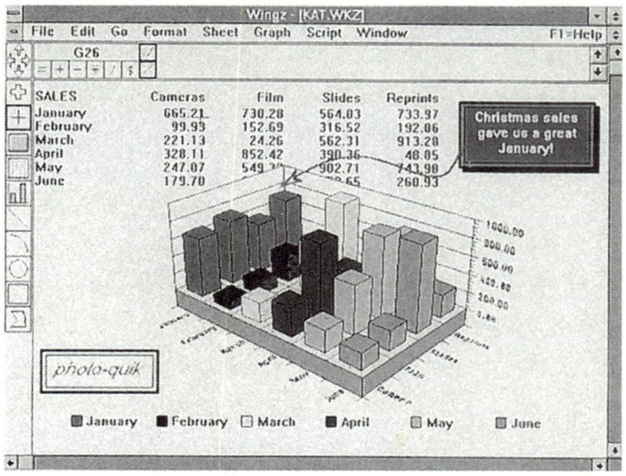

Figure 8.1

A Chart Prepared with a Presentation Graphics Program

A presentation graphics program gives you much broader options than spreadsheet graphics functions can offer, and your end product can be much more sophisticated. However, the underlying concepts are no different from those of the companion applications that come with the common spreadsheet programs, both components of integrated packages and stand-alone packages. All graphics programs allow you to represent numbers pictorially and thus increase the effectiveness of your communications.

Prerequisites for Graphing

In order to prepare a graph or chart, you must meet several criteria. First, of course, you must have data to graph—a completed spreadsheet. In addition, unless you have a separate presentation graphics program, your spreadsheet application must have graphing capability. You must also have a **graphics card**—a circuit board that plugs into the motherboard of your computer system—in order to see the graph on the monitor. Several kinds of graphics cards are available for personal computers. However, since you are using the *Windows* interface, the computer on which you are running *Works 3.0 for Windows* probably has at least a minimal-resolution color graphics card. If you purchased your computer recently, a graphics card was certainly included with the system.

Finally, if you wish to print charts, you must have a printer that is capable of printing graphics, such as a dot matrix, ink jet, or laser printer. A formed-character printer, which we have described as a true *letter quality printer*, does not have the capability to print graphics. Ink jet and laser printers, which are rapidly becoming the standard for personal computer systems, produce high-quality graphics. Many personal computer users are opting for the newer ink jet, color printers.

Types of Charts

In most packages, the various kinds of displays for spreadsheet data are called *graphs*. *Works*, however, calls these displays *charts*, referring to the result of the graphing process. We will use that term when discussing the *Works* program.

Many types of charts are available. We will cover the basic types of charts *Works* can produce—bar charts, pie charts, line charts, *X–Y* charts (also called *scatterplots*), radar charts, and combination charts. Charts plot series of numbers on *X* and *Y* axes; there is one *X* axis, and up to six series of numbers on a *Y* axis.

Bar Charts

The **default chart** for *Works* (the chart you automatically get unless you specify another type) is the bar chart. A **bar chart** is so named because it represents data in bars, or solid columns. Each row or column of spreadsheet numbers appears as a set of bars in the same color or pattern. The chart has a horizontal axis, the *X* axis, and a vertical axis, the *Y* axis. The coordinates of the *X* and *Y* axes determine the heights of the bars. Each bar extends to the height at which its *X* and *Y* values intersect.

Variations of the bar chart that *Works* offers are the **stacked bar chart**, where the bars are stacked on top of each other and show the total of each category, and the **100 percent bar chart**, where those stacks must total 100 percent. See Figures 8.2a, 8.2b, and 8.2c for examples of the three types of bar charts that *Works* offers. The stacked bar chart and the 100 percent bar chart are available as two of the six perspectives you may choose from the 3-D chart options in *Works 3.0 for Windows*.

A bar chart can represent many different kinds of data, a fact that helps explain why it is the default choice in *Works*. The bar chart becomes impractical only when a chart must represent a great number of different categories. More than a dozen different bars, or stacks within a bar, are likely to render the chart more confusing than helpful. Otherwise, bar charts are easy to understand and interpret.

Pie Charts

Pie charts are exactly what the name implies. A pie, or circle, is divided into segments of the whole. Each segment represents one spreadsheet column or row. The pie chart is perhaps the most widely used type of chart. It is simple, easy to understand, and straightforward. The pie chart, however, is limited to one *Y* **series**. A series is a sequential or related listing of numbers or items; for example, data for 1991, 1992, and 1993; or for January, February, March, and April; or expenses for rent, utilities, and groceries. You can represent only one series with a pie chart because your aim in a pie chart is to show the proportional share of each component within the whole. For example, you can use a pie chart to show the proportion each class of household expenses constitutes of one month's total expenses; however, you cannot simultaneously represent each expense's proportion for each month of the year in one pie chart.

When viewing time is brief, or the audience is unfamiliar with the content of what you are representing, a pie chart is really "worth a thousand words." It answers simple questions about proportions, and it is readily understandable to

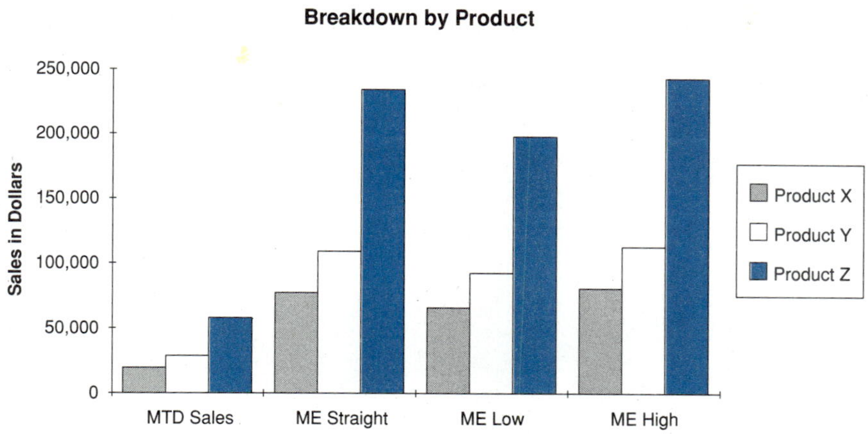

Figure 8.2a

A Bar Chart

Bar charts are the Works default chart.

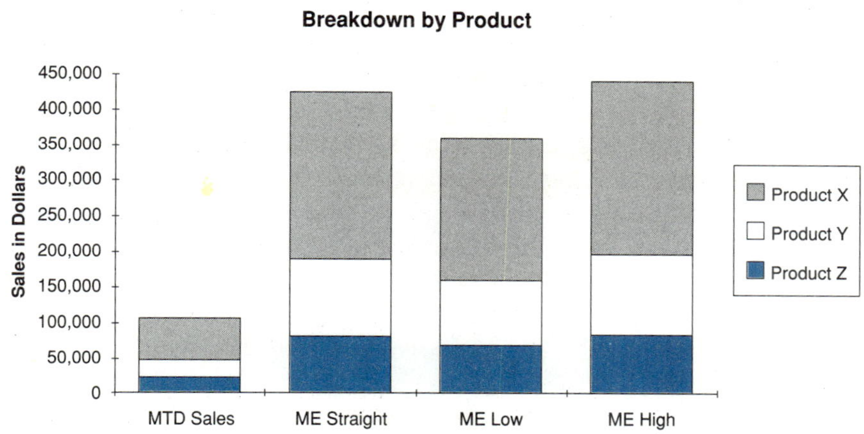

Figure 8.2b

A Stacked Bar Chart

Stacked bar charts add comparisons of Y series.

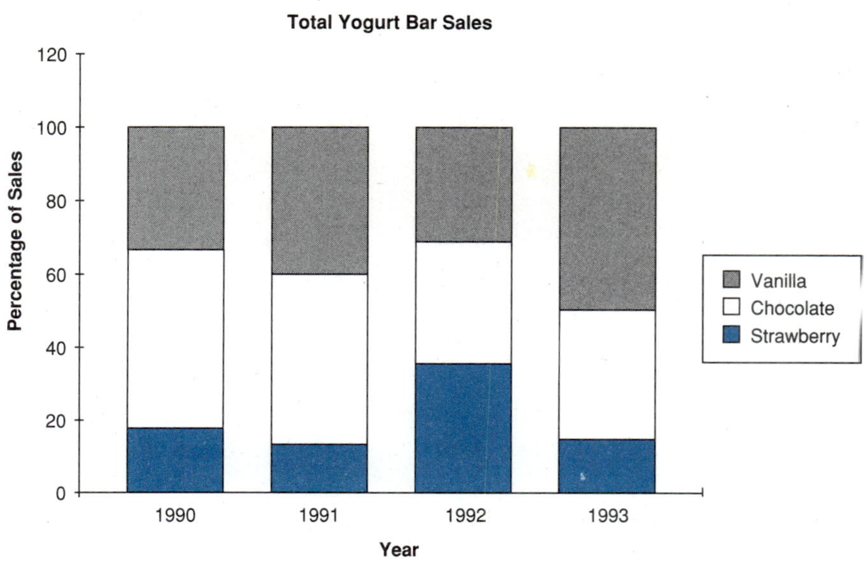

Figure 8.2c

A 100% Bar Chart

100% bar charts depict parts of the whole for multiple series.

most people. You can add emphasis to one section by **exploding** it, or enlarging it and bringing it away from the rest of the segments. Figure 8.3 shows a 3-D pie chart with an exploded segment that could be produced with *Works*.

Figure 8.3

A 3D Exploded Pie

Exploding a section of a pie chart adds emphasis.

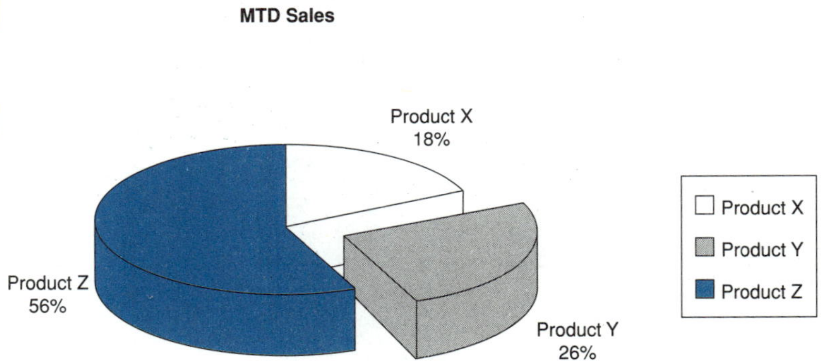

In order to maintain clarity, a pie chart should not have more than six pieces, or sections, unless the divisions are so familiar (months of the year, days of the week) that labeling is not a problem. Just like its physical counterpart, a pie chart divided into many, very small portions loses its impact.

Line Charts

When the relationship among several different items is important and you want to make a comparison or emphasize a trend (change over time), a **line chart** is a good choice. Line charts have a definite advantage over some other types of graphics in that they can simultaneously depict as many as six different data series on the *Y*-axis over a long span of time along the *X*-axis, and yet appear clear and uncluttered. In a line chart, you can compare multiple sets of data, such as earned income, interest from savings, stock dividends, and other types of income over many months or even years in one concise picture. This can represent the data more clearly than trying to glean this same information from the maze of numbers in a large spreadsheet. Thus, line charts are useful for showing trends, or changes in data over time.

Figure 8.4

A Line Chart

Line charts can provide constant comparison of series.

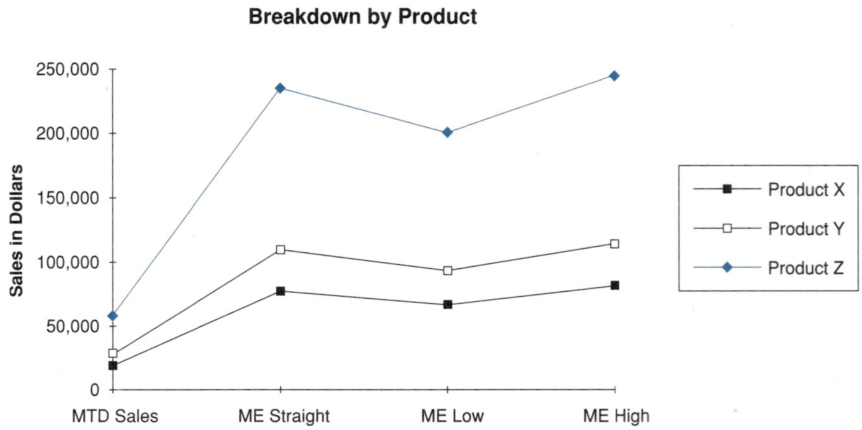

Each line pattern in a line chart is described in a **legend**, or key of patterns, and each line represents a row or column from your spreadsheet. As a result, a line chart represents much data very concisely. To represent a very large amount of data, you can change the **scale** (intervals of measurement) of the line chart along both the *X*-axis and the *Y*-axis. A representative line chart is shown in Figure 8.4.

The *Works* chart program can produce some alternative types of line charts. The **stacked line chart** presents multiple lines, stacked to show the relationships between the values of several categories and their totals. In a stacked line chart, each line's values are added to the values of the line below it, hence the term *stacked* lines. Figure 8.5 illustrates a stacked line chart. A stacked line chart can also be called an **area line chart** because the areas under the line are cumulative. This makes the effect similar to that of a stacked bar chart, but much easier to understand for an extensive *X* series, say data for each month for over several years. With *Works 3.0 for Windows* you can depict the areas as ribbons, as shown in Figure 8.5.

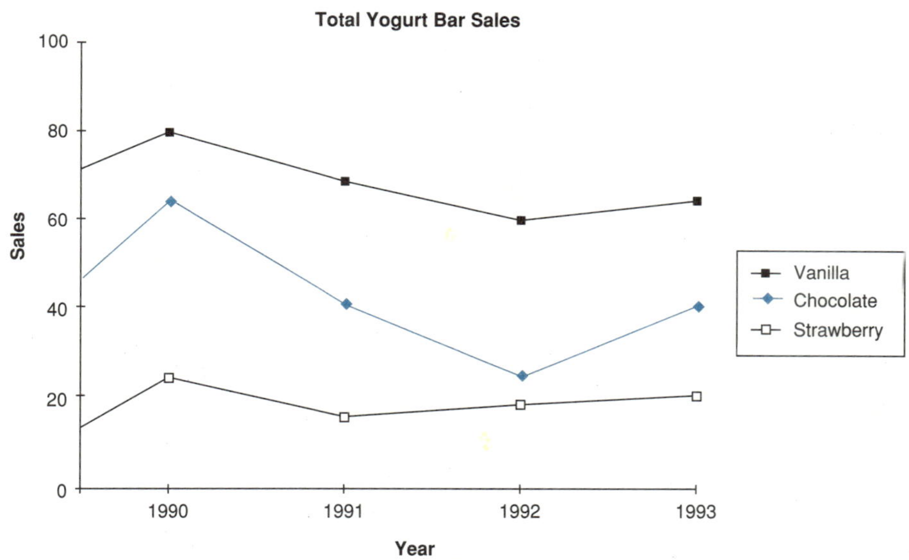

Figure 8.5

Stacked Line Chart

Hi-Lo-Close Charts

A **hi-lo-close chart** can represent a range, or spread, of values within one category. This type of chart can show ranges of many different sets of data, but it is most often used to depict stock market information. The chart presents symbols for the high price of the day, the low price of the day, and the closing price for each stock. The symbol for one category covers a range that is grouped vertically, with the high and low symbols connected to the close symbol. Hi-lo-close charts are similar to what you may have heard referred to as a *box plot*. Both types of charts effectively represent ranges. Figure 8.6 shows a typical hi-lo-close chart. *Works 3.0 for Windows* does not offer the hi-lo-close chart as an option, but most stand-alone spreadsheet programs do, and the earlier versions of *Works* offer it.

Figure 8.6

A Hi-Lo Close Chart

Hi-lo close charts depict ranges for series.

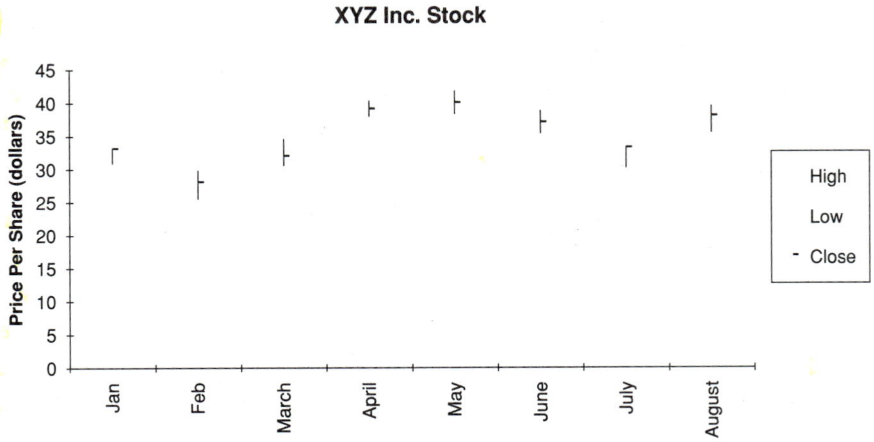

Although most beginners don't use hi-lo-close charts very frequently, they are an excellent way to clearly depict ranges.

X–Y Charts or Scatterplots

When you wish to chart the relationship between two variables on a chart, an ***X–Y* chart** or **scatterplot** is your answer. Often called a *multiplot chart*, this chart shows the association between two different variables, or changing data items. The explanatory or causing variable is scaled along the *X*-axis, and the dependent, or response, variable is scaled along the *Y*-axis. The intersection of the *X* and *Y* measures is shown as a point.

A scatterplot can depict a huge amount of data in a small space and show the general tendency of the relationship between data items. You can easily see the strength and direction of the relationship between the two variables by looking at a scatterplot. This relationship is not readily apparent to the untrained eye looking at the spreadsheet itself. Although you may never plot an *X–Y* chart, you will no doubt see them used occasionally. Figure 8.7 shows a typical scatterplot.

Figure 8.7

A Scatterplot

XY or Scatterplots depict relationships between two variables.

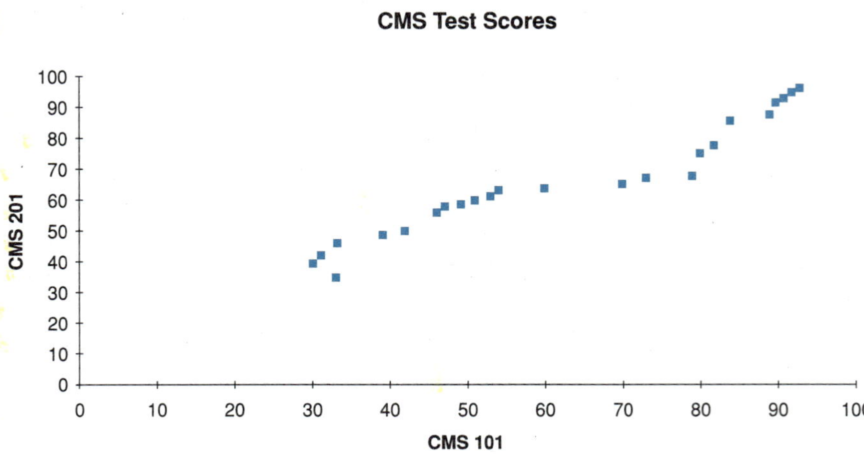

Radar Charts

The newest type of graph that *Works 3.0 for Windows* offers is the **radar chart**, or radial chart. A radar chart can depict frequencies in relation to a center point. Each spoke, or radius, radiates from a common center axis to depict values of one series. You can connect the data markers in a *Y* series on the various radii with lines, or you can depict each value with no connecting lines. Figure 8.8 shows an example of a radar chart without connecting lines in each series. Radar charts have become more popular recently, and are often used with logarithmic scales.

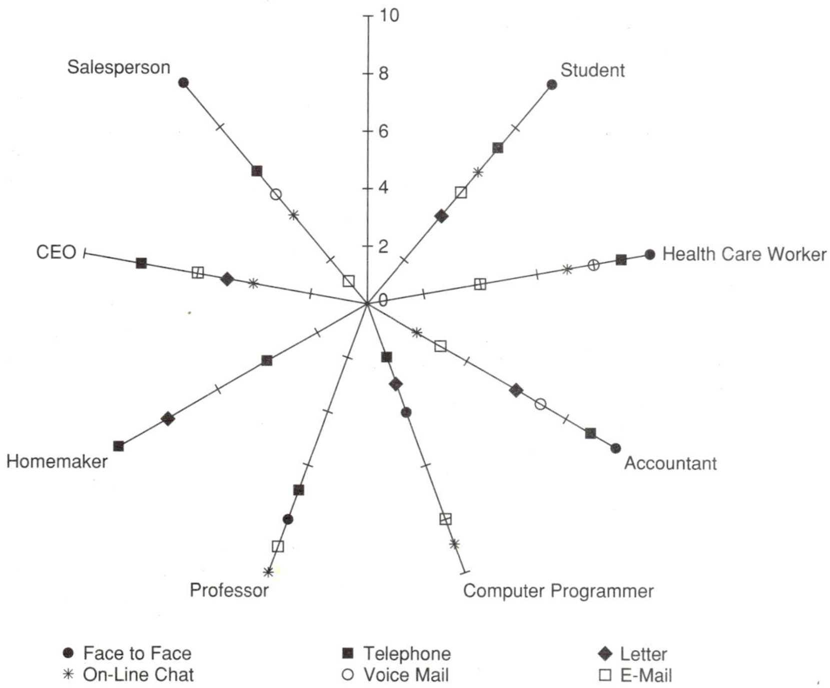

Figure 8.8

Radar charts show series relative to each other and to a central point.

Combination Charts

You can combine lines and bars in the same chart to make one of the categories stand out effectively. This produces a **combination chart**, like that illustrated in Figure 8.9.

Except for the hi-lo-close charts, all of the chart types we have mentioned are available in the charting portion of the *Works* spreadsheet application. Which type of chart you should choose depends on the situation. Try to match the type of chart with the task of representing your numbers so that the chart makes it easier for your audience to understand your spreadsheet. It is possible to combine types of charts, such as a line and a bar chart, but simplicity is the rule. Your whole purpose in using a chart is to improve your communication, so you want to present the information in the simplest, most straightforward manner possible. Even when using a presentation graphics program, you should be careful not to clutter charts with needless information or with too many colors or patterns.

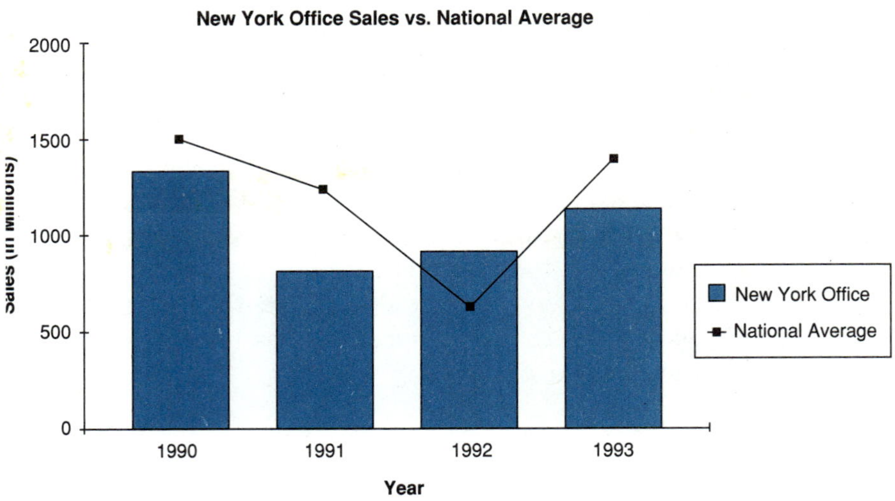

Figure 8.9

A Combination Chart

Combination charts must be carefully designed to avoid confusion.

Importance of Titles, Labels, and Legends

A picture is not worth a thousand words if you do not know what the picture represents. The cardinal rule of graphing is to document a chart to show very clearly what you are graphing (give it a **title**); what each segment, bar, or line represents (give them **labels**), and what each pattern of the bar or line stands for (provide a legend). The only chart that does not require a legend is a pie chart because it depicts only one variable. Differentiation of segments is obvious. See Figure 8.3.

Chart titles explain your graph to the viewer. You may choose to include both a main title and a subtitle for your chart. You may choose one title for the *X*-axis and one for the *Y*-axis, if you wish. The spreadsheet data for the *X* series (for example, Jan., Feb., Mar.) often is text, anyway, so those intervals on the scale will be labeled when you define the areas to be charted.

Labels are words or numbers from a spreadsheet that identify information in a chart. Category labels are displayed along the *X*-axis, and data labels are displayed near the bars, lines, or markers they identify. You can represent up to six *Y*-series within a chart, and you can label series, if you wish.

A legend resembles the legend, or key, on a map. It explains what each pattern or color in the chart represents. Like most graphics programs, *Works* arbitrarily assigns patterns or colors for you when you define the *X* and *Y* series on a chart, but you can change these patterns, if you wish. In this chapter, we will not cover hiding or turning off the legend display, although this option is available in *Works*. You may even put a border around a chart in the Options menu in *Works* and add horizontal and vertical grid lines (lines like those that separate the cells in the spreadsheet).

It is very important to describe your chart with as much detail as possible. Often the difference between a really outstanding presentation and a vague, easily misunderstood one is the attention to detail in titling and explaining graphs.

Chart Menu

The Chart menu is a submenu of the spreadsheet application. From the *Works 3.0 for Windows* spreadsheet menu, you can access the charting application through the View command, or from the chart icon in the toolbar. From the toolbar, clicking on the chart icon allows you to create a new chart. With the View Chart command, you may choose a chart that has already been created. You may define and save eight charts with each spreadsheet. It is usually not necessary to create more than eight charts for a single spreadsheet, but if you need more than eight, you can always save a second copy of the spreadsheet with a different name, then create eight more charts for the duplicate spreadsheet. The Gallery command specifies chart types; you may also change the type of a chart by clicking on the toolbar option for the chart type you want.

Charting Toolbar

Since the chart application is a submenu of the spreadsheet application, the chart toolbar is also a separate and distinct toolbar from the spreadsheet toolbar. Figure 8.10 shows the *Works 3.0 for Windows* chart toolbar. The new chart icons are described more completely below:

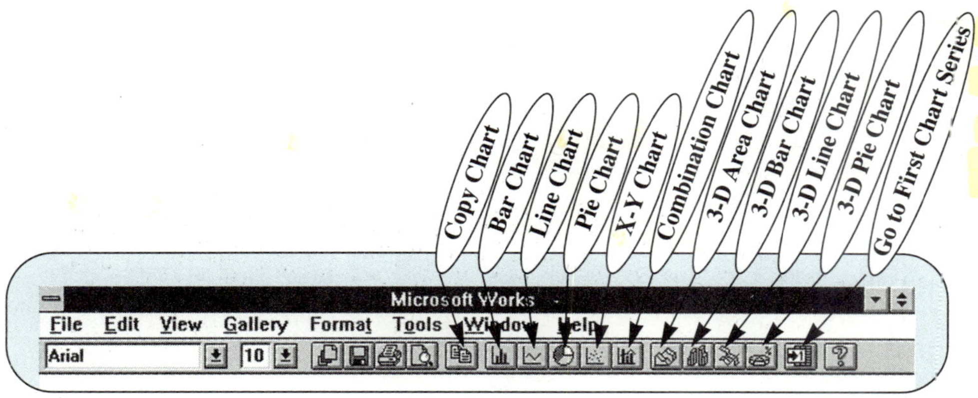

Figure 8.10

Icons on the Charting Toolbar

The Chart Toolbar conveniently provides many charting options at your fingertips.

- Two overlapping documents—Copy a chart
- Bar—Display a bar chart
- Line—Display a line chart
- Pie—Display a pie chart
- *X–Y*—Select an *X–Y* chart (scatterplot)
- Line and bar—Display a combination chart
- 3-D area—Display a 3-D area chart
- 3-D bar—Display a 3-D bar chart
- 3-D line—Display a 3-D line chart
- 3-D pie—Display a 3-D pie chart
- Arrow—Go to the first chart series

Creating a Works Chart

The entire *Works* chart application is contained within the spreadsheet application; it is not a separate application, but must be used with an existing spreadsheet. We noted that the chart menu is accessed through the spreadsheet's main menu. Since charts are saved along with the spreadsheet, you must remember to save your spreadsheet to disk after you define a chart, or you will lose the chart definition.

To create a *Works* chart, the data to be charted must first be entered into a spreadsheet and the spreadsheet file must be open. As was noted it is possible to define eight entirely different charts for each spreadsheet file. When you are charting, the rows and columns in the spreadsheet are organized into categories along a horizontal line called an X *series* by *Works*. Each row or column selected then becomes one of the bars or lines (called the Y *series*). When you change data in the spreadsheet, the chart is automatically updated to reflect that change. *Works* also automatically names each chart you create (with filenames in a series: chart1, chart2, etc.). You can later rename charts by a procedure to be covered later in this chapter. Figure 8.11 shows a typical *Works* chart with the various parts marked.

Figure 8.11

Typical Works Chart with Elements Highlighted

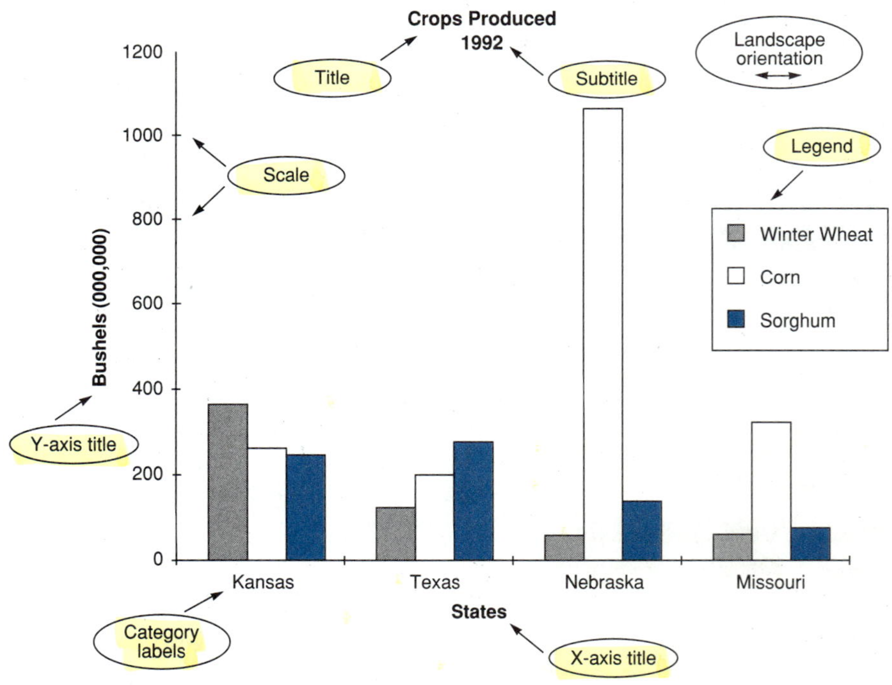

You cannot create a chart in *Works* without first selecting the cells to be graphed. After selecting the cells:

- Click on Tools.
- Choose Create New Chart.

OR

- Click on the toolbar's chart icon.

If a chart has already been created for the chosen spreadsheet, you can access it as follows:

- Click on View-Chart.
- Select the chart you want to view from the list.

These commands give you access to the Chart submenu, which looks similar to the main spreadsheet menu, but contains specific charting commands. From here, you may view the default chart defined by *Works* and modify the chart in any of various ways, including selecting cells or ranges; adding labels, titles, and legends; customizing colors, patterns, and markers; and even changing the type of chart and its name. To return to the spreadsheet program from the Chart submenu:

- Click on View-Spreadsheet.

  OR

- Click on Window and choose the spreadsheet from the list.

Selecting Cells or Ranges for a Chart

As mentioned previously, before you create a chart, you must select the cells or ranges of cells that contain the data you want to chart. When you choose View-Create New Chart, *Works* will automatically assign category labels (on the *X*-axis) if you select a row or column that contains text. Numbers under the first row, or to the right of the first column of text, become your first *Y* series. The second *Y* series is the data in the second column, and so on. You can define six *Y* series, one for each column of numbers on the existing spreadsheet. *Works 3.0 for Windows* also automatically creates a legend for each *Y* series if you select a column or row with text. If you have a large spreadsheet with many columns and you wish to choose a portion to be graphed, you can first select the area to be charted instead of accepting the default of the first six columns. To select the area to be graphed:

- Place the cursor at the beginning of the range.
- Using your favorite selection method, highlight the range.
- Select Tools-Create New Chart.

  OR

- Click on the chart icon from the toolbar.

Works names the chart and adds it to the View-Chart menu. The chart appears on your screen with default labels taken from the defined range.

- Press ESC when you finish viewing the chart.

Your chart will be defined by the range you select. When you press ESC to clear the chart from the screen, you will see the Chart menu at the top of the screen, instead of the spreadsheet menu. The Chart menu has different options that allow you to customize your charts.

Changing the Chart Type

We have emphasized that certain chart styles fit certain purposes better than others. Although a pie chart is simple to understand, a bar or line chart may more effectively plot many different kinds of expenses over a period of time. Many types of charts are available in the *Works 3.0 for Windows* program.

3-D Charts

You can even create **3-D charts** for some of the basic chart types. To change the display of data from one type of chart to another, as from a bar chart to a line chart, with the Chart menu active:

- Click on Gallery.
- Select the new chart type.

If you choose one of the 3-D chart types:

- Click on one of the six perspectives.
- Click on OK.

The new chart type with the same data series will display on the screen. The Chart menu remains at the top of the screen. Click on View-Spreadsheet to return to the spreadsheet and the spreadsheet menu.

If you are defining one of the three-dimensional types of charts, you may choose which of six different 3-D perspectives you prefer. The first is the default. You may choose from a stacked representation, a separated representation, ribbons in a 3-D line chart, all slices exploded in a 3-D pie chart, horizontal and vertical grid lines, or series labeled S1, S2, and so forth. Once you have mastered the rudiments of chart construction, you will enjoy experimenting with the three-dimensional possibilities that *Works 3.0 for Windows* offers. However, if you need hard copy keep in mind that your printer must support the chart selections you choose.

Naming or Deleting a Chart

When you first create a chart in *Works*, it is automatically named chart1, chart2, and so on. To change the name of a chart:

- Click on Tools-Name Chart.
- In the Name box, type in up to 15 characters.
- Click on Rename.
- Click on OK.

To delete a chart from a spreadsheet:

- Click on Tools-Delete Chart.
- Select the chart to delete.
- Click on Delete.
- Click on OK.

Viewing the Chart and Spreadsheet Together

By exploiting one of the great advantages of the *Windows* environment, you can see both your spreadsheet and your chart on the screen at the same time. You can resize your chart view and place it, let's say, in the upper, right-hand corner of the screen while you work within the spreadsheet. You can size both windows to fit side by side, if you wish. This windowing ability is a great help for beginning chart users because they can quickly view the effects of their actions.

To size a chart and move it to a different area of the screen:

- Click and hold down the mouse button on a corner of the window.
- The double-headed sizing arrow appears.
- Decrease the chart window to the desired size by dragging the mouse.
- Drag the entire window to the desired area.
- Release the mouse button.

The spreadsheet behind the chart will show, as well as the chart itself. The Chart menu will remain at the top of the active window for further action. If you wish to edit the spreadsheet, click anywhere outside the chart window to make the spreadsheet window active and return the spreadsheet menu. You can now edit the spreadsheet.

At this point, however, the chart window will move behind the active window. To make the chart window active again, simply click anywhere in the chart window. (If you need to review the techniques for sizing windows, refer back to Chapter 2.) Remember, if you lose a window by maximizing it or otherwise, you can always use the Window menu selection in either application's menu to activate another window.

Customizing a Chart

You may change the *X* and *Y* series on your chart independently. To do so, after allowing *Works* to define the default *X* and *Y* series automatically, and after viewing the new chart:

- Click on Edit-Series.

The *X* and *Y* series, as first defined, are displayed. You may change any or all of them:

- Enter any new *Y* series ranges you want.
- Enter any new *X* series.
- Click on OK.

Adding Labels, Titles, and Legends

As was noted labels are words or numbers from a spreadsheet that identify information in a chart. Category labels—words or numbers that identify chart components—are displayed along the *X* axis. Some examples are names of months, categories (such as *income* and *expenses*), names of people, and so on. Data labels, which show the spreadsheet values from which a category is calculated, are displayed next to or above the bars, lines, or markers they identify.

Works automatically inserts data labels next to plotted points on a chart when you define a chart that has text in the selected range. On line and bar charts, the values themselves can become labels. If you wish to change the labels, you can use the Data Labels option from the Edit menu. If you wish to summarize them, choose the Category Labels option described below.

In a pie chart, you have the extra option of defining two types of data labels. On a pie chart, you can put two labels on each slice because you are plotting parts of a whole, rather than multiple *Y* series. To place both a value and some descriptive text on each sector of a pie chart:

- Click on Edit-Data Labels.
- Type what you wish at the 1st Label and 2nd Label prompts.

  OR
- Choose Cell Content and type the range you wish to use.
- Click on OK.

Figure 8.12 shows the Data Labels window in which you create data labels for a pie chart.

Figure 8.12

The Data Labels Window

As we noted, *Works* automatically assigns labels if you select a row or column of text when you define a chart. To create category labels, you assign other cells from a spreadsheet row or column to serve as labels for one series of bars, lines, or markers. If you wish to replace the *X*-series and *Y*-series default text that *Works* defines, you may choose your own category labels. This is especially useful if your spreadsheet includes many labels that will not fit nicely on a chart. To reduce the clutter, you can summarize the labels on the chart. To add or edit category labels, if they do not already appear, add the text or numbers to your spreadsheet somewhere, then:

- Select cells with the text or numbers within the spreadsheet.
- Click on Edit-Copy.

This places the material on the clipboard. Then:

- Activate the Chart menu.
- Click on Edit-Paste Series.
- Choose Category.
- Click on OK.

Works 3.0 for Windows will now change the category labels on the chart. Likewise, if you wish to delete any category labels:

- Click on Edit Series.
- While in Category X Series, press DELETE.
- Click on OK.

You can also change only the frequency of category labels as they are already defined. To do so, from the Chart menu:

- Click on Format-Horizontal (X) Axis.
- Select the content of Label Frequency.
- Type the new interval number you desire.

  For example, type **6** to use only every sixth *X*-series entry as a category label.
- Click on OK.

You can create titles and subtitles in the Edit Titles option box. You can type in the title, or reference a spreadsheet cell to serve as a title, using the Edit Title Text selection. Each title and subtitle can include up to 37 characters. You will notice that *Works* adds double quotation marks to your title when you type it in the option box.

To create a chart title and/or subtitle:

- Click on Edit-Titles.
- Type a title (or a range reference).
- Type a subtitle, if desired (or a range reference).
- Type an *X*-axis title, if you want one on your chart.
- Type a *Y*-axis title, if applicable.
- Click on OK.

To delete chart titles:

- Select Edit-Titles.
- Select the title you want to delete.
- Press the DELETE key.
- Click on OK.

Legends in a chart are like the legends on a map; they show what the colors, patterns, and marker shapes mean. They explain the meanings of the different *Y* series. When you create a chart, *Works* will automatically create legends for each *Y* series if you select columns or rows that contain text for the titles or labels. You can add, change, or delete legends. The only chart type that does not require a legend is the pie chart, because it graphs one series. Any other chart should have a legend that explains the meanings of the various patterns and colors.

You can change the default legend through the Edit menu.

- Click on Edit.
- Click on Legend Series/Labels.

A legend series window appears to identify the selected *Y* series ranges and also offer the option of using series definitions automatically as legends. You may change these legends to more descriptive terms if you wish, or simply mark Use as Legend to use the text that is already in the spreadsheet.

Customizing with Colors, Patterns, and Markers

The Format command in the *Works* Chart menu allows you to set colors and patterns for your chart through the Patterns and Colors option. The Series box lists the *Y* series in the chart. When you select a *Y* series, the other boxes show the data format for that series. For a pie chart, the Series box is replaced with a Slices choice. The Colors box shows the colors you can choose; the Patterns box shows the patterns you can choose; the Markers box shows the marker shapes available for points on a line chart, including circles, diamonds, and rectangles. The Format option at the bottom of the box applies your formatting selections to the selected *Y* series or pie slice, and the Format All option applies your selections to every series or pie slice.

To change data formats:

- Click on Format-Patterns and Colors.
- In the Series box, select the *Y* series you want to change.
- Select Colors, Patterns, and/or Markers.
- Choose Format, Format All, or Cancel.

If you are constructing a pie graph, the bottom option allows you to explode a slice as you format it.

Scales

A scale is a set of numbered marks that measure values along an axis. To define a scale, you set a minimum, a maximum, and an interval between the marks. *Works 3.0 for Windows* automatically determines the scale when you create a chart. (You can use logarithmic scales in *Works,* but we will not discuss those.) To change the scale of an axis:

- Click on Format Horizontal (*X*-axis), or Vertical (*Y*-axis), or Right (*Y* or vertical axis), or Two Vertical (*Y*-axes).
- Place the lowest number in the Minimum box.
- Place the highest number in the Maximum box.

- Enter an interval in the Interval box.

  OR
- Type **Auto** in the boxes to have *Works* set the values.
- Click on OK.

Gridlines and Borders

You can add horizontal **gridlines**, vertical gridlines, or both. You can also put a border around your spreadsheet.

- Click on View-Chart-Name of chart.

To add gridlines:

- Click on Format.
- Choose an axis (*X*-Axis, *Y*-Axis, or Right *Y*-Axis, if any).
- Click on the Show Grid Lines check box. (Click again to delete.)
- Click on OK.

To add a border:

- Select Format-Border.
- To delete a border, remove the check mark by clicking again.

The gridlines and border options are toggle commands; you turn them off and on by selecting again.

Printing a Chart

The Print menu offers several options. You can change the page setup and margins as you did for word processing documents; you can preview your chart; you can view your chart as it will appear printed in black and white; you can see a list of the options for colors, patterns, and marker styles available on your printer. You can display a newly selected printer font on the screen (*Works* will use the original screen font unless directed otherwise), and you can change the printer specifications. You can put headers and footers on charts, as well as on spreadsheets. You can print the chart in screen size, or fill a page with it. *Works* gives you many print options to control the printouts of your charts.

To define headers and footers:

- Click on View-Headers and Footers.
- Type in the desired header or footer.
- Click on OK.

To see a list of available options:

- Click on File-Page Setup.
- Click on Margins, or Source Size Orientation, or Other Options.
- In Orientation, choose Landscape or Portrait, or change the setting for paper Width or Length.

- In Other Options, choose Screen Size, or Full Page size, or Keep Proportion.

To change the font for your titles and labels:

- Click on Format-Font & Style.

You can print a chart in either portrait or landscape mode. Use portrait mode to print a chart vertically on the page, and landscape mode to print horizontally. Landscape is the default option.

It is always a good idea to preview your chart before you print it, which can be done with the File-Print Preview option. Printing graphics uses a great deal of toner or ribbon and takes much longer than printing text, so it is wise to view and correct a chart as necessary before printing it.

Saving a Chart to Disk

As we noted, since your chart is really a part of the spreadsheet whose data it represents, you must remember to save the entire spreadsheet file before finishing your work session. To do so, return to the main spreadsheet menu and save the entire file to disk:

- Click on File-Save.

  OR

- Click on the Save icon from the toolbar.

After this, you may exit *Works* with the assurance that whatever charts you have created are saved along with the original spreadsheet.

GRAPHICS TUTORIAL NO. 1

You are going to create a bar chart from the Miscellaneous Payments section in the persfin.wks spreadsheet that you created in Chapter 7. Remember that the bar chart is automatically created in *Works* once you select the range of cells. You can view it in the preview window of your screen.

1. Open the existing file persfin.wks.
2. Save it with the file name graphics.

   Mark the data for your chart:

3. Select Cells A27:G31.

   (This includes all of the miscellaneous expenses without totals.)

4. Click on Tools.

   The Tools menu displays, as shown in Figure 8.13.

5. Click on Create New Chart.

   The New Chart screen is displayed showing your data in a bar chart similar to Figure 8.14. TAB to the Chart Title text box, then:

Figure 8.13

The Tools Menu

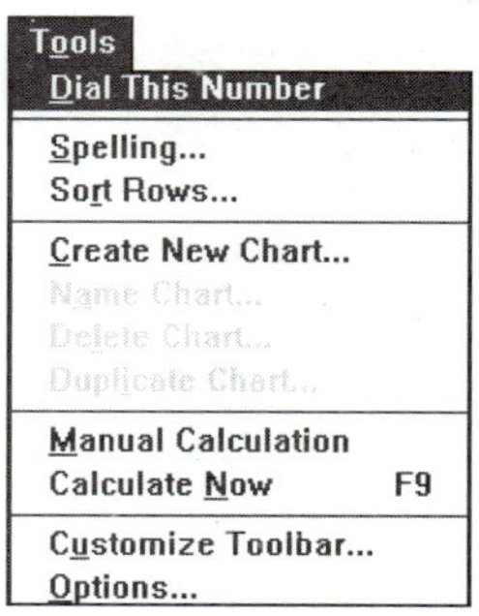

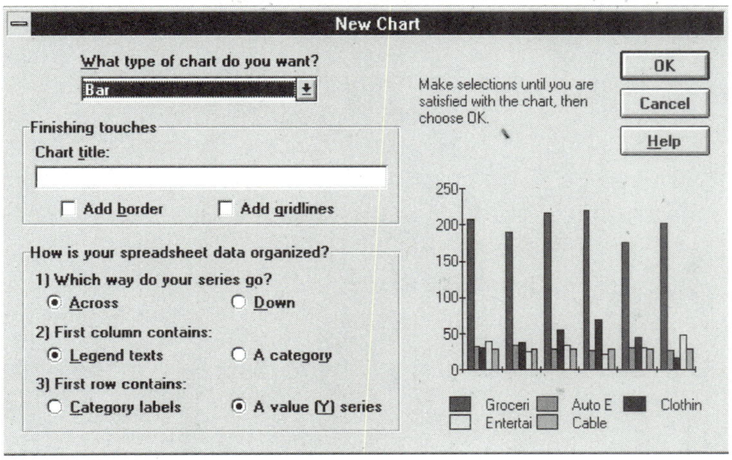

Figure 8.14

The New Chart Screen

6. Type **Miscellaneous Expenses**

   The title displays above your bar chart in the preview window. The following items should be marked under the question, "How is your spreadsheet data organized?"

   1) Across
   2) Legend texts
   3) A value (*Y*) series

7. Click on OK.

   The bar chart fills the screen. You want to add a subtitle and titles for the *X*-axis and *Y*-axis.

8. Click on Edit.

   The Edit menu displays, as shown in Figure 8.15.

9. Click on Titles.

   The Titles option box appears with the title displayed.

10. TAB to Subtitle.
11. Type **January-June, 1995**
12. TAB to Horizontal (*X*) Axis and type **Item**
13. TAB to Vertical (*Y*) Axis and type **Amount**
14. Click on OK.

    To put the names of the months on the *X*-axis:

15. Click on Edit-Series.

    The Series option box displays, as shown in Figure 8.16.

16. Click on the Category (*X*) Series text box, and type **B4:G4** (the range of cells that contain the month names).

Figure 8.15

The Edit Menu

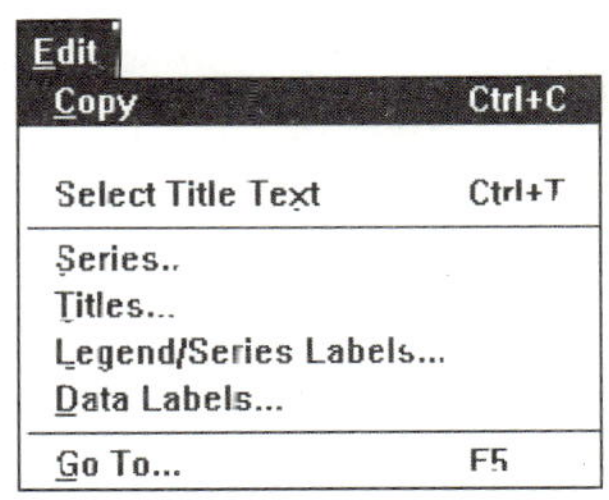

Figure 8.16

The Series Option Box

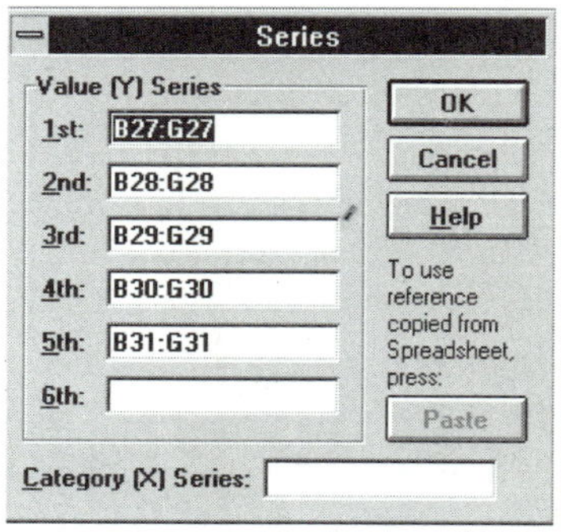

The names of the months are displayed at the bottom of your screen.

17. Click on OK.

    Now you want to change the chart name from chart1 to miscexp.

18. Click on Tools-Name Chart.

    The Name Chart option box displays, as shown in Figure 8.17.

19. In the Name text box, type **miscexp**
20. Click on Rename.
21. Click on OK.

    The name is replaced. Your chart should look similar to that in Figure 8.18.

Figure 8.17

The Name Chart Option Box

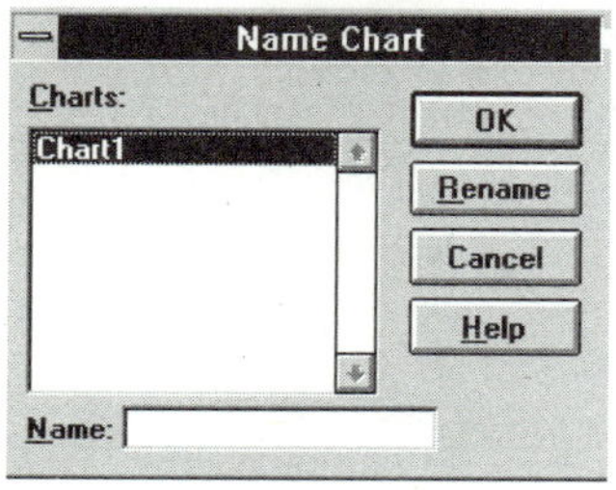

Figure 8.18

The Bar Chart with the Name Replaced

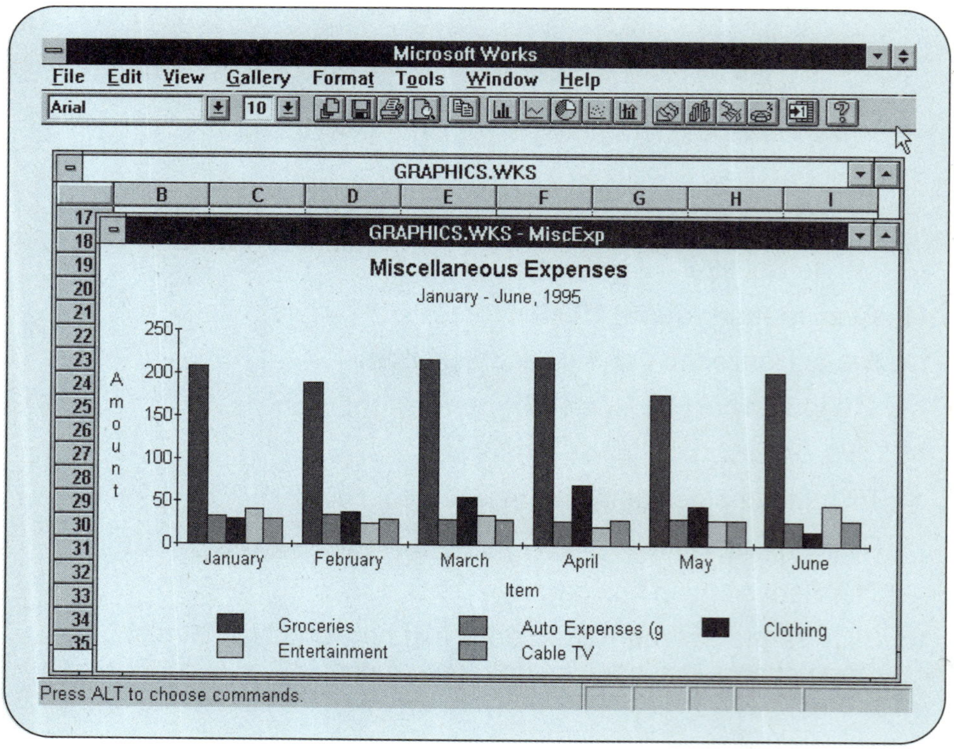

22. Click on the Save icon.

    When you save the spreadsheet, your charts are automatically saved with it. You now want to print your chart.

23. Click on the Print icon.

    Your chart will begin printing after a short pause. To close the bar chart:

24. Click on the Control menu box of the chart, and then click on Close.

GRAPHICS TUTORIAL NO. 2

You would now like to see the proportion of your monthly expenses that pay for insurance. A pie chart is appropriate for proportions as it shows the parts of a whole.

1. Select Cells A19:B23.

   You can chart data for only one month because the total must equal 100 percent.

2. Click on Tools-Create New Chart.

   A bar chart is shown on the New Chart screen. In the "What type of chart do you want?" box:

3. Click on the DOWN ARROW and select Pie.
4. Click on OK.
5. Click on Edit-Titles.

   The Titles screen displays, as shown in Figure 8.19.

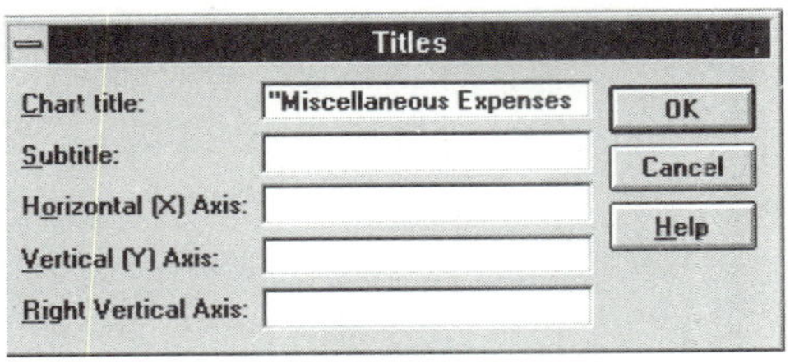

Figure 8.19

The Titles Screen

6. Type the title **INSURANCE EXPENSES**
7. Type the subtitle **January-June, 1995**
8. Click on OK.

   The titles appear on your graph.

9. Rename the chart insexp (Tools-Name Chart).

   You want to emphasize the auto insurance slice of the pie by exploding the slice.

10. Click on Format.

    The Format option box displays, as shown in Figure 8.20.

Figure 8.20

The Format Option Box

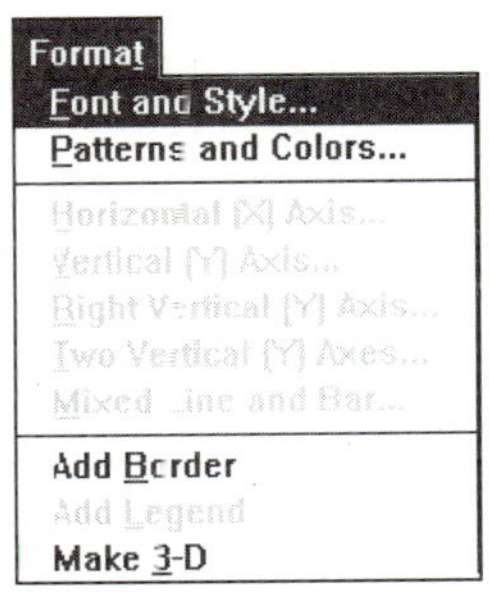

11. Click on Patterns and Colors.

    The Patterns and Colors option box displays, as shown in Figure 8.21.

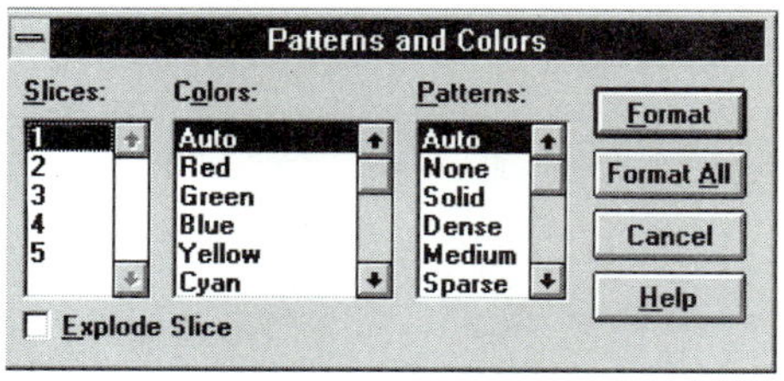

Figure 8.21

The Patterns and Colors Option Box

12. Select 2 from the Slices box.
13. Select Explode Slice.
14. Click on Format.
15. Click on Close.

    Your chart should look similar to the one in Figure 8.22. Now you want to see what the pie chart would look like in 3-D. First, replace the exploded piece.

16. Click on Format-Patterns and Colors.
17. Select Slice 2.
18. Click to remove the mark on Explode Slice.

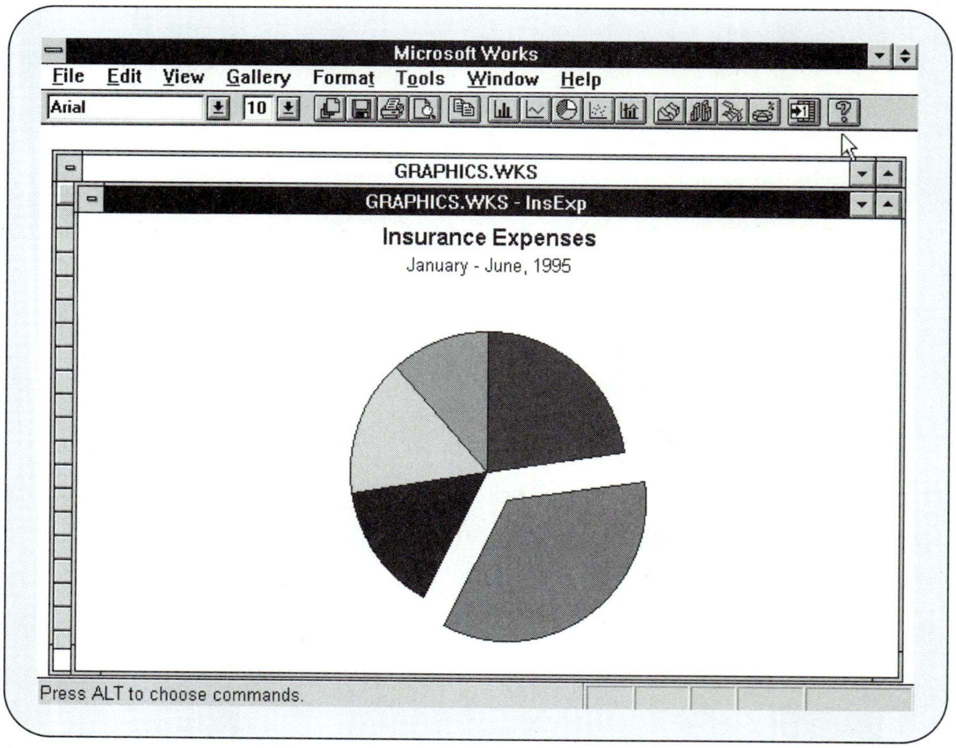

Figure 8.22

Screen Displaying Pie Chart with Exploded Piece

19. Click on Format-Close.
20. Click on Gallery.

    The Gallery menu displays, as shown in Figure 8.23.
21. Click on 3-D Pie.

    The 3-D Pie screen displays, as shown in Figure 8.24.
22. Click on 6.
23. Click on OK.

    The pie chart is shown in 3-D with labels for the percentage of each slice and the type of insurance, similar to Figure 8.25.
24. Close the pie chart.

    You wonder if the 3-D Area chart would look better.

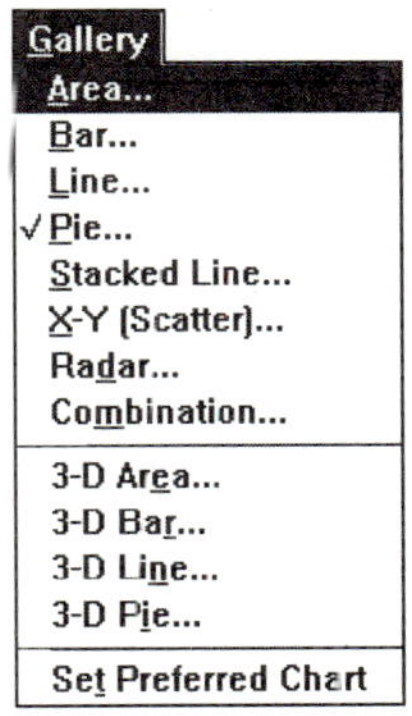

Figure 8.23

The Gallery Menu

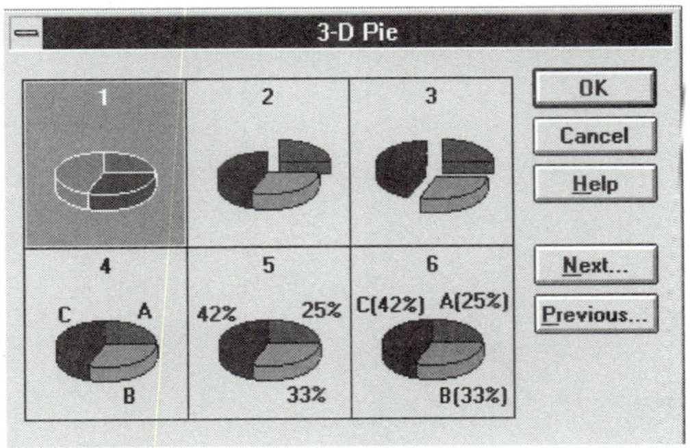

Figure 8.24

The 3-D Pie Screen

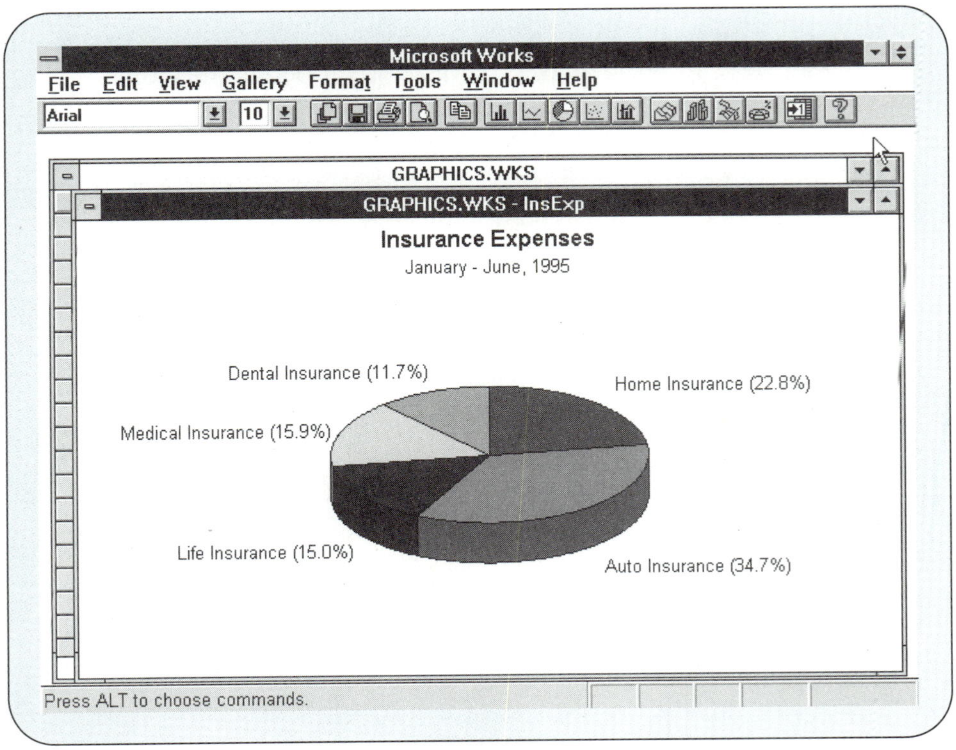

Figure 8.25

Screen Displaying 3-D Pie Chart

25. Click on View-Chart.
26. Click on insexp-OK.
27. Click on the Area chart icon (the sixth icon from the right).
28. Click on OK.

    You decide that you prefer the 3-D pie chart.

29. Click on the 3-D Pie icon.
30. Click on 6-OK.
31. Click on the Save icon.
32. Click on the Print icon.
33. Close the insexp chart.

GRAPHICS TUTORIAL NO. 3

Next, you would like to see the trend in your miscellaneous expenses over the six-month period. A line chart is most appropriate for that purpose. You want to add a border around the chart and add gridlines. To create a new line chart:

1. Select Cells A27:G31.
2. Click on the New Chart icon.
3. Select Line chart.
4. Click on Add Border.
5. Click on Add Gridlines.
6. Click on OK.
7. On your own, rename chart1 as miscline (Tools-Name Chart).

   You think the chart might be easier to read if the colors and formats of the lines were different.

8. Click on Format.
9. Click on Patterns and Colors.

   The Patterns and Colors option box displays, as shown in Figure 8.26.

Figure 8.26

The Patterns and Colors Option Box

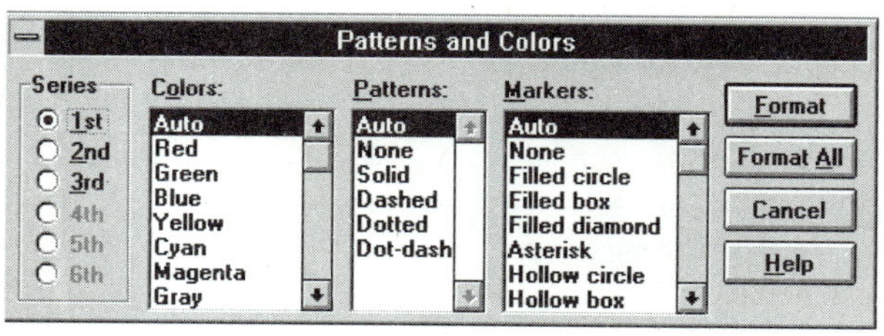

10. In the Series box, select 1st.
11. In the Colors box, select Red.
12. In the Patterns box, select Solid.
13. In the Markers box, select Filled Circle.

    Select the other four series as follows:

Series	Color	Pattern	Marker
2nd	Magenta	Dashed	Filled Box
3rd	Blue	Dotted	Hollow Circle
4th	Dark Red	Dot-Dashed	Asterisk
5th	Dark Green	Solid	Filled Diamond

14. Click on Close.

    Notice that it is somewhat easier to read with different formats for the lines and the new grid lines. If your printer cannot produce these patterns, markers, and colors, use any unique combination you choose. Now you will add a title, a subtitle, and titles for the *X*-axis and *Y*-axis.

15. Click on Edit-Titles.

    The Titles option box appears.

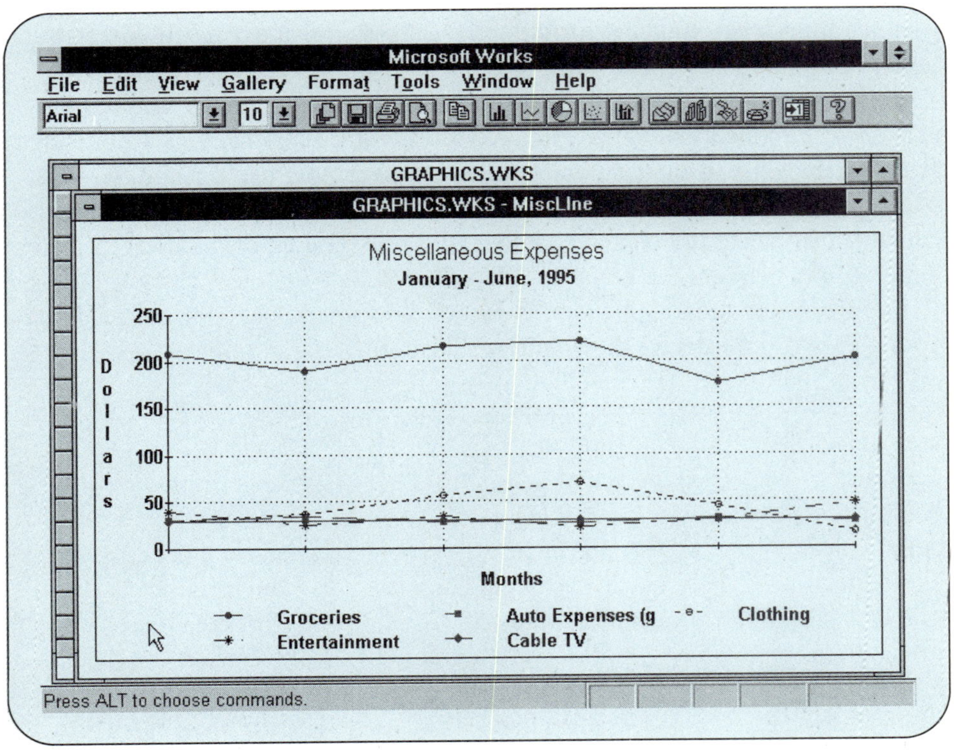

Figure 8.27

Screen Displaying Graph of Miscellaneous Expenses

16. In the Chart Title line, type **Miscellaneous Expenses**
17. In the Subtitle line, type **January-June, 1995**
18. For the *Y*-axis title, type **Dollars**
19. For the *X*-axis title, type **Months**

    Your screen should look similar to that in Figure 8.27.
20. Click on OK.
21. Click on the Save icon.
22. Click on the Print icon.
23. Close the file and exit *Works*.

Chapter Summary

Graphics software uses a computer to create, edit, display, and print graphic images. Such images enhance the effectiveness of communicating information to others, and they can be important aids in decision making. *Works* supports many popular types of charts such as bar charts, line charts, pie charts, and scatterplots. In order to make charts using *Works*, you must have a graphics card installed in your computer, and you need a completed spreadsheet. To print your charts, you must have a printer that can output graphics. Presentation graphics packages, in particular, have evolved into very sophisticated software. These products can produce high-level graphics for company reports, business meetings, and customer presentations.

You create charts by working from the Tools menu or the Toolbar of the spreadsheet application. Once you have selected the data that you want to chart, *Works* creates a bar chart automatically; however, you can change the type of chart by selecting other choices from the toolbar or from the Gallery menu. You can also customize the chart by choosing a 3-D version, or a variety of colors, patterns, and markers.

The *Works* charting application is part of the spreadsheet application. To save your charts you must save the whole spreadsheet file.

KEY TERMS

area line chart
bar chart
combination chart
default chart
exploding
graphics program
graphics card
gridlines
hi-lo-close chart
import
chart label
chart legend
line chart
100 percent bar chart
pie chart
presentation graphics software
radar chart
scale
scatterplot
series
stacked bar chart
stacked line chart (or area line)
3-D chart
chart title
X–Y chart

REVIEW QUESTIONS

1. Briefly define the term *graphics*.
2. List at least five ways a business could find graphics useful.
3. How do presentation graphics programs differ from the graphics program in *Works*?
4. List the items necessary to prepare a computerized graph.
5. List the major chart types. Briefly explain each one.
6. State the purpose of the Chart menu.
7. List the charting Toolbar icons. Briefly explain what each one does.
8. Name the steps in creating a chart.
9. Why might you want to change from the default bar chart to another type of chart? How would you do this?
10. Describe the advantage(s) of viewing a chart and the corresponding spreadsheet together simultaneously. How is this done?
11. Explain (a) what labels, titles, and legends are, and (b) what they could add to a chart.
12. Explain how to include labels, titles, and legends in a chart.
13. Review the technique for customizing a chart with colors, patterns, and markers.
14. Briefly review the purpose of a scale; how could you change a scale?
15. Explain the difference between the portrait and landscape modes of printing graphics.

SOFTWARE EXERCISES

Exercise 8.1

1. Open a new spreadsheet.
2. Widen Column A to 13 spaces.
3. Change Column B to 9 spaces in width.
4. Enter the data from Table 8.1 into the spreadsheet. Type the word **SECURITY** in Cell A1 and the word **INVESTED** in Cell B1; type **LAST YR.** in B2. Type the details in A4 through B9.
5. Select the range A4 through B9.
6. Create a new chart.
7. Change the bar chart to a pie chart.
8. Use the View menu to select the spreadsheet again.
9. Add a chart title that reads: "[your name]'S PORTFOLIO."
10. Check the Printer Setup menu under the Print menu; change the selection to the printer you are going to use if it is not already selected.
11. Choose a Title Font size of 10 or 12 under Format menu.

12. Preview your chart.
13. Print your chart if the preview looks acceptable; otherwise change it, preview it again, and then print it.
14. Rename chart1 (the default name) as portcht.
15. Save the spreadsheet as portfol.
16. Close portcht and portfol.wks.
17. Exit *Works*.

Table 8.1

SECURITY	INVESTED LAST YR.
U.S. Treasuries	35000
Stock Fund	22000
Growth Fund	18000
Balanced Fund	60000
CDs	15000
Bond Fund	25000

Exercise 8.2

1. Open the portfol.wks spreadsheet you completed in Exercise 8.1 or complete Exercise 8.1 before continuing.
2. Change Column C to 9 spaces in width.
3. Type "INVESTED THIS YR." in column C. Type the dollar amount of each investment in the portfolio, as follows: U.S. Treasuries, 50000; Stock Fund, 22800; Growth Fund, 12000; Balanced Fund, 45000; CDs 25000; Bond Fund 25200.
4. Select the range from B4 to C9.
5. Format this range as comma with zero decimal places.
6. Select the range from A4 to C9.
7. Create a new bar chart of this range.
8. Add a chart title that reads: "[your name]'S PORTFOLIO."
9. Add a chart subtitle that reads: "Last Year vs. This Year."
10. Add an *X*-axis title that reads "Investments" and a *Y*-axis title that reads, "Dollars."
11. View the chart often as you build it.
12. Make certain that your printer setup is correct; enlarge the title font size to 10 or 12 and use a font of your choice.
13. Click on Auto Series Labels, if it is selected. Add the following legend for the 1st Value Series: "LAST YEAR."

14. Add the following legend for the 2nd Value Series: "THIS YEAR."
15. Rename chart2 as portcht1.
16. Save the spreadsheet as portfol1.
17. Print your chart.
18. Close portfol1 and portfol1.wks.
19. Exit *Works*.

Exercise 8.3

1. Open the indxfnd.wks spreadsheet on the student data diskette.
2. Select the range from A3 through I5.
3. Construct a bar chart.
4. View the chart often as you build it.
5. Add a suitable title.
6. Add titles for the *X*-axis and *Y*-axis.
7. Add grid lines to the *Y*-axis.
8. Add a border.
9. Rename chart1 as indxcht.
10. Save the spreadsheet.
11. Print the chart.
12. Close indxcht and indxfnd.wks.
13. Exit *Works*.

Exercise 8.4

1. Open the perfm.wks spreadsheet on the student data diskette.
2. Select the range from A6 to B11.
3. Construct a line chart.
4. View the chart often as you build it.
5. Add a suitable title.
6. Add titles for the *X*-axis and *Y*-axis.
7. Add grid lines to the *Y*-axis.
8. Make certain that the correct printer is selected.
9. Enlarge the title font size to 10 or 12 in the font of your choice.
10. Reduce the other font sizes to 3 or 4.
11. Rename chart1 as perfmcht.
12. Save your spreadsheet.
13. Print your chart.
14. Close perfmcht and perfm.wks.
15. Exit *Works*.

Exercise 8.5

1. Open the houseinv.wks spreadsheet that you created in Chapter 6.
2. Construct a bar chart for the first six items showing their costs and replacement values.
3. Add a title, legends, grid lines, a border, and series labels to your chart.
4. View the chart often as you build it.
5. Rename chart1 as invchart.
6. Print your chart.
7. Close invchart and houseinv.wks.
8. Exit *Works*.

Exercise 8.6

1. Open the persfin.wks spreadsheet that you created in Chapter 7. Note the cell address for the following ranges before proceeding: Total Income, Expenses, and Net Income for January through June.
2. Select the Total Income cells for January through June; *Do not* include the words *Total Income* along with the January through June data.
3. Construct a new bar chart. With the bar chart created, you are going to add the Total Expenses and Net Income series.
4. With the bar chart showing, click on Edit-Series.
5. TAB to the second Value *Y* Series and enter the range for Total Expenses from January to June.
6. Click on Edit-Series again.
7. TAB to the third Value *Y* Series and enter the range for Net Income from January to June.
8. Add a title, subtitle, titles for the *X*-axis and *Y*-axis, legends, *Y*-axis grid lines , a border, and labels to your chart.
9. View the chart often as you build it.
10. Rename chart1 as perfinch.
11. Print your chart.
12. Close perfinch and persfin.wks.
13. Exit *Works*.

Exercise 8.7

1. At your library, locate a recent copy of *USA Today* or a local newspaper of your choice.
2. Find a graph of interest to you in the paper.
3. Enter the graphed data into a *Works* spreadsheet.

4. Save your work.
5. Construct a graph from your spreadsheet. Include a title, legends, a scale, labels, and patterns in your chart to make it easy to read.
6. Save your chart.
7. Print it.
8. Close your chart and file.
9. Exit *Works*.

Exercise 8.8

1. Open an existing spreadsheet. This might come from your student data diskette, or from the spreadsheet exercises you completed in Chapters 6 and 7.
2. Construct a graph from your spreadsheet. Include a title, legends, a scale, labels, and patterns in your chart to make it easy to read.
3. Save your chart.
4. Print it.
5. Close your chart and file.
6. Exit *Works*.

Exercise 8.9

1. Use some personal data such as your own household budget, college budget, a collection, or any basis for a chart that interests you.
2. Build a spreadsheet with your data.
3. Choose an appropriate title for your spreadsheet.
4. Construct an appropriate chart from your spreadsheet. Include a title, legends, a scale, labels, and patterns in your chart to make it easy to read.
5. Save your chart.
6. Print it.
7. Close your chart and file.
8. Exit *Works*.

Chapter 9

Introduction to Databases

Objectives

After studying this chapter you will be able to:

- *Define the term* database
- *Explain the difference between a file management system and a database management system*
- *Explain the uses of databases*
- *List and explain the four types of data models*
- *Define the terms* file, record, *and* field
- *Plan and construct a* Works *database structure*
- *Enter data into the database structure you construct*
- *Retrieve and edit records from an existing file*
- *Query and sort your database*

Definition and Uses of Databases

A database is a special kind of data file; it is self-describing, meaning that records conform to a structure built within it. This makes a database file a very powerful way of keeping records. It is the electronic equivalent of the manual filing cabinet, but once the file is built, its operation and maintenance become much easier than the manual file system.

A database allows you to organize a collection of data in a way that facilitates retrieval and reporting of information. A **database management system** is made up of hardware and software designed to allow for the organization, storage, manipulation, retrieval, and reporting of records that are related in some way. This system is what acts upon database files.

A database program facilitates organized record-keeping, but unlike a file cabinet, it offers much more than just somewhere to store information safely and efficiently. The **database file** itself is a self-describing collection of related records—that is, records for which the structure of the file is built into the actual file data. For example, if you build a database devoted to members of your recreational softball team, all the records have a common feature—they are all concerned with the members of a team. The persons described in the **file** have individual characteristics, but they have one common characteristic, their membership in the team. A **record** is all the information that pertains to one person, object, or event. Within each record are general **fields**, or categories, by which the records can be grouped. The information within each field pertains specifically to an individual, object, or event, but the categories are common to all the records. For example, name, address, and batting average are fields that contain information specific to each player, but each record has these common fields, or places to enter the unique information.

An advantage of database software over a manual filing system is its ability to quickly retrieve individual records in many different orders, and to order records within another order (creating a nested structure) without losing the original filing scheme. If all of the softball team records are initially entered alphabetically, or even randomly, the records can be retrieved according to the players' Zip codes, batting averages, or even uniform numbers without losing the original filing system. Records can also be selected, or filtered out, to identify those that meet certain requirements (criteria) based on the contents of a single field. For example, the records of all team members who have batting averages of .200 or above can be displayed. These powerful capabilities of database software make it the foundation of business computing. Almost everyone, however, can use databases in their personal lives, as well.

There are two types of database software packages: **file management systems**, in which records from only one file can be related at a time, and **database management systems**, which allow records from multiple files to be related and manipulated at the same time. The first type of software is often referred to as a **flat file**. The *Works 3.0 for Windows* database is a flat file program, since it uses one file at a time. This kind of database software can meet most personal and some small business needs. The second type of software, a true database management system, requires more sophisticated and expensive hardware and software. Larger businesses and government organizations find these useful. The purpose of both types of database software is the same, however: to offer the user rapid, easy access to data in endless patterns.

Databases are suitable for managing an endless variety of records, for example:

- Customer lists
- Records related to hobbies or collections
- Employee records
- Inventories

- Sales records
- Student grades and information
- Catalogs of tapes or books

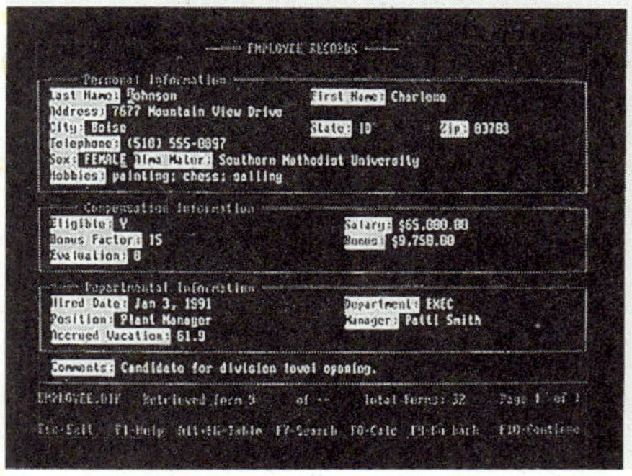

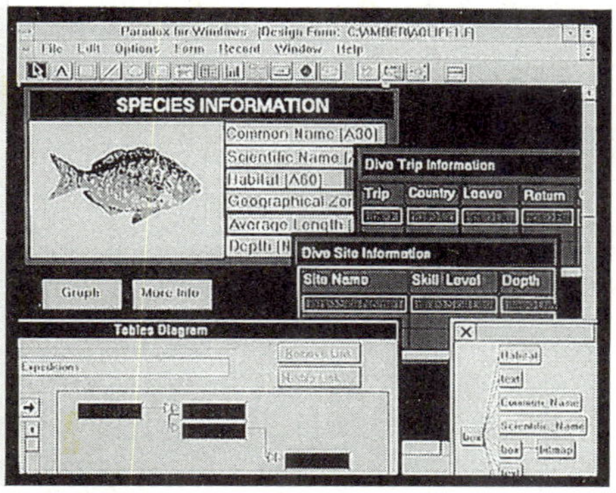

Whether you use a flat file database program like *Works*, or a relational database model like *Paradox*, the record entry screens should be easy to use.

Types of Data Models

A **data model** is a way for humans to visualize the relationships between records that are filed in a complex database management system. A number of data models have been developed over the years. No single data model is best-suited to all applications. Traditional data models include the hierarchical, network, and relational models. The newest model, which has become more popular since the growth of multimedia systems, is the object-oriented model.

The **hierarchical data model** is the oldest of the data models. Its top-down design resembles an organization chart, or an inverted tree. Each record at one level is linked to a record (has a "parent record") at the next higher level. To reach the second or third level down, you must follow a path from the highest level. These paths are established when the hierarchical database is first designed. Although predefined pathways result in rapid access to the data, they make modification of the database cumbersome. The hierarchical data model has been commercially successful for a number of years, but is gradually being phased out in favor of newer data models.

The **network data model** is similar to the hierarchical data model, except that it establishes multiple relationships between different branches of the data structure. As with the hierarchical model, network databases use pointers, to link related records. These pointers are established prior to the use of the database and help to speed access to the data in many different ways. Again, however, they make modification of the database very difficult.

The main difference between the hierarchical model and the network model is the requirement of the hierarchical model that any record (other than the root) must have only one parent record; the network model can accommodate several. The network data model was developed to meet the needs of users who required more flexibility of access than the hierarchical model allows. It, too, has been commercially successful for a number of years.

The **relational data model** is the most flexible database organization scheme. Records can be related according to the contents of **key fields**, or common categories. Files still contain records, and those in turn contain fields. The model of organization for a relational database is a table, a collection of rows and columns. In a true relational database management system, one file can be linked with any other that has a common field; a third file can be linked to the first, even if it does not have a field common to the first, if it has a field common to the second. In this manner, many very distinct files can be easily and quickly joined together.

An important advantage of the relational data model is that data relationships do not have to be rigidly defined prior to use as they do in the hierarchical and network data models (although they must be planned). Another advantage of the relational data model is the ability to add new fields as the need arises. Finally, the image of the relational model as a table with rows and columns is easily understood.

Object-oriented data models are the newest development. They link **objects** (individual entities that are not fields or records, but unique definitions). Object-oriented databases make links by association rather than by identified field types or definitions. The Macintosh program **Hypercard** allows you to build an object-oriented database with only a minimal knowledge of databases. Using a card file system, you link objects via buttons that are defined. Figure 9.1 shows a diagram of the various data models. All four models have their places in file organization, but the relational model has become increasingly popular.

Setting Up Your First Database

Within the individual fields in each record, you store the unique information for that record which you can then manipulate and retrieve. When you studied

Figure 9.1

Four Database Models

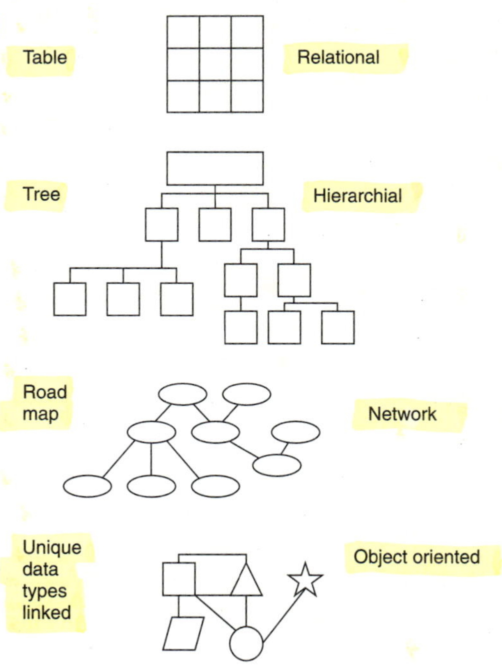

spreadsheets, you organized numerical data into rows and columns. These are analogous to records and fields in a database. Now, instead of organizing according to column and row location, you will organize according to field and record contents.

It is possible to keep database-type records in a spreadsheet program. (In fact, many spreadsheet programs have database features.) However, to keep track of both text and numeric information, it is best to use a database. Then you can search for, select, arrange, and print data by field, whether these operations require numerical calculations or not. Many of the same functions—predefined formulas—that you were provided with in the spreadsheet program are available in the database program. However, the formal reports you will learn to design in Chapter 11 are more versatile and more appropriate for printouts of text-oriented (historic) information (such as addresses, model names, or colors), even if they have some numerical elements, as well (such as prices).

Figure 9.2 shows a typical *Works 3.0 for Windows* database screen. It identifies the Menu bar, Toolbar, Formula bar, and Scroll bar, along with a field, a record, and information relating to the status of the marked fields and records.

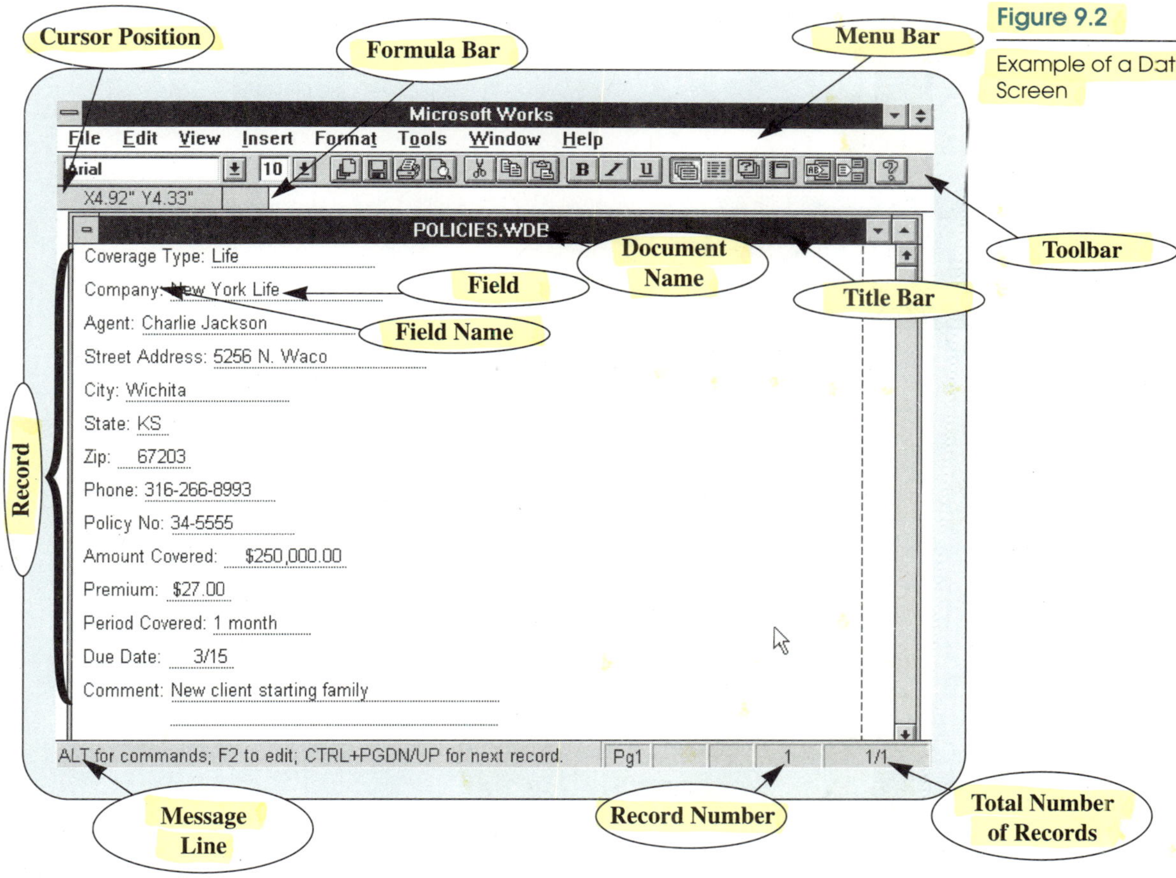

Figure 9.2

Example of a Database Screen

Works Database Toolbar

As in the other applications, the toolbar can help you to perform some commands more quickly with the mouse. It is very easy to switch to different **views** (screen displays of records) via the toolbar. See Figure 9.3 for a picture and description of the icons that pertain only to the database and report modules. The options are as follows:

- B—Make the highlighted entry bold
- I—Make the highlighted entry italic
- U—Underline the highlighted entry
- Form—Switch to form view
- List—Switch to list view
- Query—Switch to query view
- Report—Switch to report view
- Insert a field
- Insert a record
- Preview—Preview your printed document
- Save
- Cut
- Copy
- Paste

Figure 9.3

Icons that pertain only to database and report modules

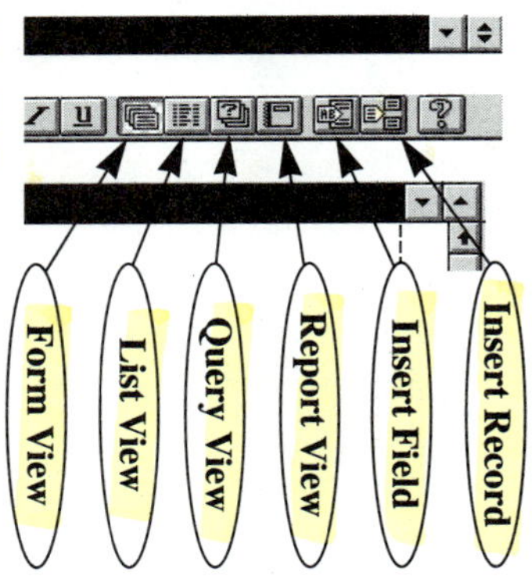

- Print
- Start the cue card display
- Choose a font
- Choose a font size
- Open a new or existing database file

As with all of the applications, you can customize the toolbar in the Tools menu of the database, adding the icons you use the most and deleting those that you rarely need. If your toolbar does not look the same as the one we have shown, it may well have been modified by an earlier user, or it may have been set up by the school lab and you cannot change it.

Defining the Structure

Planning a database is just as important as what you do with it after it is designed and the records are entered. If a database is not designed with the end output in mind, it can be less useful than a manual filing system—in fact, it may have no value at all. All of the fields or categories that you need should be determined first. The most important fields should be defined first, primarily for convenience in viewing and sorting (arranging) the records. In most of today's database programs, including *Works,* you can add fields later without losing all of your data, but it saves work to assess your needs thoroughly the first time.

You may want to add one field more than you actually need in the structure to serve as a comment, or miscellaneous, field where you can enter added information in free form with no set format. This feature is handy for additional notations in records. Having a place to store information that is not easily categorized is often useful.

Once you have determined what fields you will need and their order of importance, you can define the structure of your database. This involves deciding the names of the fields you want to enter; the maximum number of characters needed for each field; the field's type as an alphabetic, numeric, or date field; and, for a numeric field, how many decimal places should be maintained. Each record must have the same number of fields, but every field does not have to have content. With the exception of key fields (required fields that contain unique information specific to one record only), fields can be blank. They take up the same amount of space on disk as if they were filled, however.

A blank record whose structure has been defined is shown in Figure 9.4.

The database application of *Works 3.0 for Windows* can store up to 32,000 records, up to 256 fields in each record, and up to 256 characters in each field. *Works* requires a colon after each field name, and the maximum number of characters allowed for a field name is 15. The actual name of the field has no significance to the database structure. You could name them Field1, Field2, Field3, and so forth if you wish. The name of the field simply helps you to distinguish between them, but most users prefer to name fields in a way that describes their contents as an aid to memory. It is easier to tell what is in the field if its title describes the information.

In addition, you can define fields in any order, and put them any place on the page (form). You can even define more than one page of fields for each database. Databases in business applications often have as many as 50 fields per record. As mentioned above, the most important and most descriptive fields are defined first, but this is not necessary. It simply allows easier reading of the records.

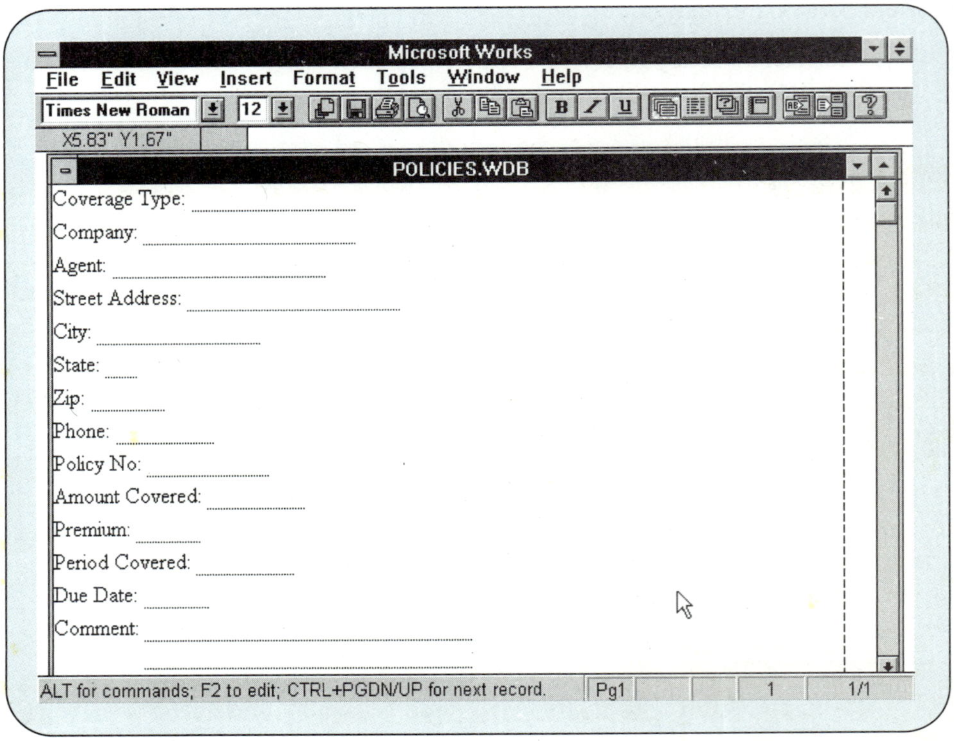

Figure 9.4

Example of a blank record whose structure has been defined.

When defining a field, just move the insertion point to the position where you want the field name to appear on screen. The position in inches from the left (the *X* coordinate) and from the top (the *Y* coordinate) appears on the formula bar at the top of your screen.

Unlike some other database programs, when defining a structure in *Works 3.0 for Windows*, you do not have to indicate the type of field you are defining. By default, the contents you type for the field when you enter the records determine the field type—numeric, character, or formula. If you type in letters, the field will automatically become a character field and *Works* will insert double quotes before the field contents. If you begin to type a number as the field contents, the field by default will become numeric. A formula or function field (sometimes called a *calculated field*) will be defined as such when you enter the formula in the first record. This process is covered in Chapter 10.

To begin defining a structure from the Startup menu:

- Click on Create New File.
- Click on Database.
- Place the insertion point where you want the field to appear (virtually anywhere on the screen).
- Type the name of the field.
- Type a colon.
- Click the mouse button, or press ENTER.

The Field Size box displays:

- Type the field width you desire. (The default is 20.)
- Click on a height choice.
- Type a field height, or accept 1 as default.
- Click on OK.

If you have the **field lines** turned on (to display outlines of the field areas in reverse video), you can actually change the size (width and height) of a field by using the mouse to resize, or move the field by dragging the mouse. (Field Lines on is the default setting in the View menu.) Take care that this is actually what you wish to do if you hold down the mouse button on the field contents area. Descriptive text from the *Works* program will appear below the field area box to indicate whether you are dragging to move or resize, and which dimensions are affected.

Continue designating fields in this way until your field definition is complete. If you wish to enter any descriptive text (called *labels* by *Works 3.0 for Windows*) on the database form, you simply enter it where you want it on the screen, omitting the colon. Labels are usually titles or instructions for completing a form. They appear in every record of a database, but are not part of a field, and they are not displayed in **List view**, which displays multiple records. If any text does not end with a colon, it is merely descriptive, and not a field definition.

Entering Data and Editing Entries

After the database is defined, you may enter data into the records. Since this process is time-consuming, you should enter data carefully so that it will not have to be corrected unless the information truly changes, such as when a record of the database has a change in address. Databases are dynamic; they are always changing. Indeed, if information never changed and records were never edited, added, or deleted, you could hardly justify the complicated process of creating a database! Maintaining the database (keeping the data current) is an ongoing job; however, editing is easier with an electronic database than with a manual one.

The information you store in each field, such as a name, an address, an inventory part number, or a salary amount, is known as the *field contents*. You can enter text, a number, a date, a measure of time, or a formula as a field's contents. Each field's contents can have up to 256 characters or numbers of text. Unlike other database programs, the information you enter into a *Works* database field is not lost if it exceeds the width you set when you defined the structure.

To enter field contents:

- Select the record in which you wish to enter data.
- Click to the right of the name of the field, or TAB to highlight this area.
- Enter the desired text, number, date, time, or formula.
- Press TAB, or click on the next field area.

You will notice that it is easier to use the TAB key to move to a field because your fingers are already on the keyboard; pressing the TAB key after entering data in a field positions you at the next field. You can enter many records in the **Form view** (which displays a single record or page on screen) by keying in the contents and pressing TAB to move to the next field, then moving smoothly to the next record without lifting your fingers from the keyboard.

To edit a field (change its contents) in *Works*:

- Use the TAB key to move to the field (or SHIFT+TAB to move backward).

  OR
- Select the field with the mouse or directional arrows.
- Retype the entry.

  OR
- Press F2 and make corrections using the arrow keys.
- Press ENTER to complete the correction, or click on the next field area.

Displaying Data

Works 3.0 for Windows allows four different views, or displays, from which to view data from the database: (1) the Form view, (2) the List view, (3) the **Query view**, and (4) the **Report view**.

The form view, as already noted, shows one record at a time, displayed as if it were a filled-in form. In fact, you can design the screen form to match a printed form. You move from one record to another by pressing CTRL + PAGE DOWN (to move to the next record) or CTRL + PAGE UP (to move to the preceding record). In the form view, you can enter and modify data or edit field names. You can edit labels (descriptive text), change the sizes or formatting of fields, and move or copy fields or their contents. You can also insert or delete fields or labels. To display the form view:

- Click on View-Form.

  OR
- Click on the Form icon.

The List view displays your records in a grid of rows and columns, similar to the display for a spreadsheet. This multiple view of records is often called the *table view* by other programs. Each row is a record, and each column is a field.

List view allows you to use the cursor to work with several records at one time. However, only a few of the fields may be visible at once, and only ten characters of a field are displayed. To see the rest of the fields, you must scroll to the right with the arrow keys. CTRL + HOME will always take you to the first record on your screen. In the list view, you can also enter and edit field names or contents and change the sizes or formatting of fields. To create a new field in list view, type the field name (it must be unique) in an empty column. To display the List view:

- Click on View-List.

  OR
- Click on the List icon.

To toggle between the Form and list views, you can also press the F9 key.

The query view is the display that results from specifying criteria and directing the program to show only the records that meet those criteria. Querying is a filtering process, where only certain records are selected for viewing. *Works* offers both a query view and a query definition screen called *New Query*; these are separate commands.

To display the query view:

- Click on View-Query.
- Choose a query to select the records you wish to view.
- Click on OK.

  OR

- Click on the query icon.

The display of the active query view shows the conditions that were defined for the particular query you are viewing. Notice that *Works 3.0 for Windows* converts query sentence directions to operators and operands for the query as it was defined. If you wish to edit the query from this query view, you may. However, you need to know how to insert the proper relational and logical operators (listed later in Table 9.3) and enter the proper prefix for the type of data in the selected fields. Character-field contents are preceded by double quotes (“) and dates and times by single quotes (‘).

In query view, you can create compound queries that check for more than one condition within each field, such as querying for all names that are either Smith or Jones (“Smith” #or# “Jones”). We will cover the procedure for defining queries in a later section. The view of the criteria, however, will be displayed in the query view. The query view is just that—a view of a query that has already been created.

If you wish to define a query and view its results, you access the Create New Query command. Instructions for a new query are described later, under the heading *Data Manipulation*. You can also use the query view to designate records to include in a report that you design with the Tools-Create a New Report command. If your report is selective, showing only certain records in the database, you define a query to select records and complete the report.

The report view shows you a report definition and lets you edit it and specify how you want your report to look when it is printed out. As in the query view, if you know the operators and functions allowed for *Works* reports, you can enter titles, subtitles, column headings, summary headings, and so on. You may also use the standard *Works* report generator. Chapter 11 will show you how to format and run reports from the *Works 3.0 for Windows* database. To display the report view:

- Click on View-Report.

  OR

- Click on the report icon.
- Select the report whose definition you wish to see.

The report view shows you the report definition. To see the actual data in the report:

- Click on View-Report.
- Select the report by name.
- Click on OK.
- Click on Preview.
- Print from the Preview or click on Cancel.

PC User in the Work Place

You can print database contents from any view. We will cover database queries in this chapter and the next, and we will give detailed instructions on defining and printing reports in Chapter 11.

DATABASE TUTORIAL NO. 1

Now you will have a chance to apply some of these database concepts by creating a file to track insurance policies. You will fill in eight records and manipulate the records in some basic ways. Then you will retrieve selected records and print them. In Chapter 11, you will learn how to retrieve these records in a more formal, permanent manner through the use of reports.

You will design a database screen by typing in field names, specifying field widths and heights, and formatting nontext fields. You will then enter data into the database. You can use either a mouse, the TAB key, or the arrow keys to move your insertion point to the desired locations.

To start, enter the *Works* program and proceed as follows:

1. Click on Database.

   The Database screen appears in form view, as shown in Figure 9.5.

The fields will all begin at the left margin, even though it is possible to place them anywhere on the screen.

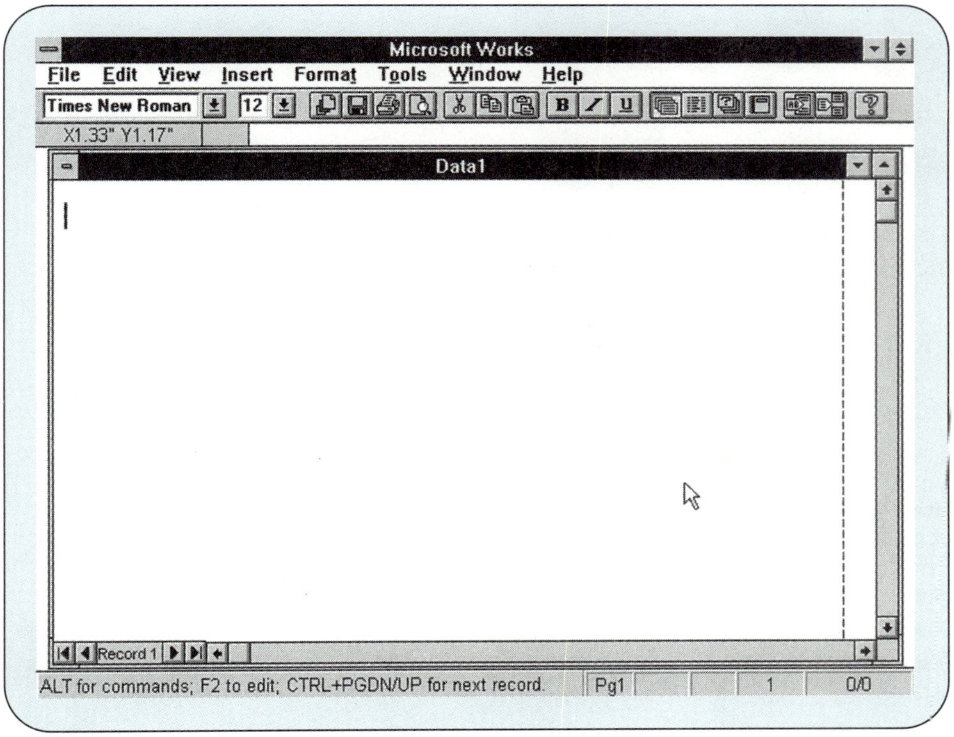

Figure 9.5

Form View

The font is Times New Roman 12 point. Your default may be Arial 10 point, or another font, depending on what your printer supports. When you use a proportional font such as Times New Roman or Arial, you must put in more spaces than you need in a monospaced font. For example, two spaces is not enough for a state abbreviation because some characters take more than two standard spaces.

Place the insertion point at the top of the screen, at the left margin.

2. Type **Coverage Type:** (Don't forget the colon.)
3. Press ENTER.

The Field Size dialog box appears, as shown in Figure 9.6.

4. Press ENTER or click on OK to accept the default width of 20 characters, and the default height of one line.
5. Type **Company:**
6. Press ENTER.
7. Type **26** for the width.
8. Press ENTER or click OK to accept the default height of one line.

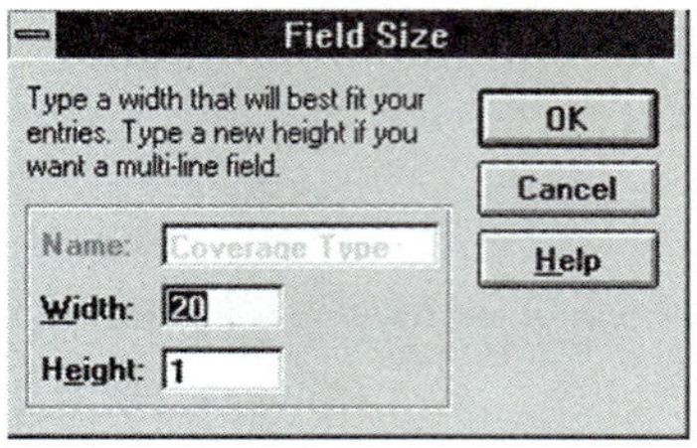

Figure 9.6

Example of the Field Size dialog box

Continue to type in the rest of the field names and their widths and heights as shown in Table 9.1. Note that when you create the Comment field, you will TAB to Height and change the line height to two lines.

Table 9.1

Field Name	Width, Height
Agent:	26, 1
Street Address:	26, 1
City:	20, 1
State:	4, 1
Zip:	9, 1
Phone:	16, 1
Policy #:	15, 1
Amount Covered:	16, 1
Period Covered:	12, 1
Premium:	10, 1
Due Date:	8, 1
Comment:	40, 2

9. Save the file as policies. (*Works* will add a .wdb extension.)

   To format the fields that are not character (text) fields:
10. Click on the line to the right of the Amount Covered field.

    Notice that the size of the highlighted bar covers the width of the field as you defined it. You are going to designate dollar signs with no places to the right of the decimal.

11. Click on Format.

    The Format menu displays, as shown in Figure 9.7.

12. Click on Number.

    The Number option box displays, as shown in Figure 9.8.

13. Click on Currency.

    A Decimal option box appears.

14. Type 0 to replace the default of 2.
15. Click on the line to the right of the Premium field.

Figure 9.7

Example of the Format Menu

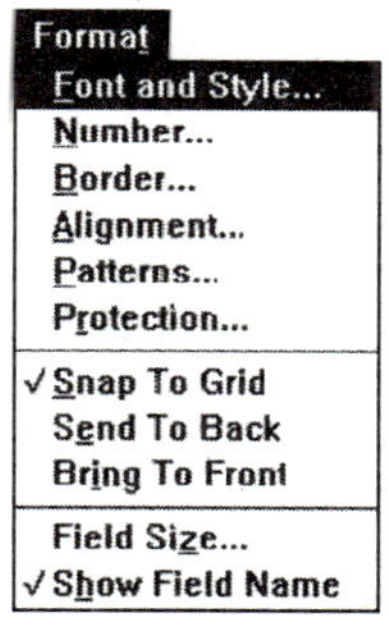

Figure 9.8

Example of the Number Option box

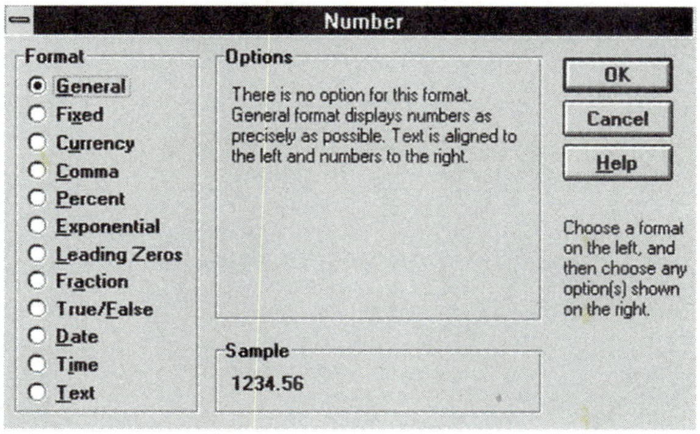

16. Format it as currency, with no decimal places.

    To select the format for your date field:

17. Click on the line to the right of the Due Date field.
18. Click on Format-Number.
19. Click on the Date radio button in the Format list.
20. In the Date list box, select the Month, Day, as 3/11.

    Remember, the current date will be used in the examples.

21. Click on OK.

    You can now begin entering the data for the eight records. Press TAB to move from one data entry area to the next. Save frequently.

22. Click to select the Coverage Type line and type **Life**
23. TAB to the Company field and type **New York Life**
24. TAB to the Agent field and type **Charlie Jackson**
25. TAB to the Street Address field and type **5256 N. Waco**
26. TAB to the City field and type **Wichita**

27. TAB to the State field and type **KS**
28. TAB to the Zip field and type **67203**
29. TAB to the Phone field and type: **(316)266–8893**
30. TAB to the Policy # field and type **34–5555**
31. TAB to the Amount Covered field and type **250000**
32. TAB to the Period Covered and type **1 month**
33. TAB to the Premium field and type **27**
34. TAB to the Due Date field and type **3/15**
35. TAB to the Comment field and type **New client starting family**
36. Save the file again.
37. Press CTRL + PAGE DOWN to get to the next blank record.
38. Enter the information for Records 2 through 8 from Table 9.2.

Table 9.2 Data for Records in policies.wdb

Record 1: Life, New York Life, Charlie Jackson, 5256 N. Waco, Wichita, KS, 67203, (316)266–8893, 34–5555, 250000, 1 month, 27, 3/15, New client starting family

Record 2: Auto, Farmers Insurance, Bob Thomas, 5593 E. Central, Wichita, KS, 67207, (316)687–4566, 135–34–3555, 10000, 6 months, 162, 12/15, Goes up 30 percent with each moving violation

Record 3: Home, State Farm, Tom Sullivan, 2578 E. Cresthill, Littleton, CO, 80121, (303)798–7080, 34–55–6666, 100000, 1 year, 300, 7/1, Includes home alert discount and is paid by mortgagee

Record 4: Medical, Prudential, Lea Stevenson, 5322 S. California, Sunnyvale, CA, 94087, (408)735–5344, 34–9087–444, 1000000, 1 month, 87, 1/5, $250 deductible annually

Record 5: Dental, Blue Cross/Blue Shield, Cindy Wilson, 3848 Walnut, Orange City, FL, 32763, (813)335–9382, 45–195–333, 6000, 1 month, 12, 1/1, 80 percent restorative work

Record 6: Boat, State Farm, Jane Alexander, 8922 W. Louisville, Aurora, CO, 80013, (303)693–9821, 345–5525–24, 30000, 1 month, 12, 8/15, Interested in financing another boat

Record 7: Art, Lloyd's of London, Sue Pledger, 8922 N. St. Francis, Danville, CA, 94506, (510)736–9236, 34–78684, 2000000, 1 year, 450, 8/14, High-priced art work

Record 8: Computer store, Allstate, Craig Killian, 8200 E. 41st Street, Wellington, KS, 76152, (316)326–8295, 344–55–05553, 940000, 1 month, 223, 9/30, Contents and facility coverage

39. Print, save, and close the file.

Data Manipulation

Once you have records in your database, you can manipulate and retrieve the data in various ways. The outstanding advantage of an electronic filing system such as a database program is the ability to retrieve specific records from your file quickly, without the need to refile all of them when you have finished viewing them. What is more, you can retrieve records in any order by the contents of any field.

For example, you can retrieve records of all the people whose addresses are in Colorado, or all the people who owe you more than $500, or everyone whose last name is Smith; you can select records based on virtually any criterion that you have entered in the database. You can even define complex queries and retrieve records that meet more than one criterion, as long as a field has been defined for each.

As we noted, most databases are **dynamic**; they change frequently. Part of the convenience of a database is the ability to change, add, or delete records as needed. In the example database from the tutorial, insurance agents may change, or they may move offices. Certainly, the premiums will fluctuate. All of this change requires editing of the records.

A very small database, such as the one you have just created, can easily be viewed in its entirety on the screen in the list view. However, most databases become quite large. When you need to edit certain records, you don't want to have to use a mouse or directional arrows to search for them through screenload after screenload.

For these reasons, you will often want to filter out certain records to view or print with a **query**. You may also want to rearrange, or **sort**, the database to list records in a different order, such as by premium due date. All of this can be done without permanently altering the database.

Querying

Every database program has specific rules for querying, or questioning, the database file in order to retrieve desired records. The query is normally accomplished by entering, on a blank query form, a condition or conditions for field contents. The program checks this condition against the contents of the corresponding field in all of your records and gathers those records that match.

Queries in *Works 3.0 for Windows* are accomplished by entering the desired filtering conditions on a query form. You can use the standard query window that uses sentence form, or you can define your own query in the query view. You can name this query form and save it, to be used again and again. You can delete or rename queries, as well. You can access all of the query functions from the view menu, or from the toolbar icons.

To define a query sentence:

- Click on Tools-Create New Query.

  OR
- Click on the query icon.
- Select the name of a field for which you want to define the criterion.
- Select relational or logical conditions by scrolling through the available choices.
- Click on the conditions you want to impose.
- Type in the required value contents for the field.

To define a complex query that evaluates the contents of more than one field:

- Click to mark the And or the Or choice.
- Click on the next field for which you want to define a criterion.

Continue building the **query sentence** until you have specified all of the conditions you need to retrieve the records you want. You may use the three fields and any combination of contents for each field. When the query sentence is complete:

- Click on View-Apply Query.
- Select the query you wish to apply. (The menu will list just one if this is your first defined query.)

  OR
- Click on the list or form view icons.

The records that meet the conditions of the query sentence will appear on the screen. You can clear this query and further define the same query or begin anew if you wish, with an entirely new query. After applying a query, you should return the display to include all of the records in the database before you query again, or close the file. To display all of the records:

- Click on View-Show All Records.

The entire database returns for viewing.

Once you have created a query, you can access it and apply it again, through the View menu.

- Click on View-Apply Query.
- From the list, select the query you wish to apply.
- Click on OK.

The results of the query will display on the screen.

Works 3.0 for Windows has a standard query definition screen based on sentence definitions. If you do not specify more than three criteria, you don't have to type in relational and logical operators, or specific instructions for field types. However, a basic understanding of logical and relational conditions is necessary to successfully query a database and filter out just the records you wish to see. Further, you cannot construct a compound query that tests for multiple conditions within each field unless you master these operators. You can use **relational operators** and **logical operators** to select records that match multiple conditions or to query for records that fall within certain upper and lower limits. Table 9.3 lists the relational and logical operator symbols you see in the saved queries and their text equivalents.

Table 9.3 Relational and Logical Operators for Use in Queries

Relational operator	Meaning
=>	Greater than or equal to
>	Greater than
=<	Less than or equal to
<	Less than
<>	Not equal to
=	Equal to
Logical operator	
#AND#	And
#OR#	Or
#NOT#	Not

When querying for records, you must specify conditions carefully. Enter the exact form of the criterion as it exists in the database records, or you will receive a "No Records Match" message. If you receive this or another error message, and you know that certain records meet your condition, check the information in your query sentence. The query screen when you view a query shows records for exactly what is entered in that query sentence. Your error may be that you failed to choose the right condition, or typed in the wrong value. If you type in conditions manually in query view instead of using the query sentence method, you may have omitted necessary quotation marks (double quotes for character data, single quotes for dates or times). You may even state a criterion for the wrong field name. For example, a dollar sign ($) may be part of the format of a field and not part of its actual contents. (Field contents of 56 may display as $56.)

If you use the Create New Query option box that *Works* provides for you, you needn't worry about enclosing field values in quotes. *Works* will insert them for you. However, when querying for character data by editing in the query view, you must surround the string of letters with quotes (as in "Smith, John"). Using the query view, you can set as many conditions for a query as you have fields in your records. With the New Query option box method, you can query on up to three fields, though it is possible to query within a query. (We will cover this technique in Chapter 10.) In the query view, you can also combine conditions (such as =="Smith, John #OR#="Jones, Bill").

When you are looking for either John Smith or Bill Jones, the query begins with two equal signs (==) to indicate a multiple condition. Be careful about the logic involved here. You could not enter =="Smith, John" #AND# ="Jones, Bill" because one person cannot be named both Smith and Jones.

When querying for numbers, quotes are not necessary, but you must take care that the query criterion does not contain dollar signs ($), commas, or any other characters that might be part of the format of the field and not its contents. The system looks for an exact match of what you enter. When defining a query in the Query View form, be sure to leave fields on which you are not querying blank. You can clear them, if necessary:

- Position the cursor on the desired field.
- Click on Edit-Clear.

This chapter and the next will lead you to query in many different ways.

Sorting

Sorting a database involves rearranging its records in a different order. It rearranges the entire database, not just selected records. It is like shuffling a deck of cards.

You sort a database by indicating the fields on which you wish to sort. *Works 3.0 for Windows* can perform a **nested sort**, which arranges records within a larger arrangement, such as sorting by days of the month within a sort by months of the year. You can sort on as many as three fields, if you wish.

Sorting can be very useful for rather general searches, where you don't want to impose an exact match, but you need to see records that fall within a more general range, such as names that begin with the letter *S*. If you were uncertain what records you wanted, but you knew you wanted all of the most expensive items in a file, for instance, you could sort on a price field.

You can sort a database, alphabetically or numerically, in ascending or descending order. Ascending order starts with *A* and ends with *Z*, or it starts with 1 and ends with 99,999. Descending order goes in reverse, from *Z* to *A*, or from 99,999 down to 1.

To sort a *Works 3.0 for Windows* database file:

- Click on Tools-Sort Records.
- The Sort option box appears.
- Scroll to select a field name.

  OR
- Type in the first field on which you want to sort.
- Mark Descending, or accept the default, Ascending order.
- Click on the second field and enter a field name.
- Repeat the selection for the third field, if desired.
- Click on OK when you finish entering sort criteria.

The records will be arranged on your screen in the order you requested. If you are sorting on more than one field, the order of the second field will be apparent only if multiple records meet the first sort condition; if so, the records that match the same first sort condition will be arranged according to the second. This is a nested sort, or a sort within a sort.

- Type in the name of a field on which you want to sort.

- Choose Ascending or Descending order.
- TAB to fill in two other fields, if desired.
- When the box information is complete, press ENTER.

It takes some practice to query and sort a database successfully, especially with multiple conditions, but it is an excellent way of retrieving just the records you wish to view in a large database.

DATABASE TUTORIAL NO. 2

In the policies.wdb database that you created earlier, you find an error in Record 6; the agent's name should be John Alexander, instead of Jane. You will now go into list view, change the field width of the agents' names, correct the name, and use the query and sort records features.

1. Open policies.wdb.

   To go to the List View screen:

2. Click on View.

   The View menu displays, as shown in Figure 9.9.

3. Click on List.

Figure 9.9

Example of the View menu

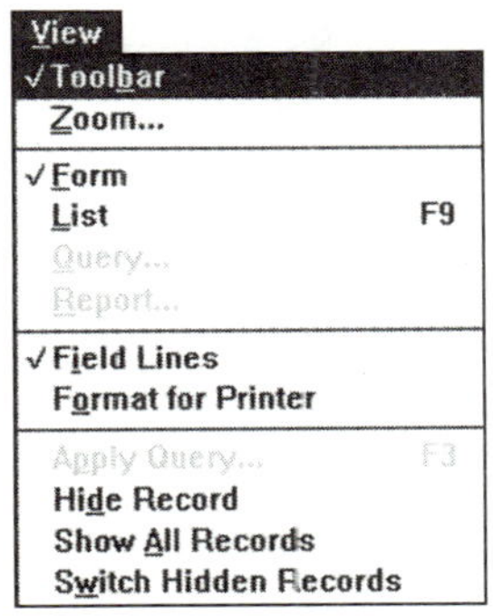

In list view, records are listed in columns across the screen. As you can see, many of the fields are not wide enough to display their entire contents. Even though you enlarged the field width for many fields in form view, all the fields in list view default back to ten characters. You will now widen the Agent field.

4. Click anywhere within the Agent column.
5. Click on Format.

   The Format menu displays, as shown in Figure 9.10.

6. Click on Field Width.
7. Change the width to 15.

   You can now see the entire list of agents' names. To see the difference between selecting a specific number and selecting the Best Fit option:

8. Click in the Agent column.
9. Click on Format-Field Width-Best Fit-OK.

   It is not feasible to change all the field widths as it would take up too much room and you will rarely print from list view. In Record 6, the agent's name should be John Alexander instead of Jane Alexander. To correct it in form view:

10. Click on View-Form.

    The numbers 8/8 at the far right of the screen designate the current

Figure 9.10

Example of the Format Menu

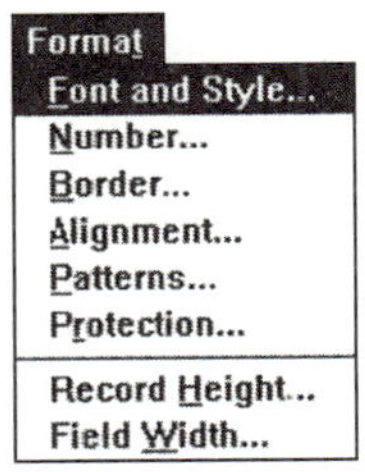

record and its place in the number of records in the file. (The number at the left shows what record is currently active.)

11. Press CTRL + PAGE DOWN or CTRL + PAGE UP to move to Record 6 (the boat insurance record).
12. Click on the field to the right of Agent (which lists Jane Alexander).
13. Press F2 to edit.

    The name displays in the upper, left-hand corner of the formula bar.
14. Use the LEFT ARROW key to move to the right of the letter *J*.
15. Delete **ane**
16. Type **ohn**
17. Press ENTER.
18. Click on the save icon.

Figure 9.11

The Tool Menu

You will now use the query command to retrieve only the records for insurance from State Farm. *Works* automatically saves each query you build so that you can use it again or modify it to find different information. You can build up to three query sentences for a single query.

19. Click on View-List.
20. Click on Tools.

    The Tools menu displays, as shown in Figure 9.11.
21. Click on Create New Query.

    The Query option box displays, as shown in Figure 9.12.

Figure 9.12

The Query Option Box

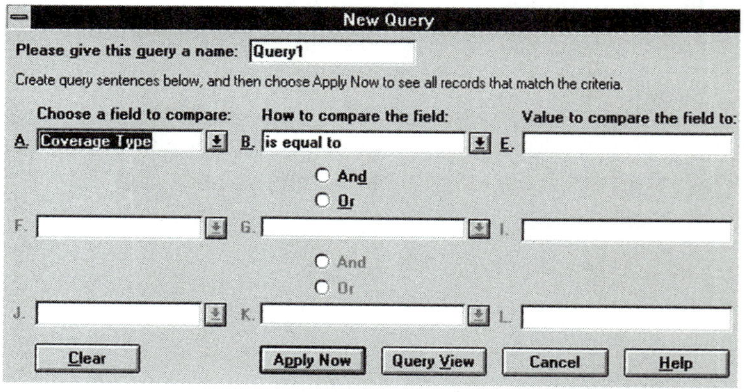

22. Select Query1 in the text box headed "Please give this query a name."
23. Type **Company**
24. TAB to "Choose a field to compare."

25. Click on the down arrow and scroll to select **Company**

    In the "How to compare the field" text box, the phrase *is equal to* should be selected.
26. TAB to the text box headed "Value to compare the field to."
27. Type **State Farm**
28. Click on Apply Now.

    The list screen displays the home and boat insurance records, as shown in Figure 9.13.

POLICIES.WDB

	Coverage	Company	Agent	Street Add	City	State	ZIP
3	Home	State Farm	Tom Sullivan	2578 E. Cre	Littleton	CO	80121
6	Boat	State Farm	John Alexander	8922 W. Lo	Aurora	CO	80013
9							
10							

Figure 9.13

The List Screen

When you switch to list view, your field size defaults to ten characters wide. Therefore, your view of many of your fields will be cut off at the end of ten characters. If the field is larger than ten numbers, you will see the # sign in place of the actual data. Printing from this view will yield only ten characters per field. Remember, CTRL + HOME will move the cursor bar to the first field of the first record.

To print your results:

29. Click on File-Print-OK.

    It will take three pages to print the database. Also, as mentioned before, some of the fields will not be complete. After doing a query you must be sure to return the hidden records to the screen for future action.
30. Click on View.
31. Click on Show All Records.

    The other six records redisplay on the screen. You now want to retrieve all records for which Period Covered is one month and Premium is more than $15.
32. Switch to View-List, if you are not there.
33. Click on Tools.
34. Click on Create New Query.
35. Select Query1 in the Name text box and type **Premium**
36. TAB to the field box (A.) and select **Period Covered**
37. The compare box (B.) should state *is equal to.*
38. TAB to the value box (E.) and type **1 month**

    Note: When you query your database, it is good practice to type the fields and field names exactly as they appear in your database, i.e., same capitalized letters, same cases, same numerals, and so on, even though *Works 3.0 for Windows* is not case sensitive.

39. Click on the radio button for *And.*
40. In the F. text box, click on the arrow and select *Premium.*
41. In the G. text box, click to select *is greater than.*
42. In the I. text box, type **15**

    Your screen should look similar to that in Figure 9.14.

Figure 9.14

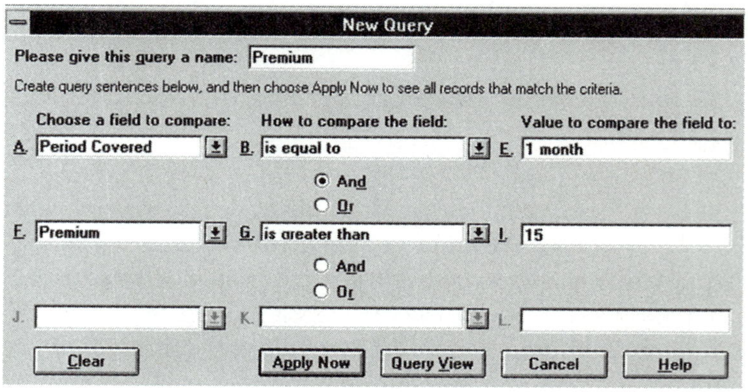

43. Click on Apply Now.

    The records displayed should cover life, medical, and computer store insurance.
44. Press CTRL + END to see the Premium and Period Covered fields.

    Your screen should look similar to Figure 9.15.

Figure 9.15

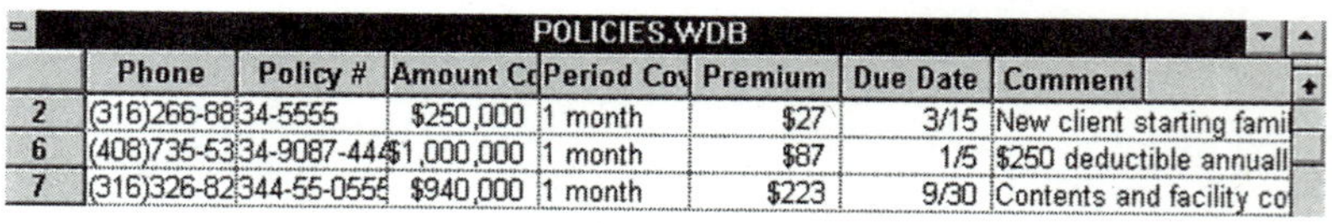

45. Click on View.
46. Click on Show All Records.

    The entire database is displayed again. You will now sort the database in chronological order according to premium due date.
47. Make sure the Due Date column is visible.
48. Click on Tools.

49. Click on Sort Records.

    The Sort Records option box appears, as shown in Figure 9.16.

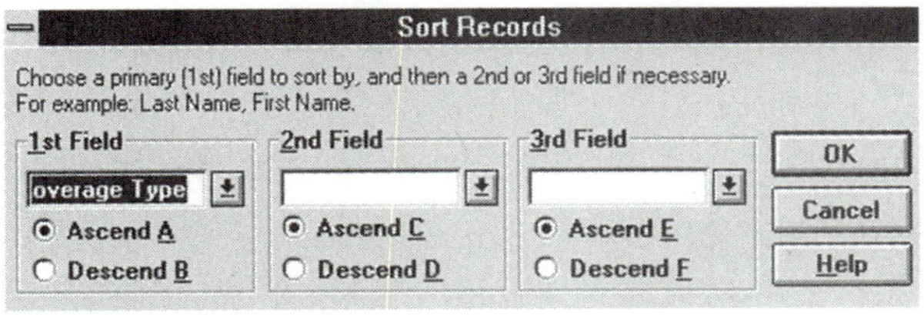

Figure 9.16

Example of the Sort Records Option Box

50. Click on the 1st Field text box arrow and scroll to select Due Date.
51. If it is not marked, click on Ascend A.
52. Click on OK.

    Your screen should look similar to the one in Figure 9.17. You now want to print only the records for the first quarter, from 1/1 to 3/30.

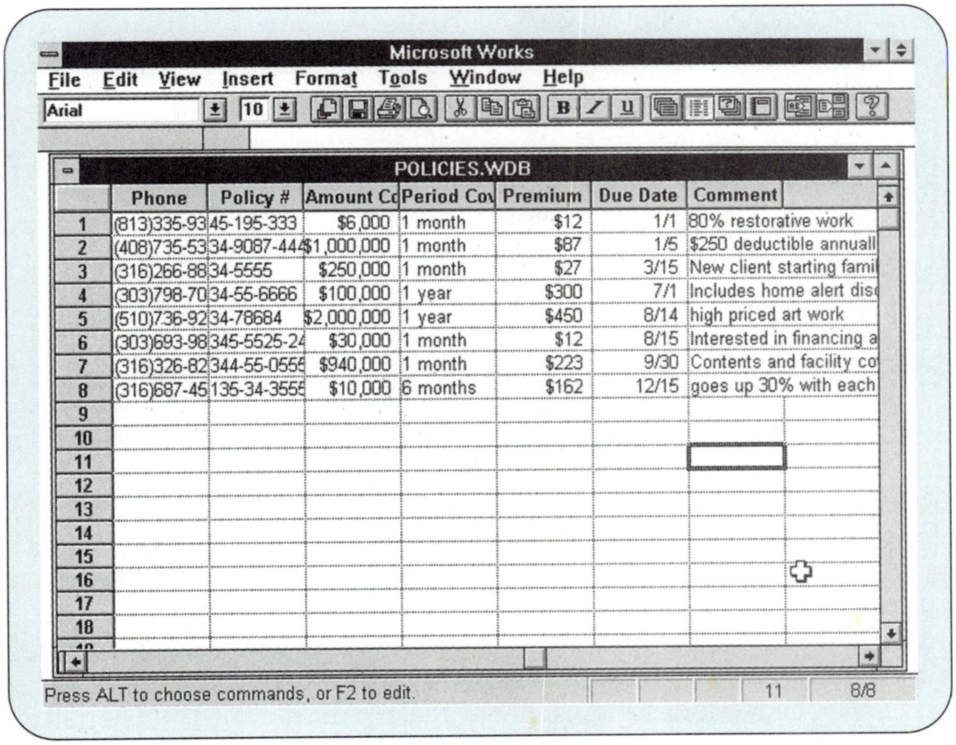

Figure 9.17

Policies Database Sorted by Due Date

53. Press CTRL + HOME.
54. Click on the number 4 to select Record 4, home insurance.

Figure 9.18

Example of the Insert Menu

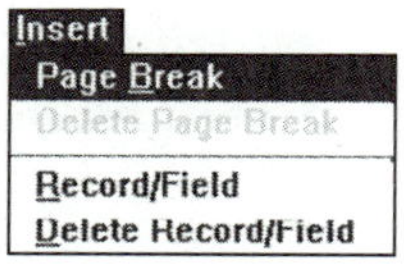

55. Click on Insert.

    The Insert menu displays, as shown in Figure 9.18.

56. Click on Page Break.

    The Insert Page Break option box displays.

57. If it is not marked, click on the Record radio button.
58. Click on OK.

    A dotted line displays above the home insurance record. To print only Pages 1 and 3 (the pages of your first three records):

59. Click on File-Print.
60. Click on Pages.
61. Type **1** in the From text box.
62. Type **1** in the To text box.
63. Click on OK.
64. Click on File-Print-From 3 To 3-OK.

    Your printout should cover the first three records with premium due dates of 1/1, 1/5, and 3/15. To remove the page break:

65. Click on the home insurance record.
66. Click on Insert-Delete Page Break-Record-OK.
67. Click on the Save icon.
68. Exit *Works*.

Chapter Summary

Database software allows you to keep records electronically in an organized, flexible way. It represents an improvement over manual filing systems because it allows you to enter records once, then edit or retrieve them in any manner without refiling.

A data model is a way of representing complex data relationships in a database management system. The four data models include the hierarchical, network, relational, and object-oriented models.

A database file is a collection of related records that are organized into fields. The individual information for each record is stored within the fields.

Database programs allow you to store, manipulate, and retrieve database files. A database file should be planned carefully before it is constructed. Once the file is designed and the records are entered, you can edit, add, or delete records. You can select certain records with a query, and you can rearrange all of the records in the database with a sort. You can search on more than one condition with a query, and you can rearrange on more than one field with a nested sort. Database software packages are among the most powerful applications available for personal computers.

KEY TERMS

data model
database file
database management system
dynamic
field
field lines
file management system
file
flat file
form view
hierarchical data model
Hypercard
key field
logical operator
list view
nested sort
network data model
object
object-oriented data model
query
query sentence
query view
record
relational data model
relational operator
report view
sort

REVIEW QUESTIONS

1. Define the term *database file.*
2. List (a) a minimum of five personal uses for a database and (b) a minimum of five business uses for a database.
3. Name and briefly describe the four data models.
4. Explain the difference between a file management system (flat file) and a database management system.
5. Briefly define *field*, *record*, and *file*.
6. Review the steps involved in planning a database structure.
7. Why can't you enter data into a database without first defining its structure?
8. What is meant by defining the structure of a database and what must a structure definition specify?
9. What is the primary purpose of the database toolbar?
10. The toolbar that displays when you create a new database offers 19 options. List and describe any nine of them.
11. Explain how you can resize a field using only the mouse.
12. Recall and briefly explain each of the field data types, *i.e.*, character data, etc.
13. Explain the importance of efficient and accurate entry of data into a database.

14. Entering data carefully and accurately into your data structure is essential. Briefly recount how to do this most easily and how you can most efficiently edit incorrect data.
15. *Works 3.0 for Windows* offers four different ways for you to view your database records. List and briefly review each one.
16. Compare and contrast the meaning of *data manipulation* in computerized databases versus paper-based records systems.
17. Recall how to define a query in *Works 3.0 for Windows*.
18. List the relational and logical operators used in *Works* and review the meaning of each.
19. Compare and contrast a sort versus a nested sort.

SOFTWARE EXERCISES

Exercise 9.1

1. Make arrangements with your instructor to familiarize yourself with the *Works 3.0 for Windows* database application tutorial.
2. Make notes about what was covered in each of the following sections:
   (a) Introducing the database
   (b) Creating a database
   (c) Working with lists
      (1) View several records at once
      (2) Change a field width
      (3) Move through a list of records
      (4) Insert fields and records
3. Use *Works 3.0 for Windows* to type your notes about what you learned.
4. Save your work as tutdb9.
5. Print tutdb9.wps.
6. Close tutdb9.wps and exit *Works*.

Exercise 9.2

1. Create a database structure for the investment data shown in Table 9.4.
2. Insert the mutual fund investment data using your choice of list or form view.
3. Click on list view, if necessary.
4. Widen the columns, if necessary.
5. Center the following title in a header: VALUE OF $10,000 AFTER TEN YEARS.

6. Format the Value field as currency with no decimal places.
7. Save the database as fndinv.
8. Print the entire database.
9. Center the following in a header: SORTED VALUE OF $10,000 AFTER TEN YEARS.
10. Sort the records on the Value field in ascending order.
11. Save the result as fndinv1.
12. Print the result of the sort.
13. Close the fndinv.wdb and fndinv1.wdb files and exit *Works*.

Table 9.4 Data for the fndinv.wdb Database

No.	Fund Name	Fund Type	Value
1	Green Fund	No load	135355
2	Today Fund	Selling charge	70630
3	Financial Fund	Low load	182786
4	New Dimensions Fund	Medium load	51937
5	Exploration Fund	No load	64404
6	Schooner Fund	No load	92272
7	Valley High Fund	Selling charge	68789
8	Equity Fund	Low load	86014
9	Brotherhood Fund	Medium load	38129
10	Safe Growth Fund	No load	84415
11	Robinson Fund	No load	66491
12	Omni Mutual Fund	No load	55632

Exercise 9.3

1. Open the fndinv.wdb file, or complete Exercise 9.2 before continuing.
2. Sort the records on the Fund Type field in descending order.
3. In list view, widen the columns, if necessary.
4. Center the following title in a header: VALUE OF $10,000 AFTER TEN YEARS BY FUND TYPE.
5. Print the result using gridlines and record and field labels.
6. Save the result as fndinv2.
7. Close the fndinv2.wdb file and exit *Works*.

Exercise 9.4

1. Open the fndinv.wdb file, or complete Exercise 9.2 before continuing.
2. In list view, widen the columns, if necessary.

3. Query the database to find all the no load funds.
4. Sort the database on the value field in descending order.
5. Center the following title in a header: NO LOAD FUND VALUES AFTER TEN YEARS BY VALUE.
6. Print the result using gridlines and record and field labels.
7. Save the result as fndinv3.
8. Click on Show All Records from the View menu.
9. Close the fndinv3.wdb file and exit *Works*.

Exercise 9.5

1. Open the Household Inventory template found under the Household Management Category of the AutoStart Personal template group.
2. Within this structure, add 12 or more records. These records can be real or imaginary, but should be items that belong in a family room or a kitchen.
3. Format the fields as needed.
4. Query the database to locate all items that belong in the family room.
5. Enter the following header on the left side of the header space: FAMILY ROOM PERSONAL PROPERTY BELONGING TO [your name].
6. Enter a centered footer with the current date.
7. Print the result of the query using gridlines and record and field labels.
8. Save the database as homeinv.
9. Click on Show All Records from the View menu.
10. Close homeinv.wdb and exit *Works*.

Exercise 9.6

1. Open addres.wdb from the student data diskette.
2. Put the database into ascending order by Last Name.
3. Center the following title in a header: MY NAME AND ADDRESS BOOK.
4. Change the left and right margins to 0.2 inches.
5. Print the sorted database.
6. Save the database as addres1.
7. Query the database to locate all friends who have birthdays in the month of March. Note: Type "Mar" to locate your friends instead of the date form of March.

8. Enter the following in a footer: March Birthday List.
9. Print the result using gridlines and field labels.
10. Click on Show All Records from the View menu.
11. Save the file as addres2.
12. Close all files and exit *Works*.

Exercise 9.7

1. Open policies.wdb, which you created in the tutorials in this chapter.
2. Put the database in descending order by premium amount.
3. Add an appropriate header.
4. Save the file as policy1.
5. Print policy1.wdb.
6. Put the database in ascending order by company name. Change the header to reflect the new order of the database.
7. Save the file as policy2.
8. Print policy2.wdb.
9. Put the database in descending order by amount of coverage. Change the header to reflect this new order.
10. Save the file as policy3.
11. Print policy3.wdb.
12. Close all files and exit *Works*.

Exercise 9.8

1. Open policies.wdb, which you created in the tutorials in this chapter.
2. Query the database to locate every auto policy.
3. Add an appropriate header.
4. Save the file as policy4.
5. Print out policy4.wdb.
6. Click on Show All Records from the View menu.
7. Query the database to locate every policy that has a premium greater than $100.00. Change the header to reflect the result of this new query.
8. Save the file as policy5.
9. Print out policy5.wdb.
10. Click on Show All Records from the View menu.
11. Close all files and exit *Works*.

Exercise 9.9

1. Open the CD/Tape Collection template found under the Household Management Category of the AutoStart Personal template group.
2. Enter a minimum of 15 records, using real or imaginary data; format the fields as needed.
3. Save your database.
4. Query your database to locate a CD or tape of interest to you and print the result under an appropriate header.
5. Click on Show All Records from the View menu.
6. Sort your database and print the result under an appropriate header.
7. Close the file and exit *Works*.

Exercise 9.10

1. Create your own database.
2. Enter a minimum of 15 records, using real or imaginary data; format the fields as needed.
3. Save your database.
4. Query your database to locate something of interest to you and print the result under an appropriate header.
5. Click on Show All Records from the View menu.
6. Sort your database and print the result under an appropriate header.
7. Close the file and exit *Works*.

Chapter 10

More on Databases

Objectives

After studying this chapter you will be able to:

- *Make changes to a database design, including adding explanatory text, adding or changing a field, moving a field, and deleting a field*
- *Insert and delete records*
- *Copy a record, a file, or the database design*
- *Make backups of your database structure and database file*
- *Lock and protect selected database fields and data*
- *Select a record or an entire file, perform nested sorts, and make complex and compound queries*
- *View different parts of a large file through split windows*

You have already seen in Chapter 9 that database programs are powerful tools. Record-keeping with a database program is simpler, faster, and more efficient than any manual system could be. The proliferation of databases used to store everything from customer mailing lists to voting records for a precinct is proof of the widespread use of databases by microcomputer users. In a particularly important trend for personal computer users, the number of on-line databases offered by information services (covered in Chapter 12) has increased dramatically within the last few years.

In this chapter, we will deal with some advanced database design concepts, but we will also delve more deeply into the use of the database after it has been designed and filled with records. The manipulation of the database after it has been created is added proof of its value. Whether you query or sort a database as a temporary measure to retrieve information, or design a formal report to retrieve information and print it (see Chapter 11), the underlying reason for maintaining a database is to retrieve swiftly information desired in any arrangement.

Modifying a File

Most database programs produced today allow you to modify a file structure after it has been created and records have been entered and saved to file. This was not always the case. In the past, database applications, especially ones without true relational data models as explained in Chapter 9, often did not allow you to modify the original structure—the names and lengths of fields, for example. This either left you with what you had designed initially, or with a lot of work to copy the contents of the records to another temporary file, change the structure of the database, and then move the record information back into the new file structure. Today, most database systems give you the freedom to change your mind and to adapt the database to your changing needs. This does not preclude the need for care in designing a database initially; it simply gives you a flexibility that increases the dynamic nature of the database.

Works allows you to change your file structure without risk of losing current records. Naturally, the contents of the database, or the data stored in its records, change constantly. Records are added, unneeded ones are deleted, names are changed, and so forth. You may also change the order in which the fields appear on the entry screen. You may change the name of a field, or delete a field that is no longer needed. You may even add new fields that you did not anticipate the need for when you first created the database. It is this last option that is most frequently used.

Mailing labels can be obtained from a customer database.

Changing the Design and Layout

Changing the design of a database file means actually altering the structure. Since a database file is self-describing, its structure is saved right along with the contents, or records. If you wish to change the definition of the field categories, you must change the design of the database.

In *Works*, if you wish to make such a change, or perhaps add a field or two, you do so from either the Form view or the List view. You can use the Edit menu to make necessary changes to the layout of the Form view on the screen. The *X*, *Y* coordinates on the top left of the Form view screen indicate your horizontal and vertical position to help you position your changes. You use the Insert menu to add a field; if you are in the list view, you actually name the field that has been inserted using the Edit menu.

Adding Text

You may have noticed by now that the main menus in the Form view and the List view are slightly different. You must be in the Form view (viewing a single record) in order to protect the form from being altered (as the discussion later in this chapter will explain). In the form view, you may also change the layout (appearance) of the entry screen by adding text, explanatory titles, or messages intended to guide the person who inputs the records.

Since you do not intend to change the structure of the fields in the file, it is simply a matter of positioning the cursor and typing the desired text in an area that is not currently occupied by field contents. Information such as your name and assignment number entered at the top of the screen would not be part of the file structure; it would only identify the assignment. You could easily insert explanatory matter to make data entry clearer and easier—for example, "Press TAB to move from field to field." You may position this type of text anywhere on the screen as long as it doesn't interfere with field widths in the existing file structure.

To add explanatory text:

- Move the cursor to the desired location.
- Type the text.
- Press ENTER.

Be certain not to overlap text and field content areas when modifying a form in this way. If Field lines are not already present, it is a good idea to turn them on from the View menu before modifying a form view. It is easier to determine a layout with this toggle option activated, (indicated by a check mark to the left of the option).

Adding a Field

Although you can't add explanatory text in List view, in both Form and List views you can add fields. As mentioned in Chapter 9, your *Works* database file can have up to 256 fields in each record. When you add new fields in the List view, the existing ones move to make room for the new ones. In Form view, you can enter a new field simply by typing the name of the field in the desired location with a colon after the field name.

As in the spreadsheet module, *Works* shows ##### if a number or date is larger than the field width. In Form view, a field can be from 1 to 254 characters wide and from 1 to 254 lines high; in list view, a field can be from 1 to 79 characters wide and only 1 line high. In List view, you can choose the Best Fit option and let *Works* determine the size of the field to accommodate the longest entry.

Before changing the design of your database file, make sure that Protection is not turned on in the Format menu. (When Protection is toggled on, you can't change the file design. We will discuss protecting forms and data in a later section.)

To insert a field in List view:

- Move the cursor to the field *after* the spot where you want to insert the new field.
- Click to select the entire column.
- Click on Edit-Insert Record/Field.

A new field is inserted to the left of the highlighted field. Now name the field:

- Click on Edit-Field Name.
- Type a name up to 15 characters long.

The new field size will be the default (10 characters long) if you do not change it. To change the field size:

- Click on Format-Field Width.
- Type in the desired size.
- Click on OK.

To insert a field in the Form view is even easier.

- Position the cursor where you wish to place the field.
- Type the name of the new field, ending with a colon.
- Press ENTER.
- Enter the desired field size or accept the default of 20 characters long and 1 line high.

You can also invoke the Insert Field menu when your cursor is at the desired spot in the Form view to add a field, or you can click on the Insert Field icon from the Toolbar.

When you add new fields to a database structure, you can make the same choices as when you design the database for the first time. That is, you can choose the alignment and width of the field, and whether it should extend more than one line in height.

When you add fields to a database, the original contents of the records remain; the new fields in existing records will be blank until you enter the new field information. You may speed data entry for the new fields that all hold the same data by entering field contents with a default or **ditto command**. For example, suppose that you wish to add a time/date field, and to repeat one date in all of the records of your database; you would enter the date (01/01/95, for example) in the new Date field of Record 1 from the list (multiple record) view. Then you would move to the next record and simply press CTRL + " in the same field of Record 2, and repeat this procedure through the database. As an alternative, you could designate the contents as a default value by entering =01/01/95 in the new Date field of the first record. This is similar to calculated field contents, as explained later in this chapter.

Deleting a Field

If you decide that you want to delete a field from the database structure, you can do so either from the Insert menu in the Form view or from the Insert menu in the List view. Be aware, however, that when you delete a field, you lose all of the contents of that field in all of the records in your existing database file. The same is true if you change the name of a field. A dialog box warns that you will lose the contents of the existing field, and asks you to confirm that choice by selecting OK.

To delete a field:

- In either view, select the field.
- In Form view, click on Insert-Delete Selection.
- Click on OK.
- In List view, click on Insert-Delete Record/Field.

In the first case (Form view) you were asked if you wish to delete all data in this field. In the second case (List view) you receive no such warning.

Moving a Field

You may even change the locations of fields in the Form or List view to improve the screen design. Perhaps the person entering the records is reading from a stack of manual forms whose entries do not currently correspond to the field locations on the screen. To move a field, you first select it, then invoke the Edit-Cut and Edit-Paste commands, or simply drag it with the mouse pointer, if you are in the form view. However, in Form view, be careful not to put a field in an area of the screen that is already occupied by another field's width. You will receive no error message if you attempt to do this; the fields will simply overlap, and data entry will then be convenient only in the List view.

In the Form view, you may also turn off the Snap to Grid toggle command from the Format menu to align fields precisely on the screen. Let's say you wish to print out the contents of fields on a preprinted form loaded in your printer, such as a tax form. With the Snap to Grid option off, you can temporarily reposition the field in the Form view, and then print only the contents of the field to place them in the exact location of the correct blank on the preprinted form. We will not cover this process in the tutorials, but it is a very useful feature if you regularly use a database to complete preprinted forms. The Snap to Grid and Slide to Left options (in the Format-Alignment menu) allow you to print database records one time only, without the trouble of formatting a more permanent report (the topic of the next chapter).

Always turn on the Field Lines option before changing the form design, or you may end up surprised at the result. To move a field in form view:

- With Field Lines preceded by a check mark, position the cursor on the chosen field's name.
- Hold down the mouse button and drag the field to the desired area.

  OR
- Click on Edit-Position Selection.
- Move the highlight to a new location.
- Click the mouse button or press ENTER.

To move a field in List view:

- Select the entire area to be moved.
- Click on Edit-Cut.
- Move the cursor and select the field that follows the desired new location.
- Click on Edit-Paste.

In List view, all columns shift position to allow for the relocation of the moved column. Instructions for designing the original database structure suggested that you position related fields together, with the more important fields listed first. However, you can always edit your structure design if your evaluation of the importance of your fields should change after building your database.

Changing a Field Name

If, after assigning field names, you decide that another field name would be better (perhaps because you misspelled a field name), you can change a field's name without losing all of the data in that category of your records. To change a field name in the List view:

- Select the entire field column.
- Click on Edit-Field Name.
- Type the new name, but do not type a colon.
- Click on OK.

The name of the field will be changed in your structure definition. (Make sure to save the file to disk after the changes to permanently record the new name.)

Inserting and Deleting Database Records

You have already had experience, in Chapter 9, with adding records in the Form view. You can, however, add or delete records in either Form view or List view, and it is often more convenient to do it in the List view. In addition, you can delete either selected records or the whole file.

Inserting Records

Most of the time, when entering new records in a database, you simply go to the last existing record and append records to the file. If you then wish to see the selected records in, say, alphabetical order by last name, you can easily sort the file. Sometimes, however, you might want to insert a record into a database file somewhere within the existing order without having to sort again. For example, maybe you entered everything in order by date, but forgot one record; you could insert that record in its chronological place in a large database using the Edit menu.

When you insert a record into a database, the records that follow the new record are renumbered to the end of the file. (Similarly, when a record is deleted, the records are renumbered from the point of deletion to the end of the file.) To insert a record, you must first go to the record following the place where you wish to place the new record. *Works* always inserts above (or preceding) the selected area. To insert a record:

- Move to the record you want to follow the new record.
- Click on Insert-Record in Form view.

  OR
- Click on Insert-Insert Record/Field in List view.

In List View, if you selected a record (Edit-Select Record), a blank record will be inserted above the selected record. If you did not highlight a record, *Works* will present you with a window asking whether you wish to insert a record or field. Click on the proper radio button, and then click on OK. A blank record will appear in the location where you want it, and you can proceed to enter your data.

Deleting Selected Records

When deleting a record, you must first select the record to be deleted, and then delete it using the Edit menu. To delete a record in List view:

- Select the record (row) to delete.
- Click on Insert-Delete Record/Field.

To delete a record in Form view:

- Go anywhere in the record you want to delete.
- Click on Insert-Delete Record.

Always be very careful when you are editing, deleting, and inserting records in a database file. When you are in the middle of a database instead of at the end, it is all too easy to inadvertently write over an existing record for which you have not turned on protection. Pay attention to where your cursor is!

The database application of *Works* now offers an Undo Delete Record command if you should inadvertently delete a record. To recall a record immediately after deleting it:

- Click on Edit-Undo Delete Record.

The record will reappear. However, if you perform another operation after deleting a record, you will see the message "Cannot Undo Command" when you click on Edit.

If you are in the middle of the database instead of at the end when you begin entering data, it is very easy to simply type over data that is already in fields, instead of entering entirely new records, as you intend. You must use the Insert Record command to add new records in the middle of a database. Otherwise, always go to the last record and append new records there.

Never correct your database by entering a new record instead of editing an existing record. If you correct an error by entering another record, you will then have two records for the same person, event, or object in your file—one correct one and one incorrect one.

Deleting an Entire Database File

If you have no more use for any of the records in your database, but you want to preserve the structure, you can select the entire database file and delete all of the records in one simple command. You must be in the List view to access this command from the Edit menu.

To delete all of the records in a database, but retain the structure:

- Click on Edit-Select All.

  OR

- Drag the mouse to select all of the records in list view.

  OR

- Press CTRL + SHIFT + F8.
- Click on Insert-Delete Record/Field.

All of the existing records are removed.

When you issue the Select All command, it selects all 32,000 possible records in a *Works* database, so be certain that you wish to delete everything. This command is appropriate for deleting an entire database, but just as in spreadsheets, it is NOT appropriate to use this method to select blocks for other commands. An Undo command in the Edit menu can reverse this large-scale deletion if you should change your mind.

You can remove all records from a database, but usually it is better to copy the form to another database file and then **clear** all of the records, that is, delete their contents. You can then type new information into the empty records.

Clearing Field Contents

The Clear command is a convenient way to empty fields in one or many records. It does not remove the record; it merely blanks the fields so you can enter new information into them. You can clear one or more fields, one or more records, or the entire database.

The Clear command is accessed from the Edit menu in either Form view or List view. To clear a record:

- Select the record(s) or field(s) to be blanked.
- Select Edit-Clear.
- The selected area is cleared.

Copying a File

The *Works* database application includes many copying options. You can copy all of a database file, or just certain records. You can copy the whole file to another location, or you can use the Copy command from the Edit menu to copy a portion of the database into another database file using the Window menu. You can also copy records from a database file into a word processing document or a spreadsheet using the Copy command (a topic discussed in Chapter 13).

To copy a record in the List view:

- Insert a blank record (or more than one).
- Select the record(s) you want to copy.
- Click on Edit-Copy.
- Move the insertion bar to the area where you want the copies to appear.
- Click on Edit-Paste.

To copy a record in form view:

- Select the record you want to copy.
- Select Edit-Copy.
- Move the insertion bar to the spot where you want the new data to begin.
- Click on Edit-Paste Record.

Copying a Database Design

The Form (single-record) view and the List (multiple-record) view have slightly different Edit menus. If you wish to copy the design or structure of a database file, you can invoke the Edit-Copy choice in the Form view. You can then copy the form to another open database with the Window command. (Review the procedure for an external copy in Chapter 5, if necessary.)

To copy a form to another *Works* database file:

- Select the fields to copy.
- Click on Edit-Copy.
- Click on Window, and then click on the database to which you wish to copy the form.
- Open the window, where the form will be received (specified by window name and number).
- Position the cursor at the desired *X*, *Y* coordinate or column.
- Click on Edit-Paste.

Chapter 13 explains still more procedures for copying from the *Works 3.0 for Windows* database to the word processor.

Copying Records

By a single process, you can copy certain records, or even portions of records, to the same database or another database, or to a word processing document or a spreadsheet. If the material to be copied includes entire records, you may use the Copy Records command in the Edit menu in the List (multiple-record) view. (Remember, the Toolbar icon or the F9 key toggles between the two views.) If you wish to copy only certain fields of certain records, select the fields to copy, and then choose the Copy command in the Edit menu.

To copy records, or portions of records, in List view:

- Select the records or fields to copy.
- Click on Edit-Copy.
- Switch windows to another *Works* file.
- Move the insertion bar to the location where you want the copy to appear.
- Click on Paste.

Before you copy entire records to another location in a single database file, think carefully about the results. Exact duplicates of a record will not add much. However, to save time entering records that will be near duplicates, you may want to copy an entire record or two and then change only those fields where differences occur.

By contrast, copying entire records to another database file is often very helpful. You could use the records of one database as a foundation for a different database that is a modification of the first. In other words, if you want to make a new database that duplicates the first one except for the addition or deletion of one or two fields, copying the first database will be the fastest way to accomplish your goal. It may well be easier simply to open a database file with its structure defined and records entered, and simply Save As to a new file, then modify the structure of the second file. As an alternative, you could use the *Windows* clipboard operation to cut and paste fields and records.

Backing Up and Protecting Your Work

Whenever you decide to alter a database in any way, you should back up the existing file (that is, copy the entire file) to a separate floppy disk before altering the design. The data in the backup will be invaluable if something should go wrong. If you inadvertently lose the contents of some fields, you can always return to the original version and restore the lost data. Altering the structure of a database is not the trauma that it once was, but it is still good computing practice to make a duplicate of any database file before you embark on major modifications.

Backing Up the Structure

When you design a database and do not store any records in it, it is a shell. That shell makes your database file self-describing. The fields, how they are formatted, how long they are, the text that appears in the form view, and so forth are all stored along with the database records.

Any empty file structure is valuable in itself. You may decide to return to the original structure, after devising newer versions, or to use that same structure for another set of records. You may wish to enter one **dummy record** with sample data, and then save the database design to disk before copying the file as a work file and entering records in it. A copy of the shell, with all of the design, and even the report specifications that are discussed in Chapter 11, can eliminate the need to **purge** or remove all records to reuse the database design for a recurring event. If your database will be used by more than one operator, this is a precaution that should not be ignored.

Protecting the Form and the Data

Both the form and the contents of your database can be protected so that someone cannot alter them by mistake. While it is almost mandatory to protect your form or design if more than one person works with your database, it is also a good idea for a single user. The benefit of protecting the form or design of the field structures is evident. It is easy to unintentionally alter the structure of a database that you have spent many hours designing.

To make the database contents—the actual data in the fields—secure, turn on Protect Data. You can choose to protect specific fields to allow changes to the contents of some fields (such as a person's name), while still protecting the contents of others (such as a balance due) to prevent change. As with spreadsheets, protecting either the form or the content of a *Works* database file is a two-step process. Before you can turn on protection, you must lock the field.

When fields are designed in a *Works* database, they are locked by default. You may remove this lock by entering the Format-Protection menu and removing the check from the Locked option. If you have not turned off this Locked option, you may select the field and then turn protection on by accessing the Format menu. You must be in the form (single-record) view to access the Format menu that contains the choice to Protect Data or Form. The list (multiple-record) view offers only the Protect Data option in its Format menu.

To lock or unlock a field in the list view:

- Select the field you want to lock or unlock.
- Click on Format-Protection.
- Click on the radio button to lock or unlock.
- Click on Protection.

Only in the form view can you turn on Protection for your structure, or form. In form view:

- Select the field you want to lock or unlock.
- Click on Format-Protection.
- In the Protection area, click on the radio button Protect Form.

You must use caution when protecting calculated fields. A **calculated field** is a field whose contents result from a formula or function; the next tutorial contains an example. You can use some of the functions from the spreadsheet application in the database application of *Works*. You will be using these functions in the next chapter, when you learn to create reports for your database files.

However, you may also use your own formulas or functions to determine the contents of a particular field in a database file. For instance, to include a field for the balance due for each customer who purchases an automobile, you could enter a formula that takes the difference between the selling price and the down payment and automatically enters that amount in the Balance Due field. The contents of that field might be =Price-Payment. (The contents of a calculated field must begin with an equal sign, just as a formula or function in a spreadsheet cell also begins with an equal sign.)

To protect this formula from being altered, you would select the Protect Data option from the Format menu, rather than the Protect Form option. Thus the balance due would be automatically calculated by the computer, and the user could not change it manually. If you were to select Protect Form, you would be unable to alter the field name, size, format, and so forth, but you would still be able to alter the contents of the field, the formula. In this instance, you would probably want to protect both the data and the form of the Balance Due field, to keep anyone else who has access to your database from inadvertently changing either.

The important thing to remember when protecting fields is to protect each field's form or data after the field has been locked. Invoke the Format-Protection command to check the field status before turning on protection. The Locked option should show a check, signifying that it is turned on. If you turn on protection and the field is not locked, *Works* will not issue an error message, but the field will not be protected.

DATABASE TUTORIAL NO. 3

You are in the process of buying a new car, and you want to gather information in a database about the cars in which you are interested. You are going to start with only 1994 cars.

1. Open *Works.*
2. Click on Database.
3. Your insertion point should be located at *X*1.33 inches, *Y*1.17 inches.

   You do not want the field lines to display. To remove them:
4. Click on View.
5. Click on Field Lines to remove the check mark.

You will now arrange the fields down the screen, entering each one on a separate line and indicating the field widths as you go. Steps 6 and 7 remind you to press ENTER after each item that you type; you should continue to do so in the following steps.

6. Type **Make:** and press ENTER.
7. For the Field Width, type **30** and press ENTER.
8. Type **Model:** and **25**
9. Type **Year:** and **6**
10. Type **Price:** and **12**
11. Type **Ins:** and **10**
12. Type **Uninsmot:** and **10**
13. Type **Totalins:** and **10**
14. Type **Color:** and **10**
15. Save the database as **cars**.

    Your screen should look similar to Figure 10.1.
16. Click on the space to the right of the Make field and enter the information from Table 10.1, saving frequently as you go.

Remember that you can TAB from one field to the next. Also, press TAB to go to the next record. If you make a mistake, use F2 to edit the field and press ENTER; use CTRL + PAGE DOWN/PAGE UP to get to the next or previous record. After entering the first record DO NOT enter 1994 and 22.80. Since the year is 1994 and the cost of the uninsured motorist insurance (Uninsmot) is 11.20 for

Figure 10.1

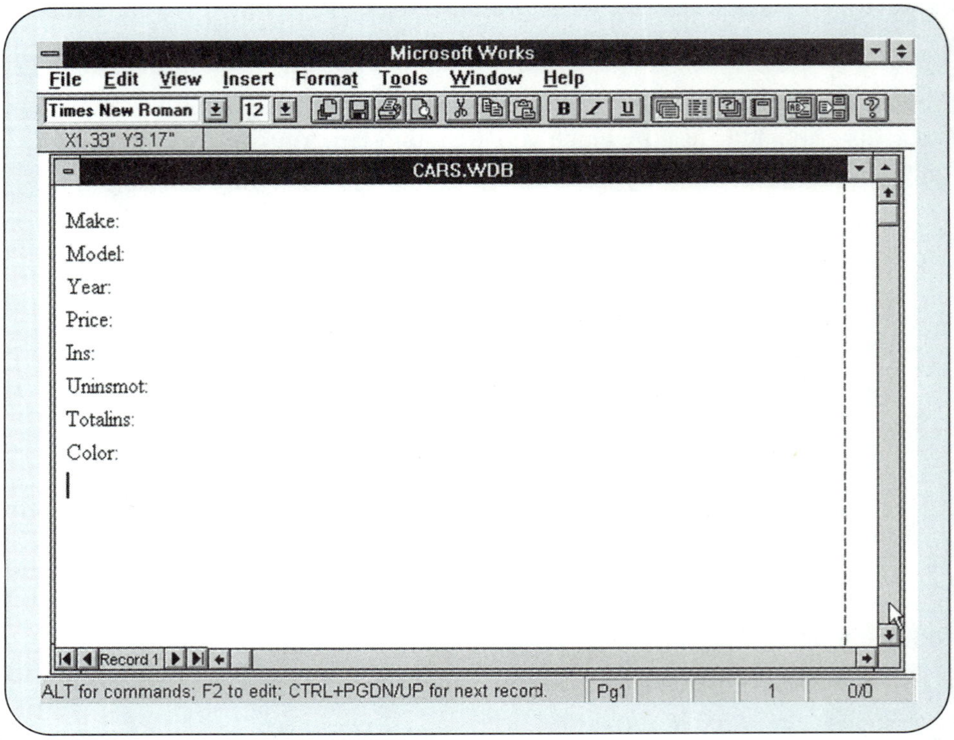

every car, you will use Fill Down to specify in Table 10.1 these fields after all records are entered. (Those two fields are not in boldface to remind you not to type them.) The table provides no data for the Totalins field. Totalins is a calculated field—the total of Ins and Uninsmot; you will enter the formula to calculate that field when you enter the first record; the amount will then be automatically entered for all following records.

Table 10.1 Data for cars.wdb Database

Record 1:	**Alfa Romeo, 164LS,** 1994, **36000, 569,** 11.20, **=Ins+Uninsmot, White**
Record 2:	**Hyundai Elantra, Sport Coupe,** 1994, **13385, 270,** 11.20, **Maroon**
Record 3:	**Infinity, Q45,** 1994, **47500, 669,** 11.20, **Maroon**
Record 4:	**Bentley Continental Coupe,** 1994, **262290, 1300,** 11.20, **Silver**
Record 5:	**Jaguar, XJS Convertible,** 1994, **60730, 950,** 11.20, **Bronze**
Record 6:	**BMW 325i, Sedan,** 1994, **29389, 569,** 11.20, **Blue-Gray**
Record 7:	**Mercedes-Benz, S320 Sedan,** 1994, **46200, 669,** 11.20, **Teal**
Record 8:	**Suzuki, Swift,** 1994, **8844, 235,** 11.20, **Green**
Record 9:	**Jeep Cherokee Laredo, 4X4,** 1994, **23395, 385,** 11.20, **Black**
Record 10:	**Cadillac Deville, Sedan,** 1994, **30450, 850,** 11.20, **Gold**
Record 11:	**Eagle Talon, 4X4,** 1994, **12995, 439,** 11.20, **Silver**

To enter 1994 as the model year for each car:

17. Click on View.
18. Click on List.
19. Click on 1994 in the Year column and select the first 11 records in that column.
20. Click on Edit.
21. Click on Fill Down.

    The year 1994 will be entered for all records.
22. On your own, enter 11.20 in the Uninsmot field for every car.

    The Totalins field is now correct, also.
23. Go to the top of the screen (CTRL + HOME).

    Notice that the descriptions for Make and Model are too wide for their fields.
24. Click on the Make title bar.
25. Click on Format.
26. Click on Field Width.
27. Click on Best Fit-OK.

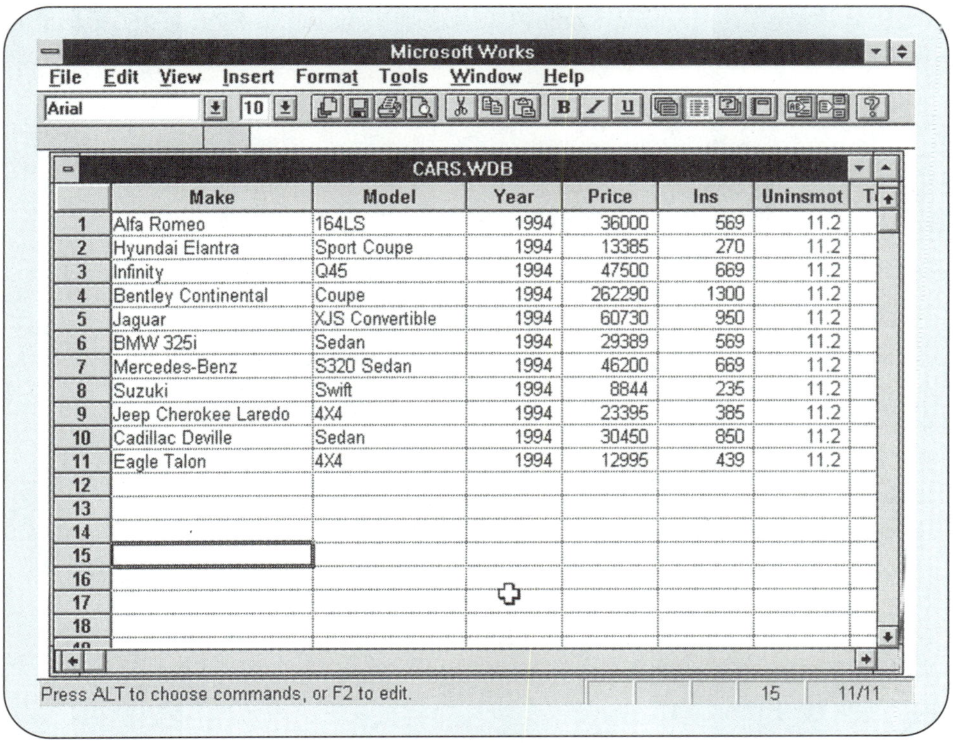

	Make	Model	Year	Price	Ins	Uninsmot
1	Alfa Romeo	164LS	1994	36000	569	11.2
2	Hyundai Elantra	Sport Coupe	1994	13385	270	11.2
3	Infinity	Q45	1994	47500	669	11.2
4	Bentley Continental	Coupe	1994	262290	1300	11.2
5	Jaguar	XJS Convertible	1994	60730	950	11.2
6	BMW 325i	Sedan	1994	29389	569	11.2
7	Mercedes-Benz	S320 Sedan	1994	46200	669	11.2
8	Suzuki	Swift	1994	8844	235	11.2
9	Jeep Cherokee Laredo	4X4	1994	23395	385	11.2
10	Cadillac Deville	Sedan	1994	30450	850	11.2
11	Eagle Talon	4X4	1994	12995	439	11.2

Figure 10.2

cars.wdb Database Records

28. On your own, widen the Model field with the Best Fit option.

    Your screen should look similar to that in Figure 10.2. (The extra record shown will be added in the next steps.) You now want to format the appropriate fields as currency. Be sure you are in List view.

29. Select the fourth field (Price) in any row.
30. Click on Format-Number.
31. Click on Currency.
32. Type **0** for number of decimal places.
33. Click on OK, or press ENTER.
34. Repeat the same process for the Ins field because it is a whole-dollar number; for the Uninsmot and Totalins fields, select Format-Number-Currency and specify two decimal places.

Now you want to print as much of the database as you can on each page. If you do not use condensed print or landscape mode (reversing page length and width, as covered in Chapter 7), you will have a two-page printout. To expand the width of your printing area on each page, be sure you are in List view and proceed as follows:

35. Click on File.
36. Click on Page Setup.

    The Page Setup option box displays, as shown in Figure 10.3. In the Margins area:

Figure 10.3

Example of the Page Setup Option box

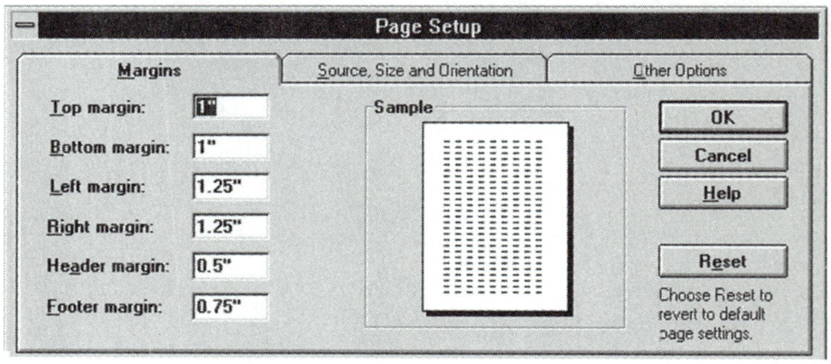

37. Change the left margin to .3".
38. Change the right margin to .3".

    Now you will instruct the system to print the record numbers, field names, and gridlines.

39. Click on Other Options.
40. Click on Print Gridlines.
41. Click on Print Records and Field Labels.

42. Click on OK.

    To print the records:

43. Click on the Print icon.

    The database prints on one or two pages with the records numbered on the left, the field names across the top, and lines separating the fields. You decide to add a record for one more Suzuki car, and you want to place it with the other Suzuki record. When you insert a record, it precedes the selected record. The existing Suzuki car is Record 8.

44. Click on the Form view icon.
45. Click on Edit.

    The Edit menu displays, as shown in Figure 10.4.

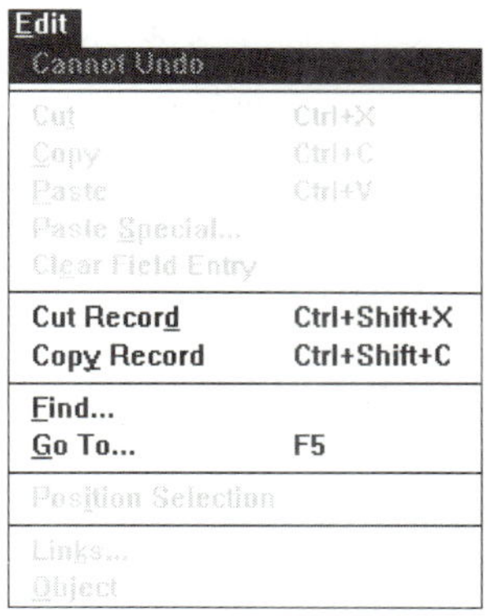

Figure 10.4

Example of the Edit Menu

46. Click on Go To.

    The Go To option box displays, as shown in Figure 10.5.

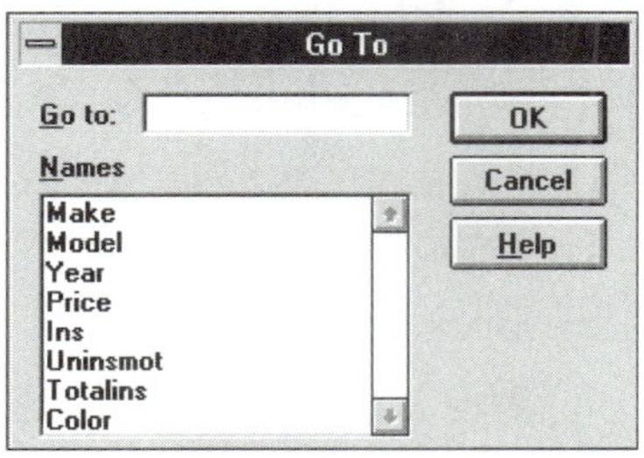

Figure 10.5

Example of the Go To Option box

47. Type **8** and press ENTER.

    Record 8 (the existing Suzuki) displays.

48. Click on Insert.

    The Insert menu displays, as shown in Figure 10.6.

Figure 10.6

Example of the Insert Menu

49. Click on Record.

    A blank record is displayed in which you can enter the new data.

50. Type **Suzuki, JX 4X4, 1994, 12994, 425, 11.20, Red**

    The new Suzuki record becomes Record 8 and the old Suzuki drops to 9.

51. Click on the Save icon.

    You feel pretty sure that you won't buy the Bentley Continental, so you want to move it to the bottom of the list.

52. Click on the List view icon.
53. Click on the number 4 to the left of the name *Bentley* to select the record.
54. Click on the cut icon.
55. Select Cell A12.
56. Click on the Paste icon.

    You decide to delete the Jaguar.

57. Click on the number to the left of the name *Jaguar*. (It should now be Record 4.)
58. Click on Insert.

    The Insert menu displays, as shown in Figure 10.7.

59. Click on Delete Record/Field.

    After careful consideration you realize that you cannot afford a 1994 car; you now want to add some used cars to your database. However, you must first add a new field called Mileage.

60. Click on the Form view icon.
61. Move the cursor bar to the last field after Color, in any record.

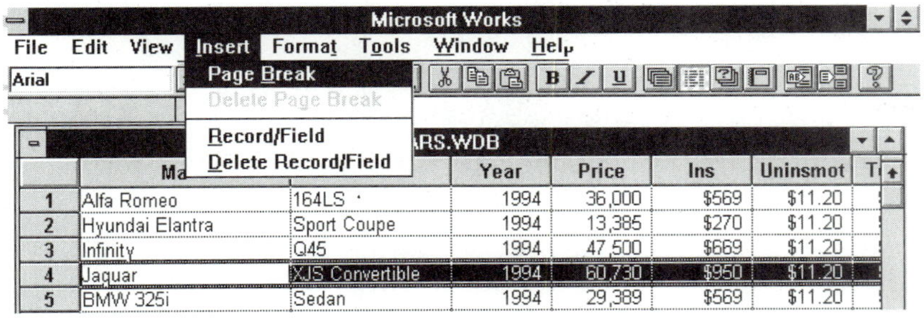

Figure 10.7

Example of the Insert Menu

62. Type **Mileage:** and press ENTER.
63. Type **10** for field width and press ENTER.

    To make the fields consistent, you will enter zeros in the Mileage field for the 1994 cars.
64. Click on the List view icon.
65. Select the Mileage field in Record 1.
66. Type **0**.
67. Press ENTER.
68. Press F8 and select down through Record 11.
69. Select Edit-Fill Down.
70. With the 11 records still selected in the Mileage field, format the field for Commas with zero decimal places.
71. Move the cursor to the bottom of the database (Record 12).
72. Enter the records shown in Table 10.2. (The Totalins field will fill in automatically, and you can use Fill Down to enter 11.20 for each car's Uninsmot field.)

Table 10.2 Data for Additional Records in cars.wdb Database

Record 12: **Honda Accord, LX, 1988, 7000, 246,** 11.20, **Blue, 85000**
Record 13: **Ford Taurus, GL, 1993, 13888, 316,** 11.20, **Black, 12000**
Record 14: **Toyota Camry, LE, 1988, 7988, 246,** 11.20, **Red, 89000**
Record 15: **Mercury Topaz, GS 2-door, 1993, 8993, 257,** 11.20, **Brown, 300**
Record 16: **Ford F250 Super Cab, 4X4, 1993, 24145, 332,** 11.20, **Red, 6000**
Record 17: **Mercury Tracer, 4-door, 1993, 9993, 301,** 11.20, **312.10, Tan, 5000**
Record 18: **Jeep, Grand Cherokee, 1993, 25988, 412,** 11.20, **Bronze, 3250**

73. Save your database as cars2 before you start entering the new data.

    Note that you can enter the data in either List or Form view. ctrl + left arrow or home is a fast way to get to the left margin in list view.

74. Print your new database from List view.

    Your printout should look similar to that in Figure 10.8.

75. Save and close the cars2.wdb database.

Figure 10.8

(Page 1)

	Make	Model	Year	Price	Ins	Uninsmot	Totalins	Color
1	Alfa Romeo	164LS	1994	$36,000	$569	$11.20	$580.20	White
2	Hyundai Elantra	Sport Coupe	1994	$13,385	$270	$11.20	$281.20	Maroon
3	Infinity	Q45	1994	$47,500	$669	$11.20	$680.20	Maroon
4	BMW 325i	Sedan	1994	$29,389	$569	$11.20	$580.20	Blue-Gray
5	Mercedes-Benz	S320 Sedan	1994	$46,200	$669	$11.20	$680.20	Teal
6	Suzuki	JX 4X4	1994	$12,994	$425	$11.20	$436.20	Red
7	Suzuki	Swift	1994	$8,844	$235	$11.20	$246.20	Green
8	Jeep Cherokee Laredo	4X4	1994	$23,395	$385	$11.20	$396.20	Black
9	Cadillac Deville	Sedan	1994	$30,450	$850	$11.20	$861.20	Gold
10	Eagle Talon	4X4	1994	$12,995	$439	$11.20	$450.20	Silver
11	Bentley Continental	Coupe	1994	$262,290	$1,300	$11.20	$1,311.20	Silver
12	Honda Accord	LX	1988	$7,000	$246	$11.20	$257.20	Blue
13	Ford Taurus	GL	1993	$13,888	$316	$11.20	$327.20	Black
14	Toyota Camry	LE	1988	$7,988	$246	$11.20	$257.20	Red
15	Mercury Topaz	GS 2-door	1993	$8,993	$257	$11.20	$268.20	Brown
16	Ford F250 Super Cab	4X4	1993	$24,145	$332	$11.20	$343.20	Red
17	Mercury Tracer	4-door	1993	$9,993	$301	$11.20	$312.20	Tan
18	Jeep	Grand Cherokee	1993	$25,988	$412	$11.20	$423.20	Bronze

(Page 2)

	Mileage
1	0
2	0
3	0
4	0
5	0
6	0
7	0
8	0
9	0
10	0
11	0
12	85,000
13	12,000
14	89,000
15	300
16	6,000
17	5,000
18	3,250

Organizing and Manipulating the Database

When a database is small, the benefits of organizing the file and rearranging it in any order are not readily apparent. However, only when a database is small enough to fit on a screen or two is it practical to search it manually. The dynamic nature of a database eventually makes it large enough so that all of the records, and perhaps even all of the fields, no longer fit on one or two display screens. Rearranging the order of the records or querying for just the desired records becomes essential to get only the records you wish to see.

Nested Sorts

You learned in Chapter 9 that sorting involves rearranging the database records. In a sort, the system temporarily rearranges the records for the desired view, but it retains their original order unless the database is saved to disk with the new order. It is possible to use a nested sort to arrange within another sort. *Works* even allows you to sort on up to three fields to produce a triple-layered arrangement. You could sort the cars.wdb database on the Make field in ascending order to arrange all of the records in alphabetical order by car name. Within each alphabetical classification, you could sort on the Year field in ascending order to arrange all of the cars within a make, from the Bentley down to the Toyota, ordered from oldest to newest. Within that order, you could sort again on the Price field in ascending order to list the cheaper cars for one year a single make category before the more expensive ones.

This ability to **concatenate** (link together) fields for a tri-level sort enables you to sort a database in fine detail. Figure 10.14, later in the chapter, shows the cars data sorted first by make, then by year, and finally by price. A group must include two or more items before that group is ordered within the first order, and no extra information affects the sort, such as Tempo or LX, as it looks at each field in its entirety.

Works can sort on up to three fields, but other database programs allow you to nest sorts even more deeply than three fields. This feature is very useful to view or print just a portion of a large number of records. The records on which you want to concentrate will all appear together in one place on the screen. After your records have been sorted in this fine detail, you can insert a page break just below the last record you want to view, and print just that page for a hard copy to help you zoom in on the chosen records. You have involved the entire database in a sort, but you can concentrate on just a few records, placed in one specific order.

You may enter field names by typing them (be sure to use exact names) in three designated windows. To execute a triple-nested sort in *Works*, go into the List view and then:

- Click on Tools-Sort Records.
- Type in the name of the first field on which to sort.
- Click on a radio button to select Ascend or Descend.
- Move to the second field and type the field name.
- Click to select Ascend or Descend.
- Move to the third field and type the name.
- Click to select Ascend or Descend.
- Click on OK.

The entire database will be reordered in the desired triple-nested sort. The records will be reordered by the third field within the second field, and then within the first field.

If you wish to print just a portion of your database, for example the first 15 cars, you can insert a page break below the last selected record (Record 15) and print those records:

- Select the record below which to place a page break.
- Click on Edit-Select Record.
- Select Insert-Page Break.

On the screen, your page break will be indicated by a dotted line before the first record on the new page. Now you can print just the portion of the database you wish by marking the radio button for the Pages option in the Print Range area of the Print window. As always, however, a sort reorders all records in a database; it cannot substitute for a query to select specific records. We'll look at that process next.

Complex Queries and Compound Queries

Chapter 9 explained that queries filter out certain records to view or print. You also learned that you could query on as many fields as necessary. A query on multiple fields is referred to as a **complex query**. As you saw in Chapter 9, filling in the query window with the criteria you want to match is relatively simple with the sentence form of the Create Query command from the Tools menu. You merely type one or more instructions in the appropriate field windows, using logical or relational operators selected from the list supplied by *Works*. *Works* then selects and displays the records that meet all of the specified criteria. You must be sure to enter the correct information in the selected field, however. (Remember, though, that *Works* does not distinguish between upper case and lower case in a query.) For example, the query to find all CMS majors with a grade point average above 3.5 who live in Chicago would look like this:

- Field: Major Comparison Criteria: = Value of Contents: CMS
- Field: GPA Comparison Criteria: > Value of Contents: 3.5
- Field: City Comparison Criteria: = Value of Contents: Chicago

The relational operators greater than (>) and less than (<) and their combinations can identify ranges of numbers and letters that are more than or less than a specific number or letter. To display all the students over 25 years of age in the same database, you would select the Age field, select the phrase *is greater than* in the How to Compare the Field option, and type the number 25 in the Value to Compare field to option.

Querying on more than three fields, or more than three conditions within one field, is also possible in *Works 3.0 for Windows*, but this requires the Query View instead of sentence form to activate it:

- Click on Tools-Create New Query.
- Fill in as many conditions and fields as you wish.
- Click on the Query View button.

A Form view of the query, as *Works 3.0 for Windows* defines it, displays on your screen. You may now edit and complete the query, using as many special characters for criteria in as many fields as you wish. Finally, you apply the query.

In contrast to a complex query, which queries on multiple fields, you can also query on multiple conditions for one field. This is referred to as a **compound query**. Suppose that you are searching for data within a range of values, or for either of two possibilities, or even for all values greater than a certain value. Such conditions require a compound query, which checks one field for several possibilities. Of course, you can also define a compound-complex query, to identify records in which more than one field match multiple conditions. In fact, using the query view method, you can combine query instructions until you completely lose your way in a myriad of compound-complex conditions. When you find yourself combining many logical and relational operators in a query on one field, it is time to rethink your logic. There is usually a simpler way to query.

The logical operators AND (#AND#), OR (#OR#), and NOT (#NOT#) can help you to perform multiple comparisons. When doing a compound and/or complex query from the query view, rather than in sentence style, the process is somewhat more complex. There are two methods for defining the query in query view. You can put all of the instructions in one field and begin it with an equal sign (=), or you can divide up the query and enter individual values in their appropriate fields. Although we will not cover the process, you can even insert mathematical operators (+, -, *, /) into query conditions and filter out records based on computations on multiple fields. (For example, you may want to find a record in which the sum of the contents of the Price and Commission fields exceed $5000. The query would be:

=(Price+Tax)>5000

When you invoke the query view, you will notice that *Works* interprets your instructions using the first method of putting all the instructions in one sentence. Using this method of defining a query within one field imposes several rules:

1. The field name and an equal sign must precede each alternative choice, as

   Make:=Make+"Suzuki"#OR#=Model="4X4"#AND#=Color="Red"

2. Numbers must be preceded by the term VALUE and enclosed in parentheses and double quotes, as

   Price<VALUE("15000")

3. Any field that contains a date, such as year, must be surrounded by single quotes as '1994'

To state a query in one field to find all CMS majors with GPAs above 3.5 living in Chicago, you would type:

=Major="CMS" #AND#GPA=>VALUE("3.5")
#AND#City="Chicago"

Note that you place quotes around the criteria but not the field names.

When using the second method of placing the criteria in several different fields, the following rules apply:

1. The VALUE function need not precede the numeric fields, and quotes and parentheses need not surround the numbers, as

   Major:="CMS"
   GPA:>3.5
   City:="Chicago"

2. The criteria must be stated in the applicable field.
3. The query statement for Compound queries must begin with two equal signs, as

   Major:=="CMS"#OR#="ACC"

In both methods, logical operators must be surrounded by pound signs and be in all capital letters, as #AND#, #OR#, #NOT# and text must be surrounded by double quotes.

Two other operators can be quite helpful: not equal to (< >) and NOT (#NOT#). When using the sentence query method from the Tools-Create New Query menu, all of the logical and relational operators take the form of text that you select in the Comparison Criteria area of the query window.

Figure 10.9 shows a query using *Works* Query Screen. Figure 10.10 shows how *Works* would write that query in sentence form. Figure 10.11 is an example of a query generated on the form screen.

Queries in a *Works* database can use wildcard symbols (? and *) to substitute

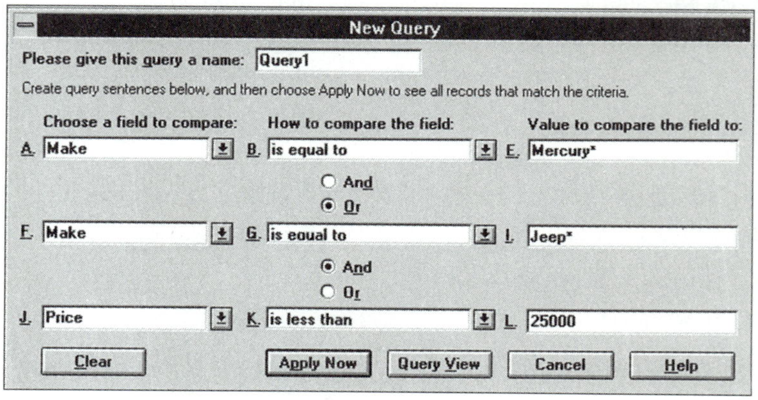

Figure 10.9

Example of a Query using *Works* Query Screen

for unknown data. The question mark stands for a single character and the asterisk stands for any number of characters. For example, if you were looking for the name *Larsen*, but you did not know if it spelled with an *o* or an *e*, you could enter "Lars?n"; you could enter "A*" to find all the states that begin with *A*. In queries of the cars.wdb database, you would have to specify "Alfa*" and "Bentley*" as conditions because extra text identifies some cars that meet these conditions. None of the cars would match based on their entire field contents. (Remember that you are looking for an exact match when querying. You could do a search from the Select menu to find a certain text string, but you could not combine conditions into a complex or compound query. Also, such a search will not find numerical information for you—only text.)

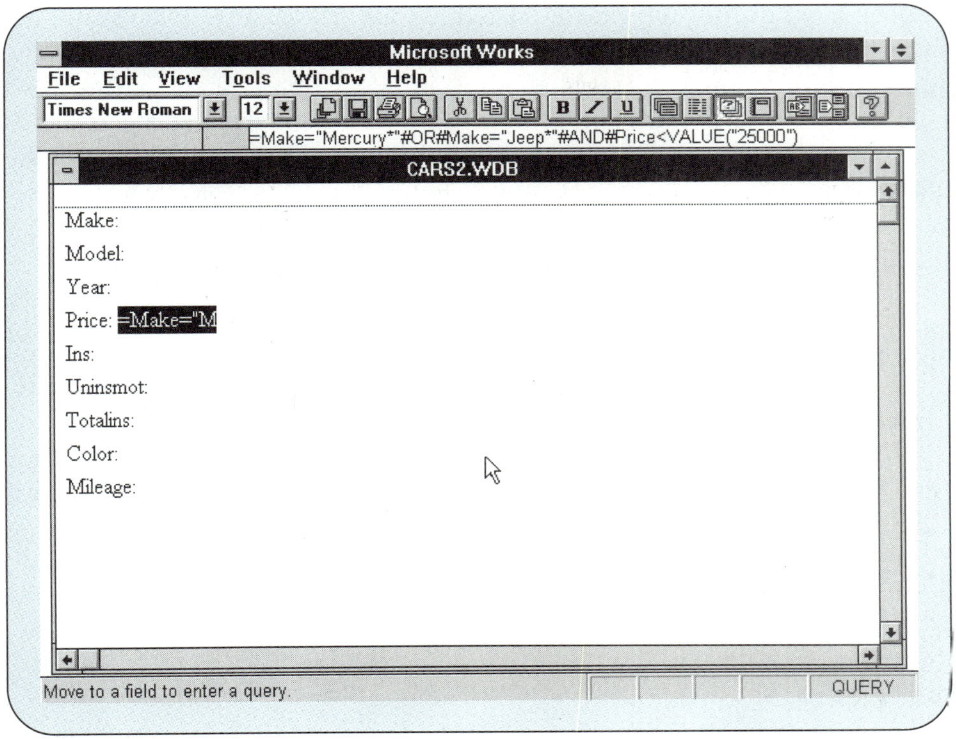

Figure 10.10

Example of how *Works* would write a Query in Sentence Form

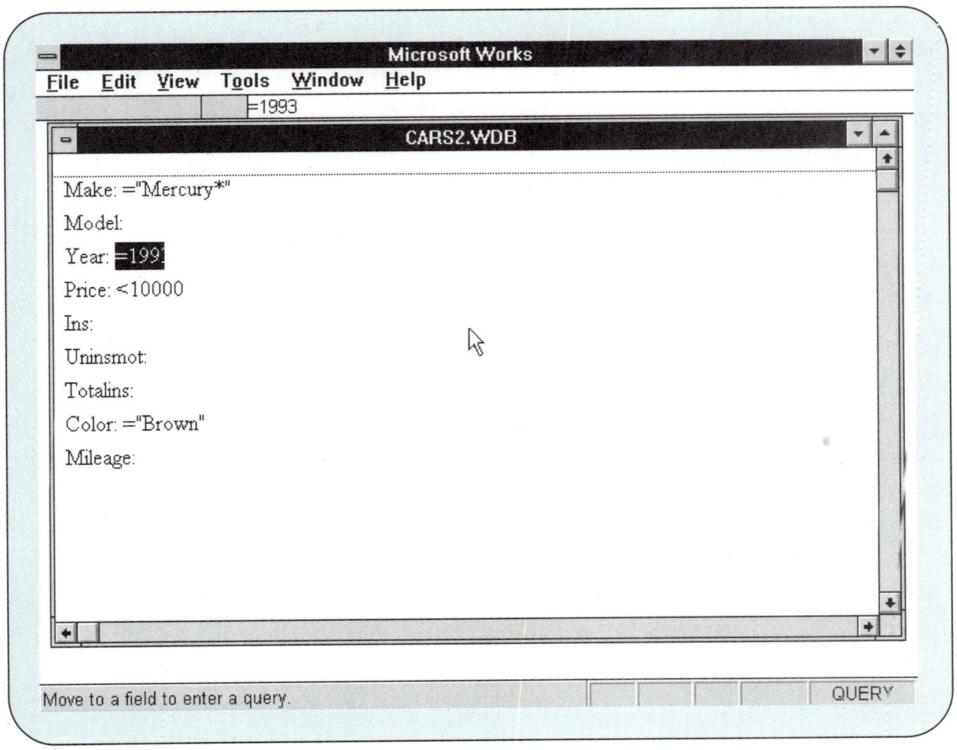

Figure 10.11

Example of a Query generated on the Form Screen

Compound queries on Time/Date formats are particularly troublesome because you have to use single quotes (‘) and colons (:) for times, as well as the AM/PM designation with the 24-hour clock. *Works* stores data in a Time/Date field based on the 24-hour military clock. If you state a query as a correct 12-hour time, the query will automatically be converted for you. Time and date queries should be done with the Create New Query menu's sentence method because *Works 3.0 for Windows* will convert your sentence into the proper query rules, and you needn't be concerned about single quotes and other designators.

The results of a compound or complex query can be printed out after the query has been applied. Click on File-Print-OK to print the selected records with all of their fields (or click on the Print icon). Printing the field names and record numbers along with the selected record is especially helpful. To do this:

- Click on View-Apply Query.
- Click on List view, if necessary.
- Click on File-Page Setup.
- Click on the Other Options area.
- Click on Print Record and Field Labels.
- Click on OK.
- Click on File-Print-OK.

The results of your query will print, with field and record labels included.

Before exiting the *Works* program, remember to redisplay all of the records in the database (View-Show All Records). Otherwise, the next time you open the database, only the results of your last query will display; you may mistakenly think some of your records are missing from the database, when in fact they are only hidden from sight.

Being able to save your queries and assign them descriptive names is a very powerful addition to *Works 3.0 for Windows*. Now you can define a particularly difficult and involved query once, and then save the query sentences and use them repeatedly, no matter how much the database changes. To apply a saved query:

- From the List view, click on View-Apply Query.
- Choose the name of the query you wish to use.
- Click on OK.

To assign a more descriptive name to a frequently used query:

- Click on Tools-Name Query.
- Type a descriptive name (up to 15 characters).
- Click on Rename.
- Click on OK.

The saved query will now have a descriptive name, making it much easier to apply it over and over.

It is also possible to delete queries that are no longer necessary. To delete a saved query that is no longer useful:

- Click on Tools-Delete Query.
- Select the query to delete.
- Click on the Delete button.
- Click on OK.

The query is deleted.

It is possible to save eight queries for each database. If the query concerns complete records that are viewed frequently, and not printed out for reference, a saved query will often suffice, and a formal report is not necessary. If you do not name your query, *Works 3.0 for Windows* assigns it a default name, as Query1, Query2, etc. Since a query can be printed, you can keep a hard copy of the query, as well. This can often eliminate the need to define a complicated formal report, as discussed in Chapter 13.

Viewing a Large Database

A small database containing only a few fields rarely creates a problem when you need to see the most important fields and records. However, as your database grows, all of the records cannot be displayed at once because only 23 records will fit on one List view screen. Also, if each record has many fields, or the fields are very wide, they extend off of the List view screen, so you must scroll right to see more than the first few. *Works* offers a couple of ways, however, to maximize your views of a large database.

The first way is to split the screen display into four panes, and then to scroll up and down or left and right within each pane. Pressing the F6 function key will move the cursor from pane to pane in a clockwise rotation. You can also move fields from one location to another to juxtapose fields in the most desirable way.

You were cautioned in Chapter 9 to design your database with the fields placed in order of importance so the critical fields would display on one screen. If you have neglected to do that, however, you can move them together through the Select and Edit-Cut or Edit-Paste menus, as described earlier in this chapter.

To split your screen display into panes:

- Select the column or row where you wish to divide the screen.
- Click on Window-Split.
- Move the bars to the desired location.
- Release the mouse button, or press ENTER.

Your screen will split into the desired panes, either horizontally, vertically, or both. To return to a single window, reverse the process.

DATABASE TUTORIAL NO. 4

You want to do a nested sort of your cars2.wdb database on the Make, Year, and Price fields.

1. Open cars2.wdb.
2. Start in list view.
3. Press CTRL + HOME.
4. Click on Tools.

   The Tools menu displays, as shown in Figure 10.12.

Figure 10.12

Example of the Tools Menu

5. Click on Sort Records.

   The Sort Records dialog box displays, as shown in Figure 10.13. The first field should read "Make" and the radio button for Ascend A should be marked.

Figure 10.13

Example of the Sort Records dialog box

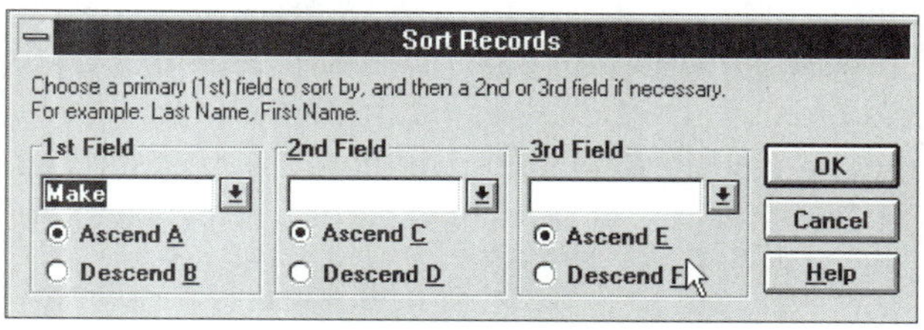

6. TAB to 2nd Field, click on the down arrow, and select Year.
7. Click on Descend.
8. At 3rd Field, select Price and mark Ascend.
9. Click on OK.
10. Save the file as carssort.

    Check to see that the File-Page Setup menu still has the Print Gridlines and the Record and Field labels marked.

11. Print the first page of carssort.wdb.

    Your printout should look similar to Figure 10.14.

Figure 10.14

	Make	Model	Year	Price	Ins	Uninsmot	Totalins	Color
1	Alfa Romeo	164LS	1994	$36,000	$569	$11.20	$580.20	White
2	Bentley Continental	Coupe	1994	$262,290	$1,300	$11.20	$1,311.20	Silver
3	BMW 325i	Sedan	1994	$29,389	$569	$11.20	$580.20	Blue-Gray
4	Cadillac Deville	Sedan	1994	$30,450	$850	$11.20	$861.20	Gold
5	Eagle Talon	4X4	1994	$12,995	$439	$11.20	$450.20	Silver
6	Ford F250 Super Cab	4X4	1993	$24,145	$332	$11.20	$343.20	Red
7	Ford Taurus	GL	1993	$13,888	$316	$11.20	$327.20	Black
8	Honda Accord	LX	1988	$7,000	$246	$11.20	$257.20	Blue
9	Hyundai Elantra	Sport Coupe	1994	$13,385	$270	$11.20	$281.20	Maroon
10	Infinity	Q45	1994	$47,500	$669	$11.20	$680.20	Maroon
11	Jeep	Grand Cherokee	1993	$25,988	$412	$11.20	$423.20	Bronze
12	Jeep Cherokee Laredo	4X4	1994	$23,395	$385	$11.20	$396.20	Black
13	Mercedes-Benz	S320 Sedan	1994	$46,200	$669	$11.20	$680.20	Teal
14	Mercury Topaz	GS 2-door	1993	$8,993	$257	$11.20	$268.20	Brown
15	Mercury Tracer	4-door	1993	$9,993	$301	$11.20	$312.20	Tan
16	Suzuki	Swift	1994	$8,844	$235	$11.20	$246.20	Green
17	Suzuki	JX 4X4	1994	$12,994	$425	$11.20	$436.20	Red
18	Toyota Camry	LE	1988	$7,988	$246	$11.20	$257.20	Red

Notice that when the database lists more than one car of a specific make, like the Jeeps, they are sorted in ascending order by year. When the years match, as for the Mercury and Suzuki cars, the prices go from low to high. You now would like to know how many 4X4 vehicles cost less than $15,000.

12. Start in List view.
13. Click on Tools.
14. Click on Create New Query.

    The New Query screen displays.
15. Type **4X4** to name the query.
16. In the A field, select Model.
17. The B text box should state "is equal to."
18. In E, type ***4X4**

When extra text may either precede or follow the specific criterion, you add a global symbol—an asterisk (*). No spaces can surround the *X*, as none appear in the data.

19. Click on the And radio button.
20. In F, select Price.
21. In G, select "is less than."
22. In I, type **15000**

23. Click on Apply Now.

    Your screen should look similar to Figure 10.15.

    To return all records to the database:

Figure 10.15

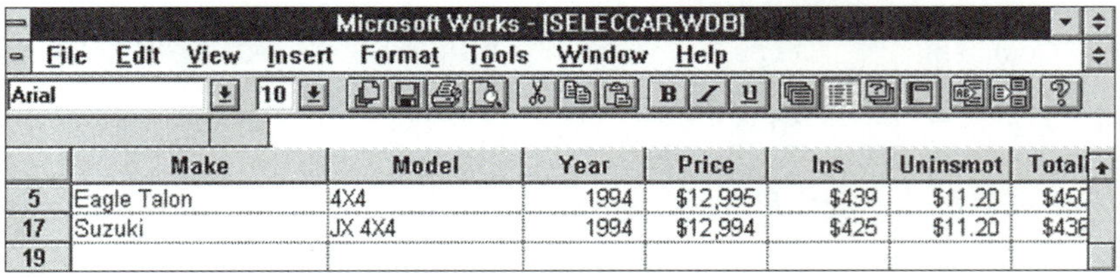

	Make	Model	Year	Price	Ins	Uninsmot	Total
5	Eagle Talon	4X4	1994	$12,995	$439	$11.20	$450
17	Suzuki	JX 4X4	1994	$12,994	$425	$11.20	$436
19							

24. Click on View-Show All Records.

    The hidden records are returned to the screen. (You may have to press CTRL + HOME.)

25. On your own, create a query with the following conditions:

    Name of query: **seleccar**

    Year: **> = 1988**

    Price: **<15000**

    Totalins: **<400**

26. Save the file as seleccar.

27. Print the first page of this file.

    Your printout should look similar to that in Figure 10.16.

Figure 10.16

	Make	Model	Year	Price	Ins	Uninsmot	Totalins	Color
7	Ford Taurus	GL	1993	$13,888	$316	$11.20	$327.20	Black
8	Honda Accord	LX	1988	$7,000	$246	$11.20	$257.20	Blue
9	Hyundai Elantra	Sport Coupe	1994	$13,385	$270	$11.20	$281.20	Maroon
14	Mercury Topaz	GS 2-door	1993	$8,993	$257	$11.20	$268.20	Brown
15	Mercury Tracer	4-door	1993	$9,993	$301	$11.20	$312.20	Tan
16	Suzuki	Swift	1994	$8,844	$235	$11.20	$246.20	Green
18	Toyota Camry	LE	1988	$7,988	$246	$11.20	$257.20	Red

28. Close the seleccar file.

When you want to query the database in *Works* using more than the three criteria allowed by the Create a New Query dialog box, you must enter the conditions in the query window. Remember AND and OR are surrounded by pound signs (#), text is surrounded by double quotes (“), and times (such as years) are surrounded by single quotes (‘). You will now write a query statement for more than three conditions.

29. Open cars2.wdb.

30. Click on Tools-Create New Query.

    To delete the last query:

31. Click on Clear.
32. Click on Query View.

    The query view screen appears with a blank record.

You have just inherited some money and you can afford to pay up to $25,000 for a car, and up to $450 for insurance; you want at least a 1993, either red or black in color.

33. Type the following criteria in the area beside the field names:

    Year: = **>1992**

    Price: **<25000**

    Totalins: **=<450**

    Color: **=="Red"#OR#="Black"** (You must begin a compound query with two equal signs.)

34. Save the file as newcar.

You could create all of these queries in cars2.wdb, but we are instructing you to save each as a new file in case you make a mistake and want to go back to a specific file. Also, we have not had you select the Show All Records command in each query, although you would do so if you were to create another query on the entire database. You now want to name your last query.

35. Click on Tools-Name Query.
36. In the Name text box, type **newcar**
37. Click on Rename.
38. Click on OK.
39. Print your newcar.wdb file.

    Your printout should look similar to that in Figure 10.17.

Figure 10.17

(Page 1)

	Make	Model	Year	Price	Ins	Uninsmot	Totalins	Color
6	Suzuki	JX 4X4	1994	$12,994	$425	$11.20	$436.20	Red
8	Jeep Cherokee Laredo	4X4	1994	$23,395	$385	$11.20	$396.20	Black
13	Ford Taurus	GL	1993	$13,888	$316	$11.20	$327.20	Black
16	Ford F250 Super Cab	4X4	1993	$24,145	$332	$11.20	$343.20	Red

(Page 2)

Mileage
0
0
12,000
6,000

40. Save the file as newcar.
41. Close the file.
42. Open cars2.wdb.

You will now protect all fields in the database except Make, Model, and Color to prevent writing over them. The Protect Data command keeps all locked fields from being changed. As a default, all fields are locked, so you will unlock Make, Model, and Color.

43. Press CTRL + HOME.
44. Click on the Form view icon.
45. In the first record, select the Make field.
46. Click on Format-Protection.

    The Protection dialog box displays, as shown in Figure 10.18.

Figure 10.18

Example of the Protection Dialog Box

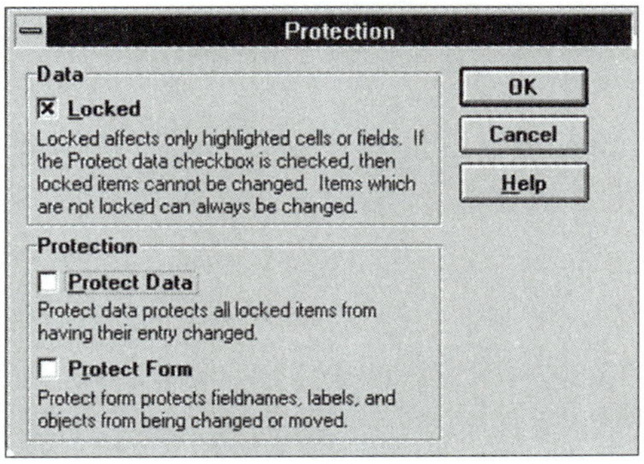

47. Click on Locked to remove the lock.
48. In the Protection box, click on Protect Data.
49. On your own, unlock the Model and Color fields.

    Now, when you press TAB, the cursor will go only to the three unlocked fields.
50. Move the cursor to Price, enter a new number, and press ENTER. The screen displays “Cannot change: locked.”
51. On your own, unprotect the data; lock Make, Model, and Color, or just close the document without saving the changes.

Chapter Summary

This chapter covered some advanced database concepts, such as changing the database design and layout, inserting or deleting a database record, copying a file, backing up the database structure and contents, performing a nested sort, posing a complex or compound query, and viewing selected parts of large databases through split windows.

KEY TERMS

calculated field
clear
complex query
compound query
concatenate
ditto command
dummy record
purge

REVIEW QUESTIONS

1. Compare the ease of modifying a database in the previous generation of flat file databases or database management systems with the same operation in modern database software.
2. Explain why adding explanatory text to a database structure is desirable and how to do this in *Works*.
3. List two reasons you might need to add, change, or delete one or more fields in a database. How do you add, change, or delete a field in *Works*?
4. Once you have laid out your database, why would you ever want to move an existing field? How is this accomplished in *Works*?
5. Under what circumstance would you want to precisely position fields on a form for printing? How is this accomplished in *Works*?
6. List a few reasons for wanting to change the name of a field and then explain how this is accomplished in *Works*.
7. Explain how to insert or delete a record in (a) form view, or (b) List view.
8. Suppose you accidentally delete a record. What should you do immediately to get it back?
9. What would cause you to get the following message: "Cannot Undo Command"?
10. Enumerate the copying options available in the *Works* database application.
11. Recall the primary justification for taking time to back up an entire database file.
12. Explain the importance of protecting the form and the data in a database and how this is accomplished in *Works*.
13. What is a shell and why would you ever consider making a copy of an empty database shell?
14. Why is it considered almost mandatory that you protect a database form and its contents? How do you accomplish this goal of protection?
15. Illustrate the concept of a three-level nested sort to reorder the third field within the second field, and the second within the first.

16. What is the difference between a complex and a compound query? Give an example.
17. Splitting the viewing screen horizontally and vertically is possible in *Works*. Identify several occasions when you might do one or both of these splits.

SOFTWARE EXERCISES

Exercise 10.1

1. Make arrangements with your instructor to familiarize yourself with the *Works 3.0 for Windows* database tutorial.
2. Make notes about what was covered in the section headed working with lists (with the subsections (1) insert fields and records and (2) delete fields and records).
3. Use *Works 3.0 for Windows* to type your notes about what you learned.
4. Save your work as tutdb10.
5. Print tutdb10.wps.
6. Close tutdb10.wps and exit *Works*.

Exercise 10.2

1. Use the *Works* form view to create the structure for a small test database that has about five fields.
2. In the Form or List view, input about five test records into the database.
3. Experiment with all of the following operations on the test database and make notes about what happened:
    (a) Adding explanatory text
    (b) Adding a field
    (c) Changing a field
    (d) Moving a field
    (e) Deleting a record
    (f) Deleting a field
    (g) Locking and protecting selected database fields and data
    (h) Copying the structure
4. Use *Works 3.0 for Windows* to type your notes about what you learned.
5. Save your work as expermt.
6. Print expermt.wps.
7. Close expermt.wps and exit *Works*.

Exercise 10.3

1. Create a database structure for the notebook computer comparison data in Table 10.3.

Table 10.3 Data for Notebook Computer Comparison

Make	Model	List Price	RAM	Hard Disk	CPU Speed	Disk Speed	Weight	Battery Life
ABC Anywhere	120A	1953	6	120	:48	:55	6.60	5:54
System D	320CX	1899	4	120	:47	:37	5.90	6:33
MasterMate	200AB	1499	4	80	:33	:39	6.10	5:43
Verylite	2000CD	1998	4	80	:44	:33	7.00	5:43
TravelMate	3001EF	2199	4	80	:35	:47	5.00	6:01
PortaComp	220X	1578	4	80	:38	:38	4.75	8:19
SigmaNote	4000Z	2300	8	160	:25	:28	4.30	8:30
NoteBook	123ABC	1995	6	120	:32	:40	5.30	6:50

2. Insert the data in your choice of List or Form view. Put the following title at the top of your database Form: NOTEBOOK COMPUTERS COMPARED.
3. In List view, increase or decrease the field widths to completely display the entries and to leave one or two spaces between columns and/or field names.
4. Change the format of the List Price field to currency with no decimal places.
5. Add a centered header that reads: NOTEBOOK COMPUTERS COMPARED.
6. Print the entire database, using gridlines and the Print Record and Field Labels options from the File-Page Setup menu.
7. Save the database as notcomp.
8. Perform a nested sort by battery life, in descending order, within list price, in ascending order.
9. Change the existing centered header to read: BATTERY LIFE WITHIN LIST PRICE SORT.
10. Print the result of the sort, using the Print Record and Field Labels option from the File-Page Setup menu.
11. Save the result as notcomp1.
12. Close the notcomp1.wdb file and exit *Works*.

Exercise 10.4

1. Open the notcomp.wdb file completed in Exercise 10.3, or complete Exercise 10.3 before continuing.

2. In List view, increase or decrease the field widths to completely display the entries and to leave one or two spaces between columns and/or field names.
3. Perform a nested sort in which the first sort field is CPU Speed (descending order), the second field is Disk Speed (descending order), and the third field is List Price (ascending order).
4. Enter the following header on the left side of the header space: NESTED SORT.
5. In a footer, enter the current date on the left side, the word *PAGE* with a hyphen in the center, and the file name on the right.
6. Print the result of the sort, using the Print Record and Field Labels option from the File-Page Setup menu.
7. Save the result as notcomp2.
8. Close the notcomp2.wdb file and exit *Works*.

Exercise 10.5

1. Open the notcomp.wdb file completed in Exercise 10.3, or complete Exercise 10.3 before continuing.
2. In List view, increase or decrease the field widths to completely display the entries and to leave one or two spaces between columns and/or field names.
3. Perform a complex query to identify the computer(s) that weigh less than six pounds and have battery lives greater than seven hours.
4. Enter the following header, centered in the header space: LIGHTER WEIGHT, LONGER LIFE.
5. Print the result of the query, using the Print Record and Field Labels option from the File-Page Setup menu.
6. Choose Show All Records from the View menu.
7. Save the result as notcomp3.
8. Close notcomp3.wdb and exit *Works*.

Exercise 10.6

1. Open the notcomp.wdb file completed in Exercise 10.3, or complete Exercise 10.3 before continuing.
2. In List view, increase or decrease the field widths to completely display the entries and to leave one or two spaces between columns and/or field names.
3. Perform a compound query to identify the computer(s) with CPU speeds greater than :35 and less than :48 and list price less than $1900.
4. Formulate and enter an appropriate header.

5. Print the result of the query using the Print Record and Field Labels option from the File-Page Setup menu.
6. Choose Show All Records from the View menu.
7. Save the result as notcomp4.
8. Close notcomp4.wdb and exit *Works*.

Exercise 10.7

1. Open the notcomp.wdb file completed in Exercise 10.3, or complete Exercise 10.3 before continuing.
2. In List view, increase or decrease the field widths to completely display the entries and to leave one or two spaces between columns and/or field names.
3. Add a field called Final Score. Make the field width 4 with one decimal place.
4. Add the following final scores to the database in the Final Score field: ABC Anywhere, 6.3; System D, 7.5; MasterMate, 7.8; Verylite, 6.1; TravelMate, 7.6; PortaComp, 7.2; SigmaNote, 9.1; NoteBook, 7.4.
5. Sort the database by Final Score in descending order.
6. Enter the following centered header: HIGHEST FINAL SCORE.
7. Print the result of the sort, using the Print Record and Field Labels option from the File-Page Setup menu.
8. Save the result as notcomp5.
9. Close notcomp5.wdb and exit *Works*.

Exercise 10.8

1. Open the cars2.wdb file you created in this chapter's tutorials.
2. In List view, increase or decrease the field widths to completely display the entries and to leave one or two spaces between columns and/or field names if necessary.
3. Perform a nested sort by Mileage (descending order) within Year (ascending order).
4. Query the database to find only the cars made in 1993. Name the query "1993 cars."
5. Formulate and enter an appropriate header.
6. Print the result of the sort and query, using the Print Record and Field Labels option from the File-Page Setup menu.
7. Save the result as cars3.
8. Choose Show All Records from the View menu.
9. Close cars3.wdb and exit *Works*.

Exercise 10.9

1. Open the cars2.wdb file you created in this chapter's tutorials.
2. In List view, increase or decrease the field widths to completely display the entries and to leave one or two spaces between columns and/or field names if necessary.
3. Sort the Price field in descending order.
4. Insert a page break between cars that cost more than $20,000 and those that cost less.
5. Formulate and enter an appropriate header.
6. Center the word PAGE and the page number in a footer.
7. Print the result of the page break, using the Print Record and Field Labels option from the File-Page Setup menu.
8. Save the result as cars4.
9. Close cars4.wdb and exit *Works.*

Exercise 10.10

1. Open the ptr.wdb file on the student data diskette.
2. In List view, increase or decrease the field widths to completely display the entries and to leave one or two spaces between columns and/or field names.
3. Use the Window-Split command to split the screen so that you can simultaneously see the different parts of the file on which you are working.
4. Add a formula to compute the total resolution (resolution1 * resolution2) for each printer.
5. Sort the file by cost, within a sort by Total Resolution, both in descending order.
6. Formulate and enter an appropriate header.
7. Print the result of the sort, using the Print Record and Field Labels option from the File-Page Setup menu.
8. Save the file as ptr1.
9. Close ptr1.wdb and exit *Works.*

Exercise 10.11

1. Open ptr.wdb and complete Step 3 in Exercise 10.10, or open ptr1.wdb, if completed.
2. In List view, increase or decrease the field widths to completely display the entries and to leave one or two spaces between columns and/or field names.
3. Insert a page break between the printer types.

4. Formulate and enter an appropriate header.
5. Print the result using the Print Record and Field Labels option from the File-Page Setup menu.
6. Save the file as ptr2.
7. Close ptr2.wdb and exit *Works*.

Exercise 10.12

1. Open ptr.wdb and complete Step 3 in Exercise 10.10, or open ptr1.wdb, if completed.
2. In List view, increase or decrease the field widths to completely display the entries and to leave one or two spaces between columns and/or field names.
3. Construct a query to locate any type of printer that costs between $400 and $1,300 and has a total resolution between 50,000 and 90,000.
4. Formulate and enter an appropriate header.
5. Print the result using the Print Record and Field Labels option from the File-Page Setup menu.
6. Save the file as ptr3.
7. Close ptr3.wdb and exit *Works*.

Chapter 11

Database Reporting Techniques

Objectives

After studying this chapter you will be able to:

- *Explain the difference between printing the result of a query or sort and printing a formal report*
- *Recall the advantage(s) of using a saved report format*
- *Name the six* Works *types of report rows*
- *Explain the concept of a control break*
- *Name and explain the seven summary statistics available in* Works
- *Use a control break to add summary statistics to a report*
- *Modify an existing report*
- *Delete report(s) you no longer need*
- *Use* Works *to design and print a report*

Report Concepts

You have learned how to query a database file and how to sort records in a different order. These are useful temporary means of manipulating a database file to select specific information to view. You found out that queries could be named and saved, so that once they are defined, they can be used again, no matter how often the database changes.

Along with these useful features, *Works 3.0 for Windows* gives you a more advanced means of selecting specific records for examination. It involves the same concepts of querying and sorting that you have already learned, but it takes the selection one step further by enabling you to format and permanently store selected records in a formal report. This is a more professional use of database records. Although reports are more complex to build, they are aesthetically more pleasing than printouts of queries. More importantly, the report format can be set up once, and then used to print future reports as the database changes. The report can be run without extensive knowledge of database operations.

The power of the report generator is often the difference between a good database management application and a weak one. Some integrated programs for personal computers do not include report generators.

If a good report can be formatted and saved with a database file, that same report can be used over and over again, regardless of how the database changes. What is more, another user can run that report with a minimum of effort; there's no need to know the rules of querying or sorting in order to run a report that has been saved with the database file. Even a *Works* report based on a query involves only a two-step process—applying the appropriate query, then running the related report. This is a very powerful capability.

The *Works* report generator is accessed through a submenu of the database. Once you have learned to design a report for an existing database, you can use that report (or others that you may subsequently design) for as long as the database file is active. You may design as many as eight different reports for any database file in *Works*. The time and effort involved in developing a database report is well invested because you do all of the arranging and formatting only once; thereafter, these tasks are performed for you as often as you wish, with no more effort on your part than selecting the name of a query, if needed, and the selected report from the View menu in *Works*. Reports, then, are a more permanent and convenient method of data manipulation.

Features

A report can use all, or any part, of the information in a database file and present that information in an organized and structured way. Reports are most often printed, although they can be viewed on the screen, as well. They may contain data from only a few records in the database, or from all of them. They may display all of the fields in each record or just some of them. They may even present only summary information, rather than listing each selected record.

You determine just how many records and which fields of each record you wish to see with each report you design. You could design one report to emphasize one or two fields, such as the price and description of a car. You could then design another report to emphasize the make and model of each car, and perhaps the year it was purchased. The choice is yours. Thus you can make the most out of the information in your database files by learning the basic principles of report construction.

Elements

One of the primary uses of a database is to extract information for presentation to others. The people who will receive your report do not want to see all of the information contained in the database; they want to see only the specific parts that interest them at any given time. This may be a list of all products available from one manufacturer, or a list of all customers who buy from a business. The most beneficial reports have titles, headings, subtotals, totals, and so forth that make them attractive and easy to read. Information presented with such features is called a *report* in most database software packages. However, there is a lot of variation in the way different packages let you design or set up that information.

A database package may have a definition screen with various choices from which you select. Others ask you questions regarding page length, width, number of lines and characters per inch, number of lines before and after headings, placements of titles, column headings, total lines, and so forth.

The *Works* system lets you choose which fields you want to include in the report and then inserts all but two types of report rows each time you begin a new report. The column headings for the fields and each record's data are inserted automatically. Figure 11.1 gives an example of a definition screen that shows labeled rows; you then can rearrange the fields or add summary fields and special formatting, as desired.

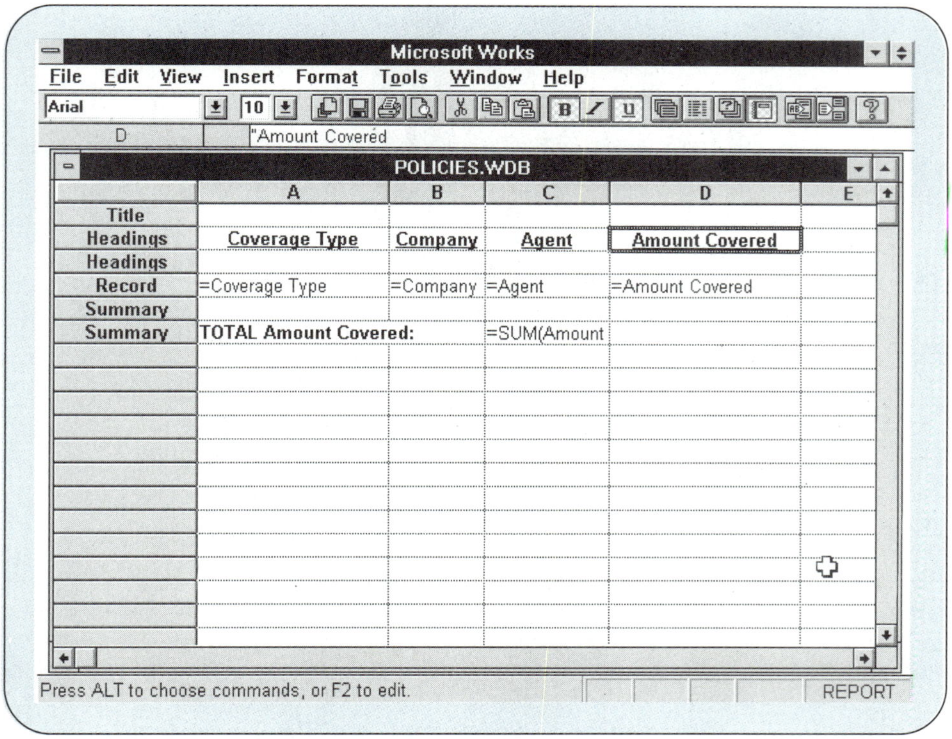

Figure 11.1

Example of a Definition Screen that shows labeled rows

You can insert several different types of rows into a *Works* report. You will hear the same basic types of rows referred to in different terms, depending upon the database program you use, but the concepts underlying them are the same.

Works labels the rows in six categories: title row, headings row, records row, intro *fieldname* row, summary *fieldname* row, and report summary row. Each of these rows has a specific function. Together, they contain the formatting instructions for the specific report that you construct. The only row types that are not automatically inserted into a new report definition are the intro *fieldname* and summary *fieldname* rows. They are both dependent upon one condition—a sorted database file. The rows and their purposes are summarized in Table 11.1.

Each **report**, then, is a customized presentation of information contained in the database. Reports that retrieve detailed information from records in a large database can be many pages long when they are printed. Figure 11.2 shows a page from a lengthy payroll report.

Figure 11.2

Payroll Report sample with control breaks and summary lines

```
                                  P A Y R O L L   R E G I S T E R

For department: 0000
For the pay period ending 09/08/90

Frequencies used on this run:  This pay period: All
Vacation check 1: None  Vacation check 2: None   Vacation check 3: None  Vacation check 4: None

------------------------------------------------------------------------------------------------------------
Dept  Emp-#  Employee-name              Salary   Reg-pay   Hol-pay    Gross     YTD-gross    FICA   YTD-FICA    CWT
      Chk-typ Soc-sec-#     Emp-typ     Wks-wrk  Ovt-pay   Vac-pay  FWT-gross   YTD-FWT-gr   SWT    YTD-SWT   YTD-CWT
                  Net-pay              Prd-start Spec-pay  Sick-pay    FWT      YTD-FWT      OST    YTD-OST   Oth-ded
------------------------------------------------------------------------------------------------------------

0000  550   BRINKMAN, TREVOR                      47.50                47.50       797.13     3.63     60.99
      Reg   017-68-0211     Hourly       1.00                          47.50       797.13     2.74     45.89
                  37 47                                                 3.66        79.39

      925   DAVIS, SALLY                          22.50                22.50       704.14     1.72     53.89
      Reg   013-56-8837     Hourly       1.00                          22.50       704.14     1.30     40.55
                  19.48                                                             62.78

      1525  FAVAZZA, DAVID                        29.75                29.75       663.82     2.28     50.80
      Reg   023-60-8542     Hourly       1.00                          29.75       663.82              27.09
                  27.47                                                             23.31

      3000  WALSH, JENNIFER                       48.00                48.00     1,469.31     3.67    112.40
      Reg   033-60-1380     Hourly       1.00                          48.00     1,469.31     2.77     84.60
                  37.82                                                 3.74       171.94
```

Table 11.1 Report Rows and Their Functions

Title	Prints designated text such as a report title, subtitle, author, and so on, at the top of the first page only.
Heading	Prints text such as a page heading and column headings at the top of each page.
Record	Each record row contains one database record; all records in the database are included and the names of fields to be printed are shown.
Intro *fieldname*	When a report is sorted in groups, this line states the fieldname by which groups are defined. A blank row separates each group.
Summ *fieldname*	When a report is sorted in groups, this line states the fieldname for each group and allows for calculations for that group, such as a subtotal.
Summary	Allows for calculations for the entire report, such as a total. (It appears once, at the end of the report.)

Designing a Report

The process of designing a report, like so many other structured computing tasks, takes prior planning. The best way to plan a report is to work backward, that is, to decide what you want to print out in the final product before you begin designing the report. In this case, the output determines the input; what you wish to see on your finished product will guide your decisions about the report definition.

What fields do you wish to print in the report? You can choose as many or as few as you wish. In what order would you like to present the field information? It is a good idea to put the most descriptive fields first, as readers move their eyes from left to right across the printed page. Also, numerical information usually follows text information to help readers more easily understand the meanings of the numbers .

You also need to plan the logical order in which you select your data. Will your report require a sort to arrange the information in a specific order? Do you wish to group specific records to separate them from the following group of records? Would you like to summarize information from each of these groups? If so, you may insert field introductory and summary lines and place group labels and subtotals on them. Do you wish to print some part of every record, or will you use a query to select certain records that meet specified criteria for the printout?

All of these points should be considered before you begin the task of actually designing the report. You can always edit a report definition after it has been created, but a planned, systematic approach is by far the easiest way to tackle this advanced database technique.

Creating the Report

Since the *Works* report generator is a submenu of the database tool, you must first open the database that contains the information for your report. You then go to Tools-Create New Report, and a report definition screen is automatically set up for you as soon as you choose fields and click on OK. You can then edit the report by adding fields, marking any calculations you want performed on each field, and further formatting the report.

You may insert extra report rows, for example, to place blank lines before and after titles, subtitles, and so on. To enter an extra line after the title row, you would select the title row line and use the Insert command. To see what the report will look like, and to toggle back and forth between the report definition and the report view screens, you can use the Print Preview feature from the menu bar, or the toolbar icon. *Works* will display the chosen fields in columns across the screen (and across the printed page) in the same order as you select them in the database field selection box.

The specific steps are:

- Open a database file.
- Click on Tools-Create New Report.

A report definition window will display with a box for the report title and a choice of fields you wish to include in the report.

- Type a descriptive title for the report.
- Select a Field in Database and click on the Add button.

The name of the field appears in the far-right, field box.

- Continue adding desired fields in the same manner.
- Click on OK when you add the last field you want.

You can select fields in any order; they will be displayed across the screen in the same order as you choose them.

To delete any fields you inadvertently add:

- Select a field that is already in the report.
- Click on the Remove button.

When the fields listed are correct:

- Click on OK.

Notice that buttons allow you to add all the fields in the database, and to remove all that have been added so far.

The Report Statistics option box displays when you click on the OK button. You can choose to report statistics on any field, and you can specify a statistical function you wish to apply to each particular field.

- Click to select a field.
- Click to mark the box for the calculation function you wish to apply.
- Repeat these steps for additional fields.

To designate the position in which calculations appear:

- Click on the radio button Under Each Column.

  OR
- Click on the radio button Together in Rows.
- Click on OK when you finish choosing statistics.

If you do not wish to use any statistical functions, you can just bypass this process by clicking on OK when the report statistics screen appears.

Works creates a sample report that contains all of the fields you have chosen. It names the report REPORT1 if you did not type a name in the introductory screen. (Remember, however, that even though it has a name, the report has not been saved. You must save the database file to save the report.) The report definition screen shows the title, column headings, row labels, selected fields, and summary or total columns. A dialog box appears to indicate that the report has been created, and that you may view it on screen by using the Preview selection.

Customizing the Report

You can customize your report in many ways. You can add subtitles, labels, and explanatory material; you can add or delete rows or columns; you can format the contents of fields, change the widths of columns, change the font styles, add headers or footers, and create specific groupings. You can insert additional rows of any type, and you can delete existing report rows, as well. If you wish to keep a type of row, but want to omit some field information, you can clear row contents by column. As you progress with your design, save the database frequently. Each time you save, your report will be saved along with the database file.

You can move from the Report submenu to the main database menu by clicking on the form view or list view icons from the toolbar. To return to the report definition screen, choose the name of the report from the View Report menu, or click on the Report icon in the toolbar. Moving back and forth from the database view to the report view is most easily done through the toolbar icons (the same icons as in the database report feature). Still, to do the same thing:

- Click on View.
- Click on either List, Form, Report, or Query.

Whichever method you use to move back and forth from the report definition screen to the database view, remember that the report menu differs from the main database menu; it has different options within the familiar commands at the top of the screen.

Sorting and Querying

Before you go any further with your report design plans, decide whether you will sort the records to show them in a specific order, and whether you will select only certain records (or their totals) to be printed in the report. You must define a query to make your report select certain records from the database. (See Chapters 9 and 10 if you need to review the process of query definition.) If you name and save the query, you can reuse it each time you run the report. You will not need to define the sort or query each time you run the report, but you will need to apply any query on which the report depends. Once you activate an already defined query, the report that filters only certain records can be run.

To sort records for a report from an open database, you make selections in an option box much like the one in the main database menu. However, in addition to selecting a field(s) on which to sort (up to three at a time) and the order (ascending or descending), you can also indicate whether, and how, to break or group the information. *Works* can insert a break each time the data in the field changes (Smith Smith Smith break Jones Jones break Allen break and so on), or it can insert a break each time the first letter in the sorted field changes (gathering all *A*s, *B*s, *C*s, etc. in separate groups).

When groups of data are separated with breaks, *Works* automatically totals each field in the group. If the field contains numbers, it adds the values; if the field contains text, it counts the number of entries. This grouping on certain fields is often referred to as a **control break**. *Works* calls it a *sort break*. For example, to break (group) a car database on the Year field, perform the sort, and

Works will insert a summary field row in the report. The printout will then separate the cars into groups based on model year, such as 1992, 1993, and 1994 cars. The total number of entries in each group will be calculated by using the COUNT() function in that summary row. Areas of the report are thus separated by breaks that are determined by field contents. The result is a better-arranged report.

As we noted in Chapter 9, sorts can be nested for a tiered effect, arranging a group within another group, within a most general group. For instance, you could order (arrange) a car database by price within year within make. For each of these group breaks, you could then insert an introductory and summary row and print out the total number of cars in each group. Even though they may be sorted on three fields, most reports break on only one. Grouping records and presenting a summary row in your report for the group is an advantage, but only the longest, most detailed report on the largest database would call for a summary row on each grouped field. When a report summarizes and totals too many fields, the result is confusion, not clarity, in the printed report.

To sort and break on a field in a *Works* database report:

- Click on Tools-Sort Records.
- Type the name of the first sort field.
- Mark Ascend or Descend.
- Mark the Break check box to create a grouping.

To group a field according to the first letter:

- Check the 1st Letter check box.

You may do this for each field sort. As we noted, however, rarely does a report break on three distinct fields, even though the report may be triple sorted.

- Repeat the process for second and third sort field boxes, if you desire.
- Click on OK.

If you choose to add one or more sort breaks, *Works* inserts a summ *fieldname* row for each break and inserts a calculation formula in each column. The sort will be saved along with the report definition when the file is saved.

To create a report that includes only those records from the database that match a specified condition, you can apply a query to the database to filter out the records you need. When you save the file, the query conditions are saved; thus you can produce the same report in the future with the two-step process of first applying the named query and then choosing the report. In list view, you can see all the records that match your query instructions; since form view displays only one matching record at a time, it is better to use list view to check the results of the query.

To use a saved query:

- Click on View-Apply Query.
- Click on the name of the saved query you want to run.

- Click on the list view icon from the toolbar.
- Verify that only certain records are selected.
- Click on the report icon from the toolbar.

The report definition screen will return. If you have not yet defined the particular query you wish to apply, you may define it now:

- Click on View-Create New Query.
- Define the query, as noted in Chapter 9.
- Click on the Apply Now button.
- Click on the report icon from the toolbar.

You will return to the report definition screen.

You may preview the resulting filtered report by looking at a preview of the report printout:

- Click on File-Print Preview.

  OR
- Click on the preview icon from the toolbar.

The report will display on the screen as it would appear printed out. To return to the report definition screen:

- Click on the Cancel button.

Now that you have selected and grouped the records you wish to show in the report, you can finish formatting the report. You specify its titles and page headers, and which fields it will display where.

Report Titles

The title of a report describes its contents in general terms. It appears in the title row in the report. *Works 3.0 for Windows* makes it easy to keep track of what is contained in each type of report row because the row type is always displayed to the left of the report definition. You specify a title by entering it in the title line: it will appear just once at the beginning of the formal report. The title can include any text you wish and it will automatically be centered. If you want it to appear in a specific font (bold, underlined, italic, and so forth), you make the choice in the report definition screen's Format menu. If you wish to add another title row for a subtitle or a blank line to separate the introductory information from the body of the report, you can insert the desired type of row through the Edit menu:

- Position the cursor on the row below the place where you wish to insert the row.
- Select Insert-Insert Row/Column.
- Click on OK to accept the default row.
- Highlight Title.
- Click on OK.

Another title row will appear in your report definition. You may leave the line blank or enter other desired information. At this time, you can change the appearance of the title with the formatting commands.

Heading Rows: Page Headers

Having completed the title, you can define the page headers, which repeat specified information on each page of the report, regardless of how many pages the finished report contains. The page headers are defined in the heading rows. They usually include column headings, which are normally the names of the fields being itemized in the record rows. Page headers can, however, include any text you wish.

By default, when you choose Create New Report, the heading rows contain the names of the chosen fields as headings, but you may change these text labels, if you wish, to make your report clearer. You can also insert additional heading rows in the same manner as title rows, creating space to separate the headings from the body of the report. Simply invoke the Insert-Column/Row choice from the menu. If you wish to type in descriptions of the field headings, you may do so directly. You may also insert the field names by using the Insert menu:

- Position your cursor where you wish to place the field name.
- Click on Insert-Field Name.
- Select the field name from the list.
- Click on OK.

The field name will be inserted in the page heading row at the column you selected.

This will print the exact name of a field. To clarify the report, you may want to enter descriptive text of your own in the heading rows, along with the names of fields in the database.

Like any other printed output, a report can include repeated text such as your name, date, etc. on every page of the printout. These text items do not need to be included in the heading row; instead, when you are ready to print, you can specify them as headers and footers in the Print menu.

The *Works* report generator is organized by columns and rows. The width of a report display, which includes field names, is set up in columns. The length of the page, which determines the number of lines to each type of report definition, is set up in rows.

To delete a field name or other contents from a report row, you must select the field (column) or row (record line) first, then use the Cut or Clear command in the Edit menu:

- Select row and column where you want to delete material.
- Click on Edit-Cut, or Edit-Clear.

The selected text will disappear. To delete an entire row (record line) or column (field):

- Click on Insert-Delete Row/Column.
- Click on radio button for either Row or Column.
- Click on OK.

The selected row or column is deleted from the report definition.

You copy, paste, clear, or delete (cut) contents of report rows from the Edit menu, just as in the Edit menus of the other applications. To move a whole column or row, you select the column or row first. If you wish to copy or move only a title or a word or two of text, select a cell or cells, not the entire column, and then proceed with your editing task.

Record Rows

The detail rows, or record rows, in a report definition print out the itemized information in a report. If you do not specify the desired **field contents** (a specific entry) beneath your column headings in a record row, your report will contain nothing but headings and, possibly, a summary. Sometimes you want to include only summary information in a report. However, if you intend to print a portion of each record, thus itemizing the information, you must define your report so that it does just that. You can place the contents of any field in the record row of the report definition.

The detailed content of a report usually appears directly below the corresponding field names (column headings) in the headings row. You use the Edit or Insert menu from the Reports submenu to add or change fields:

- Position your cursor in the record row.
- Click on Insert-Field Entry.
- Highlight the desired field.
- Click on OK.

The field name appears, preceded by an equal sign (=Field). The equal sign is the special print control character that enables the report to print the contents of a field. Be sure you understand the distinction between printing the name of a field as text and printing the content of a field, or its value. Look back to Figure 11.1 for a sample.

Formatting Columns and Rows for Layout

As we noted, although you specify records and fields to print in a database report, the report definition is set up on an underlying grid of rows and columns. When defining the layout of the report, you must think of formatting a column if you wish to change the width of a field's printout.

If a report column is too narrow to display all of the information in a field, plus a margin to the next field's contents, you can widen the display:

- Select one field in the column.
- Click on Format-Column Width.
- Type in the number or click on Best Fit.
- Click on OK.

Conversely, if a field display uses more space than it needs, you can narrow it and thus fit more fields across the width of a page of the hard copy printout. Select Best Fit and have *Works* set the width of the column, when it matches its longest entry.

You can change the style of the display to center, right-align, or left-align the column with the same Format menu. You can change the font for a column or row, as well. Working with the column and row design, you can format your report exactly as you wish it to appear.

Viewing the Report on the Screen

As a check, you can evaluate the design of your report at any time by viewing the report on the screen:

- Click on View, and the name or number of the report.
- The report definition displays.
- Click on File-Print Preview to view the report.
- Click on Previous or Next to move through the pages.
- Click on Zoom to magnify part of the report.
- Click on Cancel to return to the report definition screen.

Renaming the Report

By default, your reports are named REPORT1, REPORT2, REPORT3, and so forth up to the allowable eight reports per database file. You can choose a more descriptive name for your report at any time:

- Click on Tools-Name Report.
- An option box appears listing all available reports.
- Select the current report.
- Type a name (up to 15 characters long) in the Name window.
- Click on Rename.
- Click on Done.

The new name of the report is now listed in the View menu.

You can work on the general design of your report and its contents in any order that is comfortable for you. However, usually you should insert the detail (record) row before making any major design changes, since it is difficult to visualize how a report will look until it lists itemized data and displays the field contents for your scrutiny. This reveals how the cosmetics of the design could be improved. Of course, all design changes can wait until you have finished entering all of the specific report rows you wish. The choice is entirely up to you.

Do remember to save frequently, however. In the midst of a creative rush, it is easy to neglect to save to disk. Report definitions can become quite complex, and you don't want to risk losing a partially completed file.

Field and Report Summary Rows

For every field on which you have sorted the database, you may insert a summary *fieldname* row in your report. This allows you to summarize grouped records. When you open a new report, these summary lines may be included in the report definition if you are already using a sorted file. If you do not want them, you may simply select the row and delete it. As was noted, if you wish to include more summary rows, you may insert them from the Edit menu.

If you include control breaks or groups of records sorted on a specific field in your report, more than likely you will want to place a summary row before proceeding to list the next sorted group. Indeed, some formal reports include only summary rows and list no detailed records.

Works sorts the database that the report references. It then inserts a summ *fieldname* row in your report for every break you specify. It also inserts SUMFIELD () functions for you. You may remove these, or add to them, once you have a sorted file. The functions help you produce subtotals for each group in a report. The explanation for the calculated fields below explains the contents of your summ *fieldname* rows. Once you have sorted a file in the Report menu and indicated a break, *Works* will list Intro *fieldname* and summ *fieldname* row options when you insert a row in your report. The intro *fieldname* row specifies material that you wish to print right before each new group.

Unlike a field summary row, a report summary row summarizes the entire report—all of its records, rather than just one group. A report summary row, simply called *summary* in the *Works* report generator, accumulates whatever appears in the row and prints the total just once, at the end of the report. This type of row is explained further later in the chapter.

You insert report summary rows to format data that will appear at the end of the report. To insert either kind of summary row in a *Works* report:

- Position the cursor where you wish the summary row to appear.
- Click on Edit-Insert Row/Column.
- Click on OK to accept the row default.
- Click on the Summ *fieldname* or Summary row selection.
- Click on OK.

You may now format this row any way you wish. If you decide to enter descriptive text to explain the summary, you may enter it directly in any column, using whatever font you wish.

You may also choose to include a blank summary row just to separate groups for easier reading. More often, however, your summary rows will include one or more *Works* functions that subtotal, count, or average the contents of important fields in the grouped records. Let's see how you can put these functions to use.

Calculations on Fields

When a summ *fieldname* row or a report summary row is included in a report definition (by default or because you insert it), its content may be based on any of seven different statistical functions. You choose the function you want from the option box that displays when you invoke the Edit-Insert Field Summary menu choice. Your choices are as follows:

SUM (fieldname)	Totals the contents of a group of fields or the entire report
AVG (fieldname)	Averages the contents of a group of fields or the entire report
COUNT (fieldname)	Counts the number of records in a group or the entire report
MIN (fieldname)	Returns the smallest value in a group of fields or the entire report
MAX (fieldname)	Returns the largest value in a group of fields or the entire report
STD (fieldname)	Returns the standard deviation, or dispersion about the arithmetic mean, of a group on a field
VAR (fieldname)	Returns the variance, or difference, in a group on a field

By default, the COUNT (fieldname) function is inserted if you are reporting on a sorted database file. However, you may substitute any of the other functions for any field you wish by using the Edit-Insert Field Summary choice.

To enter a summary function in the summary row:

- Position the cursor where you wish to place the summary information (usually right below the field contents entry in the record row).
- Click on Insert-Field Summary.
- An option box appears to list field names and available functions.
- Select the field and the function you wish to use.
- Click on OK.

The name of the field and the function you have chosen will appear in the summary *fieldname* or summary row.

Subtotals and Separators

The summary *fieldname* rows that you insert in your report definition will appear in the printout after every grouping by sorted field. This feature can greatly improve the clarity of a long report. For greater clarity, you may also insert descriptive text alongside the function you have inserted, or add another summary row or two, and type in **separators** (====, ------) or leave blank lines after every grouping to emphasize the end of one group and the beginning of the next.

Report Summary Rows

Like the other definition rows, report summary rows may contain text formatted in any way you wish, and it can include statistical summaries, as well. The contents of the Summary row resemble those of the summ *fieldname* rows, except that the summary row can print grand totals, counts, or averages of the entire portion of the database included in the report.

A calculated summary operation in the summary row totals or counts the subtotals of the summ *fieldname* rows. As we noted previously, unlike the summ *fieldname* rows, the summary row will print only once, at the end of the report. It is good practice to include grand totals in this row, using one or more of the seven statistical functions.

Sometimes an extra summary row gives the message, "-----END OF REPORT-----" as a signal to the reader that the report includes all records that it should include. This is particularly helpful for a multiple-page report involving a large, queried database.

Print Options

We explained earlier how to add headers and footers to the report with the View-Headers and View-Footers options. These options allow you to include running page headings and page numbers in the report. In the Print menu you can also adjust the margins and the paper width and length if you need to fit more information on the page. You can print up to 132 characters of a very detailed report by using wide-carriage paper (which is 15 inches wide) or using a condensed font, if your printer has one.

You can see the exact layout of the report with the Print Preview choice, but your purpose in defining a formal report is, ultimately, to print it out. To print a report:

- Click on File-Print.
- Click on OK to accept the default and print all pages.

The report will begin to print as you have formatted it. As with all *Works* print commands, you may change the default settings to print only certain pages or to print in draft mode.

Modifying a Report

A formal database report requires more complex preparation than a simple printout of records selected via a query or sort; as you have seen, however, the report is worth the effort because it allows you to customize your presentation. The report is highly structured and includes only the parts of the database you wish to print. It can be printed as often as necessary to reflect changes in the database.

A report format, once it is saved to disk with the database file, can be modified as often as you like. If you find that you need to add more detail or delete some fields, modifying the report definition is as simple as entering the Report menu. To modify a report:

- Click on View-Report.
- Select the name of the report you want to modify.
- Click on OK to enter the report definition.
- Edit as necessary.
- Save the database file and the accompanying report.

Deleting Extra Versions of a Report

Often working with a database and defining custom reports over time leaves you with several versions of the same report. Keeping all of these versions is confusing, and it reduces your allotment of eight reports per database. However, you can easily delete any unneeded versions. Before you do so, preview them on the screen to be certain of what they contain. When you are sure which versions you wish to delete, remove them one by one using the Delete Report option in the Tools menu. It is good practice to assign each version a unique name as you create it to simplify deleting it later, if necessary.

To delete a report:

- Open the database file.
- Click on View-Reports.
- Highlight the number of the report you wish to delete.
- When the definition displays on the screen, click on Tools-Delete Report.
- Select the desired report.
- Click on Delete.
- Repeat these steps for another report, if necessary.
- Click on OK when you finish.

After deleting the extra versions only those you wish to keep are listed.

Finally, save the cleaned-up version of the database file and its accompanying reports:

- Select File-Save.

REPORT TUTORIAL NO. 1

You want to create a report showing all the black cars in your cars2.wdb database; the report should print only the Make, Model, Year, and Color fields. Start by loading *Works*. Be sure that all 18 records are displayed (View-Show all Records).

1. Open cars2.wdb.
2. Click on Tools.
3. Click on Create New Report.

   The New Report option box displays, as shown in Figure 11.3.
4. In the Report Title box, type **ALL BLACK CARS** (Do not press ENTER; instead, press TAB or DOWN ARROW.)
5. In the Field list box, click on the down arrow and select Make (if it is not already selected).
6. Click on Add.

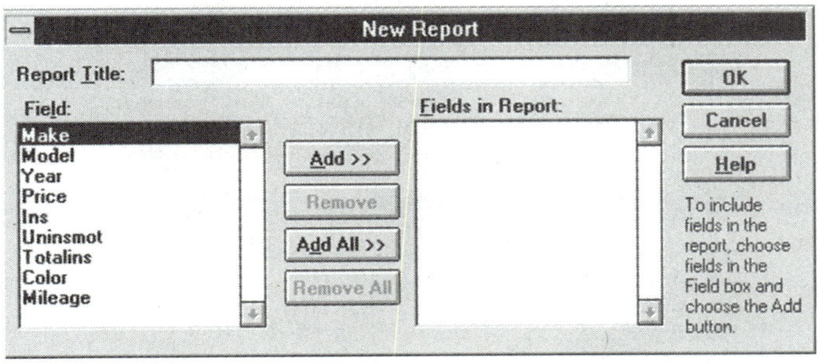

Figure 11.3

Example of the New Report Option Box

7. Select Model.
8. Click on Add.
9. Add the Year and Color fields in the same way.
10. Click on OK.

    The Report Statistics dialog box displays, as shown in Figure 11.4. You do not want any calculations in this report, so to bypass the Statistics box.

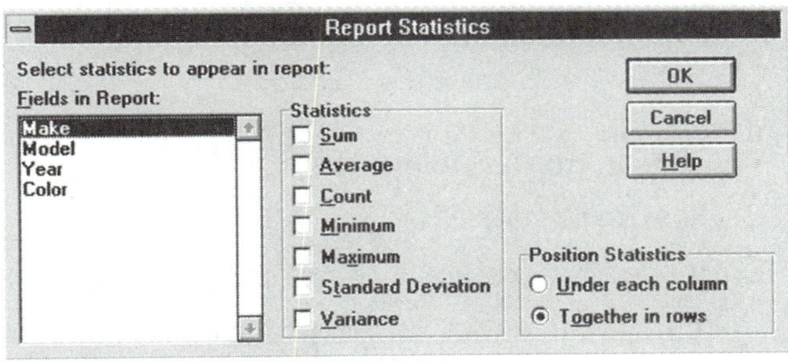

Figure 11.4

Example of the Report Statistics Dialog Box

11. Click on OK.

    A modified report definition displays only the Make, Model, Year, and Color fields, as shown in Figure 11.5. A message box tells you that a report definition has been created, and to select Print-Preview to see what the printed output will look like.
12. Click on OK.
13. Click on the print preview icon.

    You notice that the data is not aligned well.
14. Click on Cancel.

    To align the data under the headings:
15. Go to list view.
16. Select a row under the Model field.

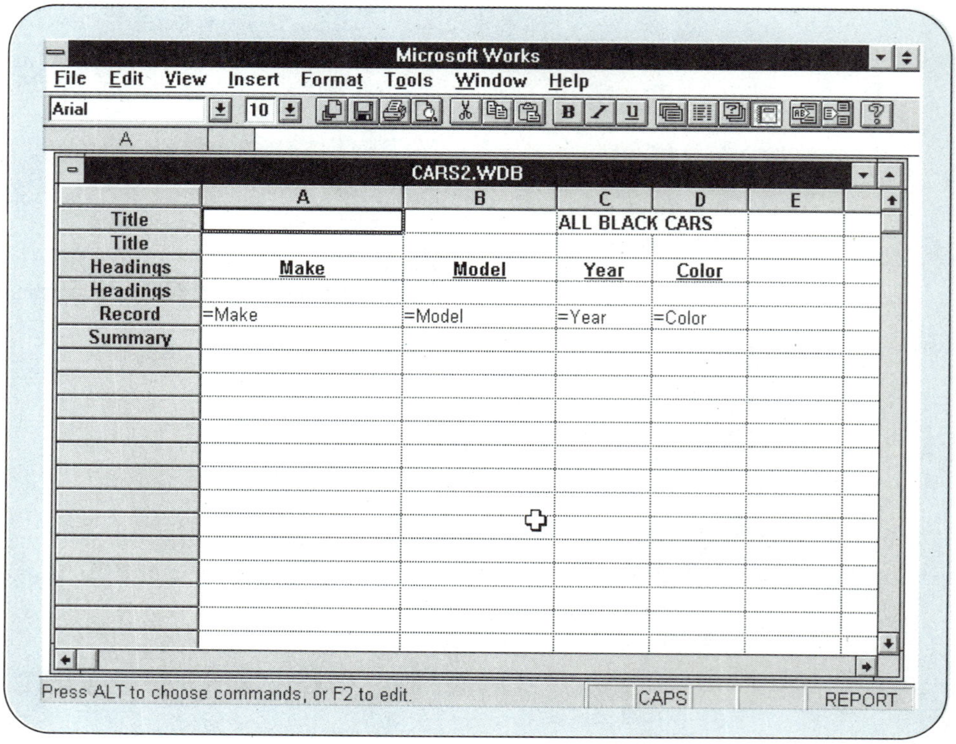

Figure 11.5

Modified Report Definition

17. Click on Format-Alignment.
18. Click on Center-OK.
19. Repeat these steps for the Year and Color fields.

    You want to select only the black cars in the database. This calls for a query.
20. Click on Tools-Create New Query.
21. Name the Query *Black Cars.*
22. In the first field box, click on the down arrow and scroll to select Color.
23. The Compare box should state *is equal to.*
24. In the Value box, type **Black**
25. Click on Apply Now.
26. Click on Preview-Zoom in.

    You can see that two black cars are contained in your database.
27. Click on Print.

    Your printout should look similar to Figure 11.6. You now want to rename your *Report1* as *Black Cars.*
28. Click on Tools.

Figure 11.6

ALL BLACK CARS

Make	**Model**	**Year**	**Color**
Ford Taurus	GL	1993	Black
Jeep Cherokee Laredo	4X4	1994	Black

29. Click on Name Report.
30. In the Name text box, type **Black Cars**
31. Click on Rename.
32. Click on OK.
33. Click on View-Report.

    Notice that your first report is named *Black Cars*.
34. Click on Cancel.
35. Save the database file.

    Your report will be saved with your database file. You must be in list view to show all records.
36. If you are not, click on the list view icon.
37. Click on View-Show All Records.
38. Do not close the file.

REPORT TUTORIAL NO. 2

Next you want to create a report showing the makes, years, prices, and total insurance premiums of the cars in your database. You want a list of the cars for each model year, the value of the cars for each year, and the total value of all of the cars. The database cars2.wdb should still be open.

1. Click on Tools-Create New Report.
2. Type this title for your report: **PRICE OF CARS BY YEAR**

   Remember not to press ENTER until you are finished.
3. Select and Add the Make, Year, Price, and Totalins fields.
4. Click on OK.
5. Click on OK to bypass the Report Statistics screen.

   You will now sort by groups, and *Works* will automatically insert field summary rows to total each group. In the report definition screen:
6. Click on OK.

   To perform the sort:
7. Click on Tools.

Figure 11.7

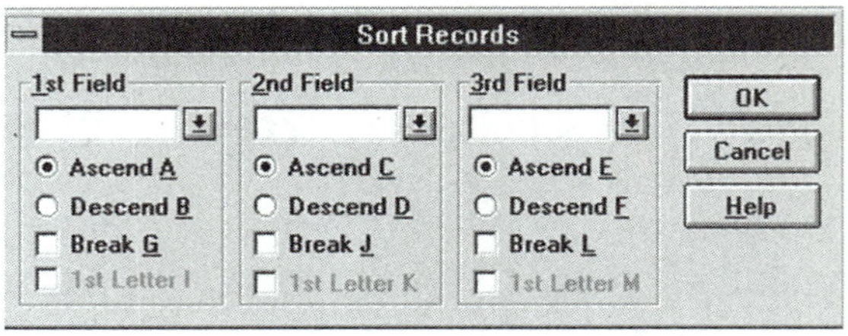

8. Click on Sort Records.

   The sort dialog box displays, as shown in Figure 11.7.
9. In the 1st Field box, click on the down arrow to select Year.
10. Click on the radio button to mark Ascend A (if it is not marked).
11. Click on Break G.
12. Click on OK.

    The system inserts a summary row called *Summ Year* (because you sorted on Year) with a summary notation under each field, as shown in Figure 11.8.

Figure 11.8

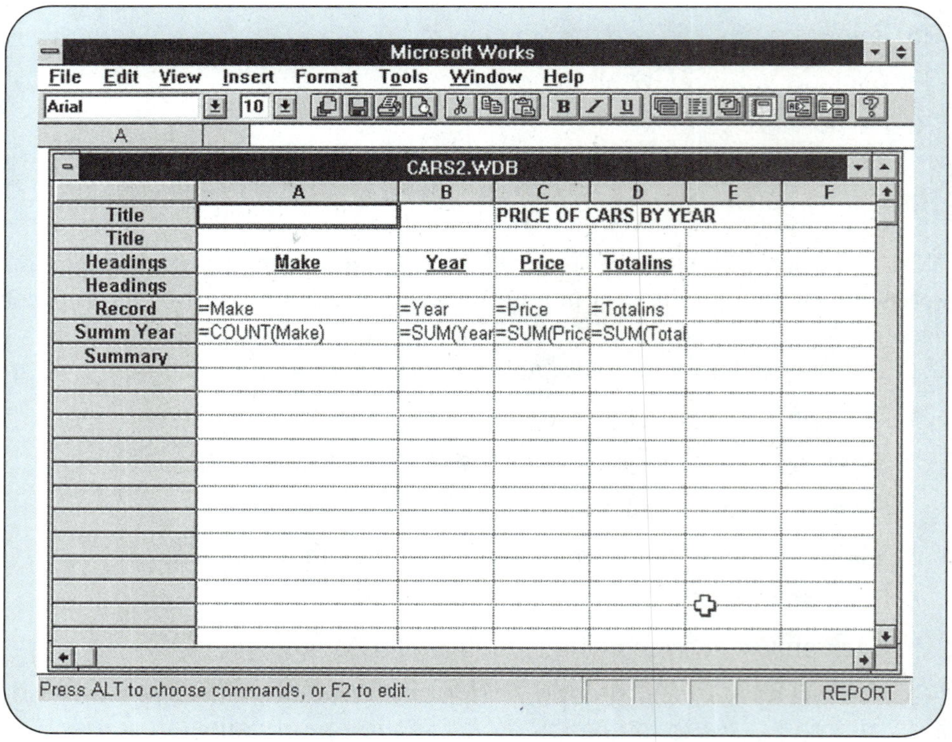

After you create a report and save your database file, you can exit and return to the report later by clicking on View-Report-name of report-OK. You want to add another title row and center your name in it, and then add blank title rows before and after your name.

13. Move the cursor to Column A in the second title row.
14. Select the first title row in Columns A through F.
15. Click on Format-Alignment-Center across Selection-OK.
16. Type your first and last names.
17. Press ENTER.
18. Deselect the cells.

    If the title of the report does not look centered, delete it and select the first title row in Columns A through F. Choose Center across selection and type **PRICE OF CARS BY YEAR,** then press ENTER.
19. Leave the cursor on the second title row.
20. Click on Insert.

    The Insert menu displays.
21. Click on Row/Column.
22. Select Row (if it is not marked)-OK.
23. The Insert Row list box displays, as shown in Figure 11.9.
24. In the Insert Row Type box, select Title-OK.
25. On your own, insert a blank row after your name. (Select the first heading row, but insert a new title row.)

    You decide to change the column heading from *Totalins* to *Insurance Premium.*
26. Move the cursor to the cell where *Totalins* appears.
27. Press F2 to Edit.
28. Delete *Totalins* and type **Insurance**
29. Press ENTER.
30. Press the DOWN ARROW once.
31. Press CTRL + E (for center) and type **Premium**
32. Press ENTER.

    Premium is not bold and underscored, as are the rest of the headings.
33. Click on Format.

    The Format menu displays, as shown in Figure 11.10.

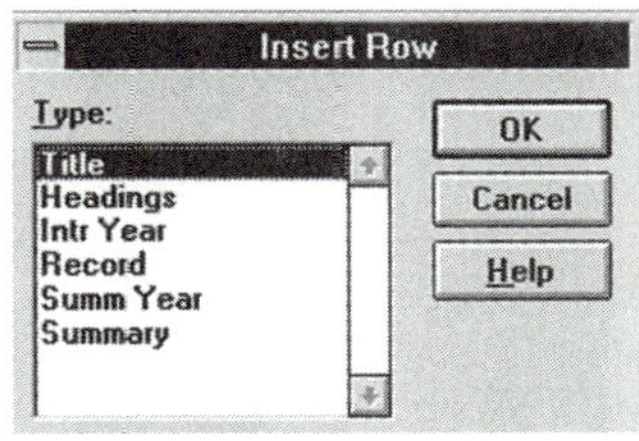

Figure 11.9

Example of the Insert Row List Box

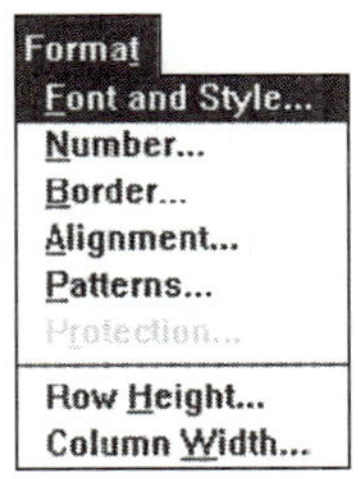

Figure 11.10

Example of the Format Menu

34. Click on Font and Style.
35. Mark Bold and Underline.
36. Click on OK.
37. Insert a blank headings row.

    (Hint: Move your cursor to the record row first.)
38. Leave the record row as it is.
39. Rename your report *Cars by Year* (Tools-Name Report).
40. Click on the Preview icon, then click on Zoom In.

    Notice that the entries are totaled by year, the years are totaled, the price is totaled, and the insurance premiums are totaled. You decide it doesn't make any sense to total the Year and Insurance Premium fields.
41. Click on Cancel.
42. In the Summ Year row, select =SUM(YEAR) and press DELETE.
43. In the Summ Year row, select =SUM(TOTAL and press DELETE.
44. Insert blank Summ Year rows before and after the current Summ Year row.

    Remember that the blank row inserts above the row in which you place the cursor. You would like to have a total count of all the cars in the database and their combined cost. (*Works* automatically totals only the individual groups.)
45. Select Column A in the summary row.
46. Click on Bold and type **Total Cost of all Cars**
47. Press ENTER.
48. Select Column B.
49. Click on Insert-Field Summary.

    The Insert Field Summary dialog box displays, as shown in Figure 11.11.

Figure 11.11

Example of the Insert Field Summary Dialog Box

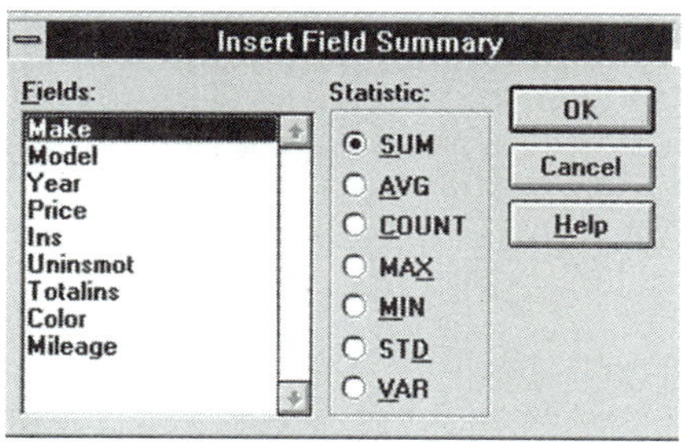

50. In the Fields list box, select Year.
51. In the Statistics box, select Count.
52. Click on OK.
53. Select Column C.
54. Click on Insert-Field Summary.
55. Select Price, and then select Sum as the desired function.
56. Click on OK.
57. Select Column A in the middle Summ Year row.
58. Select =COUNT (Make).
59. Click on the Cut icon.
60. Select Column B in the middle Summ Year row.
61. Click on the Paste icon.
62. Select Column A in the middle Summ Year row.
63. Type **Subtotal** in bold, then press ENTER.

    Your field definition screen should look similar to Figure 11.12.
64. Click on the Preview icon, then click on Zoom in.

    Your screen should look similar to Figure 11.13. The report looks pretty good, but you don't like the alignment of the headings.

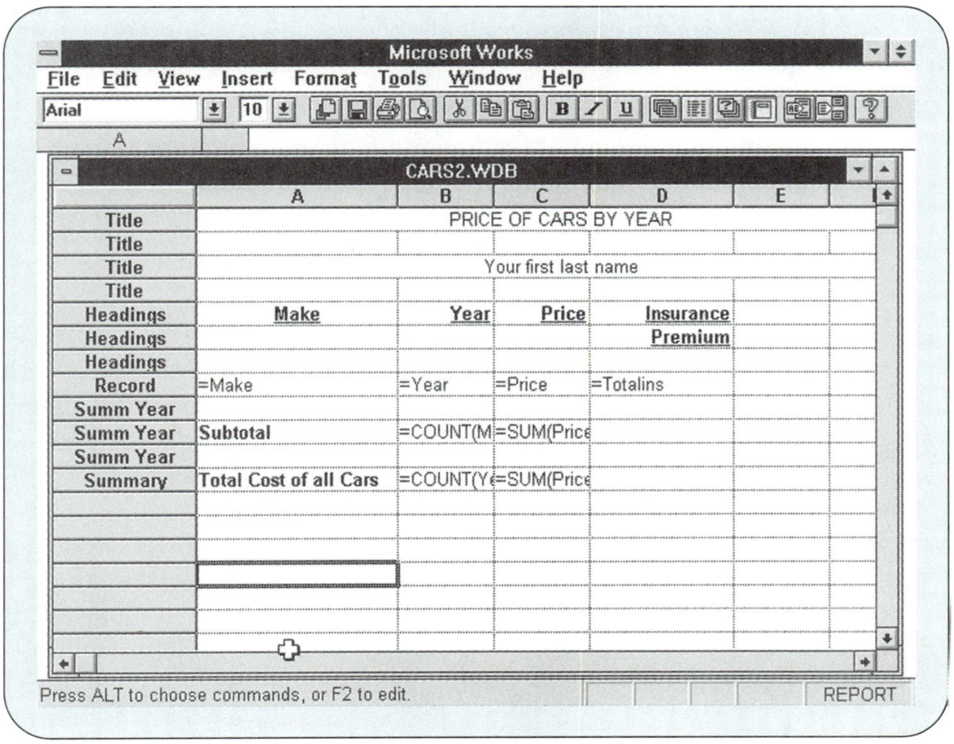

Figure 11.12

Field Definition Screen

Figure 11.13

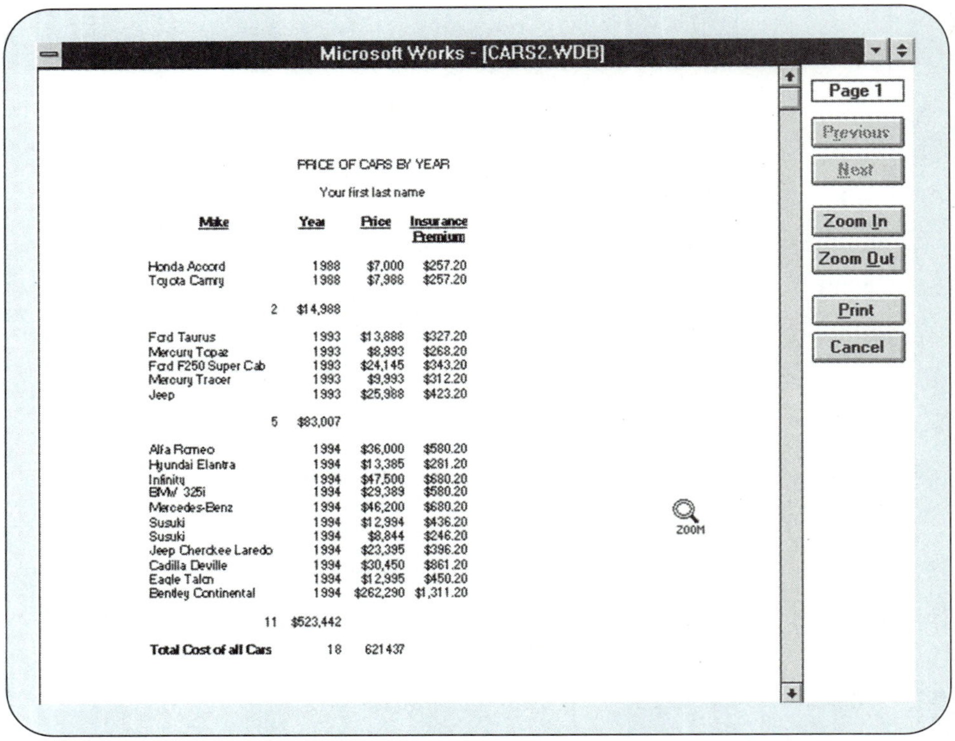

65. Click on Cancel to exit the preview screen. Click on the headings *Year* and *Price* and format them to right-align. Click on the heading *Insurance Premium*, change the column width to 15, and right-align the heading.
66. Print the report.

    Your document should look similar to the one in Figure 11.14.
67. Save the cars2.WDB file.
68. Close the database file and exit *Works*.

Special Kinds of Reports

Database users create many different kinds of reports. You can experiment with reports that print just summaries of each group in a sorted database by including only summary *fieldname* and summary rows, omitting any record rows. You can clarify long reports that have many control breaks by repeating headings in intro *fieldname* lines. You can expand the widths of columns to 79 spaces, or change print fonts for emphasis. You can format a report for a nonstandard width and length of paper, such as an invoice or statement form. You can insert page breaks in a report to put each group on a separate page with headings and subtotals for each page.

Figure 11.14

PRICE OF CARS BY YEAR

Your first last name

Make	Year	Price	Insurance Premium
Honda Accord	1988	$7,000	$257.20
Toyota Camry	1988	$7,988	$257.20
Subtotal	2	$14,988	
Ford Taurus	1993	$13,888	$327.20
Mercury Topaz	1993	$8,993	$268.20
Ford F250 Super Cab	1993	$24,145	$343.20
Mercury Tracer	1993	$9,993	$312.20
Jeep	1993	$25,988	$423.20
Subtotal	5	$83,007	
Alfa Romeo	1994	$36,000	$580.20
Hyundai Elantra	1994	$13,385	$281.20
Infinity	1994	$47,500	$680.20
BMW 325i	1994	$29,389	$580.20
Mercedes-Benz	1994	$46,200	$680.20
Suzuki	1994	$12,994	$436.20
Suzuki	1994	$8,844	$246.20
Jeep Cherokee Laredo	1994	$23,395	$396.20
Cadillac Deville	1994	$30,450	$861.20
Eagle Talon	1994	$12,995	$450.20
Bentley Continental	1994	$262,290	$1,311.20
Subtotal	11	$523,442	
Total Cost of all Cars	18	$621,437	

The report generator in *Works* is a powerful tool. It limits you to printing the contents of one database file at a time, but it gives you many additional specialized techniques to create highly customized reports. As you become more proficient with database operations, and as the sizes of your database files increase, you will want to investigate some of these possibilities.

Chapter Summary

A database report generator helps the user to construct custom output formats. Once you have constructed and saved a given report format, you can use it again and again. You can gather part or all of the data in a database file and present that information in an organized and structured way.

Six different kinds of report rows enable you to tailor each report to meet specific requirements. You begin designing a report by pinpointing your desired output and work backward from there to select from the contents of the database.

A control break occurs when the field contents in a sorted set of records change. At such a break in the stream of similar data, *Works* will print summary statistics. These statistics are useful for summarizing a group of data and for dividing the report into clear sections.

Reports can contain headers and footers; they can be modified to meet current needs or deleted if no longer needed. Up to eight different report formats can be saved for each database file.

KEY TERMS

control break
field contents
report
separator lines

REVIEW QUESTIONS

1. Explain how the output from a simple query or sort differs from that in a formal report.
2. What features make reports attractive and easy to read?
3. Saving a report format has several advantages. List them.
4. Name and explain the functions of the six types of report rows in *Works*.
5. Creating a report is relatively simple in *Works 3.0 for Windows*. Describe the steps that would lead to a successful report.
6. List and describe a few of the ways you can customize a report.
7. Review when you would or would not query or sort report data.
8. Explain the concept of a control break. Why is this concept important? How can you accomplish a control break?
9. The text suggested that the best way to design a report was to work backward from the desired output to the database itself. Why do you think this recommendation was made?
10. How many reports can you define for each *Works* database file, and what are they named by default?
11. List and explain the seven summary statistics available in *Works* reports.
12. Explain the concept of a break field. How is it used in *Works*?
13. Relate how unwanted versions of a report are deleted.
14. The text suggests several special kinds of reports. List at least three.

SOFTWARE EXERCISES

Exercise 11.1

1. Create a database structure to store the consumer debt inventory data in Table 11.2.

Table 11.2 Data for the Consumer Debt Inventory Database

Debt Type	Creditor	Monthly Payment	Balance
Auto	Bank West	199.58	9500.83
Auto	Jefferson Bank	267.21	3569.21
Auto	Wheatland Bank	127.00	985.00
Education	U.S. Bank	59.00	9999.00
Education	Bank of Lincoln	79.00	7989.00
Home	Continental Bank	149.00	35789.43
Credit card	Discover	29.00	798.23
Credit card	Visa	35.00	978.14
Credit card	MasterCard	49.00	2459.34
Credit card	American Express	15.00	255.00

2. Insert the consumer debt inventory using your choice of list or form view.
3. In list view, increase or decrease the field widths to completely display the entries and to leave one or two spaces between columns and/or field names.
4. In list view, format the Monthly Payment and Balance columns as currency with two decimal places.
5. Create a new report as follows:
   a. Enter *CONSUMER DEBT INVENTORY* as the report title.
   b. Include all of the database fields included in the report.
   c. Include no statistics in the report
6. Preview the report as you build it.
7. Center your name across Columns A through D on the second title row.
8. Add a blank title row between your name and the first heading row.
9. Center the *CONSUMER DEBT INVENTORY* heading across Columns A through D.
10. Separate the *Monthly Payment* heading into two heading rows. Center, bold, and underline the word *Payment* on the second heading row.
11. Add a blank line between the last heading and the first record row.
12. Save the database as debtinv.
13. Name the report debtrpt.

14. Print the report.
15. Close the debtinv.wdb file and exit *Works.*

Exercise 11.2

1. Open the debtinv.wdb file you completed in Exercise 11.1, or complete Exercise 11.1 before continuing.
2. Create a new summary report as follows:
   a. Enter *TOTAL CONSUMER DEBT INVENTORY* as the report title.
   b. Include only the Monthly Payment and Balance fields in the report.
   c. Include the =SUM statistic to total the Monthly Payment and Balance fields; position the statistics together in rows.
3. Move the heading so it spans Columns A, B, and C in the first title row.
4. Center *FOR* followed by your name on the second title row across columns A, B, and C.
5. Delete all headings and record rows.
6. Format the Balance and Monthly Payment totals as currency with two decimal places; increase the width of Column C to 11.
7. Preview the report as you build it; print it when you finish.
8. Change the name of the report to debtrpt1.
9. Save your changes as debtinv1.
10. Close the debtinv1.wdb file and exit *Works.*

Exercise 11.3

1. Open the debtinv.wdb file you completed in Exercise 11.1, or complete Exercise 11.1 before continuing.
2. Create a report shell as follows:
   a. Enter *CREDIT CARD DEBT* as the title.
   b. Include All database fields, but no statistics, in the report.
   c. Change the heading *Monthly Payment* to *Payment.*
   d. Underline, center, and bold the new heading, if necessary.
   e. Center the *CREDIT CARD DEBT* title across Columns A through D.
   f. Center your name on the second title row across Columns A through D.
   g. Add a blank title row between your name and the first heading row.

3. Formulate a query that will locate only the records for credit card debt; name the query *credit.*
4. Sort your card debt on the Balance field in descending order.
5. Add a new summary row.
6. Enter the words *TOTAL CREDIT CARD DEBT* on the last summary report row.
7. Enter a formula in the Balance field of this last summary row to sum your credit card debt; format this entry as currency with two decimal places.
8. Preview the report as you build it; print the report when you finish.
9. Change the name of the report to debtrpt2.
10. Save your changes as debtinv2.
11. Close the debtinv2.wdb file and exit *Works.*

Exercise 11.4

1. Open the debtinv.wdb file you completed in Exercise 11.1, or complete Exercise 11.1 before continuing.
2. Create a new report as follows:
   a. Enter *CONSUMER DEBT SUMMARY* as the title of the report.
   b. Include all database fields in the report.
3. Make the following changes:
   a. Change the heading *Debt Type* to *Debt.*
   b. Change the heading *Monthly Payment* to *Payment.*
   c. Underline, center, and bold the new headings, if necessary.
   d. Center the *CONSUMER DEBT SUMMARY* title across Columns A through D.
   e. Center your name on the second title row across Columns A through D.
   f. Add a blank title row between your name and the first heading row.
4. Sort on the Debt Type field in descending order and break on this field, marking the 1st Letter box.
5. Delete the summ Debt Type entries from the Debt and Creditor columns. Leave the =SUM statements in the Payment and Balance Due Columns.
6. Enter the word *Subtotal* in Column A on the summ row for the Debt column.
7. Insert a blank line before and after the summ *fieldname* row.
8. Total the Payment and Balance columns for the entire report.

9. Enter the word *Total* in Column A on the summary row that prints this total information.
10. Print the report.
11. Change the name of the report to debtrpt3.
12. Save your changes as debtinv3.
13. Close the debtinv3.wdb file and exit *Works*.

Exercise 11.5

1. Open the cars2.wdb file that you created in Chapter 10.
2. Create a new report as follows:
   a. Enter the title *CARS REPORT*.
   b. Add the Make, Year, and Price fields.
   c. Do not include any report statistics.
3. Make the following changes:
   a. Center the title *CARS REPORT* across Columns A through C.
   b. Center your name on the second title row across Columns A through C.
   c. Add a blank title row between your name and the first heading row.
4. Sort on the Price field in descending order.
5. Query the database to locate all cars priced less than $50,000.
6. Add a second summary line.
7. On the second summary line, enter *AVERAGE CAR COST* in the Make column and the average cost of the cars statistic in the Price column.
8. Name the report Avg Car Cost.
9. Format all prices as currency with no decimal places.
10. Print the report.
11. Show all the records again.
12. Save the file as avgcost.
13. Close avgcost.wdb and exit *Works*.

Exercise 11.6

1. Open the cars2.wdb database file that you created in Chapter 10.
2. Create a new report with the following features:
   a. Title the report *CARS INSURANCE REPORT*
   b. Add the following fields: Make, Year, Price, and Ins.
   c. Do not include any report statistics.

3. Make the following changes:
   a. Center the title *CARS INSURANCE REPORT* across Columns A through D.
   b. Center your name on the second Title line across Columns A through D.
   c. Add a blank Title row between your name and the first heading row.
4. Put the records for Insurance (Ins) in descending order.
5. Add a second summary row.
6. On the second summary row, enter *AVERAGE INSURANCE COST* in the Make column and the average cost of the cars insurance statistic in the Insurance column.
7. Format all dollar amounts as currency with no decimal places.
8. Name the report Avg Ins Cost.
9. Print the report.
10. Save the file as avgins.
11. Close avgins.wdb and exit *Works*.

Exercise 11.7

1. Open the outbrd.wdb file (on the student data diskette).
2. Create a report with the following features:
   a. Title the report *OUTBOARD MOTORS*.
   b. Include the following fields in the report: HP, Manufacturer, Cylinders, and Price.
   c. Do not include any report statistics.
3. Make the following changes:
   a. Center the title *OUTBOARD MOTORS* across Columns A through D.
   b. Center your name on the second Title row across Columns A through D.
   c. Add a blank title row between your name and the first heading row.
   d. Change the heading HP to Power.
   e. Underline, center, and bold the new heading if necessary.
4. Sort the report by HP in ascending order.
5. Name the report Horsepower.
6. Save the report as power.
7. Print power.wdb.
8. Close power.wdb and exit *Works*.

Exercise 11.8

1. Open the outbrd.wdb file (on the student data diskette).
2. Create a report with the following features:
   a. Title the report *OUTBOARD MOTORS—BY HORSEPOWER*.
   b. Include the following fields in the report: HP, Manufacturer, Cylinders, and Price.
   c. Do not include any report statistics.
3. Make the following changes:
   a. Center the title *OUTBOARD MOTORS—BY HORSEPOWER* across the columns containing data.
   b. Center your name on the second Title row across the same columns as selected in 3a.
   c. Add a blank Title row between your name and the first heading row.
   d. Change the heading HP to Power.
   e. Underline, center, and bold the new heading if necessary.
   f. Widen Column B, if necessary.
4. Sort (ascending) and break on the HP field.
   a. Insert a blank line before and after the Summ HP Field row.
   b. Delete =Sum (HP), Cylinders, and Price from the Summ row.
   c. Move the =Count (Manufacturer) statistic to the Price column.
   d. Type *COUNT BY HORSEPOWER* to the middle Summ HP Field row in the first column.
5. Name the report HPCOUNT.
6. Save the report as pwrcount.
7. Print pwrcount.wdb.
8. Close pwrcount.wdb and exit *Works*.

Exercise 11.9

1. Use *Works 3.0 for Windows* to complete a report based upon work you have completed in this course to date or for an outside of this class assignment.
2. Use all of the techniques you have learned to enhance the appearance of your report.
3. Save your file as OUTRPT.
4. Print outrpt.wdb.
5. Close outrpt.wdb and exit *Works*.

Chapter 12

Communications Module

Objectives

After studying this chapter you will be able to:

- *State the importance of the data communications age*
- *Explain how digital characters can be transmitted over analog channels from one computer to another*
- *Recall the history of computer communications*
- *Explain the difference between a wide area network and a local area network*
- *State the purposes of a wide area network*
- *Identify the remote access connections you can make via wide area communications*
- *Identify the hardware and software required to connect to a wide area network*
- *State the purposes of a local area network*
- *Identify the hardware and software used in a local area network*
- *Explain LAN topologies*
- *List and explain uses you can make of the* Works *communications software module*
- *State the default communications settings and know how and when to change them*
- *Recall the steps you take to begin a communications session, use an existing .wcm file, set up a new .wcm file, or enter new settings*
- *Explain the connection process in terms of what you must do and what you will see and hear*
- *Recall how to send and receive files, pause during data transmission, and save transmitted data*
- *Use the* Works *program to communicate with other computers*

Communications Concepts

The final type of application that you will study in learning to use a microcomputer for your personal use is computer-to-computer communications. Human communication via computers is the newest application for personal computers, yet the technology that allows us to transmit information from one person to another electronically has, at its roots, telecommunications principles that predate computers. Computer users have simply borrowed the technology of telecommunications and developed a computer application from it.

The result—the opportunity to exchange information quickly via computers—is as powerful and revolutionary as Gutenberg's development of the printing press was in the mid-1400s. It has opened a whole new era in which communication may be neither entirely written or oral, but a marriage of the two. We have entered the age of computer communications. Within the last decade, personal computer communications has grown into another of the most useful applications a beginning computer user can learn.

Telecomputing is a general term that describes using computers for communications of any type. This includes **data communications**, involving transmitting data files between computers, and **computer mediated communication (CMC)**, which describes human communication between individuals using computers.

Communications Technology

With the invention of the telegraph by Samuel F. B. Morse, it became possible to send messages over great distances by encoding letters of the alphabet and sending that code over electrical lines. When Alexander Graham Bell invented the telephone, it became possible to transmit the human voice over those same lines using patterns analogous to those that vocal sounds produce. The **analog mode** of transmission was born. An analog signal shows a continuous wave pattern, rather than distinct pulses of energy. Analog transmission can be compared to the time display on a traditional watch, where the hands move continuously from one number to the next.

Telecomputing can use analog telephone lines, **microwave transmissions** (which depend on electromagnetic waves), or **fiberoptic transmissions** (which depend on pulses of light traveling through glass strands) to pass information from one computer to another. The binary system represents data through patterns of 0 and 1 bits. Such a pattern forms a series of on/off signals that allow communications in the **digital mode**. In the digital mode each signal is discrete; that is, each is sharply defined as either on or off, rather than flowing from one state to the other, as analog signals do. A light bulb with an on/off switch could be said to operate in digital mode. A watch with a liquid crystal display reports the time in digital mode; the displays of successive times are discrete, not continuous.

Figure 12.1 shows the differences between analog and digital signals. Computer communications can change back and forth from digital to analog, and analog to digital, by means of a **modem**. The word *modem* means modulate/demodulate. This is a mechanical device that translates digital signals to analog signals and vice versa. Although many telecommunications lines are digital, many others are analog. Computer communications can use both types of lines.

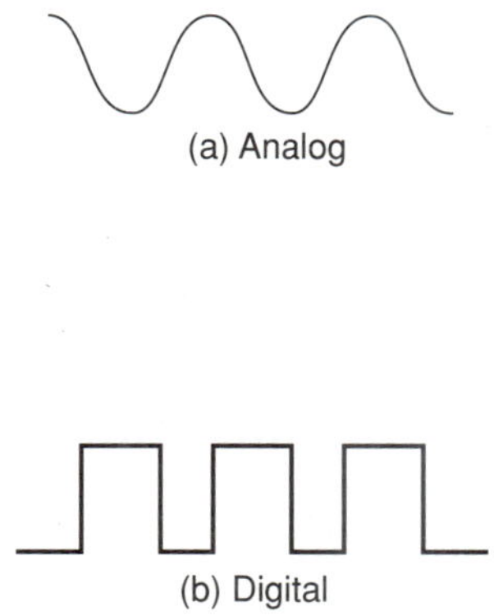

Figure 12.1

Analog/Digital Signals

History of Computer Communications

Borrowing from the telecommunications industry, data communications involve transmitting information in the form of coded bit patterns over channels of some type. Computer-to-computer connections over geographic distances usually involve leasing some telecommunications equipment. Computer-to-computer connections over shorter distances, as in local area networks (explained in the next section), are based on the same principles but they do not require leasing the means of transmission from a telecommunications company. The same type of cable used in phone lines can wire computers together in a local area network.

All computer communications, however, are indebted to the inventions of Samuel F. B. Morse and Alexander Graham Bell. You would not be able to **download**, or retrieve, data from a central computer onto your own personal computer disk without the technology they introduced, nor would you be able to **upload**, or send a file from your computer's floppy disk to a centrally located mainframe computer. All computer communications depend on the telephone technology that has been used for more than a century.

Types of Networks

A network is a path, or connection, from one place to another. A computer **network** can be defined in two ways. First, it can consist of a single computer connected via communications links and equipment to two or more terminals that have no CPUs. It can also consist of two or more independent computers connected together with communications links and equipment.

The **Internet**, which is the backbone of the information superhighway that is connecting computer users around the world, is a network of networks—a main path that connects many smaller, interconnected computer paths. With enough paths, or networks, you can connect throughout the country, and even the world, via your personal computer. More than 12 million Americans regularly access the Internet for its various services, from supporting research to finding user groups, or to chatting with fellow users or sending E-mail to them.

A network can make use of privately owned lines, satellite microwave transmission (shown in Figure 12.2), lines leased from a communications company, or even private, "in-house" lines that physically connect one computer to another. Some systems allow transmission in only one direction at a time, but almost all computer-to-computer connections involve **full-duplex lines**, which can carry transmissions in both directions at the same time, like a two-way street. Computer communications travel over two types of networks. **Wide area networks (WANs)** span great geographic distances using established transmission paths and modems. **Local area networks (LANs)** connect computers to other computers within a few kilometers of each other by physically wiring them together, or through infrared, wireless systems that can span limited geographic areas. The hardware and software needed for each type of network are different.

Figure 12.2

Satellite/Microwave Transmission

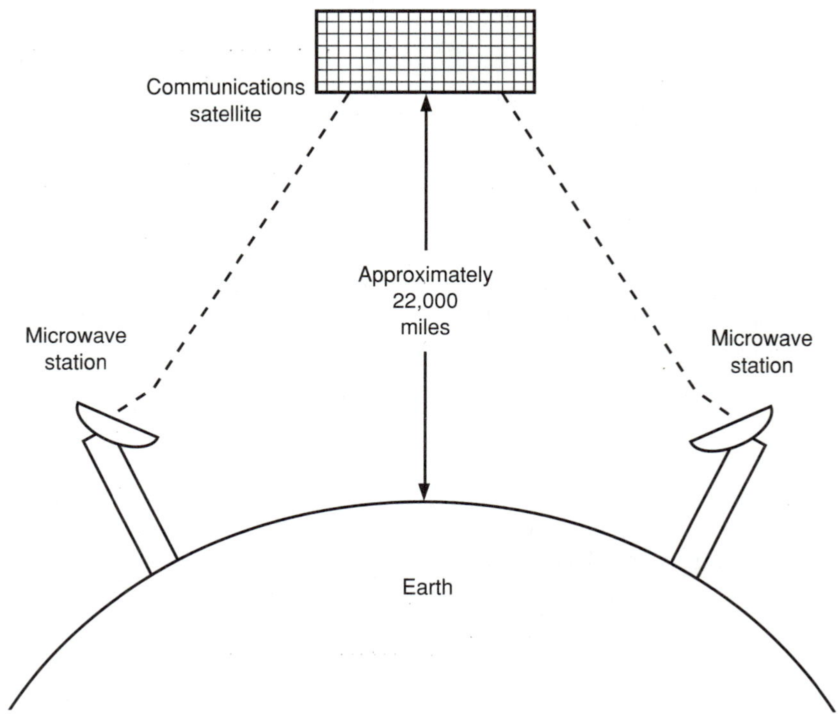

Wide Area Networks

The older of the two types of networks is the wide area network. This type of linkage has been used for several decades to tie **dumb terminals** (computer monitor and keyboard units with no central processing units or disk drives) to powerful minicomputers and mainframe computers. Data is transmitted over telephone lines to enable many workers to share the resources of a large central computer; the workers can be in many different buildings geographically distant from each other. Personal computer users rely on this same type of remote communication to access information from some central source. When your personal computer is using remote communication to access the power of a central computer located elsewhere, it is **emulating**, or imitating, a dumb terminal, even though it has its own central processing unit. It can then function as an **intelligent terminal** once you tap its own processing power.

Remote computer communication has many purposes. One is to share the power, data, and resources of a larger central computer. Another is to obtain information from a central source. Another is to communicate over geographic distances to another computer user via **electronic mail**. Electronic mail, or **E-mail**, as it is frequently termed, is a cross between the telephone and the mailbox. Each computer user on an electronic mail system has a mailbox, or section of a central directory, where messages can be left. As with the conventional postal system, messages can be left in your mailbox to be retrieved and answered at your convenience. Yet, as with a telephone, the communication is not delayed, except for the few seconds it takes to transmit the message; there is little time lag between sending and receiving. If you are **logged on**, or connected to your E-mail system, at the time a message is sent, you can read it immediately and respond to it as soon as you wish.

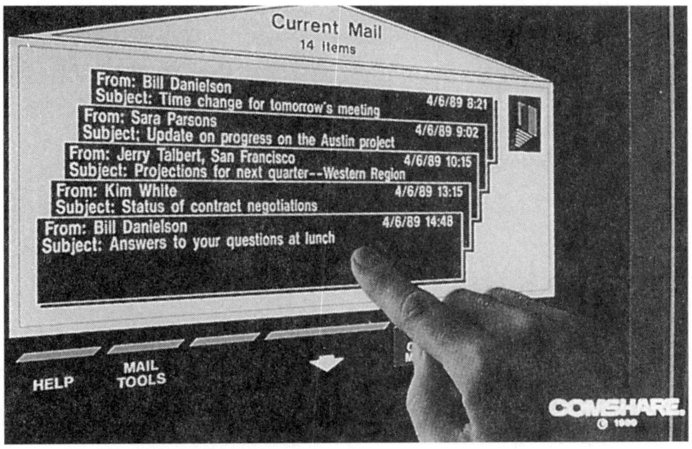

E-mail combines post office and telephone technology as a means of linking individuals.

Single users also take advantage of remote communications to access **information services**. These privately owned commercial services usually offer members access to several large databases of material for a fee. Information services have different types of memberships. Most of them require fees to join, and then charge users for **on-line time** (time spent connected to the service) for the accessed information. CompuServe, America On-Line, and Prodigy are all examples of national information services. Many such services are available to personal computer users and business computer users alike. You also may access free information services, such as on-line library catalogs that can provide titles, call numbers, and periodical issue references for books and articles you wish to read.

Another popular interactive service is the electronic bulletin board. Unlike E-mail, electronic bulletin boards are topic specific.

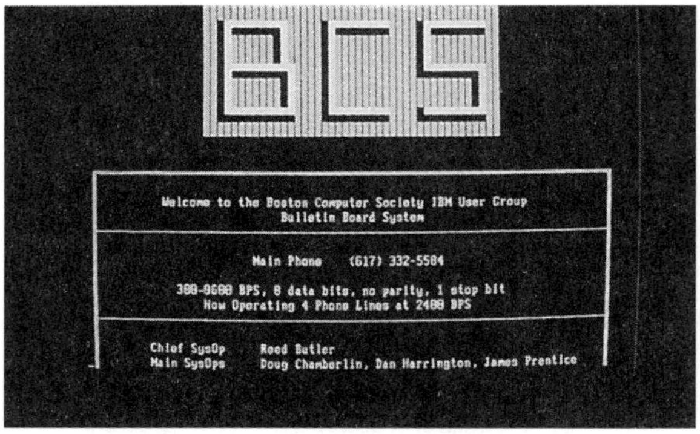

Bulletin board services (BBSs), another popular use of remote access, have developed since the growth in the ownership of personal computers. These are bulletin boards open to the public, some of them for **special interest groups (SIGs)**. They are usually set up by private individuals or organizations. Most bulletin board services are free to users. They are maintained by volunteer **sysops** (system operators) who monitor the lines, issue user identification names and passwords, and maintain the bulletin board material. Like their physical namesakes, bulletin boards are general clearing houses for information—word of new computer developments, tips for users, and other matters of interest to PC users. They can also provide much **shareware** (software that is not commercially marketed and can be used by anyone for a nominal, voluntary user's fee). Although bulletin board services often have limited incoming lines, and lack the professional quality of information services, they are interesting and valuable links between personal computer users. If you have a modem, one of the first things you will want to explore with the *Works* communications application is a bulletin board service in your local calling area.

WAN Hardware

In order to use a wide area network, your personal computer system must include a modem connected to an available telephone line. As we noted in Chapter 1, a modem, or modulator/demodulator, is a piece of hardware that converts digital signals to analog signals, and vice versa, so that you may use telecommunications lines to transmit information. There are several types of modems. Many personal computers are sold today with **internal modems** installed in available slots on their motherboards. This type of modulator/demodulator is mounted on a circuit board, like many other optional enhancements you can purchase for your computer.

An **external modem** is a small peripheral that plugs into a serial communications port on your computer's system unit. This separate unit, like an external disk drive or a printer, takes up more **footspace** (area on the desktop), but it works in much the same way as an internal modem. The Hayes or Hayes-compatible modem is the most common type of modem. After attaching the unit's cable to one of your serial ports, you plug in the phone line to a telephone jack, connecting your computer to an available telephone line. The hardware for your computer-to-computer connections is complete.

The **acoustic coupler** was the first type of modem developed. This device required a telephone handset placed in two rubber rings. The digital-to-analog data transmission was converted through the telephone receiver's signals. Acoustic couplers are still convenient for portable computer users or anyone who wishes to access a public telephone line, perhaps in a phone booth.

Figure 12.3 shows all three types of modems. The internal modem is most commonly used today, although acoustic couplers are re-emerging due to the growth of FAX transmissions. Facsimile machines enable one to transmit hard copies of a document. Fax modems are available for personal computer users.

(a) (b) (c)

Figure 12.3

Selection of modem types is often determined by need: a) an external modem, b) an acoustic coupler, c) an internal modem.

WAN Software

In order to establish computer-to-computer communications via a wide area network, you must have appropriate software to tell each computer involved how fast data is being transmitted and how it is coded. The needed software can be included in an integrated program, such as *Works*, or it can be one of many standalone communications programs. (*Procomm, Smart Talk*, and *Bit Comm* are a few.) Some are even shareware programs. Your version of the *Windows* interface already includes communications software in the Terminal portion of the Accessories module. *Works 3.0 for Windows* also has its own communications module, however.

Communications software allows you to set the transmission speed, most often referred to as the **baud rate**, although you may also see it referred to as **bps**, for *bits per second*. Modems are available to transmit data at 300 baud, 1200 baud, 2400 baud, 9600 baud, and 14400 baud. Regular, voice-grade telephone lines like those you lease for your home phone can transmit up to 14400 baud. A **smart modem**, a modem that can sense transmission capability and adjust for line noise (interference or white noise on the line), can transmit reliably at much higher rates. *Works 3.0 for Windows* allows you to transmit up to 19200 baud if your modem supports such a speed. The most common transmission speed today is 2400 baud, however. You must transmit and receive at the rate for which your modem is set. The receiving computer adjusts the rate at which it receives data; you cannot, however, transmit at a higher speed than your modem can accommodate.

Any communications software will allow you to set the **data bits** (how many bits to a character, 7 or 8) and **start/stop bits** (where one character ends and another begins) that are used in computer-to-computer connections. When you sign up for an information service or establish a link with a mainframe, you must get these settings and record them in your communications program before you attempt a computer-to-computer connection.

Some communication links also conduct **parity checks** that test whether each character transmitted is being received correctly. This requires an extra bit, added to the seven or eight data bits for each character, that serves as check bit. The extra bit can be set for odd or even parity. While most of the links that personal computer users establish involve no parity checks, some programs, such as *Works*, provide masks over whatever the setting is. (A mask allows one computer with an odd parity setting to communicate with another computer with an even parity setting; the setting is "masked over" during communications. This is the default *Works* setting.)

The data code can be ASCII or binary. ASCII (text) files contain only characters with no formatting; binary files include formatting codes, formulas, graphics, and so on. Users can now exchange even audio and video files between computers. Such files are very large, even for a minute or two of sound or video, but they can be successfully transferred with a high-speed modem and enough hard disk space.

If all of this sounds a bit technical for a beginning computer user, you can rest assured that the *Works* communications tool has default settings. Although the communications settings vary from one link to another, the default settings are the most common. You will be given the proper settings at the time you enroll in a service or join a bulletin board group. You will soon learn how to record these settings in the *Works* communication menu once and save them in a **.wcm file** for future use.

Setting the **protocol**, or the way each character is packaged when it is transmitted from computer to computer, is often referred to as *handshaking* between computers. The protocol assures that both the sending and receiving communications will be transmitted the same way. The protocol depends on the type of line used. Almost all personal computer communications involve the **Xon/Xoff protocol** with full-duplex lines, although there are other protocols. For file transfer, a user must also set **file transfer protocols (FTPs)**, which set the standards for how an entire file is uploaded or downloaded. *Works* supports **Kermit, Xmodem, Ymodem,** and **Zmodem** file transfer protocols for uploading and downloading files.

If you encounter some transmission problems in your communications with other computers, you can experiment with other settings, or ask the receiving computer for transmission advice. Usually, the default settings of *Works* will serve you well. Setting the baud rate and identifying which communication port you are using are the most important items to change, if necessary. Many times when you purchase your modem you receive detailed instructions for setting the transmission. The *Works* communication program assumes that you have a Hayes-compatible modem. The second half of this chapter gives you detailed instructions to explain how to use the *Works* communication software to establish a remote connection.

Local Area Networks

Besides a WAN, the other type of network or path for computer-to-computer connections is the local area network (LAN). A local area network is a linked system of computers (predominantly microcomputers, but always intelligent terminals with their own CPUs). These computers are physically connected to each other within a relatively short distance, and also to a central, more powerful computer called a **file server** that serves as a repository for shared data, programs, or peripherals. Figure 12.4 illustrates a small local area network that is set up in a ring configuration.

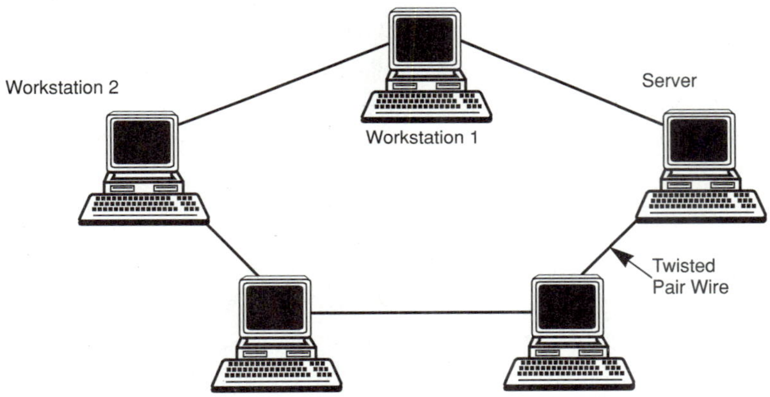

Figure 12.4

A simple Local Area Network (LAN) with server and nodes.

Although it is possible to cable a series of computers together over a few kilometers, most LANs involve contiguous buildings, one floor of a building, or even one office in a building. Most LAN connections are limited to a couple of thousand feet. This type of network does not require a modem because it involves strictly digital transmissions over a limited area. No leased telephone line is required; a LAN is a privately owned and operated group of computers that are hard-wired together. LANs are becoming increasingly popular with businesses and colleges that use microcomputers. The new microcomputer operating system, *Windows NT*, was developed specifically for LANs.

There are several reasons to set up a local area network. Since all of the **nodes**, or individual connection points on a LAN that access the server, are intelligent, each station can operate independently. Each is a smart terminal that has its own, individual central processing unit and its own RAM. This means that a LAN can do double duty. The work station nodes can function as independent, stand-alone computers for their own processing jobs; they can tap the server and share in its power; they can even communicate from one to another, passing messages along the network without using telephone lines. This last capability, often termed

in-house communications, is one of the major reasons for setting up a LAN. Electronic mail can be used in much the same way as on a wide area network, but much less expensively and more quickly than with leased telephone lines.

The key term to remember when thinking about LANs is *sharing*. These networks are set up to share things, such as E-mail messages, hard disk storage space, database files, other software programs, or peripherals like laser printers. The ability to allow computers to share resources and still operate independently has made LANs the most efficient use of networking yet.

LAN Hardware

To set up a LAN, you need two or more individual microcomputers, one of which may be a central, more powerful server computer. Each machine needs a network card and cabling of some type. A network interface card plugs into an expansion slot and allows the individual stations to transmit and receive. The cabling that connects the individual computers together could be the same type of wire used for telephone lines—**twisted pair cable**. You could also use **coaxial cable**, like television cable, to transmit more quickly, in greater capacity, and over longer distances. Today, LANs in business settings often use fiberoptic cables. This cabling passes pulses of light down glass strands to transmit signals. Fiberoptic cable is still somewhat expensive, but it is extremely secure and very fast by comparison with the copper wiring of traditional telephone technology. It is not as easy to modify once installed, however. Splicing wiring is less complicated than reconnecting glass fibers.

The configuration or arrangement of a local area network is often referred to as its **topology**, meaning the specific way in which the nodes are cabled to each other and to the server. LANs employ a number of different topologies, but the **ring, star,** and **bus** are the most common. These three topologies are shown in Figure 12.5.

A ring topology wires the individual nodes together and to the server in a circular arrangement or closed loop. Traffic on the LAN is routed from node to node to server, in one direction only. Most often the traffic is managed by what is called **token passing**. The capability of transmitting is shared in round-robin fashion. If the token contains a message, it continues around the ring until it reaches its destination. There it is delivered, and then it continues around the ring empty so that subsequent nodes may transmit in turn, if they wish. Software on the server manages this traffic. The IBM token ring system is the most common ring configuration.

In a star topology, a hub computer lies at the center, and connections radiate out to nodes. In the past, the hub or center computer was the server, but most newer star configurations, place the server not at the hub, but alongside the other nodes. If, for some reason, the hub computer is down, the nodes cannot pass data from one to another, as they can in the ring topology. However, in the star topology a node can communicate directly with the server without going around a ring, so the arrangement is often more efficient. Since all traffic must pass

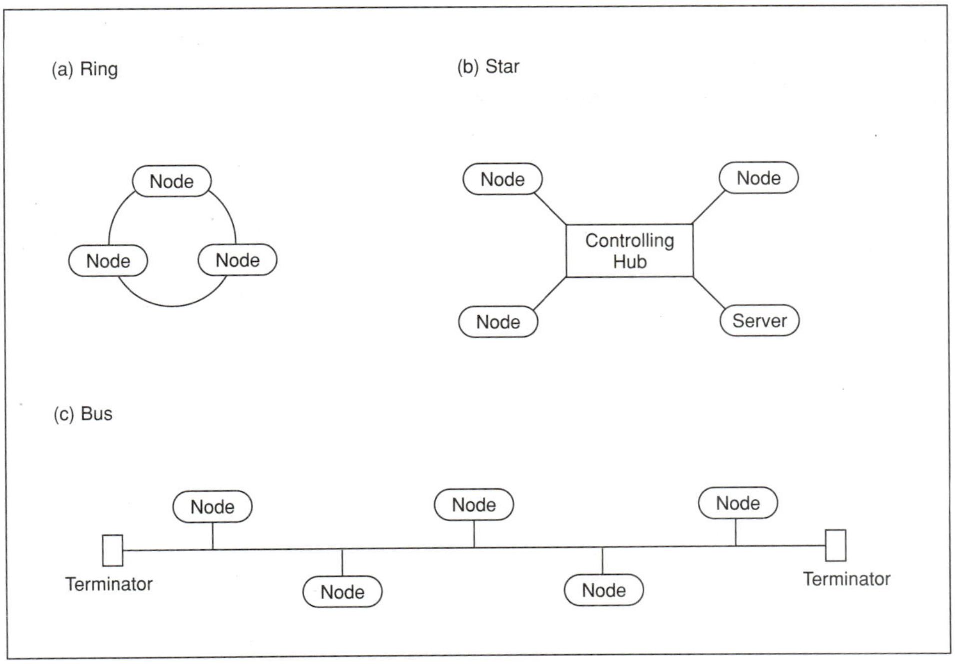

Figure 12.5

The a) ring, b) star and c) bus are the three most common topologies.

through the central server, even if it is intended for another node, a star network offers greater control than a ring topology. Arcnet is the most common system to create a star topology.

The bus topology is the simplest and least expensive arrangement. It is very easy to add nodes to a bus topology, cabling them to the existing network in a line like socks on a clothesline. All nodes have equal access, and messages are sent down a straight line to the intended receiver; a bus topology is thus similar to a party line on a telephone. Transmissions can run in both directions. Since the bus topology is simple, the server does not have to be as powerful as it would for the other topologies. Ethernet is the most common bus configuration system.

LAN Software

You have probably guessed that a local area network requires special software to operate. Since LANs are based on sharing resources, a program must control who accesses what and when to prevent a confused jumble of transmissions. The network software controls access.

One system gives access based on **contention**. A node attempts to transmit, and if the path is clear, the message is sent; if it is not, the sender backs off, waits an allotted period of time, and tries again. Access can also be based on token passing programmed into the software. An electronic token is sent from node to node along a ring or bus topology. Messages are sent and retrieved from the token sequentially. Token passing is a linear management method. The network software manages access to and from the nodes and server, regardless of which method is used.

Local area networks also require LAN packs of application programs. The same application program that an individual uses with a stand-alone PC will not suffice because many users must access the same application programs, and perhaps the same data files, stored on the server. Local area network versions of most popular software programs are available. You buy them to match the size of your LAN. You could get a LAN pack of a program for as few as six stations or for as many as several hundred. Network versions of software programs are more expensive than single-user versions, but, of course, not as expensive as if you had to buy one program for each microcomputer on the LAN.

The operating system for a LAN must necessarily be more complex than the operating system for a single user. Of several LAN operating systems available, Novell's NetWare is currently the most popular. LAN operating systems also require DOS or another operating system software package for system management within each workstation.

LANs are multiuser environments. Although they are more complex, they require less knowledge on the part of the individual user. In many cases, the LAN is transparent to the individual user; you are virtually unaware of any difference between using the microcomputer as a node accessing the central server, or using the software and the central processing unit of the microcomputer as an independent unit—until the server experiences "down-time," that is.

Although we have discussed wide area networks and local area networks separately, it is possible to use both types of networks in one operation. For example, a LAN node might access the server to use a modem for wide area communications with an information service.

Using Works Communications Software

The *Works* communications tool is written to accommodate computer-to-computer communications via a modem and telephone lines. You may use the program to communicate over distances with national and local information services. You may send electronic mail messages if you have access to an E-mail program. You may upload and download files to and from other computers. You may engage in paperless banking with an **EFTS (electronic funds transfer system)** and thus manage your checking account if your bank offers the service. You may even chat on-line with a fellow member of a special interest group. (**IRC, Internet Relay Chat**, has become a favorite pastime of many personal computer users.) The communications module of *Works* can link your computer with another computer, regardless of its size and type.

If you have the necessary hardware and software that we have discussed, all it takes is a few minutes to adjust the settings in the communications module. These settings enable you to dial up another computer. We will discuss a few of the most common settings in a moment, but all modems differ slightly, and settings for phone connections with other computers can differ significantly. Successfully connecting with other computers may require some experimenting and some adjustment on your part.

If you get confused when trying to set up your modem, remember that *Works* has default settings that duplicate the most common communication settings. More than likely, the only settings you will need to adjust are the baud rate and the phone number. All of the other settings can often be left on the default settings.

The meanings for the toolbar icons for the *Works* communications program are listed below and identified in Figure 12.6:

Figure 12.6

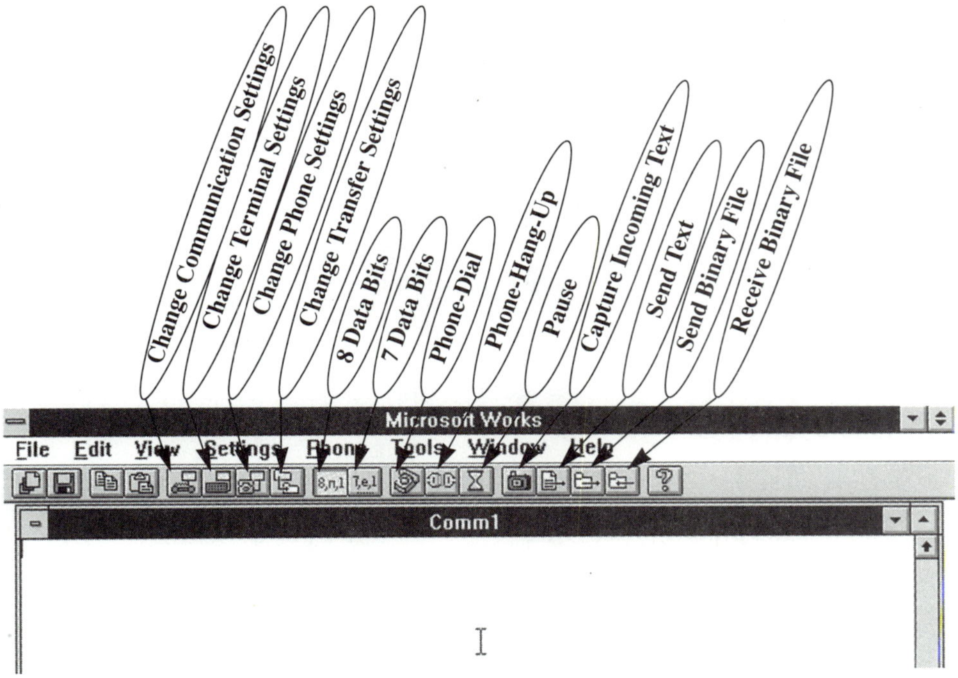

- Communications settings
- Terminal settings
- Phone settings
- Transfer settings
- 8-N-1 setting (8 bits, no parity, 1 stop/start bit)
- 7-E-1 setting (7 bits, even parity, 1 stop/start bit)
- Easy connect (dials the phone number in an open .wcm file)
- Dial/hang up (dials the current number if the computer is not connected, or disconnects if it is already connected)
- Pause (stops transmitting temporarily)
- Capture text
- Send text
- Send binary file

- Receive binary file
- Cue cards

Beginning the Communications Session

In order to connect to another computer, you need to plug your modem line into the telephone outlet. If you have an external modem, you may have to plug it into an electrical outlet as well, and switch it on. An internal modem draws power from the system unit. To begin communication, activate the *Works* program:

- Click on Create a New File-Communications.

The Easy Connect window appears:

- Enter the phone number.
- Name the service.

If you click on OK, the number will be dialed immediately. However, you want to save the file (with the phone number) for future use:

- Click on File-Save As.
- Name the file.

Figure 12.7

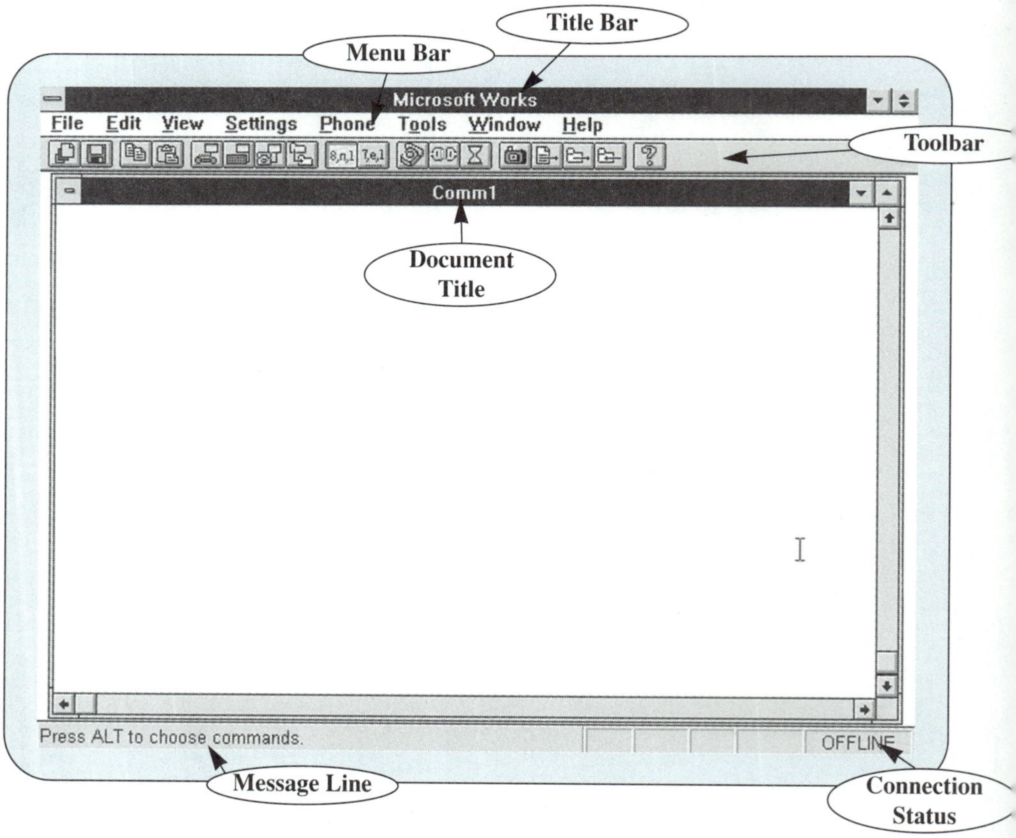

- Click on OK.

The Communication screen displays, as shown in Figure 12.7. It is similar to other program screens, except for the different toolbar icons, as illustrated in Figure 12.6.

Using an Existing Communications File

If you have a .wcm file stored on disk that has all of the proper settings for your connection, *Works* will dial the number using the Easy Connect box when you open that file. In this case, you may wish to dial immediately and not change any settings. To open a communications file:

- Click on File-Open Existing File.
- Select a file name.
- Click on OK or press ENTER.

As was noted, *Works* presents the Easy Connect window to confirm that you wish to connect to another computer. After you select OK, you will hear the number being dialed. Storing all of the settings in a file automates the connection process. Still, you need to know how to choose these settings in the first place. Before entering a phone number and naming a file, learn how to adjust the communication and terminal settings.

Setting Up a New File

For your first computer-to-computer connection with *Works*, we assume that you do not have a communications file (.wcm file) saved. Once you have all of the settings and the phone number entered, you can save them in a .wcm file.

Entering New Settings

To enter new settings:

- Click on Settings-Phone.

The Settings window appears, as shown in Figure 12.8. Type in the telephone number, taking care to type *1* and an area code for a long distance number. The program can interpret dashes and parentheses. On a PBX (private branch ex-

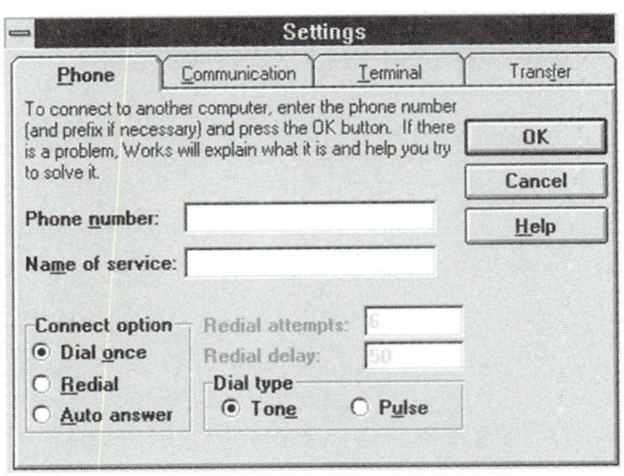

Figure 12.8

The Settings Window

change) phone system, often a *9* must precede the phone number to get an outside line. You can separate it with a comma to instruct the computer to pause while you get an outside line. *Works 3.0 for Windows* will recognize normal phone number punctuation.

To continue entering settings:

- Click on the Communication area of the window.

Another list of options is displayed. Figure 12.9 shows the choices that must be made. Set the communications port and the baud rate by scrolling, or typing in the correct settings. Adjust the other settings, if necessary. To complete the communications settings, you must know the baud rate of your modem, the port to which it is connected, and the data bit and parity settings of the computer to which you are connecting. Obtain these settings from your user's manual, or from the instructions that came with the telephone number you are calling.

Figure 12.9

Additional choices

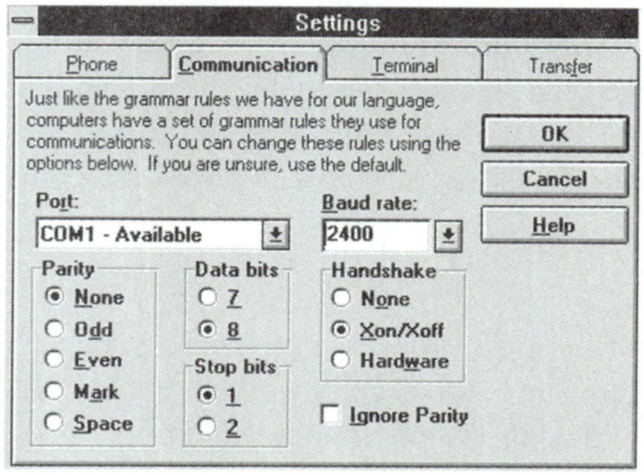

With these settings at hand, from the communications options:

- Type in a new COM port, or scroll and highlight the correct choice.
- Type in a new baud rate, or scroll to find the right one.
- Click on other options, changing them as necessary.
- Click on OK or press ENTER when your settings are complete.

Recall that the baud rate is the speed of transmission at which your modem is sending information to the receiving computer. This depends on the modem that you have. If you have a 2400-baud modem, type the number 2400 to reflect this.

Leave the data bit setting on 8 if you are not sure whether each character sent from the other computer contains seven or eight bits. The handshake is usually the Xon/Xoff full-duplex protocol. If you know that the system you are contacting conducts a parity check (a transmission check for each character), you can change the parity to odd or even, or choose none. However, the default Mask setting will usually work with either parity check. If you are certain that your modem is connected to a communication port other than COM1, you can change it to COM2, COM3, COM4, or COM5 by scrolling down the list of COM ports to find the proper one. If you are not certain, leave the setting on COM1.

The Settings menu in the communications module gives you two other choices, Terminal and Transfer, as shown in Figure 12.7. The Terminal option box allows you to change your terminal emulation mode from VT100, the default, to VT220, ANSI, VT52, or even TTY, the generic dumb terminal emulation mode. For the time being, do not access the Transfer portion of the window, or the Modem selection in the Settings command. (The latter allows you to test your modem and COM port.) In the Terminal command, you can change the carriage return, line feed, wraparound, and echo settings but this is seldom necessary with microcomputers, which generally emulate VT100 terminals.

Figure 12.10 shows the Terminal default settings. Don't change these unless you are certain you need to. Just be aware that this is how to change the terminal settings, if necessary. The Transfer command is shown in Figure 12.19 in the tutorial.

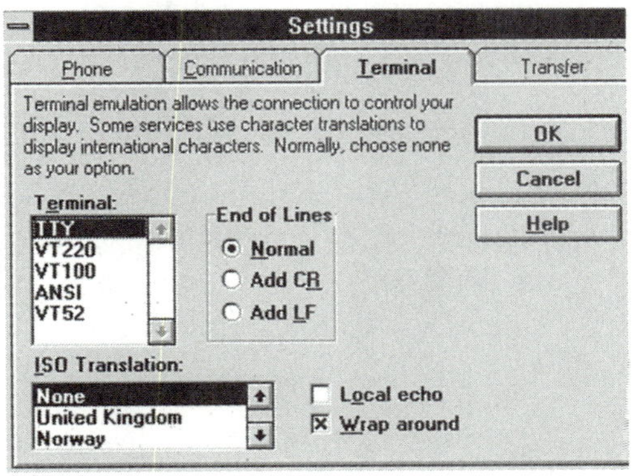

Figure 12.10

Other Communications Settings

You can select other phone and terminal options in the Settings and Tools menu. For instance, you may set your computer to automatically answer incoming calls and capture text while unattended by changing the settings in the Phone command in Settings, and the Capture Text command in Tools. The Settings-Phone or Tools-Option menus also allow you to change the dialing mode of your phone line from touch tone to rotary (or pulse) mode. You may also change your serial port (COM port) setting here. We will not discuss the changes you can make in the Options menu, since the defaults are relatively universal. Unless instructed otherwise, do not change the default settings in Tools-Options.

Automatic answer can be turned on to answer an incoming call when you are not at the terminal, but the computer is on and in the *Works* communications module. You can mark choices to redial a number if it is busy, and to specify the number of attempts and the time in seconds between redial attempts.

After setting all of these features (or accepting the defaults), you are now ready to connect to the receiving computer.

Connecting

When all of the preparatory settings are made and the telephone number is entered, you are ready to make the actual connection:

- Click on Phone-Dial.

  OR

- Click on the Dial/hangup or Easy Connect icons.

The characters *ATDT* and the number appear on the screen. You will hear the number being dialed. (*ATDT* stands for "Attention Dial using a Tone.") You will hear a high-pitched tone when the phone is answered, and the word *CONNECT* will appear on the screen. Usually the baud rate is also displayed. For example, when the connection occurs, you will see "CONNECT 2400" if the modem and program are using the 2400-baud rate.

To continue:

- Press ENTER.

The sign-on appears, and you are in business.

If you hear a busy signal, you may dial again:

- Click on Phone-Dial Again.

If you fail to connect, you may either Break or disconnect. To disconnect:

- Break is an alternative signal to a computer service, forcing an interruption. It is an unusual telecommunications signal to break all transmissions so one can begin anew. A break is a clean slate, a true "break" in the transmission path.
- Select Phone-Hang up.

A dialog box asks if it is OK to disconnect.

- Click on OK or press ENTER to confirm.

Logging on to a Service

Once you have connected, if you are calling an information service, its menu will take over, asking you for your user name and PIN (personal identification number). If you are using CompuServe, Prodigy, America On-Line, or another popular national information service, you will receive an instruction booklet when you subscribe. Most information services allow you to access the functions you want by choosing from a series of menus and key words that allow you to move quickly from one topic to another. These are often called "jump" words. Moving more quickly through the menu system can reduce your charges for service connect time and long distance services from your telecommunications company. Only when you wish to transfer a file, capture text, or end the telecomputing session do you need to return to the *Works* menu.

If you must go through a lengthy sign-on process when connecting with your information service, you can record the sign-on commands and save them in the .wcm file you maintain for that service. These commands will be repeated automatically when you invoke the Sign on command. To complete the sign-on process, first save the steps, as follows:

- Click on Tools-Record Script.
- In Type of Script, click on Sign-On.
- Click on OK.
- Type in the keystrokes for the sign-on process.
- Click on Tools-End Recording.

Save the communications file, as usual. The next time you use this .wcm file, your log-in process will be automated. You can also record other types of scripts, such as the commands to get to a certain directory or menu within an information service. You name the script and then choose the stored steps in a later on-line session:

- Click on Tools-Record Script.
- Under Type of Script, click on Other.
- Click on OK.
- Type in the necessary keystrokes.
- Click on Tools-End Recording.

You may now use this series of commands:

- Click on Tools.
- Click on the name of the saved script.

You can use the scripts after opening the appropriate communications file and responding that you wish to connect. *Works* will automatically follow the sign-on process you have saved with that file after you see the CONNECT response. You may then invoke the other scripts at any time in your session. Just be sure to save the communication file after you have defined these types of scripts.

Pausing During Transmission

You may temporarily halt the flow of data and perform on-screen editing while you are still connected to the other computer. If you wish to pause during a transmission:

- Click on Phone-Pause.

  OR
- Choose the pause icon (the hourglass).
- Use the editing keys to move about the work area.
- Click on Pause to continue.

The checkmark next to Pause will disappear and your session will resume. You may not move about the work area of the screen during a session until you Pause it. If you need to edit something quickly, or you wish to clear a jumble of characters you have received, you can do so by turning on Pause. Be aware, however, that if you are connected to a long distance number, charges accumulate while you Pause and temporarily halt transmission.

If you choose an icon from the communications toolbar at an inappropriate time, *Works* responds with the error message: "The toolbar is currently unavailable." Simply press ENTER or click on OK to clear the message.

Saving a Session

If you wish to retain information that you receive from another computer, you may save it to a file with the Capture Text command. You can then review it later at your convenience. If you are simply reading bulletin board information, or chatting on-line with another person, you usually won't want to capture the session. Sometimes you will find valuable information that you will want to save, such as research database information or call numbers of library books you will wish to check out. To do so, at the point when you wish to begin:

- Click on Tools-Capture Text.

  OR
- Click on the capture Icon (the camera).

  OR
- Type a name for the text you are saving.
- Click on OK.

Your text will be saved to a file for future reference.

Until you turn off the Capture Text command, incoming information will be saved to file. If the file name you have typed already exists, you will be given the opportunity to append material to the existing file, or to replace the original file. If you were gathering library information on call numbers of books for a research project, for instance, you could append information from several sessions with the on-line catalog into one file on disk.

To cease saving incoming data:

- Click on Tools-End Capture Text.

The incoming information will no longer be saved. Once you have captured text, you may edit the file, print it, or reread it as often as you like after you have ended the communications session.

Transferring Files

One of the most useful features of telecomputing is the ability to transfer files back and forth, regardless of the sizes and makes of the computers. You can send and receive files between microcomputers, minicomputers, or mainframes. You can send a whole file or part of a file, and you can type your text in the word processor module and spell check it before you transfer it through communications.

It can be especially helpful to transfer files between a Macintosh and an IBM or compatible computer, since the type of personal computer is irrelevant with computer-to-computer connections. If you send a text file that was prepared with *Works* and saved in ASCII text format to a Macintosh computer, it can be received and edited with a different Macintosh word processing program. ASCII files (or text files) don't contain any special formatting codes for features such as bold, underlined, or italic type, and so on.

When sending a file from *Works* to someone with a different application package, you will want to send an ASCII file. You can save an ASCII file by using the Text option in the File-Save As option. When sending a file to someone who also has the *Works* software, you should send a binary file, which includes formatting codes. If you are sending a highly structured file, or one that contains audio or video, you must also send it binary.

To send a file in the *Works* communications module, first connect to the other computer. Instruct it to get ready to receive a file. (You may have to issue a Kermit or Xmodem command, or another file transfer protocol command, to advise the receiving computer of your file transfer before you begin the process in *Works*.) Don't change the default carriage return (CR) or line feed (LF) settings in the Send or Receive File unless you are certain that you need to add them.

To send part of a *Works* file:

- Open an existing communications file or create a new file.

  OR
- Open a word processing, spreadsheet, or database file.
- Highlight the information to be copied.
- Click on Edit-Copy.
- Click on Window.
- Select the communications file.
- Click on Edit-Paste.

The text is sent to the other computer. To send an entire file:

- Click on Transfer-Send File.

  OR
- Click on the send file icon.
- A window of file listings appears.
- Select the file you wish to send from the list.

  OR
- Type the name of the directory and file (with its extension).
- Click the radio button for the Text choice, if desired. (The default is Binary.)
- Click on OK or press ENTER.

Receiving a file while connected to another computer (downloading) reverses the process. When you are advised by the sending computer that it is beginning a transfer with a command in the Kermit, Xmodem, or any other file transfer protocol:

- Click on Tools-Receive File.
- Type in a drive designation and file name for the received data.
- Change the default file type, Binary, to Text, if you wish.
- Click on OK or press ENTER.

The transfer process begins. If you wish to save the file to a drive other than the default drive, be sure to include that drive's designation in the file name you enter (for example, B:hobby.txt).

If you choose to receive the file as Text instead of Binary, *Works* will add carriage returns and line feeds as necessary when the file is transferred to your computer. A Transfer in Process dialog box will appear on the screen. It will advise you when the transfer is complete. Of course, the text file will not have any special formatting, but will be a straight ASCII file that you can edit as you wish.

Final Hints

You may choose from a variety of activities when using the *Works* telecomputing tool. Whether you are accessing a local bulletin board service, calling an information service for stock quotations, or sending a file to a colleague three states away, as you use the Communications program more, the process becomes easier. If pausing during a transmission doesn't clear up strange symbols that appear on the screen, you can disconnect and establish the connection again. You can experiment with different settings or change the terminal mode from the default to VT52 or ANSI. Often the quality of transmission lines has a bearing on the success of the connection.

Also, remember that you must both log off from whatever service you are calling and disconnect the phone in the *Works* program when you finish a telecomputing session. If you don't log off from an information service, you will incur additional on-line charges for the minutes during which the service does not recognize that you are no longer connected. Simply disconnecting with Phone-Hang up is not enough; be sure to first log off from the service or BBS, and then break the connection.

As we have indicated, recording sign-on procedures can help you to quickly get where you wish to be in an information service. You should be cautious, however, if you are not the only one using your computer and the *Works* communication program. An automatic sign-on procedure could make it possible for somebody to run up large on-line charges and long-distance telephone charges to you without your authorization. We will discuss this danger at greater length in Chapter 15.

Finally, bear in mind that any data that you transmit over a network is no longer private. The *Works* communications tool is simple and fairly powerful. It is adequate for most communication needs of personal computer users. It does not, however, have the sophistication of larger, more powerful software programs that allow **encryption** (coding to protect the confidentiality of transmitted data). Anything that you transmit over a wide area network, or even a local area network, is public information, susceptible to interception.

COMMUNICATIONS TUTORIAL NO. 1

The following tutorial is composed of several exercises that involve dialing a long-distance number if you are not in either the 303 or 708 area codes. Also, the tutorial assumes that you can connect to some system that offers E-mail software. If you have access to America On-Line or Prodigy or an information service such as CompuServe, you can use these organizations' mail services. If you have access to your campus network's E-mail service, you may use that.

You could try to find a local bulletin board number and access that service if you cannot make long-distance calls. Check with your instructor if you are not sure of your authorization for long-distance calls, and to learn what mail services are available to you.

Denver Freenet Bulletin Board

To start, load *Works* and proceed as follows:

1. Turn on your modem.
2. Click on Create New File-Communication.

   The Easy Connect dialog box displays, as shown in Figure 12.11.

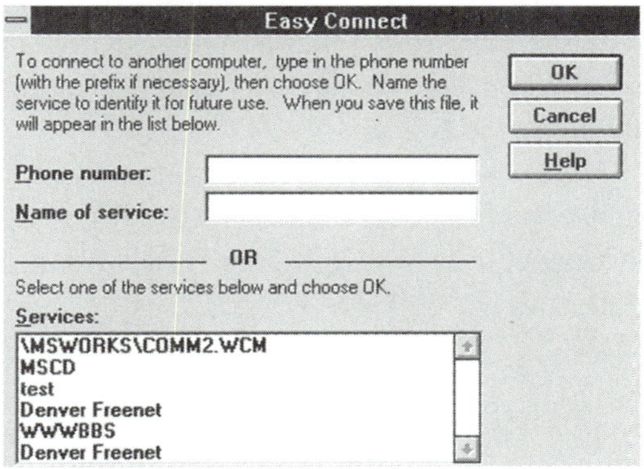

Figure 12.11

Example of the Easy Connect Dialog Box

You are going to access the national Denver Freenet Bulletin Board Service as a guest to experience the BBS process. Freenet is organized around a town theme, with a Post Office, a Health Administration Building, a Science Building, an Art Museum, and so on. Freenets around the country began with the opening of Cleveland's Freenet in 1989 at Case Western Reserve University's Medical School.

The Denver information service was opened in 1993. You will look at its menu and choose a topic. The protocol for the Freenet is either 1,200 or 2,400 baud, 8 bits, 1 stop bit, and no parity, so your *Works* default settings should work.

3. Click in the Phone Number text box, and type the number:
   1–303–270–4865

In the Denver (303) area, just type **270–4865**. [Several Freenets are in the process of being activated in Buffalo, New York, Chicago, Long Beach, Santa Barbara, Salem, and Tallahassee as we write this section. Check for the number if you are in any of these areas. If you are near any of the following areas, substitute their numbers for the one in Denver: Cleveland, Ohio, (216)368–3888; Heartland, Peoria, Illinois, (309)674–1100; Medina County, Medina, Ohio, (216)723–6732; Youngstown, Ohio, (216)742–3072; Tri-State, Cincinnati, Ohio, (513)579–1990.]

4. In the Name of Service text box, type **Denver Freenet**

   You will be transferred immediately to the screen and the number will be dialed. You want to save the file for future use.

Figure 12.12

Example of the Phone Menu

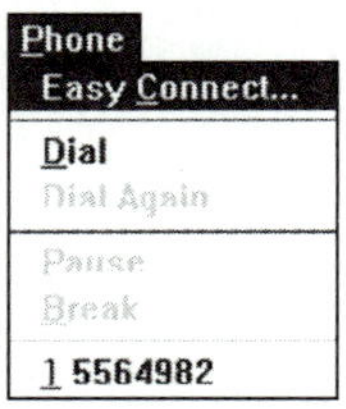

5. Click on Cancel before it answers.
6. Click on File-Save As.
7. Type **Denfree**-OK.
8. Click on Phone.

   The Phone menu displays, as shown in Figure 12.12.

9. Click on Dial (or click on the Phone icon).

This is a very popular bulletin board and you may get a busy signal during the day. When you connect a *T* and the number appear on the screen and a high-pitched tone is heard.

After you have saved a communications file, the next time you want to use that number, select Communication and open that file; the system will prompt, "Connect to Other Computer?" Select OK, and the number will be automatically dialed.

10. Press ENTER. (You may have to hold it down for a second or two, or press ENTER a few times.)

    An Initial Welcome screen appears, as shown in Figure 12.13. Several disclaimer paragraphs appear and then the screen shown in Figure 12.14 displays.

11. To answer the login prompt, type **guest**

    The Main Menu displays, as shown in Figure 12.15.

12. Select the Health Care Building by typing its menu number.

    The Health Care menu displays, as shown in Figure 12.16.

13. Select Food and Nutrition by typing its number (or select any other topic you desire).

    If you select Health Care Newsroom or Nutrition Discussion Newsgroup from the Food and Nutrition menu, you will see messages about various items of health news contributed by users. You can

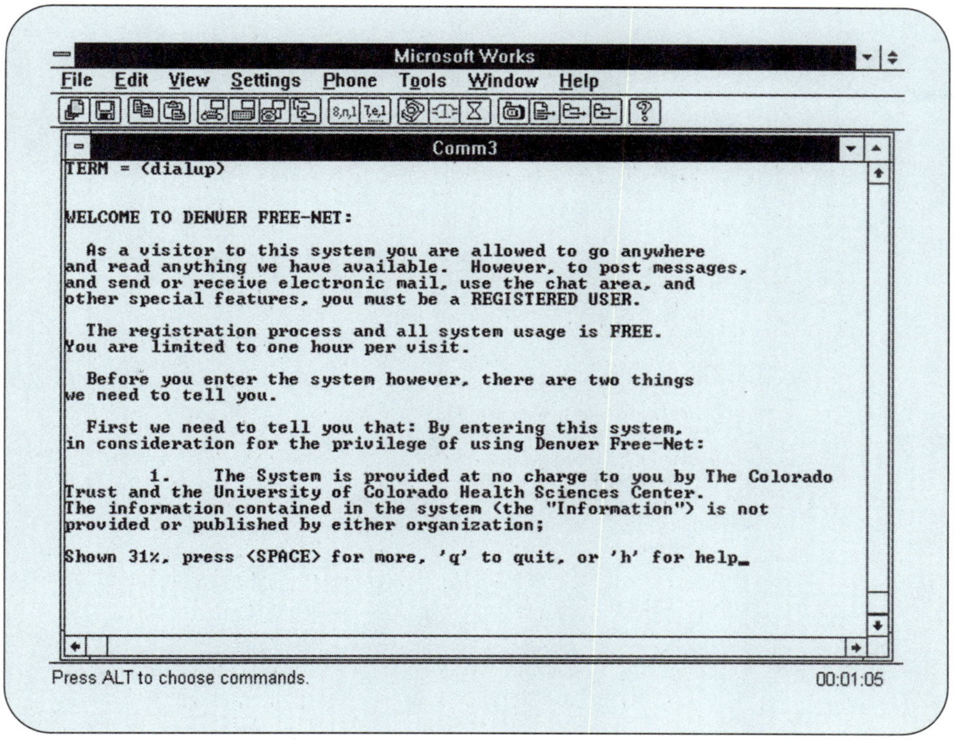

Figure 12.13

The Initial Welcome Screen

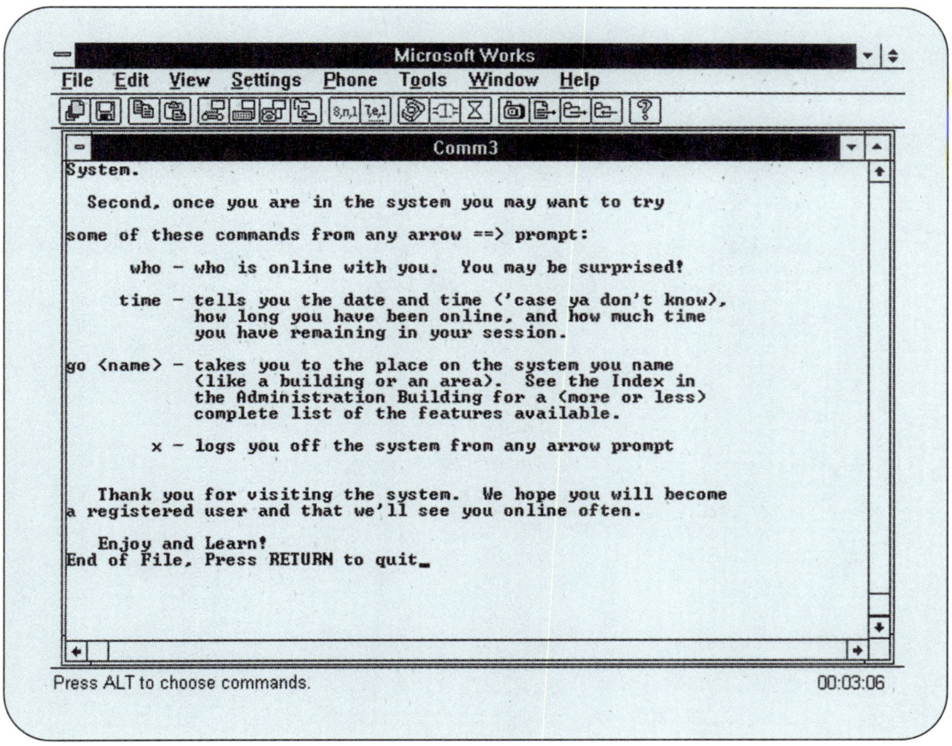

Figure 12.14

Disclaimer Paragraphs

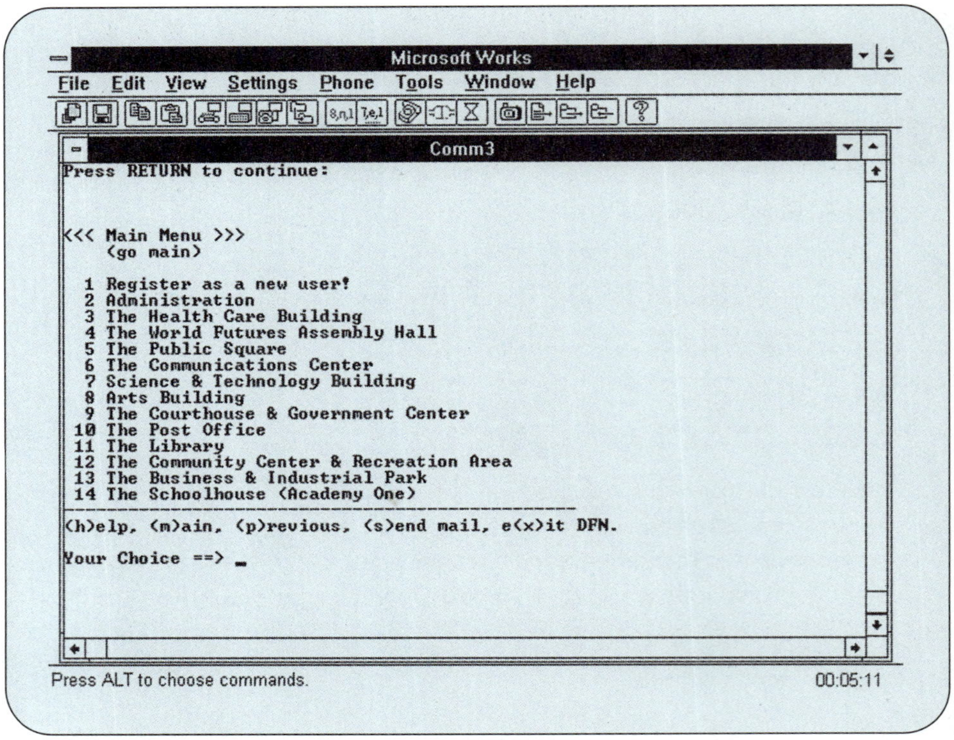

Figure 12.15

The Main Menu

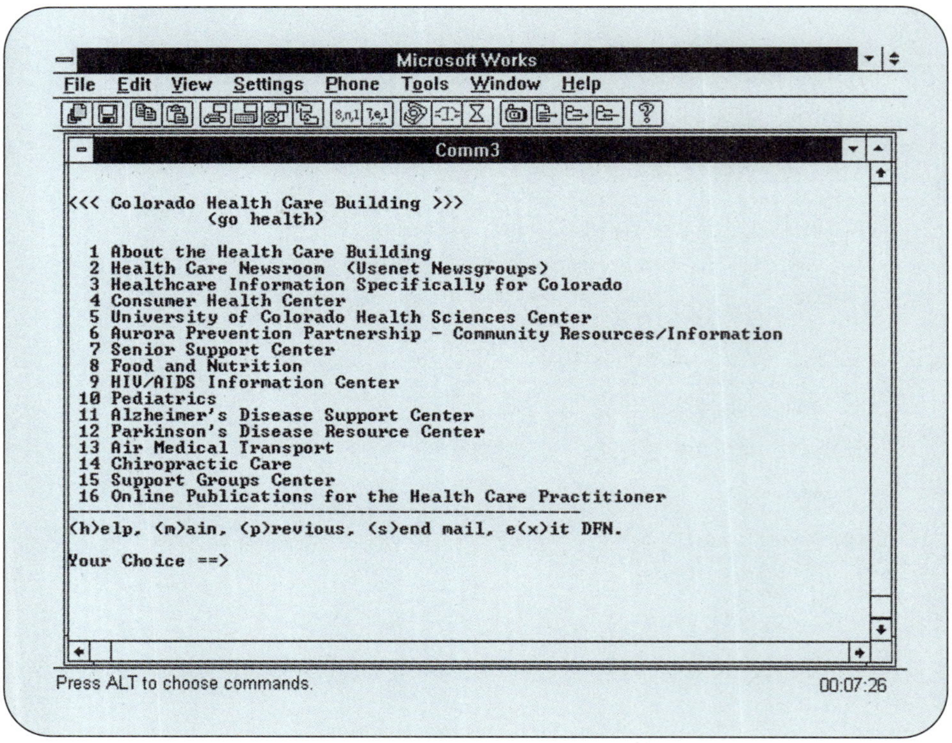

Figure 12.16

The Health Care Menu

also send a message to the bulletin board. Follow the prompts. To go to another area, *M* returns you to the Main Menu, *P* returns you to the previous menu, and *go Library, go Nutrition*, etc. moves you within the bulletin board.

14. Type **Q** to quit an area.
15. Type **X** to exit Freenet.
16. Type **Y** to end the session.

    A sign-off thank you message and the elapsed time appear.
17. Click on Phone-Hang up to disconnect.
18. Press ENTER.

E-Mail on the Internet

For your next computer communications exercise, you may send one of us a mail message using your own E-mail network or a national service. The mail service must be connected to the international Internet network; virtually all campus networks have this capability. Check with your instructor for a user name and password and for your system's commands to enter and exit the function E-mail.

1. Open a new communications file.
2. Type the phone number of your electronic mail service.
3. Type **E-mail** for the name of the service.
4. Click on Cancel and save the file as email.
5. Click on Phone-Dial, and then Select the number.
6. Click on OK.
7. Enter your assigned user name and password.
8. Type **Mail** (or whatever the correct command is).
9. Type **Send**
10. At the To: prompt type one of the following addresses:

    IN%"Larsen@mscd.edu"

    IN%"Marold@mscd.edu"

    IN%"Shaw@mscd.edu"
11. Press ENTER.

    Note: Some services such as Prodigy don't require the **IN%** portion of E-mail addresses.
12. At the Subject: prompt, type **Works Student**
13. Press ENTER.

When the system gives you an opportunity, type a brief message of your choice. (Limit it to two sentences; you may have to repeat the process if something goes wrong and you abort the mail exercise.)

14. Use a control sequence to end the message (usually CTRL + Z, or CTRL + D) and send it on the Internet.

When the mail prompt appears again, your message has been sent via a national network with specific **gateways**, or routing paths. The message will be delivered to one of our mailboxes at Metropolitan State College of Denver. You can also send a message to a student at another college anywhere in the world that has access to Internet if you have that person's Internet address.

15. Exit the Mail System (exit, quit).
16. Exit your system (*log out* or *lo*).
17. Click on Phone-Hang up.
18. Click on OK in response to the "OK to disconnect" prompt.

Transferring a File

You are now going to send your instructor the inslet.wps letter that you prepared in Chapter 4 to practice transferring a file. Be sure that the file is available on a drive on your computer and that your instructor has an electronic mailbox.

1. Open the existing word processing file named inslet.wps.
2. Click on File-Save As.
3. In the Save File as Type text box, click on the down arrow.
4. Select Text and, if necessary, type inslet.txt in the File Name text box as shown in Figure 12.17.
5. Click on OK.

Figure 12.17

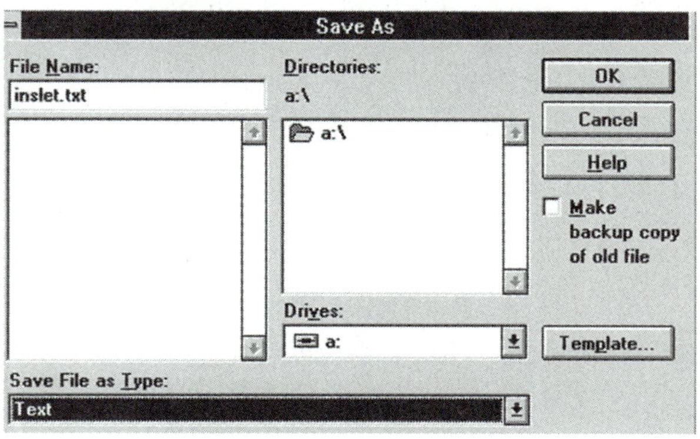

You wish to resave the letter as a plain ASCII text file with no formatting. You can then upload (copy) it from your floppy disk to your directory on the school's computer. Finally, you can send the file to your instructor.

6. Click on OK in response to the "OK to Save without Formatting?" message box.
7. Open a new communications file and select your E-mail number.

   If you are connecting to a Unix operating system, you will use *Works* default protocol, which is Kermit. At the % prompt:
8. Type **Kermit -r inslet.txt**
9. Press ENTER.

Figure 12.18

Example of the Settings Menu

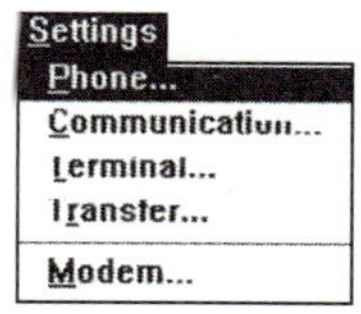

As an alternative, if you are using a MVS or VMS operating system, you would first replace the Kermit protocol with XModem as follows:

1. Click on Settings.

   The Settings menu displays, as shown in Figure 12.18.
2. Click on Transfer.

   The Transfer menu displays, as shown in Figure 12.19.

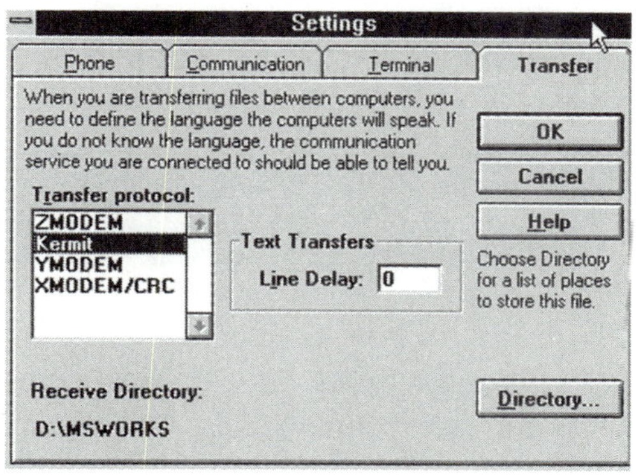

Figure 12.19

Example of the Transfer Menu

3. Select XModem/CRC-OK.

You can then replace Step 8 above with the following:

8. Type **XModem rt inslet.txt**

Now return to the sequence:

10. Press ENTER to return to the other computer.

    You get a message telling you to send your file.
11. Click on Tools-Send File.
12. Select the drive and file name (inslet.txt), then click on OK.

A dialog box will relate the attempt to transfer, detailing the number of bytes being transferred. If the file must be retransmitted, a Retries: prompt will indicate the number of times transfer is attempted. You may cancel the transfer process at any time by pressing ENTER. The message will change when the transfer is successfully completed.

At this juncture the inslet.wps file will reside in your directory on the school's system. You want to send that file to your instructor. Get into the mail subsystem.

13. Type **Mail**
14. Type **Send inslet.txt**
15. Press ENTER.
16. At the To: prompt, type your instructor's name.
17. At the Subject: prompt, type **WP File**
18. Press ENTER.

Your instructor will receive the inslet.wps file in his or her mail box. The prompt from the receiving computer will reappear on the screen. The file is now also on your directory with the E-mail service.

19. Exit from the mail directory (usually by typing the word *exit*).
20. Log out (LO).
21. Click on Phone-Hang up-OK.
22. Exit from the *Works* program.

Chapter Summary

This chapter discussed telecomputing, the final application in the *Works* program and one of the most useful ones a beginning computer user can learn. Whether your communications involve data communications or Computer Mediated Communication (CMC), the computer networks you to other computers.

The two main types of networks used for data communications are wide area networks, which span large geographic distances using established transmission paths and modems, and local area networks, which connect computers to other computers by physically wiring them together, usually in an office or a floor of a building. A LAN can facilitate the sharing of hard disk space and peripherals such as printers.

Computer communications have many useful purposes. The primary ones are electronic mail, access to information services, and access to bulletin board services. All of these permit you to upload files from your computer to another one, or to download files to your computer from another one.

Hardware requirements for remote communications include a phone line, an internal or external modem, and a computer or terminal. Software requirements include the *Works* communications software, a new or existing .wcm file that contains settings applicable to your situation. This file enables you to connect to another computer. That connection may include logging on to a service, transferring files, pausing during the transmission of those files, and saving files that have been transmitted to you.

KEY TERMS

acoustic coupler
analog mode
baud rate
BBS
bps
break signal
bulletin board service
bus topology
CMC
coaxial cable
computer mediated communication
contention
data bit
data communications
digital mode
download
dumb terminal
EFTS
E-mail
electronic funds transfer system
electronic mail
emulating
encryption
external modem
FAX
fiberoptic transmission
file server
file transfer protocol
footspace
FTP
full-duplex line
gateway
in-house communications
information service
intelligent terminal
internal modem
Internet
Internet relay chat
IRC
Kermit
LAN
local area network
logged on
microwave transmission
modem
network
node
on-line time
parity check
PIN
protocol
ring topology
shareware
SIG
smart modem
special interest group
star topology
start/stop bit
sysop
telecomputing
token passing
topology
twisted pair cable
upload
WAN
.wcm file
wide area network
Xon/Xoff protocol
Xmodem
Ymodem
Zmodem

REVIEW QUESTIONS

1. Define the concept of telecomputing.
2. Summarize the technology advances that have made data communications possible.
3. Compare and contrast analog and digital transmissions.
4. What is the difference between uploading and downloading?
5. What is the meaning of *baud rate*?
6. Explain WANs in terms of their (a) hardware, (b) software, and (c) intended uses.
7. Explain LANs in terms of their (a) hardware, (b) software, and (c) intended uses.
8. List the most important purposes of remote communications.
9. Review the hardware and software requirements for data communications.
10. What does the term *modem* actually represent?

11. Describe the role played by a modem in data communications.
12. List and explain the major local area network topologies.
13. Summarize the differences between token passing and contention access methods in a LAN.
14. Explain the meaning of each communications toolbar icon.
15. Explain (a) how to use an existing communications file, (b) how to enter new settings, (c) how to enter and save a phone number, (d) how to connect to another computer, and (e) how to log on to a service.
16. What are the steps to (a) pause during a session, and (b) save a communications session?
17. What are the advantages of file transfer using data communications?
18. Explain how to transfer a file from your computer to another computer and how to receive a file on your computer from another one.

SOFTWARE EXERCISES

Data communications facilities vary widely from one environment to another. Before attempting any of the following exercises, check with your instructor regarding their feasibility. Remember to use the *Works* help facility as needed. Also, substitute your own settings for the ones suggested if you know of a difference.

Exercise 12.1

1. Make arrangements with your instructor to familiarize yourself with the *Works* communications tutorial.
2. Make notes about what was covered in each of the following sections:
   a. Introducing communications
   b. Preparing for a communications session
3. Use *Works* to type your notes about what you learned.
4. Save your work as tutcom12.
5. Print tutcom12.wps.
6. Close tutcom12.wps and exit *Works*.

Exercise 12.2

This exercise will determine which COM port your computer uses (i.e., COM1, COM2), if any.

1. Open a new communications file.
2. Perform the Modem Setup test; note whether or not you have a COM port and, if so, what its number is. If the Modem Setup test doesn't automatically appear on your screen, click on Settings-Modem.

3. Locate the menu and change the COM port selection, if necessary.
4. Use *Works 3.0 for Windows* to type notes about what you learned; include a discussion about the importance of correct COM port identification and selection to your overall success in establishing communications connections.
5. Save your work as comport.
6. Print comport.wps.
7. Close comport.wps and exit *Works.*

Exercise 12.3

Assume that you want to set up Works to communicate with a bulletin board which has the following specifications: Phone number: (303) 469–4954; Dial type: Tone; Connect option: Dial once; Title: The Four Wheeling BBS; Description: Jeeping/Camping/Outdoors; Computer: IBM; Modem speed: 2,400; Handshake: Xon/Xoff; End of line: Normal; Operator: Bill Schockley; Data bits: 8; Stop bit: 1; Parity: None; Terminal emulation: VT100; Transfer protocol: Kermit.

1. Open a new communications file.
2. Enter the settings given above.
3. Make notes on the contents of each screen on which you enter data.
4. Use *Works 3.0 for Windows* to type your notes.
5. Save your communications file as data1.
6. Save the word processing file as wpdata1.
7. Print wpdata1.wps.
8. Close data1.wcm and wpdata1.wps and exit *Works.*

Exercise 12.4

1. Enter the settings and phone number for a bulletin board service in your authorized calling area.
2. Connect and log on to the bulletin board.
3. Acquaint yourself with some of the bulletin board's features.
4. Spend 15 or 20 minutes exploring.
5. Use the Print Screen feature along with Accessories, Write, Edit-paste, and File-print to periodically capture what you are doing and seeing.
6. Log off from the bulletin board.
7. Use the *Works* word processor to type some notes about your experience.
8. Save your file.
9. Disconnect and exit from *Works.*

Exercise 12.5

1. Enter the settings and phone number for a bulletin board in your authorized calling area that particularly interests you.
2. Connect and log on to the bulletin board.
3. Acquaint yourself with some of the bulletin board's features.
4. Spend 15 or 20 minutes exploring.
5. Locate one or more interesting file(s) to download to your computer.
6. Download the file(s).
7. Log off from the bulletin board.
8. Use the *Works* word processor to type some notes about your experience.
9. Save your file.
10. Disconnect and exit from *Works*.

Exercise 12.6

1. Enter the settings and phone number for an information service (such as Prodigy) in your authorized calling area.
2. Connect and log on to the service.
3. Spend 15 or 20 minutes getting acquainted with the various menus and services offered.
4. Use the Print Screen feature along with Accessories, Write, Edit-paste, and File-print to periodically capture what you are doing and seeing.
5. Log off from the service.
6. Use the *Works* word processor to type some notes about your experience.
7. Save your file.
8. Disconnect and exit from *Works*.

Exercise 12.7

1. Enter the settings and phone number for the computer on your campus that handles E-mail.
2. Connect and log on to the campus E-mail computer.
3. Use the E-mail facility to send messages to your instructor or several classmates.
4. Make yourself a copy of the messages you send to others.
5. Print out your own copy of the messages you send.
6. Log off from the campus computer.

7. Use the *Works* word processor to type some notes about your experience.
8. Save your file.
9. Disconnect and exit from *Works.*

Exercise 12.8

1. Enter the settings and phone number for the computer on your campus that handles E-mail.
2. Connect and log on to the campus E-mail computer.
3. Use the computer to (a) upload a text file from your computer to your instructor's or a classmate's account, and (b) download a text file from the campus computer to your PC.
4. Log off from the campus computer.
5. Use the *Works* word processor (a) to format and print the downloaded file, and (b) to write some notes about your experience.
6. Close the file and exit from *Works.*

Part 3

Putting It All Together

Chapter 13

Integrating the Applications

Objectives

After studying this chapter you will be able to:

- *Explain what integration is and why it is a powerful concept*
- *Explain the difficulties in combining stand-alone applications and why a package like* Works *makes this integration simpler*
- *Speculate upon the future of integrated software packages*
- *List the most common integrated tasks*
- *Use the Window command to size one or more windows*
- *State the meanings and uses of the terms* target file *and* file type
- *Copy parts of files from one or more* Works *applications into another* Works *application*
- *Create and print form letters*
- *Integrate* Works *ClipArt, WordArt, and Drawings into a document*
- *Move your work between* Works *and other programs*
- *Use* Works *to create integrated documents*
- *Use the* WorksWizards *tool or Templates to quickly design integrated documents*

In the first 12 chapters of this book, we have dealt primarily with individual software tools or applications for personal computer users. As a beginning user, you have progressed from the initial stages of understanding operating systems, windows, and application programs, through the basics of word processing, spreadsheets and charts, databases, and communications. We have presented these tools as individual applications with very specific uses for each. When you wanted to generate text, you used the word processor. When you needed to keep records, you used the database application. If you wanted to perform mathematical computations, you constructed a spreadsheet. If you needed to communicate from computer to computer, you used the communications tool.

These individual lessons are necessary learning steps on the road to full integration. Sooner or later, a specific task will make you wish to combine two or more of the applications to produce an integrated file. Now that you have mastered the individual applications, you can explore the power of integration.

Power of Integration

In the world of computers, **integration** refers to the use of two or more specific software applications to generate a finished product. This is an extremely powerful capability. You can call upon the best characteristics of individual applications and combine them to produce better work in a shorter period of time. The finished product of the typical integrated task is a document, but this needn't be the case. Whether you want to move a chart from an existing spreadsheet to a word processing document, or insert names and addresses from a database file into a form letter (mail merging), integration makes short work of sometimes complex tasks. It is a valuable skill to learn for personal efficiency. Even as a beginning personal computer user, mastery of the skills of integration can give you a competitive edge. Figure 13.1 illustrates an integrated document.

Future of Integration and Integrated Programs

We noted in Chapter 1, and again in Chapter 2, the movement in the personal computer world toward a standard user interface, that is, a common appearance to all microcomputer applications, whether they be word processing or database programs. Also, we noted that the *Windows* environment has accelerated this move toward a common interface.

Since the phenomenal growth of *Windows*-based personal computer systems, more and more software is written to conform to the *Windows* "look." Programs that previously had very distinct characteristics, with their own unique menu systems and function keys, have gradually begun conforming to what is generally termed **CUA**, for *common user access.* They use the same menu selections, and most make their interfaces conform to the *Windows* conventions. Today, the newest versions of the independent application programs look pretty much the same.

With the first version of the *Works* program (1.0), onward to the latest *Works 3.0 for Windows*, this integrated program has presented the CUA as it was envisioned by Microsoft Corporation. If the *Windows* interface will become the standard user interface (which seems likely as of this writing), users of the best-selling integrated program for microcomputers (*Works*) will have a distinct advantage. They will already be familiar with the *Windows* look. Those who have already taken advantage of the integration capabilities of *Works* will find it

Software Inc.
123 W. 99th
Golden, CO 80401

Dear Mr. Marshall:

We appreciate your interest in Software, Inc. We have been in business in Golden since 1978 and have built a reputation based upon an honest relationship with our customers.

As you can see from the data below, software sales have been significant.

Software	Hardware	Service
130,000	500,000	60,000

From a Database

To provide a better picture of this data, I have charted it for you below:

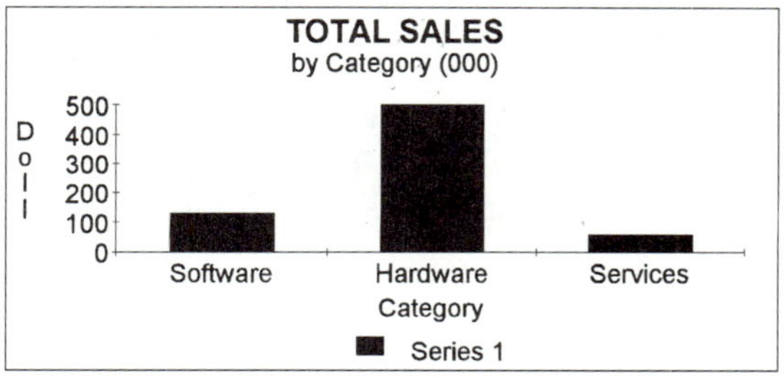

From a Database to a Spreadsheet

We appreciate your business and look forward to working with you in the future.

Sincerely yours,

Ken Shaw
Branch Manager

Figure 13.1

Integration allows you to pull together the best features of several different applications, thereby creating a highly sophisticated finished product.

a small step to learn to integrate files from independent, stand-alone applications.

Learning to integrate applications in *Works 3.0 for Windows* will not only help you to easily produce integrated files, but it will also serve as a training ground for common tasks in the future—integrating applications with stand-alone programs. Integration of files from different software packages will become increasingly common. The future of personal computer software may feature independent applications, or suites of independent applications from one publisher, rather than integrated programs. You will be able to accomplish the same thing with independent applications, and the interfaces of each program will look much the same. In the meantime, however, learning integration in *Works* will help you perform seamless file combinations.

Combining Individual Applications in Works

Personal computer software has allowed integration for a long time. In *Works*, the process is as simple as moving the pertinent files into RAM and cutting and pasting them together through the use of the Window command. You can now even view portions of each open file on the screen at the same time. Although practically speaking, it is awkward to work with more than four files at the same time, you can open as many as eight, depending on how much main memory you have. (You will receive a message that "Too many files are open" when you try to exceed your limit.) You can then work with each open file in turn.

What is more, the specific format of each file is converted when the material is moved into a file from a different application. This makes the whole integration process a lot simpler to master. It is as easy as selecting material from the active file and moving it with the Edit-Copy or Edit-Copy Special command into a target file. You can develop better presentations as a beginning computer user, and have that same competitive advantage that a seasoned microcomputer user has.

As you know, each *Works* tool has a common look; the way each application is presented to you, the user, is the same. The main menu that appears at the top of the screen looks the same in each application you choose. Choices within each of those main commands may differ; Tabs appears in the Format menu of the word processor, while Time/Date appears in the Format menu of the spreadsheet. Yet each tool has the File-Edit-Tools-Insert-Window-Help text line series. You move between the menu and the workspace in the same way, and many commands are common to each tool. This similarity speeds the learning process and greatly simplifies integration.

We have already mentioned that most products of the integration process are documents, that is, word processing files. The foundation upon which the end product is built is usually some sort of text. It is just as easy, however, to move records from a database into a spreadsheet to make projections or chart some data. In this case, the end product would not be a document, but a spreadsheet with data arranged in columns and rows. This is the second most common integration task.

You are not limited to just two applications in an integration project. For example, after you move records from a database into a new or existing spreadsheet, you might proceed to create a pie or line graph and insert it into a word processing document for the final product. A graph that visually represents the numbers in a spreadsheet within a word processing file can give your finished document a more professional appearance and make it more effective. Integration thus allows you to use your microcomputer as the ultimate tool for personal productivity.

In this chapter, we will emphasize procedures for moving portions of other files into a word processing document because this is the most common integration task, and also the easiest for a beginner to master. As you will see, you can produce superior presentations with minimal skills.

Working with the Window Command

We mentioned that each file to be used in the integration process is first opened, or loaded into main memory. The Window command lets you move from one open file to another. The open files are listed in the pull-down Window menu in the order that they were opened. Selecting one of the choices makes that file active. The active file displays more brightly and has a double horizontal bar at the top border of its display area, so that you can always distinguish which open file is the active file.

As you open one file after another, the newly opened file occupies the work area, and the previously opened files underlie it. The identifying borders of all open files remain visible, cascading one on top of another. If you would like to see a portion of each open file, *Works* will arrange them on the screen for you. Once you have opened the appropriate files:

- Click on Window-Cascade or Tile.

Works will arrange a display of all files on your screen similar to what *Windows* did in Chapter 2.

You can move and resize each of these windows by using the mouse to drag the pointer across the screen. You have already had experience in Chapters 2 and 8 with maximizing (enlarging the display area) and minimizing (reducing the display area). This involves selecting the Size corner of each window and enlarging or shrinking the outline of the window until it is the size you wish, or holding down the mouse button and dragging the window's corner to the selected area of the screen. The active window will be surrounded by a black border, and the title bar will be highlighted in blue, indicating that the file is ready to be used. With the mouse, you can change the dimensions and location of one window at a time. To confirm the size and position of the window, release the mouse button.

Target File and File Type

One important concept affects all integration: the target (receiving) file determines the data type. When you move figures from a spreadsheet into a word processing document, the spreadsheet figures become text—alphanumeric symbols. They are no longer values that can be calculated and manipulated as if they were still in the spreadsheet file. For example, columns and rows of numbers in a letter to stockholders may look like values, but they are really text, and can no longer be manipulated in calculations. Records and fields moved from a database file also become text, separated by tabs, when you move them into a word processing document. Even a chart, when moved from a spreadsheet into a document, only graphically represents the values present in the cells of the spreadsheet. Therefore any manipulation of values, retrieval of records or fields, or charting needs to be performed in the original application before you move it to another file type. Once you have moved the material into another application, you cannot change formulas, add Time/Date or Currency formats, or change data field types without repeating the entire integration process.

You gain some advantages when an integrated file takes on the properties of the target file. When cells are moved into a word processing document from a spreadsheet, or when records are moved to a spreadsheet from a database, they are arranged as a table in which the columns or fields are separated by tabs. When spreadsheet or database data becomes text, you can use all of the word processing features that were not available to you in the spreadsheet or database menus. You can use different paragraph and margin formats, run the spelling checker and the thesaurus, search and replace, double-space, use many different fonts, create footnotes, and generally concentrate on the appearance of your finished document.

Similarly, if you wish to chart some numeric data from a database, you can move the fields into a spreadsheet, where they become columns of values that can be charted. If you wish to query and easily filter out just certain information from a large payroll spreadsheet, let's say all of the employees who have been with the company longer than ten years, you can move the spreadsheet cells into a database, where they become fields and records, and you can apply a query to the information. The power of integration is simpler to achieve with *Works* because its integrated features allow easy movement between applications.

Specific Uses for Integration

As you have seen, many occasions warrant preparation of an integrated file. Sometimes it is the only way to get the information you want together in one place; sometimes it is simply the easiest way. We will discuss only the most common uses of integration. As you become more proficient at the integration process, you will find more and more uses for it.

Personalized Form Letters

Probably the most common use of integration today is the preparation of **form letters** to be sent to persons on a mailing list that is usually stored in a database file. When you prepare a boilerplate document and insert fields from a database in appropriate places to personalize each letter, you are using **mail merge**. Each letter that is sent out contains the same basic information, supplemented by unique information such as name, address, and so forth to personalize the mailing. Much of the business bulk mail that advertises products is mail-merged. It can be so sophisticated and smoothly done that it seems like a personal appeal. This is one of the most useful integrated tasks that a beginning computer user can learn.

Sometimes merged documents are sent only to a portion of the names in a database. In such a selective mail merge, only the records that meet a certain query criterion are merged with the boilerplate document. For example, if you are sending letters only to one city, or only to clients with balances due, or perhaps only to alumni who have contributed to a scholarship fund in the past, you are making use of selective mail merge. You query the database to filter out the records that meet your criteria, and merge only those records with your boilerplate document. With *Works 3.0 for Windows*, you can quickly apply a query that has been previously saved in the database program, then merge the database with the boilerplate letter and very easily produce personalized, custom mailings. In addition, the Database Designer, Letterhead, and Form Letter features of WorksWizards make creating form letters a simple task.

Mailing Labels

Although some database report generators offer label reports, it is very easy to prepare a label template in a word processing application and to merge that template with a database file to produce sheets of mailing labels. The logic is the same as in a mail merge, but the document in this case is just a label with name and address placeholders. The *Works* Envelopes and Labels tool, located in the Tools menu, allows you to print several labels across a sheet with the same format. You choose how many labels to print across and down the page, and *Works 3.0 for Windows* automatically sets the printer for you.

A refinement of this integration task is to sort the database by Zip code first, then print the labels in that order for sorted, bulk mail labels. The U.S. Post Office requires that you presort letters to qualify for comparatively cheap bulk mail rates. If you sort the database first, and then merge the labels in order, the job is already done for you.

The process for printing labels in *Works* is:

1. Open the database you want to use.
2. Set up a word processing document with database placeholders, as shown in the mail merge directions on page 483.
3. Set up label dimensions in the Mailing Labels area of the Envelopes and Labels window in the Print menu of the word processing application.
4. Load the appropriate labels in your printer and put it on line.
5. Preview and/or test the labels in the Mailing Labels menu.
6. Print the labels with File-Print-Print Merge in the word processing Print menu.

Envelopes

Almost all printers, from dot matrix to ink jet to laser printers, allow you to print envelopes. Although you can purchase envelopes already mounted on tractor-feed strips for dot matrix printers, they are very expensive. Laser and ink jet printers are page printers and always use single envelopes. Most dot matrix printers allow **cut sheet feeding** of envelopes (moving single sheets with a friction feed mechanism instead of tractor feed) if the software allows for a pause between printing each envelope. *Works* allows you to pause between printing to feed another envelope into the printer to make mail merge with envelopes possible by taking the printer on and off line. This approach produces a more personalized mailing, even though it will take more time, than simply printing many labels and affixing them to envelopes before mailing.

Presentations and Reports

Formal presentations and longer report documents can also benefit from the integration process. You can prepare a report with both text and columns of numbers that are totaled and summarized; you can even include several different charts, all appropriately sized, with borders and distinctive print fonts. Headers and footers can appear on each page, and margins can allow for binding.

You can produce a high-quality document from several different applications relatively simply with the *Works 3.0 for Windows* package. In today's competitive and technologically advanced markets, appearance is often the difference between a presentation that is well-received and one that is not. Today you can produce a fairly sophisticated document that only a professional printer could have produced a decade ago.

Customized Art Products

In Chapter 5, you learned about combining text and graphics in desktop publishing, and you learned that the clip art and custom drawing modules in *Works 3.0 for Windows* offer some of the same functions that desktop publishing packages offer. Also, in Chapter 8, when you mastered charting, you saw that *Works* allows three-dimensional and combination graphing similar to what many presentation graphics programs provide. The ability to integrate highly formatted text and special graphics into a finished document, and to add personal artwork as well, allows you to produce customized material that rivals the products of desktop publishing packages.

While *Works* does not offer the ability to produce a true multimedia product, with sound and video, it does allow you to approach a rapidly emerging standard in computer-generated art products. The paintbrush tools within the newest software programs have provided drawing tools and electronic sketch pads. The Word Art, Drawing, and Clip Art modules of *Works 3.0 for Windows* also allow you to create a highly customized and individual product. More and more, mere text is not enough for today's readers. We are moving from a text-based culture to one that focuses on pictures and icons. Compare the publications of a generation ago to current publications and you will see the dramatic change that has taken place in our culture. The move to multimedia and electronically generated art products is accelerated by the availability of the electronic paintbrush programs and color printers. You have these same art tools at your disposal in *Works*, and their output is easier to combine with other files because of the integrated nature of the program.

Additional Works Features

Works 3.0 for Windows has several features that can make integrated document production easier and faster, with better looking results.

WorksWizards

The 3.0 version of *Works* introduced some added features to help you accomplish certain tasks more easily. The **WorksWizards** program allows you to complete some integration tasks much more easily than you ever could before, even with an integrated program. It does this by asking you questions. If you read the screen (RTS) carefully, you can accomplish remarkably complex integration tasks by simply supplying the answers to the questions. WorksWizards includes several specific tools including: Address Book, Business Contacts, Business Inventory, Customer Profile, File Organizer, Footnote, Form Letter, Home Inventory, Letterhead, Membership Tracker, Quick Database, and Student Profile.

Letterhead Designer helps you to create personalized stationery by inserting clip art, borders, and custom pictures. You can easily create your own logo and reuse it as often as you like.

Database Designer helps you to create an address book, an inventory, or a special collection by entering names, addresses, phone numbers, and other information you want to store.

Form Letters provides a document created in the word processor that uses information from an existing database file or address book to create individual letters. This simplifies the mail merge process we discussed earlier. Automating the process allows the beginning user to proceed without detailed knowledge of database concepts and merge techniques.

Footnote Generator is a new option that organizes and presents citations in any of several accepted styles. You provide only the raw information.

File Organizer will search your directories for a specific file; it also allows you to copy files, rename them, and so forth without resorting to DOS or *Windows* commands. Many stand-alone applications have been developed to perform similar feats in the past few years. The File Manager in *Windows*, and the *Magellan* program perform similar operations.

AutoStart Templates

A **template** is a document that contains predefined formats such as margin and tab settings in the word processing application, labels and formulas in the spreadsheet, and field names in the database. You learned in Chapters 6 and 7 that spreadsheet templates are shells with labels and formulas, but no specific values; recall that you can purchase all kinds of special purpose templates rather than creating your own.

AutoStart templates are of different kinds. You can save a template and use it every time you need its settings without having to enter them again. Some of the software exercises in earlier chapters used these templates. The AutoStart templates come with their own set of cue cards to guide your use of them. When you use a template to complete a file for later reuse, *Works* refers to it as a **master document**. Other programs may refer to these files as boilerplates, style sheets, or library files.

Works 3.0 for Windows offers many predefined templates, or you can create your own. It groups templates together, and defines categories within each group. Tables 13.1, 13.2, and 13.3 list the templates by group and category.

The Custom group of templates stores the templates you create. When you use a *Works* template to construct your own version of a template, it is stored in this group, on the hard disk where your *Works* program resides.

Table 13.1 *Works 3.0 for Windows* Business Templates

Application	Category	Template
Database	Billing	Accounts receivable
Spreadsheet		Sales invoice
Word processing		Past due statement
Spreadsheet		Service invoice
Spreadsheet		Account statement
Spreadsheet	Planning	Budget
Spreadsheet		Breakdown analysis
Spreadsheet		Cash flow statement
Spreadsheet		Personal financial statement
Spreadsheet		Income statement
Word processing	Documents	FAX cover sheet
Word processing		Three-column newsletter
Spreadsheet	Expenses	Mortgage and loan analysis
Spreadsheet		Purchase order

Table 13.2 *Works 3.0 for Windows* Personal Templates

Application	Category	Template
Database	Addresses	Membership roster
Database		Personal directory
Word processing	Document	Three-column newsletter
Word processing		Resume
Database	Household management	Book collection
Database		CD/tape collection
Database		Household inventory
Database		Recipes
Database		Video collection
Spreadsheet	Personal finance	Mortgage and loan analysis
Database		Credit cards
Database		Check register
Spreadsheet		Personal financial statement

Insert a Picture

Another feature of *Works 3.0 for Windows* is the ability to insert a picture—a graph, screen image, clip art, or your own drawing—into a word processing document. As you have already learned, **clip art** consists of predefined pictures that are ready for insertion into documents. *Works* furnishes a number of these pictures, as do most independent word processing programs. *Works 3.0* accepts several file formats including: PC Paintbrush (files with .pix extensions), clip art from other *Works* versions (.pcx extensions), Tag Image File format (.tif extensions) and encapsulated PostScript files (.EPS extensions). After inserting a pic-

Table 13.3 *Works 3.0 for Windows* Education Templates

Application	Category	Template
Database	Classroom management	Book collection
Database		CD/tape collection
Database		Student records
Database		Video collection
Spreadsheet	Productivity	Grade book
Word processing		Three-column newsletter
Database		Personal directory
Word processing		Resume
Spreadsheet		Class schedule
Word processing	Testing	Multiple choice
Word processing		True/false test
Word processing		Essay test

Table 13.4 *Works* Clip Art

bells.wmf	santa.wmf	recycle.wmf
camping.wmf	cakeslic.wmf	soccer.wmf
celtic.wmf	cat.wmf	splat.wmf
compass.wmf	checkmrk.wmf	spring.wm
disk.wmf	deco.wmf	star.wmf
evergren.wmf	drink.wmf	summer.wmf
firework.wmf	fall.wmf	sun.wmf
hardhat.wmf	globe.wmf	tropics.wmf
lightblb.wmf	heart.wmf	wheelchr.wmf
music.wmf	luggage.wmf	winter.wmf
phone.wmf	notes.wmf	
pushpin.wmf	present.wmf	

ture, you can change its size, alignment, and placement, and the space around it. The clip art provided by *Works 3.0 for Windows* has the file extension .wmf. The files are listed in Table 13.4.

To insert a clip art selection in a word processing document:

- Click on Insert-Clip Art
- Click on the category in the Gallery list from which you wish to select.
- Scroll to select the picture you want.
- Click on OK.

The picture is inserted at the spot your insertion point indicated. You may use the picture as it is, or you may edit the clip art by copying it from the Edit menu, then using the draw program described below. You may size the clip art to suit you, or drag it to another location. As you learned in Chapter 5, you can wrap text around clip art.

Microsoft Draw

This is the separate drawing, or paintbrush, module that is included with *Works 3.0 for Windows*. You can create custom artwork using a palette of colors and drawing tools. You can modify the clip art explained above, or make your own drawings. This module is very similar to the Paintbrush application in the Accessories window of the *Windows* interface. However, using Microsoft *Draw* saves you the trouble of switching from one independent software application to another; you do everything within *Works*.

The program presents a palette of colors, a set of drawing tools, and a special menu that allows you to manipulate your creations in many different ways. You are limited to inserting a drawing from this module into either a word processing document, or a database form screen. The tools for Microsoft *Draw* are listed in Table 13.5.

Table 13.5 Microsoft *Draw* Tools

Arrow	Zoom
Line	Ellipse/Circle
Arc	Rounded Rectangle/Square
Free form	Rectangle/Square
Text	

To create a custom drawing in Microsoft *Draw*, position your insertion point in the document or form where you wish the drawing to appear, then:

- Click on Insert-Drawing.

The *Draw* window appears, with the tools on the left and the color palette below.

- Click on a tool, then click within the frame and begin creating with that tool.
- Click on another tool to change shapes or figures.

When you finish drawing:

- Click on File-Return to Document (name).
- Click on OK to Update Document.
- Click on Yes.

The drawing is inserted into the word processing document or the database form.

Moving Between Applications Within Works

In this section we will explain the procedures for moving between *Works* modules in order to create integrated products like those we have described.

From Databases into Word Processing Documents and Spreadsheets

We have said that information from a *Works* database file is copied to another *Works* tool as a table. When you copy the data to the word processor or the communications module, fields are separated by tab stops and each record ends with a paragraph mark. If you copy the data to a spreadsheet, each field appears in a column and each record defines a row. You use the List view when copying from the database to another *Works* tool.

Whether you wish to copy certain records, or even portions of records, to another spot in the same database, to another database, or to a word processing document or spreadsheet, the process is the same. If the material to be copied includes entire records, you may use the Select Record command in the Edit menu while you are in the List (multiple-record) view. (Remember that the Toolbar icon can move you quickly between the two views.)

You can copy only certain fields of certain records, in the same way. After you select the fields or records to copy, you use the Copy command in the Edit menu:

- Select the cells to copy.
- Click on Edit-Copy.
- Switch windows to another *Works* file using the Window command or by clicking with the mouse in another window.
- Move the cursor bar to the new location.
- Click on Edit-Paste.

The database records, or parts of records, will be moved into the document or the spreadsheet.

From Charts into Word Processing Documents

You can easily insert a chart that you created with the spreadsheet into a word processing document and print the result. Because *Works* gets the chart from an open spreadsheet file when you print the document, your chart will always reflect the latest changes made in the spreadsheet. Both the word processing document and the spreadsheet file must be open to insert a chart.

To insert a chart into a document:

- Open the appropriate spreadsheet file.
- Click on Window.
- Select the appropriate word processing document.
- Move the cursor to the desired location.

- Click on Edit-Insert Chart.
- Select the appropriate spreadsheet file.
- Select the appropriate chart.
- Click on OK.

The chart will be inserted into the document at its original size.

You can now resize this embedded object, if you wish. To change the size of a chart:

- Click on a corner of the chart until the border and handles appear.
- Click on a handle until the resize arrow appears.
- Hold down the mouse button and drag the object to the desired size, then release the button.

  OR
- With the border and handles visible, click on Format.
- Click on Picture/Object.
- In the size window that appears, type in the new height and width measurements.
- Click on OK.

The object will be resized.

When you print the word processing file, the chart will print with the document. You should preview the finished product before printing. Once you have inserted a chart, you can select the chart and move it, or even delete it, as needed. To insert a different chart, repeat the chart insertion steps above.

Inserting Pictures into Word Processing Documents

To add a picture to a document:

- Place the insertion point at the desired position.
- Select Insert-Clip Art.
- If necessary, move to the correct category.
- Click on the desired picture.
- Click on OK.

The picture will be inserted at the point indicated by the insertion point. You can size it in the same manner as a chart. After inserting the picture, you can change its size either by changing the height and width measurements or by specifying a percentage change, such as a 200 percent increase, or a reduction to half size (by specifying 50 percent). You do this in the Format-Picture/Object menu. When you print the document, *Works* will size the picture to fit the space defined by the measurements you have specified.

You can use the Word Art option to wrap text around charts and pictures, as you did in Chapter 5. If you include a border in a chart or picture before moving it into the document or database form, the task of setting off the artwork from surrounding material will already be accomplished.

From Spreadsheets to Other Works Tools

You can copy spreadsheet cell contents to a word processor document or to a database file. The spreadsheet data is copied as a table; when going to a word processing file, the cells are separated by tab stops and each row ends with a paragraph mark. If spreadsheet cells go into a database file, each column defines a field and each row defines a record.

To copy spreadsheet data:

- Select the cell or range to copy.
- Select Edit-Copy.
- Choose an open *Works* file from the Window menu or click on the desired window in the cascade or tile arrangement.
- Place the insertion point in the desired location.
- Click on Edit-Paste.

Creating Form Letters

A form letter is a standard letter that is sent to any number of people on a mailing list. As we have noted, this is often called *mail merge*. Preparing such a mailing is simple with *Works*. First, if you do not have a database file containing the names and addresses that you want, you need to set up one. You can do this with the WorksWizards, the *Works* templates, or by defining the database and entering the records through the database tool.

On the word processor, draft your standard letter. In the word processing document, you simply insert placeholders at each place where you want database information to appear. Each placeholder represents one field of a database file, such as a Name field, or a Street Address field. Once you've inserted a placeholder, you can copy, move, or delete it as you revise your draft letter. You can format both text and placeholders by selecting them and choosing commands from the Format menu. When you are done you print the form letter file using the Print-Form Letters command from the Print menu.

To create a form letter file:

- Design and create a database file.
- Enter the individual data into the records.
- Create a word processing file containing the letter's standard text.
- Move the insertion point to the location for the first item of variable data.
- Click on Insert-Database Field.
- Select a database.
- Select the desired field.
- Click on the Insert button.

- Repeat as desired for other fields.
- Click on the Close button.

Placeholders will be inserted in the word processor file. You may repeat these steps for each item of variable data that you wish to insert in the form letter, then:

- Click on File-Save As and assign an appropriate file name.

Printing Form Letters

Works will print one copy of a form letter for each displayed record in the database file. To print a form letter:

- Open the database file and the word processor file.
- Click on File-Print.
- The Print Merge option should be marked; mark it if it is not.
- In the Databases box, select the desired file.
- Click on OK.

To print just one copy of the form letter with the database field placeholders:

- Select File-Print.
- Click to turn off the Merge option.
- Click on the OK button.

To cancel printing:

- Press ESC.

You can also use WorksWizards to create a form letter:

- Click on WorksWizards.
- Scroll to find the desired tool.
- Click on OK.
- Follow the screen directions specific to the chosen file.
- Save as a new file.

At this point the WorksWizards file will be copied to a personal custom file; you can add, edit, move, copy, and delete material. You can go to the different views, and you can create a report if the file is a database file.

If you wish to use one of the form letter templates that *Works* provides, such as the memo template, it is a simple process. To use a template to create a new document, from the Startup menu:

- Click on Use a Template.
- Select the type of group and category.
- Select the specific template.
- Click on OK.

A new file named word1.wps or data1.wdb will be opened with all the text and settings defined by the template.

- Insert and delete material, as appropriate.
- Save the file with a new name.

You may wish to create individualized templates and store them in your personal library of master templates. To create a new template:

- Click on New and Recent documents.

A new file will be created. To insert a template into it:

- Click on File-Templates.
- Select the appropriate template.
- Enter your information in new template.
- Click on File-Save As.
- Click on the Template button.
- Type in a new name for the newly created custom template.
- Click on OK.

Works adds the new template you have created to the available templates. The next time you wish to use this template, you can access it from the Startup menu, or from the File-Templates menu:

- Click on File-Templates.
- Select Custom from the template group.
- Select the new template from the list of specific custom templates displayed.
- Click on OK.

Your custom template will be open, and you may use it to design your form letter, or any other type of file you wish.

Moving Between Other Programs and Works

As you learned in Chapter 2, you can import the files that you create with other programs, such as *Lotus 1-2-3*, into *Works*. You can also save *Works* files in formats that will allow you to export to those other programs.

When you open a file from another spreadsheet or database application, *Works* recognizes fields or cells (separated by either commas or tabs) and records or rows (separated by carriage returns). To open a text file from another program:

- Click on File-Open Existing File.
- In the File to Open box, type the file name and extension of the text file you want to open.

  OR

- Scroll through the File Types window until you reach the type of file you wish to see.
- Click on the proper type.

The File Names window will display all files of the type you chose on the current directory.

- Click on the file you wish to open.
- Click on OK.

Works will import the file, giving you a message that it is being converted to a *Works* file in the best manner possible. In conversion to the database or spreadsheet, *Works* assumes that the first line of the opened file contains the first row or record, rather than column labels or field names. If you have labels or fields names in that first position, they will appear as records or rows.

The name of the *Lotus* file will appear in the File Names box.

- Select the proper file
- Click on OK.

By saving a *Works* file as a text, or ASCII, file you can use it with many other programs—not only word processors, but other database and spreadsheet programs, as well. You have already seen in Chapter 12 how convenient it is to upload and download text files in computer communications.

When you save a *Works* spreadsheet or database file as a text file, the cell contents are retained as values, not as formulas. For example, if you type the number *3* in a cell formatted as Currency with two decimal places, then $3.00 is displayed in the cell and retained in a text file. If the display of $3.00 is the result of a formula, such as =B1+B2, only the value $3.00 is retained in the text file, not the formula. In spreadsheet and database text files, the contents of fields or cells are separated by commas, and the contents of rows or records are separated by carriage returns and line feeds.

In a text file, the *Works* error values, labels, and numbers in the Currency, Percent, or Time/Date formats are enclosed in double quotation marks ("); numbers in General, Fixed, Exponential, or True/False formats are not. This is because most database programs, including *dBASE*, recognize numbers only in General, Fixed, Exponential, or True/False formats. Spreadsheet column designators and database field names are not retained in text files.

To save a *Works* spreadsheet or database file as a text file:

- Choose File-Save As.
- Select Text.
- Type the appropriate file name.
- Click on OK.
- Click on OK again to accept the loss of formatting.

The text file will be saved on your disk. Your original file is still displayed and is not replaced or altered.

INTEGRATION TUTORIAL

In the following exercises you will (1) select the Resume template and enter your individual information, (2) create a new letterhead template composed of a piece of clip art and your name and address, (3) create a database file using WorksWizards to store names and addresses for your application letter, and (4) generate job application letters by merging your new letterhead with the database file.

Template

1. Start *Works.*
2. From the Startup menu, click on Use a Template.

   The Use a Template menu displays, as shown in Figure 13.2.

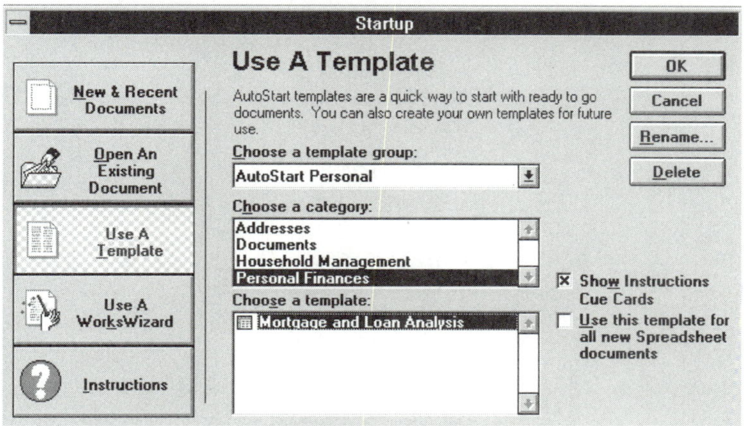

Figure 13.2

The Template Menu

3. In the Choose a template group option, click on the arrow and select AutoStart Personal.
4. In the Choose a Category option, click on Documents.
5. In the Choose a Template option, click on Resume.
6. Click on OK.
7. Before you continue, save the file as resume94.
8. Print the Resume so you'll have it for reference.

   Your printout should look similar to that in Figure 13.3. (Note: If the cue cards function is activated you may want to close it.)
9. Replace the name, address, objectives, work history, and so on with your own data, as appropriate. If any of the items aren't applicable, select them and delete them.

   (Hint: Select the text, then type your information to replace it.)

Figure 13.3

Resume Template

Your Name
Street Address
City, Prov/State, Postal Code
Phone Number

OBJECTIVE

In this section describe the job you are applying for, your employment goals, your personal strengths, reasons why you feel qualified for the position.

WORK HISTORY

Describe your last job (the company, your position, responsibilities, etc.)
Type the beginning and ending dates
Tell about your work and accomplishments.
Describe your job before that
Type the beginning and ending dates
Tell about your work and accomplishments.
And the job before that
Type the beginning and ending dates
Tell about your work and accomplishments.
And the job before that
Type the beginning and ending dates
Tell about your work and accomplishments.

EDUCATION

Latest Certificate or degree
Name of school and accomplishments.
Training before that
Name of school and accomplishments.
Training before that
Name of school and accomplishments.

AWARDS/COMMUNITY SERVICE

Describe personal accomplishments in community clubs, church, service groups, etc.
Other personal accomplishments.
Other personal accomplishments.

10. Save, print, and close the file.

    The new document is saved as a regular file and the resume template remains intact, to be reused another time. You will now create a letterhead for your own personal use.

11. Click to create a new word processing file.

    To insert a centered clip art picture:

12. Click on the Center icon.
13. Click on Insert.

    The Insert menu displays, as shown in Figure 13.4.

14. Click on Clip Art.
15. Click on the picture of the disk-OK.

Figure 13.4

The Insert Menu

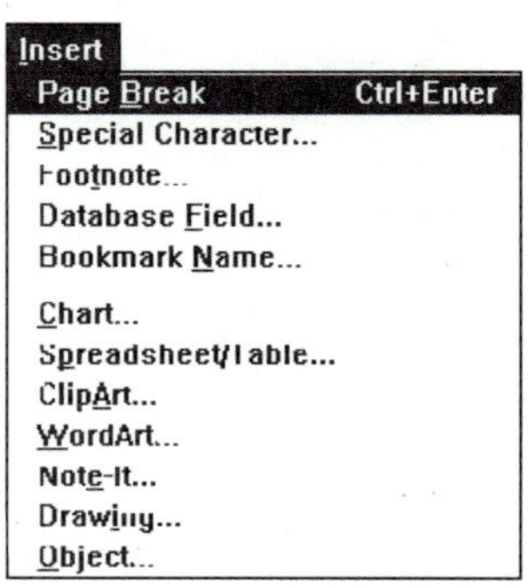

16. Move the insertion point to the right of the disk picture.
17. Press ENTER twice.
18. Select a 14-point or 16-point font. (Remember the fonts you can use depend on your printer. Adjust your choice as necessary.)
19. Mark the Bold option.
20. Click on OK.
21. In all caps on three lines, type your first and last names, your street address, city, state, and Zip code.
22. Press ENTER twice.
23. Click on the Bold icon and change the font back to the default.
24. Enter the date code (Insert-Special Character-Print long Date).
25. Press ENTER five times.
26. Click on the Left-Align icon.

    You will save this work first as a regular file on your own diskette, and then as a template on the hard drive of the machine you are working on. (Check with your instructor to see if your school allows this.)
27. Select File-Save As.
28. Type A:LTRHEAD or B:LTRHEAD.
29. Select File-Save As again.
30. Click on the Template box.

    The Save As Template box displays.
31. In the Template Name box, type **LTRHEAD** then click on OK.

    Because other students may have done this same assignment, the message "Replace existing template?" may display. If it does:
32. Press ENTER.
33. Close any files that remain open.

If you return to the Startup menu, click on Use a Template, and click on Custom in the template group to see LTRHEAD added as a template.

WorksWizards Database

To create a database file using WorksWizards:

1. Click on Use a WorksWizard from the Startup menu.

   The Use a WorksWizard list box displays, as shown in Figure 13.5.
2. Click on Business Contacts.
3. Click on OK.

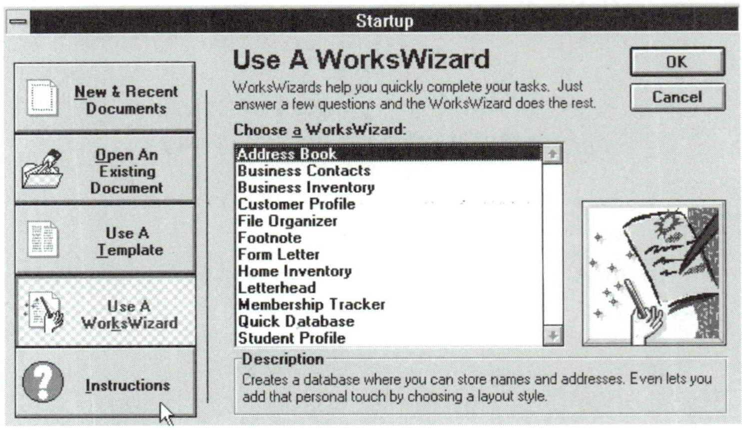

Figure 13.5

The Use A WorksWizard List Box

4. The Business Contacts Welcome menu displays, as shown in Figure 13.6.

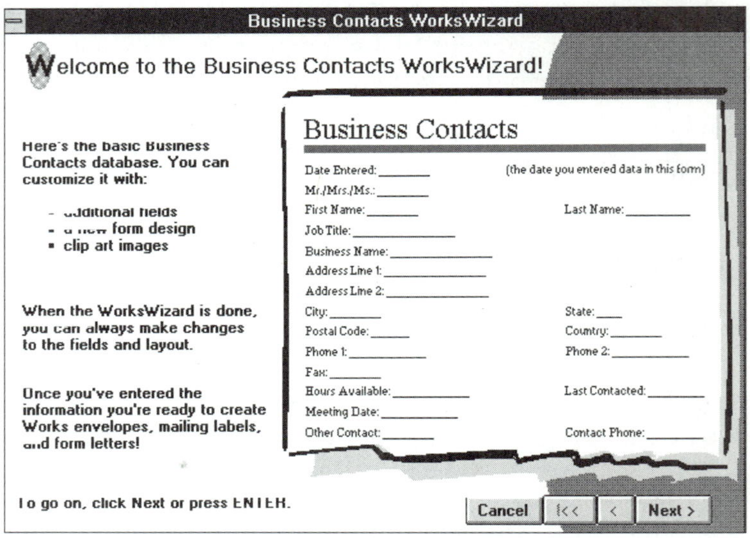

Figure 13.6

The Business Contacts Welcome Menu

5. Click on Next or press ENTER.
6. Click on the Comments box.
7. Click on Next.
8. Click on Cubed (for the database style)-Next.
9. Accept the option to add Art to your form on the left by clicking on Next.
10. Click on the arrows to see more clip art and select the clip art you desire.
11. Click on Next.

12. Click on Create.

    After a few seconds you may get a dialog box; click on OK. Your screen should look similar to that in Figure 13.7.

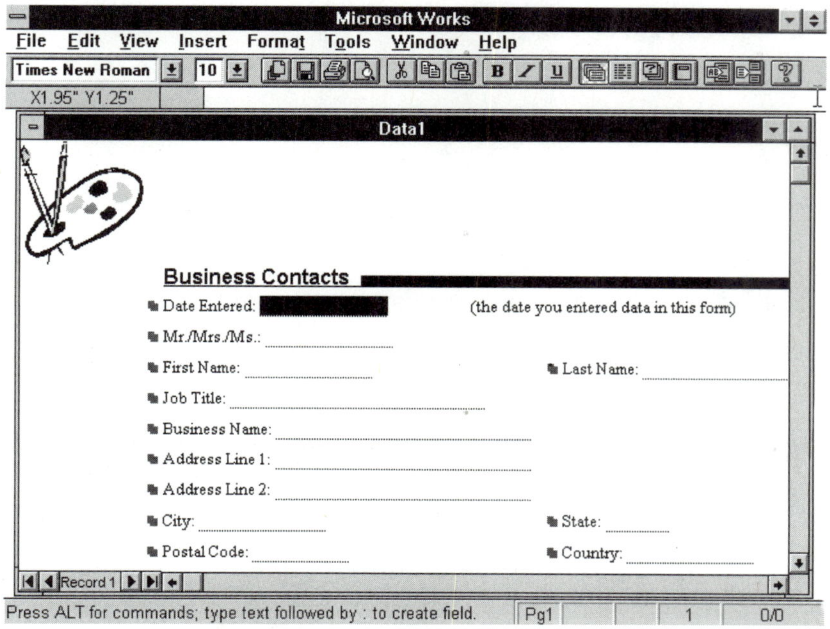

Figure 13.7

Business Contacts Database Shell

13. Save the file as buscont.

    A .wdb extension will be added as the file becomes a database file.

At this point your file becomes a standard database file and you can add, delete, move, copy, and edit fields; you can go to the Form, List, Report, and Query views. You have created a custom database in a few quick steps with the aid of WorksWizards.

14. Enter the records in Table 13.6, pressing TAB to go to the next record.

Table.13.6 Data for Business Contacts Database

Record 1: 12–25–94, Mr., Steve, Sundahl, Personnel Director, IBM Corporation, 727 N. Waco, Wichita, KS, 67203, USA, (316)266–8800, (316)555–4253, 8 a.m.–5 p.m., never, none, none, none, Job involves a lot of traveling

Record 2: 10–31–94, Ms., Elizabeth, Johnson, Marketing Director, NCR Corporation, 4124 S. Washington, Littleton, CO, 80122, USA, (303)770–2344, (303)324–5593, 7 a.m.–12 p.m., never, none, none, none, Good chances for advancement

Record 3: 11–24–94, Mrs., Jane, Beals, MIS Director, Amdahl Corporation, 3445 W. Matilda Avenue, Sunnyvale, CA, 94087, USA, (415)933–3555, (415)533–5532 cellular, (415)355–5542, 9 a.m.–4 p.m., 11–24–93, 1–5–94, Mr. Bill Snyder, (415)554–3342, Fly to California for interview

15. Save buscont.wdb when you finish entering records, leaving it open.

    You will now print the three records to check for accuracy, after changing the margins to zero and the orientation to Landscape to get as many fields on a page as possible.

16. Click on List view.
17. Click on File-Page Setup.
18. In the Margins area, enter 0" for all margins.
19. Click on the Source, Size, and Orientation choice.
20. Click on Landscape Orientation-OK.
21. Click on the Print icon.

    If you get an error message stating "Form too wide, Print anyway?" press ENTER for OK. Your file should look similar to that in Figure 13.8. Do not close the file.

Figure 13.8

Business Contacts

(Page 1)

12-25-94	Mr.	Steve	Sundahl	Personnel Director	IBM Corporation	727 N. Waco	Wichita	KS	67203	USA
10-31-94	Ms.	Elizabeth	Johnson	Marketing Director	NCR Corporation	4124 S. Washington	Littleton	CO	80122	USA
11-24-94	Mrs.	Jane	Beals	MIS Director	Amdahl Corporation	3445 W. Matilda Avenue	Sunnyvale	CA	94087	USA

(Page 2)

(316) 266-8800		(316) 555-4253	8 a.m.-5 p.m.	never	none	none	none
(303) 770-2344		(303) 324-5593	7 a.m.-12 p.m.	never	none	none	none
(415) 933-3555	(415) 533-553	(415) 355-5542	9 a.m.-4 p.m.	11-24-93	1-5-94	Mr. Bill Snyder	(415) 554-3342

(Page 3)

job involves lot of traveling
Good chances for advancem
Fly to California for interview

Form Letters Now you will integrate the data from your buscont.wdb database file with a form letter to accomplish a mail merge. After inserting the fields you need from your database file into your letter, you can merge the three records from your buscont.wdb file with the letter and then print the result. To begin, you will create a form letter in your letterhead template to send with your resume to prospective employers.

1. Click on File-Templates.
2. In the Choose a template group, click on Custom.
3. Click on LTRHEAD-OK.

   If the letterhead template that displays is not yours, return to the Template section of this chapter's tutorial and create one of your own.

4. Press ENTER six times after the date code.
5. Click on Insert-Database Field.

   The Insert Field box displays, as shown in Figure 13.9. (If it does not display, click on Database and select buscont.wdb.)

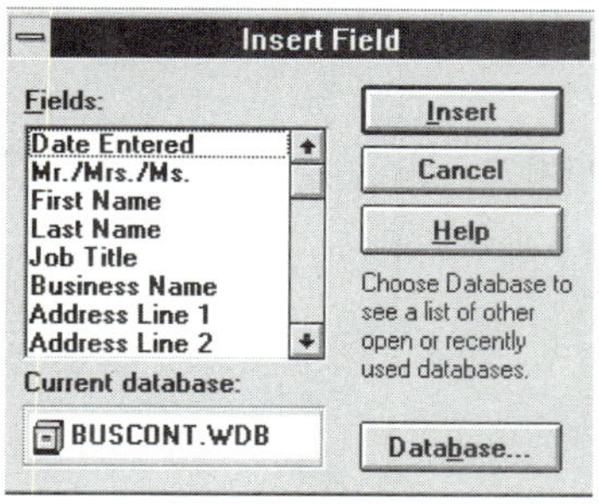

Figure 13.9

The Insert Field Dialog Box

6. Click on Mr./Mrs./Ms.
7. Click on Insert.
8. Click on Close.

   The first field appears on your screen, surrounded by placeholders.
9. Press the spacebar once.
10. Click on Insert-Database Field-First Name-Insert-Close.
11. Press the spacebar once.
12. Insert the Last Name field.
13. Press ENTER.
14. Insert the Business Name field and press ENTER.
15. Insert the Address Line 1 field and press ENTER.
16. Insert the City field followed by a comma and space once.
17. Insert the State field and two spaces.
18. Insert the Postal Code field and press ENTER twice.
19. Type **Dear** and space once.
20. Insert the Mr./Mrs./Ms. field and space once.
21. Insert the Last Name field.
22. Type **:**(a colon).
23. Press ENTER twice.
24. Type the following material:

    After considering many different companies in the information systems arena, I have narrowed down my selection to three. I am sending you my resume for your review and I will be calling you in a few days to see when we can set up an appointment to discuss possible career opportunities with your firm. I graduated with a 3.95 grade point average from [your school] **and feel I would be a great asset to your company.**
25. Press ENTER twice.

26. Type **Sincerely yours,**
27. Press ENTER four times.
28. Type your name.

    Don't forget to spell check.
29. Save the master form letter as appltrs.
30. Click on File-Print.

    Your form should look similar to Figure 13.10. To check a mail merged letter first before you print:

Figure 13.10

The Application Form Letter

YOUR FIRST AND LAST NAME
YOUR STREET ADDRESS
CITY, STATE ZIP

July 08, 1994

«Mr./Mrs./Ms.» «First Name» «Last Name»
«Business Name»
«Address Line 1»
«City», «State» «Postal Code»

Dear «Mr./Mrs./Ms.» «Last Name»:

After considering many different companies in the information systems arena, I have narrowed down my selection to three. I am sending you my resume for your review and I will be calling you in a few days to see when we can set up an appointment to discuss possible career opportunities with your firm. I graduated with a 3.95 grade point average from **Your school** and feel I would be a great asset to your company.

Sincerely yours,

Your name

31. Click on the Print Preview icon.

    The Choose Database option box appears, as shown in Figure 13.11. Your screen may differ from ours.

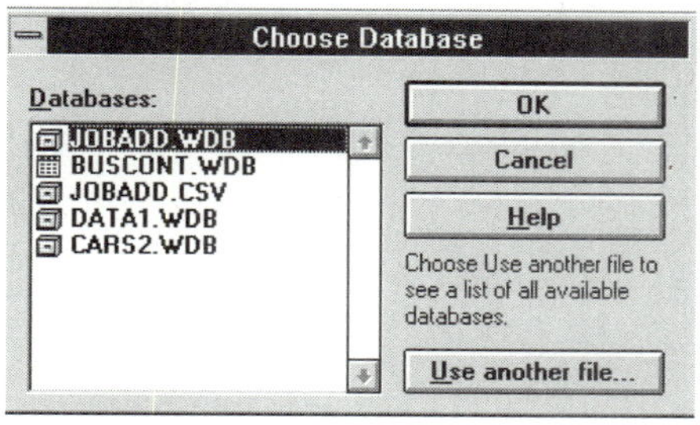

Figure 13.11

The Choose Database Option Box

32. Click on buscont.wdb-OK.

    If everything looks right:

33. Click on Cancel.
34. Click on File-Print.
35. Click to mark the Print merge option.
36. Click on OK from the Print dialog box.
37. Select buscont.wdb-OK.

    An individual letter with a specific name and address prints for every record in buscont.wdb. Your documents should look similar to the one in Figure 13.12.

38. Close any open files.

Integration

For your final integration exercise, you want to create a graphics portfolio of sample documents. You will use the WorksWizards footnote feature and create a document with a couple of samples of clip art and a drawing you create yourself. To accomplish all this, you will create a new word processing document with a title page and insert documents into it.

1. Create a new word processing file.
2. Click on Format-Font & Style.
3. Select a proportional 14-point or 16-point font (if your printer is capable) and mark Bold.
4. Press ENTER 15 times.
5. Center and type (double spacing after each line):

    Works Portfolio

    by

    Your First and Last Name

Figure 13.12

A Form Letter

YOUR FIRST AND LAST NAME
YOUR STREET ADDRESS
CITY, STATE ZIP

July 08, 1994

Mr. Steve Sundahl
IBM Corporation
727 N. Waco
Wichita, KS 67203

Dear Mr. Sundahl:

After considering many different companies in the information systems arena, I have narrowed down my selection to three. I am sending you my resume for your review and I will be calling you in a few days to see when we can set up an appointment to discuss possible career opportunities with your firm. I graduated with a 3.95 grade point average from **Your school** and feel I would be a great asset to your company.

Sincerely yours,

Your name

6. Press ENTER.
7. Return to your normal font and left justification.
8. Save the file as portfoli.
9. Press CTRL + ENTER to create a page break.
10. Press ENTER twice.
11. Open the file abstract.wps from your student data diskette.
12. Click on Edit-Select All.

13. Click on Edit-Copy.
14. Click on Window.
15. Click on 1portfoli.wps.

    Be sure your insertion point is two lines from the top of the new page.
16. Click on Edit-Paste.
17. Press CTRL+END to move to the bottom of the document. Place the insertion point just after the sentence that ends: ". . . academicians."
18. Click on File-WorksWizards.
19. Click on Footnote-OK.

    The Wizards Footnote screen displays, as shown in Figure 13.13.

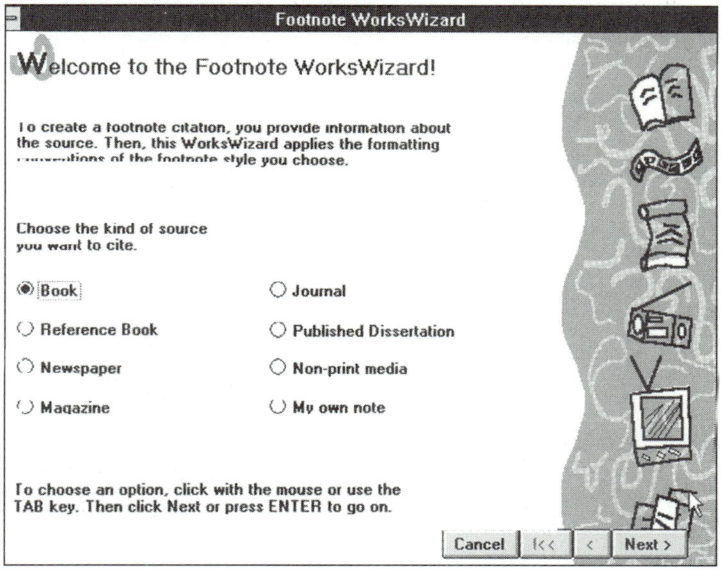

Figure 13.13

The WorksWizard Footnote Screen

20. Click on Journal.
21. Click on Next.

    The Journal screen displays as shown in Figure 13.14. Type the following material in the designated text boxes (noticing the tips that appear at the bottom of the screen as you click in successive boxes):

    Title of Article: **Presentation Graphics Theory and Use**

    Name of Journal: **Collegiate Microcomputer**

    Author: **Edward M. Cooper**

    Date of Publication: **Spring, 1992**

    Volume/Issue No: **Volume 10 Number 1**

    Pages: **15–19**

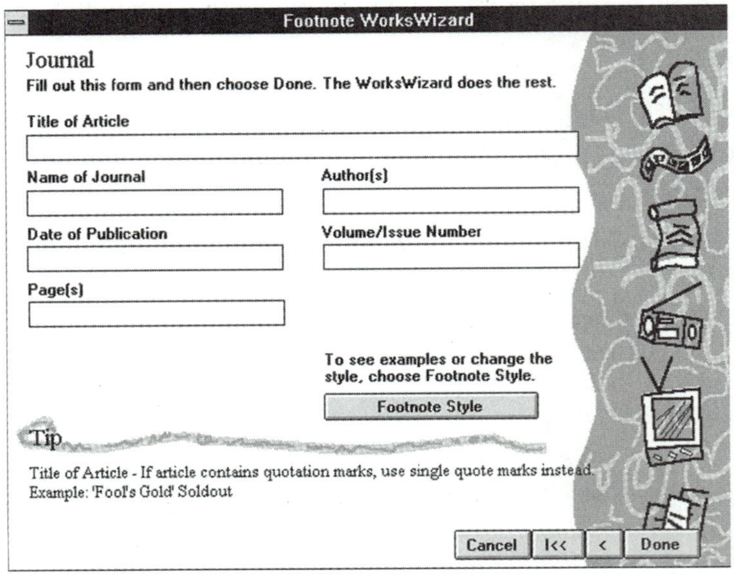

Figure 13.14

The Journal Screen

22. Click on Done.

 Your screen should look similar to that in Figure 13.15. It is divided into two sections and you don't know how to close the footnote screen.

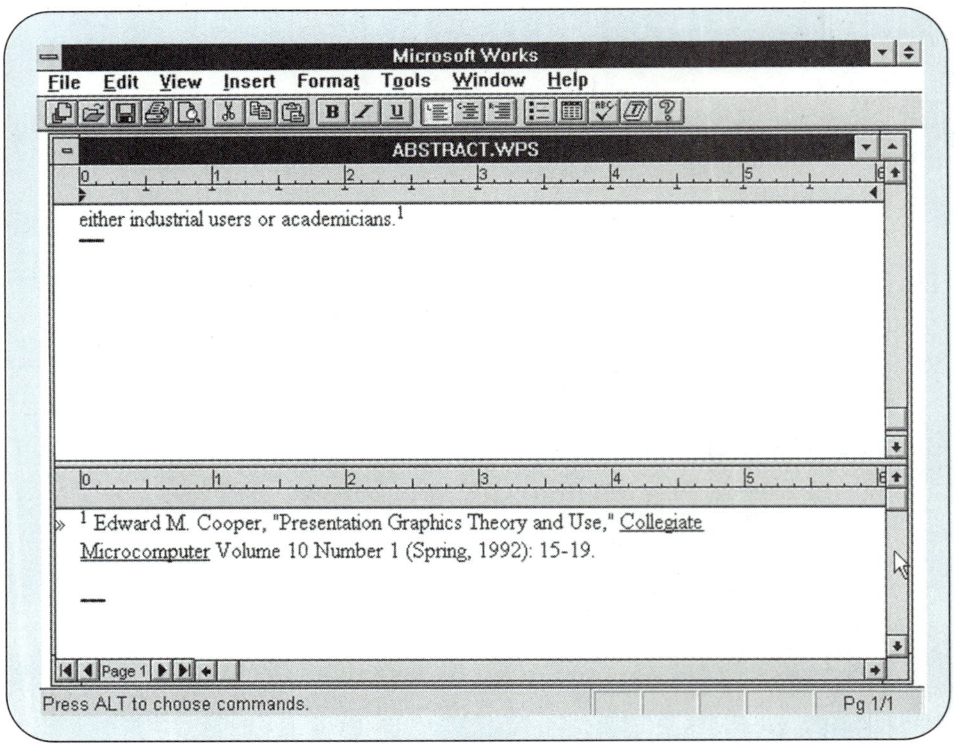

Figure 13.15

The Footnote Screen

23. Click on Help-Cue Cards.
24. Click on I want help from Cue Cards.
25. Click on Typing or revising text (incl tables and footnotes).
26. Click on Work with Footnotes.
27. Click on Open or close footnotes.
28. Click on OK.

    The cue card states, "To look at or close footnotes, click the View menu and click Footnotes."
29. Click on Done-Close-Close in the cue card.
30. Click on View-Footnotes.

    You return to your original screen.
31. Save portfoli.wps.

    You will now open your graphics file and insert a chart into your portfolio.
32. Press CTRL+ENTER for a new page.
33. Press ENTER ten times.
34. Open an existing file named graphics.wks you previously created.

    A new window opens containing the graphics.wks file. To go back to your portfoli.wps document:
35. Click on Window-1Portfoli.wps.
36. Click on Insert-Chart.

    The Insert Chart option box displays, as shown in Figure 13.16.

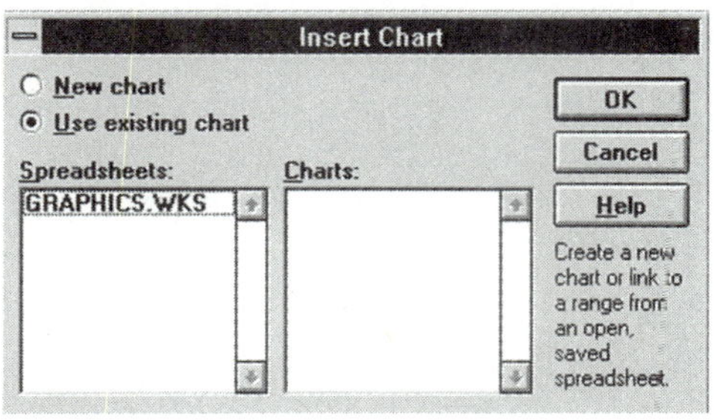

Figure 13.16

The Insert Chart Option Dialog Box

37. If it is not marked, click on Use existing chart.

    In the Spreadsheet list box:
38. Click on graphics.wks.

    The three charts you created in that file are listed in the Charts list box.

39. Click on insexp-OK.

    The insurance pie chart appears in your document. You want it on a page by itself.

40. Press CTRL+END, then CTRL+ENTER.

    You will now create a title in WordArt, bring in two clip art pictures, create a drawing of your own, and add a header to the document.

41. From the top of the page, press ENTER four times.
42. Click on the Center icon.
43. Click on Insert.
44. Click on WordArt.
45. In the Enter your text here text box, type **Art Samples**
46. Click on the Plain Text icon at the far left.
47. In the second row, click on the second text style from the left.
48. Click on the down arrow of the font size icon (marked "Best Fit") and select a 16-point and 18-point font (or whatever size your system will support). If asked, select Yes to Resize.
49. When finished, click outside the text box and your title will appear at the insertion point you defined.

Note: If you want to edit the WordArt, click within the text to select it, and click on Edit-WordArt. Now you will add a clip art picture.

50. Move the insertion point to the right of the Art Sample heading.
51. Press ENTER three times.
52. Click on the Left-Align icon.
53. Click on Insert-ClipArt.
54. Select the palm trees. (You may have to scroll to find them.)
55. Click on OK.
56. Press ENTER four times.

    You want to draw a whale in the middle of the page.

57. Click on Insert-Drawing.

    The Draw program opens, as shown in Figure 13.17. Note the Freeform icon.

58. Point to the Freeform icon and click the mouse button.
59. Place the pointer where you want the drawing to start and hold down the left mouse button as you draw the picture. The pointer changes to a pencil as you draw. To stop drawing and place the pencil some place else on the screen, double click the left mouse button.

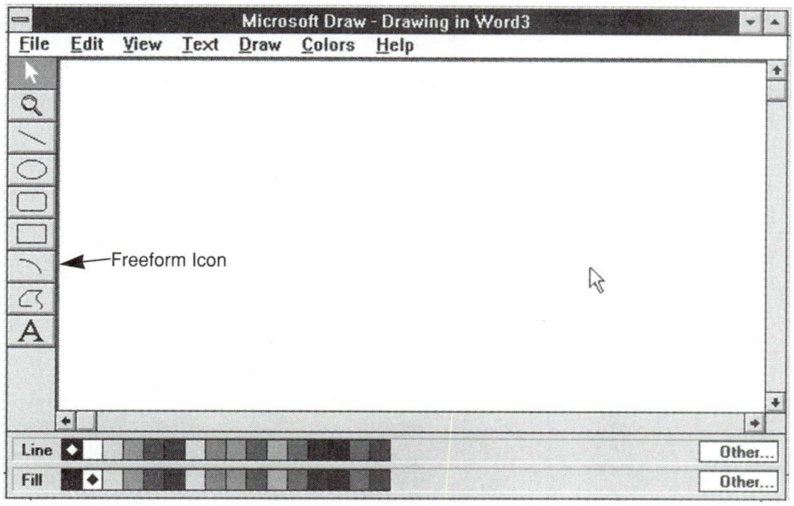

Figure 13.17

The Microsoft Draw Module

60. To continue drawing in another place, click on the Freeform icon and repeat the process. To delete some of your drawing, click on an area to select it and press the DELETE key.
61. After you finish the drawing, press ENTER four times.
62. Click on the arrow at the top of the list of icons to get the mouse pointer back.
63. Click on File-Exit to return to your document.
64. Click on Yes in response to the "Update?" query.
65. Click in your document to display the drawing.
66. In the bottom, right-hand corner of the page, insert a clip art picture of a sailboat. (Insert-Clip Art-Sailboat-OK.)

    To add a header that reads "Portfolio" at the left margin and page numbers at the right margin:
67. Click on View-Headers and Footers.
68. In the Header text box, type **&LPortfolio &rPage - &p**
69. Mark No header on the 1st Page.

    Be sure Use header and footer paragraphs is not marked.
70. Click on OK.
71. Save and print portfoli.wps.

    Your file should look similar to that in Figure 13.18.
72. Close all the files and exit *Works*.

Figure 13.18

Your Portfolio

Works Portfolio

by

Your first last name

Figure 13.18 Continued

Your Portfolio

Portfolio Page - 2

PRESENTATION GRAPHICS THEORY AND USE

Abstract

Computer use is being required in an increasing number of courses in the business school curriculum. A plethora of graphics packages is available for use in the business world to enhance the presentations by corporate users. With the advanced capability of graphics software and the necessity to accurately and graphically depict data, the question arises, "Are there guidelines and theories that should be introduced in business courses that offer graphics and in the training of business college faculty who teach those graphics courses?"

The ability to create graphics is possible in several different types of software packages. There is a wide array of graphics displays available. Graphic presentations are becoming more prevalent in the business world and are being taught in more courses in colleges. The mere numbers of graphics being used, however, do not necessarily mean that the graphics are well designed. A study was undertaken to determine the amount of theory and information about graphics design that is known by industrial uses and designers of graphics packages and by the college faculty members who teach graphic courses. It was found that a substantial percentage of both industrial users and academicians are familiar with some of the graphics theory that is available. However, there is much more graphic information in scholarly journals that is not being utilized by either industrial users or academicians.[1]

[1] Edward M. Cooper, "Presentation Graphics Theory and Use," Collegiate Microcomputer Volume 10 Number 1 (Spring, 1992): 15-19.

Figure 13.18 Continued

Your Portfolio

Portfolio

Page - 3

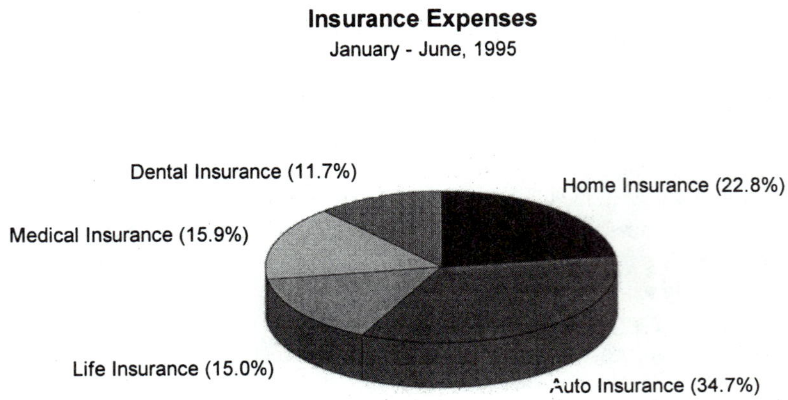

Figure 13.18 Continued

Your Portfolio

Chapter Summary

Up until now, this text has dealt with each *Works* application individually. In this chapter, we discuss the power of integration and compare the difficulty of combining output from stand-alone applications with the ease of combining output of applications within the *Works* integrated software package. This ease of use comes from the common interface—the main menu that appears at the top of the screen, which looks the same in each application. It also comes from using the Window command to move easily from one application to another, or to view files from several applications at the same time.

When you move records from one application to another, the target (receiving) file determines the file type. Therefore, any necessary data manipulation must be completed before the move is made.

The WorksWizards feature of *Works 3.0 for Windows* makes it simple for the novice computer user to develop an address book, write a form letter, create mailing labels, create a footnote, find a file, or find specific data in a database.

Templates are also useful in *Works 3.0 for Windows*. A number of templates have been created for every application except communications. They provide skeletons for particular applications, leaving the user the simple task of filling in blanks or changing existing data to suit an individual situation.

ClipArt and WordArt have been added to the latest version of the program. They supplement the Drawing module and further enhance your ability to customize your work.

Common uses for integration include personalizing form letters, producing mailing labels and envelopes, and importing charts, pictures, drawings, database records, and spreadsheet information into formal presentations and reports.

KEY TERMS

clip art
cut sheet feeding
CUA
Data Finder
Database Designer
File Organizer
Footnote Generator
form letter
integration
Letterhead Designer
mail merge
master document
template
WorksWizards

REVIEW QUESTIONS

1. Explain the meaning of the term *integration*.
2. Illustrate the power of integration.
3. Identify the factors that cloud the future of integrated programs.
4. Explain why combining files from stand-alone applications is difficult and how an integrated program like *Works* simplifies this process.

5. List several specific uses for integration.
6. Explain the meaning of the term *common interface*.
7. Describe the steps you would take to view three files at the same time on the screen.
8. Which application determines the file type when a file is moved from one application to another?
9. Explain the meaning of the term *mail merge*.
10. Our culture has become visually oriented. What modules in *Works 3.0 for Windows* address this orientation and what do they do?
11. List and briefly describe the purpose of each of the WorksWizards tools.
12. What is a template? How do you make use of one?
13. List and briefly describe the purpose of each of the *Works* templates.
14. Describe the steps you would take when moving records among each of the *Works* applications.
15. List the steps for creating and printing form letters and mailing labels in *Works*.
16. Give some examples of files that are not in the *Works* format when you import or export them.

SOFTWARE EXERCISES

Exercise 13.1

1. Make arrangements with your instructor to familiarize yourself with the *Works Using Tools Together* tutorial.
2. Make notes about what was covered in each of the following sections:
   (a) Introducing the tools together
   (b) Sharing information
   (c) Strategies for using *Works 3.0 for Windows*
3. Use *Works* to type your notes about what you learned.
4. Save your work as tutint13.
5. Print tutint13.wps.
6. Close tutint13.wps and exit *Works*.

Exercise 13.2

1. Open a new spreadsheet file in *Works*.
2. Create a four-year budget headed State College Costs using the data provided in Table 13.7.
3. Create a bar chart of your total annual costs.
4. Save your spreadsheet as colbud.
5. Open a new word processing document.
6. Enter the text of the letter in Table 13.8.

Table 13.7 Sample Spreadsheet

ESTIMATED COSTS TO ATTEND
FOUR-YEAR PUBLIC COLLEGES AND UNIVERSITIES
IN THE UNITED STATES

1995–1996

Area	Tuition & Fees	Add'l Out-Of-St. Tu.	Books & Supplies	Room & Board	Trans-portation	Other Costs
Nat'l	1948	3086	522	3495	508	1198
New E.	2377	3676	535	3787	299	1075
Middle	1979	2866	539	3969	443	1063
South	2024	2595	532	3272	514	1015
M'west	2290	2711	472	3108	422	1288
S'west	1311	2933	527	3281	764	1300
West	1524	4675	566	4181	630	1386

Table 13.8 Sample Letter

9850 W. Alameda
Lakewood, CO 80226
July 2, 1995

Dear Tammy,

I have just completed research into the cost of attending a four-year state college. Those figures are graphed for you below.

Based on these projections, I am priced out of the market unless I decide to move back home with my parents and attend a local college for the first two years.

I don't want to move back home, but that may be the only way that I can begin attending a college next term. What would you do?

How about your situation? Have you made a decision yet? I'm anxious to hear from you.

Your best friend,

[your name]

7. Place the cursor two lines below the sentence that reads, "These figures are graphed for you below."
8. Copy and edit your college costs chart.
9. Preview the letter and chart; resize the chart as necessary.
10. When you are satisfied with the chart and letter, save the word processing document as colltr.
11. Print colltr.wps.
12. Close all files and exit *Works*.

Exercise 13.3

1. Open the colltr.wps file created in Exercise 13.2, or complete that exercise before continuing.
2. Click on No to the update links question, if asked.
3. Delete the existing return address.
4. Use WorkWizards to create a letterhead with your name and address. Use any style that suits you.
5. Cut and paste your letterhead to the top of colltr.wps.
6. Preview the letterhead, letter, and chart; resize the chart and change the margins as necessary to keep everything on one page.

   You are going to use Draw to draw a sad face. Move your cursor 2 tabs to the right of "Your name" at the bottom of the letter.
7. Click on Insert, Drawing.
8. Draw a sad face.
9. Click on file, exit (within Microsoft Draw) to colltr.wps.
10. Click on yes to update colltr.wps.
11. Save the document as colltr1.
12. Print colltr1.wps.
13. Close colltr1.wps and any other open files and exit *Works*.

Exercise 13.4

1. Open the colltr.wps file created in Exercise 13.2, or complete that exercise before continuing.
2. Add the following paragraph to the letter, positioned one blank line below the chart: "This chart was created from the data that appears just below."
3. Open the spreadsheet colbud.wks created in Exercise 13.2.
4. Select all of the budget categories and their numbers.

5. Copy the selected data to your word processing document. Insert it one blank line below the sentence you inserted in Step 2.
6. Preview the letter and chart; resize the chart and change the margins as necessary to keep everything on one page.
7. Save your document as colltr2.
8. Print colltr2.wps.
9. Close colltr2.wps and colbud.wks and exit *Works*.

Exercise 13.5

You will set up a form letter with automatic inside addresses printed from the insfrmlr.wdb database on the student data diskette. The basis for the form letter is the inslet2.wps letter you typed for the Chapter 4 tutorial.

1. Open the existing word processing file named inslet2.wps (from the tutorial in Chapter 4).
2. a. At the top of the letter, add your own return address; delete any remaining blank lines between your return address and the date.
   b. Delete the inside address.
   c. Replace the date in the letter with the current date on the line below your city state, and Zip in the return address.
   d. With the cursor on the line below the current date, press ENTER three times.
3. Open the insfrmlr.wdb file (from the student data diskette that accompanies the text).
4. Return to inslet2.wps.
5. Put the company name placeholder on the fourth line below your return address. (Click on Insert-Database Field-Database . . . -insfrmlt.wdb-OK, coname, Insert.) (Note: You should see the <<CONAME>> placeholder.)
6. Put the company address placeholder on the line below the company name. You should see the <<COADDRESS>> placeholder.
7. Put the company city, state, and Zip placeholder on the line below the company address. You should see the <<COSTZIP>> placeholder.
8. Check to see that only one blank line remains between the COSTZIP placeholder and the salutation; delete any surplus lines.
9. Delete the existing salutation and type the following one: **Ladies and Gentlemen:** (Note: The salutation should be one blank line below the company city, state, and Zip placeholder and should have one blank line following it.
10. Change the date in the next to last paragraph so that it is 1 week later than the date of the letter.

11. Put a period after the date and delete the rest of the sentence which reads, "at the following address:" along with your name and address.
12. Save the file as insltr.
13. Close insltr.wps and insfrmlr.wdb and exit *Works*.

Exercise 13.6

You will print the form letter you set up in Exercise 13.5.

1. Open the database file called insfrmlr.wdb (from the student data diskette).
2. Open the insltr.wps word processing file you created in Exercise 13.5 or complete that exercise before continuing.
3. Click on File-Print Preview.
4. In the Choose Database box, click on insfrmlr.wdb-OK.
5. Preview each letter; if they all look correct, click on Print; otherwise make any needed corrections and repeat Step 5.
6. When the form letters have all been printed, close both files and exit *Works*.

Exercise 13.7

1. Open spreadsheet file called HOUSEINV.WKS (created in the Chapter 6 tutorial).
2. Select all items, costs, and replacement costs.
3. Choose Edit, Copy.
4. Open a new *Works* database file.
5. Click on the List view icon.
6. Click on Edit, Paste.
7. Increase the Field1 size to 16.
8. Put the file into descending order by Replacement Cost (Field 3).
9. Format the number fields with a comma and no decimals.
10. Copy the sorted database file to a new word processing file.
11. Create a report with an appropriate title and appropriately named fields.
12. Print the document.
13. Save your file as hsinvrpt.
14. Close hsinvrpt.wks, houseinv.wks, and Data2 and exit *Works*.

Exercise 13.8

1. Open a new word processing document.
2. Type your own return address and the current date beginning on the eighth line down from the top of the page.

3. Press ENTER four times.
4. Type the following inside address:

   First Interstate Mortgage

   4582 Ulster Street Parkway

   Denver, CO 80237
5. Press ENTER twice.
6. Type **Ladies and Gentlemen:**
7. Press ENTER twice.
8. Type the following paragraph single spaced in block style:

   At your request, and in support of my new home mortgage application, my net worth statement for last year and this year follows below:
9. Press ENTER twice.
10. Open the spreadsheet file called netwrth.wks from the student data diskette.
11. Complete the heading by entering your name and the current date in the appropriate places.
12. Format the range of cells from C7 to D9 as currency with no decimal places.
13. Select Range A1 to D10 in netwrth.wks.
14. Click on Window, Tile. (Note: You should see both your spreadsheet and your word processing document on each side of the screen.)
15. Move the mouse to the edge of the selected spreadsheet columns until it changes from a cross to an arrow that says "DRAG." Hold down the left button and slowly drag the selected columns (as the arrow changes to read "COPY") to your word processing document. Release the mouse button so that your net worth data ends up two lines below the sentence that reads: ". . . my net worth statement for last year and this year follows below:"
16. Maximize your word processing document.
17. Move the cursor to the last line of the net worth statement and press ENTER twice.
18. Type **Sincerely yours,** and press ENTER four times.
19. Type your own first and last names.
20. Spell check the entire document.
21. Save the word processing file as mortapp.
22. Print mortapp.wps.
23. Close mortapp.wps and netwrth.wks and exit *Works.*

Exercise 13.9

1. Open a new word processing file.
2. Type your own return address and the current date on the eighth line down from the top of the page.
3. Press ENTER four times.
4. Type the following inside address:

   Business Computer Systems, Inc.

   1930 Sixteenth Street

   Denver, CO 80203
5. Press ENTER twice.
6. Type **Gentlemen:**
7. Press ENTER twice.
8. Type the following paragraph single spaced in block style:

   I am interested in purchasing a new printer. Please send me price quotations on the following machines:
9. Press ENTER twice.
10. Open the PTR.WDB file from the student data diskette.
11. Sort this file by cost in descending order.
12. Select the makes and models from the top two lines (the two most expensive printers).
13. Add the printer information to the letter using either the Cut and Paste commands or the mouse technique (click on Window-Tile and move the mouse to the edge of the selection to DRAG/COPY the selection from the database to the word processing document).
14. Select the makes and models from the bottom two lines of the database display (the two least expensive printers). Copy them to the word processing document, on the line just below the previous printer model entries.
15. Leave a blank line and type **Sincerely yours,** and press ENTER four times.
16. Type your name.
17. Insert the headings *MAKE* and *MODEL* above the Make and Model columns you inserted into the letter. Leave a blank line between these new headings and the lines you moved.
18. Spell check the entire word processing document.
19. Save the document as ptrprice.
20. Print ptrprice.wps.
21. Close both files and exit *Works*.

Exercise 13.10

1. Open any three files from among those you have created in tutorials or exercises, or from the student data diskette.
2. Blend parts of these files together in a way that makes sense. You may have to create a title, format numbers, create headings, or invent some connecting text to do this.
3. Use the word processing Insert menu to insert ClipArt, WordArt, or a Drawing. Size the art to fit your document.
4. Save your work.
5. Preview your completed work; when it is satisfactory, print it.
6. Close all open files and exit *Works*.

Exercise 13.11

1. Use *Works 3.0 for Windows* to complete a school assignment for another class or a task for a club or organization to which you belong.
2. Use what you have learned in this chapter and course to create an attractive, error-free document. Create or include work from a spreadsheet, chart, database, or word processing document along with a letterhead and/or ClipArt, WordArt, or a Drawing (as appropriate to the task).
3. Preview your completed work; when it is satisfactory, print it.
4. Save your work.
5. Close all open files and exit *Works*.

Chapter 14

Buying a Personal Computer

Objectives

After studying this chapter you will be able to:

- *Recall the five steps involved in a personal computer purchase*
- *Recognize your own recent gain in computer literacy*
- *Define and prioritize your own personal computer requirements*
- *Apply the software-determines-hardware rule to your next personal computer investment*
- *Determine the suitability of freeware or shareware for your own software needs*
- *Identify many sources of information about hardware and software*
- *Decide from which general hardware family—Apple or IBM—you will select a computer*
- *Decide on the memory size, CPU type, clock speed, RAM, monitor, multimedia capabilities, secondary storage, and expandability that a personal computer needs to meet your requirements*
- *Decide on the distribution channel that meets your requirements*
- *State what preventive maintenance measures you should take to prolong the operation of your personal computer*
- *Purchase a personal computer system with confidence*

Five Steps in Buying Your Own Computer

While the prices of all computers have decreased dramatically in the last decade, most personal users still see a microcomputer as a major purchase. Today, your choices are almost limitless, and you can get much more for a lot less money than just a few years ago. Within the last several years, personal computing has achieved a new plateau; first-time personal computer buyers often start with sophisticated multimedia systems that run the *Windows* interface using large amounts of primary and secondary memory. These new users are beginning with systems that most buyers of ten years ago obtained only as their second or third computers.

However, until the desktop computer is as common a personal tool as the telephone, a considerable amount of anxiety will still be associated with selecting, purchasing, and maintaining a personal computer system. In this chapter, we will break the process into steps to which certain guidelines apply. We believe that this approach will make the whole process a lot less stressful and more rewarding. Table 14.1 summarizes the five steps in the process of purchasing a personal computer.

Table 14.1 Five Steps in Purchasing a Personal Computer

- Becoming Computer Literate
- Defining Your Needs
- Selecting Software
- Selecting Hardware
- Selecting a Vendor

Step 1: Becoming Computer Literate

Why, after 13 chapters of instruction and many tutorials, do we present information on how to purchase a personal computer like the one you have been using all along? Quite simply, we do this because a prerequisite for purchasing a personal computer is **computer literacy**, knowing how to use the software and hardware to take advantage of this remarkable tool. You must know something about how the computer operates and what a personal computer system should do before you can purchase one intelligently.

Many readers may already own their own computers. These people will, no doubt, adapt to the hardware and software that they already have. After this course you should know how to make your system work the best for you. No doubt this will help you ensure that the next system you purchase will be easier to use and better suited to your needs. You are now armed with the vocabulary of computers. You are more familiar with the technical terms of the computer world, and you better understand their meanings. If you already own a computer, you probably had help selecting it; now you will be able to select your own, and perhaps help other people select theirs.

If you do not yet own a personal computer, after reading this text and/or taking a course, you should be better prepared to make that major purchase. You can confidently select a system that suits you and that fits your budget. We will highlight only a few of the many possibilities. As with all computer-related tasks, a computer purchase requires some careful thought and preliminary planning. If you want to buy a computer, you will easily find someone willing to sell you one. However, you must be computer literate in order to define your requirements properly; this will help you to invest in a computer that will satisfy your needs now, and in the future.

Step 2: Defining Your Needs

When thinking about purchasing a personal computer system, you must first define your needs and make a list of priorities. What will you do with the computer? Since the computer is such a versatile tool, this list will probably include several different tasks.

Table 14.2 shows just some of the uses for a personal computer. You may want to write school papers, keep up correspondence (electronic or printed), prepare a personal budget, keep track of job opportunities, and so on. The uses of a personal computer are many and varied.

As part of the computer purchase process, set down in a sentence or two what your needs are, and then rank those needs. You need to recognize which tasks are more important to you than others, and which applications you will use more than others. This relationship will affect the software and hardware that you purchase.

Table 14.2 Some Uses for Personal Computers

Productivity	*Education*	*Personal*
Accounting/bookkeeping	Aptitude testing	Career development
Business forms	Authoring	Cooking
Computer-aided design	Cognitive development	Diet
Computer tutorials	Composition	Electronic publications
Conferencing	Computer literacy	Financial management
Fax transmission	Early childhood development	Motivational programs
Financial planning	Economics	Distance learning
Graphics design	English as a second language	Legal matters
Investment management	Foreign language	Gambling
Mailing lists	Geography	Genealogy
Marketing and advertising	Government	Health
Project management	Grammar	Hobbies
Slide presentations	Handwriting analysis	Household management
Secretarial services	History	Library research
Spreadsheets	Reading vocabulary	Multimedia "books"
Statistics	Social sciences	Music composition/arrangement
Taxes	Speed reading	Self-improvement
Time management	Spelling	Sports
Typing tutorials	Vocational skills	Travel
Word processing		

(continued)

Table 14.2 Continued Some Uses for Personal Computers

Entertainment	*Science*	*Other*
Adult entertainment	Astrology	Artificial intelligence
Adventure games	Biology	Expert systems
Arcade games	Chemistry	Computer languages
Animation	Dry labs	Database management systems
MUDS, MOOS	Environmental science	Operating systems
Sports games	Mathematics	Utilities
Strategy games		
Virtual reality		

If you know, for example, that you will use the computer primarily for word processing, and that your word processing documents will be complex products that must have excellent print quality, you will purchase a different system than someone who must produce high-quality graphics involving large amounts of numeric data in integrated reports. To make an intelligent choice, order your priorities and select your hardware and software to meet them.

Ordering your priorities also helps define your needs more narrowly. Even if you see a great sale on a system, it's not a great deal for you unless the computer system satisfies your most important needs. If it doesn't, you should consider waiting for another sale. As with all problem solving, defining the problem is a prerequisite to implementing a solution.

There are as many computer needs as computer users. Perhaps your microcomputer will function exclusively as your own personal information system, and you will not use it to connect to your work place, run a part-time business, or keep records for a hobby. However, most computer users find more and more uses for their personal computers once they start using them. After you master your primary application, you may find yourself using the computer to play games, to dialog with other members of an on-line chat group, or even to learn how to program.

Many microcomputer systems are suitable for small business applications. You will see offers of jobs that allow you to moonlight and earn extra income with your personal computer. Record-keeping and secretarial services for others and even tutoring others are also possibilities. If you plan to use your personal computer to free you from spending extra hours at the office by allowing you to bring some work home, the system you purchase must be **compatible** with the one at work; that is, you must be able to move data and programs between the two systems.

The software at work and at home most be compatible, particularly the operating system, and the hardware must also work together well enough to allow you to move disks with files from one place to the other. You will not be able to move files from a high-density drive at the office to a low-density drive at home; moving the other way—from low-density to high-density—usually will work. In particular, be aware that you cannot move data files from a Macintosh system to an IBM system without special hardware and software. Moving files completed on a newer version of software to an older version of the same software also often poses problems. Trying to run software written for multimedia systems is troublesome for older architectures. Software written for the *Windows* environment simply cannot be run without this interface.

Whatever your priorities, order them and make no excuses for them. They are *your* priorities; they will not be exactly the same as anyone else's. Even if your main goal in purchasing a microcomputer is simply to educate yourself further with new technology, that is a perfectly valid goal. The way we process information today, including personal information, is much different from the same work just a decade ago. Keeping abreast of new technology keeps you current in an ever-changing world. Purchasing a personal computer can be an exercise in computer literacy in itself, and you will soon find myriad uses for your computer.

Step 3: Selecting Software

This third step in purchasing a personal computer is so obvious that it is often overlooked. It is an extremely important step, however. Obviously, all software does not run on the same hardware. Programs written for the Macintosh do not run on IBM or compatible machines. Within these families, all microcomputer software has specific hardware requirements. For example, each program requires a certain minimum amount of RAM and hard disk space. In Chapter 2 of this book, you learned that *Works 3.0 for Windows* requires 2 MB of RAM and 14 MB of hard disk space. If you want to open several programs at once, 2 MB of RAM will not be enough. You will find 6 or 8 MB more practical. Much of today's software requires a fixed disk, as well.

For most *Windows* software, and all spreadsheet graphing and presentation graphics programs, your system must have a graphics capability. Modems are required for communications programs. Although you could run *Windows*-based software using the ALT key and other key combinations, it is truly cumbersome to run *Windows* without a mouse or trackball. Many multimedia software packages require **CD-ROM** drives, and perhaps soundcards, speakers, and microphones. For this reason, you should choose your software packages first, then choose your hardware to match what the software requires.

This is summed up in the guideline that software determines hardware. This applies not just to choosing a general software application, such as word processing or database management. It requires choosing a specific program, like *Works*, *WordPerfect*, *Access*, or *Excel*; you must even decide which version you will use. The newer suites of applications for the *Windows* interface have very high memory requirements (8–12 megabytes).

You should not overlook many good **shareware** programs when selecting software. These programs are mostly DOS based, except for the newer communications shareware programs, which are available in *Windows* versions. Table 14.3 lists some of the most popular shareware applications.

Table 14.3 Shareware Choices

Application Type	Shareware Program
Database	PC File III+
Spreadsheet	PC Calc
	Joe Spreadsheet
Word Processing	PC Write
Data communications	QModem
	Red Ryder
Graphics	Express Graph
Utilities	PKZIP
	ARJ
	MOSAIC
	F-Prot

These programs, and hundreds more, cost as little as $5 per disk and are available from many sources. They cost nothing if downloaded locally, and just the phone charge if downloaded from outside your local calling area.

Some shareware sources encourage you to try the program before sending in a suggested donation, which ranges from $5 to $69. Registering as a user and paying the nominal fee guarantees that you will receive information on updated versions of the shareware. You may also receive a printed manual, and you may even have access to information concerning any problems, called *bugs*, that others may discover in the software.

Another kind of software, termed **freeware**, is public domain software that you are free to use as you please—no donation is suggested or required. The only expense is the cost of the disk, usually $4 to $5. Freeware is usually not tested as widely, and it is not necessarily error-free. You may encounter some problems with freeware, and you will find documentation or instructions only in a README.DOC file on the disk; still, the price is right.

In addition, hundreds of bulletin board services, which you learned about in Chapter 12, encourage you to download software from their computers to your own disks via data communications. Exercise caution, however, if you are considering downloading software from bulletin boards you know nothing about: a program that seems interesting may contain a hidden virus. The virus could multiply itself on your disks and wipe out all of the files on your floppy or hard disk system. For more about this danger, see Chapter 15.

The software-determines-hardware rule does not imply that you will never change software; you probably will. Initially, however, you should buy equipment to match the hardware requirements for a specific program, as listed in the documentation that comes with the software. You must know these requirements so that you can budget for the necessary hardware. If you are set on operating under a GUI like the *Windows* environment, you automatically enter a higher-priced, but more universal category of hardware. By identifying both the software you want and the hardware you need to run it, you will avoid big surprises when you start shopping for your computer.

If you do not know which software programs you will use, computer magazines and popular books regularly publish a wealth of information. Four popular magazines for IBM and compatible personal computers are *Windows Magazine*, *PC Magazine*, *PC World*, and *PC Computing*. *Boardwatch* and *Wired* are good communications magazines. All of these magazines perform extensive tests of computer hardware and software each month, make recommendations based upon their findings, and give awards, such as Editor's Choice or Best Buy ratings to the best products.

These popular computing magazines provide invaluable information when it comes to choosing new software and hardware

To supplement this information, you can also discuss your needs with other computer users. Many communities have computer user groups that meet periodically to discuss topics of common interest. If such a group exists near you, plan to attend. Ask your questions of knowledgeable users. Another good way to look at alternatives in software, and in the corresponding hardware, is to try it before you own it. Take an introductory course through a community program, or browse at retail stores. The time invested in testing your tentative choices of software and hardware will be well spent.

Go to a retail outlet and ask for a demonstration. The sales staff will be happy to oblige you. In general, immerse yourself in reading and talking about available programs if you are uncertain about your choices.

Step 4: Selecting Hardware

Once you have decided what software you will use with your system, you are ready to choose hardware. Despite the many fairly technical aspects of hardware, there are only a few basic types of personal computers. If you choose your system wisely and allow for expansion, you can add optional hardware as you gain expertise and funds. Aside from the choice of family (IBM or Apple), you need to consider several factors at the outset, including the type of microcomputer you want, what type of processor it will have, how much main memory and storage your software requires, and what peripherals your system will include.

You can use either a Macintosh or a DOS-based system; the choice depends on which software best suits your needs.

If you have proceeded systematically, you already know which family you will choose, Apple or IBM and compatibles. Your software has dictated this. We will discuss IBM personal computers because that is the family dealt with in this text. However, many excellent programs are available in the Macintosh world.

Size Personal computers come in several sizes, each with its own advantages. A regular desktop model is still the most common size. You can however, choose from portable computers, laptop models, and even very small notebook models that fit inside your briefcase. The smaller computers offer optional battery-powered operation—a real advantage that allows you to compute anywhere for several hours without access to an electrical outlet.

Many of the smaller models have just as much processing power as desktop models. Such a computer probably has a fixed disk and internal modem, a mouse or similar pointing device, and even a small printer. Some desktop computers have docking stations that allow you to plug in your notebook computer to your larger main system when you return from a field computing session. It is even possible, with an inexpensive piece of hardware, to connect your notebook computer, through its parallel port, to a LAN. In the past, poor-quality screen displays have made portable computers annoying for extended use, but color liquid crystal display and gas plasma screens have remedied this.

On the other hand, a portable computer that has the same capabilities (CPU, RAM, fixed-disk size, floppy drives, and keyboard) as a desktop model will be more expensive. Weigh the difference carefully. Will you need to use a computer in different places? If so, a portable personal computer may be a wise choice.

A notebook computer weighs from two to six pounds, fits in your briefcase, and has enough battery energy for at least two and a half hours of computing before it must be recharged. Figure 14.1 shows the different sizes of personal computers that are widely available today.

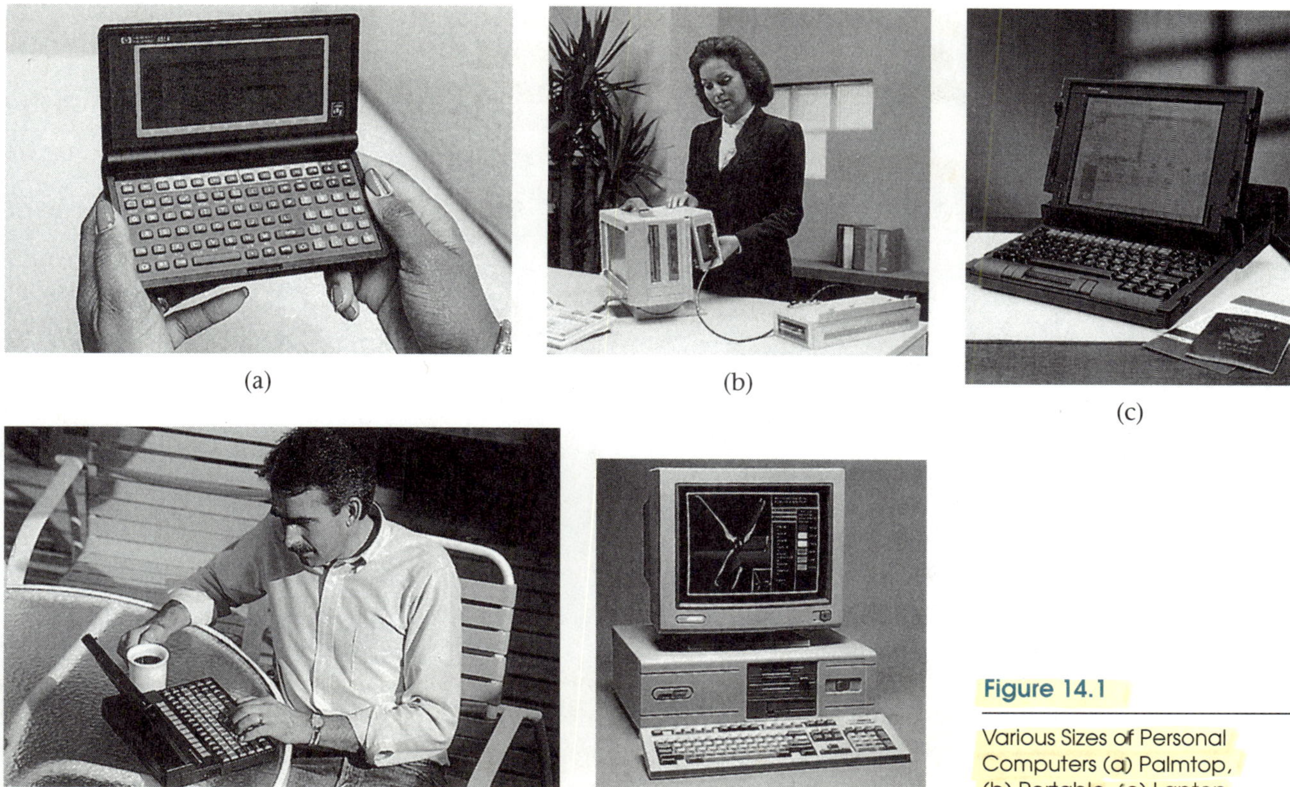

(a) (b) (c) (d) (e)

Figure 14.1

Various Sizes of Personal Computers (a) Palmtop, (b) Portable, (c) Laptop, (d) Notebook, (e) Personal

Many experts predict that eventually everyone will access a **PCN**, a **personal communication network**, through a single device that combines a computer, a telephone communication device, and a video display. As small as a cellular phone, you will carry this individualized, all-purpose tool with you everywhere to help with many different tasks. The Apple Computer Corporation recently introduced its Newton, a **personal digital assistant (PDA)** that is a first step toward the PCN of the future.

Central Processing Unit Since personal computers have become common, we have seen the development of several generations of central processing units, each with increasing power and speed. The CPU, you remember, does the actual computing for a microcomputer. The first PCs put out by IBM in 1981 relied on the Intel 8088 chip. It had an internal data bus (path of the data flow) of 16 bits and an external bus of 8 bits. Its word size of 16 bits transferred data 16 bits at a time instead of just 8 bits at a time, the standard for earlier microcomputers.

The speed of a processor is measured in **megahertz**; one megahertz (MHz) is 1 million cycles a second. A processor's speed in machine cycles is referred to as its **clock speed**. The clock speed of the first IBM CPU was 4.77 megahertz. A common system today might have an 80486 central processor with a clock speed of 66 megahertz or higher. Generally, faster clock speed, hard disk access speed, and data transfer speed produces better overall performance. Table 14.4 shows how CPU microchips for personal computers have improved.

Table 14.4

Date	Name	MHz	MIPS*	Transistors
1974	8080	2	0.64	6,000
1978	8086	5	0.33	29,000
1979	8088	5	0.33	29,000
1982	80286	8	1.20	134,000
1985	80386DX	16	6.00	275,000
1988	80386SX	16	2.50	275,000
1989	80486DX	25	20.00	1.2 million
1991	80486SX	20	16.50	1.185 million
1992	80486DX2	50	40.00	1.2 million
1993	Pentium	66–100	112.00	3.1 million

* Millions of instructions per second—the speed at which a computer performs instruction cycles.

The first DOS personal computers served an estimated 20 million users worldwide. In 1984, IBM introduced its AT (Advanced Technology) personal computers with 80286 microprocessors. This machine was faster (8 megahertz) and much more powerful than the previous computers, allowing software that was more user friendly and much more sophisticated to run at a higher speed. The AT was an introduction to the most common fixed-disk system that users purchased for the next several years.

Microcomputers with 80386SX and 80386DX chips were then introduced. The 80386SX has an internal bus of 32 bits and an external bus of 16 bits. Typical clock speeds range from 16 to 20 MHz. The 80386DX model has an internal and an external bus of 32 bits. Typical clock speeds begin at 16 MHz and climb to 33 MHz. The microcomputer of choice has now become the 80486DX or 80486DX2. Clock speed for an 80486DX ranges from 25 to 50 MHz; the 80486DX2 runs at speeds from 33 to 66 MHz, and the 80486DX4 reaches a clock speed of 100MHz.

The outcome of these advances in bus width and clock speed is increased **throughput**. Throughput measures the amount of work a PC can do in a given time period. The software you want to run dictates the hardware to assign to the task. The price of an 80486 system is now affordable, even with the addition of multimedia hardware like a CD-ROM drive, high-resolution VGA monitor, speakers, sound card, and microphone.

Multimedia Decision Just as you must decide whether to operate under the *Windows* environment before you select hardware, your desire to exploit **multimedia** capabilities also affects your hardware decision. Like all hardware decisions, it depends upon what software you wish to use. You can always use software without multimedia elements of sound, graphics, video, and animation on a multimedia system, but you cannot do the opposite—run multimedia software on a traditional system. You will get operating system error messages if you try to run multimedia software on a system that lacks the necessary hardware. It is important to purchase a more powerful CPU and enough main memory (8 to 16 MB of RAM) if you plan to use multimedia software. The very latest DOS family technology, Intel's **Pentium** chip, is still quite expensive; an 80486-based computer will run multimedia software adequately, however.

Today, the 80386DX is about the lowest system to consider if you want to run *Windows* and one or two additional programs at the same time. Memory-hungry, graphics-oriented modern software makes the 80486 microprocessor even more desirable.

Memory As you learned in Chapter 1, the amount of main memory (RAM) contributes to the power of your computer. When personal computers were first introduced in 1977, 64K was the standard amount of main memory. Now that amount is no longer adequate to run anything but the simplest text-based software. The reasons for the increase in RAM requirements are several. We are doing much more sophisticated personal computing today, and software has become larger and more complex than the personal computer pioneers dreamed would be possible. Early word processing programs for personal computers did not anticipate producing newsletters that contained clip art, nor color monitors displaying WYSIWYG interfaces. More importantly, the sophistication of software has increased so much that the added memory is needed simply to load and run the applications. Graphical user interfaces (GUIs) like *Windows*, and integrated programs like *Works*, make the user's job much easier, but the trade-off is a much higher RAM requirement.

With the 8088 computers, the maximum amount of RAM that you could install was 640K. That amount of memory will still suffice for beginning computing tasks, and most versions of DOS will run on it if you do not install *Windows*, as well. However, you should have at least 6 megabytes of RAM for *Windows* and the *OS/2* operating system (8 MB or more is preferred). Trying to run the newer, more sophisticated application programs with less than 4 megabytes of RAM is virtually impossible, and with less than 6 to 8 megabytes, they run fairly slowly.

Secondary Storage Secondary storage has also changed since personal computers were introduced. It was not until 1983 that hard drives of 10 MB were included in personal computer configurations. Up to that time, 5.25-inch floppy disks that held 360K or less were standard. When the IBM XT appeared with a 10 MB hard drive, we thought, "How will we ever use that much space?" Today, 80 MB is barely adequate for personal use, and the original 10 MB hard drive of the IBM XT is far too small.

Moreover, scarcely anyone plans to purchase a new computer without a fixed-disk drive. It is not possible to run *Works 3.0 for Windows* without a hard drive with at least 14 MB of storage space free. As you learned in Chapters 1 and 3, the 3.5 inch, high-density disk drives can store up to 1.44 MB of data. New personal computer systems often include 200 MB hard drives today. Each software package in the *Windows* environment takes from 10 to 35 MB of disk space.

The important goal is to match the drive capacity and size to your needs. The 1.4 MB floppy disk drive can read and format 720K diskettes. The 1.2 MB floppy disk drive can read and format 360K diskettes. Naturally, there is a small difference in cost between 360K and 1.4 MB floppy disk drives. The 5.25-inch drive is being phased out in favor of a system with a CD-ROM drive and a 3.5-inch floppy drive. Remember, however, if you still have much software and many important files on 5.25-inch floppy disks, you will want at least an external 5.25-inch floppy drive until you can convert all of your software to the smaller disks or copy it onto the hard drive.

Sophisticated multimedia software such as encyclopedias or atlases require CD-ROM secondary storage, but much simpler multimedia software can use 3.5-inch diskettes. One minute of stereo-quality sound takes 8 MB (8 million bytes) of storage. The typical CD-ROM disk offers a **gigabyte** (1 billion bytes) of storage, which can store more video and audio data. CD-ROM is also more resistant to viruses, as Chapter 15 will explain.

However, if your personal computing needs do not require a high-powered CPU and a great deal of RAM or secondary storage, then a used 80286 machine with 640K RAM may suit you very well. If a GUI is not important, and you can use a program like *Works 3.0 for DOS*, you may be perfectly happy with a simpler system. Numerous clones make use of the 80286, 80386, and 80486 chips to run MS-DOS. All of these machines are capable of imitating an IBM PC.

Expandability You should certainly think about expandability when you make your initial purchase. You cannot upgrade many older computers enough without changing the motherboard and spending almost as much as you would to purchase a new computer. Some of the 80386-based computers allow you to expand main memory up to 16MB, with almost unlimited secondary storage.

Consider buying a machine with at least the 80486DX architecture because it can address a variety of needs. You can add a large number of peripherals, such as a laser printer, a modem, a mouse, speakers, a microphone, and a super VGA monitor as your needs change. As a first step, map out your present and forseeable future computer requirements carefully, and purchase a computer that can expand to suit later needs.

If you purchase a system with enough available expansion slots on the motherboard, you can add an external CD-ROM drive and a soundboard with speakers later. Expanding an 80486 system to add multimedia capabilities can be intimidating because many highly technical decisions must be made. You can buy any of a range of upgrade kits, however, that offer all of the hardware you will need in several different combinations, depending upon your price range and the sophistication of your tastes. Many dealers offer multimedia software bundles to go with their hardware kits, especially if the vendor installs the hardware and software for you. This brings us to the last step in purchasing a personal computer.

Step 5: Selecting a Vendor

Choosing where to buy your personal computer is an important part of the decision, even though it is the final step in the process. This is a very individual decision that only you can make; it depends on the first four steps, and also on your self-confidence and computer literacy. You can shop at many retail stores whose only business is selling computers. Their salespeople are often helpful, they provide full service, and they require you to know less than if you were purchasing from another source, such as a mail order house. They will load your hard disk with the operating system and perhaps even the application programs you purchase. Their local presence can provide a certain sense of security and convenience that you will not find elsewhere. They may even offer training classes for new users. Of course, you pay for this convenience and service in the long run, even if the training classes are free of extra charge.

An alternative is to purchase your system from a large discount computer and/or office supply store. It may still be a local store, but it does not offer the same service. You must know more about what you want in such a store, although sales assistants can give some advice. You purchase from available stock, which may not offer precisely the brand or configuration you had in mind. On the other hand, the discount store could have exactly what you want, and the total cost of your system will certainly be lower there than at the computer retail store. To save this money, you must bear more of the burden. Also, although the discount store may offer repair service at a certain rate per hour, you can usually not rely on the same startup service that a computer retail store would provide.

Many department stores and national chain stores sell computer systems, as well. Selling computers is not their only business; computers are just one of the many items they sell. Still, you may find very knowledgeable salespeople who are extremely helpful. (You may also find someone who was in the toy department or calculator department last week!) Your choice of types and brands of personal computers will not be as wide as in a computer retail store or a discount computer store. However, a national chain offers a certain sense of security that other sources, including retail computer stores, do not. You know that the chain will probably be around tomorrow if you have a service problem or want to expand your system. In this age of quick business startups and almost-as-quick failures, this security is significant.

If you are computer literate and are brave enough to risk using a mail-order vendor, a campus co-op group, or other source that can sell computers sight unseen, you will find the most variety at the least expense. If you are fortunate enough to have a campus bookstore that offers to sell microcomputers to students at reduced rates, you will find the best of both worlds. You can see what you are ordering, yet the price will compare to that of a mail-order vendor. If no such ideal source is available, some national computer mail-order businesses are reputable and highly dependable. They advertise in all of the major computer magazines. Make sure that you have heard of the vendor, that you pay for your purchase with a charge card of some sort (for recourse in event of a problem), and that you know exactly what you want and can recognize whether that is what is contained in those boxes that are delivered.

If you use a mail-order vendor, you do not converse with one salesman to get advice, nor do you have the opportunity to have your new system assembled and tested before you accept it. Many times you cannot rely on local, after-purchase service either. Usually the vendor will correct a problem or repair your system via mail after you repack it and send it back; a few of the larger catalog vendors arrange local service through third parties.

On the other hand, a mail-order vendor can probably sell you exactly the same hardware and software as other sources offer, or a wider variety, perhaps at half the price. All of this is wonderful as long as you do not need "hand-holding" from the vendor. Most reputable mail-order houses have 24-hour customer service numbers that you can use to communicate with someone if you have a problem setting up your system. Otherwise, a mail-order house leaves you basically on your own.

A VAR (Value-Added Reseller) does more than just sell you hardware and software; he or she also teaches you how to use what you buy.

As a final source of computer systems, you might consult a special vendor known as a **VAR (value-added reseller)**. This person may be associated with a computer retail store or may operate independently, making purchases and configuring a system for you. A VAR acts as a consultant, a salesperson, a purchaser, and often a trainer, as well. This vendor offers the maximum in seller support and the most secure purchase, even though it will be more expensive. Many VARs handle **vertical applications** that offer special software for a particular field. If you operate a small business (for example, a video store) and want a microcomputer system to keep specific records, a VAR can advise you on what hardware and software to buy, including a program or templates written specifically for your business interests. With such advice, you can pick out a system even if you are not very computer literate. Often, the VAR does not charge an hourly fee; instead, the price of the entire personal computer system includes all of the extra service and training.

As you can see, the choice of vendors is both diverse and very individual. Every source has its advantages and disadvantages. All of these vendors may not be available to you, or you may find still other sources, such as classified advertisements in local papers for new or used systems. The amount of money you have to spend, the degree of service you would like, your level of computer literacy, the degree of risk you are willing to assume, the specific hardware and software you require—all of these factors will affect your decision about the source from which you will buy. However, since a personal computer is still a major purchase for most beginning users, it is wise to consider several different vendors before making a choice.

Setting Up, Operating, and Maintaining Your Computer

Once you have purchased your own personal computer, you will probably experience both joy and frustration. You now have your own system to work on as long as you wish, whenever you wish, using the software of your choice. However, you are now also responsible for setting up and operating the computer. Beginners always face a period of confusion, and you can expect some difficulty getting everything to work exactly as you planned it. Installing the mouse, the printer, the modem, and other hardware is time consuming. Although most written directions are fairly simple, you will probably make some mistakes. Perhaps you have neglected to purchase something you need, like a printer cable. If you purchase locally, your salesperson can help with these things and show you exactly how to assemble the system at the store if you ask. Then the system will be disassembled, repacked into boxes, and given to you to reassemble on your own. If you purchase from a mail-order house, usually you have recourse to a toll-free customer service number for new owners. The phone line is often busy, but when you get through, the representative is usually a good source of advice. Even though assembling the system may be a bit overwhelming, patience and a sense of humor will take you a long way.

Installing the software is the next hurdle. Many vendors partition your fixed disk and load the operating system and your copy of *Windows* for you. As we mentioned earlier, some will even load application software that you purchase from them. However, you will want to create your own directories and subdirectories to organize your hard disk, and you will most certainly obtain other software that you must install. Most software installation routines today are menu-driven. They sometimes ask a few questions about printer types, screen displays,

Unpacking a PC; once the computer is unpacked and assembled, you are on your way.

config.sys files, and so forth. Some installation routines, such as the *Works 3.0 for Windows* setup program, automatically recognize your hardware configurations so that you must merely confirm the selections. Nevertheless, you will spend a lot of time reading the documentation that comes with your hardware and software. Directions and documentation are clearer than they have ever been, but you will still have to ponder some questions. Again, you will undoubtedly make some mistakes. Just know that you can reinstall a program if everything does not function the way it should. Software houses have long-distance help lines to answer questions, sometimes without charge. The point is, you should give yourself enough time to install your software and test it before you have to use the system to meet a deadline on a major project.

Preventive Measures and Maintenance

Now that you have your own computer, you are entirely responsible for keeping it in good running order. That means practicing some preventive maintenance. You should avoid exposing the hardware and floppy disks to extreme temperatures and you should keep the equipment reasonably clean. A high-quality **surge protector** and electrical strip is important; this will protect your system from spikes in the electrical lines that supply power to your system. You may even want to use an **uninterruptible power supply (UPS)** which provides an alternative energy source for uninterrupted computing. It contains a surge protector, as well. If there is an unexpected power outage, you can continue to compute for several minutes, saving files and backing up as necessary, instead of aborting all open programs and losing everything in memory.

Dust covers are available for system units and all peripherals. Keeping the system dust-free prolongs its life. You must also clean the monitor screen (when the monitor power is off). Providing enough circulation space around the system unit is also important. Leaving a tower unit in an enclosed cabinet is not a good idea because poor ventilation may allow heat to build up to damaging levels. A few common sense precautions can prevent costly repair bills, or even the complete loss of your system.

Preventive maintenance does not guarantee freedom from problems, however. Since computers are mechanical, you should anticipate that some day, your personal computer will go down. For some reason or another, it will quit running. Hardware is very substantial today, and complete system failure is rare. If you keep the computer clean and exercise care with it, will probably serve you very well, but problems do occur. Don't wait until you have a major problem before you investigate who could service your system and how much it would cost. Reputable, well-trained technicians are common. The vendor from which you purchased your computer probably offers a repair service, unless you purchased the system by mail or from a private party. You can even purchase a maintenance agreement that guarantees to fix your computer within a certain time frame, but this reassurance is expensive.

You can keep your disk drives clean by purchasing and periodically using a disk drive cleaning kit for $5 to $10. The kits are abrasive, so they should not be used too often, but they can remove stray dust and debris from the read/write heads with a minimum of fuss. Figure 14.2 shows a cleaning kit. Of course, if you are technically inclined, you could clean the heads yourself, but leave cleaning dust from the motherboard and aligning the disk drives to a professional computer technician, who can do preventive maintenance checks and cleaning for you at regular intervals.

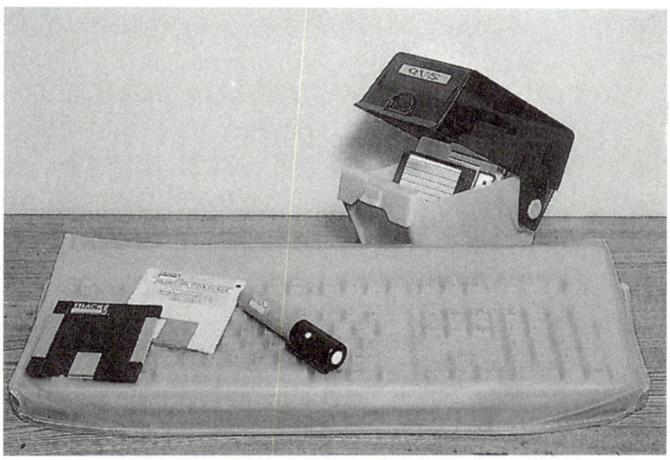

Figure 14.2

A little time and care spent on protecting and cleaning both your hardware and software is quite likely to reduce problems in the long run.

Unless your computer is running 15 hours a day, every day, in an uncontrolled environment, this is rarely necessary more than once a year. The amount of use your computer gets, as well as the kind of care it receives, often determines how much professional attention it requires. Just be aware that you are no longer in a campus lab where hired technicians do this work. Take care of your system and heed warning signs like frequent disk reading errors or data reading errors. These steps can help prevent catastrophic situations such as having the computer fail at 2 A.M. on the morning before a major research paper is due.

Once you have set up your new computer, read all of the documentation, and tested the system, you are on your way to a very rewarding experience. You will soon wonder how you ever functioned without your computer. You will find new uses for it every day. It will become a truly personal computer—an extension of your own productivity. You will now have a microcomputer that does the work that the name *personal computer* implies. In this electronic age, computers have been called "the mind tool" (Graham), the "second self" (Turkle), and many other names that suggest their value as one of our most useful tools. They can change your thinking and increase your personal productivity. Few individuals today question the worth of learning how to purchase and use a personal computer.

Chapter Summary

This chapter describes five steps in the process of purchasing a personal computer. Computer literacy—knowing how to use personal computer software and hardware—is a prerequisite to making an intelligent computer investment, as is defining and prioritizing your requirements.

Beginners often overlook an essential rule: Software determines hardware. This means that you should first choose the specific software that you intend to use, then you can identify the hardware required to run your software and add it to your budgeted costs, thus avoiding last-minute surprises.

Hardware selection begins with your choice of a general family—Apple or IBM. From there you decide on the personal computer's size, CPU type, clock speed, RAM, secondary storage, expandability, and monitor type. Deciding to work in a *Windows* environment and to exploit multimedia capabilities depends on your other software choices.

The last step is to select a vendor. Your choices include the campus bookstore, mail-order outlets, value-added resellers, and retail stores. Your budget, the amount of service you require, your level of computer literacy, the degree of risk you are willing to assume, and the specific hardware and software you require all affect your decision about the source from which you buy your computer.

After you have bought a system, you will have to deal with the initial setup, proper operation, preventive maintenance, and required repairs. Purchasing and learning to use an individual microcomputer system requires a period of adjustment that is well-rewarded once you have mastered your own system.

KEY TERMS

CD-ROM
clock speed
compatible
computer literacy
freeware
gigabyte
megahertz
multimedia
PCN
personal communication network
PDA

personal digital assistant
Pentium
shareware
surge protector
throughput
uninterruptible power supply
value-added reseller
VAR
vertical application

REVIEW QUESTIONS

1. List and explain the five major steps involved in purchasing a personal computer system.
2. Justify this statement: "A prerequisite for purchasing a personal computer is computer literacy."
3. Explain why it is essential to define and prioritize your requirements for a personal computer.
4. Explain this statement: "Software determines hardware."
5. Identify sources of software; summarize the advantages and disadvantages of each.
6. List and explain the various factors involved in hardware selection.
7. Identify several vendors of computer hardware.
8. Review the advantages and disadvantages of each vendor source identified in Question 7.
9. Identify what you must do after you make the purchase decision to put your new computer to work.
10. Summarize the preventive maintenance steps you must take to keep your personal computer running.

SOFTWARE EXERCISES

Exercise 14.1

1. Go to your school's library.
2. Compare reviews in *PC Magazine* and *PC World* magazines of 80486-based IBM compatibles that have similar configurations.
3. Using *Works*, write a report on the two machines that received Editor's Choice awards.
4. Check your report for spelling, grammar, and appearance.
5. Save your report.
6. Print your report and exit *Works*.

Exercise 14.2

1. Go to your school's library.
2. Compare reviews in *Mac World* and *Mac User* magazines of any two different Macintosh computer models.
3. Using *Works*, write a report on these two machines.

4. Check your report for spelling, grammar, and appearance.
5. Save your report.
6. Print your report and exit *Works*.

Exercise 14.3

1. Assume that you have $2,000 to spend on a computer system.
2. Go to your school's library.
3. Read reviews in *PC Magazine* or *PC World* of IBM-compatible PCs. Note the configurations of two machines that do not exceed your budget.
4. Using *Works*, write a report on these two machines.
5. Check your report for spelling, grammar, and appearance.
6. Save your report.
7. Print your report and exit *Works*.

Exercise 14.4

1. Assume that you have $2,000 to spend on a computer system.
2. Go to your school's bookstore or another campus outlet that sells IBM computers at a discount.
3. Check out the prices, and note the configuration of a machine that does not exceed your budget.
4. Using *Works*, write a report on this machine.
5. Check your report for spelling, grammar, and appearance.
6. Save your report.
7. Print your report and exit *Works*.

Exercise 14.5

1. Visit a computer store that sells primarily IBM and compatible computers.
2. Note the ten best-selling software packages.
3. Using *Works*, write a report on this software.
4. Check your report for spelling, grammar, and appearance.
5. Save your report.
6. Print your report and exit *Works*.

Exercise 14.6

1. Visit a computer store that sells primarily Apple Macintosh computers.
2. Note the ten best-selling software packages.
3. Using *Works*, write a report on this software.

4. Check your report for spelling, grammar, and appearance.
5. Save your report.
6. Print your report and exit *Works*.

Exercise 14.7

1. Make a complete list of your software and hardware requirements for a computer system. Use the five-step process from this chapter as a guide.
2. Compile a comparative price list for your requirements from three sources: a mail-order vendor, a retail computer store, and your campus bookstore (or a second retail computer store).
3. Using *Works*, write a report on your findings. Use the integrated features of *Works* to produce a spreadsheet with the comparative prices; move this data into the word processor to complete the report.
4. Check your report for spelling, grammar, and appearance.
5. Save your report.
6. Print your report and exit *Works*.

Exercise 14.8

1. Using *Works*, write a report that compares each of the four integrated *Works* tools with a similar well-known stand-alone program.
2. Check your report for spelling, grammar, and appearance.
3. Save your report.
4. Print your report and exit *Works*.
5. Give the report to your instructor.

Exercise 14.9

1. Do some research into shareware.
2. Using *Works*, write a report on the following shareware topics: the shareware concept, the numbers and types of shareware programs available, and the five shareware best-sellers.
3. Check your report for spelling, grammar, and appearance.
4. Save your report.
5. Print your report and exit *Works*.

Exercise 14.10

1. Load *Works* into memory.
2. Choose the word processing program.
3. Open the file require.wps on the student data diskette.
4. Print the require.wps file.
5. Close require.wps and exit *Works*.

6. Use the resources of your school's library and community to configure and price a computer system that best meets the requirements given for each of the situations.
7. Use the integrated features of *Works* to construct a report that lists your recommended software/hardware configuration along with its cost.
8. Check your report for spelling, grammar, and appearance.
9. Save your report as require1.
10. Print require1.wps.
11. Close require1.wps and exit *Works*.

Exercise 14.11

1. Form into teams of three each.
2. Make an appointment with the administrator in charge of the PC resources at your school or at the place of business where one member of your group works.
3. Find out:
   a. How many computers of each type the administrator manages
   b. What software is available
   c. What changes to hardware and software the administrator anticipates for the next year and the next three years
4. Use *Works* to create a report based on your research.
5. Check your report for spelling, grammar, and appearance.
6. Save your report as research.
7. Print research.wps.
8. Close research.wps and exit *Works*.

Exercise 14.12

1. Write a report that uses your major as a basis for examining the ways you now foresee using the *Works* integrated software in connection with your present or future job. Include a discussion of other software you foresee needing to know.
2. Check your report for spelling, grammar, and appearance.
3. Save your report as future.
4. Print future.wps.
5. Close future.wps and exit *Works*.

Chapter 15

Computer Security And Ethics

Objectives

After studying this chapter you will be able to:

- *List and explain the major types of computer crime*
- *Recall the measures software companies take to combat piracy*
- *List the major types of computer viruses*
- *Explain the effects the major types of computer viruses have on personal computer hardware and software*
- *Identify the major virus prevention and cure techniques*
- *Summarize the protection given to individuals by the 1974 National Privacy Act and its 1986 extension*
- *Identify privacy issues for users of E-mail*

Computer Crime

The intrigue, suspense, and drama that accompany electronic crime make it one of the most interesting computer-related topics. Everyone likes a good mystery story, it seems, and computer crime, although it is a huge problem that costs us billions of dollars annually, is fascinating to almost everyone. Tales of an exotic computer virus spreading through thousands of business and personal computer systems become the cover topics of national news magazines. Rumors of a bank employee accumulating thousands of dollars by transferring the rounded-off portion of pennies from individual bank accounts (the so-called *salami-slicing technique*) become the topics of everyday conversation. Admiration for clever, bored hackers who can break into national security systems, wreaking havoc and potential nuclear war, make them the subjects for popular movies.

The computer criminal is glorified, whether the crime is intentional or not, because we are fascinated by the use of the computer for productivity, even when the product is crime. There are many types of computer crime, and although they are costly, they often go unpunished for a variety of reasons. We do not intend this chapter to be an exhaustive investigation into computer security and ethics, but only your introduction to the scope and magnitude of computer crime as it exists in America today. Nor will we address the physical theft of computer equipment for resale or for employee use. Instead, we will briefly outline the major types of crime that center on misuse of hardware and misuse and/or alteration of software.

Types of Crime

There is an almost endless variety of computer crime, but most computer crime fits into a few categories: unlawful access to information, manipulation of information for unwarranted gains, vandalism of hardware and software, and sabotage of systems. This includes the deliberate theft or criminal destruction of computer data or services. Use of computer hardware, software or data for illegal activities is part of computer crime, as is the illegal use of computers for legitimate purposes.

You will often see the topic of computer crime divided into five major types. First is **manipulation of computer input**, resulting in unlawful gain for an individual. As an example, a computer operator might change a data entry to reflect a lower charge for a friend's account. Implanting a **Trojan horse** program that looks innocent on the surface and runs normally the first few times, but then runs amok and destroys data to be processed is another example. The field of computer security has spawned passwords, **data encryption** (recoding data to protect its sensitive nature), and call-back procedures to verify access as a means to protect data and programs in the business environment.

Changing computer programs is another type of crime. The **salami-slicing** technique is one example; a programmer might alter computer code to transfer all of the leftover fractions of cents from rounding of calculations to a personal account. Computer **viruses** (programs that quickly spread through all exposed computer systems, destroying data or causing the systems to become congested and perhaps fail to run) also fall into this category of changing or destroying computer programs.

A third type of computer crime, **stealing data**, is also prevalent. Someone who sells the company mailing list of customers without authorization commits this type of crime. Someone who simply obtains unauthorized access to electronic records for gain, such as a competitive edge, is also guilty of computer crime. **Stealing computer time** can be just as insidious. Using the company computers for your own profit, or perhaps using someone else's Compuserve or Prodigy account without permission would be an example of stealing computer time.

Software Piracy

The final type of crime, **stealing computer programs**, is perhaps the most common type of computer crime, and the one that is least prosecuted. The field of computer ethics is primarily a response to the problem of unauthorized copying of computer programs. The futile attempt of software companies to impose **copy-protection** on their software (to prevent duplication of any part of the programs) was a response to this enormous problem. The practice was abandoned because it punished the legitimate user and added significantly to the complexity and cost of programs.

The **end-user license** you receive when you purchase a software program allows your individual use of the program. Often, you do not own a program that you buy. The company that produced the program actually owns the **source code**—the lines of programming instructions; you own only the medium on which the code is stored (the disk), not the program itself. By opening the package when you purchase a software program, you agree to abide by the end-user agreement to run the program for your own use on one system.

A copy of the end-user license and a registration number are always included with a legitimate software purchase. Copying the program and treating it like shareware or public domain freeware is computer crime. The practice of duplicating and disseminating unauthorized copies of registered software is referred to as computer **piracy**. The growth of the computer virus problem has succeeded in slowing the practice of pirating software somewhat, but it is still an enormous problem that costs software publishers millions annually. Piracy is as much a computer crime as the other illegal acts mentioned earlier. This blurs the stereotype of the computer criminal as a bright, bored, anti-social **hacker** (person who gains unauthorized access to a computer network for profit, criminal mischief, or personal reasons) who feels unappreciated and seeks revenge.

Recent surveys of personal computer users reveal that many users see no crime in using pirated software or giving away copies of their software to others unless they profit monetarily from it. Nevertheless, violating the terms of the end-user license can result in criminal prosecution. As with so many other types of computer crime, however, violations often go unpunished. A large business may fear the negative publicity surrounding knowledge that someone has tampered with the company's data or programs; the high cost of litigation may also prevent a business from vigorously punishing the computer criminal. To publicly admit to a security failure or a theft of vital records or programs may affect a company's credibility. To avoid further damage the firm quietly discharges the criminal, who may go on to the next job and repeat the crime.

Most certainly, the cost in money and time of pursuing an individual computer pirate is simply not cost effective for a software publisher. Educating computer users about their rights and responsibilities is one means of combating the problem of piracy, but it remains a severe problem. The five major types of computer crime are summarized in Table 15.1

Table 15.1 Five Types of Computer Crime

Type of Crime	Example
Manipulating computer input	Lowering charge account balances
Changing computer programs	Salami-slicing
	Trojan horse
	Viruses
Stealing data	Selling mailing lists without authorization
	Using access to gain a competitive edge
Stealing computer time	Using company computers for personal profit
	Using someone's Compuserve or Prodigy account without permission
Stealing computer programs	Making unauthorized copies of software programs

Viruses

Definition and Types

Viruses emerged as a problem after computers became commonplace for a good portion of the population. Such programs are simply computer instructions—code—that have been written to act in a destructive way after invading a system surreptitiously. Viruses are sometimes written for revenge, sometimes just to create mischief. At their best, they are a time-consuming nuisance; at their worst they are destructive and costly. They have become such a problem that 1988 was dubbed "the year of the virus." The plague began with the transmission of literally hundreds of varieties of computer viruses that could be attached to electronic files. When transmitted and triggered by a preplanned event, such a program might multiply itself and fill the memory and secondary storage capacity of a system. A **file virus** attacked executable files—those with the extensions .com or .exe—and rendered those programs unusable. The year climaxed in November when Robert Morris, a graduate student from Cornell, infected the Unix-based Arpanet computer network (the precursor of the Internet network), which in turn infected several thousand computer systems in a matter of hours. Even though the virus destroyed no information, the cost of removing it from all systems and the resulting **downtime** (the period when the computers cannot be used) was estimated at $100 million by the Computer Virus Industry Association.

Viruses can be distinguished as **boot viruses** (which attach to the boot sector of formatted disks and reside there) or file viruses, as described above. **Signature viruses** are recognized by identifiable strings of code they contain.The most common boot virus is a signature virus called "Stoned." It spreads from personal computer to personal computer by hiding in the boot sector of a disk in the A: drive. It then spreads to the hard disk, reassigning the original boot sector to other tracks and sectors on the hard disk. It can also write over data that resides there, such as the file allocation table (see Chapter 3). A common signature virus that propagates as a file virus is called "Jerusalem."

Sometimes viruses are classified by the damage they do. A **worm** virus like the one the Cornell student used infects systems that run multiple sessions, taking advantage of security flaws in the operating system. A **bomb** is a virus that is triggered by a date or event; it may be activated, for example, when the computer's internal calendar indicates a certain day. The virus named "Michaelangelo" is one of these bombs. A Trojan horse sits complacently along with another useful program that performs correctly a specified number of times. As its historical name suggests, a Trojan horse appears to be a gift, but instead bears destructive forces within itself. Suddenly it activates and destroys data on the hard disk.

Regardless of how you classify viruses, they are all violations of computer security. States such as New Hampshire and Texas have already passed antivirus legislation; other states are in the process of doing so.

The First Virus

The first documented virus was written in 1983 by a student, Fred Cohen, at the University of Southern California. For his doctoral dissertation on the lack of computer security in America, he proved that a tiny (4K) string of computer code could replicate itself, growing exponentially and changing the behavior of the computer's operating system. Since that time, hundreds of different viruses have been developed, many just as mischievous exercises to test a system. Frequently, however, they get out of hand, and they have proven to be as tough to cure as their biological counterparts. Table 15.2 lists some of the more common viruses.

Table 15.2 Common Viruses

Virus Name	Characteristics	Consequences
Red Cross, also called Ambulance Car	Infects .com files	Causes a siren noise and displays an ambulance driving along the bottom of the screen.
Dark Avenger-B	Installs itself in memory and attaches itself to .com, .exe, .sys, or overlay file	After every 16th infection, it writes "Eddie lives . . . Somewhere in Time" to a random sector on the disk. This sector is irretrievably lost.
Stealth, also called 4096, FroDo, the Century Virus, and 100 Years	Attacks .com, .exe, .sys, overlay, and even some data files	Alters the disk files to the point where they become unusable.
Joshi	Locks the system on January 5	Displays a message and unlocks when the user types "Happy Birthday Joshi." Joshi damages nonstandard hard disks and floppy disks that do not use the 360K format.

(continued)

Table 15.2 Continued Common Viruses

Virus Name	Characteristics	Consequences
Stoned	Nondestructive signature virus	Announces "Your computer is now stoned" when activated.
Michaelangelo	Activates annually on March 14	Destroys files on the hard disk
LoFro	Hides from antivirus checkers	Alters operating system interrupts
Dedicate	Polymorphic; resistant to virus checkers	Mutates using a Dark Avenger Mutation Engine (DAME)
Jerusalem	File virus	Destroys .com and .exe files
Twin-351	Lives as a hidden file; nondestructive	Does not change modification date when it attaches to a file
Grand York File	Destroys partition table on the C drive	C drive no longer exists when the computer is rebooted.

Sources: *PC Magazine*, October 29, 1991, p. 271; March 16, 1993, pp. 209–218.

Virus Scanners and Cleaners

Many antivirus scanners and removers have been developed to combat known viruses. They can be purchased at retail stores, but many are available as shareware, as well. Symantec, Central Point, Norton, Certus, and many other companies have antivirus programs that you can purchase, entitling you to all future **upgrades**. An upgrade is a newer version of a software program; keeping antivirus software current is critical because every new virus requires new code to detect it and remove it.

You use a virus protector program to first scan a disk for any number of different virus varieties. You then run a program to clean the disk of a particular virus if one is detected. If the file allocation table of a disk has been deleted, it can often be restored. Utility programs can reconstruct hard disks.

Antivirus software that can scan and remove a virus before it is triggered requires that you use the scanner immediately upon turning on power to the computer. The price of this constant vigilance is time; scanning for different viruses can take several minutes. Also, you must continue to acquire updates of the virus checker for it to be effective against new strains.

Also, some newer viruses are clearly written to elude antivirus programs; they are extremely difficult to detect and they resist cleaning. **Stealth viruses** can avoid detection, and **polymorphic viruses** constantly mutate; every time they replicate, the code is altered, but it still remains destructive.

Checksum techniques by which virus checkers find the unauthorized code entails a mathematical calculation on each file checked, followed by a comparison to the original sum the next time the file is checked. This electronic fingerprinting comparison technique is called **integrity checking** of files. This is just one of the ways that virus protection programs work to help you avoid the serious consequences of a destructive virus. No virus checker and cleaner is completely effective, however. Once a virus has done its damage and you are unable to retrieve lost clusters and sectors, often your only recourse is to begin anew after cleaning the virus from the hard drive. This entails reformatting the hard drive and reinstalling all of your software programs and any data that you have on backup disks.

Prevention

The best medicine for viruses is prevention. Like their biological equivalent, viruses are most often transmitted by contact, perhaps with public bulletin board software, unauthorized copies of pirated programs, and unauthorized use of your personal computer by others.

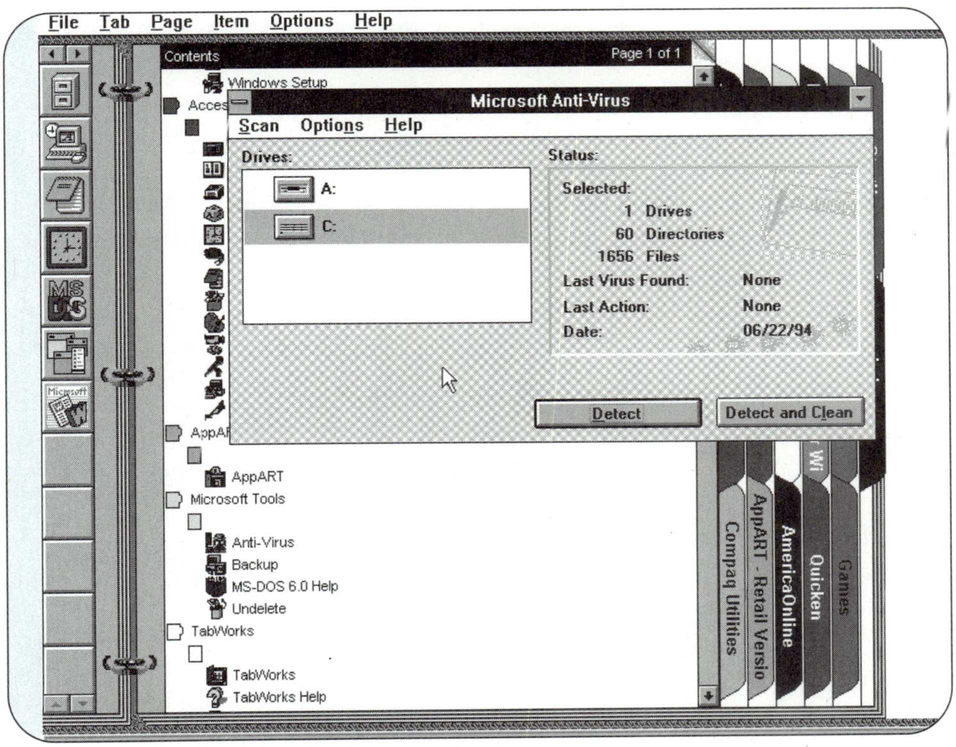

Figure 15.1

Virus Prevention

We mentioned that viruses have slowed the flood of pirated software. Wise users have learned not to accept copies of popular software at ridiculously low prices. Make sure the package includes a registration number and an end-user license when you purchase software. Public domain software and shareware are particularly prone to viruses planted by malicious individuals. Know your source of shareware or freeware. If you download software from a bulletin board, it is a good idea to isolate the new program by storing it on a floppy disk rather than your hard disk. Then use any antiviral software you have to scan the disk for known viruses before you use the program. If you use public bulletin boards and data communications a great deal, installing a virus scanner that checks every time you turn on the computer might be worth the investment.

Above all, keeping current backups is important. Throughout this book, we have stressed the value of backup copies of programs and personal data that you value. You should always keep the original disks from which you install your software programs. Store them away from your computer, ready to be retrieved to reinstall the programs if necessary. Don't use these originals as working copies; use copied disks instead. The possibility of a virus infecting your software programs is only one of the many calamities that can face beginning and seasoned users alike. Keep second copies of important documents, spreadsheets, and databases, as well. Losing valuable software to a virus or to any other cause is disabling once you have begun to depend on your computer as the helpful tool that it is.

Finally, unauthorized use of your computer is dangerous. You should know at all times who is using your personal system, and for what means. Employers often allow their employees to take work to finish on their home computers. Employees often bring software into the workplace. If you know exactly who uses your system, and what programs are affected, you can guard against viruses and other unforeseen calamities, as well. A fellow worker can unwittingly transmit a virus to your machine without even realizing that one exists on an executable file. If only you use your personal computer, you know that your software is virus free, and if you do not frequently access public bulletin boards, you are reasonably safe from computer viruses.

Computer Security Legislation

Since the 1970s computer technology has raced forward, leaving computer security techniques and legislation to protect your privacy far behind. Some laws do seek to punish computer crime, such as the national Computer Fraud and Abuse Act. As we mentioned, however, in reality computer crime often goes unpunished. Bringing a computer criminal to trial is difficult, time consuming, expensive, and potentially embarrassing, so most businesses choose to avoid it. Some of the federal legislation on computer crime is listed in Table 15.3.

Table 15.3 U.S. Computer Crime Legislation

Privacy Act (1974)	Applies only to federal records; protects you from unauthorized individuals using your records.
Right to Financial Privacy Act (1978)	Certain government agencies cannot search your bank records.
Electronic Communications Privacy Act (1986)	Electronic messages on public networks are protected; those on private networks are not.
Computer Matching and Privacy Act (1988)	Agencies cannot cross-check files from another government agency to verify eligibility; has many loopholes.
Video Privacy and Protection Act (1988)	Your video rental records cannot be accessed without a court order or your consent.
Fair Credit Reporting Act (1970)	You have the right to inspect your computerized financial records.

Some laws protect personal privacy, as well, but there are too few of them, and they are not strictly enforced. Interpretations of laws often ignore your right when using electronic mail to the same privacy as when mailing a letter. The national Fair Credit Reporting Act protects your credit records from unauthorized access.

Although there is a federal Electronic Communications Privacy Act, this law hasn't yet prevented employers from viewing E-mail correspondence between employees. In 1986, Congress passed this law extending the existing 1974 Privacy Act protection for oral and wire communications to electronic communications. The act prevents government agents and third parties from intercepting electronic mail, but it has not been held to cover interception of business electronic mail messages by private parties. Most companies have staunchly defended their right to monitor all computer activity within their company, if only for the security of the company.

Providing Computer Security

Computers were used for business before personal systems became available. Naturally, therefore, any current computer security practices have come from the business world. Log-on procedures, passwords, and personal identification numbers (PINs) have long been used to protect hardware and software in the business world. The physical hardware has often been isolated and well-protected on a single floor of a building. Even desktop microcomputers in business settings today often are locked in cases when not in use to prevent unauthorized access or theft.

When businesses gained the ability to process data at a distance with distributed processing and teleprocessing, they developed data encryption to protect sensitive material as it was transmitted across public telecommunications systems. Even small, personal computer accounting programs today lock out a user who unsuccessfully gives a password three times. Some information services and bulletin boards follow **call-back procedures** that verify a user's access by returning the call to be certain the connection comes from the proper computer system.

All of these safeguards help, but no computer system is completely secure. The moment a communication signal passes over remote connections, the danger of violation of security increases. Software for microcomputers does not have the sophistication of the software for larger systems. Although we have borrowed many practices from larger systems, generally microcomputer systems have less security than minicomputers and mainframes. Computer security is becoming a major concern with the move toward the information superhighway that many envision will network our nation together.

Privacy and E-Mail

In Chapter 12 you learned that electronic mail is a means of correspondence from user to user via a computer network. E-mail has become widely used by microcomputer owners in the last few years. Some electronic mail systems transmit messages via a local area network (computers connected via cable over a limited

Figure 15.2

Popular E-Mail Software

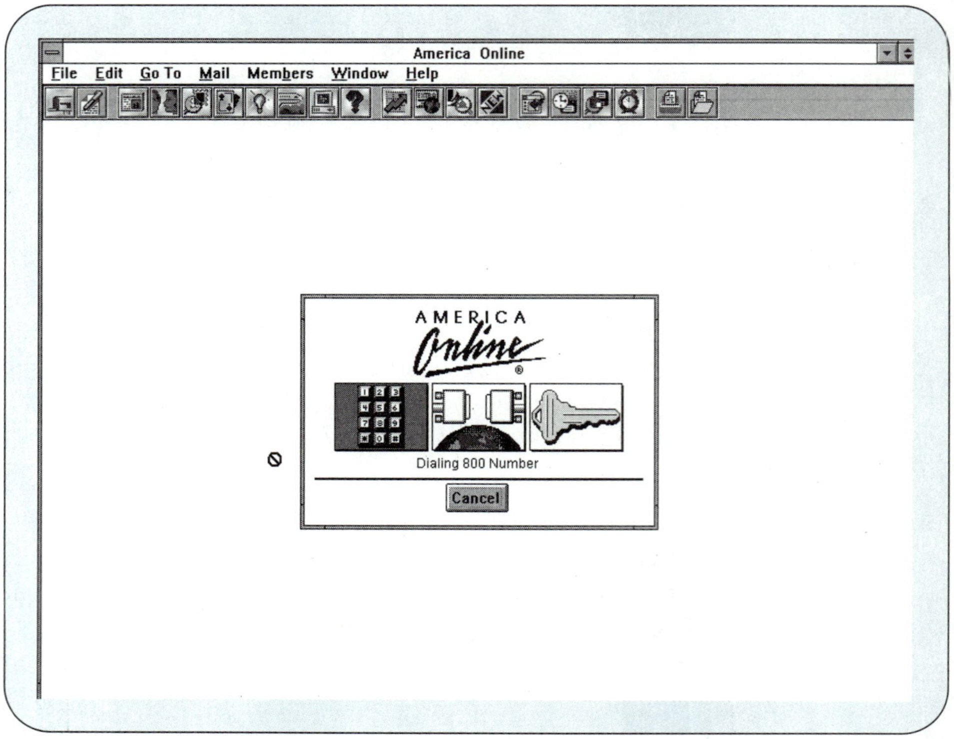

area); others send them over wide area connections (computers connected via phone lines over the entire country), as was noted in Chapter 12.

Many different kinds of E-mail software packages are available, for large systems and personal systems alike. IBM's PROFS became famous during the Oliver North trial (copies of E-mail documents thought to be deleted still existed). *WordPerfect Office* has an E-mail system for microcomputer connections, as does Microsoft's *Office Professional*. Most software suites, or bundled sets of applications from one software publisher, include mail applications. Some popular E-mail software is shown in Figure 15.2.

More than 40 million people in the United States are using some form of E-mail. The Internet that we discussed in Chapter 12 is emerging as the backbone of the information superhighway, and more and more personal users are accessing it. The E-mail community has become very broad. It includes not only the people in your company's other offices, telecommuters working at home, and employees using laptops in the field, but also the company's suppliers and customers.

In recent years, the rights of employees to use E-mail without employers and superiors having access to their messages has been tested. Can a company enter the electronic files of an absent employee to obtain vital company data? Can a company legally intercept and read electronic mail messages to ensure adherence to its policies? Some companies believe that employees should realize that E-mail messages generated from company computers and stored on company media are company property. United Parcel Service reminds its employees on the screen that they should use the system for UPS business only and that the company retains the right to monitor messages. No current federal law specifically addresses the rights of E-mail users and owners over private E-mail networks.

Basing their case on the Electronic Communications Privacy Act workers from two different major corporations took their companies to court over the privacy issues involved in E-mail communication. The employees felt that they had the right to privacy to protect their messages from being monitored by management. In one case, the systems manager responsible for managing the company's minicomputer systems systematically read electronic mail sent via MCI Mail from the 700 employees at headquarters to people outside the facility. The employees considered electronic mail to be their private property, just as their personal letters, and they used it to write notes to their coworkers about their personal lives; sometimes they made derogatory remarks about their supervisors.

Management said that as owners of the E-mail system, they had the right to monitor employee accounts and identify abuse. How much access should employers have to employee workspace, and how much freedom should employees have to use the workspace for their own purposes? These questions have no definitive answers as of yet.

Ron Plesser, former general counsel for the U.S. Privacy Protection Study Commission, suggests that companies make sure that the, "ground rules are explicitly clear." If a company intends to monitor E-mail, it should notify employees of that intention from the beginning. As of now, some companies have informed employees that their electronic mail could be read at any time. Others have assured employees that their E-mail will not be read. The Harvard Law Review has suggested that a federal law should be enacted to require that employees be notified that their messages could be monitored, and prohibit the secret interception of employees' E-mail messages. Many other lawsuits have been filed after employees have been fired because of E-mail messages in the workplace. The issue of personal privacy in electronic communication is growing more important as more and more people use E-mail, voice mail, and fax machines.

You should be aware that any electronic communication, by its very nature, is susceptible to invasion. It is apparent that legislation has not kept up with technology. Computer security and computer privacy are still great problems begging our attention. We believe that future policing of electronic communications in America is inevitable.

Chapter Summary

This chapter is an introduction to the scope and magnitude of computer crime in America. It generally includes unlawful access to information, manipulation of information for unwarranted gains, vandalism of hardware and software, and sabotage of computer systems.

A computer virus is a program written to act in a destructive way. The most benign viruses are time-consuming nuisances that are difficult to remove from your files. The more destructive ones destroy files. Viruses are distinguished by where they attach themselves. A boot virus attaches itself to the boot sector of any formatted disk. A file virus attacks executable files rendering them unusable. Viruses can be classified in many different ways.

Viruses are combatted by antivirus scanners and removers. Prevention is the best defense. Knowing the source of your software is paramount. The ultimate precaution against catastrophe is to back up all of your software.

Several laws have been passed to protect individual privacy. The National Privacy Act of 1974 was passed to protect federal records from unauthorized access. The Electronic Communication Privacy Act of 1986 extended the 1974 legislation by making it illegal for government agents and third parties to intercept electronic mail. However, no law prevents your employer or supervisor from reading E-mail you send through company computers. Computer ethics, computer security, and computer crime will demand our attention in the next decades.

KEY TERMS

bomb
boot virus
call-back procedures
changing computer programs
checksum
copy-protection
data encryption
downtime
end-user license
file virus
hacker
virus integrity checking
manipulation of computer input
piracy
polymorphic virus
salami-slicing
signature virus
source code
stealing computer programs
stealing computer time
stealing data
stealth virus
Trojan horse
upgrade
virus
worm

REVIEW QUESTIONS

1. List the five major types of computer crime.
2. Explain each of the five major types of computer crime.
3. Define the term *computer virus.*
4. Identify the characteristics that distinguish the two major types of viruses.
5. Explain the worm, bomb, and Trojan horse types of viruses and the damage they do.
6. Suppose your system contracts a computer virus. Relate the method(s) you would use to eradicate it.
7. Explain this statement: "The best medicine for viruses is prevention."
8. Detail the legislation aimed at computer security.
9. Explain the measures businesses take to provide computer security.
10. Discuss the privacy of E-mail.

SOFTWARE EXERCISES

Exercise 15.1

1. Go to your school's library.
2. Look up at least two current articles about computer crime.
3. Take careful notes on each article.
4. Note the references completely.
5. Use *Works* to write a report on your findings. Include footnotes and references at the end of the report.
6. Check your report for appearance, spelling, grammar, and content.

Exercise 15.2

1. Go to your school's library.
2. Look up at least two current articles about computer viruses and their causes and effects on computer hardware/software.
3. Take careful notes on each article.
4. Note the references completely.
5. Use *Works* to write a report on your findings. Include footnotes and references at the end of the report.
6. Check your report for appearance, spelling, grammar, and content.

Exercise 15.3

1. Go to your school's library.
2. Look up at least two current articles about computer virus detection, prevention, or cure.
3. Take careful notes on each article.
4. Note the references completely.
5. Use *Works* to write a report on your findings. Include footnotes and references at the end of the report.
6. Check your report for appearance, spelling, grammar, and content.

Exercise 15.4

1. Obtain a copy of Buck Bloombecker's book entitled *Spectacular Computer Crime*.
2. Read the book.
3. Write a report using *Works* on the two most interesting computer crimes reported in the book.
4. Add a section to the paper to detail your suggestions for how each of these crimes could have been prevented.
5. Check your report for appearance, spelling, grammar, and content.

Exercise 15.5

1. Obtain a copy of Cliff Stoll's book entitled *The Cuckoo's Egg.*
2. Read the book.
3. Write a report using *Works* on the two most interesting espionage activities reported in the book.
4. Add a section to the paper to detail your suggestions for how each of these crimes could have been prevented.
5. Check your report for appearance, spelling, grammar, and content.

Exercise 15.6

1. Obtain a copy of the software license agreement found on personal computer software.
2. Read the agreement.
3. Write a report using *Works* that covers the following points: the number of backup copies that may be made, on how many computers you can install the software, and who owns the software.
4. Check your report for appearance, spelling, grammar, and content.

Exercise 15.7

1. Suppose that you have just purchased the latest software package of its kind. It cost you $350. You proudly display your new purchase to your best friend, who is impressed and wants you to make a copy of the program.
2. Prepare your response to your friend's request for class discussion.

Exercise 15.8

1. Suppose that you know of someone who uses a company computer after hours to process personal part-time business records. No one else is around the office and the computer is normally idle at this time.
2. Prepare your response to this situation for class discussion.

Exercise 15.9

1. Suppose that you use the company E-mail system regularly to send messages to your colleagues. You sometimes use the E-mail system to write uncomplimentary remarks about your supervisor to your close friend. You have just read an article that declares that E-mail is company property and that management has the right to read mail you have sent.
2. Prepare to discuss your feelings about the present privacy laws for class.

Exercise 15.10

1. Start up *Works*.
2. Choose the word processor program.
3. Open the file survey.wps from the student data diskette.
4. Complete the survey of opinion on computer ethics by typing your response to the questions in the space provided.
5. When you have answered all the questions, spell check the document.
6. Print the document.
7. Save survey.wps and exit *Works*.

Appendix A

Shortcut Keys for Keyboard Users and Menu Trees

Formatting

bold	Ctrl+B
center	Ctrl+E
italics	Ctrl+I
font size	Ctrl+K
left align	Ctrl+L
justify	Ctrl+J
open fonts	Ctrl+F
right align	Ctrl+R
underline	Ctrl+U

Menu selections

undo	Ctrl+Z
cut	Ctrl+X
copy	Ctrl+C
paste	Ctrl+V
repeat paste	Ctrl+V
repeat search	F7
print	Ctrl+P
preview	Alt+F+V
save	Ctrl+S
ss autosum	Ctrl+M
close window	Ctrl+F4
quit Works	Alt+F4

Moving

top of document	Ctrl+Home
end of document	Ctrl+End
next window	Ctrl+F6
previous window	Ctrl+Shift+F6
next option	Tab
previous option	Shift+Tab

Menu Trees for Word Processing

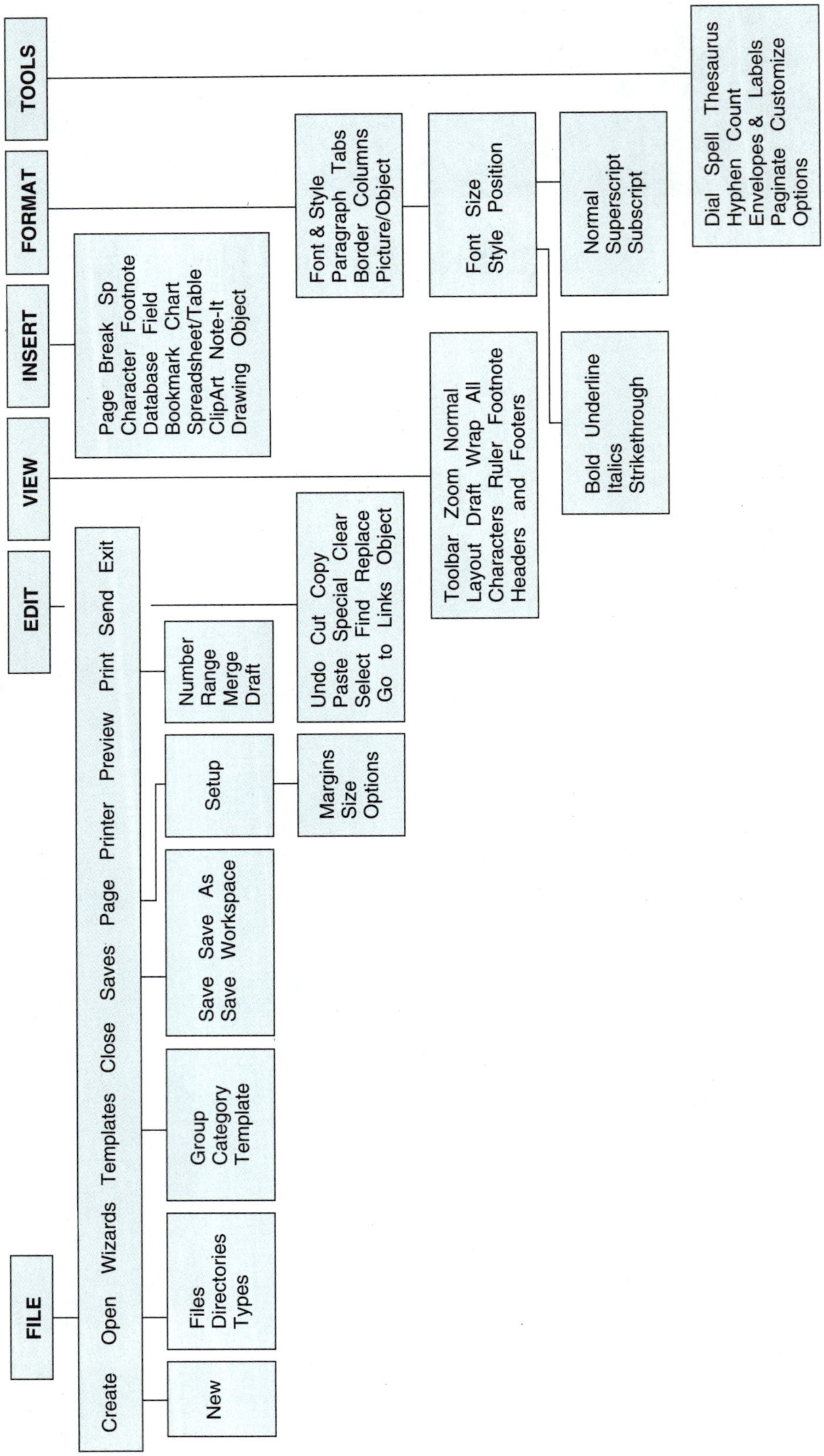

Menu Trees for Spreadsheet

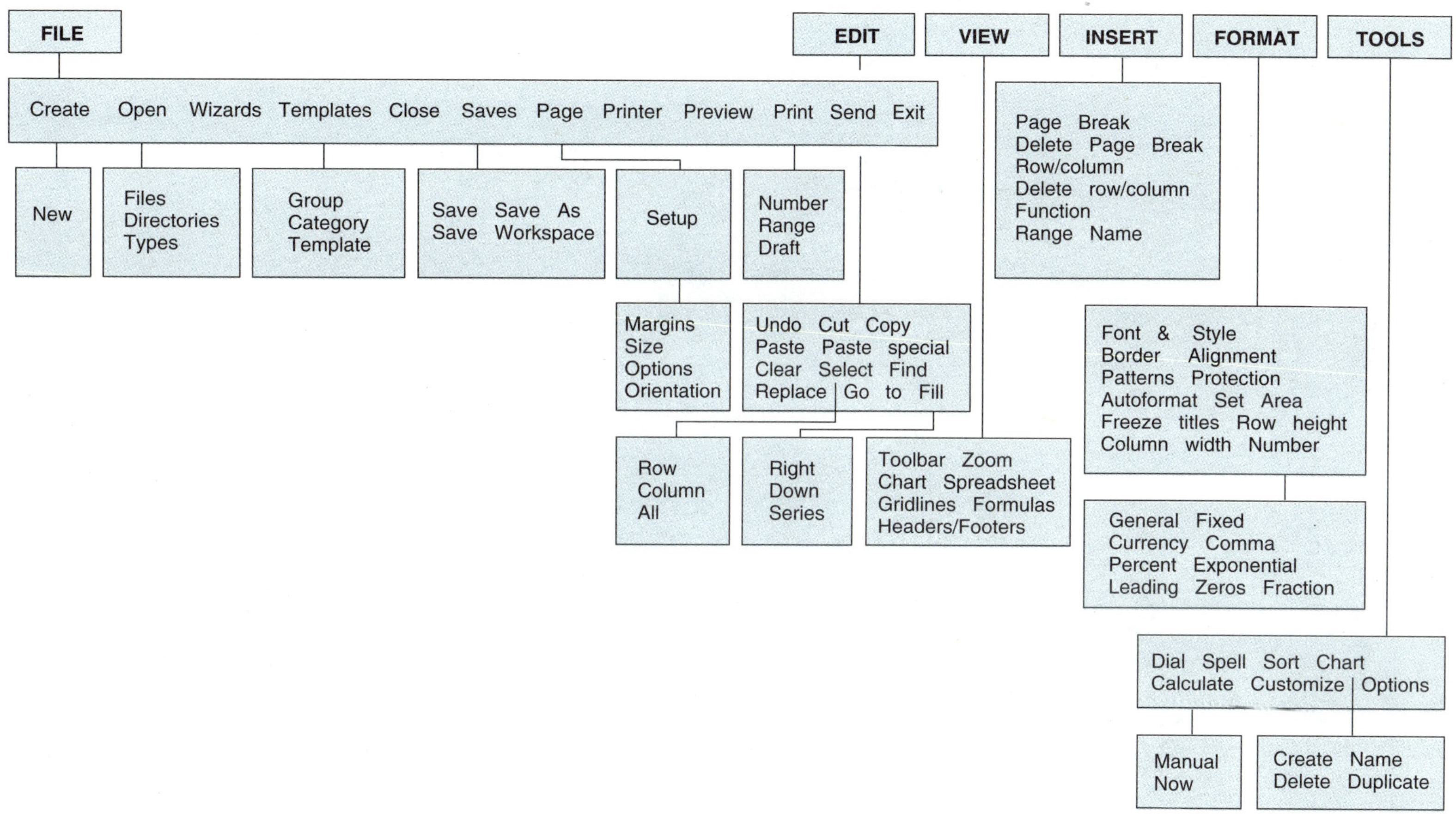

Menu Trees for Charts

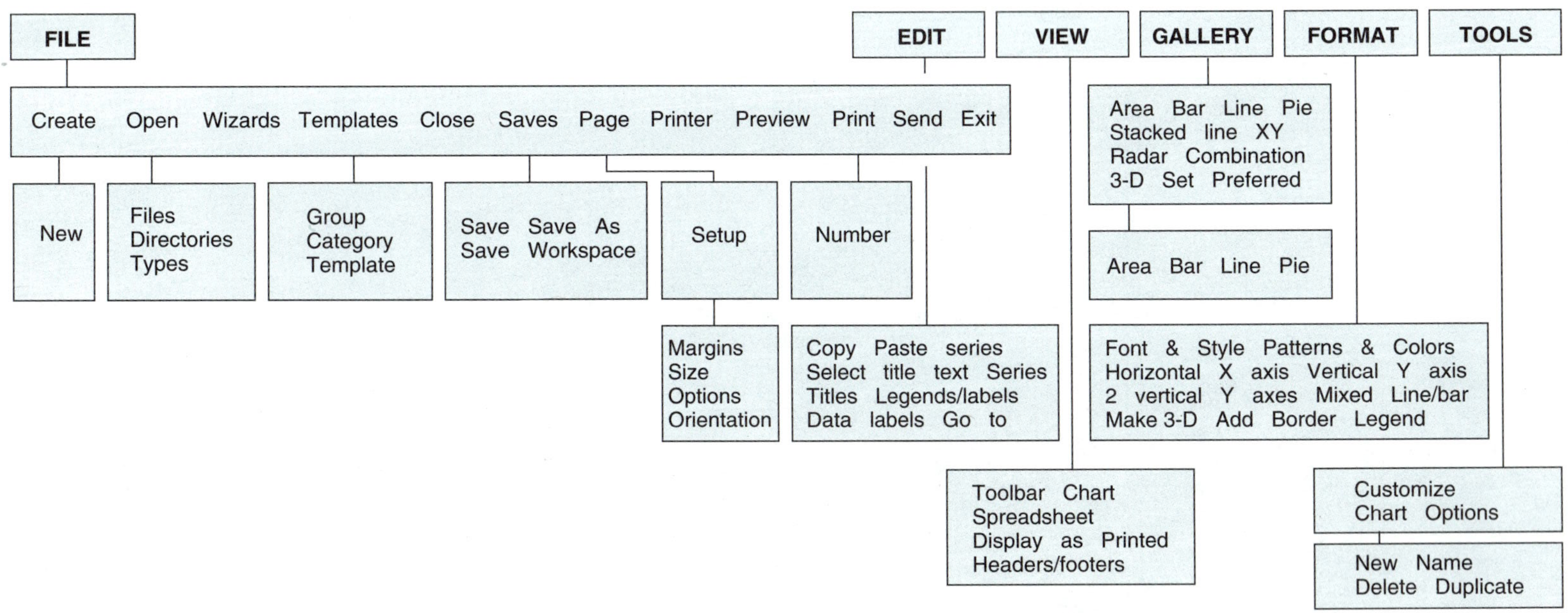

Menu Trees for Database List View

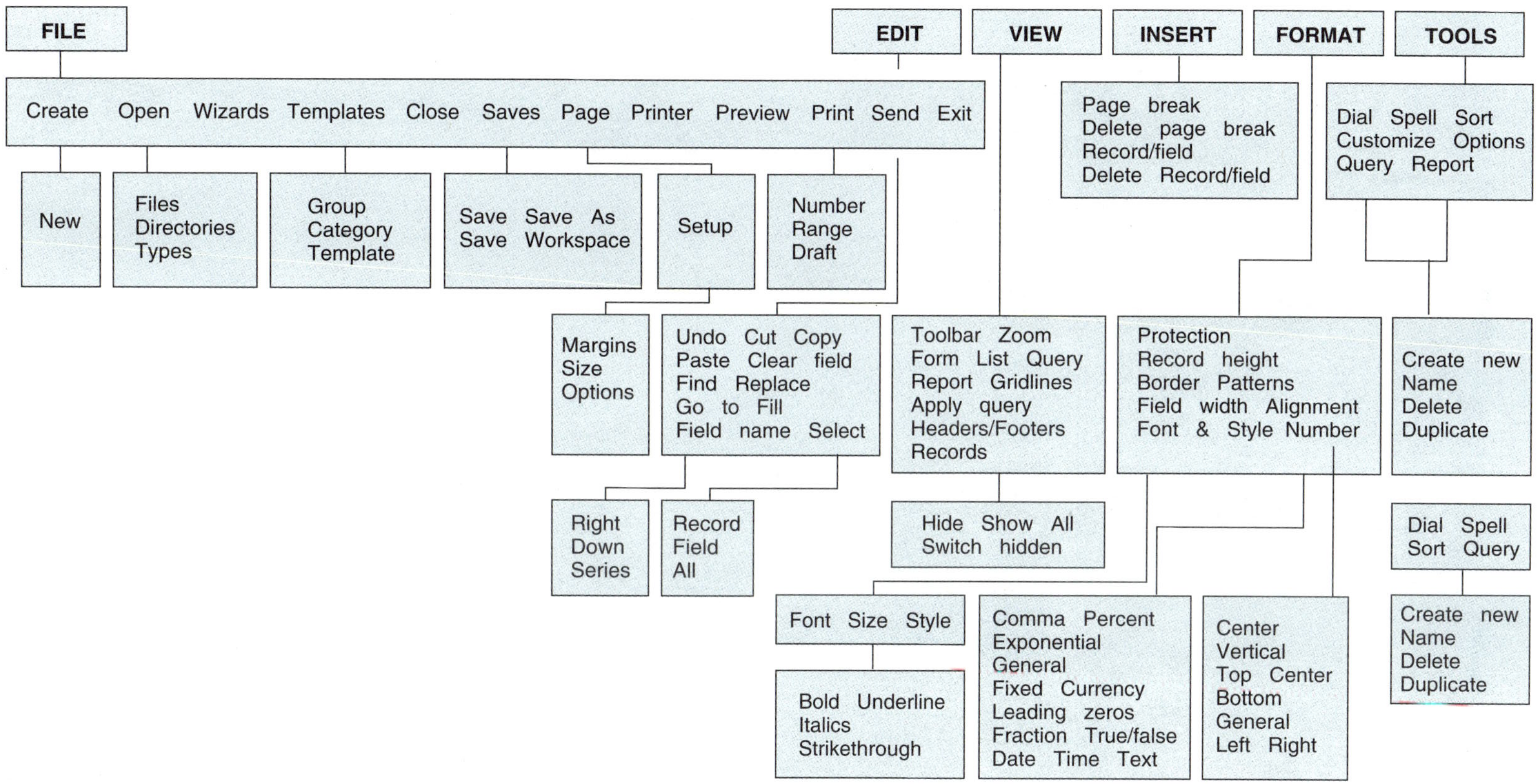

Menu Trees for Database Form View

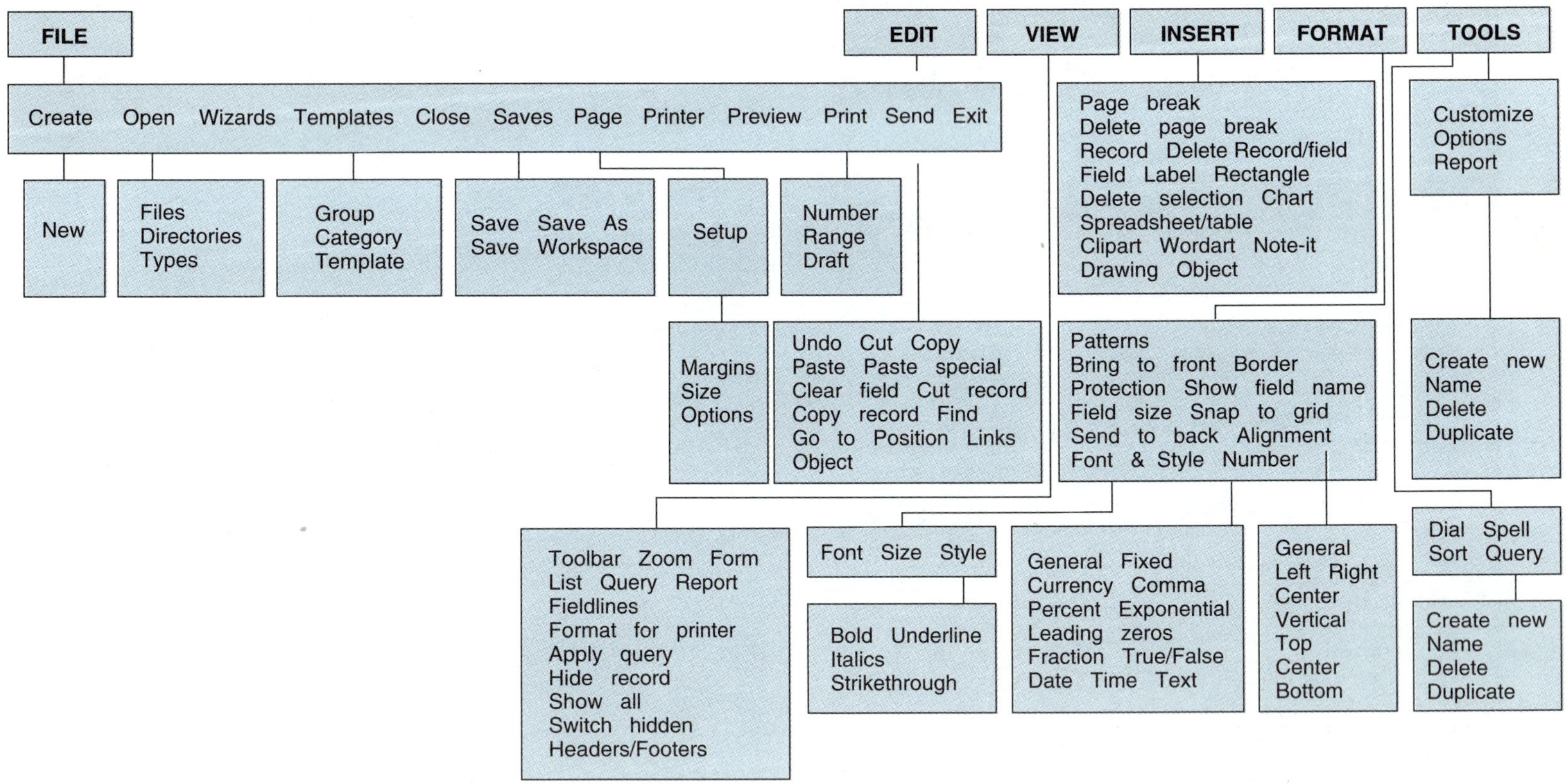

Menu Trees for Database Query View

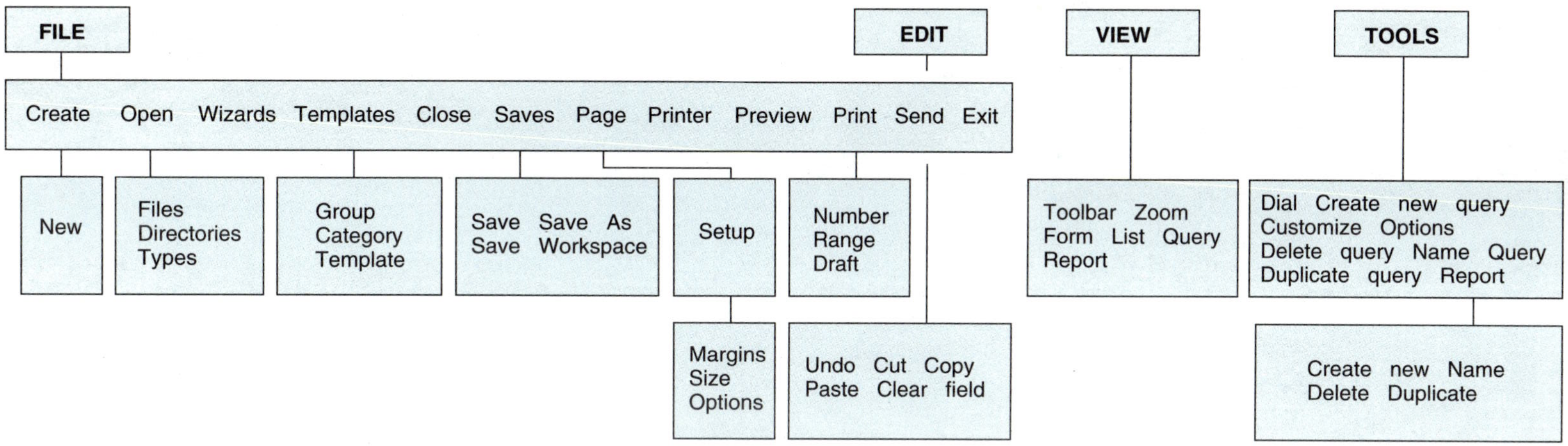

Menu Trees for Database Report View

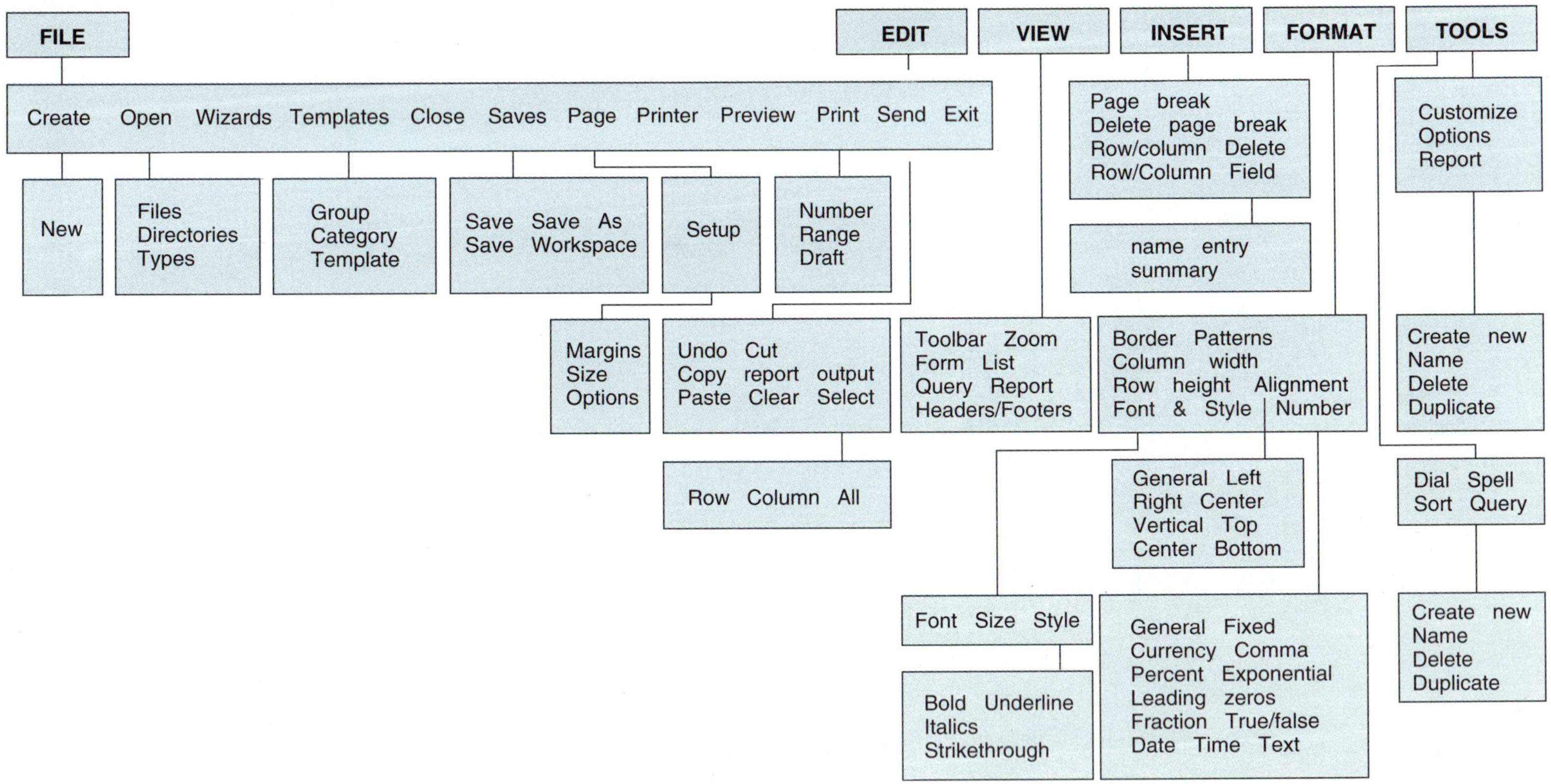

Menu Trees for Communications

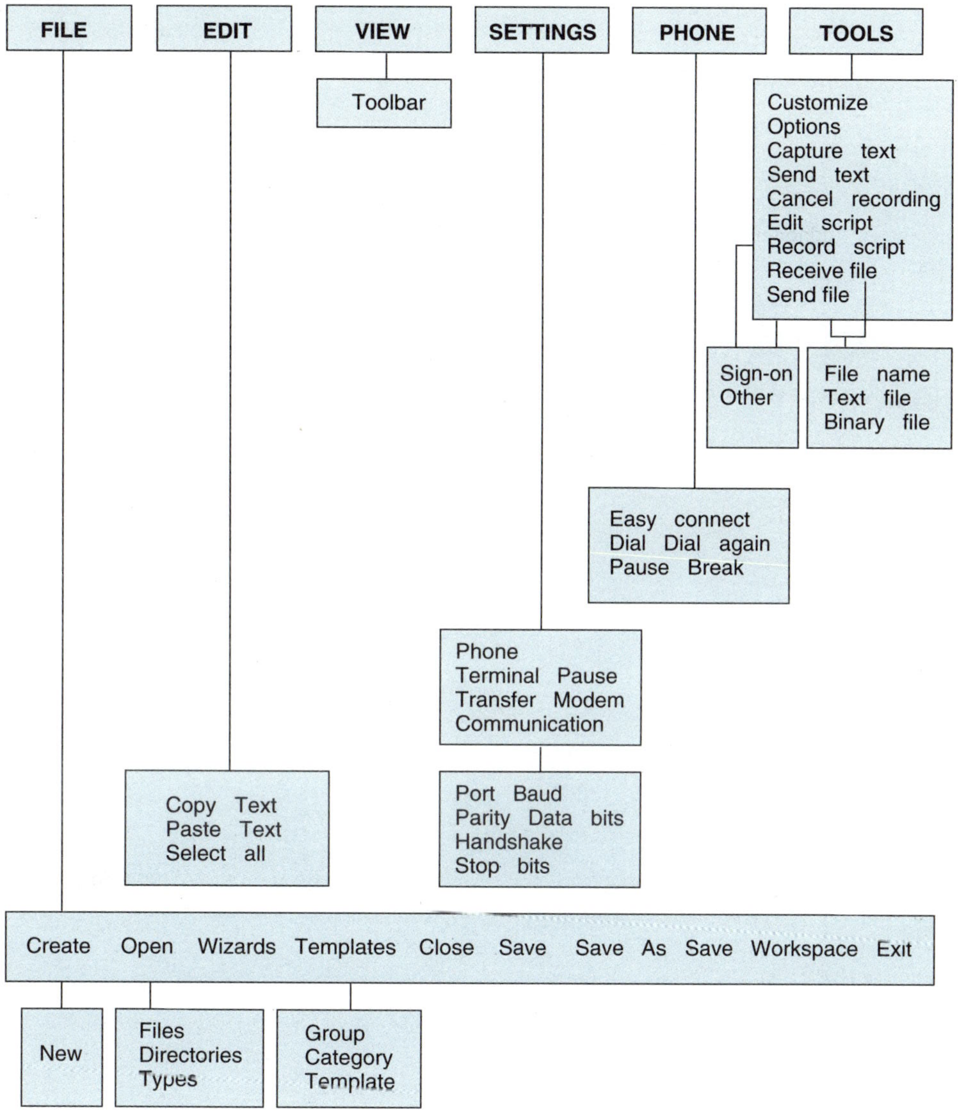

Menu Tree for Draw

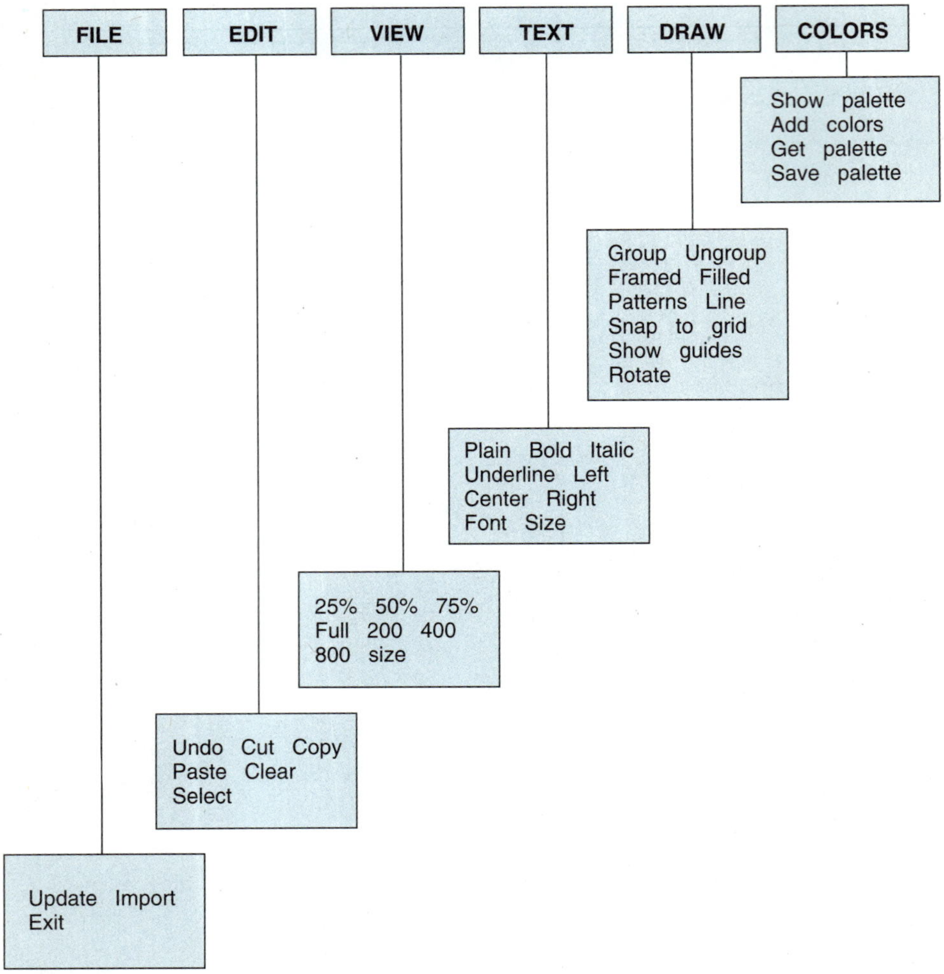

Menu Tree for Clip Art

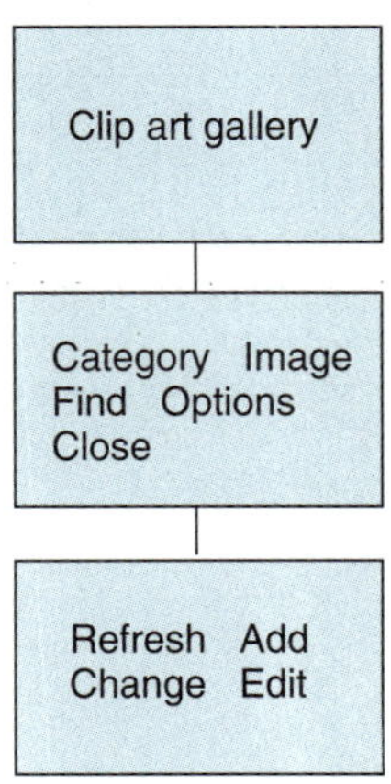

Appendix B

Functions for *Works 3.0 for Windows*

ABS (n)	Returns the absolute value of *n*.
ACOS (n)	Returns the value of the arc cosine (the angle whose cosine is n). The result will be in radians for an angle of 0 through 180 degrees.
AND (1, 1, . . .)	Return 1 if all arguments 1 are true; 0 for false if at least one argument is false.
ASIN (n)	Returns the value of the arc sine (the angle whose sine is n). The result will be in radians for an angle of -90 through +90 degrees.
ATAN (n)	Returns the value of the arc tangent (the angle whose tangent is n). The result will be in radians for an angle of -90 through +90 degrees.
ATAN2 (x, y)	Returns the value of the angle of the line from (0, 0) to (x, y). The result will be in radians for an angle of -180 degrees to +180 degrees.
AVG (r)	Returns the average of the range *r*.
CHOOSE (c, o 0, o1)	If the choice is False, returns the value of option 0; if the choice is True, returns the value of option 1.
COLS (r)	Computes the number of columns in range reference r.
COS (n)	Returns the value of the cosine of n, an angle measured in radians.

COUNT (r)	Counts the number of nonblank cells in range r.
CTERM (r, v, i)	Returns the value of the term (number of compounding periods) needed for investment i to grow to value v at interest rate r.
DATE (y, m, d)	Computes a *Works* date number for the date specified by year y, month m, and day d. *Works* dates are represented by numbers from 1 to 65,534, which denote the days from January 1, 1990 to June 3, 2079. (*See also* TIME.)
DAY (d)	Returns a number from 1 to 31 for the parameter d, a *Works* date number.
DDB (c, s, l, p)	Returns the value of depreciation for period p using the double declining balance method. Parameter c is the cost of an asset, and s is its salvage value at the end of lifespan l. For tax purposes, l and p are usually stated in years.
ERR ( )	Forces a cell to display *ERR*, indicating that an error has been made in a calculation. Any calculation that uses this value will result in *ERR*, as well. Used to catch erroneous calculations.
EXACT (t, t)	Returns 1, for True, if text in one location matches text in a second location.
EXP (n)	Calculates the base number of natural logarithms to the *n*th power. The base number of natural logarithms is 2.71828.
FALSE ( )	Returns 0 for False.
FIND (t, t, #)	Finds the location of the first text t within the second t and returns a number corresponding to the start character #.
FV (d, r, t)	Returns a future value of a deposit d earning interest at rate r for term t. Used to compute the effect of compound interest.
HLOOKUP (v, r, row)	Searches by row for value v found in the table of range r.
HOUR (n)	Returns a value of n from 0 to 23 for a *Works* time number.
IF (c, v1, v0)	Returns *v*alue 1 if condition c is True, or value 0 if it is False.

INDEX (r, c, r)	Returns the value of the cell at the intersection of column c and row r.
INT (n)	Returns an integer (whole number); since this includes only digits to the left of the decimal point, the function truncates decimals.
IRR (g, r)	Returns the value of the internal rate of return in range r.
ISERR (n)	Returns 1 (for True) if n is the value ERR; otherwise, returns 0 (for False).
LEFT (t, n)	Returns the leftmost n characters in string t.
LENGTH (t)	Returns the length of phrase t.
LN (x)	Returns natural logarithm of x.
LOG (n)	Returns the base 10 value of natural logarithm n.
LOWER (t)	Converts specified text t to lowercase.
MAX (r)	Returns the maximum value in range r.
MID (t, o, l)	Returns text t for length l starting at o.
MIN (r)	Returns the minimum value in a range.
MINUTE (n)	Returns value of n, a *Works* time number, from 0 to 59.
MOD (n, d)	Returns the value of the remainder (modulus) for the division n/d.
MONTH (n)	Returns the number 1 to 12 for n, a *Works* time number.
N (r)	Returns 0 if range r contains text.
NOW ()	Using the internal clock and calendar of the computer, computes the time and date as a *Works* time and date number. (*See also* HOUR, MINUTE, SECOND; DAY, MONTH, YEAR.)
NOT (l)	Converts True of logical l to False, and vice versa. Returns the opposite equivalent.
NPV (r, range)	Returns the net present value for a cash flow series in the specified range at rate r.
OR (l, l, . . .)	Returns False (0) if all of the logical arguments l, l, . . . are false; returns 1 if at least one logical l is true.

Pi	Returns the constant number 3.14159.
PMT (p, r, t)	Returns the value of the payment for a loan with principal p, rate r, and term t.
PROPER (t)	Capitalizes the first letter of text t, converting it to a proper name.
PV (p, r, t)	Returns the present value of a series of payments in the amount of pv, at interest rate r, for term t.
RAND ()	Returns the value of a random number between 0 to 1. Multiply or divide RAND by another number to get larger or smaller random numbers.
RATE (f v, p v, t)	Returns the value of the fixed interest rate needed to achieve future value f from present value p over term t.
REPEAT (t, n)	Repeat text t, n number of times.
REPLACE (ot, #, l, nt)	Replaces old text ot starting at number # for length l with new text nt.
RIGHT (t, n)	Returns the rightmost n characters in string t.
ROUND (n, p)	Round n to p digits. Uses decimal portions of n to round. If p is negative, digits to the left of the decimal point are rounded. If p is 0, n is rounded to the nearest integer.
ROWS (r)	Returns the number of rows in range r.
S (r)	Returns the text in the first cell of range r; returns a blank if the cell holds a value.
SECOND (t)	Returns a number from 0 to 59 for a *Works* time number.
SIN (n)	Returns the sine of n measured in radians.
SLN (c, s, l)	Returns the value of c using the Straight line method depreciation for cost, with salvage value s, and life l.
SQRT (n)	Returns the value of the square root of n.
STD (r)	Returns the value of the standard deviation (spread about mean) for the population in a range.
STRING (x, d)	Converts value of x as text, with d decimal places. Changes data type to character.
SUM (r)	Returns the sum of the cells in a range.

SYD (c, s, l, p)	Returns the value of depreciation for cost c using the sum of the years' digits method and salvage value s, life l, and period p.
TAN (n)	Returns the tangent of n.
TERM (p, r, fv)	Returns the number of periods needed for equal payments of p, earning interest rate r, to reach future value fv.
TIME (h, m, s)	Returns a number for the time specified by hour h, minute m, second s.
TRIM (t)	Removes blanks from text t.
TRUE ( )	Returns 1 for True.
UPPER (t)	Converts specified text t to uppercase.
VALUE (t)	Converts text t to a numeric value for computation. Changes data type to numeric.
VAR (r)	Returns the variance of range r.
VLOOKUP (v, r, col)	Finds v in the leftmost column in range r. The values located by v should be in ascending order by row for HLOOKUP and by column for VLOOKUP.
YEAR (n)	Returns the value of the year for n, a *Works* time number.

Photo Credits

	Page	Source/Credit
Chapter 1	4 (a)	Digital Equipment Corporation
	4 (b)	Cray Research, Inc.
	4 (c)	Hewlett Packard Company
	4 (d)	IBM Corporation
	5	Fredrik Bodin/Offshoot
	11 (a)	Logitech, Inc.
	11 (b)	Kensington Microware, Inc.
	11 (c)	Gabe Palmer/Stock Market
	11 (d)	Logitech, Inc.
	11 (e)	Gnd Systems, Inc.
	14 (a)	Hewlett Packard
	14 (b)	Hewlett Packard
	14 (c)	Epson, Inc.
	15	IBM Corporation
	19	Fredrik Bodin/Offshoot
	20	Compaq Computer
	22	John Curtis
Chapter 3	86	Fredrik Bodin/Offshoot
Chapter 4	124	John Greenleigh/Apple Computer Corp.
	125	Fredrik Bodin/Offshoot
	126	Fredrik Bodin/Offshoot
Chapter 5	203	Aldus Corporation
Chapter 6	222	Fredrik Bodin/Offshoot

Chapter 7	258	Fredrik Bodin/Offshoot
	268	Fredrik Bodin/Offshoot
Chapter 8	294	Peter Le Grand/Tony Stone Worldwide
	295	Informix, Inc.
Chapter 9	329 (a)	Fredrik Bodin/Offshoot
	329 (b)	Borland International
	338	Don Smetzer/Tony Stone Images
Chapter 10	360	Laima Druskis/Stock Boston
Chapter 12	435	Comshare, Inc. Ann Arbor, MI
	436	Fredrik Bodin/Offshoot
	437 (a)	Supra Corporation
	437 (b)	Barbara Alper/Stock Boston
	437 (c)	Hayes Microcomputer Products, Inc.
Chapter 14	521	Fredrik Bodin/Offshoot
	522	Stephen Swimburne/ Stock Boston
	523 (a)	Hewlett Packard
	523 (b)	Compaq Corporation
	523(c)	Grid Systems, Inc.
	523 (d)	Peter Beck/Stock Market
	523 (e)	Compaq Corporation
	528	Spencer Grant/Stock Boston
	530	Liane Enkelis/Stock Boston
	531	Fredrik Bodin/Offshoot

Index